TIMING THE FUTURE METROPOLIS

TIMING THE FUTURE METROPOLIS

FORESIGHT, KNOWLEDGE, AND DOUBT
IN AMERICA'S POSTWAR URBANISM

PETER EKMAN

CORNELL UNIVERSITY PRESS
Ithaca and London

Copyright © 2024 Peter Ekman

All rights reserved. Except for brief quotations in a review, this book, or parts thereof, must not be reproduced in any form without permission in writing from the publisher. For information, address Cornell University Press, Sage House, 512 East State Street, Ithaca, New York 14850. Visit our website at cornellpress.cornell.edu.

First published 2024 by Cornell University Press

Library of Congress Cataloging-in-Publication Data

Names: Ekman, Peter, 1985– author.
Title: Timing the future metropolis : foresight, knowledge, and doubt in America's postwar urbanism / Peter Ekman.
Description: Ithaca [New York] : Cornell University Press, 2024. | Includes bibliographical references and index.
Identifiers: LCCN 2024000035 (print) | LCCN 2024000036 (ebook) | ISBN 9781501778384 (hardcover) | ISBN 9781501778391 (paperback) | ISBN 9781501778407 (pdf) | ISBN 9781501778414 (epub)
Subjects: LCSH: Joint Center for Urban Studies—Influence. | City planning—United States—History—20th century. | Cities and towns—Research—United States—History—20th century. | United States—History—1945–
Classification: LCC HT167 .E393 2024 (print) | LCC HT167 (ebook) | DDC 307.1/216097309045—dc23/eng/20240412
LC record available at https://lccn.loc.gov/2024000035
LC ebook record available at https://lccn.loc.gov/2024000036

Contents

Introduction: Urban Times ... 1

1. Centers and Their Edges: Formations of Urban Knowledge in Postwar America ... 17

2. The Atmosphere and the Network: Organizing Expertise at the Joint Center for Urban Studies ... 54

3. "Our Retrospection Will All Be to the Future": History, Inference, and the Temporalities of Planning ... 87

4. "A Documented Experience": Cambridge on the Caroní ... 130

5. Reoriented: The Conservative Center and the New Politics of Expectation ... 176

6. The Belated City: Forgetting the Future Metropolis ... 209

Coda: A Forward Signal ... 246

Acknowledgments 257

Notes 263

Index 365

TIMING THE FUTURE METROPOLIS

Introduction
Urban Times

"Is it going to be a new time—is it really going to be a new time?" Alfred Kazin, aged thirty, jotted these words in his personal journal and dated them March 22, 1946.[1] The war was over. All around him, Kazin found a city, New York, "that had never been richer, smoother, more expansive." Midtown Manhattan would soon be studded with metallic office towers that, to him, "resembled the massed file cabinets and coded systems they were built to hold."[2] Postwar America was becoming "a society that is based on the future [and] discredits all links to the past."[3] Kazin could relate. "How wonderful it would be," he wrote that day, "not to look back anymore."[4]

And yet, look back he did. His reputation as a critic secure on the basis of *On Native Grounds* (1942), a rhapsody to what he asserted was a uniquely American literary inheritance—penned by the son of working-class Jews from Eastern Europe, as many reviewers noted or found ways to insinuate—Kazin spent the war's immediate aftermath plumbing the depths of his childhood in Brownsville, the ragged East Brooklyn neighborhood he would exalt in a series of intensely nostalgic memoirs. He had written his breakout book unhappily domiciled in the industrial Long Island City section of Queens, dense by American standards but, in Kazin's view, a "raw, makeshift suburb" with little to tell him about the past, present, or future of America's alpha metropolis.[5] Now he began imagining a memoir, *A Walker in the City* (1951), and to do that, he had to return to Brownsville.[6]

To hear Kazin tell it, his newfound fixation on the past—his, New York's, and all the ways in which one could stand in for the other—caught him by surprise. It overtook him. He had not meant to look back, much less board the train, walk the streets, and actually look around the neighborhood he had long since abandoned. He was not a historian in any accredited sense. Although he spent it safely on the home front, the war had been traumatic, and it had overlapped with a spate of marital drama he would just as soon forget.[7] Even Brownsville's built environment seemed to offer mute confirmation that its past was beyond retrieval. "There was something in the everyday look of the streets that reproached me," he wrote of Pitkin Avenue, Rockaway Avenue, Chester Street, and the neighborhood's other unprepossessing seams; "they seemed to know I had come back to them unwillingly."[8]

Three years into his walks, Kazin had an encounter with the "granite force" of the Brooklyn Bridge. The date was May 8, 1949. As Kazin tells his journal, in breathless tones, "I am threaded through, caught up and threaded through, by millions of lines [i.e., bridge cables]. . . . I am led on. Into the thousand thicknesses and coiled strength of the lines, I am led on. . . . It is in me that they do their work."[9] As ontology, this vision of suasive bridges and buildings, stone and steel, would be peculiar enough if its effects were confined to the present tense, merely redistributing the agency that most post-Cartesian thought has assigned to humans alone. For Kazin, though, the built environment also has the capacity to induce a kind of time travel. It transports its subjects across tense, from the postwar present into the deep recesses of the past. Nowhere is this more evident than in the bridge episode. "Glistening monads of imagery" stayed with him in the aftermath. On the bridge and for months thereafter, "the city before my eyes in 1950 lifted me back into another city; one level of being swept me into another." Kazin began to see every present landscape as a sedimentation of its past. To a degree that surprised him, his walks ignited a genuine obsession with "Old New York," whose traces he began noticing in disused factories and warehouses, the debris of a large-scale deindustrialization that began right after the war, not in the 1970s as many Americans presume. Old buildings "shut in a world from time"; they encase temporal process, freezing it for consumption and inspection, and if a "gigantic dead clock" happens to perch above the old mill yard that first caught his eye, so much the better.[10]

Many critics found these lines embarrassing. Kazin seemed to have become a celebrant of the urban past for its own sake: "The past, the past was great: anything American, old, glazed, touched with dusk at the end of the nineteenth century, still smoldering with the fires lit by the [I]ndustrial [R]evolution." Yet he was not on a search for antiquity per se. According to his schema, for reasons he tried to rationalize but finally had to chalk up to personal taste, old was great, but oldest was not necessarily greatest. "The present was mean, the eighteenth century too Anglo-Saxon, too far away."[11] Kazin seized specifically on the period after the Civil War, a "dark revolutionary time" that Lewis Mumford, writing in 1931, had called the Brown Decades and exemplified architecturally in H. H. Richardson's imposing take on the Romanesque.[12] "I had made a discovery," he announced with great solemnity: "walking could take me back into the America of the nineteenth century."[13] In the five years after the war, Kazin coped with the new, futurist America, victorious but ahistorical, by going back in time.

Yet what Kazin finally found admirable about that sliver of American history complicates his atavistic gesture. The 1880s, he claimed, were notable chiefly for their time orientation—their shared sense that "everything was about to occur."[14] Never the simple nostalgic who seeks to wallow and restore, Kazin sounded out a complex nested tense for the writing of history. Never content to stop the clock, he sought to reinhabit and retrieve how people at a specific moment in the past perceived time's passage and imagined the onrushing urban future—the better to reignite a sense of continuity among his readers in the present day.

This attraction to bygone articulations of the future became only stronger after the publication of *A Walker in the City*—in rough proportion to postwar liberals' elevation of "planning" as a central motif in urban governance, social policy, public morality, and political economy. In 1959, for instance—in the journals again—Kazin wrote that "the feeling for history is the sense that the intelligence of man, a foreseer, really works to carry man into an imaginable—not always imagined—future."[15] He too, sub rosa, was a foreseer: "All my life I had lived for the future, had anticipated everything in terms of some overriding idea."[16] That was why he had bothered to write the memoirs: "To be an initiate again, to write the story of youth"—his own, the block's, the city's, the nation's—"to look forward to everything."[17]

In July 1960, in the Pocono Mountains of northeastern Pennsylvania, on the grounds of a summer resort established by New York's Rand School of Social Science and popular since the 1920s with left-facing urban Jews, a group convened for the Tamiment Conference on the Metropolis. The meeting, which had been in the works since 1958, was the initiative of the MIT city planner Lloyd Rodwin, who had recently joined the American Academy of Arts and Sciences and—a first for someone of his professional background—the editorial board of its generalist organ, *Daedalus*. Rodwin had cycled through several possible titles for the event, the themed issue that would go to press in early 1961, and the related book that George Braziller would bring out later that year. Passing over "The Metropolitan World: Nature and Potentials" and "Mastering the Metropolis," he settled on "The Future Metropolis."[18] The papers, Rodwin believed, demonstrated by simple adjacency the promise of a fully interdisciplinary urban studies, and although they pursued a range of specific goals, certain sentiments recurred. All were animated by an optimistic, basically liberal faith that the American city was amenable to expert-led improvement over time. The future was metropolitan; metropolitan growth, both upward at the core and outward into the suburban hinterland, was all but assured; and the major intellectual and political challenges for that future would orbit how best to ensure degrees of "technological freedom," particularly in the realms of transport and communication.[19] "Since they live in a time of change," Stephen Graubard wrote of the amassed scholars by way of preface, "they are conditioned to expect change, even prepare for it."[20]

The volume's proposals were perhaps something other than utopian. "It is the utopian process that should be emulated rather than the utopian product," opined the city planner Martin Meyerson, based across town at Harvard, for "very rarely has a first-rate mind invented a utopia."[21] Yet, in all, *The Future Metropolis* broadcast a confidence about the future-facing temporality that, as the contributors pointed out, would always inhere in the task of urban and regional planning. "Only rarely do we find a contemporary plan that anticipates the future with pleasure," Rodwin wrote, with Kevin Lynch. "The spirit of hopeful intervention should prove at least as effective as the desire to escape present discomfort." He called for "cautious projection, utopian fancy, and pragmatic recommendation" to proliferate in roughly equal measure.[22] Meyerson echoed these calls: "If they are recognized as caricature," he wrote, utopian schemes "can be extremely useful in posing potentially desirable ends and in testing these ends with a logical model."[23] To think seriously about urbanization, they agreed, was to think ahead. The future metropolis was a place worth imagining before it came to fruition. Urbanism had to be understood as a futurism, and the future, until further notice, was open.

Between his first proposal to the American Academy and the event at Tamiment, Rodwin's institutional obligations had become more complex. In late 1959, he and Meyerson began serving as the inaugural directors of the Harvard–MIT Joint Center for Urban Studies, a novel interdisciplinary contraption, years in the making, that joined faculty from both ends of Cambridge. The Joint Center was seeded with ample Ford Foundation money and was, in important respects, the prototype for that philanthropy's incursions into urban studies, a new field-of-fields forged at the intersection of several disciplines and professions. It brokered partnerships and attempted to organize the heterogeneous endeavor of urban research, quickly becoming critical infrastructure in far broader networks of scholarship, policy making, and public intellect. On a scale unknown to any of its peers, within or without Ford's sphere, it sought to supersede inherited tensions between those dedicated to the physical design of cities—architects, planners, some landscape architects, and increasingly those aligned with the new field of urban design, in which Harvard had just opened the first degree program—and those enacting the social research needed to make those designs credible, grounding the unknowable future in methodically registered facts about cities present and past.[24]

Alfred Kazin was on the original list of invitees to Tamiment. Rodwin had imagined him speaking on natural landscape and the city, in what would have been the company of an eclectic group featuring numerous philosophers, literary critics, and other humanists. Kazin himself paid social science little respect. He was suspicious of its attempts to describe behavior in terms of its regularities, disinclined to heed its calls to quantify, and forever put off by what he saw as its penchant for wooden prose. His attempts at urban time travel might well have found a receptive audience among the urbanists. With the Joint Center up and running, however, Rodwin rewrote the invite list so that the resulting conference would better reflect its membership and prerogatives at the borderlands of planning, design, and, above all, social science. *The Future Metropolis* broadcast the center's arrival on the scene and served as its first collective, programmatic statement. Rodwin and Meyerson understood it to be submitting for public consideration their vision of broad-based but method-bound urban expertise rendered in an anticipatory key. Their agenda, voiced in ways partially consonant with the "new rigorism" then ascendant in the social sciences and humanities alike, offered a different response but was a product of the same period of breakneck change that had led Kazin, for a moment, to believe that a "new time" could exist.[25]

This book addresses a broad network of interdisciplinary initiatives that between 1945 and 1985 engaged in codifying the methods and mores of organized urban research. It does so at multiple scales but works chiefly through the career of one unusually dense, connected, and consequential node in that network. The Joint Center for Urban Studies advanced styles of inquiry that Ford and its new cadre of self-styled experts deemed necessary edification and preparation for those who would mount attacks on a host of "urban problems," in the parlance of the time: unchecked suburbanization, industrial flight and large-scale abandonment near traditional urban cores, violent conflicts spiraling out from the racialized encounters between darker-complected postwar migrants to American cities and their extant populations, and the purported erosion of what Lynch called clear mental "images" of those cities, cognitive gestalts that, properly maintained, might induce a sense of belonging, orientation, stewardship, and comity. Assessing urban and metropolitan change in real time and, crucial to how it achieved prominence, devising new methods by which to infer its probable futures, the Joint Center incubated a remarkable variety of basic and applied research (and reflected on how to balance those impulses), theorized how localized acts of urban inquiry might equip inferences about "the city" writ large (although it only occasionally looked beyond the United States), and kept the network of knowledge producers in working order. Indeed, the roster of those who populated or in some way engaged the Joint Center reads as a nearly complete census of the urbanist establishment that emerged to face what many of them, by the middle 1960s, were routinely, and in the singular, calling the *urban crisis*.

Planning must be understood as a form of temporal reasoning. City and regional planners specialize in foresight: they discern where present trends are heading and make interventions that might redirect their course. Planners work in the future tense. On one level, this point could not be more banal: *to plan*, the verb, by definition, includes some orientation to the horizon of the not-yet. Even so, remarkably few scholars concerned with the planning of urban space have reflected systematically on urban time, temporality, or tense with the conceptual or historical detail they merit.[26] Planning constitutes an attempt to exercise power over the urban future, and, in the name of the future, it becomes an exercise of power on cities of the present. Simply by centering attention on the politics of planning's timescale, this book offers a revision to the prevailing historiography, which tends to phrase debates on postwar urbanism in terms of either spatial scale (large versus small units of analysis) or the directionality of planning power (top-down versus bottom-up). The confrontation between the "big urbanism" of a Rexford Tugwell—or a Robert Moses, Le Corbusier, Daniel Burnham, Baron Haussmann—and the "vital little plans" of a Jane Jacobs has had pride of place, and it has settled into a familiar set of dichotomies that orient but can ossify.[27]

The future tense, however, also has a history. The methods by which planners articulate it with other tenses, bringing knowledge about past and present to bear on the as yet unknown, have undergone dramatic changes in their own right. Planners inherit and account for the urban past; they acknowledge the present but treat it as a filter onto what lies ahead.[28] They manage transitions (or try to), regulate the pace of urban change (ditto), warn the public of approaching problems, and work to realize some alternatives and stave off others. Twentieth-century planners took pains to conjoin and cross-reference the tenses—and to give the sense that they alone had devised methods to do this work methodically, subject to none of the speculative whimsy of the prophet, the seer, or the fabulist, who would just as soon cut the future loose from its moorings in the already-so.

City planning, with roots in nineteenth-century sanitary reform, was institutionally secure, and growing, as a discipline and profession by the time of the First World War.[29] That war's exigencies further consolidated planning expertise and brought leading practitioners into sustained collaboration, chiefly around projects involving the selection of industrial sites for shipbuilding and other wartime production; the retooling of existing manufacturing complexes, many of them already sited on the suburban fringes of large metropolises; the improvement of rail and road infrastructure that would keep these new state spaces provisioned and bring their products to the theater of war; and above all, via the rapidly organized United States Housing Corporation and Emergency Fleet Corporation, the construction of whole new neighborhoods to house defense workers, spaces received and routinely cited as object lessons disclosing the latest thinking in "subdivision science."[30] After the war, metropolitan or regional planning—meaning essentially the central city plus its suburban hinterland—became the dominant framework, a response to patterns of dispersal that had roots deep in the nineteenth century but, abetted by widespread automobile use, had altered planners' sense of the minimum scale at which decision-making had to operate in order to manage expansion. The Regional Plan Association, chartered in 1922 in New York, was perhaps the best-known group by that name, but there were many others nationwide—some little more than chambers of commerce accustomed to coordinating across municipal lines.[31]

In the 1920s, it was possible to dissect the finer points of spatial planning, single-city or metro-regional in scope, without seriously debating the category of *planning* as such: whether to do it, how to allocate the task between state and market forces, what sort of power planners held (or should, in a notionally free capitalist economy), and what time horizons it involved (or ought to). During the Depression and New Deal, however, political discourse broached the question in newly direct, frequently antagonistic ways. The Soviet counterpoint loomed in the background of Western politics, its Five-Year Plans stacked end on end, mocking and unnerving those for whom the short-termism of capitalism was one of its virtues.

Increasingly by 1934, the political left and right, so labeled, could be distinguished in terms of their positions on the desirability of planning. The British sociologist Barbara Wootton could intelligibly title a volume of comparative political analysis *Plan or No Plan* (1934). However stark, these were the decade's terms of debate—these the maximal stakes that seemed to haunt even the most workaday, neighborhood-level dispute over zoning.[32] In 1937, the German-émigré sociologist Hans Speier, noting that opportunities to exert rational control over economy and society tend to increase when the overall social structure seems to be under threat, bristled at hearing "short-cut argumentations for and against planning" invoked without any apparent middle ground.[33] That same year, Findlay MacKenzie was able to convene thirty-five "economists, sociologists, and statesmen" in a symposium devoted to *Planned Society: Yesterday, Today, Tomorrow* (1937), based on his Brooklyn College course on economic control. Speier turned out, as did Harold Lasswell, the philosopher Sidney Hook, the celebrity anthropologist Margaret Mead (documenting economic control in "primitive societies"), Wesley C. Mitchell (national planning), George Soule (general economic planning), and Rosalind Tough, the one participant to address the planning of urban space: William Penn's 1682 grid for Philadelphia, the rectilinear 1811 Commissioners' Plan for Manhattan, tenement reform, war housing, and more. MacKenzie's volume included a foreword by Lewis Mumford, by then the *New Yorker*'s architectural critic and a long-standing font of opinions on urbanism at scales larger than the single building. Mumford, citing the Scottish polymath Patrick Geddes as his "master," defined planning as "the art of simultaneous thinking," a generalist form of inquiry uniquely able to achieve "integration" of disparate perspectives into one "single picture." "Specialists, as such, cannot plan."[34] By the mid-1930s, the characteristic problems tackled by city and regional planners appeared ever more clearly to be a subset of all-or-nothing debates on the political economy of planning as a state capacity and habit of mind.

Mumford's reference to "simultaneous thinking" stressed planning's synchronic dimension and de-emphasized its future-making qualities. During the Second World War, however, a new "shared temporal imagination" took hold. The war effort involved quite a bit of top-down planning, and in its aftermath, as Andrew Shanken has deftly shown, a respect for administered forethought ran far deeper: a "culture of expectation" pervaded public life, and planning became legible as "the great temporal art form."[35] By the end of the 1950s, it was possible for the regionalist John Friedmann—Austrian-born but based in US universities since the war—to claim that "the great debate about planning," which had roiled since the New Deal, was resolved. The planners had won. "We live in an age of analysis," Friedmann wrote. Its temporal dimensions were clear: "For the planner, the present is already history."[36] The future took precedence.

Friedmann spoke primarily for what Lionel Trilling was quick to identify as "our educated class"—which by the 1950s partook of a "political feeling," so pervasive as to be seldom justified out in the open, that was "predominantly liberal." Postwar liberalism, American style, tended to include "a ready if mild suspiciousness of the profit motive, a belief in progress, science, social legislation, planning, and international cooperation."[37] Such was the climate in which Kazin filed his dissent. It was against this backdrop, too, that organized interdisciplinary research on urban life came together on a scale unknown before the war. No institution discloses its ambitions, intellectual range, internal tensions, and eventual collapse more clearly than the Joint Center for Urban Studies.

Quite a number of writers have mused retroactively on the temporal condition of what it could mean to be *post*war, or in any sense future-oriented, in a world so profoundly disfigured. Intellectuals "had to make do with a life among ruins," Leo Raditsa wrote from the vantage point of 1974—"ruins whose overseeing presence grows palpable" in the era's visual art, literature, and other expressive culture.[38] The war had left its physical signatures in cities all across the world: jagged, unpitying ruins in Europe and Japan; American military bases stretching across a new global archipelago; and, at home, new facilities equipped to produce arms, distribute them, and house the vast workforces so engaged. If the war had been "a sacrifice to progress," as Kazin wrote two decades after Hiroshima, using the language of the grand strategist, its ending was anything but clear-cut. Looking back "in embarrassment, many laughed" and promptly averted their eyes, but "the war, in the form of permanent rearmament, goes on and on."[39] The critic and sociologist Daniel Bell, aged twenty-six when hostilities formally ceased, also worked out a complex temporality of endings and beginnings, of pasts that interlace with futures and haunt the present, when diagnosing the outlook characteristic of his intellectual milieu. "Ours, a 'twice-born' generation, finds its wisdom in pessimism, evil, tragedy, and despair. So we are both old and young 'before our time.'"[40] Any apparent break with history, clearer-eyed critics understood, was illusory. How, then, to think the future? How to imagine cities—worlds—configured otherwise?

"It was the Present tantalizingly sublimated," the Welsh itinerant Jan Morris wrote forty years after the events reconstructed in her *Manhattan '45* (1986). "It was the Future about to occur." *About to*—from 1945, Americans occupied not only a "new time," Kazin's provisional hope, but a new tense. "For the first time in the city's history the place was poised rather than headlong, eyeing the future rather than plunging into it."[41] Morris, too, was writing of New York, but the mood she described, a qualitatively new orientation to time, was readily palpable in American cities across the map and in a wide range of cultural and intellectual spheres that after the war proved remarkably explicit about, and invested in, reconceptualizing the future tense. What she called the city's "moment of grace," of course, eventually came to an end, and when it did, as this book will show, the resurgent profession of city and regional planning—interlocking as never before with the social sciences—would attempt to formalize many of these insights and rethink the very temporality undergirding what it is, at root, to plan.[42]

Kazin's tortured reflections on tense and the Joint Center's attempts to traverse it methodically both belong to what might be called the history of the future. A growing number of scholars have turned their attention to dissecting what Reinhart Koselleck decades ago referred to as "futures past," seeking to understand earlier moments or entire eras in terms of how people then living sought to envision and prepare for what lay ahead. Some of this scholarship has been essentially idealist in character, following Koselleck's own method of *Begriffsgeschichte*, or conceptual history, with a purity he may never have intended. More of it, of late, has asked after the specific practices and technologies by which prediction, projection, speculation, visioning, imaging, and forecasting have unfolded. Importantly, this turn has enabled historians to theorize how such attempts to know the future before it transpires—by definition, impossible in any strict sense—have constituted material interventions on the world, not only depictions or descriptions of it.[43] *Timing the Future Metropolis* seconds the impulse to historicize foresight and diverts it to the cultures of expertise attending to the multifaceted changes underway in urban form and life at the middle of the twentieth century. It pursues an intellectual history of the urban future as a concept, object, political horizon, and, at length, lever for intervention on the urban present.

A concern with the urban future is subsidiary to a more encompassing concern with the social life of time. Temporality—time as experienced, imagined, allocated, governed—itself has a history, and that history proves upon inspection to be thoroughly political. Time's passage has registered differently at different points in history: opened onto different presumed horizons, quickened or slowed, seemed amenable to technical mastery or exceeded human cognition. Moreover, distinct segments of society, as striated by class, race, and other diacritics, experience time differently: control it or are subject to it, make or follow schedules, order or carry out (or resist) accelerations in work, economic production, political change, "modernization," "progress," and other essentially temporal imperatives of an industrial and then postindustrial society. By attending to temporality, we address difference and inequality by other means.[44]

This, in broad strokes, has been the founding insight of the sociology and anthropology of time. It is perhaps telling that the midcentury moment, coterminous with both Kazin's emergence as a critic and the consolidation of a future-facing urban studies, saw those subfields first come into their own. Sociologists devised formal theories to explain the temporal ordering of society, and they did this work precisely as depression gave way to war, *planning* crested as a concept and talking point, and large-scale crisis began to call the foundations of social order itself into question. Pitrim Sorokin and Robert C. Merton coined the concept of "social time" (1937), noting on functionalist premises "the need for social collaboration . . . at the root of social systems of time" such as the calendar, the eight-hour day, the seven-day week, the agreed-upon market day (in the preindustrial period), and the felt sense of hurry that has long made metropolitan time qualitatively unlike the regimes that prevail in the small village. Even if, to coordinate society, we do resort to astronomical time—with its even, easily quantified units that the widespread use of mechanical clocks has naturalized—for Sorokin and Merton, that numerical system is simply a "time [E]speranto," a soft infrastructure, a contract to which no one has ever officially signed on.[45] Wilbert Moore's postwar syntheses of "man, time, and society" made these insights compatible with the work of Talcott Parsons, the dominant social theorist of the immediate postwar moment despite his demonstratable lack of interest in accounting for social change.[46] A raft of anthropological studies taking E. E. Evans-Pritchard's study "Nuer Time-Reckoning" (1939) as their point of departure made examples of non-Western societies to reflect on temporality's basis in social relations, distinguishing an "ecological time" grounded in natural cycles and seasons from a "structural time" keyed to collective human goals.[47] The history of planning runs in parallel with, and is enriched by, the history of time itself.

Work specifically claiming to advance the intellectual history of planning and urbanism is not plentiful.[48] This is so even as the "ability to forecast and plan," as Robert Brym notes, has for decades been considered one of the core competencies of that strange sect called "intellectuals."[49] At a methodological level, then, the present book belongs to an inchoate genre worth defending and perpetuating. *Timing the Future Metropolis* might, more exactly, be called a history of urban knowledge.[50] Even as it intervenes in the history and sociology of intellectual life, however, there are compelling reasons to move off of *intellect* as the dominant framework, if that term would confine attention to accredited scholars with clear and recognized claims to expertise. The book deals with forms of knowledge deemed technical and, indeed, attends to the arrogation and bounding of expertise. It also, however, explores and willingly trespasses the shifting boundaries of the academy. The Joint Center and its network matter to the history of public intellect—not the public intellectual as a social type, the focus of so much consternation during the twentieth century, but the manifold means by which specialists translate and mobilize their ideas to wider publics that they themselves are constantly working to assemble. The Joint Center's personnel reflected on these questions repeatedly, in the open, and sometimes in agony.

Twenty-first-century turns in the history and sociology of knowledge have called for an attention to ideas as "interventions" in a "domain composed of movements," one significantly mediated by institutions and individuals who act as "brokers." The question has become what expertise does, rather than (as in the Marxian debates that Karl Mannheim most famously tried to sidestep by positing the intelligentsia as a free-floating, classless class) who, exactly, the experts are. With this new pragmatics of intellectual life, the literature has often explored the novel configurations into which thinkers, perpetually seeking interlocutors and sponsors, have arranged their work: disciplines and professions, yes, but also the shape-shifting networks, "theory groups, bandwagons . . . and invisible colleges," the "coterie, clique, circle, cenacle, club . . . chapel, curia, and so on," all of which, Daniel Bell once mused, mysteriously begin with the letter c.[51]

The midcentury social sciences have proved quite amenable to this style of analysis. As Nils Gilman writes, through "microhistories" of "social networks that gave rise to an enduring terminology and set of ideas" by constantly referring to one another, one can reconstruct "immediate reactions to local intellectual contexts" with a richness and flexibility that analyses predicated on broad-gauge, pregiven categories such as "the intelligentsia" forgo.[52] Hunter Heyck astutely observes that the historiography of postwar social science has tended to stress flexible networks and interdisciplinary confabs in part because their members spoke this language, thinking of their own work as establishing an infrastructure of exchange that readily and by necessity punctured the boundaries of discipline. American social science prior to 1930 included nodes of interdisciplinarity—on urban topics, prominently, Robert Park's Chicago School, which occupied a department of sociology and shared terrain with its neighbors in geography, anthropology, economics, and beyond—but during that period, the fundamental impulse was to legitimate each new discipline by clarifying the uniqueness and exclusivity of its approach. In turn, the historiography of Progressive Era social science has stressed boundaries and separation.[53]

Timing the Future Metropolis entertains the thought that there must be at least some relationship between the forums of intellectual life and the forms of knowledge they generate—between institution and idea, configuration and content. The relationship resists easy closure; unambiguous causation is hard to come by. Nonetheless, the center's patrons and personnel themselves repeatedly reflected on this relationship, inconclusively but always on the assumption that the question truly mattered. As much as any specific finding or framework that crystallized out of its highly heterogeneous research, a concern with the organization of knowledge—the hunch that urban knowledge, like urban life itself, could and should be better organized than it currently is—circulated through the dense, self-referential network that the center helped call into being. Through this one center, then, a broader and entirely dynamic infrastructure comes into view.

The narrative spans six chapters. The first presents a panoramic view of postwar American attempts to organize urban knowledge, make it interdisciplinary, give it institutional standing, codify its epistemology and root it in systematic doubt, and focus it temporally on the *future metropolis* without indulging the utopian gestures that mainline social scientists had come to reject. The second and third chapters narrow to the case of the Joint Center. One begins in 1951, when preliminary conversations at MIT and then Harvard began to circle the question of forming a new and fully interdisciplinary unit, and discusses the group's first conflicted attempts to serialize a body of basic research. The other, beginning in 1963, follows the center into its complex interface with urban policy and explores how it negotiated new uses for the historical imagination in an age dominated by compulsive forecasting, much of it quantitative in character. The fourth chapter details the center's involvement with a New Town project sited in South America, the group's one major extraterritorial engagement and salvo in the geopolitics of the global Cold War, as well as the only time it participated in directly building the future metropolis into existence rather than theorizing or projecting it. The fifth chapter follows the center's concepts back north in order to assess its role in introducing, or anyhow abetting, fractures and realignments in the politics of American urbanism—shifts evident by the later 1960s, stoked in part by critiques of its purpose-built city and others like it, and by the 1970s, resonant with a broader skepticism about planning and other forms of expertise presumed viable just a decade prior. The sixth and final chapter reckons with the late Joint Center's contorted politics of time in an age of putative urban "ruin": its newfound presentism, concomitant disavowal of the future as a horizon of expectation, embrace of doubt (once the epistemological hallmark of its non-Modernist liberalism) over certainty, and increasingly disconsolate attitude regarding the solubility of any of the problems that had first motivated the conjunction of theoretical with applied urban knowledge. A brief coda, without fully instrumentalizing this history, nonetheless articulates the generative place of these postwar tales in urban debates of the early twenty-first century.

At midcentury, there was an unfulfilled desire to account for the city, as such, in theoretical terms. There was also an exhaustion with previous overreaching attempts to do so. The city, however, was an abstraction, and any given city under study was manifestly a moving target. The pace of postwar urban change occasioned new forms of curiosity, and anxiety, about the *future* as both a conceptual category and a horizon of human existence. In the scholarly fields constituted to address these predicaments, time and tense themselves came under new kinds of scrutiny, and as the emerging set of urban experts sought to draw on the documented past and experienced present to infer probable future developments, the very knowability of urban problems became the subject of complex, ornately politicized dispute.

No single institution was more consequential for these debates, as infrastructure and as actor, than the Joint Center. This book pursues neither a straightforward institutional case history—of one relatively closed circle of people who remained in regular contact over a defined period of time—nor a history of urban temporality as such, if such a thing could even be accomplished in a responsible way. Precisely because of how it reframed the politics of planning, design, and social science in terms of those fields' respective claims on the *future*, the Joint Center was able to mediate, intervene in, abstract from, and alter a wider range of debates than if the group had been constituted around a simpler, more self-evident set of objectives. When its thinkers came to question the basic terms of debate, unraveling the systems of analysis that they themselves had fastened into place during the expectant 1950s, doubters everywhere saw concrete models of how to critique planners' expertise, and the apparatus splintered. By orienting their knowledge to an object, or horizon, that was by definition unknowable in any strong sense, they prepared the way for a resurgent, differently politicized skepticism from which urban studies has yet to recover.

This is a work of history, but its author is also a geographer. Even as segments of the text skew to the ideational, it is in every respect a history of urban space, one built on a granular, sustained exposure to the designed and vernacular landscapes of many American cities and towns, sensed in three and four dimensions, surveyed, mapped, visualized, and walked. In 1962, H. C. Darby mused on what he called "the problem of geographical description." If language is the geographer's leading medium, he observed—and *geo-graphy* has always literally denoted "Earth-writing"—then the simple act of describing even an entirely static landscape necessarily unfolds over time.[54] Language elapses; sentences, paragraphs, and even single words occupy durations; they take time to be either written or read from beginning to end. What Darby identified is a paradox but not, in every case, a problem. For historical or geographic writing, the very temporality of argument is one of its most basic strengths: the patience it invites of the reader and the possibility of surprise it perforce builds in. *Timing the Future Metropolis* centers on less than half a century of history, but it is a detailed account of a heterogeneous institution that sometimes acted in concert but always encouraged internal critique, privileging doubt over certainty. Its processes of fusion and fission are the stuff of this book.

In a 1955 essay, the literary critic John Kouwenhoven ventured that "America is process," precisely because, with Emerson as his witness, "becoming somewhat else is the perpetual game of nature." The same might be said of urban planning as a "manner of handling experience and materials," of the center's ways of knowing, and of its bequests to the present.[55] This book is a history not of plans but planning, not of thought but thinking—processes all the way down. It is a history of urban space, but space too, like all matter, exists only in time, becoming otherwise.

Postwar urbanists were apt—perhaps too apt—to draw correlations between specific spatial forms and the social or behavioral patterns presumed to follow from them. Let us indulge just one. Kouwenhoven noted then that Americans "are used to living in grid-patterned cities and towns." It is now commonplace for critical scholars to hold up the rectilinear grid as the decisive signature of spatial rationalization and to index its uniformities to the deadening hand of capital or state. Yet, left to its own devices, the grid itself inherently lacks either a command center—unless one has been specifically built in for, say, a courthouse or capitol—or a firm, enclosing edge that would demarcate city from non-city. It is precisely the grid's edgelessness that made it so useful for eighteenth- and nineteenth-century capitalists' speculation in land, so easily expanded as the developer attaches still more cells, publishes a map with his (usually his) name on it, and calls it an "addition." Even as it might be enrolled to entrench or clarify unequal relations of power, in the formal interchangeability of its units the grid is a nonhierarchical mode of organization through and through. For Kouwenhoven, writing as 1950s prosperity crested, the grid's very underdetermination, its essential incompleteness, said something enduring and optimistic about America's time orientation. "The past of those who live in the United States," he wrote, "like their future, is open-ended. It does not, like the past of most other people, extend downward into the soil out of which their immediate community or neighborhood has grown. It extends laterally backward across the plains, the mountains, or the sea to somewhere else, just as their future may at any moment lead them down the open road, the endless-vistaed street."[56]

That Kouwenhoven overstated the case is obvious. Yet his words find clear echoes in the styles of future-facing research that the Joint Center and its network eagerly set about codifying in the ensuing years. It is plausible but by no means certain that these scholars read Kouwenhoven's words. It matters little whether they did. Like the grid itself, in articulating their vision of properly modern urban knowledge they often spoke the language of rationality, system, order, and theoretical closure while, in practice, their work took forms that were quite open—at times improvised—and defined less by bright boundaries than by the adjacencies and serializations of disparate agendas. The center became central to postwar urbanism by forging connections and acting as a kind of relay station; the resulting interdisciplinary collage of expertise operated, in truth, without one single uncontested center or edge. Precisely those qualities allowed urban studies, for a time anyhow, to thrive—to trespass and enjamb, to suture together some inherited fields and supersede others entirely. Precisely because the *future* metropolis, its stated interest, would forever be receding over the horizon, it resisted outright capture as an object of study and target of intervention, remaining by definition open—a watchword of the Cold War as seen from the West—and perpetually replenishing demand for an entity very much like the Joint Center to pronounce on where things were headed and what might be done about it. Cities would always be changing, study would continue, plans would be laid and undercut, and there would always be a new time to keep.

CHAPTER 1

Centers and Their Edges
Formations of Urban Knowledge in Postwar America

To understand the Joint Center's emergence, and to grasp how the future metropolis came to seem like an urgent and tractable focus for such work, we must first account for its milieu. Four interlocking domains of thought and practice supply the intellectual map of postwar urban research, and this chapter, its compass points. New styles of public intellect—encouraged by new commitments to paperback publishing, urban and architectural criticism in mainline newspapers, and a set of heterodox magazines of a literary and speculative bent—engaged a growing audience, literate but unspecialized, that craved new approaches to writing the city and gauging its problems. Inside the large research-oriented American university, postwar scholars and administrators rethought the methodological bases of the human sciences and the porosity of their boundaries. New organizational contraptions seemed to promise a way to reintegrate a fractured epistemology of the social world. The most zealous orchestrators of these new forums, however, were not scholars but foundation officers. New conjugations of philanthropy with social science reshaped urban inquiry and left its stamp on some of the era's most conspicuous and controversial inquiries into urban change. Crucially, organized urban research arose from collaborations between the retouched social sciences and the professions of planning and design. The Joint Center was "the grandfather of all the urban research centers," sociologist David Popenoe would write in a 1971 state-of-the-field report.[1] Both its certitudes and its doubts took shape within an extended, highly self-referential network.

To plan is to plan *ahead*. Postwar urbanists of all stripes attended in depth to the temporality of urban development and to the forms of reasoning by which experts versed in the urban past and present might make claims on the fundamentally uncertain future. A vibrant set of postwar debates, by turns enamored of complexity and prone to simple declarations of faith in the inevitable course of things, circled the question of how to pose that future as the object of something like scientific knowledge. Urban studies, by that name, arose on the perforated border between the academy and the wider world whose pace of change so fascinated and alarmed its tribunes of expertise. It was by posing the question of the city in terms of its future that the Joint Center became legible to this network and proceeded to articulate its characteristic forms of urban knowledge. It was by navigating these postwar currents, while remaining slightly peripheral to each, that the center became central indeed.

City in Your Pocket: Paperback Urbanism and Public Intellect

Postwar efforts to organize urban expertise and center it in the university unfolded against the backdrop of new and emerging genres of urban writing that eschewed claims to expertise in favor of creative synthesis. These generalists helped render debates in urbanism visible and make them seem legitimate, urgent, and, to many, exciting. Soon, the city as an object of fascination and concern weighed on a vast reading public, who consumed marquee book-length analyses unencumbered by the parish boundaries of academic life.

This indisciplined turn was conditioned by postwar shifts in the publishing industry. By the 1950s, the major houses were intent on scaling up demand for paperback volumes in social science. Doubleday began its Anchor line of "quality paperbacks" under Jason Epstein in 1953, partly to furnish college students with affordable editions of assigned texts; Knopf and Random House began analogous lines the following year; Beacon Press and the New American Library also entered the paperback field, which was broadening beyond the fiction that Pocket Books, the American analogue to Penguin, had been offering cheaply since 1939.[2] Prices ranged from $0.65 to $1.25, with distribution on newsstands, at drugstores, at hotels, and in train stations. Typically, the first print run for such a paperback was between twenty thousand and thirty-seven thousand copies.[3] Nathan Glazer had coauthored the ubiquitous *The*

Lonely Crowd with David Riesman and Reuel Denney, and in its wake watched a market develop for non-academic social science. He spent two years as an editor at Anchor before decamping to the academy—becoming a sociologist by acclamation with no advanced degree to his name.[4] Meanwhile, Epstein became a particularly important broker of the new urban writing. His house put out *The Exploding Metropolis* (1958), a best-selling, pocket-sized collection assembled by *Fortune* magazine's William H. Whyte, and one of its essays, "Downtown Is for People," piqued public interest in its author, the Scranton-born Jane Jacobs. It was Epstein who courted Jacobs and cultivated her *Death and Life of Great American Cities* (1961)—for many readers, even in the twenty-first century, the first or only book on urbanism they would consume cover to cover.[5]

But Jacobs had not emerged ex nihilo. Since 1952, she had been well connected to circles that centered on the magazine *Architectural Forum*, first writing conventionally defined architectural criticism—treating buildings unto themselves—and then, in 1956, purposely broadening her remit to take in the urban scene in full.[6] The decade saw humanistic architectural criticism become a regular feature of several major newspapers, too. Frederick Gutheim stewarded the first regular column, in the *New York Herald–Tribune*, and by the early 1960s, he had joined the *Washington Post*.[7] Wolf von Eckardt assumed the *Post* position in 1963 and stayed on for eighteen years.[8] Also from 1963, Ada Louise Huxtable achieved broad visibility writing historically informed criticism for the *New York Times*, and she furthered the cause of preservation, especially as Penn Station's remains were consigned to unceremonious burial in the marshes of Secaucus. This was "a relatively new field in the popular press and a growing one," she wrote in 1970. "People have been looking at the environment, as environment, for only a very short time."[9] In columns for the *Louisville Courier-Journal* in Kentucky, an unlikely locale whose obscurity he relished, Grady Clay wagered that the reading public had a baseline curiosity about the city's physical build but that people still had to be taught to see what was right before their eyes, untethered to discipline or method.[10] For Clay, this was not only a question of aesthetic temperament, or morality, although it had those implications. Resistance to disciplinary specialty was a prerequisite for those looking to get an adequate grip on the urban future: "To see," he wrote, "is to believe in what is certain to come." Critics track changing fashions, emergent if short-term futures, in real time. For Clay, criticism was a mode of anticipation, and anticipation could not be precisely diagrammed, programmed, or taught.

These new varieties of urban commentary did not shun the academy entirely. Clay haunted Cambridge for a year (1960–1961) as a research associate of the Joint Center (see chapter 3). His best-loved book, *Close-Up: How to Read the American City* (1972)—an illustrated primer on curbstones, underpasses, off-ramps, brownfields, and other vernacular forms—was published by a university press.[11] Gutheim founded George Washington University's program in historic preservation. The unclassifiable Lewis Mumford, the postwar city's greatest pessimist, had never settled into a permanent academic life (or even finished college), but in the postwar era, he became a serial visitor to major universities: the Bemis Professor at MIT for three years, a popular teacher at Penn, and a visiting professor at Berkeley twice. Mumford was essentially an interwar cultural critic: his postwar fulminations on "sprawl" and the "formless" (because edgeless) metropolis were largely worked out by the 1920s, and *The City in History*—the other 1961 blockbuster on urbanism—which won him a National Book Award, was largely a rewrite of *The Culture of Cities* (1938).[12] His generalist architectural criticism for the 1930s *New Yorker* was of direct inspiration to Huxtable and her peers. If his assertions about the future—by turns, declensionist and triumphal—could seem untutored, Mumford knew enough about the disciplines to recommend blurring their lines. And the one academic field that canonized Mumford—American studies—accommodated some proudly catholic approaches to the built environment alongside the myth-and-symbol literary analyses that defined its first postwar generation.[13]

Crosscutting approaches to urban life also decorated the pages of the so-called little magazines, the preferred venues of the academy-adjacent, mostly Jewish New York Intellectuals whose literary and political criticism has commanded so much attention among historians. Sub rosa, these publications—*Partisan Review*, *Commentary*, *Dissent*—were replete with insights on the built environment. When it counted, the New York Intellectuals had quite a bit to say on the physical contours of New York and the forces unmaking it.[14] In 1961, *Dissent* brought out a number that departed "rather sharply from our usual kind of issue." "New York, N.Y." did not promise a comprehensive inventory of New York, much less seek to extrapolate to the city as ideal type. In the event, though, it brought together authors of many different competencies to illuminate urban life at a moment of metastatic growth and potential crisis. Profiles of public-housing tenants complemented exposés of "Real Estate Confidential," West Village "blight," and "Robert Moses: Glutton for Power." The celebrity socialist Michael Harrington reported from the streets of Harlem, while Eileen Diaz wrote "A Puerto Rican in New York." Robert Nichols contributed "The City: A Poem," while Irving Howe and Lionel Abel penned "remembrances" of a bygone age. Paul and Percival Goodman proposed banning cars from Manhattan and re-sorting city form on decentralist principles; Percival alone reflected on Lincoln Center, then rising atop the freshly cleared West Side whose story Leonard Bernstein set to song; Herbert Gans assessed how the Goodmans' 1947 treatise *Communitas* (just reissued in Vintage paperback) had affected the planning profession. The special issue was utterly of the moment, both responding to and stimulating a surfeit of discourse on urban change. And it sold: the initial print run of eight thousand was "so far our largest"—the final sales figure of fourteen thousand still the journal's best showing.[15] Lionel Trilling, whose preferred organ was the *Partisan Review*, wrote that the little magazines, which arose on the left in depths of the Depression, scored intellectual life an unimpeachable "victory" within the "larger circumstance of defeat."[16] Amid broad but unevenly shared affluence, not to mention a broad-gauge anti-intellectualism that of course persists in American life, big-tent assemblages of urban criticism seemed one way to renew that promise.

The most enduring experiment in indiscipline took root far from New York, closer to the dispossessed field of geography and with politics that were more difficult to decipher than *Dissent*'s. John Brinckerhoff (J. B.) Jackson, a motorcyclist and self-styled rancher with a transatlantic childhood and some aristocratic leanings, founded *Landscape* magazine, "a magazine of human geography," in 1951, as a vehicle for his own explorations of the northern New Mexico settlements to which he had moved.[17] *Landscape* quickly became a sui generis vessel for historical, speculative, and often entirely personal evocations of the vernacular landscape, urban and otherwise—*vernacular* referring to "the visible result of a confrontation between . . . aspirations . . . and the realities of the environment."[18] Jackson's own essays interpreted lawns, highway strips, billboards, gas stations, factories, and pueblos on equal footing, without the disdain most postwar intellectuals unleashed on environments that seemed either mass-produced or shambolically "primitive." Often under pseudonyms, he chipped away at the reigning Universal Style in architecture. Jackson developed friendly ties with Carl Sauer and the "Berkeley School" of cultural geography he helmed for the middle third of the twentieth century. Despite an aversion to academia's penchant for formal methodology, Jackson would often populate *Landscape*'s pages with the writings of Sauer's students: Yi-Fu Tuan, Wilbur Zelinsky, James Parsons, and many others. At his very last Berkeley seminar, in 1964, Sauer pointed to *Landscape* as one possible model of how to perpetuate "this matter of cultural geography" in public.[19] Although designs for geography's future as a fully integrative discipline had stumbled, perhaps Jackson's countermodel—always acentric, always idiosyncratic—might yet live. The feeling was mutual: "I am not a geographer," Jackson wrote later in the 1960s, but "it is a geographer's public that I most like."[20]

Along a path that only sometimes intersected the academy, a set of vernacular interdisciplinarities had cropped up. These shifts helped create a readership, a public, for new genres of informed but nonspecialist writing on urban affairs. Perhaps this was a geographer's public. But it was a public that came into focus only as that field and others in its midst became less distinct.

Recentering Rigor: Discipline and Interdiscipline in the 1950s

Urban studies, a composite field first named and propagated in the 1950s, emerged in the context of many other attempts to rethink the methods, mores, and optimal organization of social research. In the aftermath of the Second World War, the methods, utility, public orientation, and direction of every social-scientific discipline came under renewed examination. The interdisciplinary research center soon emerged as the main alternative to the traditionally defined academic department. A wave of new organized research units (ORUs)—some, with slightly different connotations, dubbed institutes, bureaus, programs, or, on a larger scale, schools—occasioned a large-scale restructuring of many American universities. Centers *decentralized* governance into a plurality of power bases, and they incited new forms of intramural competition for patronage and prestige. They split the difference between basic and applied research, disinterested projects and those commissioned by outside funders. The most pluralistic let these tendencies fight themselves to a perpetual draw, encouraging constituent scholars to ponder their mutual affordances across years of inconclusive seminar discussion.[21] Centers either overrode the inherited disciplines or concocted new ones in their own image.

The arrival of these problem- or topic-oriented centers was, in part, the artifact of a new regime of patronage. The National Institute of Mental Health and the Office of Naval Research also supported highly scientific social inquiry. While the National Science Foundation had, at its founding in 1950, excluded social research from eligibility, by 1957, it had cracked its door to allow "hard-core" renditions—quantitative, positivist, notionally value-free.[22] As this transpired, and as social science became an increasing focus of the major philanthropic foundations, scholars wagered, correctly, that some degree of demonstrable organization—coupled with adherence to the positivist orthodoxy that federal funders rewarded—would help them seem credible when petitioning for plentiful but inevitably finite dollars. For a "large portion of the educated public," the conceptual argot of systematic social inquiry constituted an increasingly "common sense."[23] But what commanded public respect, often as not, was social science's aura of rigor—of system as such. A fixation on method—or "methods," denoting prescribed techniques of inquiry rather than sustained reflection on epistemology—underwrote the rise of behavioralism in political science, quantitative "modeling" (a term seldom used before the war) in economics, sociology's "variables revolution," and the broader transdisciplinary fetish for hypothetico-deductive and causal reasoning.[24]

In part, the new rationality could be traced to the conduct of the war itself and to the strategic uses of social science approved within that context. In the Office of Strategic Services, the War Department's Research Division, and elsewhere, social science survived only insofar as it was trained on clearly defined objectives or problems. Wartime research was instrumental research. Instrumental research, the consensus held, was quantitative research. Quantitative research, in turn, was best done in teams. Collaborative, de facto interdisciplinary social science was expressly favored.[25] Samuel Stouffer's project *The American Soldier* (1949), which pioneered survey and "attitude scaling" techniques in order to assess serviceman morale, was its epitome.[26] In the move "from warfare to welfare," as Jennifer Light has phrased it, hard social scientists domesticated for peacetime a set of values that had been forged in conflict. This work was quintessentially *post*war, but it was also and always post*war*.[27]

Certain ORUs gained national visibility and became common organizational templates. The University of Michigan's Survey Research Center (established in 1946) was widely imitated. At Carnegie Mellon, from 1949, Herbert Simon helmed the Graduate School of Industrial Administration and polarized it toward basic research. Harvard's Russian Research Center was one of dozens advancing area studies, often with transparently anti-communist motives. The defense-oriented RAND (Research and Development) Corporation of Santa Monica, California, came together in 1946 outside the university system, although its mania for modeling remade the discipline of economics and helped seed departments of political science with game theorists.[28]

Certain universities, in turn, underwent unusually profound reinvention-by-center, and, as at RAND, the Cold War context is crucial. MIT was the one most transformed by postwar imperatives to organize research. By 1951, in its new School of Humanities and Social Sciences, a Center for International Studies (variably CIS or CENIS) began to formalize staged theories of "modernization" in the developing world, after W. W. Rostow, and to equip foreign interventions of a decidedly Cold War taint.[29] From 1957, on the heels of the Sputnik launch, MIT's president, James Killian, became the first official science advisor to the White House, and the university's linkages with military power grew only tighter through the 1960s. As Roger Geiger has written, much of this scholarship helped ratify "the simple faiths of the early 1960s." At home, this meant explaining and maintaining the "affluent society"; abroad, enforcing systems other than Communism.[30]

The ambient Cold War is a necessary ingredient in any account of postwar intellect. Even the classically liberal pretense of value-free knowledge, as Carl Schorske suggested in the 1990s, gathered steam as a way to preempt the McCarthyite aspersions then being cast on social science as just the newest form of sedition. And yet, casually invoking *the* Cold War is also insufficient to capture the complexity of postwar debates. There were only Cold War rationalities, not Cold War rationality in abstracto. "The existence of a currency," Paul Erickson has noted, "does not imply the existence of a central monetary authority."[31] The "ideology of basic research" seems to have been even more entrenched and consequential than anti-communism.[32] Postwar social science was a recombinant repertoire of methods and mores, not an articulated whole that rose or fell in unison.

Harvard also sprouted new centers, aided by the fact that each of its constituent schools was empowered to create its own set of research units.[33] The University of California, Berkeley, led in absolute number, among which a special fascination attended the Institute of International Relations, Bureau of Public Administration, and Survey Research Center. Clark Kerr, who coined *organized research unit*, directed the Institute of International Relations from 1945 to 1952—an experience that directly informed the model he would dub the "multiversity," both as campus-level chancellor and then, from 1958, as president of the statewide University of California system.[34] Instrumental in its remit and public in its intended audience, the multiversity—"a series of processes producing a series of results"—was the university of many centers.[35]

There were prewar precedents. Kerr himself called attention to Johns Hopkins, which from the 1870s had adopted a Germanic model that privileged graduate training and faculty research. The hybrid fields of public administration and industrial relations followed trajectories toward instrumental "organization" that began in the 1910s.[36] And yet the impulse to decenter and recenter the entire research university around these new trading zones was unique to the postwar moment.[37] When was a center genuinely central? What was a bureau, anyhow? (Did it court accusations of bureaucracy, that Weberian bugaboo?) Were programs necessarily programmatic in their work, and, if so, would that unity of purpose squelch academic freedom? Did schools actually specialize in schooling, and, if so, who were their ideal pupils? Much discussion swirled around these questions. Emotions ran high, and some of the most ardent advocates of the ORU model came from unexpected quarters. By 1957, the celebrity anthropologist Margaret Mead was calling for the construction of entire new cities—sited just outside existing ones—designed to host interdisciplinary conferences. These "small centers of research and practice" would draw from eclectic found models: the Mayo Clinic in peri-urban

Rochester, Minnesota; Harvard's Salzburg Seminars in American Studies; numerous research units already in place at Ann Arbor; the conference facilities at Cornell's Statler Hotel; Bread Loaf in Middlebury, Vermont; Yaddo in Saratoga Springs, New York; Arden House in Orange County, New York; the Pittsburgh Airport's dedicated meeting spaces; and still more.[38] That she rooted intellectual discourse in its geographic conditions is telling. Centers were spaces of exchange, both literally and figuratively.

In *Reforming the University* (1972), Sam Sieber reviewed the postwar track record, convinced that "a good theoretical contribution requires a larger team," and portrayed the new centers as having reintegrated universities that had been tending toward fragmentation—centers as saviors, redeemers of institutions in crisis.[39] Paul Lazarsfeld, the sociologist and longtime head of Columbia's Bureau of Applied Social Research (BASR), introduced Sieber's volume and took a more technocratic tack. His bureau had achieved "integration" only at the behest of a new sort of "marginal man" (Robert Park's term): the "managerial scholar." He (always a he) did the work of integration, holding forces in balance and titrating the center's different components to maximum effect. A new role in academic leadership had emerged. (Lazarsfeld had made a similar case in his 1962 presidential address to the American Sociological Association, as well as in a report that same year to the United Nations Educational, Scientific, and Cultural Organization.)[40] In principle, the recentering of the university promised the collapse of old hierarchies and a commitment to exploration and brokerage across the crumbled ramparts of the disciplines. In practice, new hierarchies took their place.

Some centers circled the wagons around a particular topic or theme; others derived their identity from a commitment to theory or method; still others functioned essentially as data-processing facilities for faculty who remained department-bound. Lazarsfeld's BASR was of the second kind: it posed social questions in only the broadest terms—"reasons for action," "effects of context"—and existed to quantify them. Much of its work could be assigned to the field of social psychology, but the same survey methods ended up powering studies of Puerto Rican migration, the John Birch–era radical right (by Daniel Bell), television coverage of the Kennedy assassination, the rise of mass audiences for media (by the exiled Theodor Adorno), and even one of Alan Lomax's forays into Americana and musicology.[41] At the University of Chicago, a panoply of centers coexisted with departments, but as faculty aligned with the new units, they often became estranged from colleagues who remained discipline-bound. Chicago's distinctive "experimental college," founded at midcentury by President Robert Maynard Hutchins to shore up a core curriculum amid specialization, recruited high-profile sociologists such as Bell, Riesman, and Lewis Coser but kept them penned off from the sociology department, which remained committed to the approaches promoted since the 1910s by Robert Park.[42]

At Harvard, social research underwent postwar realignments quite unlike the experiences at Columbia or Chicago.[43] In 1946, sociologists, psychologists, and anthropologists (but not economists or political scientists) aggregated into a new Department of Social Relations. This was indeed a department, not a center or bureau. It nonetheless belongs to the history of organized research units that includes Kerr, Lazarsfeld, and Cold War MIT. In designing "Soc Rel," Talcott Parsons, its figurehead, paid visits to shops including the BASR, the National Opinion Research Center in Denver, and Yale's Institute of Human Relations, which had interwar roots.[44] The leading entrepreneurs of interdisciplinarity were mobile, intellectually promiscuous, and hungry for examples to absorb and amalgamate, and the network of similar centers thrived on relentless cross-referencing. If, on his watch, the sociologist's fundamental quarry was the "common-value elements of systems of action"—never has a research agenda been more general—Parsons could argue that his seemingly impossible theoretical synthesis had already been "worked out on the organizational level." *Toward a General Theory of Action* (1951), Soc Rel's first collective statement, was the result of a specially convened 1949 conference on theory (and a prolonged visit by Edward Shils, always an outlier among Chicago sociologists). Synthesis seemed within reach.[45]

That comity, however, was short-lived. The preexisting fields chafed and once again diverged. Graduate students still entered a market that rewarded people who had been trained and made legible within disciplines. Even among the Harvard sociologists there was dissent, with George Homans's also-classic *The Human Group* (1950) advancing a program of inquiry based on disparate, carefully observed case studies rather than reasoning from first principles, and thus in contradiction with Parsons's party line.[46] By 1962, only Parsons and Gordon Allport, the psychologist of prejudice, remained from the original circle. In 1970, the department dissolved. If Soc Rel is paradigmatic of the ORU circuit, it also points up the challenges involved in constructing an interdisciplinary formation that blurred some boundaries but did so within the scope of a single department.

Similar stresses beset the field of geography. More so than sociology, its American fate affords insight into the ambiguities of discipline and department in the age of the center. It invites a narrative of erosion, dispersion, and (partial) supersession, all visited upon a field that might well have done some of the same work of integration that urban studies eventually took on.

Geography had a far smaller institutional foothold than did sociology, anthropology, history, political science, or economics. In 1945, only thirteen universities offered PhD degrees in geography.[47] Even so, since the nineteenth century, it had been common to hear geographers self-identify as the academy's great synthesizers. Lacking either methods (ethnography, archival work, statistics) or topics (cities, dwelling types, natural resources, agriculture, climate, and landforms) that were uniquely their own, geographers instead touted their field as the consummate interdiscipline. Committed only to a dimension of human existence—space—leading geographers such as Isaiah Bowman intoned that they alone could comprehend the relationships binding together disparate social and environmental phenomena. From Darwin forward, as David Livingstone has written, "the geographic experiment" set about to explain both nature and culture, environments found and made, within a single conceptual framework.[48] Human geography cleaved into more and less humanistic subfields, and due to an accident of history, the whole lot found themselves sharing stationery but precious little intellectual terrain with physical geographers—effectively geologists. Synthesis-as-vocation proved to be a weak rallying cry.

In the postwar era, this fragile status quo collapsed. Geography had been amply put to work in the war: mapping, field survey, and the still-young technologies of aerial photography were instrumentally valuable in combat. All were domesticated for peacetime use; all were perpetuated to some extent by the familiar patrons of Cold War social science.[49] Geography seemed well positioned to expand its institutional profile, not least given the rising interest in cities, which with the discipline's own "quantitative revolution" had elevated urban economic geography as a subfield, industrial production and distribution as topics, and neoclassical location theory—rebranded as "regional science"—as an outlook.[50] Then, in 1948, Harvard closed its department. The internal politics were complex, and they have become well established as disciplinary lore in a field that since the late twentieth century has been notably shame-faced about its own past. Bowman's personal contempt for the chairman Derwent Whittlesey's sexuality—and the initiative he took to intervene, even from his outside post at Johns Hopkins—was at least part of the calculus. But this bigotry intersected with a broader scientistic backlash against humanistic, historical, interpretive, or just descriptive geography as an intellectual pursuit. The "geographer's public" that J. B. Jackson envisioned was on the wane.[51] Paradoxically, the successes of applied wartime geography, viewed from within a world of only cold war, now called into question the field's legitimacy as a philosophically coherent, more-than-instrumental endeavor. The field's tentative unity, along with the compromised notion that a single department, rather than a new-style

ORU, could somehow fuse its components into a supradiscipline, finally broke down at Harvard.

Over the next forty years, most private universities and many publics followed Harvard's lead. They closed departments, reassigned faculty, and discontinued degree programs if a set of protean bureaus, institutes, committees, laboratories, and centers could achieve the same research quotient. Every Ivy League school but Dartmouth eventually dissolved its geography department. Penn's withered in the late 1950s under the leadership of economic geographer Lester Klimm.[52] Michigan's folded in 1982, a wrenching event for many in the Midwest, which had become a hotbed of precisely those quantitative approaches ascendant after the war.[53] (Its flat terrain, some thought, inclined scholars to distance-decay models and the Cartesian abstractions of central-place theory.) In 1986, with talk of restructuring afoot, the cultural geographer Marvin Mikesell wrote that he very much hoped his University of Chicago would arrive at something "better than unconditional surrender . . . a better-than-Michigan fate." Perhaps it did: in October of that year, Chicago's storied Department of Geography became the Committee on Geographical Studies.[54]

Elsewhere, the trajectory was more complex. Citing the war as a reason to expand capacity, Yale founded a proper department in 1945, having subsisted since 1919 on only one tenured geographer, the arch-determinist Ellsworth Huntington. The department dissolved in the 1970s, but not before enjoying a period of growth.[55] Cornell had offered degrees in the absence of a department. In the 1960s, noticing that "interest in Geography at Cornell is increasing," it organized a lecture series, blessed by the Association of American Geographers, to "illustrate" the field's "variety" and explore possible institutional forms.[56] Columbia had maintained an informal geography program but, as of 1965, awarded only two doctorates; interdisciplinary centers and studies programs dominated the scene, while card-carrying geographers were scattered across campus, including in the business school. A bona fide Department of Geography appeared in 1965, but it verged on becoming a service station for other faculty in need of customized maps or fitted spatial equations. The "smell of death" was perceptible by the late 1970s, and closure came in 1986.[57] Centers would suffice.

Thus, by the end of the 1950s, clear incentives were in place that favored interdisciplinarity as an ethos and organized research units as the vehicle for that ethos. In the abstract, the notion of interdisciplinarity was necessarily flexible—an incitement to debate, an open-ended license to reframe and reshuffle. To grasp the pacing and spacing of a changing world, its partisans believed, a nimbler, more adaptive intellectual kit of parts would be needed. New forms of knowledge required new forums, especially if they were concerned with objects, such as the city, that just would not stand still.

On New Foundations: Programming Urban Studies

The large philanthropic foundations—principally, Carnegie, Rockefeller, and, at length, Ford—were prime movers behind the ascent of the center model in social science and a new hybrid field, urban studies, to which many centers were oriented by 1960. They, not universities, proselytized hardest for new units of specifically urban research, anxiously scanning the nation's metastasizing urban regions and growing convinced that their inequalities, especially between newly built suburbs and freshly abandoned slums, would be ignored at society's peril. Ford, far more than any of its peers, worked to delimit urban studies and secured its place in the instrumental university. In the process, it consolidated the intellectual infrastructure that, later in the 1960s, would loudly diagnose a "crisis" developing at the heart of urban life and prescribe a range of programs and policies designed to stave off total collapse.

The imprint of Carnegie, Rockefeller, and Ford on the shifting postwar map of disciplines is indelible. Where there was a center or its equivalent, there was quite often a major foundation, only slightly off camera, keeping it solvent and setting some of its terms. Social Relations at Harvard entered its imperial period on the strength of a grant from the Carnegie Institution. The 1949 seminar series addressing "social action" was the Carnegie Project on Theory, designed so as to be compatible with the foundation's understanding of team research. In 1954, a major Ford grant came in; the Rockefeller and Field Foundations also supported the department before its closure.[58] BASR at Columbia relied integrally on Ford support beginning in the late 1950s. Lazarsfeld's first professional travel to the United States, in 1933, was on a Rockefeller grant—before it became clear that the rise of the Third Reich would obligate him to stay away indefinitely from his native Austria—and the purpose was to visit universities in search of models of effective cooperation among the disciplines.[59] Foundation-supported centers formed around area studies, American studies, survey research, economics, and assorted social science being pursued within new-look business schools. The foundations especially liked funding "small teams in large places." Indeed, some 48 percent of Carnegie–Rockefeller–Ford dollars flowed to units at Harvard, Columbia, or Chicago. Since the 1920s, Rockefeller had adhered to a policy by which its goal would be to "make the peaks higher."[60]

It is tempting to see the big foundations operating as an undifferentiated bloc, one consensus-governed system of patronage that together counterbalanced the federal programs (and, for five crucial years between the war's end and the establishment of the National Science Foundation, backed social science when federal funding had fallen off).[61] Yet the *social* is a broad, elastic category, and each foundation had its own distinct emphases and styles. Carnegie's giving focused on education, citizenship, American studies, and international relations. It dialed up its involvement in area studies in the late 1940s and was the key patron of Harvard's Russian Research Center.[62] Yet it did its giving with a light touch: as Parsons would reflect in 1967, Carnegie "does not operate any more than it feels is necessary" and often gave through other organizations such as the Social Science Research Council. Unlike at Ford, he felt, "catholicity . . . finesse and balance" defined Carnegie's permissive, unprogrammatic forays into "somewhat risky fields."[63] Amorphousness and improvisation, not a mania for "organization," were Carnegie's hallmarks: once the money had been allocated, said David Riesman, "very mild commissars," known for an "easy-going refusal to monitor" progress, made only periodic contact with scholars. *The Lonely Crowd* (1950) and Riesman's subsequent studies of American leisure benefited from this "free-wheeling spirit. . . . They're not worried, they're not anxious, they don't over-monitor their grantees. . . . They expect that between a grant and its fulfillment great changes and variations will of course occur." The foundation never signed on to a settled theory of interdisciplinarity. Rather, by acting as a "switchboard" among researchers, it helped enact interstitial work. It also led Carnegie to de-emphasize work concerned mainly with theory and method—Parsons very much notwithstanding. To Riesman's mind, this was in its way intellectually "subversive."[64] The disciplines would find other ways to get along.

The Rockefeller Foundation pursued slightly different pathways. It strongly favored institutions over individuals and displayed a clear preference for ORUs.[65] Yet *Rockefeller philanthropy*, the term of art, names a cluster of shifting and semi-autonomous programs. From its 1913 founding until 1921, public health was the near-exclusive focus. In the 1920s, under the youthful Beardsley Ruml, it was the Laura Spelman Rockefeller Memorial, not the foundation per se, that spearheaded work in social science. Large-scale reorganization in 1928 eventually created a Social Science Division coequal with those covering natural science, medical science, medical education, and the humanities.[66] Rockefeller money assisted interdisciplinary work at Harvard, Columbia, and especially Chicago—the latter university having enjoyed a special relationship with the family since its founding. Rockefeller established extra-academic bodies such as the Brookings Institution and the National Bureau of Economic Research, shaped the London School of Economics in the image of the American research university, and backed Yale's influential Institute of Human Relations. The Institute for Research in Social Science, founded in 1924 at the University of North Carolina by the regionalist Howard Odum, was the Laura Spelman Rockefeller Memorial's other major beneficiary and the leading example based outside the country's northeastern quadrant.[67] Ruml and his colleagues were somewhat skeptical of the academy for its habitual remove from civic engagement, and in personality they were less likely to inspire the devotionals to free inquiry and the appeal of "crazy millionaires" that Carnegie inspired in Riesman.[68]

By 1957, in one of the first sustained works of scholarship on American philanthropy—a literature whose very appearance testified to the new power of foundations in American life— the intellectual historian Merle Curti could assert that "the movement commonly referred to as urbanization" had become the leading topic for funded research.[69] Rockefeller was the first of the three to make serious postwar incursions into urban matters and give credence to Curti's claim. Its brief, potent engagement came closest to becoming an urbanist rendition of the Carnegie approach—freewheeling, miscellaneous, and conducted with a sense of fun. It supported this research through its Humanities Division, not as a subset of the social sciences, and its aim was not to funnel urbanists into new or existing ORUs. From 1952 to 1962, it backed a number of big books on urban form and life—big in ambition, explanatory scope, and, often, physical size. These appeared well into the 1960s as Studies in Urban Design: richly illustrated hardcovers such as the morphologically exacting *Man-Made America: Chaos or Control?* (1963) by Canadian landscape architect and Yale professor Christopher Tunnard, with Boris Pushkarev; *The American Landscape: A Critical View* (1965) by Ian Nairn, the British Jeremiah of "subtopian" sprawl, who drove ten thousand miles for the cause of research; and Philadelphia planning director Edmund Bacon's colorful, transnational *Design of Cities* (1967).[70] Together with the little magazines and the new urban criticism, these works helped further consolidate a public audience for idiosyncratic work on cities. Issued by a mixture of trade and university presses, these were humanistic inquiries, pretending to system and precision, perhaps, but attuned to aesthetics and the form of the built environment in a way that most postwar social science did not even attempt. Their authors were architects, architectural critics, and, in the case of Bacon, planners with an architectural orientation that was swiftly losing ground in academic planning departments.[71]

These works homed in on *urban design*, which named a cluster of new, ostensibly more humane attempts at comprehensive planning that arose amid mounting critiques of Modernism. The Congrès Internationaux d'Architecture Moderne (CIAM), the coordinating group that had brought Corbusian theorists together since 1928, held its last congress in 1956 and disbanded by the end of the decade. Harvard opened the first graduate degree program in urban design in 1960, and still others claimed the mantle of *environmental design*, which came to synthesize and augment the usual tripartite of architecture, landscape architecture, and planning.[72]

The new Harvard curriculum followed directly from four years' worth of exploratory Urban Design Conferences convened by the Rockefeller Foundation, attended by Jane Jacobs—whose *Death and Life* had been supported by that foundation—and many others named thus far in this book.[73] Yet the 1958 conference, organized by urbanists from Penn and held in tony Rye, New York, was not fixated on rethinking the academic division of labor: it convened a who's who of "urban design criticism," or "urbanism in journalism."[74] Whereas the lasting institutional legacy of the Urban Design Conferences resides in the academy, with departments, disciplines, degrees, and chairs renamed as testimony, their public impact was more readily apparent in the pages of newspapers, little magazines, other heterodox journals, and a broader archipelago of venues making intellect public. Together, the liberties afforded by these organs helped urbanists redraw or simply flout inherited boundaries.

Other works of foundation urbanism pursued the ideal of a humanistic social science without capitulating to placeless quantification for its own sake. The Twentieth Century Fund committed its money and name to Jean Gottmann's *Megalopolis: The Urbanized Northeastern Seaboard of the United States* (1961), a volume of nearly a thousand pages replete with maps but none of the photos that so defined the Rockefeller library.[75] Gottmann was a geographer by training, with significant ties to French regionalists such as Albert Demangeon, epigone of Paul Vidal de la Blache; Carl Sauer at Berkeley, where Gottmann was a visiting scholar in 1961; and Isaiah Bowman, his former chair at Hopkins, whom he attempted (following a chance encounter aboard a transatlantic ship) to dissuade from hastening the departmental closure at Harvard. Russian-born, Gottmann spent the 1950s and 1960s between France and the United States; in 1968, he decamped to Oxford. Throughout, his work was thoroughly embedded in the foundation world. Twentieth Century counted *Megalopolis* as its major urban coup: the book was much discussed, and its title entered the lexicon, even if most converts were disinclined to read every page. Rockefeller contributed funds—it was not uncommon for multiple foundations to cosponsor—and Gottmann would also tap the Mellon Foundation when preparing a regional survey of Virginia, the southern extreme of his 118-county conglomerate.[76] The foundations had come around to the city.

The decisive force in the reorganization of urban research, however, was the Ford Foundation, and its initiatives marked a clear departure from Rockefeller's acentric approach. In the academy, Rockefeller's footprint was urban design; Ford's, by contrast, was urban studies. These intersected less often than one might imagine, given the strong winds of interdisciplinarity then blowing. In 1950, the foundations' preferred approaches to urbanism were yet to be determined—forked between humanistic and scientific casts of mind, grants to individuals and institutions, and other binaries that simplify but were routinely invoked in period debates. A decade later, Ford had made its choice. The field of urban studies was central to its own reinvention during the 1950s, and in the Ford worldview, the habits of mind necessary to understand and administer changing cities were those of the social scientist, not the humanist. True, Ford allocated some money to support arts "of broad national significance." It made some room for avowedly humanistic scholarship, assisting the work of thirty-five university presses (with $2.7 million), the American Council of Learned Societies ($8.27 million), and the Humanities Center at Johns Hopkins, so crucial in importing "French theory" for the study of literature.[77] In general, though, Ford parted company with the example set by Rockefeller. By 1972, it would commit a total of $3.9 billion to 6,283 organizations and individuals in eighty-three countries and all fifty states.[78] Its endowment dwarfed Rockefeller's, and its campaign in the social sciences was so overwhelming that, by 1955, both Carnegie and Rockefeller decided to stand down, ceding those fields to Ford alone.[79]

The Ford Foundation had been in operation since 1936, but it was the death of the conservative Henry Ford Sr. in 1947 that made room for activism and experimentation. September 1950 saw trustee H. Rowan Gaither and a study team issue a very public document announcing that Ford would from then on "advance human welfare" in all its programs. The "Gaither Report" laid out an aggressive new agenda, public in orientation, interventionist in intent, and vigorously international in scope. ("A sacred text," the in-house historian would write.) Its stated "areas" were fivefold: irrespective of discipline, Ford would promote peace, democracy, economic growth, education, and, most unusually, the sciences of "individual behavior and human relations," a far cry from Rockefeller's loose, writerly urban agenda in every case. A veteran of MIT, RAND, and the National Defense Research Committee, Gaither served as the foundation's president from 1953 to 1956. Ford's ties to Cambridge ran deeper still. The physicist and MIT president Karl Compton joined the board in 1946. Donald K. David of Harvard Business School joined in 1948.[80] The list of Cambridge connections could be multiplied many times over. "Whatever the purpose," one historian wrote, "Harvard would most likely be judged the most effective vehicle."[81] MIT was a close second. This was the climate for organized research in which those two universities would form a Joint Center at decade's end. First, however, *urban studies* had to be defined.

The foundation's new orientation to the outside world was much discussed—the stuff of *New Yorker* cartoons and literate gossip. Paul G. Hoffman, the key figure directing implementation of the Marshall Plan in Europe after the war, was the first post–Gaither Report president, serving from 1950 to 1953 and expanding activity in area studies. Henry T. Heald assumed the presidency in 1956, after Gaither, and made official a shift beyond study and toward direct intervention in international affairs. Heald held the office until 1965, when it fell to McGeorge Bundy, another Harvard professor, one-time dean, and statesman. New grant programs and pronouncements tumbled out, one after another, in a cascade that both fascinated and bemused observers. Importantly, the foundation departed Pasadena in 1953 for New York—Hoffman had, for personal reasons, insisted they take root in Southern California—and from its Midtown perch (figure 1.1), Ford could directly liaise with, learn from, and encroach upon its peers.[82] Its "programmatic support of good men" accounted for 70 percent of the foundation dollars granted to social scientists between 1946 and 1958, and for 80 percent between 1954 and 1958.[83] Confine the data to the years beginning with 1956, and Ford's share would be greater still.

Ford's incursions into urban research built on organizational precedents it had established in encouraging other kinds of social science. During the early Gaither era, the Behavioral Sciences Program (BSP) had pride of place. This was the fifth area indicated in the Gaither Report, and the most outré by far. The BSP was explicitly theoretical where the other four were applied; its relation to human welfare could be difficult to intuit. Ford endowed numerous centers of behavioral sciences whose very existence would help make the case that such a field at least existed and might even have a unified logic of inquiry all its own—crosscutting psychology, sociology, and anthropology (but at first excluding political science, as had Parsons). (*Behavioral* could easily have been restated as *social*, but in 1951, enough officers felt that the latter term would connote socialism.)[84] Over the coming decade, mostly at Ford's urging, the behavioral sciences became something like an organized movement. While its essential content could be hard to define precisely, the BSP learned from the existing network of interdisciplinary experiments and fed its development in turn.[85] Parsons's unit secured funds, as did Lazarsfeld's—outcomes surely aided by the fact that the principals served on the BSP's advisory board,

FIGURE 1.1. The architect Kevin Roche affixes windowpanes to a scale model of his Ford Foundation headquarters, enclosing the vegetated atrium by the landscape architect Dan Kiley that won the building such renown from its opening in 1967. Courtesy of Kevin Roche John Dinkeloo and Associates.

alongside a social-scientific king's court that included Robert Merton, Edward Shils, Samuel Stouffer, Herbert Simon, the economists Kenneth Arrow and Kenneth Boulding, Harold Lasswell, and the MIT political scientists W. W. Rostow and Ithiel de Sola Pool. For Ford, the BSP was a theater and incubator of new templates for interdisciplinary social research.[86]

Tensions beset the program internally. Broad-gauge interdisciplinarity was not for everyone. Paul Hoffman admitted he "did not understand" what behavioral sciences were. Chicago's Robert Hutchins, a trustee, called the program "utter nonsense." Karl Compton, who "detested" Hutchins, finally ensured its survival through an appeal to Rowan Gaither.[87] As the 1950s elapsed, the program became steadily more instrumental and applied, and in 1957, it was abolished. Still, the BSP experience provides a critical prologue to the manner in which Ford, in the same decade, would plot its interventions on the conduct of urban research. It was through this program that Ford committed to the research center as the proper cradle and agent of interdisciplinarity, the organizational form best equipped to sense the interconnectedness of contemporary problems, assess their dynamics, and glimpse their future. Crucially, Ford not only rewarded existing centers but created them from scratch. Only a minority of twenty-first-century social scientists, if pressed, could give a precise definition of behavioral science, but the vast majority know Stanford's Center for Advanced Study in the Behavioral Sciences (CASBS), Ford's marquee example then and still its most enduring monument to six heady years.[88] These centers were largely autonomous entities—their quality control performed through gentle monitoring from New York and periodic bouts of foundation-funded "self-study."[89] For those intent on seeing things whole, urban problems seemed to hold the key.

Interdisciplinary urban research entered Ford's viewshed for good in 1954. The first grants came from within its Public Affairs Program; a dedicated Urban and Regional Program (URP) started up in 1955. In 1956, to much publicity, Ford suddenly made $500 million in grants directly to colleges, universities, and hospitals rather than to individual researchers or teams. A number of these addressed urban questions.[90] Soon, the foundation was eagerly planting centers of urban studies in universities. Each had broad latitude to select scholarly emphases, devise publication programs, allocate the block grant, hire and fire, pick battles in public life (or withdraw from them), and otherwise navigate the thickets of discipline and its aftermath.

Ford's urbanism hinged on making "attacks at strategic points"—so claimed *Metropolis* (1959), a public-facing brochure summarizing half a decade of activity. It led off with the words of H. G. Wells, for whom the American city (already by 1901) had "burst an intolerable envelope and splashed," and then paired Wells's contention with an aerial photograph of ostensibly "formless" sprawl, a visual genre ubiquitous in the late 1950s. The target of Ford's interventions was not only the city per se, but the "Great Urban Region," a complex agglomeration that, regrettably, tended to contain "several Not-So-Great Cities" spaced at semi-regular intervals. Ford's scalar vocabulary was not always consistent—city, metropolis, and (urbanized) region appear in oscillation—but persistent visions of disorder, of crises already present or just visible on the horizon, always haunted the URP agenda. The afflictions of both "slums" and suburbs would be channeled into "orderly growth," and the perpetuity of growth was never seriously put in question.[91] Urban knowledge in the new style would indirectly help redress these ills—and restore that elusive order.

Through it all, Ford's urbanists routinely spoke of *the urban problem* in the singular or *urban problems* in the plural. No consistent definition or comprehensive list ever emerged. Problems were easy enough to litanize, and Ford's culprits were not unusual choices for the time: congestion and sprawl, runaway population growth and inadequate means of distributing it (and resources, services, justice) equitably across space. Although their rhetoric could conjure an atmosphere of crisis, the so-called urban crisis, as object and preoccupation, would not define philanthropic or political discourse until the middle of the 1960s. In the 1950s, research posited a world of problems, soluble until further notice.[92]

Ford's emphasis shifted from project to project, brochure to brochure. At times, it seemed that urban form, or the seeming loss thereof at metropolitan scale, was their main topic, and orderly growth purely a physical matter. By 1962, Paul Ylvisaker, the URP's charismatic officer, was pondering opportunities for Ford to bankroll "experimental" building projects: "a major suburb or suburban ring, a regional airport complex, an education and research complex." In the Space Age, he noted, specialized "new cities are sprouting," but they need not "continue to take the sprawled happenstance form of Canaveral."[93] In a 1957 report, Ylvisaker seemed particularly galled by the "linear cities" developing unbroken between Boston and Norfolk, Los Angeles and San Francisco, Detroit and Toledo (a rather shorter distance), Cleveland and Pittsburgh. Their miscellany and mess were an affront, he wrote, foretelling societal decline in passages that could easily have come from the pen of Lewis Mumford. There were problems upon problems. And yet, the problem of the city somehow remained constant: "New York and New Delhi, Los Angeles and São Paulo, Boston and London," he wrote, "are basically alike."[94] The task for researchers was to organize "some systematic inquiries in the tradition of [Robert and Helen Lynd's] *Middletown*: microcosmic counterparts of [Hoover's] *Recent Social Trends*."[95] The essence of system, in other words, was to devise instruments that could bridge general and particular, finding glimpses of the former in the latter.

At mid-decade, Ford emphasized conducting finite projects, not setting up centers or other durable organizations. They distinguished three classes: "demonstration," "regional demonstration," and "specialized area" projects. Each was tied to a particular city and hinterland, and its scope was defined narrowly. In Boston, Kansas City, Peoria, and Dayton, Ford sponsored demonstrations whose outputs comprised a mixture of survey research, proposals for educational reform, and newly drafted city plans. Under this heading, the foundation also helped organize seminar series; the Boston College Citizens' Seminar, which began in July 1955, attracted notice. Regional demonstrations numbered only two. The six-county Southeastern Michigan Metropolitan Community Research Corporation convened scholars from four Detroit-area universities and readied them for fifteen years of continual study, while the cumbersomely named group Penjerdel (that is, Pennsylvania, [New] Jersey, and Delaware) attempted both the "face-lifting and lifting-by-the-bootstraps" of greater

Philadelphia—"the most Pecksniffian of American cities," Ford's unnamed copywriters added with evident relish—through a range of conferences, publications, and campaigns. "Specialized area" projects numbered a dozen by decade's end. They touched down in gargantuas on the order of New York, and in more thinly spread "clusters" or "tentacles" of development including the Carolina Piedmont and the Southern Appalachians, where a New York City–sized population of eight million people spanning "230 mountain counties" came under study, with Kentucky's Berea College the main institutional partner.[96]

The single-city project that most excited Ford's officers was the Metropolitan St. Louis Survey. It had its origins in 1953, when a reformist Washington University professor, Raymond Tucker, was elected mayor. By 1955, on Tucker's watch, talk of city–county consolidation was afoot in hopes of rejoining a notably fragmented, racially segregated, deeply unequal metropolitan region comprising 149 separate political units. A team of researchers from Washington and Saint Louis Universities, headed by political scientist John C. Bollens, approached Ford and proposed a "non-political, objective" study that would help inform the public as they decided the case. This initiative came about at the exact moment that the URP was emerging as its own entity in the interstices of Public Affairs. Urban questions were newly and vividly on the agenda, partly due to the 1954 passage of the second federal Housing Act, which had liberalized the terms of Urban Renewal, dramatically expanded the range of eligible projects, and enabled condemnation of large sections of St. Louis. In 1956, each university received $125,000 to proceed. The survey's progress was widely reported in the local press. More than a simple opinion poll, it set up a series of public conferences where the city–county issue saw fine-grained debate; it made a study of the region's universities, it assessed regional capacity for medical care, and, most modishly, it developed educational programming that ran on local television, "not to reorganize or remake the life of the community," but to teach.[97]

The outcome is simply stated: the researchers' August 1957 report recommended a new level of governance to be overseen by a fourteen-member Metropolitan Council, but that very month, a public referendum shot down the proposal. As a work of advocacy, the project failed. As an act of social science, and an entry in its intellectual history, it has a more complex afterlife. While consolidation fell, the project itself maintained broad public support. The mayor became convinced that it should serve as a prototype for other cities looking to inject social science into the routine conduct of politics, and evidence suggests that it indeed became a reference point. A number of large cities floated consolidation plans in 1957 and 1958—Miami and Toronto successfully, Cleveland not so—and in those debates, the names John Bollens, Henry Schmandt, Werner Hirsch, and Scott Greer (to say nothing of Paul Ylvisaker and Ford) were routinely heard in the halls of power. The foundation itself was oddly noncommittal as to whether the survey afforded a plausible prototype, microcosm, or model of the urban condition and how to study it. St. Louis, it stated, was "neither typical nor atypical of a large American city"; it was a "big city" in absolute size, "but most people [there] live real small-town lives." *The Ford Foundation and St. Louis* (1958), its executive summary of the project, was prepared only as "a way of cross-cutting the variety of Foundation activities" in urbanism to make them intelligible to the public "and pinning them down *by random choice* to a particular community." The imperative of "human welfare" was identical "whether carried out in St. Louis, Boston, New Delhi, or Beirut." And yet, for a few years, St. Louis seemed to be very nearly the city for the Ford Foundation. St. Louis figured in fully a third of its twenty "major programs." The city, readers learned, was far more than its prewar conjunction of "hot weather, cold beer, wild jazz, black slums, and purple sin."[98] It had become—Ford had made it—a laboratory of the urban future.

In mid-1957, the foundation expanded its remit and established university programs dedicated to training future urban planners and policy makers. It embarked on an eight-year program at the University of Pennsylvania's School of Design and endowed a rotating research professorship first occupied by Lewis Mumford. At Columbia, under the supervision of Wallace Sayre, a Ford program set out to train twenty-five to thirty new PhDs and postdocs versed in urban politics. "Until recently," asserted a 1960 Ford brochure titled *The Apprentice Experts*, "urban problems have been almost a no-man's-land in political science." To ensure New York's survival was not the program's reason for being, the foundation admitted, but that metropolis was a useful "laboratory" and any new knowledge on its workings would be a "valuable byproduct."[99] (Results were mixed: Ylvisaker wrote that, unlike in St. Louis, he saw "no 'sparks'" flying from Columbia.)[100]

The foundation's next venture was to develop urban extension programs, modeled quite explicitly on the agricultural field stations attached since the late nineteenth century to land-grant universities located well outside anything that could pass for a metropolis. As one North Jersey columnist wrote, the idea was "to do for the city what the Agricultural Experiment Station did for the tomato."[101] Rutgers's extension program, opened in 1959, was the occasion for William Caldwell's quip. The Universities of Delaware and Wisconsin–Madison rounded out the first crop. Programs opened also at Purdue, Illinois, Missouri, Berkeley, and Oklahoma—state universities all, and, per Ford's preference, situated in towns or cities no larger than two hundred thousand residents.[102] Also from 1959, across an eight-year program that very much respected existing disciplinary boundaries, Ford endowed six new university-based centers, various chairs, and entire courses of instruction that would expand the subfield of urban economics according to the latest theories and methods, especially Walter Isard's regional science. Its partner on this was the group Resources for the Future, founded in the 1950s at Ford's behest and for many years a producer of research at the intersections of economy, ecology, and planning.[103]

Into the 1960s, Ylvisaker grappled with the question of how to focus Ford's urban agenda intellectually. In warning of the intellectual mess that would ensue without a clearly defined plan of attack, he often drew analogies between the metropolis and the academy, both formless if left unchecked. "The hop–skip–jump technique of grant-making is . . . not attractive on a continuing basis," he wrote in a 1962 prospectus, in language that echoed critiques of "leapfrog" patterns of suburban development.[104] He contrasted the URP's "early sprawl of interests" to its now-explicit foci. During 1958, Ylvisaker rethought Ford's uses of the university. The Metropolitan St. Louis Survey had revealed the relationships that let the "whole community" cohere as a unit. Perhaps the university, too, was structured like a city; perhaps both were in crisis, both in need of renewal. Perhaps, he thought, centers of urban studies—which would impinge on the practice of planning but set it within a broader commitment to the methodologies of social science—could bring "the whole university" together.[105]

Ylvisaker was an outsized character. For many Americans attuned to the sector, he was "the heart and soul of organized philanthropy," its leading ombudsman above and beyond whatever particular projects were exciting him intellectually at the moment. He had come of age in Mankato, Minnesota, as the son of Norwegian immigrants, and made his name as a student of political economy, teaching briefly at Swarthmore and then working in the office of Joseph Clark, Philadelphia's pro-planning mayor in the age of Ed Bacon.[106] He also wrote and spoke prolifically on his work's guiding assumptions. "The mood of a philanthropoid"—an original coinage he used often—"oscillates between satisfaction and disappointment, between boldness and caution. Half of him wonders whether he has missed the big chances because of timidity, lack of imagination or skepticism; the other—and sophisticated half—keeps saying that the big ideas are rare, bad[,] or half-baked." This was as true of the URP as of Public Affairs or any other subdivision of Ford's empire. Ylvisaker was forthright, too, about the difficulty of evaluating all the work Ford was now backing. "Are we dealing with intractable realities where our effects, if any, will be measured with calipers, not yardsticks—over decades rather than in years?"[107] If the dynamics of urban change, rather than the statics of the city as an object, were primary, then some intellectual concern with urban temporality was inherent to the work. Change over time, moreover, would have to be studied over time, indefinitely, and as Ylvisaker came to this understanding in 1959, the center struck him as the organizational form best able to complete the pivot from commissioning one-off projects to institutionalizing programs of perpetual research—the better to keep time on the future metropolis as it emerged. Urban studies had found its form.

"Science Plus": Organized Urban Research and the Question of the Future

At first, Ylvisaker was ambivalent about the promise of these centers. In early 1958, he wrote to Dyke Brown that the future seemed to belong to more "area projects" on the order of the Metropolitan St. Louis Survey. As far as he knew, "advanced urban institutes" with their own autonomy and momentum "turn out to be little more than personal aspirations" on the part of their directors. Yet Walter Isard, along with Luther Gulick of Columbia's Institute of Public Administration, had lately made the case to him in a persuasive way, and the terrain had shifted: "now . . . the field is crackling with energy and diversified activity." Ford would be remiss not to harness that energy into new combinations. Although there were orthodoxies emerging with respect to method—Isard presided over one of them—Ylvisaker was loath to force researchers into a "prescribed form." More than a dozen years had passed since the war, and it was time to declare independence from its fully instrumental logics of inquiry. In establishing centers of urban studies, Ford's "first criterion is that their setting be one where there is readily available a full 'smorgasbord' of library and intellectual fare. The Harvard–MIT complex is clearly one such possible setting."[108] Beyond that, concrete requirements were few. By mid-1959, Ylvisaker was convinced that Ford's duty was to "restore the balance" upset by the positivistic National Science Foundation: establish at least six "model" centers and "give the social sciences a shot in the arm." "These softer sciences," he wrote, "have always been the poor relations in the academic family; and with Sputnik, they are being even further depressed." Again likening the university to a city, he promised uplift for the "slum-dwellers of the campus." This time, he meant it literally: at colleges and universities across America, students of the social world had gradually been consigned to obsolescent laboratory buildings that filtered down as Big Science moved on to eye-catching new facilities.[109] By the end of the year, Ford committed funds to the cause. "Model" centers of urban studies received $4.5 million between 1959 and 1966. A second series of grants, made between 1968 and 1970, disbursed $23 million to nine universities.[110]

With this, urban studies—by that name—fully entered the world of organized research toward which other social sciences had been moving for at least a decade. These centers were interdisciplinary, yes, but each became so in a different way. Theoretical advance and policy upshot, quantitative and qualitative lines of attack, and, residually, the ongoing territorial aggressions and cessions of the disciplines—different centers struck different balances, and not always without acrimony. The key oscillation, though, was between an orientation to the practice of planning—building, designing, or otherwise configuring physical space—and to the social science that would subtend, prepare the way for, justify, translate, and evaluate that work. As a field, urban studies set out to fuse the two. This was social research in, on, and for planning.

There were again prewar precedents that Ford and others drew on when working out the terms of the new organized urban research. Some were federal. Herbert Hoover had convened a Research Committee on Social Trends in 1929, and its 1933 report was widely read.[111] Roosevelt's New Deal had led to a superabundance of new social science. In urbanism, the National Resources Committee's compendium *Our Cities* (1937) best exemplified team research on a large scale. The National Resources Committee and the National Resources Planning Board persisted into the 1940s amid opposition from the right.[112] The Tennessee Valley Authority sponsored extensive research to vet prototypes for the housing it was building in its model New Town, Norris, and other riverine sites; the authority also maintained a Department of Regional Planning Studies from 1937 to 1941.[113]

Other precedents were university-based. At the University of Chicago, the political scientist Charles Merriam oversaw an array of research activities and in 1940 wrote one of the first English-language treatments naming urbanism—from *urbanisme*, the term of art for Francophone Modernist architects looking to scale up their practice beyond the stand-alone building—as an approach to knowledge.[114] The university lacked a department or school of planning, but even so, the implication was clear: social science should comment on and inform that practice. Harvard's School of City Planning, the first such, had secured Rockefeller funds and from 1929 officially added a research component to supplement its course of instruction. Its main organ of publicity was the Harvard City Planning Series, which published several classic monographs with the university press and achieved visibility during the New Deal. At Princeton, which also lacked a planning program, the Bureau of Urban Research opened in 1940 under the direction of Melville C. Branch Jr. and was productive until about 1945, when it was crowded out by the war effort.[115]

After the war but prior to Ford's interventions, centers proliferated with an orientation to planning and urbanism. This had become a populous region of the ORU world. By 1953, Robert Lillibridge, the chief land planner at the Chicago Land Clearance Commission, could register "major research activity" in progress at several dozen institutions. Since 1948, Columbia had hosted Leo Grebler's well-connected Institute for Urban Land Use and Housing Studies. Wisconsin had a respectable operation doing research in regional (though not mainly city) planning. The University of North Carolina's Department of City and Regional Planning now had a research wing, Odum's Institute for Research in Social Science touched on the city, and a new Institute for Government had joined the fray. At Chicago, a group called Social Science Studies counted Charles Merriam as a member, while urban research went ahead in the sociology and geography departments alike (with less interaction between them than some historians have assumed). With the neighborhood's "renewal" in the offing, the Chicago Community Inventory brought the university into closer contact with its South Side neighbors. MIT's own planning department had formally taken on a research orientation. Harvard had active research afoot in its Department of Regional Planning, School of Public Administration, Bureau for Research in Municipal Government, and elsewhere. "Special sections" focusing on urban topics existed at Cornell's Housing Research Center, Yale, Northwestern, New York University, American University, the Illinois Institute of Technology, the College of William and Mary, Ohio State University, and the Universities of Alabama, Oklahoma, Maryland, and Virginia. Lillibridge also noted "independent research institutes with professional staff," such as New York's enduring Regional Plan Association, the development-friendly Urban Land Institute, and the Social Science Research Council's Committee on Housing Research. Merriam, one of the council's framers, also managed the warren of public administration–focused agencies known as "1313," for its address on Chicago's East 60th Street. There were dozens of other examples, some of them explicitly keyed to urban topics, others supporting such work within a more general social-science frame.[116]

With so many nodes in the network, organized urban research was arguably disorganized in the aggregate. The 1950s struck Lillibridge as high time for the emergence of a "clearing house" that would "reduce duplication and achieve a coordination of effort." But the field, he felt, was less disorganized than urban America itself, which was riddled with the "maladjustments" these centers were "belatedly attempting to correct." Lillibridge sounded a note of melancholy about the efficacy of their research: "It is plain that what we have done has been too little and too late."[117] And yet, the essential belatedness of this work—its asymptotic creep toward solutions for problems that were themselves always growing in complexity and receding from experts' grasp—was its own motor and justification. There would always be more to know.

Philadelphia emerged as a particularly important node. The University of Pennsylvania opened its Department of City Planning in 1951 and made an earnest attempt to overtake Harvard and MIT as the profession's intellectual lodestar. To do so, the department constituted a semi-autonomous body, the Institute of Urban Studies (IUS), to execute empirical research on planning that, over time, would feed into and modify the department's working theory of planning. (Penn's well-established architecture program also made use of the IUS.) Robert Clair Mitchell and G. Holmes Perkins, the key administrators, were quite explicit about this division of labor, and in the case of Mitchell, the applicability of this research was self-evident: he sat on Philadelphia's planning commission.[118] Shortly thereafter, in 1954, a group known as ACTION (the American Council to Improve Our Neighborhoods) formed with funds from Ford's Public Affairs Program. Formally, it was based in New York, but it was directed for many years by Martin Meyerson, Penn faculty in planning since 1952 and a resonant voice in national debates. Its work of advocacy included a commitment to research. ACTION acted, but only upon the advice of social scientists. In an early agenda-setting memo, the planner Reginald Isaacs of Harvard took pains to distinguish the "functions of a research division," "relation of reference function of research division to action divisions," and so on. The group maintained a small library of planning literature and prepared technical manuals, up-to-date bibliographies, and summaries of breaking research that readers could seek out at the nearest university.[119]

These were the centers of activity that Paul Ylvisaker surveyed between 1955 and 1958. During that period, he also followed the progress of an upstart Study Group on Metropolitan Problems, national in scope, that involved many prominent figures—Isard, Merriam, Coleman Woodbury in Madison, MIT's John Tasker Howard—and eventually applied for Ford funding. In the summer of 1956, Ylvisaker conducted a tour of "representative cities" that struck him as ripe for study. Over the following academic year, he attended a two-day conference that the study group organized, and on the advice of Woodbury, he investigated a dozen universities with research infrastructure already in place—the better to assess where the URP might direct its next round of funding. The application from the Study Group on Metropolitan Problems was unsuccessful, but three years of acquaintance with its conversations had opened Ylvisaker's mind to a vibrant, varied, coherent (if loosely structured) network with broadly shared intentions and methods. "Is there common ground on which we can build an attack on the urban problem?" "What kind of expert or kinds of experts" are we producing? "Are we presently producing these experts in sufficient numbers?" Luther Gulick posed these questions to the 1956 conference, and by way of Ylvisaker's purse, they guided the next several years' worth of attempts to recenter urban research.[120]

From 1959, the label *urban studies* was further codified, and many new centers emerged, both directly through Ford and, as its work gained publicity, in imitation of the units to which it had already committed funds. Some stood at a remove from the system of higher education. The para-academic Washington Center for Metropolitan Studies began work in 1960 under the direction of the critic Frederick Gutheim. It had contact with the Urban Renewal Administration and the Housing and Home Financing Agency—precursors to the cabinet-level Department of Housing and Urban Development (HUD)—but was less obviously a policy shop than most groups based in the capital. It developed ties with George Washington University but was never subsumed within the school.[121] The New York–based Committee for Economic Development had existed since 1942, but in the Ylvisaker era, it undertook even more encompassing research projects dwelling on "area development" as such.[122] Resources for the Future bridged the academy and the public sphere, taking an urban turn under the leadership of Harvey Perloff and then Lowdon Wingo.[123]

Other centers, per Ylvisaker's preference, were housed securely within the university. The Institute for Urban and Regional Studies (IURS), at Washington University in St. Louis, exemplified the new type. In its early days, usually through a conference and often through a book based on the proceedings, a new center tended to issue some sort of collective, exceedingly general statement concerning the nature of the urban and how best to study it. In 1961 and 1962, the IURS ran a Faculty Seminar on Foundations of Urban Life and Form; the volume *Urban Life and Form* (1963) ensued. The collection was a command performance of interdisciplinarity. Werner Z. Hirsch, a veteran of the Metropolitan St. Louis Survey, presided over the volume, and while it emphasized built form to a greater extent than would come out of most centers aligning themselves with urban studies, its generality and ambition were very much of a piece with prevailing trends. *Form* was the conceptual totem, and, like *structure*, the word could describe entities made up of either animate or inanimate matter—bodies or bricks. Urban studies invoked these binaries even as it punctured them. The sociologist Leo Schnore addressed them in an entry informed by Chicago-style human ecology; the lawyer William Weismantel made a well-illustrated inquiry into how "word law" and "map law" should relate in a world governed by zoning codes; and Joseph Passonneau of Washington University's architecture school, drawing on the ideas of his colleague

Fumihiko Maki, made a lyrical plea for "open form" that, in the cities of an "open society" (after Karl Popper), would be able to accommodate "built-in change."[124] Indeed, wrote F. Stuart Chapin Jr., director of the University of North Carolina's new Urban Studies Program, without some attention to the two- and three-dimensional extent of "structure and form," urban studies would become "little more than a behavioral science specialty in public administration." Planning was perhaps a science, he wrote—a contention that dated at least as far back as the profession's consolidation during the Progressive Era—but by 1963, it had taken on "a 'science plus' aspect." Aesthetics had a place. Both there and in the political realm, Chapin argued in the volume's closing statement, the task was not only to observe forms of life, but to modify them. A "sixth sense" for those governing and designing cities, planning required an analytic "vision of the city in the round," but also, and inseparably, "a sense of timing, a knack for picking the right moment in time to act."[125]

What was the urban? What distinguished a studies orientation from other methodological credos? In real time, David Popenoe of Rutgers took an interest in the rollout of urban studies and in the center as its organizational vehicle. In a trio of articles (1963, 1969, 1971), he puzzled over these conundrums. Centers had enacted various answers, but without resolving the questions in the abstract. Centers, he wrote in 1963 with Robert Gutman, were "concerned more than incidentally with the term 'urban.'" They, by definition, had at least some interest in urban theory, even if their day-to-day business consisted mainly of dry empirics. *Urban* seemed to have a force of its own: as Ylvisaker had imagined, the term had, in fact, oriented "heretofore unrelated academic approaches toward a common goal." The work of interdisciplinary brokerage hinged on positing a common object around which scholarly collaborations could take shape.[126] Perhaps. But *studies*, its counterpart, was a devilishly open-ended term. It presumed a mixture of political attachment and scholarly detachment, Popenoe wrote in 1969. It also connoted an interest in "Modern Society" more readily than did the traditional -ologies and -ographies.[127] Just how to relate the city's past, present, and emergent—but necessarily unknown—future was a question that urbanists would mull, inconclusively, for many years. In an era of unremitting socio-spatial change in the American city, organized research compelled increasingly intense reflection on the very temporality of that change—its pace, direction, rhythm—with results that often unsettled its captains. What, after all, did it mean to be expert on urban lives and forms that did not yet exist?

So far, the narrative has steered wide of the most influential pre-1959 attempt to bridge urbanism and social research. No longer. From 1947 to 1956, the

University of Chicago maintained a short-lived planning program that was the first to be housed outside an architecture school. Despite suggestions that they partner with the Modernist phalanx then active at the nearby Illinois Institute of Technology, its directors noted a "deep cognitive division" with the design professions and found a home in their own university's Division of Social Sciences.[128] The interdisciplinary Program for Education and Research in Planning (PERP) came first under the direction of Rexford Tugwell, the heterodox economist whose top-down leadership of the Resettlement Administration—responsible for the three Greenbelt towns built during the New Deal—had won him notoriety and a subsequent job as governor of Puerto Rico. PERP's ranks drew in sociologists, economists, political scientists, geographers, scholars of public administration, and some faculty who had trained in city or regional planning, such as a post-Princeton Melville Branch and a pre-Penn Martin Meyerson. Among its organizational models was Johns Hopkins, which early in the century had adopted the policy that the training of medical doctors had to occur within an environment oriented also, and always, to research.[129] From 1951, leadership passed to Harvey Perloff, and the intellectual focus narrowed somewhat. PERP increasingly converged on the notion that planning was at root a style of rational decision-making about policies of all sorts, urban or not. Land use itself became more and more peripheral—the bailiwick of "physical planning" approaches (phrased this way, a new distinction) that now met with scorn.[130]

PERP's self-appointed agenda was to carry out research on the planning process—to adumbrate it with precise data and empirically supported theories at the Mertonian middle range of abstraction. Its unifying interests, wrote Perloff in *Education for Planning* (1957)—a book looking back on the program's nine years just after Chauncy Harris, the dean of social sciences and an urban geographer himself, closed it down amid budgetary strain—were in planning theory (also a new designation at this time) and "planning-in-general." Neither one dealt with maps or elevations, or with buildings, roads, or rails as its raw materials. And neither, Perloff felt, was adequately perpetuated in the program's wake, even as its faculty and trainees dispersed throughout the country: Meyerson to Penn and then, in 1957, to Harvard; John Friedmann, its first PhD, to advisory work in Latin America and then, in 1961, to MIT; Perloff to Resources for the Future and eventually UCLA; and still others to Penn's research-minded IUS.[131] Ford's late-1950s turn toward university-based centers of urban studies can be understood, in part, as an attempt to rehabilitate PERP's vision, with a difference.

This nine-year period at Chicago cast long shadows. If PERP eschewed grand theories of urban form, it still had a tendency to issue pronouncements on the nature of planning, of research, of science, and, indeed, of knowledge itself. Its scholarly output was plentiful, comprising a set of programmatic articles and a few key books, and a great number of them operated at this second order of abstraction. As other university planning departments remade themselves on the model of the social sciences, ex cathedra statements from Chicago were taken seriously as rules of thumb. "Planning... is not a science," Tugwell wrote in a 1948 article. "But the *study* of planning may be scientific."[132] For PERP, this was the first crucial distinction to uphold. Planning itself had inarguably emerged from the design disciplines, Martin Meyerson wrote in a 1954 article, but planning research had not. The latter offered the more fundamental truth. "To make planning decisions effectively," he continued, "requires vastly more knowledge and vastly more accurate knowledge about a huge variety of factors." Researchers would thus commit to building a "fact inventory." Planners would tap that inventory, submitting their own decision-making to perpetual examination.[133] In a 1946 address titled "What a Planner Has to Know," Meyerson was more insistent still: the proper approach would advance "a kind of wisdom by which to distinguish the expert from the quack, and the better from the worse expert."[134] Meyerson further developed these insights on planning and/as knowledge in the influential monograph *Planning, Politics, and the Public Interest* (1955), written with the Chicago political scientist Edward Banfield. Perhaps total rationality was never attainable, they argued, but practitioners could still work in ways that erred on the side of more research and more reflection, rather than less. Of the warring interests seeking to decide where in Chicago public housing would (and would not) be located—the authors' central case study, shot through with a racial animus they only began to explore—Meyerson and Banfield were blunt: "No one knew." There was "no real evidence" to draw on.[135] In practice, planning was not yet a way of knowing. In theory, it could be.

Second, the PERP conclave also repeatedly took pains to define their key term, *planning*—not only how it should be done, but what, if anything, it really was. Banfield was the first to admit that the word had a "bewildering variety of meanings." Socialists planned; economists planned; engineers planned; the followers of Frederick Winslow Taylor streamlining production on factory floors were undoubtedly engaged in planning, too. City planning had its own history; regional planning overlapped it, but not entirely. (And what was a region, anyhow?)[136] *Planning* was a "generic term," Perloff admitted. It named many different ways of "trying to see things whole."[137] It did not, however, name a thing. If decision-making took precedence over design (and even if it did not), then planning was a process. In a 1950 article, "Coordinative Planning and the Architect," Melville Branch, the PERP faculty member best versed in visual analysis, invoked Alfred North Whitehead to emphasize this point: whereas architects imagine "static, three-dimensional form," planners know that "the process itself is the actuality." "Dynamic . . . forces" have to be planners' targets, he counseled, and they "are not less vital because they cannot be seen and touched as directly" as, say, a concrete façade.[138] An orientation to process became basic to PERP's oeuvre. Planning takes time. "One of the characteristics of a good plan," Meyerson wrote, "is that it could not conceivably be realized in its entirety the morning after it is produced."[139] Planning research had its own temporality; planning knowledge was a knowledge of process. And, wrote Meyerson in "Building the Middle-Range Bridge to Comprehensive Planning" (1956)—a classic, difference-splitting statement of theory—this was a knowledge that required continual self-correction. "Perpetually scan the community," he instructed his readers, "for indications of maladjustment" between program and reality.[140] Then research some more.

Third, and most critically, for the Chicagoans, planning was not simply process-oriented; it was future-oriented. To be sure, wrote Branch in 1950, "comprehensive" planning had its synchronic dimension: "seeing things whole," integrating disparate places and parts, brokering peace among the disciplines, and so forth. "All planning involves multiple components." But its diachronic dimension was the decisive one: "Planning, of course, is projectional in nature." If planning entailed its own genre of knowledge, it was knowledge about the future. Planners needed, in a sense, to be theorists of temporality; at the least, they needed to retain such people on staff. The interesting questions then became how to exercise foresight, what kind of object *the future* was, and what degree of certainty this work would ultimately yield. Branch mused, inconclusively, on planning's resonances with a variety of other probabilistic fields: weather forecasting, actuarial science, population projections, and more.[141]

Planning as futuring—this was an ontological question, but, as Tugwell himself had been pointing out since the 1930s, that ontology entailed political commitments all its own. In a widely read essay of 1939, he called for a new government agency to assume "directive power" over a wide range of affairs. His locution cut two ways: planners, as he understood them, would "point out" the direction in which things were currently heading, and they would also give direction, new direction, to those tendencies. "The Fourth Power," designed to augment the existing three branches of government, was defined by its "persistent orientation to the future, a future discovered by charting the trends of the past through the present." "A power is needed," Tugwell wrote, "which is longer-run, wider-minded, differently allied": planning had, respectively, a temporal horizon, a spatial scope, and an essentially political bent.[142]

Tugwell wrote from the left, without apology, but midcentury shifts soon inculcated the will to plan at various levels of government—and according to political logics totally inimical to the man conservatives branded "Rex the Red." Outlook studies became common in the 1920s, as did economic forecasting by that name, at the Rockefeller-backed National Bureau of Economic Research and elsewhere.[143] Then, in the postwar moment, as Timothy Mitchell has written, "the future entered government" on another scale entirely.[144] Following the Employment Act of 1946—which codified a federal role in ensuring labor and price stability—and sustained by the new Council of Economic Advisors and its annual statistical reports, "governmental institutions for discovering and objectifying the future" entered the (Keynesian) American state at its very heart. So wrote Tugwell and Banfield in 1951.[145] Planning was a matter of knowledge and intellect, theoretically motivated while data-rich. It was also a profession with its own codes of conduct and a history one could embrace or disavow. It also, however, proposed a politics of—a power over—the future. As Chicago's short-lived experiment made clear, postwar urbanism would be transacted in a new tense.

Tense, indeed, became a central conceptual issue for urbanists in the years after PERP's disestablishment. The temporal demarcations of past, present, and future themselves seemed to be in flux, entering and leaving new operational relationships according to the demands of the day. In their writing, planners and the social researchers in their service began creatively shuttling among the tenses in order to shed light on the nature of urban change. Paul Ylvisaker was a key rhetorician in this regard. Ylvisaker relished a clever turn of phrase, and by 1957—before Rodwin had cause to conceive the Tamiment conference—he often dwelled on the coming of "the future metropolis." In an address titled "The Brave New Urban World" (1961), he picked up where PERP had left off. "Planning is politics," he wrote, "but it is even more than that. Politics has the job of reconciling the known past with the known present; planning has to make both the past and present compatible with an unknown future. If politics is the art of the possible, planning comes close to being the art of the impossible."[146] The complex relation of the tenses, not the mere assertion of some future state, was top of mind. In "Conscience and the Community" (1964), Ylvisaker's theory of planning's temporality developed further still, keyed to a postwar world in which the onrush of novelty was the overwhelming fact and challenge: "The new community we live in has no precedents . . . and [yet] its future is so immediately caught up in its past and present that we don't know what tenses to use when describing it—except we do know that whatever the time, it's imperfect."[147] In a scholarly article, "Innovation and Evolution: Bridge to the Future Metropolis" (1957), his approach was even more experimental. He addressed contemporary America as if looking back from the year 1980: "The tenses used are the simple present and past of an obscure future as a contemporary historian might one day write them." Ylvisaker's stance, he clarified, was the paradoxical one of "projection . . . in the guise of retrospect." And what did his notional historian discern about 1957? That its denizens were looking ahead: "In or around 1957 . . . Americans became aware of the city. Really aware of it in the sense that they finally accepted the fact that life in an urban environment would be their permanent destiny."[148] Surely the time was (or had been?) right to unleash systematic inquiry into these questions.

Sometimes Ylvisaker's reshufflings of urban tense worked in the service of observations that were banal—musings on modernity as speed-up and not much more. Writing for an audience of broadcasters in 1964, he asserted, "Time in our generation is moving so fast that the present is fifty percent future" (a line he reused the next year in "Quality of Life in 1980," yet another attempt at projection). "Someone" on the cutting edge, he winked to the media men, "has to help keep future time."[149] He pressed similar points at a 1961 New School conference, "The Shape of the Future: Urban Life."[150] Clichés, however, can be diagnostic. Their perpetuation depends on the existence of an audience that is receptive or at least tolerant. By 1957, solidly by 1961, and still to some extent in 1965, many Americans, interested in the future metropolis but unsure of the forces hastening its arrival, processed that uncertainty in ways that called attention to futurity itself and, to manage the unknowable, tried to explain it in terms of present and past.

Theoretical ingenuity, however, was only part of it. These expert urbanists thought across the tenses in order to compel action on the future, which, strictly speaking, meant action in the present. Perloff made this claim in his own mild way: "The setting up of a vision or image of a future state of affairs," whether via linear regressions or artists' renderings, "in practical terms can serve as a 'pulling' force in the making of policy."[151] Tugwell put it more dramatically: a plan is "not a prediction" languishing arbitrarily on some distant horizon, but "a successfully functioning Gestalt in the present." "Present conjuncture," he continued, "is the *result* of projection into that future." The future, in other words, has to be primary; it both precedes and inhabits the present, drawing it out, infusing it with force and urgency. (This could all sound jarringly abstract—it echoed classic Heideggerian themes on the authentic finitude of life as a being-toward-death—and Tugwell was indeed prepared to work from ontological first principles. Planners, he wrote, are always "joining" elements "into a time–space–volume whole.")[152] In turn, as Ylvisaker and many others pointed out, this collapse of the future into the present defined planning's most basic political temporality. To compel action that would realize desired futures and stave off unacceptable alternatives, the task was to "confront the community today with its emerging tomorrow."[153]

Both in circles that called themselves expert and those with a more glancing relationship to the research apparatus built up since the war, talk of the future metropolis (and variants on that phrase) was widespread. Despite this chapter's focus on the country's northeastern quadrant, the network it has sketched did reach the shores of the Pacific, where in 1963 a Conference on the Metropolitan Future, held at the University of California, Berkeley, brought together dozens of its most vocal members. A partial roll call would include Ed Bacon of Philadelphia, James Rouse of Baltimore, Meyerson, Hirsch, Perloff, Branch, Grebler, and Greer. (Berkeley had opened its Institute for Urban and Regional Development the previous year under the direction of Penn veteran William Wheaton, and the Institute for Governmental Studies, formerly the Bureau of Public Administration, had been working on urban topics since the chancellorship of Clark Kerr.) Although discussion ranged far afield, the official topic was California's own future: the state had just become the nation's most populous, with no end in sight to its low-density urbanization, and the governor had convened a series of meetings in order to look ahead systematically. Ford Foundation dollars supported the conference, chaired by the versatile "houser" Catherine Bauer Wurster, a seasoned regionalist and, it must be said, one of the few women occupying positions of prominence in this overwhelmingly male intellectual network. Kerr introduced the conference, expressing confidence that, in matters of the future, "he"—"Man"—"has the power to control it." Optimism ran high, both about future outcomes and about the organizational model that the conference itself exemplified. Martin Meyerson exulted that the interdisciplinary crowd in attendance had "already made the bridge of understanding" that the best ORUs advanced and the past generation of funders and administrators, himself included, had set out to build.[154]

Yet the shape of this metropolitan future was anything but certain. In order to sound a warning, one participant reshuffled urban tense in ways legible to Ylvisaker and his milieu. Earl Warren, a former governor and current Chief Justice of the Supreme Court of the United States, had returned to California for the occasion. He, too, professed anxiety about California's heedless sprawl and the specter of "one [unbroken] mass of people from Crescent City to San Diego." His next move was the critical one. Dystopian images of a formless future led him not to nominate a utopian future in its place, but rather to burrow into the deepest recesses of the past in search of lessons. As

Warren told the assembled audience, he had toured ancient cities in Mesopotamia, Egypt, and Greece—all of them reduced to ruin. They were "victims of strangulation," and he traced their fate to one specific cause: "they grew without regard to the problems of the future."[155]

Now, a kind of expert had determined, the task was to find other, better ways of thinking ahead. How to conceptualize the urban and metropolitan horizon in light of history but without simply projecting observed trends forward, unchanged? How to anticipate, or anyhow accommodate, ruptures, divagations, and swerves? How to plan for them? How to know the future to a satisfactory degree, and with what methods? Such were the stakes of postwar urbanism. Such were its politics of time. This was the terrain on which years of rich, conflicted debate went ahead, and it was never too soon to ask these questions.

CHAPTER 2

The Atmosphere and the Network
Organizing Expertise at the Joint Center for Urban Studies

From its founding in 1959, the Harvard–MIT Joint Center for Urban Studies became the crucial node in the emergent network of expert and organized research on cities. The Joint Center took shape within that milieu and in so many ways bore its stamp. The group's main funder, until 1970, was the Ford Foundation, who charged it, foremost among its urban centers, with "the building up of intellectual resources and capital" that might then circulate beyond New England and model the forms of scholarly coordination appropriate to the next decade of urban change.[1] Affiliated faculty enthusiastically spoke the language of interdisciplinarity, and they tried to split the difference on virtually every major binary into which the urbanist establishment was so often riven: disciplinary persistence and a robust generalism, social science and humanistic commitments, academic agenda-setting and an unabashed public profile, theory and practice, basic and applied research, quantitative and qualitative methods. It arose in context, but, more than any other unit of its kind, once constituted it became a broker, a relay, and a transformer of intellectual currents both established and inchoate. It is not enough to say that the Joint Center legibly reflects, expresses, or otherwise encapsulates the network. Rather, the center was critical infrastructure: it kept the network in working order, maintained its circuits of exchange, and remade urban expertise in its image.[2]

The Joint Center worked steadily to broadcast the arrival of a new and distinctive brand of urban research. Its seal, formed of two interlocking puzzle

FIGURE 2.1. Official seal of the Joint Center for Urban Studies. It depicts two puzzle pieces interlocking: Harvard and MIT, social science and physical planning, and other binaries purportedly folded together by the jointure. This logo appeared on the majority of the center's publications and correspondence, beginning in 1959. Courtesy of Joint Center for Housing Studies, Harvard University.

pieces representing the two universities (figure 2.1), was recognizable on the spines of its book series, on stationery and business cards, and on dozens of published reports, some widely consulted in the making of urban policy. In the substance of its work, by contrast, the Joint Center was a good deal more miscellaneous than its peers: Chicago's PERP with its narrowly procedural theories of the planning process and the authority of social science, Penn's IUS with its orientation to the practice of redevelopment, and other shops that had elected to specialize in economic modeling, survey research, or another methodological sliver of hard social science. Precisely in its malleability, its arguable lack of central tendency, the Joint Center becomes an effective index of broader intellectual and political shifts that remade the United States between the 1950s and the 1970s. The story of the Joint Center very nearly is the story of postwar urbanism.

"Urban problems," the Joint Center announced, had, paradoxically, arisen amid prosperity, "unleashed by increasing income, technological innovations, and rising expectations." Prosperity had set less privileged populations on the move. African Americans and "the poorer white population from rural regions" had remade the cities of the Northeast, Midwest, and West—disproportionately "the" American city said to be under study—and a host of "tensions," they wrote, had followed in turn. Many midcentury research centers invoked *problems* to justify their own efforts. Most kept the term nebulous or shrouded in euphemism, but the Joint Center was prepared to enumerate: their work addressed, among other issues, the widening gaps in urban transportation systems, the "decline" of central business districts, the "rise" of suburbs, the political economy of what would soon be called deindustrialization, the attendant demographic shifts and strains—signally along lines of race and class—and the "cold war carried on by local governments within metropolitan areas" over tax base and service provision.[3] In a metropolitan age, they sensed, the city, conventionally defined, was losing its form. Or was it that new technologies were bringing greater regimentation, thereby tamping down the drift and informality that make urban life what it is? These were substantially the same concerns that had motivated the foundations to ramp up support for urban research in the first place. Problems required research; research required problems.

"If interdependent people create interlinked problems," the center's leadership wrote to Ford in 1965, then "perhaps interdisciplinary scholarship is a prerequisite for effective action." The Joint Center was more explicit than any of its counterparts in advancing this claim—that the complexity of the urban, as an object of knowledge, had to call forth a new complexity in the intellectual division of labor. "The function of a center is to serve both as a partner of and as a gadfly on the traditional academic departments."[4] Beyond that, the group's remit was almost entirely elastic, defined as much by the personalities and agendas of its constituent faculty as by any statement of purpose they might turn out in order to maintain foundation support. Interdisciplinarity meant different things in different places. A close-range historical engagement with one center, in one place, is necessary to add precision to the generalist grandiloquence that marked so much of postwar intellectual life.[5]

Some of the center's work touched down in the neighborhoods of greater Boston. This was not the Ford Foundation's first contact with New England. It had seeded research in and on Boston in the early days of its Urban and Regional Program—and had promptly mocked the city as "our historic fortress," wrapped around a pre-industrial warren of streets first laid out to follow cow paths and now absolutely hostile to automobiles, "which, their harassed drivers remark, make about the same speed as their bovine predecessors." On the downtown, Ford deferred to the words of John Hynes, Boston's mayor: "a strait jacket from which even a modern Houdini would have difficulty extricating himself."[6] And this was to say nothing of the Hub's ossified social order or—MIT's scientific frontiersmen aside—its lordly intellectual life that often chafed against the priorities of organized research. Boston, among large American cities, seemed uniquely old, uniquely obsolescent—which made it a very peculiar laboratory in which to hatch visions of the future.

If the goal was to comprehend urban life in full, in practice, those efforts proved fragmentary. The case of the Joint Center, located at the very heart of the postwar establishment in organized research, affords unique perspective on the instabilities and tensions that forever beset this style of expertise. It exposes spirited postwar debates over how to know, and how much could be known about, urbanization—and what it would take for information about cities, in the plural, to adumbrate an account of the city as a recurring form of human settlement.

"Interlinked Problems": Improvising a Jointure, 1951–1959

By 1951, MIT had a full-fledged planning department and a president, James T. Killian, who was keen on regrouping faculty research on the center model. Standalone urbanists worked away in a variety of departmental contexts: the School of Architecture and Planning partook of the Modernism that was cresting in the profession, given new sanction under Urban Renewal, and the year-old School of Humanities and Social Sciences happened to be under the direction of a broadly trained architectural historian, John Burchard, who was eager to link specialists into larger interdisciplinary colloquies.[7] In June of that year, a group began meeting as the Committee on Urban and Regional Studies (CURS), with Lawrence B. Anderson, chair of architecture, leading the discussions. Lloyd Rodwin and Kevin Lynch, young faculty members in planning, both participated, forming part of a shifting cast that included Burnham Kelly, John T. Howard, Catherine Bauer, and others. It was the age of the ORU, and that they might "consider establishing a center" was all but assumed. A center would "enlarge" the work of the Department of City and Regional Planning, the CURS held, and "build bridges" with the social and otherwise human sciences.[8] How to achieve center status was less clear, and the question was tabled.

In October 1952, some sixteen months later, "it was emphatically agreed that there [still] should be no formal organization at this time." The committee clearly enjoyed ruminating on organizational form, its possibilities, and its pitfalls.⁹ Rather than using the committee primarily as a vehicle to share members' work, or to divine the common methodologies underpinning their diverse research agendas, for the first two years, CURS dedicated considerable time to matters of organization—of the center as a distinct mode of inquiry—collecting extant examples from farther afield that might illuminate their path. Leo Grebler's Institute for Urban Land Use and Housing Studies at Columbia met with praise, not least for the cross-campus linkages it had forged with Paul Lazarsfeld.[10] Walter Isard, based at Harvard less than two miles to the west, had begun collaboration with the RAND Corporation, and this, too, appealed to the committee as one potential model of extramural engagement.[11] Some working models had emerged from outside the university system, most especially in New York, where the Regional Plan Association had issued the massive, multivolume, and substantially implemented *Regional Plan of New York and Environs* (RPNY) in 1929.[12] Rexford Tugwell remarked in one of his PERP-era essays that the RPNY "has . . . never been allowed to die," and indeed, Rodwin observed that it provided a model for all further attempts to blend a "research base" with "practical application": an eight-volume regional survey had officially prepared the way for the two-volume plan. The RPNY was, in effect, a "large-scale proposal for . . . outside groups." Present company was included: Frederick J. Adams, MIT's chair of planning since 1944, was the son of Thomas Adams, lead author and coordinator for the RPNY, and into the 1950s, his faculty had maintained ties with practitioners in New York. (For his part, the father proposed an Urban Redevelopment Field Station for Boston in the early 1940s and lectured in the son's department in his last years of life.) Those present at the first CURS meeting also cited examples of what they saw as disorganized social science. Charles R. Walker's book *Steeltown* (1950), a study of "industrial relations" in an anonymized factory town, they felt, "might have been improved by cooperation with . . . a center" of specifically urban research. At meetings of the committee—or was it a "laboratory," Anderson wondered—the ever-denser national network of centers, programs, and units was itself a leading topic of interest.[13] The larger infrastructure loomed, spectrally present and at issue.

By 1951, then, MIT had entered the terrain of organized urban research, even as its precise line of attack was undecided. In late 1952, representatives from several outside centers came to town to consult on organizational form: among others, Stuart Chapin from the University of North Carolina, Harvey Perloff from Chicago, T. J. Kent (an MIT alum) from Berkeley, Robert C. Mitchell from Penn, C. McKim Norton and Henry Fagin of the Regional Plan Association, and three men (Walter Isard, William Wheaton, and Coleman Woodbury) representing the Graduate School of Design (GSD) at Harvard.

CURS was a committee, but as a proper center, they wagered, it would achieve permanence and prestige.[14]

Yet there were obstacles in place. Every postwar citadel of organized research contained reservoirs of disorganization and plenty of internal dispute; every center had dissenters, and they could exert a centrifugal force on the whole. What, for instance, should be the committee's intellectual focus? There was considerable debate on this point. Growth was one encompassing concern: how to quantify it, how to appraise it, how to forecast and intervene on its distribution in space. Would this concept, though, be sufficiently broad (or sufficiently interesting) to justify the group's existence? Rodwin thought not, and it was de-emphasized.[15] Was community the key concept? Catherine Bauer, steeped in the left-regionalist tradition that Lewis Mumford and Clarence Stein were still pushing after the war, thought it might be: study the "community as a [whole] community . . . not . . . as a series of problems," and intellectual synthesis could not be far off.[16] (Bauer was leaving MIT for Berkeley with William Wurster, her husband and MIT's architecture dean from 1944 to 1950, but her ideas still held sway, particularly with Rodwin, who had taken "Housing 7," a course she offered at Harvard and, as early as 1945, proposed opening to cross-enrollment by MIT students.)[17] But which community? How closely to tie CURS to its surrounds? Was the group obligated, or even curious, to accept greater Boston as its bedrock case study? If so, further analytical problems lay ahead. Rodwin and Lynch puzzled over where CURS could plausibly set the boundaries of its study area: Boston proper represented a minority of the metropolitan population, eight hundred thousand of some three million, and once beyond the city limits, there seemed no consensus on the outer bounds of the region, always an elastic unit in geographic thought. Rodwin was doubly ambivalent, concerned that an orientation to the local would lead to dully instrumental, politically dubious work: "We must expect that people [in government] will dump specific projects in our lap."[18] Draw a larger circle, and even more claimants on CURS's time, resources, and patience would emerge.

Toward the end of 1951, Boston-centrism almost seemed to be winning the day, with a critical caveat: the city would furnish researchers with "primary materials," but these were intellectually valid only if they offered "convenient and representative models for urban growth, change, and decay" in general. The local and the particular had a certain dignity—gown felt at least some obligation to town. Increasingly, though, CURS's remit became more abstract, grazing local affairs but only in the name of extrapolating theoretically to the city writ large. "We live within a system of metropolitan regions," read its progress report of November 1951, "a system marked by a complex structure and a high specialization of human activity and physical locality. Existence depends on a great web of communications and interdependent functions. The metropolitan environment is all-pervasive.... It is urgent that we understand the structure of these regions, and the processes through which this structure changes." Idioms of *community* had lost out to *communications*; the holist interwar regionalism of a Bauer or a Mumford had given way to a highly impersonal language of *location*. The whole system "functioned" until proven otherwise. The report's send-off was also in character: "The answers must be sought by joint effort."[19] The Joint Center, by that name, was a creation of the late 1950s. If it eventually put forward a unified front, it arose only at the end of a decade of improvisation with the norms and forms of urban research.

Out of these discussions, Lloyd Rodwin emerged as a decisive figure. He was a planner by trade, and a historian of urban form, but his interests were more diverse still. Indeed, his intellectual biography indicates the extent to which these running meta-commentaries on method bore the stamp of a broader concern with the philosophy of science and knowledge. Rodwin was one of several urbanists who had come to MIT from New York City. He had come of age in Brownsville, Brooklyn, one of the city's major interwar Jewish hearths with roots in Eastern Europe, and, like Alfred Kazin, made the increasingly familiar passage to City College in upper Manhattan. There, he developed intense interests in American philosophy and political thought, reading George Santayana, Oliver Wendell Holmes, Charles Sanders Peirce, and many others under the tutelage of Morris Raphael Cohen. Cohen was forever undervalued as a scholar, but he was a mentor and hero to that subset of the student body who would win postwar notoriety as the New York Intellectuals, fed on four years of perfervid political argument between the cafeteria's Alcove 1 and Alcove 2: party-line Stalinists versus mere socialists. Rodwin emerged from this milieu, entranced by Cohen's seminars on epistemology, the social and natural sciences, and the importance of "systematic doubt" as the essence of method and the only way to attempt the "interconnection of facts into a unitary system." Cohen's "encyclopedic interest" in ideas stayed with Rodwin as he entered more instrumental circles focused on urban affairs: "My mind was prepared," he reflected later in life, and his own exploits "always reflected" this approach to history, philosophy, and social research as science-like enterprises defined by a skepticism toward their own production of certainty.[20]

Rodwin's intellectual base only broadened as he wound through the academy and profession. After City College, he took his first courses in housing and planning at the New School for Social Research—the cheapest offerings in the catalog, Rodwin would plead—and he developed a lasting bond with his teacher, the famed housing specialist Charles Abrams. Abrams brought him on as an assistant in 1940 ("the equivalent of an Abrams Fellowship"), secured him an internship focused on defense-worker lodgings during the war, and after 1945 steered Rodwin to MIT, which the elder deemed "much more alive" than Harvard.[21] Well into the 1960s, Abrams embodied yet another lasting, powerful link to New York for MIT's urbanists, as well as to Jewish communities for a planning profession and an academy that could still seem the province of Anglo-Saxon Protestants.[22]

Rodwin also kept up ties with members of the New York–bred Regional Planning Association of America (RPAA), the informal interwar group that had advanced decentralist solutions to urban ills—at Sunnyside Gardens in Queens, Radburn in North Jersey, Chatham Village in Pittsburgh, Baldwin Hills Village in Los Angeles—instructed Franklin Roosevelt in the need to see things regionally, and, during the New Deal, exerted influence through the Tugwell-run Greenbelt program. In fact, Rodwin had first made his scholarly reputation by writing a withering critique of such ideas. In "Garden Cities and the Metropolis" (1945), he urged more migration into cities, not less, and skewered Bauer as a "sentimental" back-to-the-land advocate. Ebenezer Howard, the Garden City movement's British father figure, was brilliant, he wrote, but his vision had hinged on "faith, accident, or prophecy," not analysis. It offered mere "inspiration" where skeptical, empirical "spadework and wisdom" was needed. "Prophets," he wrote, "should never be taken too literally."[23] Rodwin continued in this vein in *The British New Towns Policy: Problems and Implications* (1956), his first monograph and a full-scale critique of the UK's postwar program of population dispersal, whose design hewed close to Howard's original template. The towns' record was mixed at best, he wrote, and would have turned out better if animated by more "research and research-mindedness." "There was a complacent assurance" among Patrick Abercrombie and his subordinates, and among the RPAA theorists who cheered them on, "that the basic answers were *known* and that research was expendable."[24] Doubt had played no part in their methodology, as Morris Cohen, no urbanist himself, would instantly have recognized.

Rodwin's politics were broadly progressive but never utopian. He increasingly bristled at the management of housing built with public funds.[25] Lewis Mumford was quick to rebut Rodwin's 1945 article—the author had conflated different types of dispersal and, despite his youth, was stuck in the "dead past"—but he ended up blurbing the 1956 book: "so important." Rodwin deemed Mumford and Bauer "very good friends."[26] Although the RPAA had splintered in the postwar era, most of its members kept up the same lines of critique, and when Bauer began organizing a replacement group, the Regional

Planning Council of America, in 1948, she proposed Rodwin's name for inclusion.[27] Later, for *Daedalus*, he would enthusiastically edit a "self-review" Mumford wrote to mark the twenty-five–year anniversary of *Technics and Civilization* (1934), a piece Rodwin felt "deserve[d] to become a part of history."[28] Urban research at MIT, on Rodwin's watch, reached back in historical time, beyond provincial Boston, and across rival intellectual traditions, doubting at every step but seeking higher synthesis.

By the end of 1956, CURS had gotten serious about becoming something more formal than an exploratory committee. The acronym persisted, but as of 1957, its referent would be the Center for Urban and Regional Studies.[29] The question of its essential purpose remained entirely unresolved, and over the course of that year and the next, a number of seemingly incompatible answers emerged. A research orientation was de rigueur, a fact related to the establishment of MIT's new doctoral program in planning, which admitted its first students in 1958.[30] The main internal division—never acrimonious, but real nonetheless—was between social-scientific approaches focused aspatially on human interaction and those that refused to sacrifice attention to the city's physical pattern and form. Kevin Lynch, on faculty since 1949, pushed hardest to compel a focus on form. He had raised this issue at the first CURS meeting in 1951, and with a more structured proposal in 1957, he redoubled his efforts. "The three-dimensional environment" deserved pride of place: "How does it work?" he asked. "How can we change it?" Various centers of urban studies had sprouted nationwide and, hastily perhaps, looked to the social sciences to provide their grid of mutual intelligibility. This may have made sense for those based at universities without robust architecture programs (or any at all, as at the University of Chicago). But MIT had one, Lynch noted, and the center ought to treat it as an asset, not a pleasant distraction from the pursuit of behavioral science. He enumerated many potential foci and sub-foci for the new CURS, and inevitably some dovetailed with the PERP approach honed at Chicago: MIT's urbanists would address "the planning process" as such, "social values," and "intensities of activity and communication." But all these facets of life, Lynch held, invited consideration only as bound up with the city's "spaces, silhouettes, masses, color, detail," and "the dynamic interrelation between these elements and the beholder." Lest this seem like an unsystematic swerve into the aesthetic realm, a focus on the physical fabric helped specify "the way in which the city communicates messages to the observer." This all added up to "urban landscape," the report asserted, in a richly interactive sense, very close indeed to how J. B. Jackson, himself fond of Lynch's work, used the word. The word *landscape* went almost entirely unuttered at centers that championed *system* and *organization*, but as late as December 1958, the fledgling CURS seemed ready to commit to a definition of the felt, experienced city that would have broken with recent orthodoxy in urban studies.³¹

These suggestions had not bubbled up at random. They emerged from intellectual currents that Lynch had been encouraging for several years, and that linked MIT not to Ford but to Rockefeller, the other major strand of urbanist philanthropy. In April 1954, Lynch and György Kepes, an MIT colleague and an unclassifiable Hungarian-emigré theorist of vision and aesthetics, had secured a five-year grant from the Rockefeller Foundation for a project originally pitched as "The Perceptual Form of the City." Lynch attended all of Rockefeller's Urban Design Conferences; Kepes joined him in 1956.³² The summation of their work was Lynch's *The Image of the City* (1960), after Jacobs's *Death and Life* probably the best-known volume of Rockefeller urbanism. In addition to interviewing passersby—in downtown Boston, Jersey City, and Los Angeles—Lynch and his assistants had them rapidly sketch maps, by which the author then purported to take stock of ordinary urbanites' cognitive "orientation" in space and the extent to which the "paths" and "landmarks" punctuating recently "renewed" downtowns might be eroding it.³³ (The method was pitched as replicable, and many American cities' departments of planning implemented versions of it later in the 1960s.)³⁴

During the 1950s, to rather less fanfare, Lynch was working out a heterodox vision of what truly basic research on cities could be. His first attempt to delineate this vision had appeared in *Scientific American*, of all places, the same month his Rockefeller grant came through. "The Form of Cities" (1954) proposed a novel classificatory method that would allow researchers, whatever their intentions, to first redescribe the city in terms of five aspects: size, density, grain, shape, and internal pattern. Each contained subdivisions. There were four major shapes: "annular accretion," (i.e., concentric rings); "ribbon" or "corridor" development; the star-shaped "metropolis," in which a titular "mother city" anchored various outlying sections; and the polycentric "constellation." "Internal pattern" also turned out to be many-splendored: the medieval "capillary mass"; the "axial" or "nodal" option found both in Baroque European cities and industrial Chicago; the all-important grid form, definitive of nineteenth-century America and its Western settlement; and the "open," curvaceous anti-grid regnant in the twentieth century despite its "'flat' taste." A city, "this complicated piece of equipment," enfolds and affects us, whether we realize it or not. The task was to assess how built form gave form to everyday life. Form was the cause; what were its "effects"?³⁵

In "A Theory of Urban Form" (1958), his second attempt to make headway on these questions, Lynch brought Lloyd Rodwin on as a coauthor. The

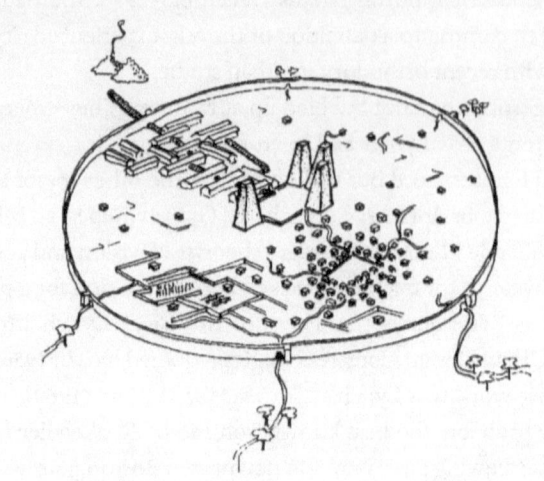

FIGURE 2.2. Lynch and Rodwin's hypothetical city called Pone, a composite meant to help readers grasp the six aspects of their 1958 general theory of form: element types (e.g., houses), quantity (of those elements), density, grain, focal organization, and generalized spatial distribution. Kevin Lynch and Lloyd Rodwin, "A Theory of Urban Form," *Journal of the American Institute of Planners* 24 (1958): 201–214. Courtesy of Taylor & Francis.

assumptions remained the same: form affects life (somehow); form has effects (of some sort); urban research had, in turn, to be "a study of the goal–form relationship." Even more than before (was this Rodwin's influence?), Lynch insisted that he was setting up an analytical system, one beyond the reach of "palliative knowledge and rules of thumb." This was theory, and theory had to be general in scope, applicable anywhere, and an aid to comparison (figure 2.2). "Upon it hangs all the rest." But, Lynch clarified, this was theory "formulated operationally." Only then could it be "tested, revised, and ultimately verified." Only then was "elementary knowledge" within reach.[36]

Just as CURS came into its own as a full-on research center, Lynch and Rodwin, its director, had come together in a partnership that was, if not quite interdisciplinary, a fusion of approaches so often at war within planning departments and their appurtenant research divisions. The MIT milieu had brought together precision social science with a rich, many-sensed appreciation for the atmospheres and affects of the city built. "Basic" research, impelled by the right kind of "theory," could join these tendencies into what Anna Vallye has called a "deferred instrumentality"—willing to speculate a bit and capacious enough to bring almost every subgenre of urban research within its fold. A common urban "image," on Lynch's telling, had the capacity to galvanize social solidarity. Kepes, nodding to Gestalt psychology, maintained hope that shared ways of seeing would help "overcom[e] a generalized condition of isolation or fragmentation" that accompanied capitalist modernity.[37] Cities themselves were being physically prised apart day by day. Visual experience of those cities, and of life itself, had fractured. Social solidarity was probably never as intact as classical theorists had hoped, but it, too, seemed on the verge of collapse. Kepes, Lynch, and Rodwin were less declarative just yet about the forms of organization best able to produce knowledge on these coincident crises. What they were proposing, however, was a richer interdisciplinarity, a joint center of equal opposites, with stakes far higher than those suggested by the desiccated treatises issuing from other units whose first and last commitment was to method.

Ultimately, at the Joint Center for Urban Studies, the materiality of urban form became one, but only one, topic for research. Lynch's vision lost out, first tempered by Rodwin's trace scientism and soon overshadowed by many other scholars more instrumental than he. The mainline social scientists were more numerous, assertive, and, likely, marketable in the policy-making circles the center eventually courted. Yet the Joint Center always remained a composite, not an alloy. MIT's urbanists were themselves an intellectually diverse group. To appreciate this complexity, it is necessary to migrate to the western part of Cambridge, consider Harvard's entreaties, and at length reflect on the meanings and predicates of intellectual jointure as they stood in the last years of the 1950s.

In 1957, Harvard's GSD established its own research unit, unimaginatively dubbed the Center for Urban Studies (CUS). Martin Meyerson was its director, a job for which the GSD's dean, Josep Lluís Sert, specifically poached him from Penn. (Meyerson was also appointed as a professor of planning.) By this time, Meyerson was firmly entrenched in the network of those who would organize the study of urban life, and he had borne witness to a majority of the episodes related in the previous chapter. He had been on faculty at Chicago beginning in the late 1940s and become a core contributor to the theoretical literature laid down by PERP. He had extensive experience in planning practice: with the American Society of Planning Officials in 1940s Chicago; on that city's South Side, exploring housing questions under Illinois's pre–Urban Renewal redevelopment law; with the Chicago Housing Authority beginning in 1949, the year federal funds first freed up; and in Philadelphia, where he worked in 1944 and returned in 1952, after being hired away from Chicago when Penn's planning department and IUS were beginning their imperial period.[38]

Like Rodwin, Meyerson was a New Yorker who came of age politically and intellectually in the interwar period. Like Rodwin, he had contact with many of the thinkers reared at what some called the Harvard of the proletariat: Nathan Glazer, Seymour Martin Lipset, and other budding New York Intellectuals with sociological leanings. Unlike Rodwin, he had attended not City College but Columbia. There, he liaised with a different subset of the city's Jewish intellectual scene, one more steeped in aesthetics and high culture (as part of their day jobs—Glazer and others were certainly not inattentive). He studied literature with Lionel Trilling and art with Meyer Schapiro, and even came to know the photographer László Moholy-Nagy as a tutor. Once installed at Harvard and its CUS, Meyerson considered lobbying for a Great Books–style core curriculum within the design school.[39] A planning polymath of sorts, he had a friend in David Riesman, whose *Lonely Crowd* benefited from the assistance of Meyerson's wife, Margy.[40] He had made contact with Charles Abrams in the 1940s, seeking advice on organizational form and citing the example of the Telesis group based in Berkeley.[41] He had friendly-enough relations with Bauer, Stein, and the successor institutions to the RPAA.[42] He attended the third and fifth Rockefeller Urban Design Conferences. By the end of the 1950s, he had also consulted on urban issues in Japan and Indonesia. Meyerson was invested in compelling reflection on the urban future and planners' capacity to improve it. In 1949, he had even proposed a Museum of the Future for Chicago, based at least in part on the Bacon-designed Better Philadelphia Exhibition of 1947, and on Patrick Geddes's Outlook Tower in Edinburgh before that.[43] Meyerson was, however, like Rodwin, a critic, a "pragmatic utopian" at most who was fundamentally skeptical of prophecy as a habit of mind.[44] Harvard was well stocked with research centers by 1957. If its administrators were late to arrive at that model for urbanism specifically, in Meyerson they had selected an almost perfect distillate of urban studies as a burgeoning field-of-fields.

Each university, then, had a center of its own. Each was already interdisciplinary, and each bridged designers of urban space with observers of the people inhabiting that space. The resulting Harvard–MIT Joint Center for Urban Studies joined not only two universities but two existing research units. Jointure was in the air, and if the concept was not perfectly synonymous with interdisciplinarity, their affinities were clear enough. In his widely read 1956 article on "middle-range" planning—quite possibly the piece that clinched his case to head the new CUS—Meyerson had called for an even deeper sort of jointure, one that would reside within each individual urbanist: "Joint designer–planners, statistician–planners . . . and other dually trained personnel," he wrote, "will be necessary."[45]

Formal talks on the possibility of merging the MIT and Harvard centers began in the fall of 1957. It became apparent to Rodwin and Meyerson that each of the groups was independently preparing an application to the Ford

Foundation. Paul Ylvisaker processed both requests, noted the overlap, and initiated a pair of meetings that December with the two directors. At first, Rodwin and Meyerson's impulse was to preserve the two separate centers and keep each somewhat informal in its agenda.[46] They would collaborate on seminars and other activities, and improved lines of communication would "avoid unnecessary duplication and competition for personnel and funds," as Rodwin wrote.[47] But there already was competition. It was Ylvisaker who proposed their consolidation into a single center, Ylvisaker who wrote independently to MIT's new chancellor, Julius Stratton, another convert to the center model. It was the "incorrigible" Ylvisaker who in early 1958 convened, in one room, Rodwin and Meyerson, the directors; Pietro Belluschi and Josep Lluís Sert, the respective architecture deans; Stratton and, standing in for Harvard's president Nathan Pusey, the prominent dean McGeorge Bundy.[48] Ylvisaker entertained doubts about the Harvard side of the jointure: in February 1958, he felt he still needed "to get from Harvard more than a superficial protestation of interest in the field. They have managed to recruit some of the country's top urbanists this past year primarily, I think, by their 'Harvard' appeal."[49] By the end of the month, however, Ylvisaker had resolved these doubts and persuaded the group that one joint center would be enough. There would be only one director, Meyerson; Rodwin would chair the faculty committee. In March, the presidents signed a Memorandum of Agreement. On September 22, the center officially got its name. Four days later, Ford internally approved the grant of $675,000 "for approximately five years." In October, they notified all parties. (The scholars had sought an eight-year grant comprising $4.8 million.)[50] In January 1959, Stratton and Pusey signed yet another agreement and thus began the work of actually organizing the center, allocating funds, and giving the work direction and form. Fall 1959 saw the center begin operations in an inconspicuous second-floor space at 66 Church Street, a moment's stroll from Harvard Yard despite the lingering sense that the impetus and intellectual ballast had for so long come from MIT.[51] Mentally and physically, the Joint Center was on the map.[52]

"To Make Studies Additive": Serializing Urban Knowledge, 1959–1963

Organization is a process, not a state. For the nascent Joint Center, the year 1959 was only an inflection point in what became a protracted, unwinnable game of self-definition. The first five years, in particular, were marked by ceaseless drift and debate over the very terms of engagement. What were the purpose and function of this thing they had worked so long to constitute? What were its intellectual foci? What was a center, anyhow—the perennial question—and how did this one differ from others in Ford's viewshed? How to divide up the labor? How closely to supervise research in progress? Was the Joint Center even one coherent entity—a research unit in the truest sense—or was it a shape-shifting kit of parts?

Meyerson and Rodwin never stopped posing these questions. Indeed, one condition of foundation-supported work, and a boon to those who write its history, is that grantees periodically have to take stock of what they are up to, committing their rationales to writing and so performing their own legitimacy, on demand, in the form of progress reports, digests of completed research, memos of all kinds, and applications for continued support (which the center made, successfully, in 1962 and 1965).[53] Their answers evolved without any clear telos. The center turned out research but was also "a discoverer and collector of talent," as Meyerson wrote to his visiting committee in 1963. It was "a recruiting and training ground" for scholars new to the study of cities, or for seasoned scholars, from whatever field, who were new to urban studies so called.[54] This did not mean annulling the disciplines. They persisted. As "partner" and "gadfly," though, the Joint Center "tries to create an atmosphere in which work is encouraged that cuts across traditional disciplines."[55] Simply achieving dialogue, in other words, was insufficient: the center set out to broker interactions that would themselves give rise to new and interstitial habits of mind.

Discoverer, collector, recruiter, trainer, partner, gadfly, active broker, passive atmosphere—plainly, it was difficult to choose just one role. A 1964 report produced for public consumption (and to attract funders, especially if the next round of Ford money should fall through) styled the center a "stimulator . . . a generator of ideas, and a clearinghouse for scholars and funds." Whereas most of its counterparts defined their missions far more narrowly and instrumentally, the Joint Center in its first half-decade was proudly "exploratory." It eschewed "large, focused projects" except in the case of "special financing," and even then, proposals for applied work came under serious consideration only if they had conceptual "significance beyond the particular area" addressed.[56] The center was avowedly "permissive," Meyerson wrote, willing to admit different styles of work into the fold while remaining convinced that such work "can also be structured." How? "Our effort has been to make studies additive by getting an exchange of ideas, methods, and knowledge."[57] Unlike a Parsons, the early Joint Center did not deduce first principles and shoehorn its members into prosecuting one unified agenda.[58] *Additive* did not mean *total*. In fact, there was no total system to add up to. There was only the one added on to, iteratively, through the accretion of small and medium-sized projects by basically independent-minded scholars. The center set out to establish the trading zone through which these urban studies, in the plural, became mutually intelligible.

Formally, the Joint Center had three distinct goals: It existed to "improve fundamental knowledge" about urban and regional issues, broadly conceived—the classic postwar ideal of basic research. It sought to "build a bridge" with the craft of urban policy—its applied or instrumental face. It also served to "enrich" the "educational purposes" of Harvard and MIT both—undergraduate and graduate courses had emerged with its assistance, even as the center offered no instruction of its own. By 1970, the center claimed, each university had inaugurated a hundred new courses. But these broad ambits, useful as subheadings in a progress report, do little to transmit what defined the early Joint Center, much less what distinguished it from the dozens of come-lately ORUs sprouting at the peak of that model's popularity. The center's deliberate rejections were every bit as important. This was not, or not only, big social science drowning in its own data and collectivizing authorship: "Both the individual scholar and the team effort are supported." A responsible center "ought not commit" to just one topic, be it housing, redevelopment, migration, industrial location, suburbanization, or any other likely candidate. The center insisted on "maximum flexibility" in the use of its resources. (In fact, resisting overspecialization and preserving a "broad-gauged program" counted among Ylvisaker's stated requirements.) The language of *exchange* and *transaction* punctuates its statements of purpose, economistic in flavor but decoupled from any obvious conversion of these ideas into a monetary return on investment. *Communication* was a third watchword. Discussion would unfold, foci would emerge, and work would ensue. The center's primary task was to coordinate these new sorts of interchange at seminars, conferences, and weekly luncheons that among select circles became the stuff of legend. And, to a degree unknown elsewhere in the wider world of ORUs, at the Joint Center, "individuals" were said to undertake this work. Even as they entered collaborations, the thinking went, affiliated scholars remained idiosyncratic, reared in but not bound to the disciplines or their successors, and always academically "free" from any acephalous will of the collective: "In the case of the ablest scholars, the Joint Center ought not to substitute its judgment for theirs as to what constitutes significant research. Fostering such diversity enhances the intellectual vigor and imaginativeness of urban studies at a university. It also minimizes the conflict between the individual scholar and the research center which is a source of friction and concern at many institutions."[59] *Ought not*—the rationale behind Ford's newest center was, in part, a critique of existing formations that, promising to revitalize knowledge, had come to regiment it, producing only a bland new orthodoxy. The Joint Center tested, updated, expanded, and to some extent undid the dominant model used during the 1950s to organize and govern urban research.

The work that gestated at the Joint Center those first few years under Meyerson and Rodwin was miscellaneous. It encompassed the social consequences of industrialism, the technological underpinnings of urbanization, commerce and retail space, transportation systems, Urban Renewal and the expanded field of housing policy, speculative development on the urban fringe, the architecture of ordinary dwellings, social and spatial mobility, theories of industrial location, race and ethnicity, and many other topics, any one of which could have justified a center of its own. Many Joint Center texts were cited widely, and one gets the sense that the directors expected these first books, in tandem, to impart structure and standards to an emerging field. Some remain classics in the early twenty-first century. In many cases, an author supplied the first full monographic or comparative treatment of his (just about always his) topic. At first, the broad scatter of interests, rather than signaling incoherence, served to mark out, and then gradually advance, the perimeter of urban studies.

Some of the work was quite applied and atheoretical in character: John Delafons's *Land-Use Controls in the United States* (1962) was an early monograph, the work of a British scholar hosted by the center as a visiting associate. (The work was well timed, as New York City had completely rewritten its zoning code in 1961, famously allowing taller skyscrapers in exchange for smaller building footprints and thus more open space at the heart of Manhattan.)[60] A. Scheffer Lang and Richard Soberman, MIT civil engineers, published *Urban Rail Transit: Its Economics and Technology* (1962).[61] The same year, George Sternlieb, a former retailer on loan from Harvard Business School, completed *The Future of the Downtown Department Store* (1962) while a fellow—a term the center generally reserved for graduate students it awarded funding and office space to complete dissertations on urban topics. With store managers as its intended audience, the book compared evidence from New York, Philadelphia, Pittsburgh, and Boston and recommended policies to salvage these palaces of consumption at a time when the future seemed to belong to suburban branch stores: tax abatement, center-city transit improvements, more plentiful parking structures, and continued land clearance to accomplish all this. In one reading, this text could register as little more than an advice manual to small-time capitalists. How Sternlieb framed the work is thus diagnostic: he pitched it explicitly as "basic research," dwelled on the linkage between the basics and their application, and insisted that he had moved the study of shopping beyond "the 'gosh' and 'gee whiz' school" of historiography predicated on celebrating individual stores, painting proprietors as civic heroes, and giving voice to shoppers' memories of the early days. Writing a Joint Center monograph, Sternlieb knew that it was his duty to abstract and to generalize—*the* downtown department store.⁶² It was in this sense that such a text could appear in the company of *A Communications Theory of Urban Growth* (1962), the MIT planner Richard L. Meier's difficult, diagram-laced text that harnessed the latest in systems thinking to recast "the civic bond," "uses of time and space," "information flows and human channel capacity," and other ontological primitives of urban life.⁶³

"Monographs" and "books" were distinct categories for the Joint Center.⁶⁴ The distinction helped give form and hierarchy to the group's plentiful output. Although many of the above publications were indeed hard-bound objects bearing the name of either Harvard or MIT's university press, the latter term was reserved for works published in the center's book series, which from 1960 became a prestigious venue in which to communicate urban expertise, perform interdisciplinarity as a fait accompli, and display the capaciousness of urban studies as a field.⁶⁵ Here, too, the products were diverse in terms of discipline, method, regional focus, and historical scope (or lack thereof). William Alonso, a Harvard faculty member trained at Penn by Walter Isard, published *Location and Land Use: Toward a General Theory of Land Rent* (1964), which purported to view the city as a "featureless plain" of unimpeded transactions, each voiced in terms of quantifiable transport and labor costs per unit distance.⁶⁶ This was the argot of regional science, an approach that informed, without monopolizing, the Joint Center's assumptions about political economy. This was general theory incarnate.

The planner Charles Haar, prominent during Lyndon Johnson's Great Society period, edited the transatlantic collection *Law and Land: Anglo-American Planning Practice* (1964).⁶⁷ Charles Abrams, by this point a faculty member at MIT, parlayed decades of policy experience and numerous consulting jobs overseas into *Man's Struggle for Shelter in an Urbanizing World* (1964), a massively comparative study of housing in what were coming to be called the Second and Third Worlds.⁶⁸ Some books in the series existed mainly to communicate empirical findings, while some attempted to formulate systematic theory, at least at the middle range. The collation of those two levels, and therewith the nature of social-scientific inference itself, was an ongoing concern. Most Joint Center books addressed the issue directly, whether in the main body or in an appendix, and in-house debate at seminars and luncheons routinely turned on questions of generalizability.⁶⁹

Some work, by contrast, had a more humanistic cast. The Joint Center series drew in Kevin Lynch's *The Image of the City* (1960). The book was substantially complete by 1959—and had of course been funded by Rockefeller, not Ford—

but the center claimed it retroactively, affixed its logo to the spine, and inducted it into the series, where it would forever be listed as the first title sent to press. (A high-level 1965 progress report to Ford, making an inventory of publications to date, admitted that Lynch's *Image of the City* "would have been done anyway under different auspices." Other titles were classified as either "clearly J.C.U.S. auspices" or "greatly expedited" by the center's atmosphere.)[70] The same series that gave Alonso a platform also somehow accommodated *The Public Library and the City* (1965), the proceedings of a Symposium on Library Functions in the Changing Metropolis, held in May 1963 in patrician Dedham, Massachusetts, in tandem with the National Book Committee, and chaired by Talcott Parsons (of all people), the lone sociologist sitting on the Joint Center's faculty committee.[71] The Olympian, placeless tendencies of his social theory were nowhere reproduced in the center's output, but his neo-Durkheimian concept of social functions and the necessity of their integration was broad enough that these bedfellows were not altogether strange. Interdisciplinarity thrived on these juxtapositions and left readers to speculate on how, not whether, such dissimilar parts could fuse into a greater, more-dimensional way of understanding the changing city. This was as true of the series as of the center itself.

Joint Center affiliates were expected to publish in the series at some point, although they were not prohibited from taking their business elsewhere. The two presses split the titles equally, with no obvious division of labor imposed a priori. Harvard University Press published some MIT faculty and vice versa, although books with a more quantitative or technical orientation tended to appear with MIT Press. For each title, the Joint Center recouped royalties on the first 1,500 copies sold.[72] Joint Center faculty, not the press's editors, decided which titles belonged in the series and which did not, and this arrangement became a source of dispute in 1962, when at least one of the publishers questioned Meyerson's judgment as to quality and appropriateness. To assuage them, Meyerson agreed that three, not two, reviewers would descend upon each manuscript. The center also added the political scientist Martha Derthick, a 1962 Harvard PhD, to its staff in order to oversee the publications program and smooth out any misunderstandings.[73] By the end of that year, it was agreed that "style and form," not content or intellectual validity, would be the presses' only grounds for influencing the manuscripts.[74] Still, discontent lingered. In July 1963, just as the Harvard political scientist James Q. Wilson took over for Meyerson–Rodwin as director, the two presses severed their working relationship. The series continued to exist, but now it was a joint venture only in name. Each press agreed to continue printing the list of books approved by its crosstown counterpart in the back matter, but they would appear under two separate headings.[75]

A majority of the titles to be serialized, like so much postwar social science, were presentist in intent. They adduced just enough history to set current conditions in context and, usually, to issue recommendations for the future. They were not ahistorical, but they used history in an instrumental way that would become common among scholars claiming affiliation with urban studies. Lloyd Rodwin's first contribution, *Housing and Economic Progress* (1961), is diagnostic in this regard. He looked back as far as the nineteenth century and drew on the classic evidentiary sources of historical geography to examine the shifting fate of Boston's middle-income population—a group that, according to Rodwin, scholars had by and large neglected, lavishing attention only on the rich and the poor. Noting that "economic progress," as defined by the postwar apostles of affluence, carried with it serious "side effects," and always had, Rodwin argued that a reliance on market-based solutions to housing shortages would never be sufficient, that rent control did not hamper growth, and that decades of pro-homeownership policies had been deleterious. As evidence, he offered the case of those Bostonians caught "in the twilight zone between renting and ownership" and attempting to move outbound from the dispossessed neighborhoods that Paul Ylvisaker and others were now calling the American city's "gray areas."[76] (Ylvisaker first came to that term in a paper by the Harvard economist Raymond Vernon, a member of the Joint Center's faculty committee, whom he continued to cite as the Gray Areas Program grew into the Ford Foundation's marquee urban initiative on the domestic front between 1960 and 1967. *Gray* may well have referred to once-white neighborhoods then becoming demographically Blacker due to northward migration.)[77] Far more than the social scientists in his midst, Rodwin went into great detail on building-and-loan societies, realtors large and small, zoning codes, and Boston's vernacular building types—the better to understand how the three-decker apartment houses that blanketed the metropolitan middle distance into the 1920s had given way to open-lot homes, and how tenancy had been overtaken by ownership. Precise halftone maps, which layered data representing income and population shifts onto the jigsaw of Boston's many outlying jurisdictions, supported his case, as did a taste for local idiosyncrasy that would completely elude Alonso.

Yet, one gleaned, this was not only or primarily a study of Boston. If it supplied basic knowledge—and local color, especially via the tirades elite Bostonians had unleashed on the "flimsy, sheer ugliness" of three-deckers at the turn of the century—that knowledge was finally subservient to theoretical aims. Rodwin was determined to refute the sectoral theory of urban growth associated with the land economist Homer Hoyt. In 1939, Hoyt had posited that wealth and poverty inherently tend to sort themselves into elongated slices of land leading out from the downtown, usually along rail lines, rather than the concentric rings that the Chicago sociologist Ernest Burgess had imagined in the 1920s and committed to paper in one of the most reproduced diagrams in urban research. The fact that Boston's elite had jumped en masse from the South End to the newly filled (and western-extending) Back Bay neighborhood in the second half of the twentieth century, Rodwin contended, was evidence enough that an inertial theory of stratification in which classes "spread along" contiguous sectors or vectors of urban land and move in only one "direction" apiece could not be universally valid. More importantly, the Federal Housing Administration had adopted Hoyt's assumptions about markets, and in their hands, on questions of class and race, "the inescapable policy conclusion is to 'keep 'em out.'" Rodwin's politics as a left-of-center critic, very much contra the neoclassical economics that were ascendant at Chicago and in Alonso's work, showed through in ways that most studies with the imprimatur of the Joint Center downplayed or disputed. Sector theory, he held, made segregation, past and present, seem natural.[78]

These styles of reasoning passed down to the first generation of doctoral students supported by the Joint Center (even if Rodwin's political commitments did not). Bernard Frieden was Rodwin's advisee at MIT (and the university's first PhD in planning), and his dissertation joined the book series as *The Future of Old Neighborhoods* (1964). Like Rodwin, he asserted on the first page that "growth and decline go hand in hand." By the second page, he was invoking "Gray Areas" as a feature of the ideal-typical American city, and he would reuse the term uncritically in later chapters. The book, a study of residential preferences and the economics of redeveloping such grayspace, took pains to respect local variation. It juxtaposed case studies of New York, Hartford, and Los Angeles—dissimilar cities in every respect. The goal of this comparative history, however, was to abstract, to infer something more general about center-city neighborhoods as a spatial type, and, on the strength of their past, to propose the course of their future. Dutifully, Frieden credited the Joint Center, using their preferred language, as "a stimulating atmosphere in which to work."[79]

Yet the center proved oddly ambivalent about how much this all mattered—just how central to its existence as a nominal research unit the production of research ultimately had to be. Throughout the 1960s, an unresolved tension simmered between the center's role as a connector and the substance of the knowledge its connections were calling forth—between form and content, the network and its nodes. Books and monographs were "one measure of its accomplishment," the directors declared in a 1964 report, "but not the most important one." The center's actual value, they insisted, derived from the partnerships it had forged among departments, universities, and other centers—from its basically infrastructural work as a "communication exchange in urban affairs." (Never mind that the vast majority of that report, *The First Five Years*, was given over to summarizing its publications.)[80]

Considered purely in terms of the density and miscellany of its contacts, the Joint Center quickly became a peerless intellectual crossroads for urban studies. During 1960, it convened a conference on Urban Renewal (together with the Nieman Foundation) and one called "The Urbane City," John Burchard's attempt to braid traditional architectural history and aesthetics with the social science that surrounded him. In 1961, a conference called "The New Mayors" lined up officials from Cambridge, Boston, New Haven, St. Louis, and Nashville—the better to theorize reform-minded decision-making beyond the modus operandi of the ethnic machine. Another meeting took urban spatial structure as its object and hosted leading quantifiers from Penn, Berkeley, the University of North Carolina, and the University of Toronto. In 1962, T. J. Kent of Berkeley led a symposium on urban master plans. The next year, one meeting brought together practitioners of industrial and commercial real estate, only to be followed by the library symposium whose proceedings appeared at mid-decade. In the first three years alone, the center's Tuesday luncheons, held at the Harvard Faculty Club on the far side of the Yard, brought to town Lyle Fitch of New York's Bureau of Public Administration; Britton Harris of Penn and a newly formed interstate transportation authority for Pennsylvania and South Jersey; the planning theorist Melvin Webber of Berkeley; Constantinos Doxiadis, the Greek philosopher of ekistics and lead architect of Islamabad; Ben Bagdikian, then commissioning urban reportage at the *Saturday Evening Post*; Daniel Patrick Moynihan, then of the Department of Labor, speaking on urban crime; the development economist Bert Hoselitz of Chicago; the Penn sociologist and Meyerson student Herbert Gans, discussing suburbs as he prepared *The Levittowners* (1967); and scholars and public officials with experience in Mexico City, Delhi, London, Southern Italy, the Illinois statehouse, and again New Haven, that small-city testing ground for the nation's most comprehensive approaches to Urban Renewal. In addition to its own conferences, the center's office space often hosted other meetings, hatched at the intersection of scholarship and practice, by groups as expansive as the United Nations or as narrow as the coalition making moves to redevelop Boston's waterfront.[81] With porous borders, the Joint Center ended up piecing together a robust cross section of the urbanist establishment in and selectively beyond the United States.

Even confined to the two campuses, the roster of those who maintained at least some connection to the center sprawls almost uncontrollably. It is hard to make precise delineations as to who at any given time felt himself to be part of or based at the Joint Center. Scholars passed through, kept up ties when convenience allowed, attended events, pitched in on collaborative projects, or signed on to teach new courses. Raymond Vernon remained a force at Harvard Business School, but he departed the faculty committee in 1962. Talcott Parsons's days were numbered. At various moments during the Rodwin–Meyerson period, the faculty committee included V. O. Key, the singular scholar of Southern politics; Max Milliken of MIT's CENIS; Hideo Sasaki, the Modernist landscape architect on faculty at the GSD; and the sociologist Samuel Stouffer of *The American Soldier* fame. The roster of full-fledged "research members" and doctoral "fellows" comprises a list of eminences and eminences-in-training that would be even more tedious to enumerate.[82]

Within the wider world of urban expertise, the center became something very close to an obligatory passage point.[83] With rather less fanfare, it also took seriously its role as an exchange of information, independent of its producers, and it exhorted other universities to collect, cross-reference, and share pertinent research materials in a more coordinated way than had yet held sway. In 1961, having spent three months consulting with scholars and librarians, Helen Kistin produced a Joint Center report (for their purposes, a category distinct from either monograph or book) titled *Urban Economic Research: Improving the Accessibility and Utilization of Literature, Data, and Data Sources*. Kistin was the first woman with full standing as a research member of the Joint Center. (Martha Derthick was considered staff.) The better to pool together books, journals, reports, and the reams of raw data that modern-day centers were constantly generating, she called for a "repository, special library, and/or clearing house." Perhaps Harvard, MIT, or the Church Street office would house that collection. Perhaps not. She noted that Harvard's GSD already possessed "the largest and best collection of city planning literature at any university [that featured a] center," but also that both universities "suffer from inadequate space and equipment." The goal was to embed Harvard, MIT, and their swarm of urbanists ever more deliberately in circuits that could connect them with the world beyond Cambridge. The Joint Center never established the entity Kistin had in mind. Hers was a call to centralize information—basic information, not fully worked-over knowledge—in a way that Rodwin and Meyerson tended to eschew. Nevertheless, her report testified to the center's growing sense that it was only one node, one dense knot, within a far broader network of endeavor defined by its relations, not by its central point—if one even existed—or by its perimeter.[84] With each passing year, the early Joint Center came to understand itself as an open whole. Urban studies, as a field, itself deferred closure. It proposed a serial knowledge, one open to revision, to the recalcitrant urban world, and to the future.[85]

Basic Research and Its Discontents

From the first, the Joint Center's inner circle displayed a profound ambivalence about whether basic research alone could ever be sufficient to motivate a properly dynamic, plural, and, on some level, intellectually interesting orientation to the city—that intricate composition of buildings, infrastructures, economies, landscapes, and lives. Indeed, despite occasional bouts of grandiloquence in which one or another scholar would call for immediate severance with existing paradigms, the Joint Center evinced discomfort with programs that exalted either incremental fact-gathering or hastily general theory.[86] Both orientations coexisted at the center's founding, and both would persist in low-level conflict. Yet rather than committing to either antipode, the center seemed more interested in querying their relationship, formulating and reformulating questions about how cases and the inferences drawn from them might add up. Inference as a mode of reasoning, not theory or empirics as such, was the central conceptual issue for the center. It fostered debate on the many mutually resonant ways in which inquiry could be systematic, without presuming that all facts and findings would amount to one structured system.

Two projects organized during the Joint Center's first year of operation are diagnostic here in their divergent fates. The first came together at the behest of the political scientist Edward Banfield and had roots at the University of Chicago. Banfield had been a fixture at Chicago until 1959, when his friend and one-time collaborator Martin Meyerson arranged to hire him away to Harvard and the center. His first act as an affiliate was to set in motion a copious, multiyear series of reports on policy making and political contestation in more than two dozen American cities. Banfield deputized his own students, graduate and undergraduate alike, from Harvard and Chicago to spend the summer visiting and preparing reports on cities he assigned them. The reports were all but uniform in structure. Students answered a standardized checklist of questions, even as their literary execution of the report varied in tone. Their titles, too, were standardized: typically *A Report on Politics in* the chosen city. In many cases, the topic was the student's hometown, where he (she, in the case of Martha Derthick) would be spending the summer anyhow. (This led to some curious inclusions in the series: coequal with Detroit, Washington, and Los Angeles were Manchester, New Hampshire; Worcester, Massachusetts; and tiny

New Castle, New York.)[87] Each one included a section on religious, occupational, racial and ethnic, and other "interest groups" active on the scene, very much in keeping with the understanding of political "influence" that Meyerson and Banfield had advanced in *Planning, Politics, and the Public Interest* (1955), on Chicago. Each one itemized the discrete "issues" around which these various groups organized their claims: policing, taxation, public housing, highway construction (and route selection), zoning, city–county consolidation, and the ever-present specter of Urban Renewal. Many, but not all, led with a creditable potted history of the city since European settlement, and many included valuable maps of the city's demographics, approximate neighborhood boundaries, and recent voting behavior. Most reports dedicated a section to the "ethos" underpinning the city's political activities. These tended to be written in a breezy shorthand: Kansas City's politics were forever "westward-facing" in spirit; Milwaukee radiated a Teutonic "thoroughness," "orderliness," and "decency"; in Houston, "government is still a simple country store"; and so on. For larger, more diverse cities such as Philadelphia, Banfield wisely omitted this section.[88]

Banfield and Derthick directly oversaw a report on Boston, the longest by far, that comprised thematic chapters by several contributors.[89] Other students reported on El Paso, Seattle, Cincinnati, Denver, St. Louis, San Diego, Nashville, Salt Lake City, and Greater Miami, the only place treated in this metropolitan way. Unaccountably, one report dealt with Stockholm.[90] Alan Altshuler, who had begun his doctorate under Banfield at Chicago, spent four weeks in the summer of 1959 researching separate reports on Minneapolis and St. Paul, places he had never before visited, due to Banfield's hunch that the reformers in power there, engaged in "planning at its best," would supply a useful contrast to the machine-run (and overstudied) Windy City.[91] To each report was appended a preface by Banfield himself stipulating that the series' uniformity would "facilitate comparative analysis." These were expressly "not finished treatises. Rather, they are systematic collections of raw and semi-interpreted data."[92] They were, in other words, the quintessence of basic research.

This endeavor lasted for four years, and it stands as the Joint Center's purest example of large-scale, standardized, narrowly empirical research that was notionally collaborative in nature—although the authors were on their own, submitting work to Banfield, director and one-man clearinghouse, without ever cross-checking findings with their peers. University libraries and fifty other centers of urban research subscribed to the series, with each volume arriving on single-sided, mimeographed typewriter pages bound by three rings.[93] The reports became a public resource compatible with Helen Kistin's vision of a transinstitutional pool of common data worth amassing irrespective of its use.

In parallel with the Joint Center's hardcovers, they put forward a second serialization of knowledge, incremental by nature, that might, or might not, eventually aggregate into some larger statement about the essence of urban life.

That synthesis arrived in 1963, and it was Banfield himself who prepared it. All along, he had been commissioning these reports in order to support his own research agenda. The division of labor was clear in his mind: atheoretical canvassing could be done by almost anyone who had passed one of his seminars, whereas true conceptual synthesis awaited his hand. Research was basic until the right kind of expert drew inferences—produced scientific knowledge—from it.

City Politics (1963) was the name of the book. Its coauthor, James Q. Wilson, had joined Harvard's government department in 1961, but he was a Banfield advisee from the Chicago years who arrived during the last days of the PERP experiment and finished up in the all-important year 1959. Southern Californian in origin, he had written the report on Los Angeles—like him, politically more conservative than the New Yorkers who ran the center—and had quickly become the other leading figure at Harvard writing on the urban political process. *City Politics* acknowledged "a general debt" to the reports, of which Banfield and Wilson made "extensive use" even as direct citations ran to only a dozen. The term *ethos* was discarded in favor of political *style*, *character*, or *culture*. More explicitly than the field-workers had dared, Banfield and Wilson signaled that the time had come to generalize from case to theory. And generalize they did: "There are only a few democratic nations, and all of them differ radically in culture. But there are several hundred democratic cities in the United States, and their [political] culture is, broadly speaking, the same." The authors bracketed their almost twenty empirical chapters with high-level statements: "A Political Approach to Urban Government," "The Nature of Urban Politics," and "The Trend of City Politics" at present. (Specific approach was never owned up to in the reports.) Culture was the master explanans for Banfield and Wilson, and on their understanding, it was conditioned by class. The middle classes, they wrote, were in the habit of positing one unified public interest, in order then to speak on its behalf; the working classes in American cities, they argued, had no such pretense. More generally still, politics is a process; political coalitions form around specific issues, not abstract concepts of the good; never confined solely to administration and its metrics of efficiency, politics is a form of rough and unending play.[94] Meyerson and Banfield's 1955 book had also ended in an eruption of general theory, but there, its empirical support consisted of a single case: Chicago, they wrote, had indicated "what to look for" when studying urban politics in any guise.[95] Banfield's work of 1959–1963 marked a clear shift. Now he would not think of generalizing on the strength of just one place. The Joint Center, dwelling on the inferential process that turned various *cities* into *the city*, demanded work that made the linkage explicit. To perform that work of abstraction, however, the textures of specific places would always, and necessarily, be sheared away as so much standard variation.

A very different kind of project took shape in 1960. Grady Clay, lately of the *Louisville Courier-Journal* and newly appointed to edit *Landscape Architecture*, came to town that May for a conference put on by the Harvard-based Nieman Foundation, dedicated since 1938 to building, or repairing, bridges between journalists and the academy. Clay had been a Nieman Fellow in 1948–1949, but at that time, urban and architectural criticism had little foothold in the major newspapers. By 1960, the situation had changed, and the meeting brought together numerous writers, who ruminated on how best to tell stories about American cities as they grew in size and complexity. Clay himself focused on the question of language, which he felt should be simple and evocative. He had been waging "a running battle against gunk in our copy: that thick, mucous, oleagenous [sic], cloying, stoppaging, indigestible language which creeps out of heavy Renewal Agency documents, and seeps into our copy." His address, vintage Clay, went on in this vein. However, all was not a matter of style: "How do we say a neighborhood is going to hell without hastening the process?" Words had consequences. "How do we handle Race," he asked, "possibly the biggest story in America today," without superficially indulging "the 'Comma, Negro' fixation"? Simple answers were not forthcoming, but, within earshot of the strikingly white Joint Center, Clay insisted that the questions had to be posed.[96]

The month prior, Clay had written to Martin Meyerson with an idea. After years of lyrical columns for the *Courier-Journal*, he had decided to write a book. Would the Joint Center host him, no scholar by conventional standards, as a fellow? They would. Clay arrived in October 1960, with Ylvisaker's blessing, as a research associate obligated to produce a manuscript by the end of the next calendar year. The initial thought was that he would write on the legacy and promise of New Towns as a resettlement strategy. By the time of his arrival in Cambridge, his interests had shifted to Urban Renewal and its shortcomings. The better-connected Meyerson informed him that Jane Jacobs already had a book on the way, and Clay became convinced that he could not top her.[97] Already a public figure of sorts, he wanted to write a blockbuster, and this would require differentiating his product. He shifted focus yet again and narrowed his sights on the design competitions by which boosters, politicians, planners, architects, artists, and others made their bids—performed their

FIGURE 2.3. Critique of judgment. Grady Clay reviews entries in an architectural design competition. Such competitions were the subject of the long-suffering, and still unpublished, manuscript that Clay prepared while hosted by the Joint Center in 1960–61. Courtesy of Competitions-Archive LLC.

competency, in a sense, for the chance to renew. The book would be called *The Competitors* (figure 2.3).[98]

As he developed this project, Clay took full advantage of the Joint Center's atmosphere and its network of professional contacts. Clay was an obsessive chronicler of his own whereabouts, and his dozens of pocket-sized notebooks are crammed with the minutiae of an intellectual man-about-town. He met up with Lynch, Abrams, and many other center regulars; he took an interest in Richard Meier's theories of urban growth; he interviewed Sert and Walter Gropius, both of whom had served on juries for the kind of competitions he was seeking to explain. Meyerson egged Clay on. This was just what the center was for: "JC can help by giving intellectual xposure [sic] to what you do," Clay paraphrased, "discussion seminars + take yr MS apart + get from other disciplines." Meyerson suggested he circulate a first treatment of the project in pamphlet form. Abrams disagreed: that would be a "premature giveaway," a grave unforced error if nonfiction smash was the end goal.[99] Clay attended talks with gusto, haunted the Church Street office, and relished the academic setting. The Boston region, moreover, was of acute interest to him. Alongside San Francisco's Golden Gateway project and London's redone Elephant and Castle district south of the Thames, the third and most involved of his case studies was the majority-Irish Farm section of Brookline, a first-ring suburb that is almost an enclave of Boston. Philadelphia's Society Hill, where I. M. Pei's towers were then rising above eighteenth-century row houses according to plans supervised by Ed Bacon, was to anchor a fourth chapter, sketched out but unexecuted.[100] Attending meetings of the Boston Redevelopment Authority (BRA), Clay came to know Ed Logue, the face of Urban Renewal in that city and a deeply polarizing figure at the time. In 1962, with Clay gone from the region and the Farm project winding down, Logue even offered Clay a job as BRA's lead communicator. "Help us tell our story," he suggested. Clay replied in the negative, by this point skeptical of the will to renew and likely suspecting that Logue was looking to co-opt a potential critic: "I can think of nothing less interesting or challenging than being Ed Logue's PR man. You need a PR man like I need a hole in the head. You run too fast in a shifting field for a PR man to keep up anyhow."[101] The point of writing this book, after all, was to step back: compare, classify, conceptualize, and critique.

The book, however, never saw publication. Its disappearance has long been one of the minor mysteries in the intellectual history of postwar urbanism, and it is one of the Joint Center's avowed failures, nearly scrubbed from the historical record. For decades thereafter, biographies printed on Clay's book jackets noted that he had produced a "monograph" on these competitions, with no details given as to its title or where to find it.[102] Yet Meyerson, Derthick as editor, and virtually every other figure Clay interacted with that year considered *The Competitors* unpublishable. Meyerson began his critiques before the draft was even complete. "You've been too spare," Clay remembered him saying in the fall of 1961. "*Underplayed* very much is a description" of what Clay had done with the available evidence. Derthick, for her part, wanted him to "squeeze out" more analysis from his field notes.[103] (Clay had written 135 pages on the Brookline case alone, but the scholars found it thin gruel.) In January 1962, once Clay had left town, Meyerson passed along Derthick's thoughts on a redrafted version of the Brookline chapter. One recommendation was to come back, reembed at the Farm for a few months, and then overhaul the text completely. Clay knew he would not have time to do so, and as 1962 progressed, the Joint Center began to lose interest.[104]

From Louisville, Clay began casting about for another way to place his book in view of the reading public. To do so, he again made abundant use of the Joint Center's far-flung network. He wrote first to Robert C. Mitchell and William Wheaton at Penn's IUS to see if they might be able to take it on. (Meyerson and Ylvisaker approved; indeed, it was often Meyerson who sent out the manuscript on Clay's behalf.) Wheaton thought it might work, but not for another year or so, and then only as a hardcover—what Clay, the budding public intellectual, expressly did not want.[105] The book "must not go stale," he wrote.

"It was not written for the ages," unlike Banfield's book and so many other Joint Center treatises, "but for now."[106] Even if Jacobs's prose could not be matched in color or accessibility, Urban Renewal as a subject, he wrote, "is a hot one . . . my efforts will amount to little if it doesn't get published until late 1963," the date Wheaton had tentatively offered him.[107] Clay's book was not theory; it was, he believed, a direct intervention on the world. Timing was everything.

Clay's correspondence became even more frantic as the year wore on. Publisher after publisher shot him down. Toward the end of 1962, cutting losses, he proposed a long piece to Harper's, and this too was rebuffed.[108] Could the manuscript, Meyerson wondered, be reimagined as a Joint Center working paper? Clay insisted he had written a book, and in June 1963, Meyerson agreed to accept one more revision.[109] But Meyerson left Harvard that month to take a job at Berkeley. The decision would be in James Q. Wilson's hands, with Derthick, another system-building political scientist and an even less forgiving reader, supplying the institutional memory. By December of that year, the verdict was in: Derthick deferred to the university presses, but she herself deemed *The Competitors* unfit for the Joint Center series. Wilson was "fascinated by much of the material I found there" in the three central chapters, but the higher-level conceptualization was "difficult to follow." (Those chapters were also "seriously out of balance" in terms of length, as Clay had not appreciably cut down the Brookline bit.) There were cases, but the overarching claims seemed "not systematically related to the case studies, and [they] suffer from an imprecision of language."[110] Imprecision? Clay had staked his entire reputation as an urbanist on knowing the right words to use in order to narrate city life—to set its physical scene and evoke its human drama.[111] Wilson's position was that research and theory, evidence and inference, were just not adding up. By 1963, that was the language of urban studies as Ford had defined it. If nothing else would secure its identity, the Joint Center had to defend at least this minimum definition of method.

This is not to say that Clay became unwelcome at the center. He returned to Harvard in April 1962 for the sixth Rockefeller Urban Design Conference. This one concerned "inter-city growth," and Clay gave a talk, "New Towns for Appalachian America," that was pro forma in terms of content—this was the topic he had abandoned upon arriving as a fellow—but distinctive in its regional focus.[112] In 1964, after *The Competitors* project was confirmed dead, he attended a GSD conference on landscape architecture and called for "love of place" in "a world rapidly turning to love of process."[113] (Was the latter a veiled reference to the center itself?) He remained a major voice in urban criticism; indeed, his star only rose. But the unhappy encounter between Grady Clay and the Joint

Center for Urban Studies had thrown into stark relief the differences between two kinds of urban knowledge—differences that, by all accounts, the eclectic center had seemed poised to annul or at least ignore. That the center could accommodate both styles of work, and that it intended to fuse them into a larger assemblage, is telling. That the blend proved unstable—that Clay's impressionistic urbanism could or would not fit into the frame of systematic research, even when he tried to play comparative social scientist—is also telling.[114] Interdisciplinarity did not mean that anything goes. Indeed, urban studies seemed to have elaborated its own criteria for what counted as systematic inquiry. They were general, to be sure, and methodological in a broad sense that belonged no more to political scientists than economists, or to sociologists than geographers. But they held sway, and as a unit, the Joint Center was sufficiently organized, and hierarchical, that it could punish deviations from the norm. It could, in a word, discipline. The experiment so far had stretched and remade the center as an organizational model, but it had also revealed its limits.

On the eve of his 1963 departure for Berkeley's College of Environmental Design, Meyerson found much to commend in what he and Rodwin had overseen.[115] The Joint Center, he wrote in a final report to the visiting committee, "has once again made the study of the city and the region intellectually respectable." That pursuit "had been in eclipse for a generation" until interest revived after the war. As Meyerson periodized things, the last genuine peak had come in the 1920s with Robert Park and the Chicago School. Depression and war had not put a stop to urban work by any means, but international affairs, he felt, had overtaken the American city as the leading claim on experts' attention.[116] The Joint Center, having reset the agenda, was thus of generational import. Rodwin, too, seemed pleased with the center's first act. It had shifted the framework, he argued, from "the problem of the city" to variously scaled "problems within cities." It had successfully made the case for social science as a necessary ingredient in the theory and practice of planning. It had also counteracted the tendency, apparent at Chicago's PERP and some of its imitator institutions, to recast the planner's work in terms of "generic skills" of negotiation with no inherent connection to land use.[117]

Paul Ylvisaker, too, celebrated the early work. Ylvisaker was a man forever on the hunt for models of best practice, and he carefully monitored the contraption he had been so instrumental in setting up. By 1962, he was convinced that, in its ethos and basic division of labor, the Joint Center demonstrated how centers of urban studies outside the United States ought to look—and soon. Around the world, he wrote, there was an acute need for similar units to "gather" and "sort" the "accumulating bits and pieces of wisdom relating to the building and rebuilding of cities." This would not be easy, given "the vastness of the subject ('urban' is about as broad and permissive a word as 'international')." Yet the Harvard–MIT model was appealingly interstitial, a template for further "halfway houses between what knowledge we have and what action we are forced by necessity to undertake."[118] Ylvisaker proposed opening six to twelve of these "urban study and consulting centers." Candidates outside North America included Tokyo, Delhi, Cairo, Caracas, Athens, Berlin, London, and The Hague; closer to home were Ottawa, New York, somewhere unspecified in California, and the Joint Center itself. They would "emphasiz[e] especially the capture-and-recording of significant urban experiments." They would engage their own surroundings, but each host city would also become a case study slotted into the comparative, law-seeking, ever-bigger science of urban life.[119]

Ylvisaker spoke for himself. Others at Ford raised doubts, particularly as the time came for Rodwin and Meyerson to seek renewal of the grant. The psychologist Robert Havighurst, whom Ylvisaker called upon in 1962 to evaluate the group, gave urban studies ten years to reach maturity as a field. Of the Joint Center, he wrote, "They see their task as the production of a company of sophisticated specialists" on the model of the medical sciences. To do that, though, "a very consistent effort is necessary to bring about in the social sciences that form of integration" of training with research that Abraham Flexner had urged at Johns Hopkins.[120] The program officer Homer Wadsworth found it hard to imagine that consistency would ever be the center's hallmark. He could see that their projects were miscellaneous. "The utility of such studies is not always clear. It is not necessary that it should be," he clarified—a point on which humanists and basic scientists could find common ground—but "the price paid is a considerable diffusion of effort. It is a necessary price: no other means is available to what the interest and enthusiasm of people singularly independent of mind and spirit" were bound to produce. But in its current state, it seemed unlikely to last.[121]

The grant renewal came through at the end of 1962, and another followed in 1965 under James Q. Wilson's direction. Ford's critiques had not cut the experiment short. But all throughout the 1960s, there were tensions between what Ylvisaker's contingent thought the center should be and what it was becoming. The political scientist Malcolm Moos, Ford's director of policy and planning at mid-decade, was the harshest. He approved of the basic research Banfield had enabled with the uniform "Reports on Politics": "The Center could become something of a data bank" if it followed this path. He cheered efforts to strengthen urban economics as a subfield, although there were prejudices to contend with: at Harvard, "putting the word 'urban' before the term 'economist' . . . was like putting the word 'horse' before 'doctor.'"

Above all, whereas Wadsworth had valued the scholars' wide range of interests, for Moos it all seemed "highly diffuse." "It has been episodic.... The Center's interest in a particular problem has usually lasted only as long as that of the scholar who happened to be writing a book on the subject in question." This scatteration had been fine at first, but it was time to narrow the scope. Around 1965, Ford became far more insistent on promoting a version of systematic, empirical, incremental work that moved legibly from evidence to generalization on the model of the hard sciences. The center was "a kind of clubhouse," Moos observed, and "the importance of the clubhouse *atmosphere* as a source of *stimulation*"—he had done his reading—"cannot be denied." And yet, to him they seemed to be luxuriating in their luncheons and eccentric visitors from Louisville "rather than generating a sustained attack upon any of the problems of urban life."[122]

In its formal evaluations of what the Joint Center had wrought, Ford reprised the language of urban problems, ubiquitous after 1945 but also resonant with Progressive Era theorizations of social problems. *Problem* cut two ways. The word could denote a state of affairs that was deficient and in need of urgent redress. This instrumental sense was crucial to how the center first justified its existence and argued for continued financial support. In the postwar era, however, the term swung toward a more exploratory meaning. *Problem* meant a conceptual problem, a problem of knowledge worth dwelling on in light of or in spite of any solution yet proposed. As Ford's appraisers argued, the term *urban*, because it was so broad, denoted "not a discipline but a problem area." Hence the jointure. "These problem areas must, however, be defined. Only in this way can the Joint Center be a center and not simply an intellectual clearinghouse."[123] Six years into the experiment, the most basic questions were still unsettled: what they were studying, how, and why.

The Joint Center soon responded to these critiques, redirected its energy, and, in the process, rethought its role as an active participant in the planning process. After 1963, a set of even more fundamental intellectual shifts took hold there, and in urban studies more broadly, as it became clear that American cities were changing at a faster pace than the experts expected or, at root, were comfortable with. To remain credible, its leaders sensed, the center had to reckon with the very temporality of that change—to make urban temporality as such their topic and theme. As it did so, and as the next chapter discusses at length, the focus of its knowledge slowly drifted from *the urban* to *the urban future*: by definition, unknowable in any absolute sense and thus productive of intense, intricate debate. As the center went public, it laid bare new conflicts over the place and politics of expert knowledge.

CHAPTER 3

"Our Retrospection Will All Be to the Future"
History, Inference, and the Temporalities of Planning

In 1963, the Joint Center went public on another scale entirely. *Beyond the Melting Pot*, a study of ethnicity in New York City by Nathan Glazer and Daniel Patrick Moynihan, bespoke a series of changes underway as the center entered its second phase.[1] Quite possibly the best-known work of postwar social science after Riesman's *The Lonely Crowd*, of which Glazer was also a coauthor, it was the center's first genuine blockbuster. Considered in tandem with the center's contemporaneous incursions into both federal policy making and the hyperlocal politics of development, its reception points up a set of ambivalences that wracked the new urban expertise and colored every attempt to make basic knowledge applicable to the interlocking crises of the postwar metropolis.

In Public: Greater Boston and the Anxieties of Intervention, 1963–1970

Other Joint Center books had reoriented disciplines or subdisciplines. Lynch's *Image of the City* (1960), for instance, had broad and immediate influence, but it was largely confined to the design fields. Glazer and Moynihan conceived their book from the outset as a work of popular sociology. Indeed, at the time of writing, neither was affiliated with a university. Glazer had come of age in the City College milieu. From the 1940s, he had carved out a life in letters at *Commentary*, the most explicitly Semitic of the midcentury little magazines, and at Anchor Books, where he had a key editorial role in the "quality paperback" revolution. In Kennedy's Washington, he took up a post at the Housing and Home Finance Agency (HHFA) and dedicated himself full-time to urban topics.[2] Moynihan was born in Tulsa, but as a child, he moved to New York. He, too, claimed a basically working-class background: he made it through City College but never tired of telling tales of life as a shoeshine boy on the streets of Hell's Kitchen. Unlike Glazer, he attained a PhD in history, and by 1963 had spent a few years teaching in university settings. Most of his career, however, had been in public service: he learned state politics in 1950s Albany under the energetic Democratic governor Averell Harriman, and under Kennedy, he rose to Assistant Secretary of Labor. Both authors were accustomed to perforating the border between scholarship and politics, academe and its potential publics.[3] *Beyond the Melting Pot* did precisely that and was all the while a work of bona fide social science in a way that other conspicuous urban texts of the time—by Jacobs, Mumford, Bacon, or Tunnard—were not.

The book was a sociological inventory of five racial and ethnic groups well represented in New York City and indicated in the subtitle: "the Negroes, Puerto Ricans, Jews, Italians, and Irish." Each group commanded one chapter. Glazer had begun the project alone in 1959, and he wrote all but the Irish material—Moynihan's assignment upon signing on in 1961—and the conclusion. The main contention, repeated throughout a dense but digestible mass of empirical detail, was that full "assimilation" of (especially) white immigrant groups and their descendants "did not happen." Ethnic allegiance, crosscut with class and religion, persisted in America; indeed, as a source of identity and basis for political organization, ethnicity was "not a survival . . . but a new social form" given salience by later generations. This fact contradicted prevailing postwar ideas of consensus, obviously, but also most academic sociology, which tended to accept Milton Gordon's functionalist theses on assimilation and, indirectly, the Chicago School's naturalistic models of neighborhood "invasion and succession." Glazer and Moynihan adopted a broadly cultural approach to explaining racial and ethnic difference that was compatible with the Banfield-Wilson model. Also like Banfield and Wilson, the book hastened the Joint Center's retreat from Lynch's (and to some extent Rodwin's) vision of an urban studies committed to the analysis of physical form. Here, people in cities, their views and interests, and the organizations they contrive to pursue those interests—not houses, parks, ports, rails, autos, billboards, roads—were the field's fundamental objects. Glazer and Moynihan pieced together a mostly qualitative study that, when looked at in the right light, could pass for basic research. It was empirical, it was comparative, it made recourse to descriptive statistics when necessary, and, at first glance, it seemed to withhold judgment. Like Banfield, Wilson, and their epigones, the authors directly addressed the methodological question of how well its empirics could equip inferences beyond local context, even as their tone in doing so could be ironical: "Paris may be France, London may be England, but New York, we continue to reassure ourselves, is *not* America," precisely on account of the very diversity that was their topic. "But, of course, it *is* America: not all of America, or even most, but surely the most important single part. . . . As time passes, the nation comes more to resemble the city."[4]

Beyond the Melting Pot deepened the Joint Center's connection to New York, and it diversified the group's funding sources beyond Ford. Initially, the project's major patron was the New York Post Foundation. When one *Post* writer, reporting a series on Jewish life, found himself at a loss, Daniel Bell, a friend of the newspaper's editor, reached out to Glazer, his old acquaintance from City College circles, and suggested he "produce a quantity of background research material" for its reporters to use in their subsequent work. Martin Meyerson caught wind of it, a "complicated contract" emerged between the Joint Center and the Post Foundation, and research began under the heading "The Peoples of New York City." Having seen the first few chapters, though, the Post Foundation declared itself unsatisfied and cut off funding, leaving the Joint Center to resuscitate the project, replenish Glazer's team of research assistants, and bring the book to press.[5]

This was fully public social science. Meyerson, often technical in his own work but never hostile to popularization, had sensed the project's potential. James Q. Wilson was skeptical of the sloganeering that tended to punctuate academics' public utterances, but he, too, pushed policy relevance and civic engagement, even if those came at the expense of a fuller accounting of urban life in terms of its physical grain. But there were many different ways to go public, and by 1963, conversations at the Joint Center were dwelling ever more on the complexities and pitfalls of exposure—not whether to pursue it, but how. *Beyond the Melting Pot* saw coverage in the *New York Times* in September of that year, and the chosen reviewer was none other than Harvard's Oscar Handlin, a Joint Center affiliate and a leading student of ethnic New York (as well as its product, having come up through Brooklyn College). Glazer and Moynihan knew that he could easily disembowel the book, if he so chose, and make an example of it as having laid bare the problem with softer social scientists preening for wider attention. They also knew that when writing in the public eye, savvier academics tended to obey other norms. Glazer wrote to his coauthor, in anticipation of the *Times* review, that Handlin "would blast us in an academic journal *but not there*."⁶ When it appeared, Glazer deemed the review "so-so. It could have been better."⁷

Martin Meyerson spoke with similar nuance of his own incursions into public life. *Face of the Metropolis* (1963) was a richly illustrated, coffee table–sized volume that he authored in his capacity as the head of ACTION, the advocacy group whose work ran on a parallel track with his scholarship on the planning process. After Clarence Stein wrote him to praise the book, Meyerson's reply revealed a scholar who was becoming ever more tactical about how to package his ideas to reach plural readerships: "To a professional audience, I would have been much harder. Some of my professional colleagues do not realize this distinction."⁸ The Joint Center was learning the rules of engagement for bridging urbanism and public intellect. In time, it would rewrite them.

Moynihan was by all accounts uniquely equipped to blur the boundaries between pure inquiry and worldly intervention. He had left the Department of Labor in mid-1965 for a professorship at Harvard, in the same government department that employed James Q. Wilson. He latched on to "the Joint," seeking the sort of backslapping bonhomie that the strictures of department life, he felt, could not accommodate, and by mid-1966 was handpicked by Wilson to succeed him as director. Wilson enjoined the faculty to allow Moynihan "as free a hand as possible" in his management.⁹ Moynihan took to the role with a singular, dandiacal gusto. The weekly research luncheons became major events, known campuswide to be "very much his baby" and always prefaced by theatrical remarks from Moynihan himself—routinely more memorable, many said, than the invited speakers.¹⁰ Talks represented the usual cross section of topics, regions, methods, disciplines, and positions on the spectrum between scholarship and practice; he compelled no radical innovation in terms of intellectual content. The series became so identified with its charismatic host, however, that in 1968, when Moynihan was recalled to Washington, this time to serve Nixon, the Harvard Faculty Club discontinued it.¹¹

Although he had an appreciation for the built environment—under Kennedy, he had introduced the Guiding Principles for Federal Architecture—as director, Moynihan oversaw still further dephysicalization of urban studies as a field.¹² These trends had been gathering force throughout the postwar era; in some ways, Moynihan, a latecomer to the urbanist academy, merely shepherded them along. Whereas Rodwin had tried to keep urban studies traditionally geographic in its remit, Wilson had steadily elevated a narrower, more falsifiable social science of culture, politics, and behavior whose spatial footprint was not always precisely stated. The Moynihan period saw the Joint Center reissue the results of a 1964 conference in a book titled *Computer Methods in the Analysis of Large-Scale Social Systems* (1968).¹³ Moynihan enthusiastically published the proceedings of a 1967 conference he had convened in Washington as *Social Statistics and the City* (1968), which addressed remedies for the decennial census's habitual undercount of the poor.[14] Physical planners, urban designers, and theorists of urban form were not summarily banished from Moynihan's Joint Center; it remained an intellectually heterogeneous place. Yet their interests seemed more peripheral than ever. Kevin Lynch severed ties in 1968. Rodwin stepped away from the faculty committee in 1969—the better to focus his attention on the MIT-only Special Program for Urban and Regional Studies, which he had founded in 1967 as an alternative to the Joint Center.[15]

As a discipline and profession, planning had changed. In 1959, no funds for research on planning were specifically earmarked at the GSD; in 1967, such research commanded 38 percent of the departmental budget.[16] Comparable figures could be adduced from any number of design schools. The Joint Center had long rewarded systematicity of thought. Under Wilson, though, and then Moynihan, quantitative sophistication was finally enshrined as the decisive mark of rigor and the recipe for policy relevance.[17]

Wilson and Moynihan also ramped up the Joint Center's collaboration with policy makers at the federal level. Rodwin would look back on 1965–1966 as "the period during which the problems of cities were formally placed on the agenda of American national government," with Johnson's 1965 creation of HUD being the watershed.[18] The chairman of Johnson's National Commission on Urban Problems concurred, writing in 1968 that "the characteristic phenomenon of American politics in the 1960s will some day be seen as the emergence of the city as a political issue." Robert C. Wood, MIT political scientist, eventual HUD undersecretary, and a figure with growing clout at the redefined Joint Center, would quote this line approvingly, with a few years' hindsight, in *The Necessary Majority* (1972).[19] Rodwin contended that the Joint Center "clearly anticipated the rising national interest in urban affairs," and it "helped shape and direct that interest, if only in the limited ways of academic institutions."[20] Seen from Cambridge, the emergence of this new object of political calculation, the city, was a direct consequence of organized researchers' success in positing it as an object of study.

As the preferred locution among policy makers shifted from *problems* to *crisis*—the urban crisis—the center was a vital link in the semantic chain. The Joint Center could not have precisely foretold the "long, hot summers" of African American unrest, which began in 1964 and, with the prolonged confrontation in the Watts section of Los Angeles the following year, ratified *crisis* as the elite term of art (although the center had long insisted, without embarking on a polemic, that all was not well in the affluent society: sudden migrations and attendant racial frictions not only accompanied but were the product of prosperity). Nor was Wilson, an Angeleno and the center's director when Watts rose up, dispositionally comfortable with crisis rhetoric. A term like *blight*, imported by the Chicago School from plant ecology, always introduced "more drama than precision" into political debate. And yet, he admitted, such language, ubiquitous by late 1965, did signal a new visibility for urban questions—which, in the America of Lyndon Johnson and Paul Ylvisaker, meant a demand for more expertise. It was convenient, then, that September was the due date for Wilson to apply for a third grant from Ford. "While scholarship," he wrote in the proposal, "should not be guided by each passing whim or fad or fancy, neither should it fail to address itself to the fundamental changes in the civilization of which it is a part."[21] Riot, rebellion, uprising, unrest—the nomenclature for these episodes of (mostly) Black resistance has been contested for decades. Elite perceptions and categories had consequences for the allocation of funding and its capacity to reorganize the life of the mind.

Even before 1965, the Joint Center had begun bidding for greater influence on federal policy. Kennedy relied on the advice of social scientists as no president had before, and of the twenty-nine issue-specific task forces he established to formulate plans of attack, problem by social problem, scholars employed or trained at Harvard and MIT were the dominant presence. The pattern continued during Johnson's Great Society period. His forty-two task forces—twenty-five of them begun in 1964 alone—encompassed 411 members, of whom 167 were academics. Of the academics, 29 percent had earned PhDs from those two universities. Harvard and MIT also dominated Johnson's presidential commissions, a desirable alternative to task forces "when an especially vexing policy issue became publicly visible and the White House needed to signal its concern without committing itself substantively and politically." Urban questions had clearly crossed that threshold of visibility. The Kerner Commission, formally the Commission on Civil Disorder, was the most conspicuous, appointed in 1967 to assess the root causes of rioting. The broader-based National Commission on Urban Problems began work the next year, Johnson's last in office. From 1964, Robert C. Wood himself chaired one of Johnson's "Big Three" task forces, the group known as "Cities"—formally the Task Force on Metropolitan and Urban Problems, its name a reflection of the scalar adjustment that Wood and others had worked to compel in an age of suburban dilation. To fill out its roster, he drew from Joint Center circles and added Meyerson and Glazer (both of whom were now Berkeley-based). The Model Cities Program, which took cues from Ford's Gray Areas and proposed a less physicalist alternative to Urban Renewal, launched in 1966, also with clear Joint Center connections in the person of Harvard's Charles Haar. Haar then steered a pair of task forces set up in 1967 to address "suburban problems" and one supposed remedy, the planning of New Towns.[22]

The Joint Center also carried out a modest amount of research on contract to the federal government. Forming a center helped attract funding, whether that funding originated with a foundation or a public agency. For instance, the Senate's Subcommittee on Intergovernmental Relations commissioned a well-received report, *The Effectiveness of Metropolitan Planning* (1964), on a complex but urgent topic amid large-scale suburbanization and its attendant fragmentation of governance, service provision, and intermunicipal goodwill. Meyerson had brokered the agreement in 1963; Wilson oversaw its execution. (Moynihan was not yet on Harvard faculty at this time, but he was a Joint Center author and an obvious link to Washington, as was Glazer on account of his stint at the HHFA.) Haar headed the research team, whose report called for "orderly growth" and "more harmonious . . . relations" among the hundreds of redundant municipal corporations that made up larger metropolitan areas. It also called for an "integrated economic study," prepared by scholars, to serve as the basis for policy recommendations. It admitted, however, pace the Taylorists, that "there can be no 'one best way' to resolve the problems."[23]

Perhaps not, but as *crisis* became the new catchall signifier, Ford, the Joint Center, and the federal complex ramped up the quantity and intensity of their interactions (for a finite period, which ended around 1969, leading Wood to lament that policy makers and their experts focused on these questions only "belatedly and briefly").[24] Moynihan was the director, but Paul Ylvisaker's will was as strong as ever. New centers of urban studies were still cropping up at his urging, both at home and abroad, and not only in the expected places—one had recently been proposed at the University of Alaska. He was glad to continue channeling Ford's funds to universities, strengthening their planning curricula, investing in computing capacity, and embedding academics in their communities, as Penn's Paul Davidoff and a growing number of participatory planners were stressing by mid-decade. But Ylvisaker remained devoted to the center as an organizational form, and he was fixated on its propagation. Perhaps, he wrote, the next step was to found a research center internal to the Department of Housing and Urban Development, staff it with scholars trained in the world of ORUs, and task them with evaluating the performance of that agency's own programs.[25] Its model: the Joint Center.

The linkages were many and intimate, and more so with each passing year. The Joint Center had gone public, convinced that organized research and federal policy each had something to offer the other. Contract work was one thing. But what was the intellectual content of this work? What concepts stood behind these gambits for public exposure? Of what were Wilson and Moynihan seeking to convince Americans? Moynihan made the move into academia at a very particular juncture in his career. In March 1965, working independently but from within the Department of Labor, he had issued "The Negro Family: The Case for National Action," or the Moynihan Report, a document so widely and bitterly debated from the moment of its arrival that it is impossible to compass the Joint Center's activity, mid-1960s urban studies, the machinery of federal urban policy, the clash at Watts, or the era's moral politics of race without reference to it. The report rather infamously posited that a cultural "tangle of pathology ... capable of perpetuating itself," not material deprivation from without, was the engine behind manifold problems in African American communities. These ideas were not original to Moynihan; much other period social science explained urban life in terms of "the culture of poverty." Some of this work, by Oscar Lewis and Michael Harrington, for instance, was written from the political left, often with literary verve and often with the aim of indicting larger constellations of forces and proposing their reconfiguration. (Moynihan remained an accredited Democrat.) Yet the report, and the high-handed persona Moynihan affected in defending it, met with astonishment and derision in left-liberal circles. Surely it was assigning blame—and the onus of responsibility—to the disenfranchised. Surely this was not an expert speaking.[26]

The report loomed over Moynihan as he joined Wilson in Harvard's government department and the Joint Center passed into his protection. It was an inescapable ingredient in the center's "atmosphere" from the mid-1960s, and it informed the reception of the subset of Joint Center work that, even without openly moralizing, called for cultural approaches to the study of ethnicity, inequality, and urban life—Wilson's own writings, and Banfield's, very much included, to say nothing of *Beyond the Melting Pot* as it became a classic of sociology and the center prepared an updated second edition.[27] Writing to Morton Schussheim of the HHFA in 1964, Wilson identified "the culture and pathology of poverty" as one of the "core problems" to take up in the near term.[28] An Ad Hoc Committee on Urban Studies at MIT listed "eliminating the culture of poverty" as the first issue meriting "national priority attention." (Number two was "moving people around efficiently by a combination of improved transportation and planned residential ecology.")[29] By 1966, Wilson was requesting Nathan Pusey's help in setting up an E. Franklin Frazier Fund at Harvard to support such research—Frazier being the sociologist of Black family life whose work Moynihan had given new prominence when decrying single-parent households. "It would not be a 'Center' or a 'Program,'" Wilson clarified, but it had to be done. "The special problem of the Negro American in our large cities is a central feature—perhaps the central feature—of what is generally referred to as the 'urban problem.'" The urban crisis, on this logic, was a crisis of Black life as adjudicated by ethnically various but racially white observers.[30]

Moynihan's Joint Center fused these keywords and worked to make their congruence seem self-evident as Watts gave way to Detroit (1967), Newark (1967), Washington (1968, following Martin Luther King's assassination), and other episodes of unrest in a growing litany anxiously recited in the halls of power—whether to condemn or absolve, propose fixes or urge legislative restraint. MIT Press (but not the Joint Center series) published *The Moynihan Report and the Politics of Controversy* (1967), a compilation of primary sources, expository essays, and sociological analysis—the better to clarify and lubricate a two-year-old debate that showed no signs of abating.[31] Its primary editor, the urban sociologist Lee Rainwater, was on the faculty of Washington University in St. Louis and well connected to its organs of interdisciplinary research and public intellect, the latter via Irving Horowitz's in-house journal *Trans-Action*. Within a year of Rainwater's report-on-the-report, Harvard's sociology department poached him, and as the 1970s approached, he became a regular participant in Joint Center activities.[32] Moynihan had found ways to make controversy a strategy by which to expand his public, absorb potential critics, and, in turn, reorganize urban research.

This was all transpiring at the level of Cabinet agencies, Senate subcommittees, and national action. Moynihan had the federal scale in mind as he plotted a course of public engagement for the Joint Center. At the scale of the individual city or metropolitan area, however, the center's commitment to applied work was far more equivocal. Ford was always more interested than the center to alter Boston's landscape and lifeways. Well into the Wilson directorate, Ford sounded these notes repeatedly and acidly in its periodic reviews. Homer Wadsworth wrote to Ylvisaker in 1961 to express concern that "the great social laboratory of the Boston region" was being ignored. National and international ambitions were not bad per se, but "the corollary of serving a world interest is that one cannot serve his region at the same time."[33] Robert Havighurst, writing in 1962, noted "a very real and difficult division that separates town and gown in this region." For years, it had militated against fuller engagement, particularly by Harvard, whose name inspired deep suspicion in non-elite parts of town. The center's understandable restraint, though, now bordered on "neglect."[34] Three years later, as another grant renewal loomed and the center had still not appreciably connected with its neighbors—but had formed an "office for Boston liaison," chaired by an executive from Eastern Gas and Fuel, and considered chartering a "Boston Studies Program"—Malcolm Moos's evaluation underlined the "heritage of town–gown animosity" that predated and constrained it. "These conditions will not quickly change, and they represent substantial handicaps to any effort to use the Boston area as a laboratory for the Joint Center."[35]

Boston, simply put, was not Chicago. Neither Harvard nor MIT was the University of Chicago. The Joint Center was not the Chicago School, PERP, or any of their offshoots that had made inroads into Hyde Park. "Laboratory" was almost surely not the correct analogy, even as the principals seemed unable to resist it. "A literature on the Boston area comparable with the Chicago series . . . simply does not exist," Wadsworth observed early on. "Meyerson is acutely aware of this deficiency."[36] But Meyerson never managed to correct course. The center was "considerably more successful," Moos wrote, "with basic or 'curiosity' research" than with applied work. Its local engagements struck him as "superficial—something of a faltering, half-hearted gesture." Some studies of Boston had come together, but they were either one-off treatments, like Rodwin's book on middle-income housing, or, when more applied in nature, "a second-rate undertaking from a scholarly point of view."[37] The trade-off seemed insoluble: rigorous basic research, which Ford supported with a passion, apparently sacrificed something in the way of public responsibility, while gestures toward deeper community engagement, for which the foundation also clamored, somehow seemed intellectually unbecoming. As the skittish visiting committee warned, "You get mixed up in politics."[38] (And as the center grew by attracting new hires, was there not a contradiction involved in poaching faculty from, say, Philadelphia or St. Louis if it interrupted research agendas developed over many years of consultation with those communities?) The gulf between the scholars and the citizenry was so vast, in fact, that Moos suggested the Joint Center partner with other nearby universities if they wished to make any headway as practitioners of planning: the program in public administration at Boston College, the Catholic school in suburban Chestnut Hill to the west; Boston University, also private, just across the Charles River from Cambridge; and the new branch of the public University of Massachusetts, then located in cramped quarters at one corner of Boston Common but soon to occupy a waterfront campus at Columbia Point, on the farthest fringes of working-class South Boston.[39] In certain contexts, institutional prestige had proved to be a liability. Clearly, expertise appealed to some publics more than others.

Eventually, in response to Ford's prodding, the Joint Center entered into contracts with a range of agencies doing work in greater Boston, thereby bringing their research and practice into closer alignment. The Harvard political scientist Charles Cherington completed a study of, and for, the Metropolitan District Commission, the special district responsible for finding regional solutions to water provision, sewage disposal, and other inherently multicity problems. For the Municipal Manpower Commission, Robert C. Wood scrutinized the political economy of technological innovation as the firms of Route 128 ramped up production. "Signs of convergence are already evident," Wilson and staff wrote in 1964 with Ford's admonitions in mind. "An even sharper focus [on Boston] is being established." It was Wilson's "firm belief" that "lasting contributions" would require the accelerated development of "a tradition of inquiry in which scholars and students use the urban area of which they are a part as a laboratory for developing and testing theories, training researchers, and exploring policy alternatives," not to mention "exposing students to the illuminating realities of research and action"—again the "laboratory," again protestations that the Joint Center was willing and able to think instrumentally ("use" the urban area?). Still, Boston had finally emerged as one of the center's foci, and this, Wilson insisted, had happened organically, without the heavy hand of management making it so.[40]

Not all of the local research was cast in the mold of exact social science. In the later 1960s, the center hosted Bernard Taper—*San Francisco Chronicle* staff writer, *New Yorker* contributor, profiler of Charles Abrams—to prepare a book-length study, *The Arts in Boston* (1970). The arrangements were complex: Taper had been invited to Boston, and paid, by the Permanent Charity Fund, but he did his work under the auspices of the Joint Center. The book bore its stamp: he cited recent work by Meyerson and Banfield, who had used Joint Center funds to take out twelve full-page ads in "all of the Boston newspapers" between 1962 and 1965, propose solutions for a range of perceived ills, and compile the results as *Boston: The Job Ahead* (1966), a slim, well-illustrated addition to the series. Taper drew on Joint Center–adjacent scholarship by György Kepes to support the idea that the "drab" built environment of Boston needed to be made "more heraldic." He also nodded to more experimental ongoing work at MIT's Center for Advanced Visual Studies, which Kepes had founded in 1967. For the most part, though, Taper puzzled over the paradox that, while the city's elites had for centuries understood themselves to be "custodians of culture," they expressed their support almost solely through private charity: Boston consistently showed the lowest public expenditure on the arts of any major American city. Even the Newark Museum of Art, he noted, had a higher annual allocation than any of its Boston counterparts. The example with which he opened the book was a 1967 dispute between the Metropolitan District Commission and Ed Logue's BRA over whether to earmark for public art 1 percent of the operating budget of a new recreation center in Roxbury, the mostly African American district that became the target of many Urban Renewal schemes on Logue's watch. It was BRA policy to do so, but the Metropolitan District

Commission "flatly refused." "Art," its officer was quoted as saying, "is a waste of time." What, Taper asked, subtended the "quintessentially Bostonian attitude" of the Brahmin class, "its admirable weighing of obligations, past and future, its deferment of delight even unto the third generation"? Like his hosts, Taper proved attentive to the temporal complexities of his subject. Preservation, stewardship, custody: if these were forms of planning, on what time horizons did they operate? And what would it take, in the near term, to "desegregate" art and public life?[41]

The answers were not readily forthcoming, and these were anyhow humanistic, speculative questions. Yet, in keeping with the center's interventionist turn, Taper also made a very detailed proposal—accompanied by his only illustrations—for what he called the Hinge Block, a cultural complex abutting Boston Common that, in its enclosure, its withdrawal from the swarming nearby streets, would represent "a truly urban, twentieth-century solution" to the problem of high-cultural provision within the framework of Urban Renewal.[42] BRA had proposed this scheme in 1966; Taper's aim was to promote it and assess its prospects. In so doing, he embarked on a conceptual exploration that asked what it could even mean, in this most nostalgic of American cities, to envision the future.

The center's public turn also momentarily foregrounded those who had argued from the start that design, physical planning, and urban form should be the group's leading concerns. With his British-born MIT colleague Donald Appleyard and a third author named John Myer, Kevin Lynch resurfaced with *The View from the Road* (1964), a singular work that raised the same questions that motivated the cognitive maps made famous in *The Image of the City*—how do differently situated groups of people see and imaginatively organize their surroundings?—but reformulated the method to analyze vision as experienced in motion. "Road-watching is a delight," the authors wrote, "and the highway is—or at least might be—a work of art." It was a kinesthetic art, like "the dance or the amusement park." Or was it a sort of text? "The roadside should be a fascinating book to read on the run."[43] These lines split the difference between rumination and prescription, and they were heresy to virtually every postwar urbanist not named J. B. Jackson, apostle of the vernacular, or Grady Clay, who may not have liked the highway strip but defended to the death his contention that "the strip is trying to tell us something."[44] A ring road would soon encircle Boston's core, and the public agency tasked with selecting its route was soliciting advice from scholars and designers. The Joint Center saw an opening.

Compromise, they had learned, was in the nature of applied work; purity was not. Even so, what Appleyard, Lynch, and Myer came up with was surely about as arcane and artistic a text as Boston's highway engineers had ever encountered on the job. The winding prose was one thing; the cascading, multisensory metaphors were another. The authors also presented a wildly intricate notation system designed to transmit the direction and intensity of the average driver's gaze as hailed, reeled in, and torqued by various features of the environment: buildings, tunnels, overpasses, bends in the road, changes in elevation, signage, greenery, other vehicles. They took pains to depict automotive vision as consisting of discrete "episodes" of perception which could be narrated "like a magazine serial" and then joined into an "articulated but 'endless' composition, of the kind typified in jazz or medieval polyphony." (The average highway driver, they admitted, was a middle-class, suburban-dwelling, implicitly white driver. The average highway drive was a weekday commute or a weekend excursion. "We know nothing" about "another class or culture.") And, they insisted, this was all to be understood in the spirit of basic research: although the specific route (with segments called Riverway, Centerway, Crossing, etc.) and its landmarks (the immovable Citgo sign above Fenway Park) were uniquely Bostonian, "the problem of designing for vision in motion is everywhere the same."[45] Applied work most succeeded when it invited reapplication to other places and times. Like Lynch's mapping exercise, this one might touch down on specific roads, but it was purportedly a method by which to master the *road* as a landscape type.

In the run-up to *View*, Lynch and Appleyard also produced *Signs in the City* (1963), a collaborative effort that drew on students' work from an experimental course they co-taught at MIT. Appleyard left Cambridge before decade's end for Berkeley's College of Environmental Design, and there he adapted aspects of the viewshed methodology to street planning in San Francisco and to the burgeoning multicounty Bay Area Rapid Transit system. Lynch, too, iterated versions of the study well into the 1970s. With Michael Southworth (who also headed to Berkeley), he produced "Designing and Managing the Strip" (1974), a Joint Center working paper that called even more stridently for "intervention" on the "endless, formless, eventless" edges of the American metropolis. The regional cross section Southworth and Lynch undertook for this study had brought them only as far out as Waltham, the once-mighty textile town just west of Cambridge that now functioned as a first-ring suburb. Yet, the reader senses, they felt they had seen enough of the strip, an environment where capitalist, "necessarily short-sighted actors" clamored for drivers' attention with garish signage that just about always disrespected its context. "There is rarely any long view," they wrote, "only a formless one." This was a plea for planning as an exercise of foresight. They had seen Boston's unplanned future, and it looked like Los Angeles.[46]

Lynch chaired the Joint Center's faculty committee in 1965–1966 and, noting the "current nationwide interest in outdoor beauty" stemming from Lady Bird Johnson's advocacy, made a proposal, "Use of Design Talent in Improving the Urban Environment of the Boston Area," that went well beyond the coarse-grained schemes so many in the area had come to associate with Urban Renewal. He proposed an approach to design that could encompass sounds, smells, the lighting of public space (of interest to Kepes, a visual artist whose media included stained glass), the planning of "viewing points" from which to take in the scene, and "special occasions."[47] In late 1966, Moynihan entertained the idea of having the Joint Center sponsor a "new city," built from scratch, in either New England or the hinterland of New York; a "demonstration development of Boston Harbor, its shores and islands"; "system designs" for "crucial physical elements of the city environment," such as water, air, and again light; and other bold interventions.[48] Physical planning, for the moment, was back. Yet a larger programmatic shift was not forthcoming, and certainly not for the center as a corporate entity. Lynch and Kepes were free to pursue these projects on their own time in the studio context. The way in which their ideas were sidelined may have had quite a bit to do with Moynihan, an aesthete of sorts whose tastes skewed to the conventional. Kepes took refuge in MIT's Center for Advanced Visual Studies as Lynch withdrew his Joint Center affiliation. Rodwin assumed the chair of MIT's planning department in 1969 but had progressively less to do with the center.

The center's most prolonged and, by some measures, productive partnership engaged the Metropolitan Area Planning Council (MAPC), a nongovernmental group akin to New York's long-standing Regional Plan Association (RPA) that existed to research and advocate for equitable solutions to problems that crosscut the boundaries of Boston and the hundred or so municipalities surrounding it. The MAPC formed in 1963, at the high tide of postwar anxieties about sprawl and fragmentation, and was a natural partner for the Joint Center. Representatives of the two groups made contact at a 1964 meeting of the so-called Committee of the Cultural Ecology of Boston.[49] In the spring of 1965, together with the Urban Renewal Administration and the HHFA, the MAPC announced a series of five "working conferences" featuring papers by an interdisciplinary cast of characters.[50] Citing their findings, the MAPC then adopted a new action program at its annual meeting in 1966. Joint Center scholars were well represented, and when selected proceedings were published, the center was identified as the corporate author—not the individual scholars, and not the MAPC, which originated some research but was mainly a "promoter and catalyst" enjoining other groups to make studies on its behalf. *Economic Development in the Boston Area* (1965), which digested the second conference, grappled with

Boston's fate amid the precipitous decline of defense spending (which had been concentrated in the Western states during the war), addressed the new status of knowledge as a kind of economic product, and hazarded guesses about the region's political economy as far off as 1980.[51]

The last and most general statement was found in *Planning Metropolitan Boston* (1967). Coordinated by the MIT-trained planner Richard S. Bolan, this ambitious text put forward many specific prescriptions for the region's housing stock, transportation systems, land use, and other issues. Yet its conceptual scope was broader still. More than any of the applied work completed thus far, it dwelled at great length on the underlying temporality of planning. Here and elsewhere, the Joint Center staked its relevance to public affairs on its ability to rephrase applied questions in theoretical language, adding complexity that more mundane policy shops would always eschew. This maneuver allowed the center to hover above and outside thorny debates, drop in to adjudicate their terms, lend a sense of discipline, and keep time as the practice of planning and design charged ahead.

Planning was a process, first of all, as Appleyard, on one flank of the profession, and scholars of participatory action, on the other, were saying more and more often. Static, one-shot plans were out. This was an ontological question. "What is planning?" Bolan's team asked. It is a "method or scheme of action," irreducible to the map or rendering inserted to display the finished product of that action. The authors' next move, in consecutive sections titled "Geographical Scale in Planning" and "Time Horizons in Planning," was the really significant one. The proper geographical frame for planners' interventions was a contested matter, but in broad strokes, the MAPC, like the Joint Center itself most of the time, was committed to fostering a metropolitan and regional consciousness, even as this "will necessarily require attention to less-than-metropolitan scale" as well. Scales were complexly nested, and the nimblest planners would devise ways to traverse them, at once serving vast collectivities and intimate communities of interest. To plan was to coordinate.[52]

The question of time horizon was more complicated. "'Planning' usually connotes . . . a sense of attempting to prearrange the future," they wrote, "and to predict the consequences of alternative actions. This, in turn, implies some ability to predict the future." Predicting (an intellectual exercise) and prearranging (an intervention) were in some way joined. But what were their parameters? What was the proper timescale of action? Here, Bolan and his collaborators had quite a bit to say, colored by an acquaintance with the history of the profession and a skeptical empiricism clearly informed by Wilson and, before him, Meyerson, theorist of the middle range. Planners during the Progressive Era, they wrote, were "long-term" thinkers only: they placed their visions of the "improved" city twenty or even thirty years in the future, and, to the extent possible, they sought to compel a series of private and public commitments that, if fulfilled, would realize a "beautiful" or "efficient" city after that stretch of time. This was "sound and unassailable in theory," the authors argued, but in practice there was a problem: the "virtual impossibility of making accurate predictions 20 or 30 years in the future." If the MAPC—or really any planning agency, by extension—were to succeed, a more complex, layered temporality would have to guide the work. "Long-term" planning, which they assigned a lower bound of twenty but might reasonably extend forty years into the future, had its place. "Middle-term" planning, the Meyersonian ideal, looked six to fifteen years hence. But here, Bolan continued, temporal considerations had to be further differentiated according to spatial scale. Citywide or regional plans ought to encompass ten to fifteen years, while plans that were more local in scope should be reformulated after six years—six, while the Cold War persisted, "largely to avoid being called 'five-year plans.'" If the latest techniques in modeling were involved and assumptions could be formalized and tinkered with in real time, they wrote, perhaps channeling *The View from the Road*, this would require a series of "staged plans . . . in sequence of from two to five years, similar to the sequential frames of a movie film." The point of all this was to get planners thinking simultaneously at multiple scales, scopes, ranges, or frames. A "conventional stress on the long-range master plan . . . is still present, but substantially tempered by an equal concern for short-term planning." Only thus would the Joint Center and its beneficiaries avoid reproducing "our cartoon of Utopia"—readily on offer in the Eastern Bloc, readers were to glean, as well as in some American redevelopment agencies—which "promises payoff *only* to a future generation with, at best, obscure benefits and high costs to the society of today."[53]

Something about the crucible of applied work had induced detailed reflection on methodology, indeed on the temporal orientations definitive of planning as a mode of intervention. This was at once a practical and a conceptual problem, and its implications, the Joint Center held, had to be teased out, at the risk of tedium, well in advance of concrete action. If, strictly speaking, *utopia* names a nonexistent place, a literal nowhere, the dominant tendency in the Joint Center's work by the middle of the decade was a variegated critique of the no*when* of hastily long-term forms of reasoning—of planning cut loose from the lessons of present and past.[54] Its agonistic debates over whether, where, when, and how to intervene were, at root, debates over the best ways to glimpse the urban future and call it into being. Referring their expertise to the future meant that there would always be a use for their services. The Joint Center commanded public influence (or tried to) to the extent that its researchers could present themselves as experts on urban time itself. The claim was not that they knew the future, but that, amid rapid and multifactorial change, they had the methods: they knew how to know.

From Prophecy to Projection: A Study and Its Times

Even as the Joint Center began to address Boston, Ford could tell that the scholars' commitment was thin. The center was in but not fully of its city. Its interventions were half-hearted at best. Wilson and Moynihan corrected course up to a point, but Rodwin and Meyerson had long since eschewed the Chicago School's tendency to take the home city for granted as a "laboratory" from which to generalize. Yet the Joint Center's temporal reasoning—which led to increasingly complex takes on a simple premise, that studies of the future had to precede intervention on the future—had a specific lineage, one routed through the city that Rodwin, Meyerson, and Moynihan all called home.

The earliest discussions that worked out the terms of the jointure drew outsized inspiration from one conspicuous example of organized urban research: the New York Metropolitan Region Study (NYMRS), prepared 1956–1959 and published to some fanfare in a series of ten volumes that rolled out during the center's first year of operation. Commissioned by the well-established RPA, administered by an interdisciplinary group of scholars at Harvard, and bankrolled conjointly by the Rockefeller and Ford Foundations, the study was a product of the intellectual network consolidated in the 1950s and mapped out previously. Its core task was to make systematic projections of that area's economic development, population dynamics, physical plant, and spatial structure to 1965, 1975, and then 1985—the better to prepare those who would make designs on the long or middle term. Yet, unlike the RPA's original 1929 Regional Plan of New York, the NYMRS was quite deliberately not a plan. It was a projection: an exercise in knowing the city yet to come.

Tasked with evaluating the Joint Center's progress for Ford in 1962, Robert Havighurst pointed to the NYMRS as the latest and biggest example of social science prepared in the public interest and treating of a single metropolis. If the Joint Center were eventually to undertake robust collaborative work on greater Boston, he wrote, it surely would muster nothing "as extensive" or as focused as the NYMRS. Perhaps the center should make the effort, Havighurst reasoned, but the group's structure and ethos were already demonstrably so permissive that "there will be more scatter to its program."[55] To hold the center narrowly to the standards of this one study would have been to commit a category mistake. Still, more than any of the competing centers or units that secured footholds in the academy, the limited-engagement NYMRS supplied the Joint Center with a compelling template for how to organize interdisciplinary knowledge and key it not only to the *urban* but to the more vexing question of the *urban future*. It is worth dwelling in some detail on the NYMRS and returning briefly to the 1950s, the better to clarify the example it set.

Adrift at midcentury and obsolescent in the minds of many, the RPA wagered its own future on the success of the NYMRS. The Rockefeller Foundation granted it $240,000 to cover expenses through 1960, with matching support from Ford and additional funding from the Twentieth Century Fund, the Merrill Foundation for Financial Knowledge, and the Taconic Foundation.[56] New York, somewhat improbably, was meant to serve as the diagnostic "archetype of the American metropolitan community."[57] "A simple extension," David Rockefeller assured Harvard president Nathan Pusey, would make the insights of the report relevant to other, "similar" cities, all of them left unnamed.[58]

Raymond Vernon, the study's director, was an economist, a Columbia PhD, the child of Russian immigrants, a City College graduate at fifteen, a veteran of the Marshall Plan–era State Department, and, on his telling, "a financial-type guy" who took a 50-percent pay cut from high-profile work to choose the topics, delegate and supervise the research, and become the public face of the project, often called the Vernon Report.[59] Harold Osborne, the RPA's president, gave assurance that "the study would be clearly labeled as a Harvard U. study made for the RPA."[60] Many of the contributing scholars, significantly, were economists, and, aside from Harvard, they represented a band of universities that included Rutgers, Hofstra, and MIT. Faculty from the latter were consulted as early as 1955, when the project was still notional and funding was uncertain. An RPA official privy to one progress report of May 1955, upon reading a section of the prospectus titled "The Availability of Data," double-underlined the words "and M.I.T." and wrote, "good."[61]

The component volumes numbered nine (figure 3.1), plus one "technical supplement," *Projection of a Metropolis* (1960), that was devoted entirely to methodology.[62] Four of them—a title coauthored by Vernon and the location theorist Edgar M. Hoover, along with works by Oscar Handlin, Robert C. Wood, and Vernon alone—appeared in paperback with Anchor Books and could be called classics of postwar urban studies. Hoover and Vernon's *Anatomy of a Metropolis* (1959) was prescient in marking out the further suburbanization of industry at a time when most commentators were mesmerized by the new residential landscape of lawns and tract homes.[63] *The Newcomers* (1959), by Harvard's Pulitzer-decorated social historian Oscar Handlin, addressed recent

FIGURE 3.1. Cover art for the nine main volumes of the NYMRS as published by Harvard University Press, 1959–1961. Those by Hoover and Vernon, Handlin, Wood, and Vernon were soon reissued by Anchor in paperback with different cover designs. Regional Plan Association, *Goals for the Region Project*, vol. 1 (March 1963), 4. Courtesy of Regional Plan Association.

Black and Puerto Rican migrations to the city as compared with the experience of earlier white ethnics.[64] Vernon's *Metropolis 1985* (1960) was an executive summary of the other volumes' projections, with few data to call its own.[65] Should the RPA once again decide to issue a full-scale regional plan, the thinking went, it would have all the data points it would need. More importantly, it would have a method by which to trace trend lines off into the middle distance—with 1985, when the process would begin again, as the next Year Zero.

In *1400 Governments* (1961), Robert C. Wood puzzled over how to redress greater New York's intense fragmentation into tiny municipalities duplicative in their provision of basic services. The region's political map, he wrote, was "one of the great unnatural wonders of the world."[66] (In North Jersey specifically, this phenomenon is known as "Boroughitis," a term held over from a wave of rapid incorporations in the mid-1890s.)[67] Wood invoked the example of the "metropolitan giants" already responsible for coordinating such boundary-disrespecting utilities as water and transportation. Wood was also the only author to mention Robert Moses, if nothing else an agent of coordination, who returned the favor in a 1962 *Atlantic* article, writing that he was "appalled" at the attention given "an obscure assistant professor with no record of administration."[68]

Max Hall, a former journalist and State Department official, put together *Made in New York* (1959), thick with detail on the agglomerative garment, printing, and publishing industries, and cognizant, as were Hoover and Vernon, that "manufacturing has roving habits"; it "is always shifting on the map."[69] The economist and newly minted Harvard PhD Benjamin Chinitz visualized new geographies of trade in *Freight in the Metropolis* (1960), just as Newark was supplanting New York as the chosen port for the age of containerization.[70] A trio of titles issued forth from less prominent economists: Martin Segal's *Wages in the Metropolis* (1960); Robert Lichtenberg's *One-Tenth of a Nation* (1960), which inferred New York's economic fate from national-level data; and *Money Metropolis* (1960), on the financial sector, by Sidney Robbins and Nestor Terleckyj.[71]

There was also a lost eleventh volume, Milton Abelson's *America's Front Office*, which disappointed the directors upon its delivery but would have supplied far more detail on building types—and white-collar office space, then ascendant as manufacturing dispersed—than economists tended to.[72] A large team of researchers, many of them Jewish and Chinese American women, contributed to the study as well, receiving warm acknowledgment in the published volumes but little explicit renown. Each volume reproduced an arresting two-page map (figure 3.2) by Jeanyee Wong, who would make her name as one of the premier calligraphers, illustrators, and book-cover designers in the age of the "quality paperback."[73]

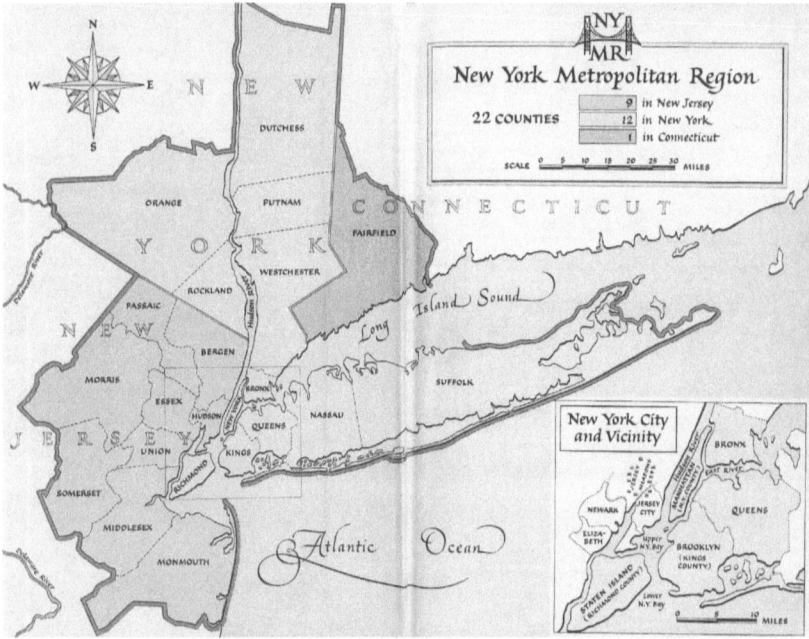

FIGURE 3.2. This twenty-two–county map by Jeanyee Wong appeared in full color in the endpapers of each Harvard University Press edition of the NYMRS, and with reduced coloration at the centerfold of each Anchor paperback. The RPA miniaturized this map and reprinted it in a range of its publications during the 1960s. Note the lettering, most especially the calligraphic treatment applied to the names of larger bodies of water. Hoover and Vernon, *Anatomy of a Metropolis*, endpapers. Courtesy of Regional Plan Association.

The study's top-line findings were essentially fourfold: increased regional dispersal of home and work; aggregate population growth for the region but a declining national share; a sectoral shift in New York City proper toward white-collar work; and a swath of decrepit or vulnerable "gray areas" (Vernon's coinage) left behind in the outer boroughs and other "core" parts of the twenty-two–county region. It was the NYMRS that put the "gray areas" concept into wider circulation, a fact that Ylvisaker acknowledged when setting up Ford's program by that name.[74]

The watchword throughout was *forces*. Forces, readers learned, were at work upon the metropolis. They might elude political capture or scholarly calculation, bend or weave in coming years, but their general tendencies could be described. "Most of the forces," Hoover and Vernon concluded, "move so clearly in the same direction"—outward from the traditionally defined urban core (figures 3.3 and 3.4)—that a metropolitan and regional perspective was essential to make sense of them. "Leap-frog" development was now normal:

Figure 3.3. Landscape and shift change at Mahwah Assembly. As had the NYMRS, the publications leading up to the Second Regional Plan made much of the new, horizontally extensive suburban workplaces that were coming to dominate the region: corporate headquarters in Westchester and Fairfield Counties, defense production on Long Island, and numerous manufacturers seeking more acreage in New Jersey. The suburbanization of industry had been occurring for decades. Ford established an assembly plant in Edgewater, New Jersey, across the Hudson from Midtown Manhattan, in 1929. (Another followed in 1948 at Edison, in Middlesex County.) Edgewater Assembly closed in 1955, and the company moved its operations another twenty miles northwest to the Bergen County town of Mahwah, depicted here. Regional Plan Association, *Public Participation in Regional Planning* (1967), 42. Courtesy of Regional Plan Association.

"there is not just one high-density commercial center but many, of different orders of magnitude.... The widening ripples come, then, not from a single pebble dropped into a puddle, but from a scattered handful of large, middling, and small pebbles, each a focus of expansion."[75] If these sounded like the beginnings of a critique of runaway postwar suburbanization, more often the reportage was roundly unpolemical in tone. "I can't afford the luxury of either

FIGURE 3.4. Spread City. The RPA directed its most critical comments at the ugliness of such postwar suburbs as Wayne and Paramus, New Jersey, in Passaic and Bergen Counties, respectively. Nassau County, on Long Island, and other automobile-oriented edge realms also came in for what by the 1960s was a predictable rebuke. Regional Plan Association, *Public Participation in Regional Planning* (1967), 58. Courtesy of Regional Plan Association.

idle optimism or pessimism," Vernon asserted in a *New York Times* profile titled "Regional Fact-Finder."[76] These forces were to be systematically projected forward, not tampered with. And if the number crunching could all seem a tedious, "mechanical" exercise, the economist Barbara Berman advised, readers were to understand that "the click of the gears is merely the sound of logic doing its work."[77]

To a significant degree, though, the jury was still out when it came to the reliability of these projections, even as the books went to press. "It is easy to slip into the use of the future tense," wrote Hoover and Vernon; "the future is so much less clumsy and so much more authoritative than the conditional."

"Yet," they continued, "no one will be deceived by the use of the future tense in this chapter. What we have stated as expectations could be set aside in reality by the unpredictable or the improbable."[78] One moment social-scientific reason takes command, and the facts are to speak for themselves; then deferral and self-doubt set in, and we enter the world of probabilities, not causal arrows. "A careful guess is better than a heedless one," Vernon counsels, but it remains just that: a guess. Statistics are "an excursion beyond the limits of reason into the realm of faith." In fact, *Projection of a Metropolis* was made public in the first place so that readers could "determine for themselves how much reliance to place on the projections" and try their hand at recalculating.[79] There is also the inconvenient "Confession and Apology" embedded in *Metropolis 1985*'s "Introduction to an Epilogue": "At critical junctures in the projection process, we had to confess that the results which these asserted relations generated were too improbable to be taken seriously. When this occurred, we did not hesitate to bend our results away from the answers which our models were producing." In other words, "if the magnitudes produced by the process offended our general expectations," they ignored them.[80]

Urban projection, as understood here, entailed a highly specific temporal imagination. *Projection* came to denote something more variegated and self-questioning than the 1940s "culture of planning" that Andrew Shanken has documented.[81] It was unlike prophecy, divine or otherwise. Projection was not mere prediction. It was more solid than a wager and less absolute than a guarantee. It could exist independent of prescriptions or plans. But it could not forgo history. The task, Handlin would write, "is . . . *to order the past from which the present grows* in a comprehensible manner."[82] And yet, so often their engagement with New York's past and present inclined the team to err on the side of inertia, to assume that present trends—absolute growth for the region, but a declining share of regional population for New York City—just would continue unhindered. "The guiding principle," Vernon wrote, "was one of simple extrapolation: what had grown fast would continue to grow, while laggards would remain laggards." "It is the salvation of the seer"—that is, it requires less skeptical reasoning to argue—"that inertia plays a major role."[83] The study's tacit growth liberalism fused a pessimism about drastic change with a comforting optimism that promised general advancement.

Only Wood openly dissented. Yes, he wrote, "While these systems continue, the economist is safe." But "the projection of trends 'as they are' may confuse rather than clarify the issue." Politics reorder—indeed create—markets in their image. "Is not the gravest danger in sketching the Region of the future that of underestimating—or even ignoring—the prospects of revolution?"[84] "'This is planning[,] is it not[?]'" interjected RPA officials when Wood raised these points during the study's organizational stage. "Taboo," they concluded. "Where did this come from? What is it?"[85] Quietly, Hoover and Vernon had conceded this point, writing at the outset of the ten volumes, "The developments which these projections foretoken could well spark greater changes in . . . policy than could have been reasonably assumed. These pages, therefore, carry the seeds of the forces which may make reality very different from the projections. In that event, in describing what *might have been*"—a new tense entirely—"this book will have served one of its major purposes."[86] Internally, matters were complex and occasionally conflictual. Outwardly, the study deflected attention from the question of political action—coordinative planning as opposed to pure projection. Vernon's neutrality was a studied performance. It was a marvel of both-and social science that fought itself to a draw over and over again.

The Second Regional Plan, which the RPA finally issued in 1968, is not the major legacy of the NYMRS—although the reports leading up to it, notably *Spread City* (1962), which took stock of the metastasizing suburbs and promised that the group would at length "pose alternatives," are underappreciated today.[87] They also came to define the region in an ever more permissive way. *The Region's Growth* (1967) scaled up dramatically, invoking "The Atlantic Urban Region," a twelve-state, thirty-nine–Standard Metropolitan Statistical Area, 150-county "urban chain" in which greater New York served as the "central link." Even *Megalopolis* had included only 118 counties.[88]

The NYMRS also modeled techniques by which the new urban experts based in Cambridge might take their research public. The RPA ran a series of five planning-focused programs on the television station WPIX, convened six hundred "special listening groups" to watch and discuss them, administered a survey (with Columbia's Bureau of Applied Social Research) to gauge viewer response, presented the results at the RPA's next annual conference, and worked them up into a companion volume to the Second Regional Plan.[89] In 1960, a photojournalist and filmmaker, Louis Schlivek of Waldwick, New Jersey, volunteered his services "to summarize and dramatize" the dry findings in visual form.[90] The end result was the popular book *Man in Metropolis* (1965), a thick tome featuring many dozens of images—always a weak suit for Vernon and his economists—and fluent prose ruminating on their implications.[91] (The RPA had considered far more provocative titles for Schlivek's book, from *The Pulse of Gargantua* to *Metropolitan Countdown* to *Dial Metropolis: 16,000,000*, but Doubleday's editors talked them down.)[92]

More durable are the ways in which the NYMRS helped further entrench interdisciplinary, often quantitative, urban studies as a pillar of the American research university. Its linkages with the emerging postwar constellation of centers, institutes, bureaus, and other interstitial units of organized research were many and tight.[93] Vernon's report further urbanized methodological trends encouraged by the NSF, by Chicago's PERP and Penn's IUS, by the Ford Foundation, by the model-happy economics profession, by so-called regional science, and by the all-important fact of wartime social inquiry and its long postwar shadow.[94]

Paul Ylvisaker deemed the NYMRS a success. He cited it often when building the case that Ford should establish a dedicated Urban and Regional Program.[95] He almost certainly had the NYMRS in mind when he posited his "Bridge to the Future Metropolis" (1957; see chapter 1) and wrote, pretending to look back from the year 1980, that "in or around 1957 . . . Americans became aware of the city. Really aware of it."[96] The Metropolitan St. Louis Survey, still in progress when Vernon's team began work, had shown what an interdisciplinary, fully collaborative investigation into a major city and its hinterland could look like. But that had been a synchronic exercise: a snapshot of a metropolis, its institutions, and its citizens at one discrete moment. Vernon's team channeled the spirit of St. Louis but rendered the task of systematic urban research explicitly diachronic: urban change, over urban time, was the critical thing to be explained. Now it was clear: the future had pride of place.

Vernon's group had operated on a scale and with a unity of purpose totally beyond the ken of the eclectic minds gathered on Church Street. The Joint Center never managed to overcome its suspicion that Boston studies, no matter how rigorously executed, would always be less significant than an urban studies with theoretical ambitions, willing to delve into the empirics of locale but always in order to enable higher-level inferences. Yet the New York study's historically informed futurism had an allure. Adopting its temporal orientation without committing to its precise division of labor, the center in so many ways picked up where Vernon left off. The steady stream of NYMRS publications furnished Rodwin, Meyerson, and their circle with concepts, data, methodologies, organizational templates, publicity strategies, a commitment to the metropolitan and regional frame, a trove of facts and suppositions about New York, license to extend these insights to Boston and other places, and, beneath it all, the very model of skeptical urban reason at work. What was this if not Cohen's "systematic doubt" on a gargantuan scale?

There was also considerable overlap in personnel. The Joint Center's book series published Vernon, now liberated from his self-imposed neutrality and ready to opine on *The Myth and Reality of Our Urban Problems* (1962). In the 1966 edition of that work, Vernon, like Ylvisaker, credited the NYMRS with having placed urban questions squarely within view of the educated public. Until the late 1950s, he claimed, "'the urban problem' was the intellectual province of a devoted and intense group. . . . The general public, so it seemed, couldn't care less."[97] Not anymore. David Rockefeller, his interest piqued in urbanism, joined the center's visiting committee as a charter member.[98] Vernon assumed a seat on the faculty committee. Robert C. Wood led the center for one year (1969) before departing to head the University of Massachusetts system and oversee the construction of its new Boston campus. When Charles Haar's team proposed a Senate-funded "integrated economic study" to allay the strain of intergovernmental competition within metropolitan regions, they cited the NYMRS as an "unusually thorough and elaborate example."[99] With the NYMRS complete but the future uses of its data still unclear, Martin Meyerson even offered to have the Joint Center—not the RPA or another group based in New York—serve as the long-term repository for its research materials.[100]

The study's affordances to the emerging world of organized urban research, then, were numerous. It forged uniquely direct linkages with Ford, with Harvard—where it helped to institutionalize urban social science prior to 1959 in a way that the noncommittal Center for Urban Studies never managed to—and with the Joint Center. More than any other of the center's precursors, it had made the case that the future of urban research belonged to research on the urban future.

Histories of the Urban Future

For postwar social scientists, the key methodological issue was the nature of inference. Whichever specific techniques authors employed to gather information about the world, the goal was to arrive at knowledge of the unknown by way of available evidence—and, more crucially still, to reflect on that relationship in plain view of their readers. The lion's share of debate concerned how best to manage, and offset, the uncertainty necessarily built into this process. The scientific maturation of urban studies, many felt, depended on the candor with which researchers could state this gap in understanding, assign it precise contours and significance, and then bridge it methodically, pivoting from case to population, from cities to the city. This was how Wilson and Derthick had drawn the line on Grady Clay's *Competitors*. By the end of the 1960s, the Joint Center would demonstrate both the force and fragility of inferential reasoning in grappling with urban change.

There was a well-developed tradition of essentially atemporal social science that the center both learned from and defined itself against. Inferential thinking can be synchronic or diachronic in character; it can generalize from part to whole at one isolated moment in time, or it can mobilize data about the past and present to bolster claims about the future. The NYMRS privileged the latter approach (and it is hard to know how seriously to take the Vernon group's suggestion that New York could plausibly serve as a prototype of any other place). Yet, earlier in the century, the first body of urban research to dwell systematically on the question of inference had almost completely removed time from the equation. Beginning in the 1910s, the sociologists of the Chicago School, superintended by Robert Park and anchored by Ernest Burgess's ideal-typical diagrams of form and process, all but assumed, without bothering to argue the point, that the city most convenient for their own research would unproblematically stand in for urban life writ large. They also assumed that deeper inquiries into the history of Chicago or other cities would do little to disrupt the law-bound ecological theory that Park's people were shoring up. "It would have been prudent to make more limited claims," Ulf Hannerz has written of the group, noting the pronounced "tendency of Burgess and others to equivocate on the question [of] whether their interpretations were supposed to hold true for Chicago only, or for any industrial city, or for any city of whatever kind."[101] If they harbored doubts, though, they never openly questioned whether observations of their own environs—flat, gridded, sited near the middle of the continent—could quickly be transposed elsewhere. Inference from locality to nation, instance to type, was the very justification for their work as a scientific endeavor.

The tradition of community studies inaugurated by Robert Staughton Lynd and Helen Merrell Lynd, also with a foothold in the Midwest, was even more explicit in its claim to have isolated typical places that could serve as the basis for generalizations about urbanization, political life, community (and its erosion), and indeed modernity as such. Their *Middletown: A Study in Modern American Culture* (1929) achieved remarkable public exposure and was quite arguably the century's first social-scientific bestseller—and, as would happen to Nathan Glazer some decades later, the prelude to academic appointments, at Columbia for the husband and Sarah Lawrence for the wife. Funded by the Laura Spelman Rockefeller Memorial and the Institute of Social and Religious Research (as part of its Small City Study), the Lynds went out of their way to advance no thesis and betray allegiance to no particular school of thought. The text was to be read as a comprehensive survey of the "average" American town, even as, as Sarah Igo has pointed out, its portrait of an industrial city's pecuniary habits, unequal economic order, and deep-seated social conformity carried the scent of critique, and their restudy, *Middletown in Transition* (1937), published in the throes of the New Deal, more clearly made the case for rational planning as a remedy. *Middletown* had an enormous stake in ensuring its site's perception as typical. It accrued power as a portrait of something called "American culture" precisely by performing its own representativeness, and "its image as an icon of the typical," noted in almost every published review, circulated widely. Their approach was also roundly atemporal. The study was hardly trying to deny the passage of time—industrialization was a process with a before and after, the Lynds included ten pages of historical background, and they addressed various "things making and unmaking group solidarity"—but the overwhelming image was of a static social unit with clear, tradition-bound, inflexible lines of command. Synchrony became an authorial strategy, a forced subtraction of one source of contingency in the name of making one's case portable.[102]

In the postwar era, overlapping the Joint Center's early period, tightly focused community studies on the Lynd model became one of the main social-scientific instruments to infer larger truths about urban life. One particularly influential set of works took New Haven, Connecticut, as its object and, atop it, retheorized the workings of urban power and political influence. The Yale political scientist Robert Dahl was its figurehead and convener. Having spent the 1955–1956 academic year at CASBS in Palo Alto, where discussion among the disciplinarily various fellows often broached "stubborn problems of concept, theory, and method," he organized a small team of researchers whose empirics might refute those scholars who saw only inertial structures of stratification, dominated by "regimes" or "elites" able to lock in power and call the shots year after year. Like Banfield and Wilson in many ways, but notably without a formalized research unit contributing funds or an acronym, Dahl and his students proposed an alternative, "pluralist" theory of urban power. For pluralists, many groups at once can claim partial influence over the political process, and coalitions of mutual interest are always forming and reforming around specific issues—notably in the New Haven of the 1950s, Urban Renewal, then overseen by Ed Logue in the first act of his career and touted far and wide by the photogenic mayor, Dick Lee. (One in six residential units in that city were demolished, the highest proportion nationwide by far, and New Haven attracted more Urban Renewal dollars per capita than any other city.) Content aside, in their methodology, Dahl's *Who Governs?* (1961) and two "closely related volumes," Nelson Polsby's *Community Power and Political Theory* (1963) and Raymond Wolfinger's *The Politics of Progress* (1973), redoubled emphasis on the microcosmic qualities of their case city and asserted its generalizability as an article of faith. Dahl struck a more measured tone than had the Lynds: Yale's backyard was "in many [i.e., not all] respects typical of other cities in the United States." Still, he wrote, in focusing on just one case "the enterprise is reduced to manageable proportions. Many problems that are almost unyielding over a larger area can be relatively easily disposed of on this smaller canvas." The opening line of Polsby's text states the faith even more baldly: "This book grew out of a study of New Haven, Connecticut, but it is not primarily about New Haven at all." (Dahl justified the approach by noting that Aristotle and Machiavelli had each begun a treatise of systematic political philosophy by registering the affairs of a single city–state.)[103] Pluralism remade mainline American political science during the first part of the 1960s and saw application to virtually every American city, but it began and remained a general theory of New Haven.[104]

Community studies proliferated in the 1940s and 1950s. They comprised an "on-going, self-conscious 'scientific' literature," Polsby wrote, in which "the community-as-a-whole is taken as the unit of study" and made to stand in for—or submit to comparison with—the complete set of American communities.[105] If systematically treated, the thinking went, smaller cities such as New Haven could be adequate proxies for metropolises the size of Boston, Chicago, or even New York. Many studies with such aspirations to generality addressed places far smaller than New Haven. And, as if to clinch the case that they had converted the mess of urban life into a kit of interchangeable parts, authors of postwar community studies had an unfortunate tendency to disguise their sites with hokey assumed names. It was revealed that "Middletown" was an alias for Muncie, Indiana, whose residents bristled upon learning that they had been observed at close range, unawares, for several years. Posing broadly similar questions about class, status, and power in "Yankee City," the anthropologist W. Lloyd Warner and collaborators produced five thick volumes (1941–1959) on Newburyport, Massachusetts, alone.[106] In *Elmtown's Youth* (1949), August Hollingshead, who chaired Yale sociology starting in 1959, was describing Morris, Illinois, a town smaller than even Newburyport with a population under ten thousand.[107] In *Community Power Structure* (1953), Floyd Hunter rechristened Atlanta "Regional City."[108] Seattle became "Pacific City" in the hands of Delbert Miller, Ernest Barth, and Baha Abu-Laban; Ypsilanti, Michigan, became "Cibola" for Robert O. Schulze; Roland Pellegrin and Charles Coates immersed themselves in Baton Rouge, Louisiana, and dubbed it "Bigtown."[109] (Digby Baltzell's immanent critique *Philadelphia Gentlemen* [1958], mercifully, resisted the urge to pseudonymize.)[110]

As with the Lynds, authors were willing to acknowledge temporality as a fact of existence. If anything, Polsby argued, pluralists foregrounded "the time-bound nature of coalitions" out of a conviction that political "issues can be fleeting or persistent."[111] Even if their theoretical frameworks were more invested in describing invariant structures of power, most community studies respected historical context. But their arguments remained ahistorical in nature: specific changes over time, while sometimes instructive as background, were simply not what the authors had set out to explain. When they did embed historical facts in wider circuits of intercity reference, it was in a basically synchronic way: a detailed picture of, say, textile production in nineteenth-century Massachusetts could be generalized to other places in the nineteenth century, but not worked up as a precondition, lesson, or warning for the twentieth century and beyond. Past did not matter inferentially to present and future, à la Vernon and the NYMRS. And the use of aliases for all persons, places, and things quite obviously prevented the authors from contributing much to the historical record—or to geographic knowledge, since accurate maps, plans, photographs, or even elevations of any but the most generic building types could blow their cover. (*Middletown* contained maps, but they were schematic, as were the attendant discussions of class and racial segregation.) In their insistence on rendering places fungible—and in their urge to abstract to the city as ideal type—aspirationally scientific community studies pushed the limits of plausibility. The Joint Center resolved to chart a new course.

In the fall of 1958, *Daedalus* published an issue titled "Evidence and Inference." *Daedalus* had begun publication under that name in 1955, in association with the American Academy of Arts and Sciences, the learned society sited blocks from Harvard's campus since the eighteenth century and a crucial gathering place in the twentieth for scholars from both ends of Cambridge. Recent issues had tended to center topics that, while broad, were substantive, not methodological, in nature: "Symbolism in Religion and Literature," "The American National Style," "Science and the Modern World View." But *evidence* and, especially, *inference* had become ubiquitous keywords of scholarly inquiry during the 1950s, and the issue sought to convince its interdisciplinary audience that these classic concerns of method were both urgent and capacious enough to bring scientific and humanistic work into new combinations. In the pages of a typical *Daedalus*, established experts would assemble to issue synthetic, authoritative-sounding statements based on decades of learning. In the "Evidence and Inference" issue, Paul Lazarsfeld spoke for the hardening social sciences. Erik Erikson, the psychologist of identity and its crises, contributed "The Nature of Clinical Evidence." Raymond Aron, the French sociologist who maintained close ties with Cold War liberals in the United States, admitted that in writing history, one only ever confronted "ensembles"; it was virtually impossible to disentangle data from the inferences being made about that data. In his preface to the volume, Daniel Lerner, an economist and one of the key modernization theorists working at MIT, concurred. To make sense of the "regularities underlying diverse events," he wrote, some admixture of "introspection" and "intuition" would be involved, even in the laboratory sciences. The task for contemporary inquiry was to harness that humanistic spark, render it "instrumental," and only then "close the gap between . . . evidence and inference."[112]

In making their urban inferences, then, the Joint Center, the NYMRS, the wave of community studies from the Lynds to the pluralists, and other instances of organized research both fed and responded to broader conversations on method. Among centers of urban studies, the Joint Center was the one most closely entangled with the *Daedalus* circle, privy to its ongoing conversations on how inferential reasoning as such, irrespective of technique—statistics, participant observation, survey research, interviews, clinical trials, the archive—could supply at once the stimulus to rigorous work, the lingua franca for disparate disciplines, and the condition for their intelligibility in public life.

Just months before "Evidence and Inference" went to press, Lloyd Rodwin had joined the journal's editorial board. It was under American Academy of Arts and Sciences auspices that Rodwin organized the 1960 "Future Metropolis" conference at Tamiment-in-the-Poconos. There, discussion turned to questions of technological change and the future it augured. A mixture of confidence and trepidation surfaced. Kevin Lynch held out hope for some degree of "technological freedom," writing against darker visions that would culminate in enslavement by the automobile, the computer, and other less-than-simple machines. William Wurster, now based at Berkeley, called the Bay Area's dispersed, polycentric pattern of urbanization—with a body of water, not a city, at its heart—"sophisticated," deeming the automobile a sensible mode of conveyance under those circumstances: "You can move it right from your house to where you are going; that is the main thing." Meanwhile, Nathan Glazer, his sensibilities formed on the streets of East Harlem and the Bronx, admitted his incomprehension—"I do not know what it is that makes the automobile what it is"—and worried that cars and computers were coming to substitute, poorly, for face-to-face contact. Reviewing the day's activities, he declared that "some of the papers gave me the shivers." Edward Banfield, an urbanite by professional necessity but a rural "Connecticut Yankee" at heart, evinced fear at the pace of change but gave cautious assent to the automobile. Above all, he said, "I would like a technology of quiet." The future was metropolitan, it was fast, and it was loud.[113]

In early 1961, Rodwin brought out "The Future Metropolis" issue of *Daedalus*, which gave the most complete cross section of the Joint Center's early period under Rodwin and Meyerson; the book version followed later that year. The papers varied in theme, but all were phrased in the same tense. The future was a metropolitan future: in "A World of Cities," Rodwin and Lynch sketched out the horizon of an emerging urban order. That metropolitan future assumed particular physical shapes: in "The Pattern of

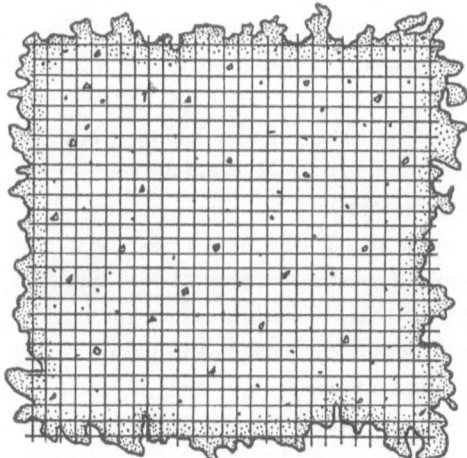

Fig. 4. The Dispersed Sheet.

FIGURE 3.5. The dispersed sheet. By 1961, this and other forms moving beyond the strictures of the monocentric, star-shaped metropolis entered Kevin Lynch's classification scheme for urban morphology. Kevin Lynch, "The Pattern of the Metropolis," *Daedalus* 90 (Winter 1961): 79–98. Courtesy of MIT Press.

the Metropolis," Lynch updated his typology and added the "dispersed sheet," "polycentered net," and acentric "galaxy," handily illustrated as always, to the set of properly modern forms (figure 3.5). There were dimensions to urban and metropolitan life that depended on but also superseded physical space: the political scientist Karl Deutsch discoursed on "social communication" and the possibility of its "overload," "the disease of cities." György Kepes contributed a rangy chapter titled "Expression and Communication in the Cityscape," Banfield test ran some of the arguments that were emerging from his students' reports on politics, Raymond Vernon pronounced on metropolitan financing, Aaron Fleisher handled the question of technology, Rodwin wrote on emerging urban patterns in the developing world, and others marked out what they saw as the advancing frontiers of urban studies.[114] Meyerson defended the utopian streak in planning but urged a more methodical approach: "delineate pluralistic urban utopias," he wrote, and "approach [them] experimentally, tentatively, consciously seeking alternatives."[115] The Joint Center rendered social-scientific inference diachronic—a form of reasoning that at its best should operate across tense, glimpsing the future metropolis but setting it on firmer evidentiary grounds.

Anticipatory thinking was clearly the dominant note on Church Street. Yet urban studies, the center argued by its own example, had to find ways to face simultaneously forward and backward in time. The field had to take equal interest in the future and the past, and it had to apply the same standards of rigor to work written in either tense. It had no license to ignore the present either, of course, but it had to understand the contemporary moment as the valve connecting its before with its after.

The very same year that *The Future Metropolis* went to press as a book, the Joint Center organized a second conference that, thematically anyhow, might seem to be proposing that volume's negation. In August 1961, at the behest of Oscar Handlin and John Burchard—the architectural historian who had served as MIT's first humanities dean and, importantly, the first editor of *Daedalus*—the center convened "The City in History." This meeting cast a particularly wide net and attracted several figures from the humanities who would have been well known to scientific Joint Center regulars as authors but not regular interlocutors. In attendance were Carl Schorske, the historian of urban Europe; Kenneth Boulding, the gnomic economist and systems theorist; Robert S. Lopez of Yale, whose paper looked backed to the medieval city as "the crossroads within the wall"; Frederick Gutheim of the Washington Center for Metropolitan Studies; the landscape architect Christopher Tunnard of Yale; the architectural historian Walter Creese of Illinois, whose work on Garden City planning would later bring him to the Joint Center as a visiting fellow; the economic historians Alexander Gerschenkron and Eric Lampard; and Sylvia Thrupp, Chicago-based and fresh off the founding of the journal *Comparative Studies in Society and History*, itself an artifact of the interdisciplinary tendency at midcentury. Participants with Church Street affiliations included Aaron Fleisher, Richard Meier, the philosopher Morton White, and Sam Bass Warner, a Harvard PhD in history and a research associate of the center. Papers took up five main concerns: cities as hearths of technological innovation and economic development; the history of urban ideas; history's purchase on the contemporary urban world; "the city as an artifact," which featured rich if traditionalist architectural histories by Penn's Alexander Garvan and Sir John Summerson of John Soane's Museum in London; and "planners and interpreters of the city," wherein Tunnard and Gutheim, historically minded critics, found their niche. If all planning worthy of the name needed history on its side, Handlin and Burchard presumed, then it also needed a common store of methods regulating the use of history. This conference, too, resulted in a book, *The Historian and the City* (1963). Its preface was blunt about the current intellectual situation: "The general works on the subject have often been interesting, but usually also speculative and tendentious; and they have neither rested on adequate data nor been rigidly disciplined in method. On the other hand, occasional monographs of value have lacked continuity and the unifying focus of common problems."[116] Drawing strength from social science, the Joint Center would impart order to urban historiography, too.

Essays by Handlin and Burchard bookended the volume. Handlin began his piece with a hypothetical survey from the window of an airplane, noting "no clear boundaries" to the American city as "seen from above": "clumps of suburban housing, industrial complexes, and occasional open spaces." He then made a quick, telling pivot: "Our difficulties with nomenclatures," he wrote, "reflect the indeterminacy of these limits."[117] Both urban form and urban studies were in need of reorganization. Burchard asserted that "the problem of interdisciplinary collaboration is *the* central organizational problem of the scholarly world and about it a great deal is still uncertain." Neither he nor Handlin was unduly prescriptive about which languages, concepts, categories, methods, or disciplines were best positioned to reform historical writing (although Handlin cited many sociologists, and the meeting perhaps overrepresented economists and economic historians). The key thing was that urban scholars be systematic in managing the interplay between particular and general—evidence and inference. "The problem of who is good and bad as between the generalist and the monographer, we did not, fortunately, tackle," Burchard wrote. "We probably need both." Each had to be willing to converse with the other, and each had to face up to the time-boundedness of all social phenomena: historians must not be "mere chroniclers too bemused by time" to reflect conceptually on its passage, while "mere philosophers or social scientists too little concerned with time" were also a liability.[118] To produce fully modern knowledge, the vocation of urban history had to include a systematic interest in temporality and tense as such.

One mere philosopher came in for especial rebuke. Lewis Mumford was not present at the conference, but it was difficult not to think of him when Handlin, at his most prescriptive, asserted, "We need fewer studies of the city in history than of the history of cities," the latter an empirical matter usually born of concern for "*a* city specifically in all its uniqueness."[119] As had been true among the NYMRS group, Mumford's name came up repeatedly—the leading example of unsystematic work. "Although Lewis Mumford was not here," Burchard remarked, "his shade was." The title of the conference was identical to that of Mumford's latest tome, released earlier that year and soon to be honored with the National Book Award. Burchard called *The City in History* (1961) "a generalized history," more "a statement of hypothesis" than a fully justified argument, and anyhow reared on "strange interpretations of science and technology" that Mumford had been voicing since the 1920s under the sign of Patrick Geddes.[120] Mumford concludes the book with "Retrospect and Prospect," a chapter in which those two temporalities are presented as if organically fused. Decline begets renewal: "the same forces that are now oriented toward death" (i.e., the past) *"will* then," in the future that Mumford's scheme guaranteed, "be polarized toward life."[121] Handlin charged Mumford with Spenglerian "exaggerations" that "distend" the insights of Simmel, Durkheim, and Weber "into a vision of imminent catastrophe."[122] Alfred Kazin would later write that Mumford "addressed himself on a large scale to every social problem with the confidence of a Victorian prophet."[123] Yet, if "Lewis Mumford talks and Robert Moses [nonetheless] disposes," Burchard quipped, then "one may wonder whether the talk matters."[124]

It was not just that Mumford could be overdramatic in his assertions, his morality, or his politics (although the latter were far more radical than those espoused by either symposiarch). He struck them as fundamentally confused about the temporal articulation of the urban past, present, and future. Mumford, the historians held, had not differentiated these categories, and distinguishing them analytically was the very precondition for adjudicating historical causation, resonance, repetition, inertia, and change. Burchard pleaded for more nuance: "Our past has surely conditioned our present; does a better understanding of our past affect *how* it might condition our present *and our future?*" He had doubts, but so did all probabilistic science: "It cannot be proved but we have to believe it."[125] Even if the goal was eventually to conjoin past, present, and future into one covering explanation, it was first necessary to demarcate them. The two key conferences put on by the early Joint Center were, in fact, intimately related. "The Future Metropolis" and "The City in History" entailed one another. They occupied the same temporal continuum; they simply pointed in opposite directions.

It was by way of this emplotment of urban time that the Joint Center's approved historians brought knowledge of the past to bear on contemporaries who would materially affect, not only project, the future. History offered both lessons and warnings for planners. Handlin was hardly a utilitarian, but even between the covers of *The Future Metropolis* (as that volume's only accredited historian), he had prefaced his chapter, "The Social System," by suggesting that "it will be useful to review the significant developments of the past with an eye to discerning the probable patterns of the future."[126] Perhaps so. But forging the linkage between urban history and the urban future, the Joint Center contingent came to insist, hinged on nothing more mysterious than securing a readership for their work. If this was public intellect they were producing—and Handlin, for one, was a familiar name in the short history of "quality paperbacks"—its intended public had practitioners at its core. "We have a right," Burchard declared, "to ask of the planners that they read history, the prose"—workmanlike empirics—"as well as the poetry"—basically, Mumford. There was a division of labor in place; historians themselves did not have to be the ones making calls on public housing, industrial location, or highway design. The problem, as Burchard saw it, was that contemporary planners and architects were very poor readers. They were unaccustomed to challenging their own preconceptions, seduced by "orations" more than logically supported "statements" and untrained in the habits of mind that would equip them to tell the two apart. "The politicians," he observed, "are learning to read faster—and many to read better." Kennedy famously kept Arthur M. Schlesinger Jr. close to hand as an advisor and court historian (and his father, also a fixture at Harvard, had written some of the first synthetic histories of urban America). All hope was not lost at the "vital center" of American politics. The next step, Burchard argued, was to put usable volumes of urban history in the back pockets of planners: "serious, detailed, even microscopic history, with only occasional peregrinations to the broad canvas or the seashore."[127] What Ylvisaker had called the "bridge to the future metropolis," it turned out, was built of books.

This was not mere exhortation. In time, the Joint Center underwrote those books. In the United States, urban history was still a young, sparse subfield when the center opened its doors. Some academic historians had touched on urban topics as early as the 1920s, and some university courses were on offer as early as the 1940s, often drawing sustenance from either Mumford's grand syntheses or Frederick Jackson Turner's intimations of the Western frontier. "A small group in the AHA [American Historical Association] known as the Urban History Group" had formed by 1957, as Blake McKelvey, the preeminent scholar of Rochester, New York, informed Lloyd Rodwin when inviting him to join.[128] Widespread interest, though, awaited the 1960s. No textbook in US urban history was available until 1967. By 1969, Bayrd Still of NYU, known for *Mirror for Gotham* (1956) and a 1948 city biography of Milwaukee, and Diana Klebanow could remark that the field now registered as "the new Frontier History."[129] In the early 1960s, the Joint Center was the critical institution sponsoring research that would soon be understood as evidence of the field's maturity—a fact that the small retrospective literature on the center has almost entirely downplayed, focusing instead on the atemporal styles of social science it also indulged.[130]

Both the center's leadership and Ford's officers valued the historical work. "Some of the greatest gaps in fundamental knowledge lie in this area," read *The First Five Years* (1964), issued under Wilson. "To reach a sophisticated understanding of the contemporary American urban situation demands a greatly increased understanding of past experience. The Joint Center takes special pride in the studies in urban history, historical sociology, and comparative analysis of cities."[131] The histories also helped give credence to the idea that the center was amalgamating not just the social sciences but also the humanities. In 1962, before the first renewal of Ford's grant was assured, Martin Meyerson had considered alternative sources of funding, and when he approached Chadbourne Gilpatric of the Rockefeller Foundation, he took care to tout the Joint Center's work in the "history and philosophy" of cities—as well as the Lynchian design tradition, Grady Clay's ongoing *Competitors* project, and other "background studies" capable of adding depth to the craft of policy.[132]

More prevalent, though, were assertions that the Joint Center had imbued historical writing on cities with scientific methods and mores. "Urban studies must develop theoretical generality," Ford's Malcolm Moos concluded in 1965. "Urban historiography may well be the real contribution of the Center, like V. O. Key's study of state politics," which demonstrated the utility of large-N interview data and deployed statistics to show variability in political behavior across the American South. The Harvard historian Stephan Thernstrom, one of the progenitors of quantitative social history and a Joint Center affiliate, told Moos that while "renaissance" was too strong a word, the center was certainly presiding over "a real boomlet in the field." Perhaps some of this work would have come to fruition without the center's coordinative efforts, "but it would have been a different *kind* of urban history, an inferior kind."[133]

The historical monographs are plentiful and heterogeneous. Sam Bass Warner published his dissertation as *Streetcar Suburbs* (1962), which decoded the "weave of small patterns" evident in the built fabric of Boston's peripheral areas constructed during the last decades of the nineteenth century by thousands of small-time speculators, each of whom dotted the landscape with a group of three or four look-alike houses a year.[134] (Learning to spot them in the wild has become a source of amusement for generations of students in field courses on vernacular architecture, and Warner's own photographs remain an essential guide.) Warner's archival labors (and Rodwin's, on a similar topic) led the Joint Center to reissue, as *The Zone of Emergence* (1962), a volume of early-twentieth-century commentary by settlement-house workers concerned with these same peripheries, suspended socio-spatially between working and middle class.[135] Robert Fogelson published *The Fragmented Metropolis* (1967), perhaps the first methodical history of pre-automotive Los Angeles—and, like Warner's book, an attempt to trace postwar patterns of suburban dispersal and capital mobility to investment decisions rendered long before the advent of that particular machine.[136] The sociologist Richard

Sennett's *Families against the City* (1970), with similar ambitions and a late-nineteenth-century focus, took the proto-suburban, once–middle-class Union Park section of Chicago's West Side as its case study.[137] Andrew Lees and Jon Peterson, who became widely cited planning historians, dissertated at Harvard with Joint Center backing. Daniel Lerner of MIT carried out historical work on urban France, as did the protean sociologist Charles Tilly, who liaised with the center while studying social relations at Harvard. Research associate Roy Lubove, the historian of Progressivism and Pittsburgh, brought out a sourcebook on housing reform while teaching at Harvard; Frederick Adams prepared a short history of planning education in the United States; Marvin Lazerson published *Origins of the Urban School* (1971), on turn-of-the-century Massachusetts; and Morris Lapidus contributed *Muslim Cities in the Later Middle Ages* (1967), a geographical and temporal outlier.[138]

Thernstrom's first book also joined the series. *Poverty and Progress* (1964) revisited the ordinary people of nineteenth-century Newburyport with the express purpose of countering the "ahistorical methodological preconceptions" that had animated W. Lloyd Warner's classic account of social mobility and its blockages. Of the Joint Center's historical monographs, Thernstrom's was the most explicit on the imperative of inferential reasoning. Like Warner, he "hope[d] to reveal something of importance about the larger society." There, Thernstrom insisted, the similarities stopped. "Inferences about 'American society' or 'American cities' based on happenings in one small city are obviously perilous," he knew, "a fact too often forgotten" by social scientists consigned to a case study but entranced by the prestige of general theory. Thernstrom closed his book with "Newburyport and the Larger Society," thirty pages querying that inferential linkage. He led off with "The Question of Representativeness." For Warner, he argued, this had not actually been a question. "Nowhere in the books was there any systematic consideration of the problem of generalizing the findings. . . . Warner simply proceeded from the unexamined assumption that . . . what was true of [Newburyport] was true of American society as a whole"—a "facile equation." Inference had simply not been of conceptual interest to Warner, who, in order to hold constant as many variables as he could, had deliberately sought a community that seemed "stable" and "well-integrated." "A latent function of the pseudonyms he applied," moreover, "was to lend an aura of typicality" that misled readers. The significance of the "Yankee City" studies as anything more than thick description hinged entirely on the movement from Newburyport to the American city writ large, but even in synchronic terms, Warner's work was clumsy, the "inferior kind" against which Thernstrom had inveighed.[139]

Thernstrom also worked hardest to justify the irreducibly temporal aspects of historical method. He included a lengthy appendix, "The Pitfalls of Ahistorical Social Science," and continued the attack on Warner. The concept of mobility implies the possibility of change over time, but here too Warner had shown a shocking preference for stasis. He had accepted at face value a sixfold scheme of class or status groups sketched out in interviews by members of Newburyport's elite and from it had posited that "relative social standing" and the corresponding set of geographical distinctions among neighborhoods were effectively fixed for all time. Like Durkheim, Radcliffe-Brown, and legions of other anthropologists before him (who usually prosecuted their work overseas in what struck them as "primitive" societies), Warner had signed on to the assumptions of a deeply conservative "equilibrium school," even if his intention had been to critique a hierarchical society by laying it bare. By his own admission, Warner had decided not to consult any "previous summaries of data collected by anyone else (maps, handbooks, histories, etc.)" if those would disturb his own intuitions about social structure. This "remarkable and revealing utterance," Thernstrom wrote, laid bare the poverty of ahistorical research. "The student of modern society is not free to take his history or leave it alone." Here he spoke for others at the Joint Center. As Thernstrom wrote—and as Handlin, Burchard, and more applied types had in very different ways asserted— "Interpretation of the present requires assumptions about the past."[140] It was not enough to preface a volume of presentist social science with a set piece supplying historical minutiae and local color. The essence of method was inference, and inference had to work dynamically, across tense.

The most humanistic of the histories was *The Intellectual versus the City* (1962), the work of the Harvard philosopher Morton White and Lucia White, his wife and a social worker by profession. (That the field, as the Joint Center defined it, could include both *Poverty and Progress* and this panoramic intellectual history speaks to its ecumenism.) This volume, for many decades the standard text on anti-urban ideas in the US (and itself a prehistory of the suburban impulse), took shape within the wider network of interdisciplinary centers and their philanthropists. The Whites began their work in the 1950s at the urging of Jean Gottmann, and like *Megalopolis*, the project enjoyed support from the Twentieth Century Fund. They spent 1959–1960 at CASBS in Palo Alto in the company of Carl Schorske. Upon their return, Martin Meyerson took a "cordial interest" in the manuscript and, to develop it, convened a Joint Center seminar that featured several intellectual historians, including Perry Miller, at least one Schlesinger, and others who would have no further contact with the center. *The Intellectual versus the City* was, in many senses, a collective product. It gestated elsewhere but became a Joint Center classic, particularly once Mentor reissued it in paperback. But aspects of its genesis remain mysterious. Though a New Yorker by birth, a student of Morris Cohen, and an exponent of a worldly philosophical outlook he called holistic pragmatism, Morton White had no obvious professional qualifications to author a volume on urbanism. He never again pronounced on urban affairs. His lengthy memoir makes no mention of the book. Its preface is signed by both authors, but whereas the book is filed under "Morton and Lucia White," there Lucia's name comes first. One begins to suspect that Morton White had, at most, a supporting role.[141]

The sundry Joint Center historical monographs are united by a set of methodological commitments and the overriding sense that historical knowledge, properly positioned, might afford glimpses of the present and future city. Thernstrom, who advised several of them as dissertations, was by far the most systematic in articulating this credo. *Poverty and Progress* found its impetus in his annoyance with "inconclusive and superficial" 1950s debates over whether the American class structure was becoming more entrenched, an inherently temporal question that was unanswerable without reference to properly formulated historical scholarship.[142] Warner, Fogelson, Sennett, and the Whites all indicate, without elaborately theorizing the point, that their work might be read as establishing a prehistory of the postwar suburb. Warner describes late-nineteenth-century Boston as a "mass suburban metropolis," a phrasing clearly informed by 1950s intellectual culture, and ends *Streetcar Suburbs* by expressing concern that, in Boston and elsewhere, "the growing metropolitan society" of the 1960s "as a whole remains shut up" in segregated, antisocial, inward-looking "units" of space.[143] Fogelson justifies his study with the claim that, since the war, "most American metropolises have duplicated, to a remarkable degree," the polycentric Los Angeles model. His case study is thus both microcosmic to the larger society and anticipatory of future events—the two desiderata of inferential urban history.[144] Sennett, writing under the influence of his advisor Erik Erikson, closes his history of Union Park, Chicago (before embarking on the "technical appendix," which during the 1960s became de rigueur in quantitative studies) with a sharp indictment of "the family disease" of compulsory togetherness, evident among his nineteenth-century subjects and "now coming to so sorry a fruition" in postwar American suburbs, where a racially cathected pattern of self-enclosure has licensed middle-class "retreat from disorder" in all its forms.[145] White and White open their book, which glosses Thomas Jefferson's agrarianism and lingers longest on the nineteenth century, with invocations of "decay," "flight," "sprawl," suburban "explosions," and other postwar keywords of an overheating public discourse on "urban problems" metastasizing to metropolitan and regional scale.[146] That was the future that the Joint Center, by reaching back in time, hoped to avert.

Both in the context of applied work and in research that could be called basic, the Joint Center compelled searching reflection on the temporality of urbanization, and of planning as a form of reasoned intervention. When the city, the stated object of this organized knowledge, proved unruly—a moving target swept up in postwar changes that self-appointed experts had not foreseen and found difficult to approve—the center shifted course intellectually and posed their questions anew at gradually higher levels of abstraction: the dynamics of urban change, then of the urban future, then of urban time itself.

Existing organizations of knowledge, they argued, had fragmented the tenses of urban life. They had parceled them out to scholarly communities unacquainted with one another and ill equipped to comprehend their interrelationship. The past was the province of historians, only some of whom respected scientific method; preservationists, who gathered force in the wake of Urban Renewal; and antiquarians of all kinds. The present was the domain of the banal, atemporal social science that an enriched urban studies needed to supersede (and a pat present-mindedness, the critics among them noted, was itself a defining malady of American life). The future metropolis, Meyerson and others protested, had too often been in the custody of utopians, whose visions failed precisely because of their inability to test the horizons of possibility against the empirics of recorded experience—not as a simple extrapolation of like from like, but as two links in a temporal chain far more complex and recursive than most practitioners were willing to admit. The center understood planning to be, before all else, a mode of thinking the future. But planning, they held, would always derive its own rationality, and motive force, from the lessons of history. This was history understood in a very specific sense, one far closer to what Reinhart Koselleck contends is the early-modern, not the high-modern, sense of *Geschichte*. The word "did not primarily mean the past, as it did later; rather it indicated *that covert connection of the bygone with the future* whose relationship can be perceived only when one has learned to construct history from the modalities of memory and hope."[147]

In its knowledge, confidence; in its orientation, something like hope—these were the affective registers in which the postwar tribunes of organized, rationalized urban research conceived their work and gave it voice. The Joint Center's first years were marked by a mood entirely of a piece with the midcentury liberalism so many of its members manifested and loosed on the city's problems. They were also, however, marked by a profound ambivalence about the efficacy of intervention. In its multiform campaign to know the city in full, the center was generally not in the habit of directly building the city anew—not durably committed to creating the futures its planners and prognosticators had judged most desirable.

There was, however, one glaring exception to this rule. The next chapter decamps some two thousand miles to the south, where the center embarked on its most prolonged experiment in physical planning, traversed new transnational circuits of expertise, glimpsed one version of utopia, and, in the process, reassessed precisely how much about the coming metropolis one could ever expect to know in advance.

Chapter 4

"A Documented Experience"
Cambridge on the Caroní

"You get mixed up in politics," the board had warned when the question of applied research came up.[1] Which politics, though? During the Joint Center's ascent, discourse on planning was inescapably bound up with Boston's forays into Urban Renewal. By 1964, Walter McQuade could write in *Fortune* that the city was a veritable "laboratory demonstration" of its techniques. Redevelopment proceeded apace downtown at the brutalist moonscape newly labeled Government Center (figure 4.1); on the "dead" waterfront by Long Wharf, whose antebellum granite warehouses were seeing conversion to residential use; and in eight outlying neighborhoods, from the "New York Streets" of the polyglot South End to the concentrated African American precincts of Roxbury. Adjusting for population, Boston was "by far the busiest of all the big cities" when it came to Urban Renewal expenditures.[2] To do urban research in public, one needed to have something to say about Urban Renewal.

Some observers projected optimism. Walter Muir Whitehill of the Boston Athenaeum, taken with the silhouettes of the Back Bay's new high-rise "insurance district" begun under Mayor John Hynes and anchored by the Prudential Center and the John Hancock headquarters, declared that a "contagion of improvement" would soon redraw the whole city's map.[3] Yet all was manifestly not well. Ringed by seventy-eight uncooperative suburbs, Boston hemorrhaged population, dropping from 801,000 in 1950 to 563,000 thirty years

FIGURE 4.1. Boston's Government Center shortly after its completion atop the former Scollay Square. Michael McKinnell's City Hall building dominates the frame. Photograph by Yunghi Kim, *Boston Globe*. Courtesy of Getty Images.

later; much of this loss occurred between 1955 and 1965. By 1960, one in four dwellings was substandard. Conditions of "crisis," Lizabeth Cohen has written, were "obvious to everyone." So, too, were the grievous failures of the city's marquee 1950s Renewal project, in the West End, which via the sociologist Herbert Gans's *The Urban Villagers* (1962) became "a textbook case, quite literally," of how not to renew. There, the Boston Redevelopment Authority senselessly scattered a rooted group of working-class Italian Americans across the metropolitan area without any methodical plan for their rehousing, interpolating aseptic solids and voids, "towers in a park," where a weave of rowhouses and narrow, peopled streets once predominated.[4]

The universities were implicated. The Boston Redevelopment Authority commanded the largest payroll among comparable agencies nationwide, and a steady stream of Harvard and MIT graduates passed through to give form to the "New Boston," a ubiquitous tagline at the time. Deans Sert and Belluschi, as well as Lawrence Anderson, took part in external design reviews after 1960, when Edward Logue, poached from analogous work in New Haven by the reform mayor John Collins, took over the authority, intent on never repeating the West End calamity. Logue attended several conferences at Harvard's GSD and, later in life, served as a lecturer at MIT.[5] The Joint Center's research agenda, including the histories, took shape with Urban Renewal as both context and referent. Indeed, Whitehill, a historian by training and preservationist by temperament, posited that it was precisely officials' penchant for the *new* that had stirred up such acute local interest in the past. That his classic *Boston: A Topographical History* (1959) saw a reprint in 1963, he surmised, was a direct result of the violence of the bulldozer. By 1968, the second edition could be filed under what he called "a fashionable academic subject": urban history.[6] The Joint Center's attempts to cross-reference the city's tenses prized complexity and circumspection in an age when the dominant developmental style was fixated quite single-mindedly on the future.

Yet their unease persisted. The center never committed to engaging the surrounding metropolis with any degree of seriousness. As professors' proposals met with evident suspicion in neighborhood after neighborhood—and as Boston's own record on redevelopment, despite Logue's best efforts, grew even more checkered—their gaze was drawn farther afield. Lloyd Rodwin had chanced upon an opportunity unprecedented in the brief, cloistered history of organized urban research. As of 1961, the city best able to withstand years of observation—and motivate high-level conclusions on the nature of urbanization and the undying question of what planners do all day—lay 2,400 miles south of the South End. If Boston would never acquiesce, never hold its pose long enough to feel quite like a laboratory, the center would build one from scratch. Along transnational circuits of its own making, urban expertise would course between The Hub and a midsized Venezuelan New Town newly dubbed Ciudad Guayana.[7] "As you say," Julius Stratton wrote to Rodwin, "Boston may not be the only laboratory or even the best laboratory for urban research."[8]

Building a Future in the Other America

Between 1961 and 1966, emissaries of the Joint Center traveled frequently between Massachusetts and Venezuela. Many faculty and students spent at least one summer in the tropics, at once building a new city and recording the process in real time. On the strength of their carefully framed microcosm, they proposed to subject urban growth and form as such to ever more precise theorization back in Cambridge.[9] Ciudad Guayana, sited where the Caroní River meets the Orinoco, was projected to house 650,000 people, roughly equal to the Boston of 1960. It rose at the heart of the country's mineral-rich East, in tandem with steel and aluminum mills, numerous extractive industries, and a hydroelectric dam. This putative "resource frontier" had justified the formation of the Corporación Venezolana de Guayana (CVG), a regional body styled after the Tennessee Valley Authority (TVA). The CVG was the creation of

President Rómulo Betancourt, a key Cold War ally as John F. Kennedy initiated the Alliance for Progress to reorganize states and economies across Latin America, anxious that the region might prove a sympathetic seedbed for Soviet ideas. Colombia, complete with its own Ciudad Kennedy on the outskirts of Bogotá, may have been the main proving ground for the Alliance for Progress, as Amy Offner has argued, but Betancourt had helped exclude Cuba from the Organization of American States and cultivated warm if instrumental relations with officially anti-communist institutions to the north. Following a coup d'état in early 1958, he won popular election later that year, assumed power in 1959, and quickly substituted an aggressive, developmentalist democracy, with clear technocratic tendencies, for the dictatorship of Marcos Pérez Jiménez that had formally been in place since 1952.[10] To 1966, across the first half of what the United Nations had declared to be the Development Decade, the Joint Center was at least as much concerned with this one slice of Latin America as it was with any single square mile of New England.

The center's ties to Venezuela predated 1961. In 1958, Lloyd Rodwin received an invitation from Luis Lander, one of his foreign students and now a minister in Betancourt's government, to visit the petrostate with a delegation of well-connected Americans. Adlai Stevenson came on the trip—"with an entourage," Rodwin recalled—and the group met with future CVG officials, including an assertive MIT graduate named Rafael Alfonzo Ravard, who would head the Corporación, and agents of Cordiplan, the umbrella agency concerned with fitting plans devised at urban and regional scales into the national context. It was Rodwin who invoked the TVA's example as one usable past.[11]

Rodwin's transnational relationships had multiplied over the 1950s. MIT recruited planning students from the University of Puerto Rico, and they too invited Rodwin for a visit; he then signed on as a consultant to the island's Planning Authority, still energized a decade after Rexford Tugwell's post–New Deal, pre-PERP stint as governor. Rodwin came away from the Venezuela trip with additional consulting contracts to his name. Yet, as a peddler of advice, as an educator, and as a planner, Rodwin sensed that he was out of his depths. His Latin American students asked that he offer a course on "the Third World," and he demurred, feeling unable to do it justice.[12] Rodwin was involved in discussions with Eric Carlson, of the Inter-American Housing Center in Colombia, that led to the establishment of a center on planning at the Universidad Central de Venezuela, but when Carlson suggested his name as a consultant to the Banco Obrero in Caracas, Rodwin admitted that "I know practically nothing about Venezuela, except what I read in the newspapers."[13] Yet the prospect of constructing a city from scratch—thus affording the space of pure inference for which social scientists, hemmed in by inherited urban forms, so often yearned—proved irresistible. It was an "entrepreneurial coup," Rodwin exclaimed; it would build his reputation—and that of the center and of the university—at the high tide of the Cold War; it was an "opportunity for professional development"; it was, at length, "an opportunity to learn."[14]

The Guayana project is diagnostic of the Betancourt era, both an icon of its geopolitical style and one of its central, constitutive matters of concern in what Cordiplan called the *ordenamiento* (ordering) of the national territory, region by productive region.[15] Ravard himself was a political survivor of the dictatorship, a basically conservative statist inclined to top-down urbanism redolent of the worst caricatures of Urban Renewal as practiced up north. Many of the CVG's top managers were independently wealthy, immovably Catholic, and philosophically quite far from the *idealistas* running neighboring Latin American states.[16] Along with his chief economist, Enrique Tejera Paris; resident director Rafael Corrada, a Puerto Rican citizen and housing scholar; and inner circle in Caracas, Betancourt heralded a broad commitment to planning that was at one with the universalist American liberalism provincialized by Banfield and Wilson but everywhere seeking to define the public interest in terms of an affluent society's further growth. "To plan," Betancourt declared, "is the unavoidable slogan of our time. . . . In our days, responsible administrative work is inconceivable without a proper articulation of objectives, coordination of efforts, and projections into the future." The future, in this sense, came first; it compelled action in the present, drawing it near. John Friedmann, then a young faculty member at MIT, would write in a 1966 study informed by his summer visits that Betancourt sought "a correlative process in which futurity and technical norms would be explicitly related to subjective events." All that planning "engendered more planning. And a marriage was contracted between politics and expertise."[17]

Crucially, while it was in every respect centralized in Caracas—a city both enriched by profits from oil and physically structured to prioritize vehicles powered by it—Betancourt's developmentalism entertained "a lively public debate on the 'where' of economic development." Intent on deploying a regional approach, the president instated a new Division of Regional Planning, tasked with distributing growth among carefully selected urban nodes or "poles."[18] The Guayana was a fertile region, and the eye-catching, orderly *ciudad* (city) at its center—the largest then rising from scratch anywhere in the world, Rodwin noted—would serve notice that a broader campaign was underway.[19] It was the country's outlying regions, in any case, that most acutely wanted for basic services. By 1970, 46 percent of Venezuela, equivalent to twice the population of Caracas, was unreliably housed.[20] In Caracas, 35 percent of the population squatted; nationwide, the number was 65 percent. And whereas thatched roofs worked fine elsewhere in the world, in Venezuela, they tended to breed the barbeiro bug, a known carrier of Chagas disease.²¹ Rodwin had backed into a complex project hyperconscious of its own significance at national and global scales.

This was by no means the first time US planners had approached Latin America as a testing ground for policies and techniques that might then be exported north for domestic use. Venezuela's first oil boom came in the 1920s, and US corporations were chief among the claimants. Venezuela's first National Planning Commission was formed in 1946 in response to the unruly development patterns that oil had wrought. Its advisors, a cross section of the Modernist establishment in American and European-émigré urbanism, informed the eventual 1955 Plan of Caracas: Maurice Rotival of Yale, a confidant of Ed Logue; Francis Violich of Berkeley's Telesis group; Robert Moses; and Josep Lluís Sert.²² Skidmore, Owings & Merrill prepared a comprehensive plan for Judibana, a company town built for the Creole Petroleum Company, a Standard Oil subsidiary.²³ Sert's firm was involved in planning three towns for US industries angling on Latin America. One, proposed in 1944, was the unbuilt Cidade dos Motores, in Brazil. Puerto Ordaz rose in Venezuela for the Orinoco Mining Company, nestled between that river and the Caroní on land that would later be incorporated into the fabric of the multinodal Ciudad Guayana. Ciudad Piar, built for US Steel, lay seventy miles south of the Guayana region's historical capital, Ciudad Bolívar. Those American employers, not the Venezuelan state, installed rail and port infrastructure, and it was they who dredged the Orinoco to a depth of twenty-five feet. If the Joint Center's board expressed misgivings about planning in and for other countries—and even Rodwin, preferring that "underdeveloped countries c[o]me to us" for education, had in the halcyon days of CURS come out strongly against "study[ing] them as one of our primary jobs"—there was ample precedent for this sort of overseas work.²⁴

American philanthropies, especially Gaither's Ford Foundation, had also, by this point, devoted considerable time and expenditure to international development.²⁵ Ford extended $141 million between 1951 and 1963, with an emphasis on "experiments which, if successful, can be adapted for use elsewhere"—substantially the same justification given for the survey of St. Louis, the NYMRS, and other ventures.²⁶ Ford came later to Latin America than to other postcolonial or decolonizing regions. It began with Asia and the Middle East, making $90 million of grants there by 1958. Sub-Saharan Africa entered the mix that year. Latin America was studiously ignored until early 1959, when Castro's Cuban Revolution forced the issue. The foundation truly consolidated its approach to international development through its work in South Asia: a master plan for

Karachi in 1952; one in 1958 for Delhi and its hinterland (New Delhi being described as "a tropical Washington"); a prolonged effort between 1961 and 1969, tapping fifty foundation staff and six hundred Indians, to entrain regional planning in Calcutta; and a congeries of rural projects with agriculture, "health, housing, and habits" at their core. In every case, spatial planning was accompanied by a wider menu of social programs: seminars on "American civilization" at Indian universities, curricula in public administration, exchange programs for students, exchange programs for art museums and libraries, and, of course, grants to American universities to carry out social-scientific work on Indian life. CENIS won a grant, naturally, but so did the distinctive Cornell–Lucknow Study, which began in 1953 with an anthropological subtlety foreign to the high priests of modernization theory.[27]

Ford's development planning both fed on and stimulated voluminous programs of research. These Indian engagements, the funders maintained, all stood as worthy instances of liberal-capitalist philanthropy in their own right, but they also had to redress "the research gap" yawning daily wider on every one of these topics.[28] The foundation was branding itself a "clearing house for developmental knowledge," not unlike what the Joint Center was trying to claim domestically in the urban realm. Indeed, Ford's leadership had begun to theorize one interconnected global "urban crisis," variegated by region but coursing along transnational pathways of influence and imitation that joined American "ghettos" with Indian "slums."[29] Each pole, improperly managed, seemed to threaten global order. On streets everywhere, by a kind of distended transoceanic domino theory, Ford saw urban opportunities to lose the Cold War.

Postwar universities also increasingly perforated national borders. MIT spent the 1950s looking abroad, not only to forecast noncommunist futures but to train administrators on the ground who might institutionalize them. Encouraged by Truman's Point Four Program—which, announced in 1949, promoted technical assistance in the service of economic development—new engineering schools spread "the MIT idea" to both India and Iran.[30] Penn and then the University of Southern California ran a program on public administration in Pakistan.[31] Rodwin took the lead on Venezuela, but Martin Meyerson embarked on global peregrinations of his own, working an urban "mission" for the United Nations in Japan from 1958 to 1962; in Bandung, Indonesia, where he and Jaqueline Tyrwhitt founded a planning school in 1958 on the GSD model; and along ekistic circuits set in motion by the abstruse Constantinos Doxiadis, whose periodic Delos symposia drew in MIT's Richard Meier and many others friendly to the globalizing tendency in urban design.[32] Doxiadis's firm alone had seven hundred employees stationed in thirty-three countries, with conspicuous involvements at Islamabad, its signature project;

Philadelphia's Eastwick district, just west of the Schuylkill River, with Ed Bacon; and, in Latin America, Rio de Janeiro, Mexico City, Santiago, and a housing project in the 23 de Enero neighborhood of Caracas.[33]

Presented with the CVG's offer in 1960, Rodwin was instantly drawn in: "I could write my own ticket." Meyerson was easy to persuade: "Bring students down there," Rodwin remembered him saying, and "have a series of books written." The Brahmin businessman Thomas Dudley Cabot, who sat on the Joint Center's board, was openly hostile, seeing in Betancourt a threatening, illiberal leftist.[34] Sert questioned whether the center, or any university affiliate, was the best choice for the job. Rodwin had been approached as a private individual. Might a private firm do the work instead?[35] Other doubts were voiced. In the end, though, the directors' enthusiasm won the day, the center agreed to five years of consultation and design in exchange for the right to publish indefinitely on the experience, and from 1961, Ciudad Guayana, future metropolis in miniature, was on the rise.

Both the northerners and the CVG, without apology, made Caracas their base of operations. They worked from a downtown office high atop the Shell Building (even as it was precisely the late-1950s drop in oil prices that had led Venezuela's leaders to diversify the industrial base and undertake Ciudad Guayana). Researchers would quest out to Ciudad Guayana on assignment (figure 4.2), but they never seriously considered making homes on the resource frontier. A futuristic metropolis in its own right, Caracas had the look and feel of an auto-age boomtown. Unornamented high-rises dominated the skyline of a city that had grown from a population of 12,000 in 1920 (immediately pre-oil) to 495,000 in 1950 and some 1.3 million by 1960. Second-tier cities such as Maracaibo, Cabimas, Valencia, Maracay, and San Cristóbal had also shot up—forty-six places first acquired "urban" status in the 1950s alone—but Caracas's primacy was uncontested.[36] From 1952, following decades of official hostility to urban living that crested during the rule of Juan Vicente Gómez (1908–1935), Pérez Jiménez inaugurated what many remember as "the bulldozer years," with the high-Modernist slabs of Caracas serving as showpiece and testament to his "Nuevo Ideal Nacional." It was from this core, and in contradistinction to it, that the CVG and the Joint Center learned to envision an urban future for the peripheral Guayana region, four hundred miles southeast and at least a day's travel from Caracas on irregular roads. (Existing rail infrastructure was in place to transport ore, not passengers.) Betancourt commissioned a study of the capital city's superblocks by Luis Lander of the Banco Obrero, declared them "costly and inhuman," and resolved to invert his predecessor's geography of state investment, distributing funds and population across the national territory.[37]

FIGURE 4.2. Developmentalist delegation at Ciudad Guayana, 1966. American-trained planners and social scientists liaised with Venezuelan counterparts, usually at the CVG headquarters in Caracas. The tallest figure, at center, is Daniel Patrick Moynihan, who assumed the Joint Center's directorship that year. James Q. Wilson of Harvard, his predecessor, stands two people to the right. Lloyd Rodwin of MIT is three people to the right of Wilson. Willo von Moltke is two to the right of Rodwin. Box I:196, folder 6, Daniel P. Moynihan Papers, Manuscripts Division, Library of Congress.

Age-old schemas positing terra incognita, unearthed from colonial times, were ready to hand when scholars and administrators ran up against the limits of their knowledge. John Friedmann invoked Sir Walter Raleigh's quest for El Dorado in the 1590s and claimed, "This is the region that gave rise to that entrancing fable."[38] The British planner Anthony Penfold, reporting in 1966, could write that "virtually unknown and uninhabited[,] the Guayana still holds the mystery that inspired Conan Doyle's *The Lost World*," adapted as a film for the second time in 1960, with Claude Rains in the lead. Yet "its true wealth," only suggested by the "drama of its scenery," lay with minerals and the river's potential for hydropower. Penfold enumerated rich stocks of iron ore; some gold, mined commercially since 1829; the possibility of manganese, nickel, chrome, diamonds, and bauxite; and, nearby, confirmed sources of oil, gas, coal, salt, sulphur, and kaolin.[39] A 1965 Joint Center prospectus, calling the population figure of 650,000 "ambitious but well-founded," focused on the manufacturing front. It augured large-scale production of wood pulp, paper, and steel. Aluminum factories powered by electricity from the Guri Dam, seventy miles upstream, would make use of plentiful nearby clay deposits and bauxite transported from the Caribbean.[40]

The place had approximated "Pittsburgh on the Orinoco," Friedmann wrote, ever since US and Bethlehem Steel's first incursions, but it had become so without any authentically regional conception of the city's insertion in a broader, functionally specialized economy. Indeed, the name Ciudad Guayana entered the language only in tandem with this more-than-urban vision: Puerto Ordaz, the twentieth-century ore port west of the Caroní; eighteenth-century San Félix, to the east along the Orinoco; and Santo Tomé de Guayana, a more general designation for the area, were the names that appeared on maps. Ciudad Guayana, by that name, was a regional city, "a hybrid of already existing formations" that comprised numerous centers.[41] The *ciudad* was to serve as ceremonial gateway to a region-spanning industrial complex focused on basic metals. (The famed Venezuelan petrochemical industry was centered on Morón, west of Caracas, while automobiles and consumer goods came from Valencia, also to the west.)[42]

If *planning* connoted growth and growth required coordination, then any scheme predicated on Venezuela's clean break with a past labeled less than modern first entailed a careful sorting of its regions and their roles. Venezuela "has suffered from the centralizing tradition," the Joint Center reported, "with its accompanying notion that nobody who is anybody ever lives anywhere except in Caracas." Redistributing the population was a leading goal, and it was an idea consonant with "a Latin American philosophy," mysteriously unspecified, that predated Betancourt and, they asserted, would endure.[43] Doxiadis had been preaching "new-centralization"—not decentralization per se, but a form of "inner colonization" that would balance out existing metropolitan giants with targeted, dramatic acts of city-building confined to specific "growth poles." It was "too late," he wrote in his oracular style, to "change the cities of the present."[44] The Guayana conclave was inclined to agree. The only option was to build the future.

Crucially, though, the team insisted that, as an object of scientific study, the city, albeit new, could not be in any strong sense *unique*. Venezuela's problems were "similar or analogous to the problems in other areas ripe for development all over the world."[45] As Norman Williams Jr., the lead American planner during the project's first stage, wrote, "The special quality which gives character to some cities as diverse as Chicago, Copenhagen, Quito—and denies it to Madrid, Los Angeles, Liverpool—is almost indefinable for an existing city; it is naturally even more difficult to define in advance."[46] The future held scholars' interest precisely because it harbored surprises. Yet even in spouting off such a list, Williams and his colleagues made sure to establish a circuit of reference within which Ciudad Guayana would become legible: a field of attractions and repulsions, like and unlike, object lessons and cautionary tales. The social scientist's task was to abstract from this mass of data—to phrase the new and unforeseen in terms of the generic. Just as the Joint Center had sought to broker a higher episcopate of disciplines, the groundbreaking at Ciudad Guayana seemed poised to yield a city-of-cities, a composite type that would illustrate something more general about urbanism as a generator of capitalist growth.[47]

In short, Ciudad Guayana was "not only a physical thing." This was the contention of the anthropologists Roderick and Lisa Peattie, disciplinary outliers and the rare center affiliates who opted to live on-site, in a northbound memo titled "Immediate Steps toward Civic Consciousness." The city had physical dimensions, but its broader remit was "to help people"—both on-site and beyond—"feel that a new entity is arising." Nomenclature (repeat: "Ciudad Guayana") was one plank of this campaign. Cartography also did important rhetorical work "[b]y showing the whole area on one map" rather than as a congeries of camps and company towns.[48] It was also critical, wrote Penfold with the Joint Center staffer Guy Kelnhofer, that there be "definite limits of settlement," a bright urban boundary marking "a sharp, clean break with the country" and, by extension, with the nation's pre-industrial past.[49]

The land was not empty of buildings or bodies. "Far from being virgin territory," Williams pointed out in a memo to his staff, some fifty thousand people occupied "a series of scattered settlements." Charles Abrams visited in early 1962 and noted a landscape "pegged by small but well-defined foci of activity and settlement."[50] Americans who saw them, however, were quick to denigrate those outcroppings as patently unplanned. "Highly disorganized both physically and socially," Williams wrote.[51] "The existing settlement suffers from formlessness and lack of character."[52] "Huts" of cardboard and tin, wrote Penfold, interspersed with "ranchos ... agglomerated in a disorganized way," defined the residential landscape as late as 1966.[53] *Organization* and its obverse—for the Joint Center, this familiar vocabulary was as likely to describe intellectual life as urban form.

What, then, to do with these found objects? The Peatties thought the CVG–JCUS team might preserve at least some of the inherited built environment in the name of tourism. Numerous forts, churches, and mills persisted—vestiges of Spanish missionary activity. Some were in ruins, and by providing contrast, they could highlight the newness of the new. "Yet, [s]o far as we could see, the European middle-class tradition of visits to ruins is not very strong here"—better, then, to write these traces out of the landscape, excise them from the maps, and photograph them only to announce their impending disappearance.⁵⁴ Kelnhofer's 1962 report was typical in this regard: "I was . . . impressed," he wrote to his colleagues, "by the vast emptiness of the Guayana area" that awaited urbanization. "It was necessary to see it in order to fully appreciate the magnitude of the problem."⁵⁵ *Future* and *metropolis* were both relative terms; neither had meaning independent of *past* and *countryside*. To argue for a new kind of city, one needed recourse to the old.

In the 1960s, contemporary with Urban Renewal, freestanding New Towns (usually capitalized in this way) became a preferred instrument by which to control the tempo and extent of urban development—to build an imagined future directly into existence rather than merely describe it. Planners applied the designation to a remarkably wide range of settlements, ranging in size from a simple Garden City of fin de siècle proportions—Ebenezer Howard had recommended capping occupancy at thirty thousand—to far more sprawling and multifarious compositions.⁵⁶ Charles Abrams felt "the breezes of Utopia" wafting through the New Town movement, noting in *Man's Struggle for Shelter in an Urbanizing World* (1964) examples completed or underway in Holland, Germany, India, Greece, France, the Philippines, and several parts of South America. National policies promoting New Town development were on the books in Israel, Singapore, Ceylon, Norway, Puerto Rico, Ireland, Poland, Hungary, Yugoslavia, and the Soviet Union.⁵⁷ Guy Kelnhofer catalogued several hundred "previous projects of this nature" and added Canada's many "single-enterprise communities"—company towns—to the list as admissible models, along with examples developed in the United States. The RPAA in New York had built Sunnyside and Radburn in the Garden City mold, and three Greenbelt towns (of Tugwell's projected three thousand) had broken ground during the New Deal, in Maryland, Wisconsin, and Ohio.⁵⁸ In the 1960s, master-planned communities were afoot most famously at Irvine, California; Columbia, Maryland; and The Woodlands, Texas—and the embattled New Towns In-Town program would soon arrive as yet another plank of Johnson's Great Society urbanism.⁵⁹ Even within the borders of Venezuela, Ciudad Guayana had company. A nationwide program of town-building, launched "to contain expansion" of existing cities, had coalesced under Betancourt. Tuy, which began in 1957, was the first of several planned industrial satellites to Caracas. El Tablazo, adjacent to the western city of Maracaibo, was a gridded, low-rise "reception city" for migrants who had come to work in petrochemicals; Richard Llewelyn-Davies and his staff divined the particulars of its physical form with EGTAC, a computer program developed at the London School of Economics.⁶⁰

Rodwin himself applied the New Town label to Ciudad Guayana, and he knew whereof he spoke, having made his name as a student and critic of the

British program that Patrick Abercrombie implemented with such purpose after the war. In carrying out that research, Rodwin admitted in 1956, he had already been looking ahead to the British model's eventual application and refinement in the United States, where national-level planning was historically weak, "and possibly even [in] overseas development." The Joint Center team was perpetually casting about for examples of how and how not to execute their laboratory city. The UK towns, Rodwin wrote, had lacked "warmth, sensory delight, surprise, stimulus, drama. . . . Like a bad painting, [they] are apprehended too quickly."[61] He attended a 1964 UN symposium on New Towns held in Moscow and toured several imperfect Soviet renditions.[62] Upon first visiting the Guayana townsite, Abrams likened the emerging regional constellation, approvingly, to the industrialized Ruhr Valley in western Germany, a multinodal basin of midsized cities frequently invoked in league with the TVA.[63] When Lisa Peattie happened to travel through Mexico with a Chicago anthropologist—not on Joint Center business—she dashed off a memo, knowing there would be a captive audience for her impressions of Ciudad Sahagún, a newly established center of automobile and railcar production that, to her, represented a considered effort to stave off congestion.[64]

The city-from-scratch that most urgently called out for condemnation, all agreed, was Brasília. Impossibly distant from Brazil's urbanized Atlantic littoral, it rose between 1956 and 1960 at the behest of the crusading President Juscelino Kubitschek, given to fervent declarations that his monumental capital, shaped like a bird (or was it a plane?) "taking off," would both reflect and constitute a break with the nation's pre-industrial past.[65] This was high Modernism incarnate, CIAM urbanism so vast and sudden that observers worldwide with no particular expertise in the history of planning were transfixed and a bit bemused. Anticipating American criticisms, Joint Center planners specified again and again that Ciudad Guayana was not Brasília. It was smaller, for one thing; its house lots were individualized where Kubitschek and architect Lúcio Costa had opted for tower blocks; a recognizably American private sector had a part to play; homeowners—and they were owners, not renters—had "ample freedom" in building and adorning their properties.[66] It eschewed any "complete 'Grand Plan,'" said Willo von Moltke—GSD faculty, German émigré, lately a collaborator on Ed Bacon's softer approach to Urban Renewal in Philadelphia, and now Ciudad Guayana's chief designer—to an audience assembled in Brasília. Instead, Ciudad Guayana would assume a "'master form' which can accommodate future changes."[67] To speak of "form" in this way obligated planners and designers to think in terms of processes and events elapsing over time. Unlike Brasília, which was transparently the work of architects (and politicians) playing city planner, the Joint Center's town, its partisans claimed, had at last brought the rigor of social science directly into the work of conceptualization and construction.

The issue was not simply that their predecessors had been utopian. Other New Towns had been *new* in the wrong way, entranced by the future as if it had an ontological standing independent of present or past. The Brazilian party line, that nations could "leap" from backwardness into modernity in the space of a single generation—"Fifty Years in Five," Kubitschek would recite—was only the most garish example of this error in temporal reasoning. The New Towns in Britain, Rodwin wrote, had shown "embarrassing failures in foresight," ignoring how their decentralist program was furthering the country's legacy of sprawl rather than reining it in.[68] Since the 1910s, European urban visionaries of the CIAM dispensation had routinely announced their intention to "work on the future," in Bruno Taut's words, and let existing cities "melt," "rot," or "wear away." Perhaps this stark rhetoric was at home in manifestoes, the favorite genre of CIAM and Marinetti's Futurists alike.[69] It entailed an orientation to the future entirely distinct from the one theorized between Cambridge and Caracas.

"Above all," von Moltke wrote in a 1963 piece explaining Ciudad Guayana to the readers of *Ekistics*, in planning, "there must be the order of growth, the dimension of time" (figure 4.3).[70] *Order*—in postwar urbanism, this watchword cut two ways. It was a primary category for Corbusian Modernists, who posited whole new cities with everything visibly in its place and located those synchronicities, intact, in a future that would in toto supersede the current state of affairs. Invoking *order*, von Moltke acknowledged the Modernists' synchronic conception and lent it some respect. For the Joint Center, however, the term indicated a consuming interest in sequence: an ordered, because ordinal, series of temporal states, interlinked and constantly cross-referenced. Whether in North America or South, the team argued, a city possessed no license to discard its past. Modernity could not be understood as mere acceleration (a motif underwriting so much critical theory of globalization and technology written since the late twentieth century). The rhythmic sequencing of urban growth was the decisive thing. The question then became one of timing: when and how fast, and with what degree of evidentiary support, to make advances toward the horizon.

Perhaps this way of phrasing the question smacked of modernization theory, whose Rostovian framework of discrete developmental "stages" toward full membership in the industrialized world exerted at least partial influence on the Joint Center—even as movements for decolonization, unignorable by 1960, had dislodged confidence that the stepwise movement from "tradition" through "take-off" to "maturity" would ever be realized automatically.[71] John

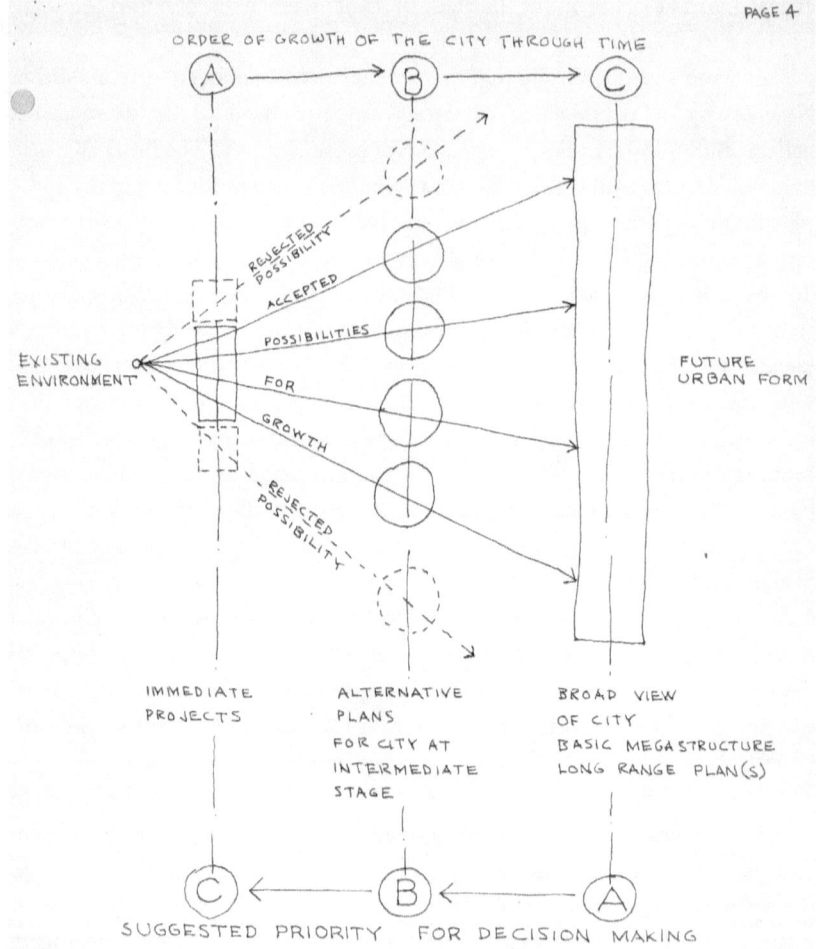

FIGURE 4.3. "Order of growth" and "suggested priority." Diagrams such as this one, drawn by a Joint Center designer reporting to von Moltke, suggest a curious temporality for planning: future states envisioned for the town take priority over conditions observed in the present. William Porter, "Preliminary Proposal for Planning Process Model for Urban Design Division," January 18, 1963 (Report E70), box 3, Joint Center for Urban Studies, Records of the Guayana Project, AC 292, Massachusetts Institute of Technology Institute Archives and Special Collections.

Friedmann suggested a rough equivalence between the Venezuelan case and Rostow's model: its mining economy was traditional, the 1920s oil strikes established the preconditions for industrialization, and manufacturing of (American) steel in the 1950s signaled take-off. Friedmann held that this last process had taken eleven years (1950 to 1961) to run its course. "Timing is a critical element here, for planned complementarities can be brought into existence only simultaneously [the synchronic order posited at Brasília] or in a predetermined sequence [the diachronic, ordinal approach]." He went on, muddying things somewhat: "Rather than a prescription for a program, [that sequence] is a prediction of the timing of certain events on the assumption that the events themselves will come to pass."[72] There was room for debate on precisely how airtight these temporal emplotments truly were—whether they were guarantees or guesses about the future, prophecies or predictions, projections or mere premonitions. At the Joint Center, however, it was beyond dispute that urbanization be understood as an articulated sequence of past, present, and future: a composite of tenses, each one of which might offer up information and be brought to bear inferentially on the others. Still, Ciudad Guayana was a built environment, a material assemblage of objects and voids, and the major question soon became how to make these temporal passages perceptible in everyday life. How to make Venezuela's approved future *present*? How to sequence urban form? How to stage physical movement in ways that would reinforce this developmental politics of time?

Intervisible: Avenida Guayana and the Temporality of Form

Extensive debate attended the question of form. From 1962, a flurry of memos, sketches, maps, graphs, and theories taxonomized "directions and types of urban growth" with a zeal reminiscent of Lynch and Rodwin's theoretical inquiries just a few years prior. By July of that year, the designers were juggling seven alternatives.[73] All presumed neighborhood units housing twenty thousand to seventy thousand residents apiece, but beyond this point, many questions remained unresolved: Where would the center of town be located? Would there be just one center of town? Should it coincide with an existing settlement of Spanish or American provenance, or was it better to construct a new focal point from scratch? MIT's Donald Appleyard weighed in: monocentric and polycentric forms produced different sorts of "exposure" to the environment, different "symbolism" of community structure, different "sensuous impact" as residents and visitors traversed the city, different degrees of formal "plasticity," intellectual "challenge," and the possibility of "withdrawal" from public space.[74] Brasília aside, could Ciudad Guayana take cues from the great purpose-built capital cities? The designers consulted "National Capital 2000 AD," the latest projection for greater Washington.[75] Or did the site merit something closer to a "twin cities layout"? San Félix, the main cluster of extant residences, was east of the Caroní; to the west were Puerto Ordaz, several heavy industries, and the plateau that, by consensus, would house the new Orinoco Steel Mill, scaled to satisfy most of the nation's demand for that metal. Writing to Norman Williams, the planner Frank Martocci invoked Minneapolis–St. Paul as a possible model. There was a caveat, though: two cities could not simply be dropped from the sky, intact. If bifocal, development had to be sequenced precisely and plotted in advance. Growth had to begin in the east, achieve critical mass, and then duplicate itself en route to the mills. Like the region's prevailing winds, it needed to have a westerly direction. The only maps evocative of Ciudad Guayana's future had to be veined with arrows. The title of Martocci's memo invoked "timing as a factor" in urban development.[76]

As late as November 1962, the designers were vetting a form proposed by Ed Bacon. Bacon had been passed over as a candidate "to run the job," but he was still a close confidant of von Moltke and glad to consult when asked.[77] Bacon's urban aesthetics, here as in Philadelphia, privileged one single center, with precious little consideration for the edges of town. "A series of radial axes" would extend out from Punta Vista, a location immediately west of the river and overlooking the waterfall that had always given the townsite its justification. "The city will have a shape more or less like a figure 8," as Williams understood it—suggesting infinite dynamism, perhaps, but without shouting "take-off" in the manner of Costa's Brasília (figure 4.4).[78] Punta Vista, Bacon showed, was exactly on axis with the junction of the two rivers to the north. A small island next to the falls—effectively what the eponymous vista was trained on—was exactly bisected by an existing bridge across the Caroní. Something about this "curious geometric relationship," von Moltke would later write, carried "a forceful emotional appeal for the designers."[79] Critics of untrammeled Modernism, the designers nonetheless entertained a design whose axiality would have been at one with CIAM practice. An unsigned memo from a Venezuelan planner dutifully explicated that group's concept of the indispensable urban *corazón* (heart) before trailing off into a long quotation from Ortega y Gasset likening peasants to vegetables.[80]

At length, however, these monocentric schemes lost out. Even in entertaining Bacon's ideas, Williams had characterized the result as "a lineal city" with several coequal centers (figures 4.5–4.7).[81] As Williams bowed out of the project, acrimoniously, and von Moltke took the helm on matters of design, this

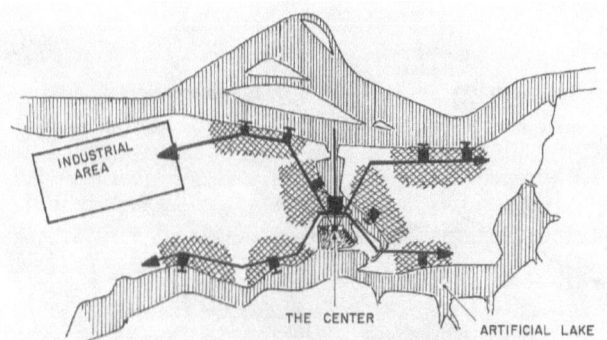

FIGURE 4.4. Edmund Bacon's unrealized plan for the center of Ciudad Guayana, 1962. The "Bacon concept" asserted one single center of town, where the two major thoroughfares would intersect in view of the waterfall that industrialists had long harnessed for hydropower. Willo von Moltke, "The Evolution of the Linear Form," in Lloyd Rodwin and Associates, *Planning Urban Growth and Regional Development: The Experience of the Guayana Program in Venezuela* (1969), 135. Courtesy of MIT Press.

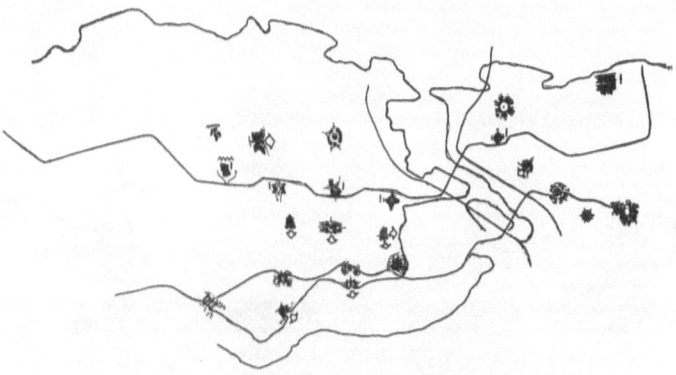

FIGURE 4.5. Centers. By 1963, a multifocal form for the city had won out. This diagram shows a variety of land uses parceled out into exclusive districts, dispersed across the fifteen-mile-wide city, and linked only by the system of highways. Donald Appleyard, *Planning a Pluralist City* (1976), 186. Courtesy of MIT Press.

conception of form—as something established by high-speed roads and experienced mainly from the window of an automobile—became the team's working consensus. "Visual continuity" over the course of a high-speed journey was the desired effect. The proper standpoint from which to assess the city was from a moving vehicle, not via the maps or aerial views that also studded official communication.[82] Von Moltke had been making similar points for years, including in his work with Bacon. In a 1957 statement of theory titled

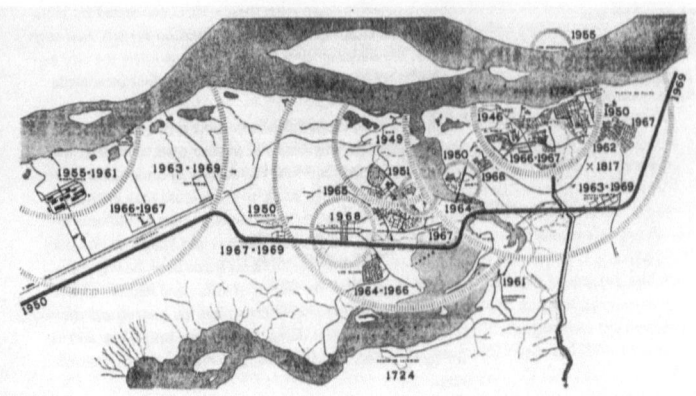

FIGURE 4.6. The firm linear foundation of an automotive city. This map spatializes Ciudad Guayana's developmental sequence, showing the compresence of Spanish colonial construction (1724, bottom center), early Venezuelan construction following independence (1817, upper right), pre-1958 industrial development by US corporations, and, from 1961, the stages of its transformation into Ciudad Guayana so called. Donald Appleyard, *Planning a Pluralist City* (1976), 203. Courtesy of MIT Press.

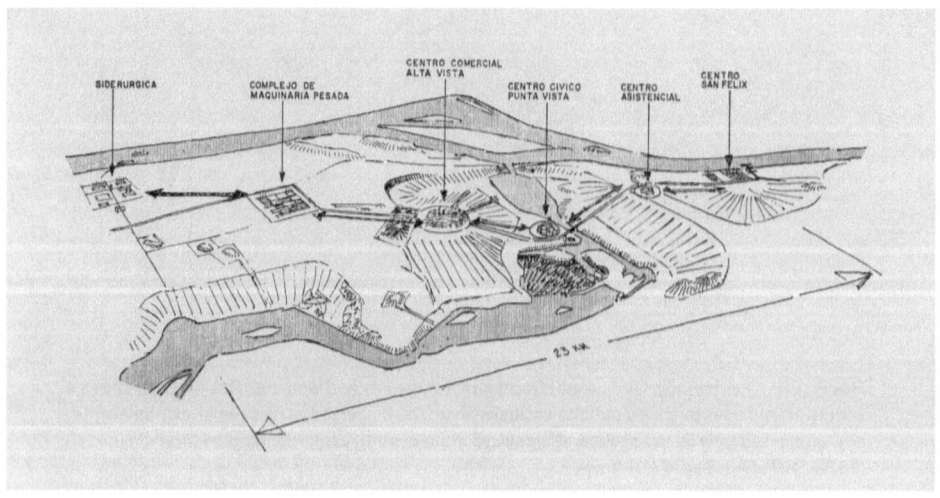

FIGURE 4.7. The nodal city. As the design process wore on, planners represented the city ever more starkly: Ciudad Guayana was Avenida Guayana, and the only districts of any consequence to them were those that straddled or flanked the road. Wilhelm V. von Moltke, "Planificación moderna en Latinoamérica, demostrada por los ejemplos de Brasilia y Santo Tomé de Guayana" (1964), Papers of the Estate of Willo von Moltke, Special Collections, Frances Loeb Library, Graduate School of Design, Harvard University. Courtesy of Frances Loeb Library.

"In Pursuit of Urbanity," they wrote that "designers must consider man's perception at all points," sketches must achieve "visual explanation" (not simply depict a future state), and a city's "scale" could be defined only "relative to [one's] movement on wheels and on foot."[83] Ultimately, the central feature of Ciudad Guayana was not any particular point on the map, any plaza, outlook, monument, building, junction, or hill. It was the new Avenida Guayana, a highway that extended some fifteen miles east to west, joining dispersed nodes of settlement, both the inherited and the imposed, into a polycentric regional unity that would have been at home in Southern California. One was either on or off Avenida Guayana. It was the sightline to which all questions of visual cohesion were indexed, and it commanded the lion's share of attention from the city's researchers, designers, and publicists as they sought "a firm linear foundation on which to develop the city's entity in depth."[84]

Whereas canonical New Town designs tended to collocate homes and workplaces, bind them into growth-limited pods of settlement, and thus enable short pedestrian commutes—the Garden City catechism committed to paper well before automobiles caught on—the situation in Betancourt's Venezuela was different. Private cars and public buses were the assumed modes of transport, rail service was not part of the equation, and while planners were thinking constantly of the home–work dyad, they did so in the context of national-level labor laws that obligated all employers to subsidize workers' commutes in full, "portal to portal." Employers themselves were still building plentiful worker housing, and to save on commuting costs, they tended to choose sites within four miles of the plant. But even in the case of government-built housing—which much of Ciudad Guayana, post-1961, effectively was—employers were on the hook and left to plead that commutes not exceed ten miles, a distance that could threaten profit margins. So wrote Charles Abrams, who investigated this issue on the UNESCO dime and concluded that a clear majority of Venezuela's workers, around 90 percent, had a preference for living apart from the factory and traveling by car.[85] An automotive city was taking shape. Correspondingly, transportation engineers rose to a new prominence in the planning process, conducting "origin–destination studies" based on interviews with residents, refining "gravity model techniques" thus far tested only in North America, projecting population distributions in light of "expected 'centre-seeking' activities" such as warehouses and truck terminals, and, by their own admission, substituting data from US cities when Venezuelan numbers were hard to find. For the Joint Center, the arts and sciences of movement came to mutually reinforce: in this future metropolis, planners would learn to simultaneously "canalize" traffic efficiently onto the Avenida, "preserve a high standard of traffic environment" in aesthetic terms, and on both fronts, wrote the MIT architect William L. Porter, reconceptualize form as something more than "large shape-making." "Fidelity to quantities," he recalled decades later, "was requisite."[86]

The team referred to Avenida Guayana as the city's "visual spine." Appleyard stipulated that researchers' first task was visual: to "discover what is actually seen from the road."[87] The CVG had made a commitment to "total design" (as opposed to merely "strategic design"), and to achieve this, Appleyard insisted, a "visual control diagram" would be necessary—effectively viewshed analysis as featured in his ongoing work on Boston's highways (figure 4.8). He cited Kevin Lynch, no expert in Latin America but, with Appleyard, firmly of the opinion that "the problem of designing for vision in motion is everywhere the same."[88] Nowhere in *The View from the Road* (1964) does Venezuela come up by name, but it is beyond doubt that Appleyard's proposals for Boston and Ciudad Guayana informed one another. The next year, to a Kepes-edited volume called *The Nature and Art of Motion* (1965), he contributed "Motion, Sequence, and the City," a work of theory that extended *The View from the Road*'s baroque system of notation. Planners needed recourse to a set of "experiential symbols," he wrote—the better to "train our senses to the complex delights of 'seeing' motion as it is. For too long we have talked only of form and space." The piece glanced in passing at the example of Boston's Northeast Expressway. On the final page, however, Appleyard shifted his focus to one lone case study of sequence design in a new city. That new city was Ciudad Guayana.[89]

Any number of Joint Center affiliates had issued scattershot complaints about the "formlessness" of extant settlement at the townsite. Appleyard and von Moltke, however, worked to reframe the debate in terms of the visual encounter with the landscape—form being something that would become sensible to the viewer only over the course of a journey (figure 4.9). The problem, for von Moltke, was that journey's "lack of visual continuity." Avenida Guayana would rectify the issue: it "connects all major existing elements, a series of nodes which are intervisible and which further continuity of activities along it."[90] A fragmentation of visual experience, he wrote, echoing early Kepes, would produce a lack of social solidarity at anything approaching the regional scale. Infrastructure did not just serve preexisting regions; it could suture new ones into existence. In a New Town, populated almost entirely by newcomers, this syncretic dimension of infrastructure had particular importance: design could "go a long way in overcoming the sense of anonymity and isolation."[91] The Avenida physically connected older nodes, such as Punta Vista—now reimagined as a district for culture and recreation—with new ones built from scratch, such as Alta Vista (or El Centro), the Modernist administrative and commercial district on the western plateau, distant from river, falls, port, or mill but still the closest

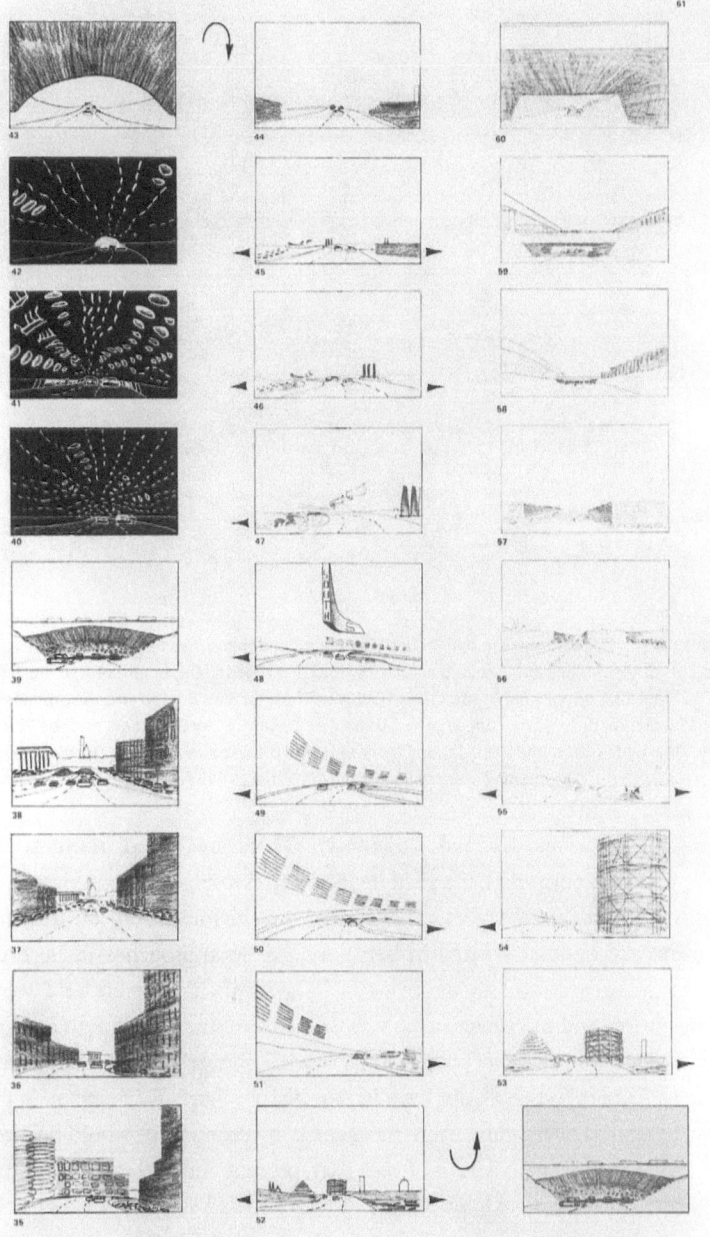

FIGURE 4.8. Vision in motion. Donald Appleyard, Kevin Lynch, and their collaborator John Myer proposed to capture—and design for—drivers' moment-by-moment visual experience along the major circumferential highway proposed to encircle downtown Boston. These twenty-seven panels, culled from several dozen on display in *The View from the Road* (1964), demonstrate the Joint Center's attempts to conceptualize urban form in terms of an experiential sequence elapsing over time. Donald Appleyard, Kevin Lynch, and John R. Myer, *The View from the Road* (1964), 60. Courtesy of MIT Press.

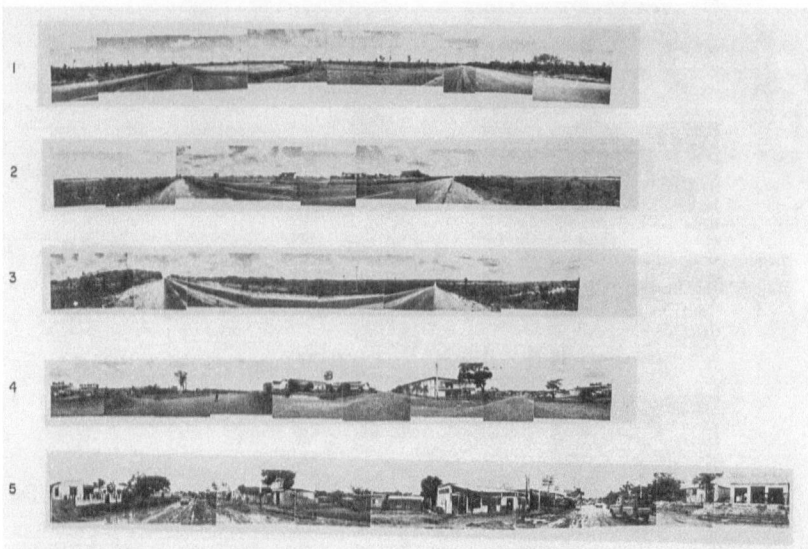

FIGURE 4.9. "Views from the main road." Appleyard had this series of 360° photos taken in 1964 "as part of the photographic record of the city" and presented them, numbered, to illustrate how a driver would experience entry into Ciudad Guayana. Research on Boston and the ongoing work in Venezuela directly informed one another. Donald Appleyard, "City Designers and the Pluralistic City," in Lloyd Rodwin and Associates, *Planning Urban Growth and Regional Development: The Experience of the Guayana Program in Venezuela* (1969), 425–427. Courtesy of MIT Press.

thing the linear city had to a downtown. There, in view of the new ziggurat-style CVG headquarters, the road divided into two one-way boulevards, six hundred feet apart, and travelers' attention would inexorably be drawn to the commercial options located in between: "As he approaches it, he must slow down and turn toward it" (figure 4.10).[92] The Avenida, planners held, would thus make visible and palpable the passage of historical time itself. Each one of these nodes was potentially a "promotional work," nonverbal testimony that tomorrow, as Robert Jungk would have it, was already here. By being seen from the road, over and over again, each node, correctly composed, would help reinforce the city's specific articulation of past with present and present with future.[93] Infrastructure became exhibition: the Avenida would stage and restage the city's own process of emergence, embedding in the texture of everyday mobilities a stepwise sequence of approaches to and arrivals at industrial modernity.[94] One of these processes operated at the scale of years or decades; the other elapsed in seconds and minutes. Both could be programmed, and the two could be brought perceptibly into correlation.

This sequential understanding of infrastructure echoed themes that had run through some of the Joint Center's pre-Guayana output as well. In "The Pat-

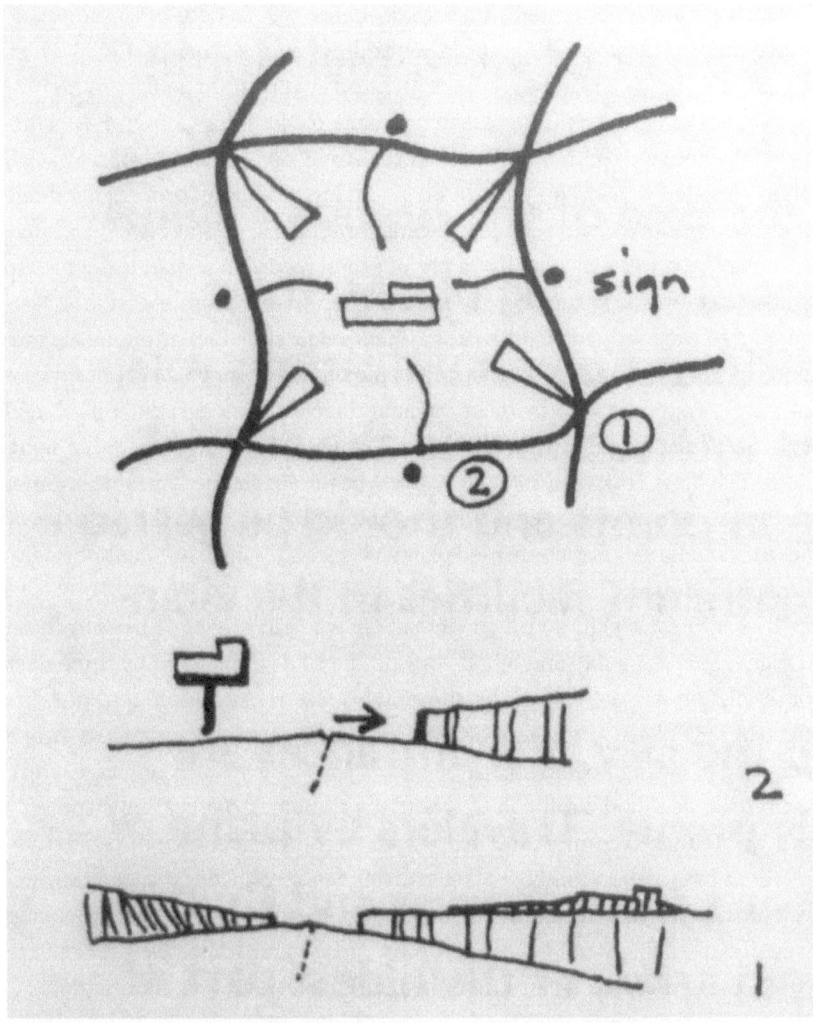

FIGURE 4.10. Choreographing peripheral vision. Appleyard's 1976 book, the last official Joint Center monograph based on the Guayana project, contains diagrams of varying complexity. This one indicates, quite roughly, how designers sought to manage drivers' sightlines, guiding the mobile eye to make it notice specific signs, buildings, or other information-bearing artifacts planted to suggest the city's path to modernity. Donald Appleyard, *Planning a Pluralist City* (1976), 139. Courtesy of MIT Press.

tern of the Metropolis" (1961), Kevin Lynch had argued that "individuals require a rhythmical alternation of stimulus and rest" and that urban form could reliably choreograph it.[95] His theoretical typology of nets, sheets, grids, rings, and stars could seem static, but Lynch was quite preoccupied with movement. The disoriented and reoriented wanderers who populate *The Image of the City*

(1960) were always potentially on the go—hence the need for the famous cognitive maps.[96] Lynch and Appleyard both drew on the work of Philip Thiel, an alumnus of MIT's undergraduate architecture program and, from his new post at Berkeley, a part-time research attaché to the Joint Center. His elaborate "Sequence-Experience Notation for Architectural and Urban Spaces" (1961) insisted that urban perception be understood as a "process involving the consumption of time" and implicating multiple senses at once: "Architecture may be 'frozen music,' like a phonograph record; but man is the pickup whose movement realizes the experience."[97] Even the traditionalist John Burchard had long argued that urban aesthetics demanded an attention to motion, speed, and angle of approach. People tended to store visual memories of a city as apprehended from a particular direction, at a particular pace, and on a particular mode of transportation. Planners could engineer these sightlines. The New York filed away in visitors' heads, he claimed in 1957, was not the one seen "across the petroleum-perfume of Bayonne and the piggeries of Secaucus," and this fact confirmed planners' successes in arranging its bridges, tunnels, and roads.[98]

Lynch himself paid a visit to Ciudad Guayana in July 1964 to consult on design. He spent a day and a half touring the *ciudad*, followed by three days of discussion with colleagues on-site, and his reactions point up tensions that the team may have grappled with but preferred not to admit out loud. Lynch admitted to having no knowledge of Venezuela or the Spanish language. From the outset, he found it difficult to ignore the climate, "so precariously poised" as it was "between comfort and misery," and recommended that the staff study methods by which to modify it: constructing outdoor shades, streamlining development patterns to allow the formation of wind channels, introducing water features that would cool nearby air, and avoiding reflective surfaces. He could also sense that, if left unchecked, durable class segregation would coalesce, with the Caroní acting as the main cordon sanitaire between the middle-class west and the eastern "slums" of El Roble, La Laja, and Dalla Costa. He questioned the project's physical scale, having seen enough of California to know that high-speed roads did not always feel like agents of unification. Ciudad Guayana was looking to be "coarse in grain, even blank and visually somewhat inhuman." The Avenida was a sound piece of engineering, but its sequencing of experience was off: too many traffic circles, "several confusions of geometry" in the route, "ambiguous turns in featureless country" out beyond the airport, and some ill-chosen landmarks to announce the trip's culmination, given the "probable inability of the heavy machinery to act as a visual dominant."[99] Were smokestacks really the future toward which all west-bound drivers wanted to be beckoned?

Lynch also argued for a density of settlement, "even congestion at first," that was anathema to most partisans of the polycentric city. In part, this was his safeguard against segregation by class: "Let them be concentrated and mixed." But even the idealistic Lynch could tell that a divided, functionally differentiated geography of land uses and users impended. "This is the 'natural sequence,'" he wrote—the scare quotes marking both distance from and resignation to the sorts of developmental telos that so often underwrote planning and design in the age of social science.[100]

Ciudad Guayana seems to have occasioned broader shifts in his thinking on temporality, regionality, and the sensory dimensions of urban life—theoretical questions that are more pronounced in Lynch's 1970s work than in his early period. *What Time Is This Place?* (1972) is the text most often cited by preservationists and their critics.[101] *Managing the Sense of a Region* (1976) contains the more profound reflections on time, and just as in that work Lynch argued for the visualization of spatial scales larger than the single city, he considered "how an active working landscape might connect us to the present time, or to the recent past, or the future—indeed, to the unending passage of time" that flows across these categories and gives them point.[102] Lynch became fixated on the temporal sequencing of life in and by urban form—the way he animates the nonhuman world here is notable—in ways codified at Ciudad Guayana a decade prior. Its central spine, domain of the automobiles that for years had been scrambling mental maps up north, did the most to elicit this turn in his thought. His critical memo from the 1964 visit concluded that, yes, this city, like so many of its peers, would inevitably be linear in form. By that year, the view from the road *was* the prevailing image of the city. "This decision having been made," however, it was vital that Avenida Guayana "be considered as a sequence in both directions." Unlike other types of journey, Lynch observed, commutes have a "tidal" quality. To design them holistically, planners needed to think of roads as "reversible flow devices," not as finite, one-way emplotments with obvious beginnings and ends.[103]

Lynch might have said the same of urban history as an elapsing temporal sequence, and of development, or modernization, as a technical process and political imperative. The future, as destination, has no existence independent of the past from which it springs; the automotive future would fail if executed in ways ignorant of its inheritance. Like those so eagerly and rapidly etching Ciudad Guayana onto the map, Lynch was inclined to relate minute questions of form, infrastructure, and design to far broader considerations on the temporality of human existence—the intervisibility of nodes in a three- and four-dimensional urban landscape to the concatenation of past, present, and future as tenses in which to think and live. Lynch came as a critic, however, and his reactions to the Avenida suggest that, in its haste to catalyze development—to bring Venezuela literally and figuratively up to speed—the Joint Center may have timed it wrong.

City as Curriculum: The Travels of Ciudad Guayana

Cities are physical volumes, built, inhabited, and moved through. Yet this city always and already had another life as an object of study. The Joint Center remained remarkably forthright about this fact, and so did the CVG, which sprouted its own Division of Studies, Planning, and Research. In consultation with it, the Universidad Central de Venezuela added a Centro de Estudios de Desarrollo (Center for the Study of Development) that would have looked familiar to any American fluent in "organized research."[104] The city was a generator of economic development, but it was also and essentially a generator of knowledge, the focal point for an interdisciplinary series of scholarly books and reports. *Planning Urban Growth and Regional Development: The Experience of the Guayana Program in Venezuela* (1969) was the summary document, an edited volume comprising selections from almost every scholar on staff, American and Venezuelan alike. In it, Rodwin admitted the center had been "self-interested" in seeking "a theater for their activities." Ciudad Guayana was a performance of planning expertise, and as the center drew "some inferences about styles of planning" and "more general questions of strategy," its audience came to span the globe.[105] Guayana knowledge traveled, and it often traveled north, recontouring American approaches to urban and regional studies in its image.

The center's leadership had expectations for this knowledge production. Memos instructed staff, again and again, that each act of research would be judged by "the extent to which the resulting volume is likely to qualify as a sociological classic." Norman Williams used this turn of phrase in January 1962, writing to Daniel Lerner.[106] Lerner repeated it in correspondence with Meyerson and Rodwin, and his "suggested researches for a sociological classic on Guayana" read as a glossary of postwar behavioral science. One set of proposed projects would address "mobility" in the metropolis: geographic, social, and "psychic" (in the sense that the city would cultivate personality types new to the developing world). Another would gloss urban and societal "stability" in all its forms, treating of "equilibrium" (or "the want:get ratio," after William James), "instruments of psychic balance," and more.[107] No Joint Center book adopted these concepts quite as robotically as Lerner seems to have preferred—he was in some ways a caricature of the modernization theorist—but his presumption that Ciudad Guayana would yield social-scientific breakthroughs of some sort, not only recapitulating established Northern truths but generating new and general ones, caught on. Lisa Peattie, whose ethnography of the eastern *barrio* La Laja was underway, bristled. The directors had begun speaking of "Great Books," and she looked askance, writing from the field, "Although I fully sympathize with the Joint Center's wish to see a series of 'great books' emerge from the present project, and although [I] have every incentive personally to write a 'great book' if within my powers (indeed, the reiteration of this phrase is not comforting), it seems clear to me that the demands of a program such as this on the participants are such as to practically insure [sic] that no 'great books' will issue."[108]

Rodwin envisioned "six or seven" books based on the Guayana experience. One monograph could not do the project justice, as the heterogeneity of the center's engagement was the "most important and unusual" thing about it. Meyerson, citing Diderot, had imagined an entire encyclopedia of urban studies issuing from the new city–laboratory, and Rodwin concurred: "The nature of our field required" such breadth "because it was a horizontal, not a vertical, field."[109] Several targeted monographs emerged. Noel McGinn and Russell Davis produced *Build a Mill, Build a City, Build a School* (1969), on the relationship between industrial life and education, while Richard Soberman completed *Transport Technology for Developing Regions* (1966), again inferring general policies and techniques from local conditions.[110] Both joined the Joint Center book series. Frank Martocci planned a book called "The Physical Regional Plan"; von Moltke prepared to write "Urban Design"; William Doebele of Harvard took on "Land Use Controls for Economic Development"; and an unnamed author would be found to address the Guayana's political organization.[111] These last four volumes never materialized, nor did work by the team's "official historian"—"one of those deceptively attractive ideas that just did not work out," Rodwin recalled, because participants were disinclined to give him interviews.[112] After the Joint Center left Venezuela in 1966, some volumes, such as Rodwin's omnibus, achieved higher priority, while others withered away. Some survived but straggled; Donald Appleyard, by then based at Berkeley, would not publish his Guayana book until 1976.[113]

It was as a case study in regional planning that Ciudad Guayana most seamlessly entered academic conversation. The work of John Friedmann was decisive in this respect. His monograph, the product of two summers spent on-site, pronounced on *Regional Development Policy* (1966) as such, complete with a textbook-style glossary of terms, but the subtitle gave away its genesis as *A Case Study of Venezuela*. Friedmann, a frequent visitor to the Joint Center during the

1960s, would claim in the early twenty-first century that this book was the very first to bring an "explicit spatial dimension" to the question of development. It helped push the dispensation of regional planning beyond its New Deal focus on river basins, although that was a component, and made the case that regionalists could chart a path beholden to neither blind advocacy of economic growth ("regional development") nor the bone-dry modeling practiced by Walter Isard and his progeny ("regional science"). Friedmann felt compelled to apologize for his book's basis in nonquantitative methods. "Many kinds of data were simply not available," he wrote, and unlike the transportation planners, he did not opt to interpose figures from the United States. Instead, he proliferated maps, most of them demonstrating the new city's role as a "counterpole of attraction to Caracas."[114] That binary—between capital and New Town, center and edge, core and periphery—lent Friedmann's inquiry its structure. It governed its reception as a classic work of regional planning, "exemplar, par excellence," Lisa Peattie wrote with hindsight, "of a successfully technocratic approach" to identifying discrete and deliberately unequal "growth poles," distributed throughout the national territory, toward which capital, industries, and all manner of planning interventions could then be directed.[115] (To speak of *core* and *periphery*, Friedmann clarified, compels intervention in a way that *equilibrium* talk does not.) This quickly became the leading spatial strategy among development planners, and precisely because of the surfeit of available studies, Friedmann wrote, the case of the Guayana "demonstrates," as nowhere else could, "the method of attack that must be used."[116]

The companion concept to *growth pole* was *resource frontier*. Friedmann did not invent this concept, but he set out to give it a more precise definition than the literature yet allowed. "Resource frontiers *are* urban frontiers," he wrote, citing the work of Richard Wade on the Ohio Valley. They "must be focused on a city." *Frontier* is always a freighted concept. At this early point in his career, Friedmann fell back on Spanish-colonial notions of Venezuela's cultural "monotony" and "tropical torpor." There are numerous moments at which his interest in the country can seem strikingly detached, as if it were only "a convenient prototype." "The spatial structure of its economy"—centralized control, clearly stated goals, little visible resistance to the developmentalist state, indeed "a surging social movement" in favor of delegating industrial development to the provincial level—"has a classical simplicity."[117]

Elsewhere, though, Friedmann took pains to give the frontier concept a history. He glanced back at overblown political rhetoric from 1940s Caracas that had seized on the Guayana as the place where "the genuine Venezuelan will emerge" in confrontation with an unforgiving natural landscape. To contextualize this thinking, Friedmann invoked Frederick Jackson Turner on the

American West, along with the example of remote Ankara's construction under Atatürk in the 1920s and Brasília more recently—cases in which nearly identical land-based ideologies of national self-creation were in play. At a more fundamental level, Friedmann intervened in debates ongoing within human geography. He questioned the ontological underpinnings of what we cognize as centers and edges, and in turn of the region as a spatial or scalar unit. Customized development agencies such as the CVG made it plain that institutions based in major cities did not just happen upon "remote" regions awaiting capitalization: policy, publicity, investment, discourse, and study all interacted to produce regions and impart "maximum" but always provisional "closure with respect to a given problem set."[118] Indeed, regional ontology and its implications for planning practice seem to have motivated much discussion among the project staff. Arthur Fawcett, for instance, wrote to Martocci that "a region does not simply exist . . . ; it is what it is defined to be, nothing more."[119] This contention, elementary to geographers active on the far side of their discipline's post-structural turns of the 1980s and 1990s, has a history, and it, too, runs through the Joint Center.[120]

Well into the 1980s, Friedmann continued to cite Ciudad Guayana in major works on the history and theory of regional planning. *Territory and Function* (1979), written with Clyde Weaver, sought to reclaim the field's "philosophical foundations," lately "dissipated" under the influence of Isard. Through Venezuela and other examples, it took a second look at the sordid politics of "growth poles" by which such "designations could be awarded like medals."[121] Friedmann did not, however, speak for the center as a whole. Disagreements gradually surfaced between him and the leadership. As the 1960s wore on, Friedmann began to theorize the tense interdependence, indeed mutual constitution, of urban, regional, and national scales in ways that struck Rodwin as disruptive to the accepted framework, which saw smaller units securely nested in and politically subordinate to larger ones. Friedmann was also increasingly interested to theorize inequality between regions, whereas the center's mainstream embraced the universal imperative (and automatic "diffusion") of growth. A longtime epigone of Karl Mannheim's *Man and Society in an Age of Reconstruction* (1935), a favorite text at Chicago's PERP, Friedmann was more convinced than Rodwin of planning as a state prerogative but warier of top-down approaches. The rift was serious enough that Friedmann left MIT by the end of the decade, decamping to UCLA in 1969 to run its newly formed planning department.[122] Ciudad Guayana brought diverse approaches into conversation, further exemplifying, or performing, the promise of interdisciplinary urban studies. It also uniquely forced the question of their incompatibility and clarified in the breach just how many different futures lay over the horizon.

After 1966, Guayana knowledge migrated once and for all into the curriculum of urban studies. Typical of its treatment was *Taming Megalopolis* (1967), a plump Anchor paperback comprising dozens of scholars' takes on different aspects of the urban question and compiled by H. Wentworth Eldredge, an urban sociologist based at the unlikely institution of Dartmouth College in tiny Hanover, New Hampshire. Numerous Joint Center affiliates appeared—Wood, Alonso, Abrams, Frieden, Banfield, Perloff, Isaacs, Rodwin—and the volume featured few if any authors unattached to the network of expertise whose circuitry these men had secured. Eldredge had visited at Harvard and come to know Ciudad Guayana as "a splendid opportunity"—so splendid, in fact, that it was the one and only case study discussed in the section headed "Aesthetics." Three selections exhausted that topic: Ed Bacon discoursed on "townscape" in very general terms; Samuel Zisman, also of Philadelphia, surveyed open-space design; and von Moltke turned up with "The Visual Development of Ciudad Guayana," a reprint. The city was small and remote, albeit in ways that justified inferences to "megalopolis" as such.[123]

Rodwin took even more explicit steps down the path from city to curriculum. He brought out *Nations and Cities* (1970) with a trade publisher and embedded his 1963 article "Choosing Regions for Development" within a broader attempt to systematize the theory of growth poles (or "urban growth centers") as strategic nodes where states could "spell out," "enlarge," and "dramatize" visions of their industrialized futures. Rodwin was aware that the Sixties had happened: "Today, if proposed, such undertakings would be labeled as mere 'show piece' psychology." "And yet," he wrote, "they actually worked." Hence the need for this book. Despite admissions that "in many ways Ciudad Guayana is unique," Rodwin positioned lesser-known Venezuela as his first case study in the national programming of urban growth. Chapters on Turkey, the UK, France, and the United States ensued.[124] The logical sequencing of *Nations and Cities* was the crucial thing: cases, inferences, and then generalities.

Understanding the transnational flow of models and ideas was of conceptual interest to Rodwin, and whereas some Cold War urbanists were entirely content to imprint US practices wholesale onto what they called the Third World, he insisted that lessons worked out in the postcolonial context be assessed for their reapplication up north. Studies either confined to the domestic context or predicated on simple north-to-south imposition struck him as "naïve and limited."[125] The nature of a laboratory, after all, requires that its results travel, persuading people who were not physically present to bear witness to the original experiment. Joint Center members, deeming this all a "rare and invaluable" opportunity to "document experiences and experiments which can be translated to problem situations arising under similar conditions" elsewhere, cross-referenced

Venezuela with a wide range of nation states deemed ripe for urban intervention.[126] In Latin America alone, Reginald Isaacs's independent consulting practice led him to Peru, Argentina, Chile, Colombia, Brazil, Mexico, Cuba, the Dominican Republic, and most of the Central American states. Isaacs also transposed many of Venezuela's lessons to the US Virgin Islands, where he occupied a seat on the planning board and instigated debate under the heading "Selection of a Future: Criteria and Method."[127] Luis Muñoz Marín, the former Puerto Rico governor, helped set up Cordiplan in the early days of Betancourt, observed the first stages of Ciudad Guayana's implementation, and drew on the experience when advising John F. Kennedy on the national planning agencies his Alliance for Progress would foment across Latin America.[128] The Joint Center's faculty committee briefly considered organizing a Chilean sequel to Ciudad Guayana that would have been executed in tandem with the city of Concepción, the ubiquitous CENIS, a company mining iron, and Pacific Steel.[129] From afar, and well after the fact, Americans had uses for Ciudad Guayana.

Pedagogy in urban studies, especially but not only in Cambridge, also regrouped around the lessons of the New Town. By 1964, James Q. Wilson's report to Ford could justify the overseas work, in part, by noting that it bolstered teaching: "Venezuelan materials are already in use in courses and seminars" and available for collation with studies of development elsewhere in the world. Teaching about Ciudad Guayana renewed the Joint Center's efforts to make their city legible within a self-curated canon of reference points. Wilson's report mentioned work ongoing in northeastern Brazil and under Colombia's Cauca Valley Authority, also modeled on the TVA.[130] Willo von Moltke taught a case-based workshop in 1971 that related Ciudad Guayana to Milton Keynes, the British New Town most adapted to automobility; Fort Lincoln, the "New Town In-Town" sited in Northeast Washington, DC; and James Rouse's Columbia, Maryland.[131] Donald Appleyard's courses at MIT and then Berkeley made routine use of Ciudad Guayana as a case study, almost always alongside examples far better known to the American public: Levittown, Canberra, Abercrombie's postwar satellites to London, and, again, Brasília. He began integrating moving images into his teaching, pointing students to 16-millimeter time-lapse films shot from cameras he affixed to moving vehicles in Boston; suburban Brookline; Chicago; Fremont, California, a postwar suburb between Oakland and San Jose; and, of course, Ciudad Guayana.[132] The Joint Center's entanglements there enabled Appleyard to make his methodologies of visual sequence more fully transnational.

What broader conclusions, however, were Americans supposed to be drawing from this cottage industry of Guayana studies? What normative appraisals did the work merit? Those guiding the project's induction into the canon and curriculum presumed that the thing had been a success and that the Joint Center's five years on-site had resulted in a stable of salutary object lessons, both physical and procedural. Consensus was elusive, however. Ford never fully came around to the project. As late as 1965, one officer was protesting that the work "might pull [the Center] too far away" from Boston; it was already hard enough to balance work at the local and national scales.[133] The issue of east–west inequalities across the Caroní also dogged the planners, to the point that a 1988 article touting the city to readers of the *Swissair Gazette* had to mention "the emergence of a 'double society,' geographically divided."[134] A 1971 review of three Venezuelan New Towns in the *Journal of Developing Areas* rated Ciudad Guayana's planning process the least flexible.[135] Many other observers likened the place to an industrial colony in the classic mold. Indeed, the "company town aspect" introduced by Sert's firm when under contract to the steel magnates, Charles Abrams wrote, would prove hard to "dilute."[136] Some critics focused on unplanned developments: the faulty population projections, the inadequate provision of housing in the face of rapid rural-to-urban migration, and the vast penumbra of shanties surrounding discrete nodes of official order. Others contended that the settlement felt too planned, too orderly to encourage the stimulating, urbane existence the designers had imagined.

Dissent also came from within the ranks. Rodwin acknowledged such conflict but tended to explain it away: there were "constraints, limited perspectives, mistakes, squabbles," yes, but also "satisfactory resolutions of most difficulties."[137] "Much too much had to be learned on the job," he wrote in *Nations and Cities*, but the center had "left on very amicable terms" with Venezuelan officials.[138] In a 1994 interview, Rodwin called Ciudad Guayana "one of the best things the Joint Center ever did . . . an extraordinary experience" and claimed that the CVG had asked him to extend the contract.[139] Others gave far more destabilizing accounts of the episode. Norman Williams's departure at the end of 1962 left the project functionally without a director, and von Moltke was not fully in command until a year later.[140] By 1963, many on staff were calling the entire project into question. Williams noted deep disenchantment even in 1962. "At the start of the project," he wrote, "we Norteamericanos were full of high hopes—but, as things turned out, rather naïve ones" in light of administrative mishaps, restive locals, and the Caracas-bound planners' evident lack of interest in ever getting too close to the site. "Rarely have glamorous hopes dissolved so rapidly on contact with reality."[141]

Over the next decade, John Friedmann came to repudiate the program's intellectual and political substance completely. This meant renouncing positions to which he himself had signed his name: the theory of growth poles, he now held, was an unacceptable "pursuit of unequal development as a matter of policy." As far as Friedmann was concerned, "a good deal of nonsense has been written (including by the present senior author) about the spatial diffusion of economic growth."[142] Failure, however, could be productive—an object lesson of its own kind if anatomized by the right analyst and mobilized in ways that might compel habits of self-criticism. The most lasting of the Ciudad Guayana books would be those committed to asking, "What went wrong and why?" Answer this question, Friedmann wrote, and "we could stop teaching the wrong theory to our students." His correspondent was William Porter, MIT's future dean of architecture but then a doctoral student researching housing and neighborhood prototypes for the New Town's *unidades vecinales*. "I can think of no better thesis topic for you than this (unless you want to get hung up on one of Kevin's image studies, which, I think, are little profitable)."[143]

Friedmann went public with his criticisms in the 1970s (although he kept his thoughts on Lynch to himself). It was in 1979, in *Territory and Function*, that he let loose on his former self, coolly citing "Friedmann 1966" as if talking about an unwelcome stranger. His memo to Porter, however, dated from 1965. Self-doubt set in early. Despite the center's stated dreams of empirically compiling an encyclopedia of best practices, Ciudad Guayana's intellectual legacy would also include a series of searching critiques—of their own foibles, but, more broadly, of the assumptions that had led so many planners in either of the Americas to think of cities as laboratories in the first place.

"This Fluid Situation": Cybernetics and the Sequencing of Intervention

What went wrong and why? One of the lasting ironies of Ciudad Guayana is that, of the many books it spawned, the one plausibly called a classic came from the project's most unsparing critic. Lisa Peattie, the anthropologist, was mystified by the CVG's "particularly damaging" decision to remain in Caracas and forfeit without contest any genuine "sense of the site."[144] In May 1962, barely three months into the thirty they had earmarked for fieldwork, she and her husband, Roderick, could sense a "total paralysis of building" resulting from the CVG's brittle chain of command. "The city will either explode or die unless it is released to grow." To this sclerotic state of affairs, the Peatties counterposed the "momentum" and "esprit" of their anthropological subjects, newly arrived rural migrants making their way in La Laja, a shantytown just downwind from San Félix that had risen during the post–World War II, pre-CVG period of industrialization: "Fire the starting gun and cut the tape. They act with great energy when they are permitted to."[145] Their labors ultimately bore fruit as *The View from the*

Barrio (1968), credited to Lisa Peattie alone; Roderick had died suddenly in 1963. This was not "research in the conventional sense," she wrote in the preface, "for I had no 'problem,' no 'research design.'" The tone had changed.[146]

In some ways, *The View from the Barrio* still operated within the conventions of mainline anthropology. Chapters constellated around well-worn topics such as economic exchange ("Getting and Spending"), the interplay between "personalism" and organic "community" (a concept of which Peattie was skeptical), and, inevitably, kinship structures—each of these treated as a discrete realm. Despite their underrepresentation at the center, she noted, anthropologists understood more than anyone else the "tendency to think small" in order to infer from case to population, neighborhood to nation. "The pages which follow," she wrote, "are in part a methodological exercise." They were far more than that, of course, but Peattie took pains to justify her ethnography as having glimpsed "the process [of development] itself on its smallest scale." "Its economic structure is Venezuelan development summarized." The part contained the whole.[147]

Peattie's approach was also compatible with the shape-shifting concept of the public interest as enshrined by Banfield and Wilson. Perhaps there was no "general interest," Peattie wrote, only the "sum of individual welfares" and provisional alliances between groups. With a population of two thousand in 1961 and forty thousand by 1968, La Laja was functionally a satellite of San Félix, and San Félix itself was fragmented and ethnically diverse: Spanish, Italian (who dominated the building trades), Trinidadian, Chinese, Lebanese. Alliances, in turn, took shape around specific political "issues." Peattie devoted an entire chapter, "The Sewer Controversy," to a conflict she observed in 1964 when the CVG, in piecing together Ciudad Guayana's water infrastructure—which already served the inherited company towns but not the informal *barrios*—put forward a plan that would have located an open sewer directly in La Laja. A vitriolic fight ensued, and Peattie herself, known locally as "Doctora," took an active role in publicizing the battle beyond the walls of the *barrio*. Peattie helped make the sewer an issue: she set in motion the very churn of political influence from which traditional pluralist social science would have taken pains to stand back, and she was often the one to drive, bus, or ferry across town to communicate with CVG agents on La Laja's behalf. When saboteurs tied to an extremist group in San Félix disfigured the construction site with dynamite, the political waters were roiled in ways that the Joint Center's apostles of method could have neither foreseen nor endorsed. Peattie, however, found the appeal of violent sabotage "understandable." "It is like the steam which cracks the closed boiler; it is a way of expressing dissatisfaction in a society which lacks the channels, the institutions, for protesting legally in any effective way."[148]

Her descriptions of La Laja's landscape added texture and atmosphere that, save for Appleyard's, other Joint Center work on Ciudad Guayana—and so much postwar anthropology, wedded to immaterial senses of "culture"—did not even attempt to conjure. Spatially, La Laja was a conundrum. It displayed the defining features of postwar "strip development," except that this strip had summarily been crumpled up and "squeezed sideways" into a triangular plot of land bounded by a combination of topography, the Orinoco, and the steel "company fence" across which a Bethlehem subsidiary, the Iron Mines Company of Venezuela, was forever visible (and audible, setting off a siren to mark the start and end of each shift). Whereas Friedmann had glossed *space* and *region* at scales best represented by two-dimensional maps, Peattie appreciated dwellings as intricate, three-dimensional volumes. She discussed their materials (cement and *bahareque*, a mixture of earth, manure, and straw); their color, ornament, and personalized "presentation" to the public eye; their détente with greenery; and the way in which *barrio* residents, by tacit agreement, had adorned façades in ways noticeably more "urban" and "modern" than the "rural," "traditional" treatment visited upon houses' rears. She also made much of Puerto Ordaz as "a visible image of the power and competence of the North American development model": a perfect likeness of "America's pre-eminent creation," the middle-class automotive suburb.[149]

Peattie's book offered at once a vivid transcript of current conditions and, like so many Joint Center studies, a prospectus for one or more urban futures. The temporal dimension of urbanization weighs heavily upon the text precisely because, according to Peattie, it weighed upon residents themselves. Ciudad Guayana "is a city which lives in the future," we learn. "It is a city of bulldozers, of engineers who wear boots and dungarees and carry shiny briefcases, of noisy bars and holes in the streets, of new traffic interchanges." Talk of *el futuro del país*, Peattie noted, peppered daily life. With this turn of phrase came several corollaries. An "idealistic optimism phrased in terms of material progress" had become "the dominant atmosphere." Peattie cited reports that 90 percent of Ciudad Guayana's workers expected to be fiscally better off in five years. More than this, though, she diagnosed a widespread sensitivity to the temporality of urbanization as a vector of social change. "There began to develop that sense of social process which makes it possible for a semieducated worker to say, 'I have had a historic life.'" Such consciousness of time's passage lent a "particular dynamism" to life in this otherwise fragmented town, comprehensively planned but palpably incomplete. "If the residents . . . often speak, as they do, of 'the future,' in a general sense aside from their own personal prospects, it is because the world has changed so rapidly in their own lifetimes that they are able to perceive the past as more than a series of events, as representing historical process, continuing into a future." Life in the *barrio* was, in this sense, "a segment of history, both because it *is* so, and because its participants *feel* it to be so."[150] Past, present, future: by inductive, vernacular means, Peattie's ethnography drew out something very much like the composite of urban tenses—fused into one articulated, cross-referenced whole—that so much Joint Center scholarship, written from the North, had held up as the modern ideal of temporal reason.

Peattie was a skeptic of "development" to an extent unknown among her colleagues. Full-scale condemnation of the CVG would await her follow-up, *Planning: Rethinking Ciudad Guayana*, issued 1987 (also with Michigan) in a climate far more accustomed to critical planning scholarship with Marxian, post-structural, or, in Peattie's case, anarchistic leanings. Even in *The View from the Barrio*, though, disaffection is apparent. Despite "its cloverleaf highways and its travertine-faced apartment buildings," she wrote, Venezuela could still feel like an updated version of a plantation economy. Massively unequal, the country found itself "in a moving disequilibrium." Ten years into the Betancourt era, the whole CVG experiment was in "jeopardy." Yet Peattie held out a dark hope. Futures, she argued, resulted not from "economic development," that "dry technicians' phrase" meaning everything and nothing, but from the thorny process of ordinary, unaccredited citizens "making the future" for themselves. "Even as the city grows under the planners' stimulus and direction, it grows only partly according to plan. . . . It is part of planning to realize this." No Joint Center monograph to date had ontologized urban change in this manner—flexible, negotiated, nonlinear—and it was Ciudad Guayana that occasioned the break.[151]

Peattie's turn toward more reciprocal understandings of the planning process dovetailed with the growing prominence of cybernetic thinking at the Joint Center. Cybernetics proposed a vocabulary in which various sorts of user *input*, sensed in real time, would *feed back* on planners' practice and iteratively modify it. By the 1960s, cybernetic concepts and catchphrases, derived from wartime anti-aircraft technologies and early computing, were discontinuously in use among planners and architects, across the social sciences, in defense and policy milieux, and in American popular culture. Robert C. Wood, of MIT, was the key figure in translating these recondite ideas for the center. He was intent on stressing the complexity of urban life and, if nothing else, redescribing it in a language of communicative, multidirectional *systems* transmitting *information* and *signals* without pause. Under Wood's influence and in the run-up to his brief stint as director, the Joint Center became one of the key research units involved in urbanizing cybernetics, both as an ontology of city life and as an epistemology for its study.

Wood's transition away from the Dahl-style pluralism that had become hegemonic in his field began in the 1950s. Indeed, it is apparent even in his contribution to the NYMRS. Much of *1400 Governments* (1961) reads as mainline political science, but already in that volume, cybernetic motifs show through.[152] In a 1963 piece later anthologized by Wentworth Eldredge, Wood could sound almost like an electrician: "There must be inputs and outputs . . . transformers to channel 'pressures' into 'decisions.'" "We must learn to deal with systems of decision making just as engineers deal with systems of weaponry and space vehicles."[153] In 1968, the American Society of Cybernetics (ASC), the main group making inroads into the social sciences, awarded Wood its Norbert Wiener Medal. By 1969, in "Science: The Good Urban Witch," he was proselytizing for a science that could accommodate citizen participation, even dissent ("'what's happening' today"), work with these "pretty volatile variables," decentralize power to the neighborhoods, and thus, Wood's long-standing goal, consolidate the metropolitan area in a more supple way, agreeable to more parties than ever before.[154] (Governance was the endgame. Wiener, the movement's unclassifiable figurehead, described cybernetics as a science of "communication and control.") "No one," Wood wrote as late as 1975, "can or should avoid cybernetics."[155]

Perhaps this turn was unsurprising: Wiener's office, just down one of MIT's long hallways, was as accessible to social scientists as to the mathematicians and technologists who had first motivated his work. And although Wiener was not chiefly an urbanist by trade, neither was he a stranger to those pursuits. In 1950, for instance, he had applied cybernetic concepts of network redundancy in a proposal for large-scale "life belts" that would ring American metropolises and allow the dispersal of critical functions outward from the core, annealing the city against air attack.[156] He coined the term (itself nautical in origin, from the Greek *kybernetes*, or steersman) and popularized it on a wide scale in *The Human Use of Human Beings* (1950), a surprise bestseller by any measure.[157] Ronald Kline has written, with a degree of bemusement, on the cybernetics craze that seized postwar America. *Life* magazine, which published Wiener's decentralist scheme, covered the twists and turns of cybernetic thinking throughout the 1950s. Policy debates on automation cited the literature, at least in shorthand. Intellectuals as disparate as Lewis Mumford, Daniel Bell, and Marshall McLuhan all saw in cybernetics a way to resolve old antagonisms between mechanistic and vitalistic worldviews. By the 1960s, its distinctive phraseology had found adherents in science fiction and among garden-variety hippies. (Kline indelibly notes the inflection some skeptics later began to apply when uttering the name of the Society on Systems, *Man*, and Cybernetics.) Virtually anyone could pass for a cybernetician if committed to its argot and willing to accept that circular causality, its central explanatory concept (figure 4.11), might not be a contradiction in terms. (With the overstatement characteristic of many cyberneticians, Magoroh Maruyama would claim that circular argumentation marked "the first major epistemological restructuring since the time of Aristotle.")[158] The Joint Center's errand at Ciudad Guayana thus participated in realignments perceptible throughout the ecology of American intellect. To many different constituencies, cybernetics seemed capable of accounting for both humans and machines by means of a theory committed to the hunch that humans were machines—or were enough like them that terms such as *system, signal, feedback,* and *flow* could describe their behavior equally without subtracting anything essential. "Like" is the key word: in urban studies as in other domains, cybernetics was, before all else, a suggestive analogy.[159]

Cybernetics' infiltration of urban scholarship was routed through but certainly not confined to the Joint Center. In *Urban Dynamics* (1969), Jay Forrester of MIT, a prominent computer scientist, pivoted from earlier work to formalize a cybernetic account.[160] The ASC featured a section on "urban systems" in its second symposium, held in 1968.[161] The hybrid field of environmental design also channeled cybernetic ideas when it promoted *fit, balance,* or *homeostasis* between spaces and their occupants. Harvard and MIT were key transformers

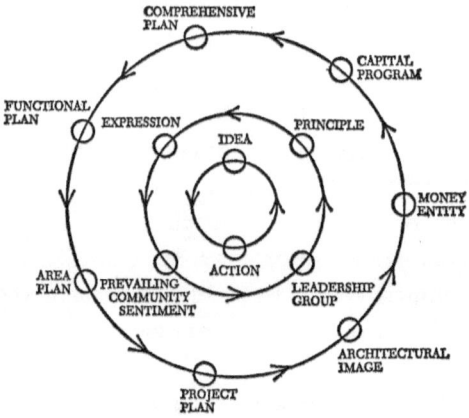

FIGURE 4.11. Planning in a world of feedback. By the late 1960s, cybernetic understandings of the reciprocal interactions between planners (leadership group) and their clients (prevailing community sentiment), and also between planners' conceptual priors (idea) and the modifications that practice (action) necessarily introduces, became commonplace. Many of Ciudad Guayana's planners, as well as their fiercest critics, began to theorize planning as a complex process without clear beginning or end. Edmund N. Bacon, "Urban Process," *Daedalus* 97 (Fall 1968): 1165–1178. Courtesy of MIT Press.

in its intellectual network as well.¹⁶² Even a veteran renewer such as Ed Bacon, in *Design of Cities* (1967) still earnestly revisiting the Rome of Pope Sixtus V to exalt its "total design idea," completely recast his working vocabulary of urban form in a swirling incantation to *forces, fluxes, processes, routes, energies,* and other watchwords that split the difference between high cybernetics and fin de siècle vitalism.¹⁶³ "Urban RAND" applied cybernetic methodologies to simulate the outcomes of proposed redevelopment schemes—would they or would they not provoke rioting?—as did the Cambridge-based consultancy Arthur D. Little on contract to San Francisco and Pittsburgh.¹⁶⁴ In 1968, the Washington Center for Metropolitan Studies released REGION, a computerized "urban systems simulation" game that had players try their hand at development strategy and, having digested users' decisions, would "feed" ever more complex obstacles "back" at them (figure 4.12).¹⁶⁵

The center never turned cybernetic in any simple or unitary sense. Only a minority of its members adopted the lingo (and most came from within MIT, not Harvard). Still, the exceptions were potent. Lynch and Kepes were both conversant with the emerging discourse on "systems."¹⁶⁶ Karl Deutsch, a sometime collaborator, elaborated a neural theory of government–citizen communication and theorized a set of "self-controls for the American megalopolis."¹⁶⁷ Richard Meier, his coauthor on the latter paper, had pitched his *Communications Theory of Urban Growth* (1962), one of the earliest publications branded with the Joint Center seal, as an entry in the general theory of information; it just so happened that, owing to infrastructural networks laid down in the nineteenth century, cities were the nodes through which the lion's share of messages perforce passed. Cities, Meier argued, were also where "communications stress" and the "imminence of the information input overload phenomenon" were becoming most apparent. He closed the book looking outward to "newly developing areas" as opportunities for American planners to establish "channel capacity" from scratch—to build new networks at a scale and with a degree of closure that was not possible on US soil.¹⁶⁸

Meier specifically championed the construction of New Towns, which he believed would bathe rural-to-urban migrants in streams of new information; surely pre-industrial society suffered from "stimulus starvation."¹⁶⁹ Meier conceived this work well before the Guayana project launched, but it is hard not to sense the resonances. Peattie and other Guayana staff were readers of Meier, and their work brought cybernetics south. Information was constantly on the move, they held, and in this blooming, buzzing world, one-shot, top-down planning would never suffice. Dynamizing things in this way did not, of course, annul hierarchies between planners and their publics—communication *and*

Computer support for the Region model.

Participants deliberate the next move.

FIGURE 4.12. The city, simulated. Here, members of the public play REGION, a game in which participants inhabit the standpoint of a developer and make locational decisions about housing, industry, and other land uses. Washington Center for Metropolitan Studies, *Region Manual* (1968).

control—but it did add more arrows to the flowchart. After the center's cybernetic turn, to plan was to traverse these circuits, over time, with destination unknown.

The cybernetics vogue privileged abstraction, but the impact of its concepts on the work at Ciudad Guayana was quite concrete. Over the course of 1962, Peattie began using the term *feedback* (or "feed-back") with greater frequency in her memos to Caracas and Cambridge, calling for a more "social planning" attuned to local needs and wishes.[170] (Her first outline for *The View from the Barrio*, then titled *People Becoming a City*, itemized "'Inputs' of ideas"— the scare quotes signaling a recent infusion of terminology.)[171] Others caught on. Friedmann would later characterize the project as having instilled a belief in process ontology: "dialogue" and "transactions" constituted the very essence of planning. This was a "genuine shift in paradigm," away from experts' urge to "blueprint" the world and then slash through neighborhoods to make the territory resemble the map. After Wiener, planning worked only insofar as the plan adapted to its environment. Recast in far plainer language, the cybernetic impulse imbued Friedmann's left-facing theorization in "Planning as Social Learning" (1981). His political reorientation—accelerated by assignments in Brazil, South Korea, and Chile—began at Ciudad Guayana.[172] Rodwin's 1969 executive summary concluded that "flexible arrangements" had proved necessary: "Groups of human beings working together develop styles of acting and valuing and conceptions of reality that suit the situations they confront, and these situations vary." This, he seemed to suggest, was as true for planners as it was for locals. At no point did Rodwin cite echt cyberneticians—he had a distaste for formalized planning theory as such, and for Friedmann's emerging politics—but he, too, spoke of "feedback mechanisms," and the upshot was the same.[173] The failures of comprehensive planning, if carefully digested, could be instructive.

Leavened by these new concepts and confronted with a recalcitrant site, the Joint Center began to retheorize the temporal parameters of what it means to plan. Their emerging critique was not simply that urban visions synchronically promising total spatial mastery were brittle and presumptuous—that much was clear. Feedback could emerge only over time: the concept obligated planners to bend their process back on itself—"adjusting ends to means," thinking harder about "sequences" and "segments of a problem," even "selecting ends and means simultaneously."[174] As Penfold wrote, a typical prospectus "makes each step appear discrete. In fact, overlapping occurs; and a continuous feedback and reappraisal of assumptions blurs the demarcation of each operation."[175] As was true of earlier, untroubled articulations of the future metropolis, the new critique of comprehensive planning entailed its own specific theory of temporality. By 1966, to oppose the view from nowhere—the much-photographed men in suits looming over scale models and gesturing toward neighborhoods they would anesthetize and cut into—was, *uno actu*, to counter with a more complex sense of timing. Information gleaned from what had once seemed like the future could circle back and intervene on the principles inherited from history and assumed true on day one.

To this end, von Moltke circulated theoretical statements on "collective form" by the architect Fumihiko Maki—who taught urban design at Harvard, alongside Jaqueline Tyrwhitt, from 1962 to 1965—and came to de-emphasize the term "master plan" in favor of "master program," as "the latter term [more explicitly] includes a time dimension."[176] Norman Williams concurred. "It is of course a truism that a master plan is not a static document," he wrote to his staff in mid-1962, "but heretofore nobody has ever done much serious thinking about following up the point." The complexities of Ciudad Guayana had finally set that thinking in motion. Its "situation is full of uncertainties," and "the machinery for making such adjustments becomes the central planning mechanism."[177] Williams would resign within six months, but his successors found ways to turn uncertainty into insight. Ciudad Guayana was never a mere arena, supine, in which to compose a city faithful to Northern doctrine. The project compelled substantial theoretical revisions. Laboratory-like in ways the center had not foreseen, Ciudad Guayana established new registers and reference points in the critique of planning's temporal reason.

At certain points in the project, the center's cybernetic flirtations led to maneuvers that could verge on the mystical, a far cry from the exact science the group so often sought to project. Peattie's memos turned poetic: cutting cybernetics together with John Dewey's pragmatism, she wrote that a plan is an "exploratory journey through a territory only incompletely known to science before its exploration by the traveller, to a destination only definitely specified at the time of arrival."[178] Friedmann also submitted to visions of planning as a winding path, and this, too, was the result of his work in Latin America and East Asia. To the 1968 Ford Foundation Seminar on Social Science, he vocalized his break with the "high, if often platitudinous ideals" that attended the "parochial profession" of planning. "Planning is a strictly Western invention," Friedmann had written in 1959. "The slogan—Man makes himself—is a Western slogan."[179] In 1968, he was quoting no less than Lao Tzu to press his case: "All things go through their own transformations." Cities, people, ecologies, matter itself—all was process, and certainty was elusive. "Tao is the wisdom of non-action," Friedmann wrote. Post-Guayana planning needed "new institutional devices" resonant with prevailing "rhythm and time conceptions in the new industrializing societies."[180] Linear, staged interventions would not do.

Maki's work in particular elicited this more speculative style of thought. His ideal, as von Moltke understood it, "is not a system. . . . The ideal is a kind of master form which can move into ever new states of equilibrium and yet maintain visual consistency and a sense of combining order in the long run."[181] J. N. Kise, another acolyte, wrote to the project staff, syllogistically, "Life is not art; it is the content of art. A city is not art; it is life . . . This process, the city, is a combination of forces. The question is, then, what forms do these forces have[?] We wish to find their forms." If he saw this particular memo, Rodwin would have bristled. And yet, whereas some at the GSD complained (with a racialized tinge) of the "inscrutable lists of issues" with which Maki would cover chalkboards, only then to propose "a differentiated spectrum of design interventions," the Guayana staff worked assiduously to "find their forms"— to translate vaporous philosophies of process into physical patterns predicated on "new kinds of order." They rejected the focal central square, the circumferential belt, the undifferentiated grid, and other inheritances. The cybernetic emphasis on informational flow, with nothing at rest and every point in the network a relay, called for "afocality" in urban design. For Kise and others, the most philosophically defensible form was that of the highway strip.[182]

When Lynch visited and jotted his critical notes, he, too, sounded essentially cybernetic themes. There were two distinct senses, he wrote, in which "this fluid situation" could be said to flow. One concerned the planning process and its dynamics of power. "Continuous design," transacted in "liaison" with locals and looping back in "continuous revision" of its prior assumptions, injected complexity and ensured "two-way accommodation."[183] Lynch also, however, used the term *feedback* to describe the movement of traffic on the Avenida Guayana—of physical things hurtling through time and space and interacting with one another. Each car fed back on other cars, reading their cues and making minute adjustments in speed or spacing. Each driver on the Avenida, moreover, was embroiled in a perceptual feedback loop with the more stationary features of the passing environment. Lynch allowed a slippage between information and artifact. So did Appleyard, who saw highway drivers perpetually "engaged in a strategy of search" amid the surfeit of "unwanted" messages, too often self-contradictory, that buildings and landscapes always nonverbally "emit." From the datum of Ciudad Guayana, with consequences for cities the world over, the Joint Center proposed a fundamentally cybernetic view from the road. "The observer," Appleyard wrote, "selects and organizes the perceptual world."[184] The Avenida's designers set out to configure things so that all this feedback would be manageable at fifty and sixty miles per hour, and that coherent signals (*modernity*, *progress*) would emerge from the ambient noise. The task was to sequence the cybernetic highway.

The cybernetic mood, then, informed the Joint Center's understanding of planning as a decision process enacted over time; of its articulations of past, present, and especially future as categories amenable to knowledge; of the hierarchies of power and rationality that attend it and might yet be flattened; and of the urban landscape as a physical artifact, traversed, seen, and otherwise sensed. For the social scientists, however, Ciudad Guayana was a site of study every bit as much as it was an opportunity to build and populate a city. As the work wore on, center staff—those dispatching memos from the field and their addressees, in a feedback loop joining the site to Cambridge and Caracas—reflected ever more critically on the city's status as a mobile object of knowledge. They debated the mechanics by which such knowledge—their memos, but also the resulting scholarship—should circulate. Here, too, cybernetic motifs both adumbrated their thinking and got retouched in the process. What kind of account best captured "the jig-saw of facts," as Charles Abrams put it on his first visit? How to narrate the recursions by which expertise morphed and self-corrected upon contact with material reality? Were "instant judgments and adjustments to unforeseen changes" worth converting into narrative, or should they be sublated in the service of a more authoritative-seeming final analysis?[185] Could the very temporality of the process, however it sputtered or spiraled off, actually become readers' primary topic of interest?

These debates were inconclusive, but the issue preoccupied the center. William Alonso spent twelve days visiting Ciudad Guayana and became convinced that "the value of this work lies in learning while doing." This was a far more processual understanding of knowledge production than New Town projects tended to incite. Static Brasília was the obvious scapegoat, but the origins of the rot lay deeper in the past. Alonso faulted the ready-made "model towns" of the Progressive Era, whether those built to "civilize" a captive industrial workforce or those conceived in the more bohemian spirit of the Garden City. "In my opinion," Alonso wrote, the finished Ciudad Guayana "should not be thought of as the source of a model for similar undertakings, but rather as *a documented experience*. . . . The documentation of the planning process," far more than any of its potential lessons as a showpiece of urban form, "would make public within the profession a great deal of insight."[186] Wood even called for the establishment of long-term "urban observatories" rather than time-limited case studies.[187]

Planning processes, in other words, had to be recorded in real time. The key question concerned method and genre. Abrams called for a "daily diary" of "events as they occur"—not moment by moment, perhaps, with planners forever stepping aside to jot down their impressions, but nightly, under cover of darkness and aided by Dictaphone. Norman Williams, responding to Abrams, urged "a more informal and [thus] effective arrangement for record-keeping."[188] Suggestions varied. That records would be kept, however, was beyond dispute. City became knowledge only once a system was in place; raw experience in the moment became a stock of experience only through its documentation.[189] The transcript was the thing.

In and around Ciudad Guayana, the most basic frameworks by which the Joint Center had gotten accustomed to organizing urban knowledge underwent profound realignment. Methodological commitments to systematic doubt gave way to the searching self-doubt obligated by an ontology of the world as a system of systems, continually embroidered by emergent feedback loops that would only ever increase in number and complexity. Over time, this emphasis on mechanisms of self-correction ended up enabling radical self-critique. Concepts introduced in the name of planning better led many at the center to question the feasibility of planning at all.

CHAPTER 5

Reoriented
The Conservative Center and the New Politics of Expectation

On August 31, 1966, a flight left for Caracas. Aboard was a seven-man delegation from the Joint Center, a cross section of disciplines and dispositions. There sat Willo von Moltke, the designer; Alexander Ganz, the economist; Russell Davis, the scholar of education still at work on his monograph with Noel McGinn; and Rafael Corrada, the Venezuelan national and one-time MIT planning student whose entreaties had brought the center to Ciudad Guayana in the first place. The plane also held three consecutive directors of the center: Lloyd Rodwin (1959–1963), James Q. Wilson (1963–1966), and, as of the summer, Daniel Patrick Moynihan, the very public intellectual, still weathering criticism for his eponymous report. The symbolism was straightforward enough. Although the Guayana data would live on, coagulating into books, reports, and curricula, the center was hereby concluding its five years of direct building of and consultation on the New Town. Moynihan's first visit to Venezuela lent him the opportunity to take stock, sign off, look back, look ahead, ponder, and posit how Ciudad Guayana's lessons might adumbrate theory and practice on the domestic scene. The group took a second flight out to the site—"Bienvenidos a Guayana," read the leaflets, the seven names printed alongside a grainy image of heavy machinery moving earth—but first Moynihan addressed the staff in Caracas. The *ciudad* had been an "ambitious effort," he said. It had projected fluency with urbanism's "state of the art." It had forged transnational ties that had not existed before. Few could deny the "unusual attraction of a unique determined pioneering development effort for scholarly research of professors and graduate students."[1]

Or so he had heard. Moynihan had heretofore played no role in the Guayana job, and his two and a half years helming the Joint Center were to be preoccupied with domestic affairs. He knew the center mainly by reputation. Ciudad Guayana had helped bolster that reputation, despite the project's many shortcomings in execution. It was during those first seven years that the crucial work of conceptualization, research, publicity, and disciplinary brokerage took place, then that the center most fully exemplified what Karl Deutsch, in "Conditions Favoring Major Advances in Social Science," a widely cited 1971 overview, called the "industrial revolution in the production of knowledge."[2] Yet, also in 1971, David Popenoe would contend that the center had entered a state of "dissolution." At the very least, it was undergoing "radical redirection." True, he lobbed similar charges at many of the institutional lodestars of urban studies, a complex totality that had lately fragmented into numerous "worlds" given to conceptual hair-splitting and some mutual antagonism—recent coinages included *urbanology, urbistics, metropology, urbiculture,* and several different glosses on *ecology*—but could no longer be called a "field."[3]

In retrospect, the experience of the center during the late 1960s and early 1970s affords a microcosm of these intellectual and political tensions. Yet, at the time, the problems unique to the Joint Center seemed to Popenoe even more consequential than those afflicting its peers. Because of the center's centrality, its struggles were not only an instance but an engine of larger and destabilizing shifts in the intellectual network that the Cantabrigians had done so much to anchor and vitalize. Cracks had appeared. They intensified under Moynihan but well predated him, and though routed through the tribulations of Ciudad Guayana, the most serious in-house conflicts over the future-facing temporality of planning surfaced in the early 1960s in discussions of the federal program of Urban Renewal. Posing the urban in terms of its future had afforded the Joint Center a forever-moving target and, with it, the ability to operate on the assumption that there would always be a demand for more of its research. This orientation to the future also, however, set the stage for broad-based disavowals of expertise, precisely because knowledge about future conditions remains, by definition, partly conjectural. On the far side of the 1960s, the center did not dissolve, but it did reorganize in ways that placed the group among the foremost skeptics pronouncing in public on planning, social science, and the risks of even attempting their synergy.

After the Planners: Urban Renewal as Waiting Game

It was inevitable that the Joint Center would address Urban Renewal in some depth. Redevelopment agencies' official rhetoric permeated public discourse on the postwar fate of cities, their funds were plentiful, and their physical impact was everywhere apparent. "The city can no longer smile," Christopher Tunnard wrote, "because so many of its teeth are missing."[4] The center had already consulted on or given cover to some federally supported redevelopment schemes around metropolitan Boston. Before long, however—notably, under the direction of James Q. Wilson, not Rodwin and Meyerson—the center began to publish work expressly, and bitterly, critical of the program.

Martin Anderson's *The Federal Bulldozer* (1964), adapted from his MIT dissertation, joined the center's book series in polemical fashion. The book did not speak for the entirety of the center—no single author ever did—but it heralded a pronounced shift toward scholarship conceived as a critique of the actual. On numerous interlocking grounds, Anderson questioned the premises, administration, and physical record of Urban Renewal. Its justificatory keywords had little meaning, for one thing. *Blight* signified whatever those bent on razing a neighborhood wanted it to signify: buildings' dilapidation, population density, barely concealed animus about "mixture" of racial or ethnic groups, or even an unsystematic street layout, as in the lesser-known case of San Francisco's thinly populated Diamond Heights district. *Revitalization*, a term less ubiquitous then than in the gentrifying twenty-first century but often used as a synonym for *renewal*, nodded to the life sciences but, Anderson held, meant even less. Planners were "implying that the city is dead or dying. How does a city die? There are no precise definitions." Anderson, a committed conservative, painted Renewal as strangely bipolar in its priorities, a strange fusion of the interests of rich and poor, those ostentatiously being of service and those supinely being served. Yet, Anderson sputtered, "today's city . . . *is the city of the middle-income group!*" Because it bypassed the concerns of the middle classes, Renewal could not stand. On his final page, Anderson called for its complete abolition.[5]

Versions of these points had surfaced in print since the late 1950s. The celebrity of Jane Jacobs, contra Robert Moses, was well established by the time Anderson finished his dissertation, Grady Clay and J. B. Jackson had jabbed at the design politics of high Modernism, Herbert Gans had anatomized dispossession in Boston's West End, and, without always publishing their criticisms in long form, a wide range of grassroots movements had enacted resistance to top-down planning through demonstration, occupation, negotiation, refusal, and sabotage. There were several intellectually and politically diverse ways of being against "the planners." But the critiques, Anderson felt, had not yet cut to the ontological core of the problem. "There is one fact about urban renewal that many of the people associated with the program would like to ignore, and which many of them do ignore. This is time." As a process, Renewal "drags itself to completion." It could only ever be "long and frustrating," "long-drawn-out," predicated on a "time lag" during which planners made no serious attempt to adjust initial designs to ambient changes in the city's "character." A typical project took nearly "*12 years*" in full. (Italics were critical to Anderson's style.) In the interim, "while waiting for the buildings to rise," officials squandered tax revenue. Urban Renewal was, in short, an unwinnable waiting game. The essence of its failures, Anderson argued, concerned pace, rate, and duration. One chapter title howled: "The Land Lies Vacant."[6] It was not enough to rail against midcentury definitions of "progress" in abstracto. Nor was it sufficient to assert, as he also did, that most of the land assembled for Renewal would have been redeveloped eventually by the free market had the state not preempted it—that clearance had come too soon. By foregrounding the bulldozer itself, and by evoking (albeit without ever depicting) the visibly transitional landscapes it left behind, demolished but awaiting recapitalization, Anderson asked the public to consider, as Francesca Russello Ammon has put it, "what 'progress' looked like when it was 'in progress.'"[7]

Anderson's book brought a new species of notoriety to the Joint Center. An "immediate sensation," *The Federal Bulldozer* was excerpted in *Reader's Digest* and reviewed in countless non-scholarly venues. The response, James Q. Wilson wrote, was "so enormous as to impair the objectivity of Solomon."[8] Anderson's premises were broadly libertarian, but even traditionalist conservatives such as John Burchard, disinclined to quantitative analysis and unschooled in economics, applauded. In 1976, George Nash, author of (still) the most comprehensive intellectual history of postwar conservatism, could lead off his chapter on right-facing critics of domestic social policy, urban and otherwise, with Anderson's "scholarly tour de force." Because it had been published by "the prestigious Joint Center . . . the book had to be taken seriously." It, Nash argued, was the reason that ensuing commentators on the right would "frequently cit[e] urban renewal as a prime illustration of liberal folly," and something about the jagged, sublime physicality of Renewal's wreckage (figures 5.1 and 5.2) had made "the welfare state" less spectral than it would have otherwise seemed.[9] Irving Kristol, the right-wing icon who proudly read no economics until 1976—the year when he latched onto the Laffer curve as having revealed a new kind of ground truth—was by 1973 nominating city planning as one of the primary redoubts of "subterranean utopianism," and he,

FIGURE 5.1. From the standpoint of human displacement, the clearance of Boston's mostly Italian West End went about as poorly as it could have. Although the archive includes some evidence of neighborhood residents posing by the ruins and grinning, critics routinely enlisted photographs of demolition—often those taken just moments after the wrecking ball made contact—to press the point that Urban Renewal was a catastrophe. Courtesy of Thomas J. Hynes Jr.

FIGURE 5.2. The West End from the air, facing southeast, late 1950s. In the age of Urban Renewal, monumental absences became a familiar presence all their own, an expected feature of virtually every American downtown. The pointed tower at top center is Boston's old Customs House. Photograph by Laurence Lowry.

too, stressed its temporal dimension. New Town builders, beautifiers, and renewers of all stripes "ai[m] to bring history to a stop"; no plan, he mused, ever happens to allot space for a cemetery.[10]

Wilson weighed in from his perch as director. He largely buttressed Anderson's claims, writing "Urban Renewal Does Not Always Renew" (1965) and venturing, outrageously, that, pace the rhetoric, "There is no urban problem in the United States except, perhaps, for the problem of urban aesthetics." Though tucked away in the pages of Harvard's alumni magazine, Wilson's piece managed to stoke further controversy. That spring, HUD secretary Robert C. Weaver declared to an audience at Harvard that "I am forced to ask what the Center is studying, and why it should not be merged with the schools of fine art and architecture."[11] Catching wind of this exchange (and collecting materials for the next grant review), Malcolm Moos of Ford noted that Weaver was "so incensed" by Anderson's book that "he is going after it"—and the whole Joint Center—"with a meat ax." Still, officially, the center took no position on these matters. Wilson had not expressly called for Urban Renewal's repeal, and Moos's colleague Francis Rourke understood him to be "disassociating the Center from [Anderson's] extreme attacks on the program" while continuing to promote the book. Moos concluded that, in the end, a conservative presence on Church Street was "a healthy matter."[12]

The battle lines were being drawn ever more clearly, but as a corporate entity, the center preferred to be the convener of these debates, not a combatant: a forum or broker of new knowledge on Renewal that would establish the priority of topics, canon of case studies, and admissible range of positions. When Dwight Macdonald, knowing few particulars on Renewal but sensing a post-Jacobs demand among his *New Yorker* readership, consulted Charles Abrams in 1961 for leads, he was referred to Martin Meyerson "of the Joint Center for Urban Studies," who had already "commissioned half a dozen people" to write on the topic.[13] Whereas the first four years' worth of Joint Center books had attempted to demonstrate the interdisciplinary comity of urban studies, with Anderson and its turn to Urban Renewal, the center rebranded itself as a theater of dissensus. The fact that these disparate styles of commentary all originated at one place, intent on coordinating such work and setting it in conversation, spoke to the shifting forms and forums of expert urban knowledge.

It was in this spirit that the center brought out *Urban Renewal: The Record and the Controversy* (1966), a thick volume of recent statements on the matter, along with some new commissioned work. Wilson, its editor, assured readers that the center "takes no position on public issues": "Neither blanket condemnations nor blanket defenses are appropriate." Most entries in the book were case-driven, and yet with Urban Renewal, "every project," Wilson argued, "seems to require a re-examination of first principles."[14] Boston's West End anchored three chapters, reprints all: a Herbert Gans article for *Commentary* summarizing *The Urban Villagers* (1962), the psychologist Marc Fried's "Grieving for a Lost Home," and the upstart planner Chester Hartman's work on "adaptation under stress" of relocation, itself funded by the National Institute of Mental Health and Harvard Medical School's psychiatry department.[15] In "Some Blessings of Urban Renewal," Charles Abrams spoke up for a program that "now makes the front page" thanks especially to journalists in Washington and Louisville, warning only that, due to drawn-out projects and ballooning costs, its temporality approximated that of "a treadmill when it should be a frontier."[16] Roger Montgomery drew on projects in Detroit, Cleveland, Hartford, and Boston to argue for "process comprehensiveness" rather than the one-shot, "make-believe world based on chancy predictions" that defined traditional top-down planning.[17]

The volume closed with an entire section organized to replay and extend the Anderson debate. Weaver agreed to contribute a reprint, using this venue to argue that the laissez-faire muckraker had "no workable substitutes" to offer.[18] Gans called Anderson an "often irresponsible polemicist" and noted that his research would have been impossible without the stock of data, some of it self-critical, that the Urban Renewal Administration itself had collected.[19] Wilson also included Wallace F. Smith's 1965 review of *The Federal Bulldozer* as "a major, though not overwhelmingly skillful, heresy." Importantly, Smith seized on Anderson's attention to pacing and lag, seeing in this conceptual focus the book's essential weakness: its author seemed "concerned only with the length of time involved" in building projects, without much to say about their actual value.[20] In the face of the bulldozer, a newly assertive conservatism had turned to the city. Wilson's Joint Center worked to put that conservatism somewhere on the spectrum of common sense. It also, however, staged debates that could invite vigorous public critiques of the very body of scholarship on which it had staked its name.

Publishing Anderson and embracing the fallout was, perhaps, a master stroke of publicity. Yet the Joint Center also backed work that made compatible points far less polemically. Bernard Frieden's first monograph, *The Future of Old Neighborhoods* (1964), operated in this vein, and it, too, issued a temporal critique of Urban Renewal, whose fixation on newness was too often left unexamined. It was "premature," Frieden contended, to clear even the "grayest" of urban areas. Sensible policy would "renovate and preserve" through "selective clearance and gradual renewal." When possible, rebuilding "should be postponed"—not discounted out of hand, but always deferred until truly necessary. For Frieden, the *when* of urban policy, not the where, was the central question. His most basic plea was for scholars and officials *"to govern the timing* of new development."[21] If one tendency united the center's disparate work on Renewal, it was this. Having worked to present the city as a dynamic entity—one liable to develop, grow, and change—they then dwelled in conceptually novel ways on the very temporality of that change and fretted over how to time their practical interventions.

Anderson's broadside was data-rich, but it was patently not the work of someone given to walking neighborhood streets or describing the built environment in any but the coarsest terms; indeed, the tone makes it difficult to imagine the author interviewing any member of a planning agency and managing to elicit much information. Frieden's book honored the specifics of his three case cities, but he undertook no sustained ethnographic work. It fell to Langley C. Keyes Jr. to produce the center's only long-form inquiry into what the renewers were doing to Boston. He wrote an MIT dissertation in planning between 1962 and 1965, concurrent with Anderson, and published it in the series four eventful years later as *The Rehabilitation Planning Game: A Study in the Diversity of Neighborhood* (1969). Keyes stressed nothing if not the complexity of Renewal's execution. He skillfully demonstrated extreme "variations in process and product" among three non-downtown parts of Boston then in the bulldozer's path: the dense, diverse South End, to which younger urbanites-by-choice had begun to flock after years of its stigmatization as a vice-ridden half-world; durably Irish Charlestown, across the river, the original referent for the slang term *townie*; and Washington Park, an uphill, middle-income segment of the city's majority-Black Roxbury section. (Washington Park, Keyes noted, was a name that residents started claiming only as a result of Ed Logue's work in the area.) Although Boston seemed like an "ideal case study," indeed a "laboratory," of Urban Renewal, Keyes insisted there was no single narrative to write; there were only contingent, contentious negotiations between planners and different fractions of their public. Lizabeth Cohen has likened Keyes to Boston's own Robert Dahl, and the comparison is apt: the hard work of planning, he argued, involved first finding project-specific partners in the community and then mobilizing just enough support, from enough little polities, to nudge redevelopment along. Who governs? Who plans? Success was by no means assured: games, of course, have both winners and losers.[22]

Keyes's book was a Joint Center production through and through. Indeed, it allows us to grasp the extent to which the center, by the middle 1960s, had self-canonized—done the conceptual heavy lifting early on, published it, and packaged it for trainees, who could then proceed apace more swiftly with their dissertations. Keyes imported the concept of the "ecology of games" from Norton Long, signed on to the definition of "politics" developed by Meyerson and

Banfield in 1950s Chicago, and assumed, with Banfield, that plans exist only insofar as they emerge from competing currents of "influence." He cited *Beyond the Melting Pot* for insight into the Irish American mind (and at one point likened Charlestown's denizens to "a tribe in the highlands of New Guinea or a clan of Kentucky mountain folk still speaking pure seventeenth-century English," sentiments that may have served him ill, whether as an observer of "the Town" or as an employee of United South End Settlements and sometime participant in the political clashes he was studying). Class loomed large in Keyes's analysis. Indeed, his ability to think its intersections with and reinforcement by race allowed for a far less monolithic account of Roxbury's internal inequalities—which spatialized neatly, poorest to richest, as Lower, Middle, and Upper Roxbury—than most white observers were accustomed to reading. Keyes noted without scorn that the "game" of planning tended to favor middle-class interests, and he took at face value Wilson's assertion that middle-class people possess a worldview essentially more comprehensive and public-regarding than that of the poor. The in-house canon, however, was not beyond critique: in his conclusion, Keyes argued for the insufficiency of class analysis, whether pluralist or (one was left to surmise) Marxist, to explain the give-and-take of planning's power politics.[23]

It was by dialing up Wilson's own issue- or object-centric approach to political mobilization that Keyes clinched his critique. *Renewal, redevelopment, rehabilitation*—used evasively, these could invoke abstract, seemingly universal processes that merely touched down in different places. Renewal, though, truly consisted of something different in each of Keyes's cases. In Charlestown, the major battle between locals and BRA officials centered on a physical site, the elevated train station that would result from a proposed extension of Boston's Green Line. (Little demolition of housing stock, however, would accompany it.) In the South End, long a haven for unattached drinkers and drifters, the main conflict concerned the issuance of liquor licenses—a social question, Keyes wrote, not a physical one. (Some demolition was planned.) In Washington Park, conflicts over the proper role and tone of Black political mobilization were primary, and in Keyes's estimation, because considerable tracts of land were going to be razed, its case had coequal physical and social dimensions.[24]

What Keyes had assembled was, by other means, a cybernetic critique of comprehensive planning compatible with Lisa Peattie's work on the *barrio*. There was no single telos that the planning process innately had to fill out, and within any single redevelopment zone, there were many possible ways of conjuring its future. Actors strategized, but every strategy ended up getting "bent, molded, and realigned." Perhaps in retrospect one could summarize the arc as having followed a "sequence," but in reality, the steps occurred "one . . . at a time."[25] Each action met with a reaction. Urban Renewal, Logue was rapidly learning, could not promise total salvation. It was instead, as Ford's Richard Magat would write, "the social application of the art of jujitsu." Progress could always loop back on itself, and it arrived only in "small amounts."[26] The Joint Center was coming to this understanding of planning's complexity in Boston and Ciudad Guayana simultaneously.

What to do with that complexity, though—what lessons to draw, which futures to pursue or foreclose—was another question entirely. Anderson's style of critique, not Keyes's, won the day. It harmonized with political currents ascendant at the center under Wilson and then Moynihan: Anderson's stripped-down catchphrases, performative expressions of disbelief, and calls for repeal simply proved more legible, or marketable, in the public sphere of the later 1960s and, especially, the 1970s. Even a measured study such as Keyes's could give empirical ballast to those on the right who would invoke complexity in order to disavow the possibility of ever identifying larger-scale solutions. If Keyes could not generalize even from his modest N = 3, except to say, in effect, that things were complicated, what hope could there be for regional or national, much less transnational, attempts to solve urban problems?

Immediacy: The Enigma of the Long Term

This new skepticism echoed shifts underway beyond Cambridge. A wide range of scholars, commentators, and political operatives began to raise pointed objections to planning—not only to top-down, comprehensive, or master planning, but to planning as such. Joint Center personnel engaged theoretical turns, in several disciplines, that resisted the ruse of the "rational" planner and embraced a different vision, most influentially sketched by the Yale political scientist Charles Lindblom, of less-than-omniscient actors perpetually "muddling through" problems piecemeal.[27] This framework appealed especially to those seeking to explain planning projects that had stalled or collapsed. In the thick of Ciudad Guayana's construction, Lisa Peattie circulated a memo to her colleagues that digested Lindblom's work with Albert O. Hirschman and urged them to think in terms of "disjointed incrementalism." This approach would yield recommendations but, crucially, "not a plan."[28]

Peattie's diction merits scrutiny. Plan or no plan—in important ways, the debate over Urban Renewal returned political discourse to the stark, foundational framings last dominant during the New Deal. But it could have been otherwise. Nothing about the many and justified critiques of bad 1950s planning led inevitably to a rejection of planning per se. (Nothing about a turn against city planning, for that matter, necessitated disenchantment with other fields exercising foresight to regulate social or economic affairs.)[29] And the critiques themselves were politically underdetermined. Although some partisans claimed otherwise, to be anti-plan is in no sense inherently a left- or a right-wing stance. Opposition to Urban Renewal proved even more varied than the program itself, and its intellectual fault lines could be remarkably hard to map.

One variety of critique took shape in confrontation with specific Renewal projects and developers, who profited handsomely but seemed never to get around to replacing the housing that "the bulldozer" had razed. During the 1960s, Boston was a hearth for this style of activism, which bore the West End catastrophe in mind but intensified at sites well beyond the city's core. Younger scholars at and adjacent to the Joint Center took part in the resistance, most bitterly at North Harvard Street in the city's westerly Allston neighborhood, where the developer was the eponymous university, and then against a highway that would have riven Lower Roxbury in two. Lisa Peattie had noticeably radicalized after returning from Ciudad Guayana—indeed, the role of La Laja *barrio* in effecting this shift cannot be downplayed—and alongside students from both Harvard and MIT, including Chester Hartman, she formed the advocacy group Urban Planning Aid. (Ed Logue disparaged the "academic amateurs" calling his bluff—Hartman, in particular.)[30] Such groups were oriented clearly to the left, and although an impatient Nathan Glazer would cough that they offered only "anti-planning and anti-architectural services for slumdwellers," their sympathies and antipathies were at least easy to define.[31]

Jane Jacobs, still most Americans' metonym for action against the ravages of Renewal, presents a more complex case. She allied with grassroots movements against displacement in New York and then Toronto, scored well-publicized victories, and often sounded much like a voice of the left. Her core ideas, though, apart from a very American dis-ease with the "curse of bigness," are harder to pin down. As Peter Laurence and many others have shown, Jacobs's "inclusive vision" appealed to seemingly incompatible camps, garnering praise from William F. Buckley in *National Review* (who listed *Death and Life* among the "great conservative books"), pleasing Irving Kristol with her celebration of older buildings and attention to their cycles of decay, and echoing the Hayekian tendency in her celebration of the ground-up, uncoordinated, unpredictable truck and barter of economic life.[32] Her Rockefeller-facilitated encounter with Warren Weaver and complexity science (on display in the last chapter of *Death and Life*), penchant for polysemous talk of "feedback," and late-period engagement with cybernetics (in *The Nature of Economies* [2000]) led Jacobs down a path that confounded settled understandings, either of rational planning's justifications or of how best to stand against them.[33] It also led her to reject the blandishments of social science, and with it the urbanist establishment for which she found the Joint Center an easy stand-in. Jacobs met with Meyerson and Rodwin at the crucial 1958 Rockefeller Urban Design Conference and made her position known. Later, Rodwin was the *New York Times Book Review*'s chosen evaluator of *Death and Life*, and despite finding her work "wittier" than Lewis Mumford's, he deprecated her "blasé misunderstandings of theory" and "amiable preference for evidence congenial to her thesis."[34] Jacobs's dissent was grounded in a divergent understanding of the temporality of urban development. Future cities, she held, were amenable to repair or adjustment, but, "like the clock business" in which she had briefly worked, they remained essentially unfinishable.[35]

As the decade wore on, arguments over how and whether to plan also reoriented the design professions and affected their articulation with urban governance. To take one example, in the San Francisco Bay Area, the landscape architect Lawrence Halprin pivoted from a Renewal-friendly language of physical *planning* to one that privileged indeterminate pedestrian *choreography* (in ways clearly informed by his wife, the countercultural dancer Anna Halprin). Fixated on movement and often sounding quite like Lynch and Appleyard—design for the "non-fixed, ever-changing viewpoint" or do not design at all—Halprin configured built environments to maximize "flexibility" of locomotion and social interaction.[36] As ever, this desideratum cut both ways, as plausibly a slogan of the left or right, united only by their preference for the small and "human-scale."

New York's first post-Jacobs general plan, issued in 1969, absorbed many of Halprin's lessons. Its authors took pains to assure the public that they understood the "futility of creating a master plan": "Our plans," by contrast, "are going to be influenced by forces that the City can neither forecast nor control."[37] The mayor who oversaw its rollout, John V. Lindsay, committed to a cybernetic-lite mantra of citizen "participation" and professed a wariness of distanced expertise. "We can never go back to the system of top-down direction," he wrote, but, like Lindsay himself—a design-conscious, liberal Republican of notably patrician pedigree—*not top-down* could encompass a considerable spectrum of political positions.[38] Cybernetic assumptions animated these politics of design. One of Lindsay's staffers, E. S. Savas, urged that physical decentralization be understood as a matter of "minor-loop control" and civil unrest a generator of "information-bearing signals" to be acknowledged and redirected. (Savas appeared in the same volume as Robert C. Wood's "Science: The Good Urban Witch.")[39] Plan or no plan?

Even studiously nonpartisan voices began talking and thinking differently in the wake of Renewal's abasement. Consider the Regional Plan Association's efforts at public outreach in the years just after the New York Metropolitan Region Study, whose last volume, by Wood, appeared the same year as Jacobs's bestseller. Veering as far from top-down schemes as they could muster, the usually establishmentarian RPA began convening focus groups, consulting with community organizations, and, most memorably, in 1963 and 1973, producing two "mass media town meeting series": television programs addressing "gut issues" that small groups of citizens, gathered in private homes by a few thousand neighborhood captains spotted across the metropolitan area, would watch, discuss, and react to via a standardized questionnaire. The RPA would record the responses, run analysis, and use their findings to inform subsequent plans. *Public Participation in Regional Planning* (1969), a report connected to the Second Regional Plan, resulted from the first series; *Listening to the Metropolis* (1974) came of the second and was issued as part of *CHOICES for '76*, a Bicentennial-adjacent campaign that repeatedly invoked the spirit of the mythologized New England town meeting.[40] Inputs, outputs, users, signals, feedback: cybernetics or something like it, wrote Horst Rittel and Melvin Webber in 1973, was "by now the modern-classical model of planning," forever "searching . . . identifying . . . forecasting . . . inventing . . . stimulating . . . evaluating . . . monitoring . . . [and] feeding back." "Now sensitized to the waves of repercussions" from many different agents in the force field of political influence, planning had absorbed the backlash against Urban Renewal and found a new language in which to present alternatives.[41] The future was uncertain after all.

The Joint Center bore witness to these shifts and firmed up the infrastructure that enabled intellectuals to interpret their significance. Figures attached to the center touched down, intervened, or otherwise engaged work from all across the spectrum of critique: the leftist organizing of Peattie or Hartman, the urban naturalism of Jacobs, the libertarian and traditionalist celebrants it attracted, the hippie (post-)Modernism of the Halprins, the friendly technocracy of Lindsay, and the non-polemical advocacy of the reimagined RPA.[42] The center hosted debates by which these divergent tendencies could mutually infect, its publication program juxtaposed the various flavors of anti-planning sentiment, and its constituency learned to consume, even seek out, a plurality of arguments both for and against planning. Its role in all this was protean, here explicit, there consigned to the wings—which made frontal critiques of the Joint Center as an institution quite difficult to set on firm ground.

One of the more colorful documents of the resistance was Robert Goodman's *After the Planners* (1971), a book fed on the author's years as a participant in development battles in and around Boston. Goodman taught in MIT's architecture department (and knew Peattie and Hartman from the North

Harvard episode) while keeping his distance from the center as a corporate entity. *After the Planners* is a hilariously unsubtle book, expressly anti-expert, broadly anarchistic, and given to polemics even more scattershot and dated than those of Herbert Marcuse, his chosen reference when indicting social science as so much technocracy. Goodman exalts a populist, agentic concept of "choice," and a sizable portion of his text comprises examples of "people housing themselves." Informal housing in the Peruvian capital city, Lima, presents one favorite example; other Latin American squatters (but notably none in Venezuela) win his praise; he peers in on Kano, Nigeria; he gives an excruciating explanation of the ad hoc dwelling tactics of Mbuti "pygmies" in the Congo; and he looks back to the towns of medieval Europe for lessons in "antiformalism." These things Goodman was for. What, precisely, was he against? Among the chief villains in *After the Planners* was the Joint Center. John Burchard, of all people, appears as an apologist for Urban Renewal and is interested in zoning only if it will "protect the big fellow." Moynihan's thoughts on federal architecture in Washington class him with Hitler, whom Goodman quotes at length. Unspecified scholars at the center, along with those at Penn's long-standing IUS, are "planning mandarins," "urban doctors," and "science mongers" whose performances of expertise only oppress the unsuspecting. Goodman singles out the Joint Center by name, alleging not only that Ford had misallocated its funds, but that urban research itself (his book excepted) was a distraction from genuine change.[43]

The point is not that Goodman's claims were inherently off base—although his noble-savage rhetoric beyond US borders embarrasses and his invocations of choice as the highest value are as compelling a demonstration as any of how anarchism and a finally rightist libertarianism, both hostile on principle to planning, can converge. Rather, *After the Planners* points up a curious paradox at the Joint Center. By 1970, it could register as both the institutional paragon of planning understood as something administered by aloof, bloodless experts, and one of the central engines giving publicity and intellectual legitimacy to a variety of foundational critiques of planning—rough, thoughtless Urban Renewal planning, yes, but with it, virtually any other formation of temporal reason attempting to grasp and direct the future before it comes to pass. The Joint Center thrived on these tensions. It organized a space for them to play out (and demarcated that space: Goodman's ill temper seemed to preclude his invitation, while Martin Anderson's did not). Eventually, the center's politics, once enamored of complexity for its own sake, tilted sharply to the right, and in its second decade, Church Street became one of the major incubators giving rise to conservative critiques of planning's very feasibility. More than any comparable institution, it both contributed to a broader conservative chastening of urban studies and took unique, decisive measures to urbanize American conservatism itself.

Emblematic of the new skepticism was Stephan Thernstrom's monograph on the anti-poverty group Action for Boston Community Development, or ABCD, a key 1960s outlet for the venerable South End–Roxbury activist Melnea Cass. *Poverty, Planning, and Politics in the New Boston* (1969) saw Thernstrom, the historian, turn his attention to the very recent past in what was intended to be one of nine separate studies of projects inaugurated under Kennedy's Committee on Juvenile Delinquency and Youth Crime. Constituted in 1961, ABCD spent four years engaged in "human renewal"—social rather than physical reconstruction—and helped strategize for the expertise-driven "New Boston" promised by Mayor Collins. Here, the Joint Center was among the actors in Thernstrom's narrative. The Church Street space had hosted Boston's "first formal meeting" on community development so named. Meyerson had advised both Logue and Collins on alternatives to raze-and-replace, and he coached ABCD on how to secure grants from Ford and the federal government—processes whose blow-by-blow consumed the first ninety pages of Thernstrom's book and must have repelled a majority of readers.[44]

What the group substantively did, however, was secondary for Thernstrom, who used the case of ABCD to mount a far more general critique of urban research, state intervention, and their mutual dependence. Everywhere he looked, Thernstrom saw contradictions and half-truths. Ford's officers "felt the need to do something," but in practice, ABCD spiraled into an infinite regress of preparatory research, "theoretical rationales" for action, and faux self-evaluation: "research now, freedom later." This was a rationalist "paint job and picture window, not the foundation" of a genuinely political program concerned with "who gets what when and how." "Action-research"—"emphasis on the hyphen"—had become a catchphrase during the 1960s, but its two components, Thernstrom argued, were clearly at odds. His was an epistemological critique written from within the very research complex that the Joint Center had codified. But Thernstrom went further. Data were fine, he wrote; tracing out trend lines was not in itself suspect. But, contra essentially the entire first generation of Joint Center scholarship, the city "is not a laboratory; social planning is not a science." "Tested knowledge" applicable to the present and future city is inherently scarce, and in its absence, social spending would be "about as sensible as investing in Czarist bonds . . . [or] giving the same ten drugs to all the patients in an experimental group." When policy makers accept fables as expertise and let them dictate goals, Thernstrom warned, the real problems begin. Indeed, there was a possibility—a "gloomy possibility," he admitted—"that feasible new ideas on what *can* be done . . . are exceedingly difficult to find, and that social-planning experts *are not capable* of providing them."[45] If non-knowledge was the starting point, inaction was the only defensible course.

Also reassessing at this time was William Alonso. Although ABCD and other programs, fearing allegations of crypto-Renewal, had avoided undertaking either demolition or construction, physical planning lived on in the federal New Towns program that materialized most massively at Irvine, Columbia, and The Woodlands, and in the embattled New Towns In-Town initiative. (In a short 1972 book published with the Urban Institute, Martha Derthick would declare the latter an outright failure and an indictment of the intergovernmental complexity of American federalism.)[46] Having soured on Ciudad Guayana in real time, Alonso lashed out, in "The Mirage of New Towns" (1970), against the penchant for "simpler, future Camelots" whose plannedness, so easy to exhibit in a single aerial photo or scale model, was supposed to be its own justification. No, wrote Alonso, sounding slightly cybernetic: planning is only an input. The task was to assess its outputs, its performance, by more meaningful criteria. He critiqued the Tapiola project executed after the war outside Helsinki, as well as the British New Towns that had been the young Rodwin's quarry. Their design had attempted "labor market closure" but failed: residents still routinely commuted beyond town boundaries, and rhetoric exalting "balance" in physical form and social composition had become code for exclusion. Alonso savaged late-1960s developments in the United States, too, crabbily calling Soul City (Floyd McKissick's novel Black Power–informed settlement in North Carolina) and the Minnesota Experimental City (the creation of scientists strongly influenced by Fuller's geodesics) "political absurdity . . . exotic residential opportunities for various minorities." Alonso knew that such towns, built from scratch in open country, were supposed to serve as tests or demonstrations of more general planning techniques, applicable to the reconstruction of existing cities, and he did not condemn this notion out of hand. He found their gains, however, "vitiated by the hyperbole and puffery of most New Town advocacy": the "sirens of utopia" emitted from HUD, the unacknowledged sclerosis of state-led planning schemes, and the total lack of clarity as to how an extraterritorial "model," hatched in Venezuela or anywhere else, was supposed to withstand travel and translation onto American soil.[47] Alonso sympathized with planners' impulse to act: "things must be said." But his dissent, like Thernstrom's, was finally epistemological: planning's essential uncertainty had to come first, and despite efforts by the "soft meta-disciplinary people" of urban studies to derive absolutes from their ersatz laboratories, the larger truths of urbanization would always prove unknowable.[48]

These anti-planning critiques swept up, and were inflamed by, a great number of Joint Center–affiliated scholars, increasingly labeled neoconservative, whose inclinations prior to Johnson's Great Society moment had been liberal if never nakedly left-wing. The term *neoconservatism* was not ubiquitous until the 1970s, but it circulated in the 1960s, often in epithet. The *neo-* prefix usually indicates little more than an update or qualified revival of an existing *-ism*. Neoconservatives, however, often used it to call attention to the fact that they themselves had changed their minds—that their conservatism was a late-breaking phenomenon, articulated amid perceptions of recent social decline brought on by specific policies and their "unintended consequences."[49] (Moynihan resisted the label, as did many others so identified, and at least one author has argued that the group is better classified as "right-wing liberals.")[50] Less a movement than a mentality, neoconservatism kept social science—and its critique of more activist tones and uses for social science—at its very core.[51] The essayist Irving Kristol, who most embraced the label and relished musing on his life as a shape-shifting "neo," in 1978 called the dispensation "basically a disillusionment with, and disengagement from, the strategy of environmental reform."[52] Phrasing the definition in this way drew in many domains other than planning and urbanism, quite obviously—he meant *environment* in the sense of social structures and contexts, not of physical milieu—but debates over the spacing and timing of urban life were far more central to the broader neoconservative turn than most historiography has emphasized. That turn, palpable in germ at James Q. Wilson's Joint Center, became conspicuous in the Moynihan period. Planning was in question. The mood had changed.

Meanwhile, the center's ties to Washington became closer and more central to its reason for being; its politics inevitably reflected campus-specific pressures but ramified beyond Cambridge. Indeed, when Moynihan left the center in 1969, it was because Richard Nixon, his hand forced by a half-decade of unrest and racialized backlash, had chosen him to head the new Council for Urban Affairs; his appointment as HUD secretary had been blocked by more steadfast Democrats for whom the infamy of the Moynihan Report could never be undone. Moynihan effectively switched places with his successor: Robert C. Wood was returning to academia from service in the Johnson administration, and he arrived at a moment when the Joint Center's internal political rifts were yawning wider than ever (and, some thought, compromising the group's public profile). From 1969, the drift to the right continued, despite the best efforts of Wood and a six-person Joint Center delegation who traveled to Washington in 1970 to inform Moynihan, in person, that they would no longer supply him with expert advice. Wood's year as director passed quickly (and at MIT, leftist demonstrators assailed him for having had any role, even a domestic one, in

Johnson's administration while the war in Vietnam ramped up). In 1970, eleven years of Ford Foundation funding came to an end, an MIT biophysicist and associate provost named Walter Rosenblith stepped in as acting director, and Wood departed to serve as president of the University of Massachusetts system.[53] The center, unmoored, was ripe for reorientation.

The center's first post-Ford leader was none other than Bernard Frieden, who in 1971 took over for Rosenblith and embarked, with the MIT-trained planner Marshall Kaplan, on what they pitched as the definitive analysis of "the major Great Society program addressed to the problems of urban slums": Model Cities. Inaugurated in 1966, Model Cities presented the latest and most complete federal alternative to the tarnished legacy of Urban Renewal: averse to physical planning pursued for its own sake, allergic (despite the confusing name) to didactic showpiece neighborhoods designed for visual consumption, committed to devolving power to community organizations, and interested in coordinating anti-poverty action across unequal administrative scales. It was precisely the sort of federal program that the Joint Center was now in the habit of talking back to, and, indeed, Frieden and Kaplan asserted in 1971 that "today there is not a single model of [its] successful operation."[54]

The center had been gearing up for such a study. Thernstrom invoked Model Cities in the preface to his ABCD book.[55] In *The Rehabilitation Planning Game*, Langley Keyes, too, had been preoccupied with the program, which he saw as Renewal's probable successor and thus the proper place to apply his findings. Although he did not indulge Thernstrom's pessimism, Keyes scored Model Cities for downplaying the variation among project areas and the many sources of social (often as not, racial) conflict they harbored.[56] Numerous Joint Center veterans contributed to the administration or evaluation of Model Cities: Wood, via the Task Force on Urban Problems, which first recommended the program in 1965; Moynihan, from his perch in Nixon's Washington, who chaired a 1969 review (one of six that year) and let the program live another day; Edward Banfield, who headed his own task force and dissented from its recommendation that the program persist; Frieden himself, who sat on Wood's 1965 task force; and Kaplan, an employee of the early HUD whose private consultancy had also conducted several evaluations on contract to the agency.[57] Upwards of 150 cities, large and small, took part. Renewal, by that name, was waning, but Model Cities could not be ignored.

The Politics of Neglect (1975) was the resulting book, a study of "the nature and limits of federal performance" and thus entirely consonant with the center's new brand of skepticism. The authors cited Lindblom to oppose "central coordination" of much soever. They praised Raymond Vernon's now-classic NYMRS books as early examples of future-oriented but planning-shy scholarship. They noted the many "specific disappointments with urban renewal" and now had an extensive in-house library on which to bolster their case: Anderson above all, Frieden's first book, Wilson, Abrams, and many more. Model Cities, they hoped, was the "last of the grand designs." Its rollout was complex, and the authors did not sacrifice detail in relating it, but in the end, Model Cities had one "single lesson" to impart: "avoid grand schemes." The authors' bottom-line prescription recalled Anderson's: "back to the drawing board." (As replacements, they favored revenue sharing and, for its flexibility, the Community Development Block Grant program.) Again, the essence of the critique turned on epistemology. It was not that the federal scale of intervention needed to be disestablished, but that the program's stewards would never know enough to know whether they were effecting legitimate change. As social science, Frieden and Kaplan wrote, Model Cities was "at best methodologically risky and at worst a technically spurious and expensive endeavor." They deplored its "still-marginal" techniques of self-evaluation. Neighborhoods were still not laboratories, there were still no control groups, and the thought leaders of Model Cities had never managed to resolve a core ambiguity: whether the program existed to serve people directly, or whether the fundamental goal was to test out approaches that might aid poverty amelioration nationwide.[58] Action on one hand, research on the other—the early Joint Center had argued that these belonged together. Now, its director insisted they break apart.

This new counsel of despair took various forms. In some hands, it was an essentially synchronic critique, predicated on historical cases but abstracting to absolutes that would transcend time or circumstance. We do not know the city; we cannot ever claim certainty; we must not act as we have. In different ways, the apostasies of Thernstrom, Alonso, and Frieden and Kaplan all followed this script. Other renditions, however, asserted planning's impossibility in an explicitly diachronic fashion, with questions of sequence, process, and tense at very their core. These are the critiques that have most endured, stoking skepticism among ensuing generations about planning's worth as a basic state capacity. The reactive wing of the Joint Center, from James Q. Wilson's ascent in 1963, advanced a neoconservative politics of time.

Here, too, the center drew strength from other voices lining up against Great Society urbanism. One crucial theorist in this regard was the reliably colorful political scientist Aaron Wildavsky, from 1963 a fixture in Berkeley's department and a curious bridge between morally oriented neoconservative thought and a purer market-oriented libertarianism. (Meyerson, Glazer, and others to grace that campus would surely have crossed his path, but there is no evidence that Wildavsky entered into any formal partnerships with the Joint Center.) In 1973, he published a book with a younger political scientist, Jeffrey Pressman—who joined MIT's faculty that year and collaborated with some center affiliates before his suicide in 1977—that drew on recent experiences in Oakland, California, to unsettle any assumption that planning could bridge the city's present and future tenses. The proximate cause was that Oakland had secured the first grant from the new federal Economic Development Administration and, from 1966, applied it to a suite of building projects: modernize the city's airport and shipping port, break ground on a thirty-acre industrial park near the docks, and build an access road to the new Oakland Coliseum. (The authors labeled these projects "internal foreign aid," and the transnational frame asserts itself, quietly, on the edges of the Oakland case. The port improvements centered specifically on the Marine Terminal, which was then becoming the major Pacific depot for arms shipments to Vietnam in standardized steel containers, a still-unproven technology whose efficiency that particular war effort helped demonstrate.) How had the programs fared? Part of the multivolume Oakland Project run out of Berkeley with support from HUD, the Urban Institute, NASA (due to the airport), and Berkeley's Joint Center–like Institute of Urban and Regional Development, *Implementation* (1973) was a study of precisely that: not the intentions behind policies and not their results (however defined), but the myriad clashes, improvisations, redirections, and costs accrued along the path from premise X to outcome Y. (The book's full subtitle, unfurled on a frontispiece-like title page in eighteenth-century typefaces, is *How Great Expectations in Washington Are Dashed in Oakland; or, Why It's Amazing That Federal Programs Work at All, This Being a Saga of the Economic Development Administration as Told by Two Sympathetic Observers Who Seek to Build Morals on a Foundation of Ruined Hopes.*)[59]

The term *policy*, Pressman and Wildavsky theorized, always encodes a hypothesis about cause and effect, and talk of causation necessarily implies the passage of time. In Oakland and other cities, however, planners seemed to have a cognitive preference for "simple sequences of events" rather than "complex chains of reciprocal interaction," and this faulty temporality kept them from ever truly learning from their environments or, cybernetically, adapting their strategies on the fly. (Social scientists, Pressman and Wildavsky argued, had been of little help, with one exception: Martha Derthick's politically congenial *New Towns In-Town*.) As a result, by cultivating an "atmosphere of crisis," interventionists had pushed "short-term expedients" into law far too fast to claim victory in either action or research. *Implementation* climaxed with what would become a classically neoconservative line of reasoning: patience is in fact a virtue, action must be deferred for as long as possible, and such restraint has its basis in the very nature of politics. The great "length and unpredictability of necessary decision sequences," the authors averred, could never be wished away.[60]

Wildavsky persisted. "If Planning Is Everything, Maybe It's Nothing," read the title of his 1973 article in the young journal *Policy Sciences*, which beneath a thick layer of sarcasm gave the most complete exposition of the anti-planning right's dissident epistemology of time. "The first requisite of rational planning is causal knowledge," Wildavsky posited. "Planning is, therefore, a form of social causation." It is also, and inseparably, "the attempt to control the consequences of our actions . . . to control the future by current acts." The only viable criterion, then, by which to support or oppose "the planners" is their degree of control: their skill in conjoining future with present, not the seeming purity of their founding ideals. Wildavsky was forthright about his assumptions: not just that planning had not worked, but that it could not work. In a tone alternately rollicking and stern, he contended that the progressive planner's modish attention to process was in fact the result of past failures at prediction: "Since the end is never in sight, he sanctifies the journey."[61] It was 1966 when James Q. Wilson, in one of his last acts as Joint Center director, posited *The Metropolitan Enigma* and, under that title, summoned a dozen sundry collaborators to probe "the urban crisis" and its limits of scrutability (figure 5.3).[62] To plan, he and Wildavsky agreed, is to make a knowledge claim. But planners do not know, and they cannot know, the future. In the 1970s, with a degree of unity that had been elusive during its first decade, the Joint Center came to endorse this pessimistic diagnosis on the temporality of urban change. The self-critique was complete.

Separate from his work with Frieden, Marshall Kaplan glossed one further concept in ways that would animate the conservative Joint Center and profoundly shape its public interventions. Kaplan had trained in planning at MIT but declined to pursue the PhD. By the 1970s, after a stint at HUD, he was based in San Francisco, helming the firm Marshall Kaplan, Gans, and Kahn and reacting to Washington from a few thousand miles off, his discontent piqued by proxies such as Oakland. In a series of essays brought out as *Urban Planning in the 1960s: A Design for Irrelevancy* (1973), Kaplan subjected issues of time horizon to a needling more direct and derisive than would surface in his monograph with Frieden.[63] The theme had come up before: Joint Center work produced by Richard Bolan for the MAPC, for instance, included rich applied discussions of the long, short, and middle range. Kaplan seized on the concept of the *long range* with a single-mindedness and sometimes a malice that fairly seeps from his pages. For one thing, he argued, planners leapt hastily to long-range thinking because acceptance of a lengthened timescale seemed also to validate a greater spatial scope for their power. "Only in the distant future," he wrote in one 1964 essay, "can the level of comprehensiveness posited [even] be defined."[64] Long-range thinking also, he charged, had an elective affinity

FIGURE 5.3. Modernist built environments erected atop the ruins became, for many on the political right, their own testimony to the insolubility of the urban crisis. This image, counterposing part of Boston's new Government Center with a colonial-era statue, appeared on the cover of James Q. Wilson, ed., *The Metropolitan Enigma* (1966). Courtesy of Harvard University Press.

with bigger, more interdisciplinary social science, a style of research he deemed both "unproven" and, in the long 1960s anyhow, "uncritically elevated" to glory.[65] He, too, enrolled Lindblom to the cause, ostensibly as proof that long-range planning "can be described" but "cannot be practiced": it "assumes intellectual capacities and sources of information" that do not exist.[66] By 1970, cut loose from HUD, Kaplan's writings increased precipitously in pitch. He was openly fuming. Agencies had recourse to an easy solution for all those urging "long-range synoptic . . . linked . . . planning": "simply fire" them.[67]

The contention was not that the future, as an object of knowledge, was itself irrelevant, or that all forms of foresight were doomed to unreason. Rather, in ways surely informed by the Joint Center's composite understanding of urban tense—of past, present, and future forever linked and cross-referenced—the Kaplan of 1970 demanded that planners "measur[e] the restrictions a current decision may place on one's freedom to choose among alternatives at a later date. This is the approach that should underlie all public policy."[68] Later social scientists would adopt the term *path-dependence* to conceptualize the present's sway over the future. Kaplan went one step further. In his most prescriptive passages, he urged a focus on the *immediate*. This, repeated ad nauseam, became Kaplan's keyword. Planners could legitimately bear the future in mind, but their practice had to "concentrate on the here and now" and supply "immediate answers for [even] the ephemeral endeavor."[69] Here and now: *immediate* signified in both spatial and temporal dimensions. It called for smaller and more localized interventions, at the scale of neighborhoods and households rather than cities, regions, or nations. It called for much shorter timescales and nearer futures than those with which 1960s planners had gotten comfortable. It also privileged a theory of knowledge that was inductive, never deductive, in character.[70] With this aggressive turn to the present, Kaplan rejected any widely held understanding of planning's unique claim on the future.

In this, he had company. In a 1968 essay critical of the interdisciplinary tendency, William Alonso foregrounded what he called *time-sense*: "incremental" planning was the way forward, and, thankfully, "the time-sense of the social sciences is shorter than the architects'." (For an economist such as him, five years counted as the long run.)[71] Alonso's politics had turned quite conservative. Langley Keyes's had not. Yet he, too, could be seen championing "the here and now at the project level. The neighborhood becomes the city. The time dimension becomes the present."[72] No single political program automatically followed from an enthusiastic present-orientation. No political theory had a monopoly on tense. Indeed, although *The Politics of Neglect* became canon for right-wing critics of social policy, Kaplan himself had roots in advocacy planning. Like James Q. Wilson, he lost patience with rationalistic liberalism that aspired to rise "above politics," but unlike Wilson, he seemed genuine in his appreciation of the "basic pluralism inherent" in urban society, differently and deeply liberal in his care for the "many culturally, economically determined differences in lifestyle" everywhere on display.[73] He came by this epistemology in tandem with a politics resistant to hierarchy: "Complex ghetto problems require an inductive approach . . . reasoned intuition and," crucially, "the veto power of our clients."[74] His immediatism took shape not a priori but out of practical encounters. Moreover, and far more directly than his contemporaries, Kaplan differentiated things along lines of class: "To the disadvantaged," after all, "the immediate present . . . is most relevant." To prioritize the long range, Kaplan argued, echoing Wilson but inverting his judgments, was a middle-class value.[75] Until planners learned to work across tense, staying with the elapsing present for as long as circumstances required, their desired futures would never arrive.

From Status to Contract: The Joint Center Recessional

The post-Ford period saw a profusion of deeply agitated neoconservative scholarship issue from the Joint Center. This heterogeneous body of work echoed or drove conversations on nearly the complete set of topics that ate at the intellectual right, both the seasoned and the recently converted, during the straitened 1970s. "In response to changing social needs," housing—not urbanization in the round—became the center's leading focus and lever of influence in the public arena.[76] Arthur Solomon, an MIT economist, brought out *Housing the Urban Poor: A Critical Analysis of Federal Housing Policy* (1974), which scaled up from the single-program critiques by Anderson, Thernstrom, or Frieden and Kaplan to argue against federal subsidies of any sort.[77] Martha Derthick continued her heterodox oeuvre on American federalism with *Between State and Nation* (1974), addressed to post-TVA forms of regional governance that spanned state lines and could easily comprise well more than 1,400 governments.[78] In 1978, Robert Schafer, a planning professor at Harvard, surveyed mortgage lending in five of New York's metropolitan areas—Albany, Buffalo, New York City (and Long Island), Rochester, and Syracuse—and concluded that while "some" discrimination had a racial dimension, "most" of it was "based on objective factors" such as income and extant property values. (Schafer left unexplored the myriad ways in which both FHA redlining and private actors' valuation practices had taken racial composition into account.)[79] Frieden, relieved of his responsibilities as director, unloaded in *The Environmental Protection Hustle* (1979), cognizant of the reality of racial segregation but caustically critical of those whose appeals to ecology held up the course of suburbanization.[80]

Also with notably conservative overtones, the majority of Joint Center publications now deflected the analytic gaze from even the merest engagement with the design of the urban landscape, a hallmark of the earlier generation. By 1975, when leadership passed from Frieden to Solomon, "demographic trends" and "social policy" had become entrenched as two of the center's three official foci, joined only by "regional and urban economics" as administrators consciously registered a break with the "early phase," which Rodwin and Meyerson had "deliberately kept flexible and exploratory."[81] Sar Levitan, presaging anxieties that would break open in the Reagan era, published *Work and Welfare Go Together* (1972).[82] With *From Welfare State to Welfare Society* (1981), Martin Rein and Lee Rainwater forecast a broader cultural slippage.[83] Mary Jo Bane, of Harvard's Kennedy School, comforted those fearful of moral atomization with *Here to Stay: American Families in the Twentieth Century* (1976). (By 1981, the Joint Center would relabel "demographic trends" as the more biopolitical-sounding "family and population.")[84] In the 1980s, in "extraordinarily influential" work later cited by the architects of welfare reform, Bane and David Ellwood prophesied a long-term slide into "dependency" as the result of existing social policies.[85]

Less polemical work continued in the interstices of the new order. A genial, noncombative administrator, Frieden himself reassessed earlier positions, but he took pains to ensure that the center remained, at root, a forum for debates in urbanism, open in principle to the interested public.[86] Well into the 1970s, the luncheon series hosted talks by a politically varied cast, from Barney Frank and Tip O'Neill, Democrats representing Massachusetts on the national stage; to Kenneth Gibson, Newark's first Black mayor; to Dick Netzer, one conservative refinancer of bankruptcy-era New York; to Ira Lowry, veteran of the post-NYMRS projection studies in Pittsburgh; to old regulars such as William Alonso, still espousing the regional science whose modeling techniques would be the topic of a series of yearly Joint Center seminars beginning in 1973. The center also began a modest amount of experimentation with media other than the written word. Television was one appealing frontier. In 1978, the center ran six programs, and planned several more, to debate Jimmy Carter's urban agenda. Work by Bane and David Marwick went public by way of a special center-convened press conference, following which marketers at *TV Guide* began using their data on family structure to predict demand.[87] The long-standing book series persisted, but it took on far fewer titles per year. Under Frieden and especially Solomon, there was a change in how the directorate understood the role of the series. In the 1960s, its prestige had been a key factor enticing scholars to affiliate with the center; under the 1970s policy, editors were left to ask already-established scholars if they might at some point, perhaps, contribute.

These shifts had many causes, as ever, but the basic parametric issue was that Ford's financial support had come to an end. Its program officers, William Pendleton above all, had sensed a "dormancy" on Church Street by 1970. (As if to mark the occasion, the center hosted a conference that year dwelling on "the role of university-based urban centers.") By 1974, although some in Ford's ranks cheered a "revival" of the center's output, it was too late: citing budget constraints amid the oil crisis and subsequent recession, the foundation was backing away from urban studies, the interdiscipline it had kickstarted but, Pendleton contended, failed ever to define clearly.[88] Federal funding had always supplemented the Ford allotment—NSF, Department of Commerce, Bureau of Public Roads—but it, too, began to drop off as early as 1971. So did support from diverse philanthropies including the Carnegie Corporation, Sloan Foundation, Olivetti Foundation, Municipal Manpower Commission, and National Book Committee.[89] Ford, for its part, shifted its giving priorities in the 1970s from the maintenance of omnibus research units to a focus on discrete research projects. The same, by necessity, could be said of the Joint Center. Only 20 percent of its $500,000 budget, from the Frieden years forward, was stably underwritten by Harvard and MIT; the remainder would have to be of external origin, and it would attach to specific industry-supported acts of research.[90] Faculty would come and go. To coordinate their efforts, a Division of Sponsored Research had formed in the later 1960s, convinced that the near future lay with "soft money" and contract work.[91] It did.

Inevitably, these formal reorganizations affected the work's content and tone. The difference was most apparent in studies of Boston and New England. The refinanced Joint Center still faced its city and hinterland, but far less critically or colorfully than before. In the late 1970s, for instance, the center teamed with scholars from MIT's Sloan School of Management to take stock of the region's deindustrialization. Capital flight had begun in earnest in the 1920s as textile firms decamped to the South, but the abandonment sped up vertiginously in the 1970s. The opportunity was there to critique what geographers were coming to call "uneven development"—the deep-seated, systematic ways in which capital at once builds up some regions and dispossesses the remainder—or at least to impart some interpretive gloss, some thematization, some drama to the process. Instead, reports on New England's paper mills (especially in Holyoke), commercial printers (Haverhill), and chemical plants (Fall River) were descriptive at best and instrumental at worst, and were conducted entirely within a framework that assumed the priorities of management, recommending plant maintenance and product specialization but no more fundamental changes.[92] A 1981–1982 series of four Boston Workshops was more diagnostic still of the center's recent capture. Its main funders were the Private Industry Council and the Greater Boston Chamber of Commerce, its focus was exclusively on economic development, its attendance was not open to the public, and the cache of data it produced became available by sale or subscription to banks, insurers, retailers, and utilities seeking advice on marketing and manpower.[93] This allowed for a kind of foresight. But was it planning?

With the great refinancing, the center adopted a new model of governance. As of 1971, a contraption known as the Policy Advisory Board (PAB), pieced together by the brash labor mediator John T. Dunlop, began to exert signal influence on the direction of research. Dunlop had trained in Kerr-era industrial relations and would later serve as Gerald Ford's Secretary of Labor. The PAB consisted of representatives from twenty private corporations, spanning real estate, banking, and insurance—but none from academia. The group would meet yearly in Washington, not Cambridge—the better to "seek a common ground" among universities, industry, and government.[94] Because the center's director would henceforth report not to the Faculty Committee—Rodwin's old bailiwick—but straight to the PAB and the two university presidents, this marked a decisive shift. Even if the center's constituent faculty chafed at the new instrumentality, and even if their politics swung well left of the average tower-builder or subdivider—and some did—the chain of command circumvented them. The PAB oversaw a turn to policy research very narrowly defined, and to a sharply economistic sense of the methodologies appropriate to the task. It was under its supervision that Joint Center scholars would come out against the formation of public urban development banks, a common proposal at the time, and take the position that the problem, mere "capital shortages caused by market imperfections," was easily rectified by the market mechanism itself. Meanwhile, the Visiting Advisory Committee added numerous figures inclined to advance the view from Wall Street. Maryland's James Rouse exerted a moderating influence. He was in the company of investment banker Felix Rohatyn, architect of New York's post-crash restructuring; prolific downtown developer John Zuccotti; and others experienced in either enacting or profiting from cuts to public budgets.[95] Market fundamentalism had touched down somewhere close to the heart of urban studies.

In part, the rightward drift reflected simple changes in personnel. The reliably centrist Meyerson had long since vacated Cambridge. He occupied a deanship at Berkeley, the presidency of SUNY Buffalo, and then, from 1970 to 1981, the presidency of Penn. (From 1967 to 1977, he served on the Joint Center's visiting committee.)[96] From Buffalo, Meyerson spoke and wrote prolifically, in "The University Community and the Urban Community" (1969) urging an ethos of public service but, as ever, clarifying that there existed a spectrum of approaches—instrumental Clark Kerr on one flank, the high humanism of

Columbia's Jacques Barzun on the other—by which to "help the larger community acquire self-knowledge."[97] The Buffalo sojourn ended less than well, as Meyerson's visions of campus expansion ran afoul of a basically working-class city and a vocal student left. He "gladly" departed for Penn, where he applied his experience with planning and design to the campus itself, reintegrating it spatially and reimagining University City's interface with the rest of West Philadelphia on the model of Chicago's Hyde Park and Kenwood.[98]

Rodwin persisted at MIT, but amid the political provocations of Wilson and then Moynihan, he became more distant from the Joint Center's day-to-day affairs. Although he was still actively thinking Joint Center thoughts, particularly on Ciudad Guayana—his volume weighing the job's successes and failures would not come out until 1969—by 1967, he was dedicating more time to MIT's new Ford-funded Special Program for Urban and Regional Studies (SPURS), launched to attract planners from developing countries for a year at a time, impart the in-house canon via a curriculum separate from either department or center, and then release trainees to apply their Northern knowledge back home. The first SPURS cohort included two Venezuelans with CVG ties. The New Town project's transnational afterlife had begun, and it steered around the ever more inhospitable Joint Center.[99]

Personnel issues and personal rivalry, however, can account for the broader right turn only in part. Neoconservatives in the urbanist academy also regrouped in reaction to specific institutional shifts apparent toward the end of the Sixties. These shakeups were vividly in evidence at Harvard and MIT, and they were driven by political agitation to a considerable degree. At once demonstrating principled sympathy with and obvious apprehension about the unrest conspicuous on Black streets from Watts to Washington, Harlem to Hough, Cairo to Chicago, and Plainfield to Pittsburgh, the Ford Foundation committed another $30 million to twelve universities in the name of addressing "the urban crisis." A litany of new centers, programs, institutes, and chairs emerged. Harvard and MIT both established new professorships "of Urban Studies," whose constituent disciplines seemed to have obsolesced in the name of properly problem-oriented scholarship.[100] In 1966, Harvard's GSD added a Program for Advanced Environmental Studies, within Sert's sphere of influence, to "produc[e] the kind of men who will be needed to lead"; such "men," the announcement lamented, were "critically few."[101] In 1968, MIT opened a Laboratory for Environmental Studies, subsidiary to its Urban Systems Laboratory. The effects overspilled Cambridge, too. Abrams had moved to Columbia, where, as of 1967, he helmed a new Urban Action and Experimentation Program, housed within the Institute of Urban Environment and intended to right the ship of seemingly "ungovernable" New York.[102] The Kerner Commission's report may not have included a section prescribing more ORUs, but that is how elite universities' funders and administrators read it.

Ford and its new cohort of centers stressed action and service, but always in a moderate, somewhat technocratic key. More radical voices calling for redress of racial and economic inequality managed to reconfigure these same institutions by other means. Rodwin had lost his grip on the Joint Center, but he became the key figure in reorganizing MIT's Department of City and Regional Planning (DCRP) into a Department of Urban Studies and Planning (DUSP). The name changed in 1969, and with formal approval the following year—and Rodwin installed as the first department chair—both the interdisciplinary mandate and the increasingly engagé mood of some planning faculty and most planning students took root. "The events of recent years," he wrote to his abiding mentor Charles Abrams, "have expanded the profession's own view of what it means to be a planner."[103] Harvard's departmental lines were not redrawn in this way, but in 1968, the GSD did establish its own Task Force on the Urban Crisis. *Crisis* was a word used by both censorious conservatives fearful of decline and leftists looking to hasten the pace of events. At the GSD, the force's task was dialogic and broadly progressive in impetus: make GSD programming available to the poor and, in turn, expose its own students to the poor—the better to enable truly participatory styles of work.[104] By 1968, there was also a Task Force on Racial Imbalance in Boston Schools, a liaison service clear-eyed about the obstacles to desegregation that the city's busing crisis of 1974 would lay bare.[105] This was the academy that conservatives old and new surveyed, quietly plotting their exit routes.

Under Wilson and Moynihan, leftist energies had surfaced via the odd Joint Center–supported graduate student or community partnership. But the center never fundamentally refashioned itself to echo the traditions of dissent that now index the Sixties for so many Americans. Its leaders found ways to accommodate the communicative or cybernetic impulse, of course, and at decade's end, its Survey Research Program, reminiscent of the RPA's politically ambiguous adventures in televising public opinion, undertook "How the People See Their City: Boston 1969," now cognizant that the experts would never know best unless they at least asked around.[106] More notable is that these deviations took place within the self-same center, which changed its tune but persisted, name and overall mandate intact, as an organized research unit of a university (or two). The center's institutional durability is particularly salient given that interdisciplinary ORUs, precisely at this moment, became a common target for conservatives. The sociologist Robert Nisbet, for instance, charged them with not only a crypto-leftism, supine before the barbarians' demands, but also an excess of intellectual cosmopolitanism that disembedded the most prominent centers from their campuses, degrading departments, canons, and pedagogies.[107]

In the early 1970s, conservatives of all persuasions began to flee universities and build up their own alternative to the ORU: the think tank.[108] That emergent network of policy research—the Urban Institute, the Manhattan Institute, the revivified American Enterprise Institute, the Heritage Foundation, the Claremont Institute, and many others—rose exactly as the discipline and profession of planning downsized. The number of graduate degrees awarded in planning peaked in 1975 and plummeted through the 1980s. Many programs closed shop as would-be planners instead pursued degrees in public policy (which increasingly meant Wildavskyan policy evaluation), education, or public health.[109] "I don't think there's much to go into now," Robert C. Weaver lamented in a 1985 interview. "It's been decimated. . . . People have been convinced largely by the neoconservatives."[110] Frieden, Solomon, and their allies linked up with the right's new intellectual establishment in the perpetual search for external funding, but to claim accredited knowledge on and against planning, they saw fit to maintain the Joint Center, to realign and redeploy expertise rather than cast it asunder.

"Planning had . . . a paradigm," lamented Ernest Alexander in 1984, "but does no longer."[111] In "The Unplanned Paths of Planning Schools" (1986), William Alonso expressed concern that the once-vital center was hollowing out as the profession polarized between a "morose and crabby neoconservatism" and mystico-political "voyages of discovery"—each in its way disdainful of careful stewardship for the city, each terminally skeptical of urban research as a guide to action.[112] Among planners, versions of this sentiment were commonplace by the 1980s. In essence, they were commentaries on the uncertain 1970s, whose fractures had roots in the conjunctions of politics and epistemology that the 1960s, reconsidering the 1950s' ossified faith in authority, had accelerated to the point of collapse. In its formation and serial reformations, the Joint Center tracks these changes as no other single institution of urban knowledge can.

What remained? The Joint Center had come into existence scanning the horizon, fixated on having something, however speculative, to say about the urban future and the conceptual apparatus needed to descry it. Although the climate for prognostication changed, the center never fully relinquished this impulse. In fact, in the 1970s, it became even more identified with the making of forecasts. In 1973, a report called *America's Housing Needs, 1970–1980*, superintended by David Birch and based on unprecedented crunching of the latest census data, attracted widespread attention, having demonstrated, among other things, that one in five American families was inadequately housed.¹¹³ The appreciative response to this enormous labor of diagnosis and prognosis convinced Frieden that narrowing the center's focus to housing would be a viable path. A follow-up report, *The Nation's Housing, 1975–1985*, arrived in 1977.¹¹⁴ These reports, along with work drawn up in partnership with Harvard's Center for Population Studies, wound up in Congressional offices, in the White House, and in the hands of major banks and developers with sway over the geography of investment.¹¹⁵ By 1981, the President's Commission on Housing was contracting with the Joint Center directly. Yet, unlike in the first decade, when the future metropolis loomed as a horizon of imaginative possibility, claims on it were by and large qualitative, and the category's abstractness was part of its appeal, under Frieden and Solomon, the center became an engine of projections: precise, quantitative, atheoretical statements about the future that experience either would or would not bear out. The housing reports marked the clearest turn yet to fully utilitarian knowledge. Moreover, while the first pair were published through standard channels, in the 1980s, the center, now "a recognized provider" of such forecasts, initiated a Housing Futures Program consisting of workshops for invited realty firms and trade associations, who had to pay in order to attend. Among the "subscription benefits" advertised to the private sector was the ability to participate in the research, and even to choose the topics.¹¹⁶ One thing had become clear: projection sells.

These high-profile studies also, however, represented the triumph of the short-term thinking that Marshall Kaplan had long been pleading for in other domains. Neither of the publications that magnetized the center to housing studies dared look more than eight years ahead.¹¹⁷ The future was foreshortened, all but closing in on the present. So, too, was the past: along with other humanistic work, historical studies of urban life essentially vanished from the center's docket over the course of the 1970s, and by 1981, Stephan Thernstrom was the only historian still affiliated.¹¹⁸ The Joint Center's time horizons were being rapidly and radically diminished. At last, by subtraction, urban studies was living in the here and now.

The Future Metropolis (1961) was the product of an optimistic moment. Genuine utopias were off the table, always, but the prevailing tone conveyed hope: study the past and present, carefully infer the probable future, and dwell intently on the possibilities for intervention and improvement. The center's critical first decade was punctuated with generalist collections of this sort, addressed to the urban scene writ large: *The Historian and the City* (1963), *Future*'s companion piece; *The Metropolitan Enigma* (1966), last testament of the Wilson era; even *The Conscience of the City* (1968), edited by the long-departed Meyerson but so dependent on Joint Center mainstays as to pass for a revival.¹¹⁹ The mood darkened year by passing year, confidence waned, horizons shrank, the group splintered politically and downsized, and across the 1970s, no single volume assumed this mantle. In the 1980s, though, the center once again spoke. Via two documents in particular, futurity as such was back on the agenda, with a difference.

One was *Future Boston* (1982), the culmination of the corporate-backed Boston Workshop Series begun under the economist David Kresge, who succeeded Arthur Solomon as director in 1980. (Both men would eventually rejoin the private sector.) In title as well as in structure, the volume bore a passing resemblance to the first generation's explorations in temporality and tense. "Past and Present Boston" was one chapter, "Future Boston" was the next, and the conclusion dwelled on various "mismatches" foreseeable on the basis of the evidence: between workers and available jobs, between quality of life and quantity of municipal spending, and, in essence, between the expected city and the one presently observed. In substance, the volume was matter-of-fact, preoccupied with growth strategy and given to none of the speculative visioning that, married with its signature commitment to empirical social science, had defined the almost-manifesto of 1961.[120]

Even more indicative of the new, dull futurism was *The Prospective City* (1980), edited by Solomon and, while informed by Boston's specific plight, inclined to generalize. The concluding chapter's title, "Shaping the Future Metropolis: The Role of Public Policy," gestured back to 1961, establishing continuity with the center's lineage and, perhaps, jogging institutional memory. In every other respect, though, the latter-day skeptics won out, sourly disavowing the viability of change. Ira Lowry seemed ready to call off the search for alternatives: "Instead of speculating about possible effects of government policy . . . examine the prospects for reviving central cities in light of *existing* conditions and trends."[121] Solomon entertained the possibility of political betterment but saw pitfalls everywhere. American federalism was too "uncoordinated" to do the job. "Government programs at any level are fragmented and inconsistent." The "indirect and inadvertent effects" of all interventions challenge the "planned, direct ones." "Policies have intentional as well as unintentional results, and," he warned, "it is difficult to measure either."[122]

The book's title alone—*prospective*, not *possible*, not *desirable*—broadcast the chastening of hopes. Solomon's executive summary marked a radicalization of the skepticism that the center's foregoing decade had introduced to urban expertise. Solomon exhumed the notion of "unintended consequences," Robert Merton's coinage from the 1930s, and echoed its recent usage by neoconservatives, who made it a bedrock concept for political defeatists. His claim about measurement was the more disabling one, and it encapsulated the late-stage, world-weary Joint Center's contorted politics of time: We do not know the effects of our interventions. We cannot understand even that which we have already and intentionally introduced onto the urban scene. We will never know enough, or formulate that knowledge with enough precision, to steer the course of urban life—to realize new worlds rather than simply project existing ones forward. Time rushes on, but we live and act in the present tense. The future of the metropolis is and will remain an enigma. Reader, lower your expectations.

CHAPTER 6

The Belated City
Forgetting the Future Metropolis

"Try to retrieve the seventies and memories crumble in one's hand," wrote Irving Howe; "nothing keeps its shape."¹ It was only 1982 when Howe published these words, looking backward on the occasion of his autobiography, *A Margin of Hope*. In the years since, motifs of dissolution and disorientation—amid factory closures, oil spikes, and generalized economic crisis—have become stock components of the historiography of the 1970s, that "age of fracture," germinally "postmodern," in which most Americans were merely "stayin' alive," haunted by "the important sound of things falling apart" and inclined to "rip it up and start again."² Disorientation takes many forms, but for a certain kind of historian, its specifically temporal variety has long been definitive, a symptom of what Jenny Andersson calls the era's onrushing "crisis of predictability."³ More than a few, leaning on lyrics from the best-known "dole-queue rock" that arose in Britain during the same era (and was sonically derivative of blues-based forms codified in the United States), will forever index that period's unmooring to John Lydon's chants of "no future," a lament but also a taunt to the growth liberalism for which such downturn had been unimaginable.⁴ The 1970s, in short, now register as a time of loss, and in countless domains other than city and regional planning, what seems to have been lost is any credible sense of a future worth anticipating.

By tracing developments within an institution so signally concerned with the timing and tensing of action, this book should by now have thrown some of these shifts into relief. Yet reorientation toward the short term was a far more pervasive phenomenon than can be evidenced by one citadel of urban research. "Time horizons shrank" in a general sense, Daniel Rodgers has written of the 1970s, and the period's resurgent popularity of "radically timeless" libertarian and rational-choice economic thought should be understood as only one instance of a broader crackup.[5] "The Future Cannot Begin," the German sociologist Niklas Luhmann would write in 1976, noting processes of "defuturization" underway in all corners of society as the "surplus possibilities" of modernity narrowed to one bleak horizon. With neo-Parsonian overtones, Luhmann urged policies of deferral to a future understood as "a kind of storehouse for decisions to be made later"—seeing deferral as structurally necessary for the maintenance of social stability in fissiparous times. (According to Luhmann, it is precisely when "loss of future" sets in that, to compensate, society needs theorists like him to devise more complex concepts of time.)[6]

To denote this emergent, future-poor mood, many scholars have made recourse to the category of *presentism*. François Hartog characterizes the late twentieth century by its prevailing sensation of an "unending now," a disjointed phenomenology of time as parceled into a succession of instants bereft of any broader narrative, logic, or direction. Hartog and others have insisted on the 1990s as the apogee of presentism—the collapse of the Soviet Union having been, if not unforeseeable, then unforeseen by the majority of those in the business of prediction. "For a moment," Rodgers writes of that aftermath, "time itself had seemed almost infinitely thin and pliable."[7] What did this mean—what could it mean—for the planning of cities?

Presentism; or, What We Talk about When We Talk about No Future

Presentism is inherently difficult to periodize: it is a recurring tendency, unrestricted to any single era or conjuncture. In the 1960s, skeptics diagnosed it in the New Left's ridicule of both administered foresight and Santayanan injunctions never to forget the wisdom of history.[8] The critic Simon Reynolds, writing in 2008, saw presentism as the dominant pop-cultural mood of the early twenty-first century, when a "retromania" for only the recent past overtook consumers crippled by "negative birthright": their sense of having missed out when it happened the first time around.[9] Others have dialed the clock back to the nineteenth or even the eighteenth century. Peter Fritzsche, for instance, has detailed the curious anomie of being "stranded in the present" that obtained in the aftermath of the French Revolution. On his telling, the presentism of modernity—a term Baudelaire would not coin until the 1860s—stems not from a loss of interest in the future, but from the perception of a temporal break that calls the past into question as a reliable fund of expectations for that future.[10]

Even if, as this book has presumed, something in temporal experience changed dramatically after World War II, must it be the 1970s that define its scope? Well before *neoconservative* was an accepted term of abuse, Irving Kristol (to take just one example) was already on his rightward path away from socialism. In an essay titled "Old Truths and the New Conservatism," he made a curious aside. The second half of the twentieth century, he found, was proving to be "a strange time, so unlike all the futures that were ever projected for us." Utopias were bunk—that much Kristol had long since decided. His prescription was more unusual, and it was couched in a specific politics of tense: the new era "offers us the invaluable opportunity to . . . be utterly committed to the present."[11] The year was 1958. A streak of presentism, inclined to disavow history and futurity at once, recurred in postwar intellectual life.[12]

The Joint Center's apostles of the short term, then, had abundant company in debasing the future as an object of knowledge, speculation, intervention, or hope. In 1975, Frieden and Kaplan drew down *The Politics of Neglect* by appealing to the "short attention span" they claimed had become dominant among the wider public, rendering Americans distrustful of "any problems that cannot be solved in a few years" but vulnerable to liberal and left "rhetoric of newly discovered crises."[13] Lloyd Rodwin, under a different political sign, closed *Nations and Cities* with a similar, amazingly general observation: "*People today* are increasingly present- and pleasure-oriented."[14] Many intellectuals sought to legitimate their newfound short-termism by invoking a broader, less tutored preference for the defuturing of American life.

Presentism, however, also provoked opposition from urbanists. In the early 1980s, not long after the first round of Reagan's budget cuts went through, a number of despairing planners penned essays intended to return their colleagues' attention, "in this period of self-doubt," to all things futural. Those by Andrew Isserman, Penn-trained and housed at the University of Illinois, were the most widely read. His interventions point up how the specter of futurelessness led some to reestablish the profession's ontological foundations of "planning in the true sense." To take the measure of what had been lost, Isserman looked back to none other than the early Joint Center. He invoked Meyerson's "bridge to the future metropolis" and quipped that "the bridge . . . now is made of pontoons."[15] Yet planning, he insisted, had a "unique claim to the future" as no other field ever would. It was an inherently temporal undertaking, forever tied to its investment in a particular tense—if no future, then no planning.¹⁶ Time, he argued, is the dimension of existence proper to the planner—and, as with space for the field of geography, it is a dimension, not an object or entity. Isserman's title was his plea: "Dare to Plan" (1985). Fiscal retrenchment was the proximate cause of the whole predicament, but he also faulted the excessive present-orientation of the outside disciplines that had colonized postwar planning in the name of technical precision: "We ape social scientists," he wrote, but "we *are not* social scientists."¹⁷

It was perhaps appropriate, then, that the 1970s should also see the arrival of the highly speculative field of "futurology" as its newest intellectual fad. The popular vogue for futurology (or futures studies) seems to have waxed precisely as a thicker sense of actual political obligation to future generations waned: it was a symptom, even a version, of presentism. Futurologists (or futurists) relished being cast as visionaries, constructing elaborate but usually data-light prospectuses on how society—nominally global but in practice Western—would operate in what we now casually label a postindustrial or post-Fordist age.¹⁸

The most gimmicky document, and the most diagnostic of its times, was Alvin Toffler's best-selling *Future Shock* (1970), the work of a former *Fortune* editor who had talked his way into some Russell Sage funding and teaching engagements at Cornell and the New School. Toffler's basic assertion was that while the direction of overall social change was not changing, its pace was, and that the impending chaos wrought by speed called for entirely new governance strategies. *Future Shock* is a portentous text. Toffler argues that the overpowering "force" of societal "acceleration" is inducing a "premature arrival of the future," which now "invades our lives" and spells "the death of permanence." His slogans fly off the page: "the throw-away society," "the new nomads," "the coming ad-hocracy," "information overload" the diagnosis, "anticipatory democracy" the only possible politics in this age of velocity. Like many less freewheeling authors, Toffler agonized over the best grammatical tense in which to write. His prose drowns in unqualified uses of the word *will*, but, as he clarifies in the otherwise breathless introductory chapter, this had been a stylistic choice: *probably* and *in my opinion* would have been unable to captivate a public hungry for any semblance of certainty as things around them crumbled.¹⁹

Strictly, Toffler was no urbanist, but in the morass of *Future Shock*, one quickly sees that urban referents were close to hand as he imagined society's epochal loss of control. Like Martin Anderson and many conservatives, Toffler invoked Urban Renewal to ask, "Why do so many well-intentioned liberal programs go rancid?" He denigrated the New York of John Lindsay as indicative of "pathetic attempts to govern our cities . . . without the least semblance of a coherent plan or policy for the urban future." Indeed, it can seem that Toffler, a Brooklynite by birth, felt that urban landscapes best concretized the "churning, goal-cluttered environment" of the 1970s. He also, in his way, seems to have recognized planning and urban studies for what they are, or had been: specialized kinds of foresight. Toffler's bibliography includes subheadings, and it grandfathers the Joint Center's own *Future Metropolis* collection into the category of "Future Studies" alongside better-known work by Robert Jungk, Peter Drucker, Kenneth Boulding, and many others. (Elsewhere, he drew on unhelpful remarks in which Moynihan had likened the United States to "an individual going through a nervous breakdown.")[20]

"Also consulted" in Toffler's preparations was a Venezuelan periodical, *Prospección del Siglo XXI*, edited in Caracas.[21] It is entirely possible that he was aware of developments at Ciudad Guayana. By 1968, Toffler was acting as a consultant on another prominent New Town project, James Rouse's Columbia, Maryland, where he proposed founding an Institute of the Future as an experiment in post-disciplinary higher education.[22] Here, too, the Joint Center proves its ubiquity. In 1966, Rouse decided that it would be beneficial to have an official historian on staff "to record the planning process" of Columbia in real time and turn the findings into a book. Put in touch with Oscar Handlin by Ford Foundation officials, Hamilton asked who the best person would be to write it. Handlin named Sam Bass Warner, Robert Fogelson, and Jon Peterson, "the three historians who had been at the Joint Center." The book never saw publication.[23]

Toffler's concrete predictions are of little consequence. In some ways, they resonate with Daniel Bell's already-public positions on the central role for theoretical knowledge in an economy structured around services rather than manufactures—in others, not. Bell's major "venture in social forecasting," *The Coming of Post-Industrial Society* (1973), arrived three years later, taking pains to distinguish its data-backed sociological theses from Toffler's word salad. He had, however, worked out its argument over the preceding fifteen years, beginning with a 1958 survey of how American behavioral scientists had navigated "the prediction of Soviet behavior" and fanning out into a 1964 article exploring "twelve modes of prediction" in social science, from Spencerian social physics to Durkheim on the division of labor to Cold War game theory and scenario planning.[24] Bell's Commission on the Year 2000, backed by the American Academy of Arts and Sciences, grew out of these interests, and the 1973 book was, in truth, a tighter and fuller presentation of ideas floated in its 1967 report *Toward the Year 2000*.[25] The group disbanded in 1974, beset by conflicts between more left-wing futurists and the immovable Talcott Parsons.[26] Still, through its activities, Bell became not just a theorist but a broker of intellectual exchange, as well as an inadvertent legitimizer, "for better or worse . . . [of] the spate of futurist studies that have flooded the American scene like the red tide in this past decade."[27] At the time, both critics and acolytes recognized "CY2000" as the futurological exercise it was.[28]

"Society's gone random," *Future Shock* submits, quoting seated Labour MP Raymond Fletcher. What Toffler proposed to organize the maelstrom, however, was expressly not more planning, and it certainly was not technocracy, a short-termism all its own which "reflects the time-bias of industrialism." Nor was it a glorification of what he dubbed the "'hang-loose' approach to the future," equally congenial to Milton Friedman and the New Left. The solution, Toffler held, involved endowing institutes of study modeled on the postwar ORU at its peak: "Multiply the future-sensing organs of society," he wrote, "spotted like nodes in a loose network throughout the entire governmental structure in the techno-societies."[29] Although its intellectual legacy is quite checkered, this generation of futurologists did manage to establish a transnational (if redundant-sounding) set of institutions: the World Future Society (1965), the Institute for the Future (1968; associated with the journal *Futures*), the World Futures Studies Federation (1973, following a years-long series of conferences), Bertrand de Jouvenel's *Futuribles* group (1974) and the state-backed "1985 Committee" in France, the British "Committee on the Next Thirty-Three Years" (1967), and many more.[30] At a smaller scale, but also in the name of fomenting "a continuing plebiscite on the future," Toffler envisioned neighborhood-level "social future assemblies" that every citizen would periodically join, his nearest analogue being the American practice of compulsory jury duty.[31]

Yet a focus on futurology's organizational imperative captures only one part of its mission. As Toffler himself stated, the fundamental purpose of his book was "to increase the future-consciousness of its reader. The degree to which the reader, after finishing the book, finds himself thinking about, speculating about, or trying to anticipate future events will provide one measure of its effectiveness": text as *inducement to*, not *transcript of*, thought.[32] What Toffler clamored to create anew, Bell listed as one of five core traits definitive of the "post-industrial" era. "Future-orientation," he argued, marked an epochal "change in the character of knowledge," and this was consequential for politics and economics alike. Yet Bell, a critic of utopias, believed that cultivating an attention to "regularities and recurrences," "trends," "directions," "rates," and "classes of events" was the only way a society could "specify the constraints, or limits, within which policy decisions *can* be effective."[33]

Although he never embraced the label without reservations, Bell found common ground with neoconservatives. For him, doubt always eclipsed certainty, and "the study of the future," more than any other topic he addressed, convinced him that "when a decision must be inferred [from incomplete data], then one is subject to many qualifying and even contradictory elements."[34] The journalist Peter Steinfels, writing in the later 1970s, described Bell as a "cautionary sage" forever searching for "a way of equitably ordering the 'no's' that must be said."[35] Toffler is seldom so identified, but his anxieties betray both a version of 1960s utopianism and the usual neoconservative graveyard of dashed hopes. Futurology had both progressive and regressive exponents; it could emphasize either throughways or roadblocks. It had no inherent or uncontested political valence on the notional left–right spectrum to which Americans so quickly appeal when confronted with new and unfamiliar movements. The futurologists sought to produce a new cohort of expectant citizens and enjoin them to look ahead, but then also to disavow responsibility if what had seemed like certainty withered in the face of events.

The questions had changed. At issue were not the contents implied when we ask what the future "holds"—anyone's guess—but the modes, methods, and cognitive styles by which populations go about collectively looking ahead. In urban studies, future-orientation became the key variable. And vary it did. In the end, the Joint Center book that most contorted debate on urban crises in the 1970s turned out to be a deeply conservative study in temporal orientation, understood as an axis of social difference and a proxy for vastly unequal relations of power. Planners work on the future, yes, but whose futures do they ensure? Whose do they disavow? These are the central concerns in any "politics of time" as Peter Osborne has defined it.[36] The point is not simply that the horizon fragments or goes out of focus. "No future" has never signified precisely or literally, and the future has never existed in a unitary sense. In his star turn as an urbanist reactionary, Edward Banfield seconded the impulse to pluralize temporal reason. He then translated it into something far more peculiar, vindictive, lasting, and disabling for the conjunction of planning and public intellect.

New Horizons: Unheavenly Cities and the "Crisis of Uncertainty"

The Unheavenly City: The Nature and Future of Our Urban Crisis arrived in 1970, and although Banfield took his business to a trade publisher, it remained a Joint Center creation through and through. Little, Brown correctly sensed a hit in the making and moved 225,000 copies of the first edition—an astonishing figure for a work of social science, especially one by an author who confessed on the first page that, for reasons of tone and content alike, he could easily be mistaken for "an ill-tempered and mean-spirited fellow." Banfield had developed his arguments in conversation with Martin Meyerson—his collaborator and closest friend since the PERP years at Chicago—James Q. Wilson, and many other Joint Center regulars. He acknowledged the Joint Center's financial support "over a considerable period." The second and ninth chapters reused material first published in *The Metropolitan Enigma* and *The Conscience of the City*. The book's one non-polemical chapter, a sturdy if determinist exposition of "The Logic of Metropolitan Growth" historically conceived, drew heavily on in-house scholarship by Raymond Vernon, John Kain, and Bernard Frieden.[37] Although he never took on a formal administrative role with the center, Banfield was a fixture from its founding in 1959. A 1999 *New York Times* obituary remembered him as one of its "intellectual leaders."[38] With *The Unheavenly City*, Banfield outgrew the senescent center and for the remainder of the 1970s occupied an entirely new plane of notoriety, "like the professional athlete who is always dubbed 'controversial' by the sports writers," one undergraduate journalist wrote in 1975. "He wears the label but few really know how he earned it."[39] Let us count the ways.

In *The Unheavenly City*, Banfield modeled a skepticism far more despairing and extreme than anything yet on offer. He set out to demonstrate that the urban crisis was neither worsening nor improving: it did not exist. Banfield posed the question as one of semantics and epistemology: "In what sense are we faced with" a crisis? The usual evidence adduced to worry the public, he pointed out on the first page, was visual in nature: "many square miles of slums and even more miles of dreary blight and chaotic sprawl." All of this had "a certain plausibility." Banfield then asked readers not to believe their eyes. He had long been involved in the broader postwar turn away from physical planning as the strategy of first resort. Yet whereas the new participatory planners rejected architectural solutions in the name of building what they called community power instead, Banfield did so in order to argue for the futility of any solution to urban ills. There was no crisis, there was no soluble problem, and "no disaster impends." Interventionist Great Society urbanism had been conceived by way of a basic category mistake. "What is to be done?" was the Leninist slogan appropriated in partial jest across the political spectrum. Banfield offered a replacement: "What *can* be done?"[40]

This was the title he appended to the penultimate chapter, and its spirit permeates the text. Banfield relentlessly minimizes crisis after putative crisis, mocking reformers, splitting hairs, and redefining ordinary words with no particular gusto. Sprawl and blight are not expansionary "cancers"—a common trope at the time, especially among those committed to organicist ontologies of the city—but something more like a "bad cold." The "inner" city—which

Banfield saw as de facto Black, plus "a few" Puerto Ricans in the Northeast and Mexican Americans in the Southwest—is troubled, but it represents "only" 10 to 20 percent of the whole. The defining feature of his rhetoric, though, is the insouciance with which Banfield lets the slightest gap in positive knowledge about urban life dilate into the deepest, most permanent gulf of unknowability. "In the absence of an adequate specification of the means by which they are to be brought about," he writes of the prevailing approaches to reform, "it must be presumed that no one knows how." There is no crisis but the "crisis of uncertainty," and Banfield is its prophet.[41]

Not every page of *The Unheavenly City* is equally inflammatory, and Banfield's core arguments, on the nonexistence of crisis and the impossibility of actionable knowledge on the urban future, well predate 1970, both in his own writings and those produced by others at the Joint Center. In *Boston: The Job Ahead* (1966)—a test run, the success of which, according to James Q. Wilson, was the direct stimulus to *The Unheavenly City*—Meyerson and Banfield had denied that Cambridge's neighbor was in "crisis."[42] Raymond Vernon had declaimed *The Myth and Reality of Our Urban Problems* (1962)—emphasis on "myth."[43] In 1966, Wilson, playing the contrarian, had written that "the major urban problem is the various and uncertain meanings attached to the phrase 'urban problems.'"[44] Moynihan was coming to think of *crisis* as a "hateful word," one that set up unrealistic expectations among the public and primed them for disappointment.[45] "Social problems are never solved," the planners Horst Rittel and Melvin Webber would write from Berkeley, having absorbed these neoconservative critiques. "At best they are only re-solved—over and over again."[46]

Back at Chicago, in PERP's aftermath, Banfield had written of the "compelling reasons which militate against planning," a "vague" and "pious" profession that "sets up a target in order to facilitate the act of shooting."[47] *City Politics* (1963) has Banfield stating that the future "cannot be foreseen," is "beyond the reach of government," and allows "nothing to be gained from speculating."[48] He, too, appeared between the covers of *The Future Metropolis* (1961), trumpeting in otherwise hopeful company the "difficulty of prediction" and "the utter impossibility within a free society of a foresighted control of such matters."[49] Banfield was already a short-termist and a conservative when he first joined the center, and he already had many adversaries, who, in addition to obvious political differences, found his personality intensely unsavory. At mid-decade, Charles Abrams complained to Lloyd Rodwin of the "stinker" who had blasted his latest book on housing. No, wrote Rodwin: this was "just plain Honest Ed Banfield, a dyed-in-the-wool ex-planner."[50]

Denigrations of cities' seeming decay, decline, obsolescence, or general turpitude had long been commonplace in American life. There are pessimists of all political persuasions. Yet, as Robert Beauregard has written, it was "still another [thing] to question the bases on which those judgments were made," extinguishing any shred of epistemological faith that problems could have solutions or could even be proven to exist. After 1970, the wider discourse on the abandonment of American cities took precisely this turn, and it was "built mainly . . . on a single book."[51] Following Banfield, a long tradition of skepticism began to look quite a bit more like nihilism. Doubt gave way to a willed disbelief. By 1976, in an *American Scholar* symposium treating of "Social Science: The Public Disenchantment," Moynihan was merely channeling Honest Ed when he asserted, "The fact of the matter is that we know little." Owing to *The Unheavenly City* and a crop of other books conceived within its force field, "life began to look awfully random, excepting that so many things never changed."[52]

The Unheavenly City also has a more positive program of study to advance. Banfield endorses cultural, cognitive, and motivational explanations for the persistence of poverty and inequality as facts of urban life. Personal discipline, not skill, differentiates strata of workers, and it manifests in different styles of dress and consumption. Income differences exist, but because they are felt as status differences, the latter must have analytical priority. Class is class *culture*. "Lower-class poverty . . . is 'inwardly' caused," Banfield writes, citing anthropologist Oscar Lewis, to such a degree that any sudden infusion of income would only compound opportunities to squander it. These qualitative forms of poverty close the poor in on themselves—Moynihan's "tangle"—and, for Banfield, are "normal representations of a class culture that is itself abnormal." In turn, "the lower-class poor cannot be organized."[53]

So much for class. Banfield disputes the primacy of race as a principle of division, and here too he is inclined to psychologize and pathologize. "Something about Negro culture" prevents the upward mobility of people who are anyhow "undesirable" neighbors. Voluntary self-segregation he deems the only kind worth acknowledging: "They got there [to Northeastern, Midwestern, and Western cities] so late and then in such great numbers" that prejudice could never have had "causal" power in allocating jobs and homes, and scholars' "overemphasis" on racism can only "raise the psychic cost" of being Black.[54]

The most original and jarring sections, by far, of Banfield's tract return questions of policy and planning to their temporal foundations. The aspect of class culture that he finds most interesting and worrisome is its time horizon. Indeed, Banfield's key innovation is to redefine three major classes—dubbed upper, working, and lower—in terms of what he sees as their divergent and incompatible ways of thinking about the future. "Ability, not performance," is his criterion: Banfield seems to believe that the poor can neither abstractly imagine a future unlike the past nor practice the self-discipline necessary to sacrifice present pleasures for future gains. The lower-class urbanite "lives from moment to moment" as impulse governs a "radically improvident" life of "action," risk, and violence.[55] At one point, he likens the adult working-class mindset to "youth culture" in its disinclination to save, invest, defer, or be anywhere but "where the action is."[56] Lest Banfield's tone leave any doubt, he clarifies that present-orientation is not only different but degraded: "In the chapters that follow, the term *normal* will be used to refer to class culture that is not lower class. The implication that lower-class culture is pathological seems fully warranted both because of the relatively high incidence of mental illness in the lower class and also because human nature seems loath to accept a style of life that is so radically present-oriented."[57] Fighting words, but how ever to assess the validity of a diagnosis that hinges on the phrase "human nature seems"?

Banfield quickly pivots from these tendentious assumptions about urban psychology to pronounce on a wide range of domains in which things just have to be left as they are. It is only through this vindictive sieve of class and time that he reengages questions of the built environment with any specificity. "Each class culture," he postulates, "implies—indeed, more or less requires—a certain sort of physical environment" to support it. Each time horizon, that is, has its own spatial correlate. "Having lots of space," Banfield decides, is a need that follows from the acquisition of upper-class culture; it would never "suit" or be well spent on the poor. "The lower-class individual lives in the slum and sees little or no reason to complain" (and Banfield's implication is that if resistance were to arise, it would be, by definition, unwarranted). "Nothing happens there by plan and anything may happen by accident. . . . Feeling that something exciting is about to happen is highly congenial to people who live for the present and for whom the present is often empty."[58] For present-oriented people, then, a present-oriented city—no future.

These arguments unfold over the course of two nonconsecutive chapters, spaced some 144 pages apart. When Banfield brought out *The Unheavenly City Revisited* in 1974, his major editorial decision in a very lightly updated text was to make the relationship between chapters 3 and 10, the ones on class, more explicit. The former, he wrote, had stressed individual psychology, while the latter stressed "several possible" causes of present-orientation that were more structural in character. Keeping them separate had only confused readers (and inflamed critics, who seized on inconsistencies in the "impatience hypothesis").[59] The two chapters had indeed differed on some particulars, but Banfield was overstating his case. In 1970, he had briefly distinguished "situational" from "volitional" present-orientation, but the brunt of his discussion circled the manifold ways in which futurelessness got drilled so deep into the poor's mental equipment as to be beyond retrieval. Even if a "stunted" time horizon is not innate, Banfield still deems it a heritable "trait," one "learned in childhood and passed on." If the ontological genesis of present-orientation is not strictly the province of nature, he understands its operation and propagation as natural, law-bound, and indeed indistinguishable from the just-so stories then surfacing in the popular literature on sociobiology. Banfield describes culture as if it were nature. "Stability" is culture's most basic property, and change "must occur very slowly."[60]

Banfield makes recourse to an extensive and entirely postwar literature on time drawn from psychology and the natural sciences. Psychotherapy, he claims, is no help for anyone but the affluent: the (lumpen)proletariat make for "bad subjects." But psychology—not sociology, not urban studies, not his home discipline of political science—holds the methodological key to his counsel of despair. He appeals at length to Basil Bernstein's "Some Sociological Determinants of Perception: An Enquiry into Sub-Cultural Differences" (1958) for confirmation that only the middle and upper classes possess the category of the "long-term" or seek to "order" space and time. Bernstein calls the (British) working and lower classes "affectual and expressive" and "volatile"—in short, irrational.[61] Banfield draws on NIMH-funded work on the Thematic Apperception Test coming out of Social Relations at Harvard—the better to distinguish time orientation (i.e., to the past, present, or future) from time span (i.e., long or short) and to justify his focus on the former. David Epley and David Ricks, its authors, had given further cover to the notion that the better-off segments of society were unique not only in forming thoughts about the future, but in knowing how to think causally and inferentially about the linkages among past, present, and future.[62]

Banfield's eclecticism of citation is one of the book's more intriguing aspects. He had read widely if not deeply, and the resulting work nicely exemplifies the interdisciplinary mandate. The *bio-* and the *psycho-* weigh so heavily on his analysis, however, that it becomes difficult to credit Banfield's denial, two hundred pages in, that "when the author uses the words 'lower class' what he has in the back of his mind is 'Negro.'" Banfield's scheme had summarily redefined class in terms of culture. Given what he presumes about culture's modes and mechanisms of perpetuation, classes, for Banfield, are discrete races of people.[63]

If Banfield had stopped there, his work might have ranked as merely heterodox, a peculiar but ambitious attempt to retheorize some of the basic categories that had long anchored social science but could always use more specification. As he converts "time horizon" into an independent variable, however, and uses the concept to weigh in on "several kinds of crime," things turn sour. The "cult of the present," he argues, includes a heightened "propensity to crime." Shorter time horizons produce an illicit "taste for risk." They also, Banfield asserts but of course cannot prove, had been the unique source of the "foray[s] for pillage" he watched unfold during the last few summers. Banfield devotes a justly criticized chapter to what he claims was "rioting mainly for fun and profit," an allegation undercut on the fifth page by his own declaration that "the culture of the lower class renders it incapable of the planning and organization that would ordinarily be necessary to start a riot by design." The question of "rioting" at once activates all of Banfield's most distinctive concepts and explodes whatever loose coherence they may have had. He continues to tread lightly when it comes to explicit racial denigration, but he also traffics in the language of nonhuman wildness and savagery, characterizing "the rampage" as "an outbreak of animal . . . spirits." Awed by visual signifiers of prosperity in ways he thought he had sworn off, Banfield proves genuinely unable to understand how Watts, built as a working-class suburb of detached homes and yards some ten miles south of downtown Los Angeles, or low-slung Detroit could ever have incubated dissent.[64]

The Unheavenly City does come around to some concrete policy proposals; Banfield was never content just to sling mud. He lists twelve feasible answers to the question, What can be done? ("Feasible" does not equate to "advisable," he clarifies half-heartedly, probably expecting the condemnation that soon rained down.) Some of the proposals seek to modify prevailing rhetoric: do not "raise expectations"; deemphasize "white racism"; substitute absolute for relative measures of deprivation. Others verge on the eugenic: "Give *intensive* birth-control guidance to the incompetent poor" and quarantine them, too, in a supervised "institution or semi-institution." The ones devised as responses to lawlessness, however, best digest Banfield's theses on time before turning them to new and punitive ends. Television coverage of riots, he insists, shall always be retrospective, never present-oriented; "live" coverage (a term he still puts in quotes) will only "provoke them." For more ordinary forms of street crime, Banfield calls a different tune: "curbstone justice" (also in quotes), "meted out on the spot," is the only way. He advocates policing on the "stop and frisk" model, and he calls for the broader justice system to "reduce drastically the time elapsing between arrest, trial, and imposition of punishment." The point is to "bring punishment within the time horizon of the most present-oriented."[65]

One strand of Banfield's temporal theory, then, leads to a renewed focus on patience, self-discipline, and the enforcement of order—classical concerns of a prescriptive, values-minded conservatism. The other strand sees creeping disorder and urges policies of non-planning that would guarantee further starvation: stall, debate, demur, disavow, and finally abandon the city to itself. The positions are not easily distinguished, the Joint Center corpus shows them to be compatible, and each entails a politics of time.

The conceptual shift signaled by *The Unheavenly City*, however, was broader still. Any number of neoconservative urbanists had over the 1960s rebranded themselves as professional short-termists, harping on the notion that it was either ill advised or impossible for experts to get a grip on the future before it came to pass. Banfield preserved this basic argument but transposed it: he insisted that it was the defective time orientations of ordinary, inexpert urban subjects that would forever constrain the options available to planners. In his own way, Banfield brought questions of social difference directly to the heart of the matter: Who can plan? Who can see as planners see? This line of questioning was one logical culmination of the Joint Center's foregoing decade of inquiry. Banfield's work was the product of an intellectual milieu committed to grappling with planning as an epistemological problem of time and tense.

A surfeit of public debate swirled around Banfield's book well into the 1970s. In both quantity and vigor, it exceeded that which had greeted Anderson's *Federal Bulldozer*. For a moment, *The Unheavenly City* was ubiquitous. It saw coverage in *Fortune*, the *Atlantic*, and *Time*, whose review ended by uncritically quoting James Q. Wilson's assertion that Banfield had written the "only serious book" on cities in recent memory.[66] It became the subject of a symposium in *Trans-Action* and mostly positive coverage in *Commentary*.[67] Numerous authors would later credit the book with having converted them to conservatism, and Patrick Allitt has argued that Banfield's work had the unique capacity to bridge the constituencies of *National Review* and *The Public Interest*, the traditionalist right and the one more solicitous of social science.[68]

Especially among critics on the left, his name became synonymous with a particular style of conservative iconoclasm, a sour naysaying pursued for its own sake. *Banfieldian* and *Banfieldesque* entered the language.[69] And the book would, in fact, quite directly affect the craft of right-wing urban policy. A decade after the fact, Robert C. Weaver singled out Banfield and Wilson for having spread "absolutely false information" on Urban Renewal in work that Nixon's people cited when announcing the moratorium that ended the program in 1973.[70] Banfield denied to the hilt that his theses on class as time had anything at all to do with race, but his "cantankerous, irritating tone," coupled with more than enough damning textual evidence, rendered his efforts unpersuasive to most.[71] In the *New York Review of Books*, freshly minted PhD Richard Sennett sensed "an emotional deadness"—an absolute inability to understand why social movements coalesce outside the usual channels of political influence—in Banfield's formulations. "I believe him" when he denies racist intent, Sennett wrote. But intent is only part of the equation. The text did racist things; it was "unspeakable naïveté" to think that this "tough-minded passivity" could simply pass itself off as "realism" when Banfield "looks at poor people as essentially a different race of beings from you or me."[72] In the first issue of the journal *Social Policy*, William Ryan, who would soon find a public profile with *Blaming the Victim* (1971), put it simply: "Is Banfield serious?"[73]

Banfield's ruthless counterintuition and tone-deaf prose led readers in a remarkably wide range of disciplines to conclude that, in fact, he was not. From UMass, Robert C. Wood escalated his attacks on the apostatic Joint Center, and Banfield was often his proxy. Wood prosecuted the case first in terms of method. "The Banfield and Moynihan contentions," he wrote in *The Necessary Majority* (1972), "are essentially essayistic," not social-scientific in any reliable sense. But method, Wood showed, inherently shades into politics, morals, and mood. Banfield's "mournful," "gloomy" texts had gone well beyond ordinary academic "detachment" or "withdrawal"—forever temporizing so as to render experts "incapable of arriving at a timely course of action." They were also, Wood noted, more than occasionally reliant on concepts of "hereditary class."[74] The biologizing impulse in *The Unheavenly City* was no peripheral concern, and it attracted critical scrutiny from some surprising quarters. Banfield's impressionistic forays into cognition and time orientation elicited reviews from the *Archives of Internal Medicine*—a notable feat for a work of urban studies—and the *American Journal of Orthopsychiatry*, which deplored his "sordid and perhaps pernicious vision."[75] A reviewer from *Perspectives in Biology and Medicine*, finding Banfield's appeals to Malthus and the birth rate racializing if not racist, could not count *The Unheavenly City* as genuine science: he "jerry-builds" his arguments out of mere "anecdotes."[76]

On university campuses, the response took yet another direction. Although Banfield had become a popular lecturer, drawing some seven hundred students (and selling them copies of *The Unheavenly City*) for his course "Urban Problems," upon the book's release, he became a target for protestors, who seized on the more eugenic-sounding parts of his twelve "feasible" if "undesirable" proposals. He was not a "fascist" in any straightforward sense, but this was the language to which period leftists defaulted, and it is difficult to imagine that when he left Harvard to join the faculty of Penn under the new President Meyerson, a decision announced at the end of 1971, it was "not because of *any* grievance or complaint."[77] When, after three years, he departed Penn and rejoined Harvard's government department, student radicalism was most definitely the decisive "push" factor. By 1973, a small group had begun traveling from city to city in order to shout Banfield down in lecture halls at Penn, Chicago, and the University of Toronto, and in at least one case to present him with a mock "Racist of the Year Award."[78] He made the trip to Chicago to give a lecture, sponsored by the American Enterprise Institute (AEI), titled "The

City and the Revolutionary Tradition"—that is, the American Revolution—and when the talk was rescheduled for a month later in Philadelphia, AEI decided to hold it at the Franklin Institute, off campus.[79]

At Chicago in the 1950s, Banfield was not yet a sought-after conservative, particularly given the long shadow of the Straussian political theorists and the neoclassicals who dominated the economics department, and he seldom pressed political positions on students.[80] It was at Harvard that he began to cultivate right-leaning advisees. One was Bruce Kovner, a doctoral student in government, who won a Joint Center fellowship to write a comparative dissertation on the "political and social conditions which encourage and limit the use of expertness. . . . The nature of expertness is discussed."[81] Kovner did not complete the project or degree, but with the windfall from his multibillion-dollar career in investing, he later became a major donor to right-wing causes and a trustee of the American Enterprise Institute. AEI had existed since the 1930s—as was true of Banfield, its original *bête noire* was the New Deal, not the Great Society—but its prominence rose in the 1970s. In 1986, it named as its new chairman a Banfieldian, Christopher DeMuth, who had sought him out while a Harvard undergraduate.[82] *The Unheavenly City* became a basic reference on urban policy in the para-academic world of Washington think tanks.

His example also charted a course for other centers of urban studies disenchanted with how Great Society policy makers had applied their work. In St. Louis, Washington University's Ford-seeded IURS took a turn in the 1970s that, though less publicized, was nearly identical to the Joint Center's. *The Mature Metropolis* (1978) was the group's major postlapsarian statement. Charles Leven wrapped up his introduction to the volume citing "what Banfield has characterized as excessive present-orientedness" in order to despair of the prospects for any city dominated by minority or female-headed households. Obsolescence was the volume's theme: its title was a slightly awkward reply to *The Exploding Metropolis* on that book's twentieth anniversary, and Leven heaped scorn on William H. Whyte's preference for "the supposedly more attractive 'Gotham-on-Hudson' lifestyle."[83] Banfield, emissary and bellwether of the changing Joint Center, had altered the terms of urban debate among the reading public, among students, in the ideas industry set up to rival the universities, and throughout the enduring network of organized research.

The scope of his claims, however, was never confined to the United States. The unheavenly city of Banfield's nightmares was a composite of American places, but to understand the provenance of his theses on time orientation, it is necessary to look across the Atlantic. In actual fact, his caricature of the present-oriented American poor had its conceptual roots in ethnographic work

FIGURE 6.1. Chiaromonte, or "Montegrano," in the interwar period. Banfield, unable to converse with his ethnographic subjects when he arrived in 1954, took numerous photographs of the town's residents, architecture, and livestock, and was drawn to environments and juxtapositions that would have been out of place in the cities of the United States. Courtesy of Universal Images Group North America LLC / Alamy Stock Photo.

Banfield carried out in Southern Italy in 1955 and published in *The Moral Basis of a Backward Society* (1958). His subject was Chiaromonte, a secluded hill town in the Lucania (or Basilicata) region that he renamed Montegrano (figure 6.1). He spoke scarcely any Italian and authored the book "with the assistance of" his American wife, Laura Fasano Banfield, the daughter of immigrants. Its title-as-argument, however, was pure Banfield: *backward* signaled a set of inflexible assumptions about the normal forward course of development toward modernity. Postwar theories of modernization always depended on counterexamples of people seemingly suspended in the atemporal world of tradition, and Banfield likened the people of twentieth-century Chiaromonte to no less than the early Indo-European culture as described by Fustel de Coulanges, "of which the Greeks and Italians are branches." In an appendix, he juxtaposed their responses to the Thematic Apperception Test—in which subjects were shown an image and asked to construct a story about its contents—with "normal" results elicited in Kansas.[84]

Banfield's understanding of *ethos*—a concept central to the reports that became *City Politics*, only later to be recoded as *culture*—began here. He delineated "ethos in principle" from "ethos in practice" and, in the final chapter,

"The Future," dwelled on "how to fix it." What needed fixing? Banfield called it "amoral familism." The townsfolk, he judged, evinced an "inability . . . to act together for their common good or, indeed, for any end transcending the immediate material interest of the nuclear family." As in the work of Marshall Kaplan and other short-termists, the word *immediate* had both spatial and temporal coordinates. Chiaromonte's poor were, in a word, present-oriented; they would not and could not envision a future world different from the one they had known. For Banfield, this was sufficient to explain their "underdevelopment": culture preceded and conditioned all economic life. His second claim was that Chiaromonte's fatalistic, futureless culture would forever depress development. He formalized this contention in a "predictive hypothesis" said to "make intelligible all of the behavior about which questions have been raised"—namely, "The Montegranesi act as if they were following this rule: Maximize the material, short-run advantage of the nuclear family; *assume that all others will do likewise.*"[85] If the poor would not project what the future held, Banfield would do it for them.

Banfield's exposure to "Montegrano" cast the die for his appraisal of all other developing countries, and it supplied him with a list of traits he could look for in American cities among migrants from those countries and their progeny.[86] Banfield had help in effecting these conceptual transpositions from south to north. By 1974, amid the resurgence of popular interest in "white ethnic" identity, the sociologist William Muraskin noticed that "Banfield 1958" had somehow become the "single most influential work" scholars were citing to shed light on the ways of Italian Americans.[87] As was true of the practice and subsequent critique of Urban Renewal, the vexed New Town movement, the phenomenology of highway design, the refinement of cybernetic approaches to power and decision, and so many other shifts that the Joint Center oversaw or intensified within the urbanist academy, Banfield's adventures in time orientation moved along transnational circuits, an infrastructure maintained by people convinced that there was a global urban crisis or none at all.

"Many Cities in One": Reallocating Urban Reason

To rephrase class or other social diacritics in terms of time orientation was never uniquely the province of conservative minds.[88] In the annals of the Joint Center, no individual thinker seems less compatible with Banfield than Lisa Peattie: critic of American development abroad, grassroots organizer, nascent anarchist, feminist, general irritant to established forms of power. Yet if

Ciudad Guayana was "a city which lives in the future," as she had written in one of *The View from the Barrio*'s more sloganeering moments, then at a finer grain of analysis, she could plainly see that the promised future was more accessible to some Venezuelans than to others. Like Banfield and Kaplan, she, too, posited the essential middle-classness of any worldview apt to "weigh" present conditions against future possibilities so as to proceed in careful "increments." Only middle-class people, she suggested, were used to "seeing connections" between tenses and calibrating present courses of action in the name of "long-term planning": study harder to secure a job, save money now to spend it later, delay gratification indefinitely.[89] Despite Peattie's prodigious political radicalization while on site in La Laja, *The View from the Barrio* began its life steeped in the culture-and-personality approaches then dominant in the Ford-delimited behavioral sciences. As of mid-1962, she and Roderick Peattie could still state that their work was signally concerned with "aspirations": how and whether non-elite Venezuelans aligned with the ideas of "progress" being projected by the CVG and its consultants. Early field notes can sound peculiarly high-handed, as if lifted from a draft by Daniel Lerner: "these psychic modes [associated with the Global North] are rather unevenly distributed; perhaps one of the requirements of an industrialized society is a certain number of 'proletarians' whose psychic mobility is limited."[90] Even as she changed her positions or found new labels for old ones, Peattie the economic anthropologist remained fixated on class and committed to redescribing it as culture, as cognition, and as orientation. A Banfieldian alchemy lay at the core of her method.[91]

Peattie and Banfield seem to have sensed their conceptual common ground (although it is amusing to imagine table-thumping seminar debates between the firebrand and the starched Connecticut Yankee). Peattie's 1968 book carries no citations, but her operational definitions of class, influence, and the public recapitulate *City Politics* almost to the letter. The appreciation was mutual. Banfield found her work legible enough to merit inclusion, among much bigger names, in the second edition of *Urban Government*, the widely adopted reader he assembled in 1969 for instructional use.[92] In his own scholarship and in his role as an educator, Banfield's attempts at general, unmarked definitions of Northern political categories routinely drew sustenance from Southern scenarios—exceptions that might yet prove the rule. Banfield never traveled to Ciudad Guayana himself, but he kept abreast of its development and embraced the project's affordances to urbanist curricula. Peattie, for her part, had presented her Venezuela work in ways that would make the "social inventions" and "body of organizational techniques" it documented applicable to US cities amid what Lyndon Johnson had taken to calling the War on Poverty.[93] The transnational portability of her findings is not asserted on every page of *The View from the Barrio*, but it does show through. Discussing kinship and economy in the *barrio*, for instance, Peattie invites readers to consider "many societies, ranging from some Mexican Indian villages to the American young-corporation-executive suburb," in which a cognate "game of status" holds sway. Some of the same phenomena seem visible "in La Laja as in Harlem."[94] Peattie revisited the New Town's saga a generation later and issued *Planning: Rethinking Ciudad Guayana* (1987), a far more radical rejection of central planning than *The View from the Barrio* ever advocated. In the later text, she noted a curious vogue among the critical Venezuelan planners and social scientists she met: they were all studying the 1960s United States, combing through the Kennedy and Johnson eras—the administrators as well as their antagonists—for solutions to the dilemmas of Caracas and its satellites.[95] Northern knowledge flowed south, and it continued to flow south even two decades after the Joint Center's delegation had cut ties. What the record on Banfield, Peattie, and many of their peers makes clear is that the arrow always pointed both ways.[96]

One final example must round out the center's extraterritorial work, and it arrives belatedly in more than one sense. The last official monograph on Venezuela was Donald Appleyard's *Planning a Pluralist City: Conflicting Realities in Ciudad Guayana*. Its completion was severely delayed, not least because of Appleyard's departure for Berkeley in 1967. The book did not go to press until 1976, a full decade after the center had ended its contract with the CVG, and six years after the Ford funding dropped off and the turn rightward accelerated.[97] He had carried out the main body of research, however, in 1964. An article Appleyard published in 1970 (and later reproduced as the core of *Planning a Pluralist City*'s eighth chapter) identified its author as "presently completing" the book. It could have arrived sooner; this distinctive study is, in a strong sense, a document of the Sixties in its ambition and experimentalism, and core elements of its argument were fully formed by the end of that decade. The work continued to evolve into the 1970s, however, and it changed with the times. As published, it was the Joint Center's first avowed, full-scale statement on "urban knowledge and its implications for urban design." It affords a unique opportunity to take stock of the inbuilt tensions and transnational travels of urban studies at a moment of profound reorganization.[98]

By "urban knowledge," Appleyard means primarily the sensory perception of cities. His debt to Lynch is frankly stated, and at the core of his empirical research stands a body of long-form, exacting interviews with inhabitants of the city under construction. Appleyard questioned locals on their overall "perceptions of change"; on the city's four main districts (Puerto Ordaz, San Félix,

El Roble, Castillito) and the "kinds of people" (in quotes) they associated with each; and, before anything else, on the city's overall spatial structure. Each respondent drew him a map and narrated, from memory, what it felt like to make a journey down the Avenida. "Many subjects," an appendix reads, "had never drawn a map before and were either reluctant or unable to attempt one. Consequently, ways were developed to assist them."[99]

Appleyard is on the trail of vernacular ways of perceiving, reasoning, and knowing—not unitary urban expertise. The pluralism to which his title refers is a cognitive pluralism, and, indeed, Appleyard points up profound incongruities in how different populations process the same landscape. He also states them far more baldly than Lynch had done in *The Image of the City*. Two axes organize the analysis. One, as in Peattie, counterposes top-down planners to the collectivity of on-the-ground locals; the other makes a finer-grained, within-city accounting of perceptual variations by class, education, and other criteria that tacitly become proxies for racial, national, or civilizational difference. "Ciudad Guayana was many cities in one," Appleyard states on the first page. "Different people knew it in different ways." Yet whereas Banfield had catalogued differences and inequalities in order to naturalize the separation of classes, Appleyard's conviction is that it ought to be possible to bridge them. He proposes to integrate this very diversity into the process of environmental design: "to structure an entity to be comprehended at different levels [at once] and to sustain attention—and affection—after repeated contact." Systematic acquaintance with multiple "urban vocabularies" and "cognitive and life-styles," he writes, can enable a vital "imaginative pluralism" and strengthen the city as a collective artifact. Too often, "the chosen ignorance of the elite . . . an almost deliberate turning away" from mess and complexity, has undercut these hopes. "The city's future sometimes seemed more real [to them] than the present."[100]

In the execution, though, Appleyard finds reasons for concern. Perhaps designers should not be consulting locals for thoughts on the city's future, as "they might not understand" which options are actually feasible. "Evidence of individual perceptions" is of course welcome in the name of basic research, but it also "may reveal a degree of ignorance that may be limiting opportunities. . . . In these cases, policies of changing perceptions and expectations may be justified." As in *The View from the Road*, "the city environment itself" is "analogous to movies, dramas, and poetry"; it could be choreographed, Appleyard believes, in ways that would induce rich participation in imagining Ciudad Guayana's future. But Appleyard also proves amenable to "the diffusion of information about future change" that experts have decided on in advance: "shift the citizens' perceptions toward . . . development," he writes, and use "environmental means" such as fences, plantings, and signs to indicate where the city is headed.[101] As the MIT architect William Porter wrote of Ciudad Guayana, the object world "could make evident not only what is happening but also what had happened and, perhaps, some of the more important things that *are going to* happen."[102] The built environment can inhabit the future tense, even if its inhabitants do not yet. The gap between Appleyard's two pluralisms widens as the text elapses. *Planning a Pluralist City* gradually incites searching reflection on the compatibility of the Joint Center's 1960s ambitions with its 1970s self-critique—of expertise with other, less quiescent ways of knowing.

Appleyard deals with perceptions of space and time in two separate chapters, "The Spatial Structure" and "Change." His conceptual apparatus could be seen as Lynch's *Image of the City* exported to a developmentalist Latin American context. He highlights Ciudad Guayana's real and imagined spatial fragmentation, on one hand, and its fuzzier zones of illegibility, on the other, devoid of memorable landmarks or "structural clarity" that would aid navigation. He is noticeably concerned about the differentials in power and mobility that the cognitive maps are laying bare—as was Lynch, particularly in his early-1970s work for the City of Los Angeles—and he enters impassioned pleas that designers first ascertain and then expand the "environment of common knowledge" defined by those areas where the sketches produced by Ciudad Guayana's disparate groups, every bit as segregated as Lynch had feared on his visit in 1964, overlap. (No citywide map was on display in any public place at the time of Appleyard's research.) For guidance, he looks back to the idealized medieval city, where "people actually met each other," and socializes von Moltke's key concept in plotting out Avenida Guayana: for Appleyard, the aim of the designer must be to make different groups "intervisible" to one another.[103]

In developing these arguments, Appleyard draws richly and eclectically on literature in the psychology of perception. He taps several texts that would have been familiar to Banfield: Magdalen Vernon's general treatment of perception; sundry Gestalt approaches to "cognitive economizing," after Fred Attneave; Jean Piaget on children's understandings of space; and Edward Tolman's contribution to the Parsons and Shils volume positing *A General Theory of Action*.[104] In ways clearly beyond Banfield's ken, Appleyard also engages the psychology of art and aesthetics (Rudolf Arnheim, Ernst Gombrich); a budding literature in environmental psychology (Kenneth Craik, Harold Proshansky); the latest theories of cognitive mapping worked out by human geographers (David Lowenthal, Roger Downs, Peter Gould); and even Aldous Huxley's 1954 psychedelic memoir *The Doors of Perception*.[105]

Appleyard divides his respondents' maps into two broad styles of perception (figure 6.2). One he dubs "sequential" and associates empirically with the city's

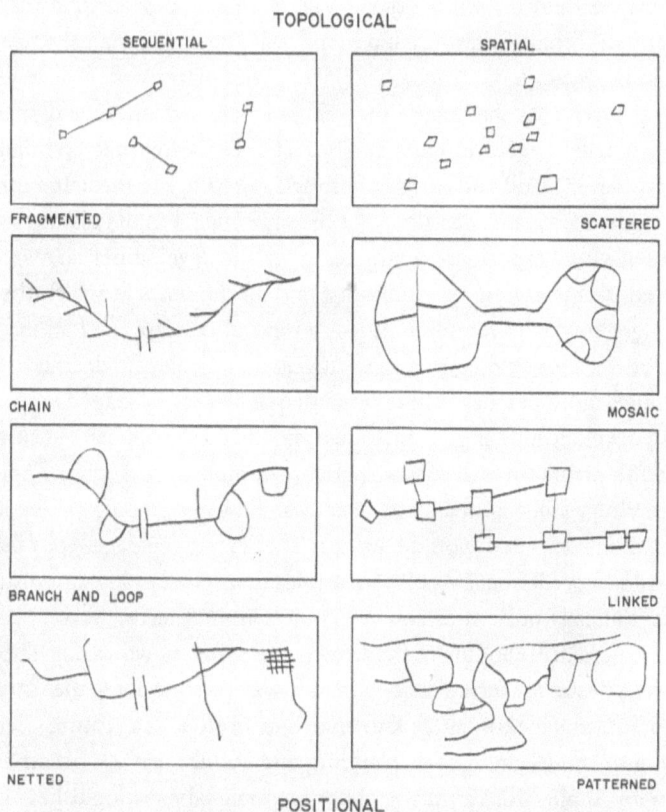

FIGURE 6.2. Sequential and spatial perception. At Ciudad Guayana, elaborating methods of cognitive mapping made famous by Lynch, Appleyard classified residents' imaginative geographies into two overarching styles, each of which he broke down into four types. Note that both major styles concern the physical space of the city; Appleyard introduces unnecessary confusion by using the term *spatial* to mean, effectively, synchronic. Donald Appleyard, *Planning a Pluralist City* (1976), 158. Courtesy of MIT Press.

working and lower classes. A sequential map hangs together by virtue of its paths: it represents a remembered journey through the city, by a moving observer, in which there is one overall directional trend. To this, Appleyard opposes "spatial" perception (an awkward coinage, as both types obviously concern physical space). If paths, roads, passages, and flows define the former style, the latter is grounded in the rather more static landmarks and district boundaries that tend to register on most official maps in the Western tradition. Appleyard sees spatial maps as "more objectively" rendered, as if drawn from high above the city rather than within it. He associates them with the educated, the affluent, and planners themselves. At this juncture, Appleyard's text becomes visually quite complex, and his will to typologize is apparent: sequential maps have "fragmented," "chain," "branch and loop," and "netted" variants, while spatial maps can be "scattered," "mosaic," "linked," or "patterned."[106] Like any self-respecting typologist, he grants that, in practice, sequential and spatial approaches usually appear in combination. The socioeconomic coordinates he assigns, however, stand undisturbed: abstraction belongs to the better off.

Sequence, of course, was already a central concept in the planners' understanding of visual experience on the highway, the developmental march from purported backwardness to modernity, and all the ways in which these two levels might mutually reinforce. It is a temporal concept, and an incautious reading of the above evidence might suggest that Appleyard deemed ordinary *guayacitanos* more persuasively attuned than elites to the staged emplotment of urban development. In fact, he took a version of the opposite position, and as the book pivots formally from spatial to temporal perception, Appleyard enters territory still claimed by the estate of Edward Banfield. There is no citation of Banfield—that would have sent the wrong message—but the arguments are nearly identical. Appleyard argues that society's lower registers are, in effect, radically present-oriented: "They seldom inferred beyond their immediate experience, clinging to the known and concrete world. . . . There was, therefore, a desire for future change but no way of conceiving the future." Inference about the incompletely known urban world and its future—leitmotif in the Joint Center's merger of planning and social science—becomes a key concern for Appleyard. Venturing one more binary, he distinguishes "inferential" from merely "responsive," which is to say passive, "modes" of perception. He finds examples of the latter in disparate and unlikely places: George Santayana's naturalistic *The Sense of Beauty* (1896), a progenitor of affective approaches to aesthetics; Huxley's popular mescaline narrative; and just "accepting what is there—the viewpoint of Taoism." Under properly inferential perception, by contrast, "Our direct and indirect sources of information are matched with each other. The environment is viewed as a communications medium, and we infer beyond the information given," probabilistically. The educated and the comfortable will "begin to infer, extending his action and thought beyond the visible field. His awareness of motivation and choice increases, as does his planning behavior."[107] The middle classes, in short, can see into the future. They alone can see the world as planners do.

Planning a Pluralist City is not a vindictive text. Appleyard is careful to note that "planning behavior" seems to increase with formal education—not just that it is unequally distributed at the time of writing, but that it can be taught and might yet expand. He also considers far more "differentiating variables" than does Banfield. Appleyard accounts for perceptual differences by sex, occupation, habitual mode of transport, and the primary medium by which respondents acquire "urban information": official meetings, official maps, newspapers, radio, television.[108] And yet, owing to its immersion in psychology, its transnational ambitions, and its theses on the unequal distribution of urban reason, Appleyard's book could easily be read as giving empirical ballast to the "denial of coevalness" that Johannes Fabian would soon identify as the hallmark of pre-critical anthropology. Anthropologists and their subjects, Fabian famously argues in *Time and the Other* (1983), share space and time during the fieldwork experience—ethnography, inherently present-oriented, is about being there—but anthropological prose is almost without exception ahistorical, committed to the unending present tense supposedly inhabited by "the people without history."[109]

Within the design fields, Appleyard's statement on Guayana has been overshadowed by his other late-period writings: a book on the preservation of European cities, a diffuse corpus on environmental symbolism and behavior, and, above all, *Livable Streets* (1981), a plea for pedestrianism made especially poignant after he was killed by a motor vehicle the very next year.[110] *Planning a Pluralist City*'s belated arrival in print meant that what was supposed to be an immersive report from within a fast-developing city became, in effect, a work of recent history. Still, Appleyard's compendium throws the temporal politics of the Guayana project into stark relief. It demonstrates an acute interest in non-Western temporalities and draws them out inductively. Appleyard adds complexity to the radiant, too-neat futures promised by the CVG and their American adjuncts, even as his critiques exist alongside language and imagery that entrench racialized notions of a cognitive separation between industrial society's future-oriented upper stratum and its present-oriented underclass, inert and abandoned to itself (figures 6.3 and 6.4).[111]

Appleyard's text also demonstrates the abundant conceptual transpositions that linked the Joint Center's northern and southern theaters of operation. Perhaps Appleyard, no social scientist in any conventional sense, was channeling Banfield as he designed his research into Ciudad Guayana and processed the data it bore—even as he himself celebrated the plurality of urban life to a degree that Banfield, the arch-pessimist, never would. Perhaps Banfield, in questioning the crisis of the *Unheavenly City*, was reinscribing Venezuela onto a domestic canvas. Perhaps "Montegrano" and Ciudad Guayana, *Moral Basis* and *Pluralist City*, were both offshoots of a growing, right-led but politically promiscuous rejection of the certainties encoded into prevailing postwar styles of urban redevelopment and indexed by the figure of the bulldozer, federal

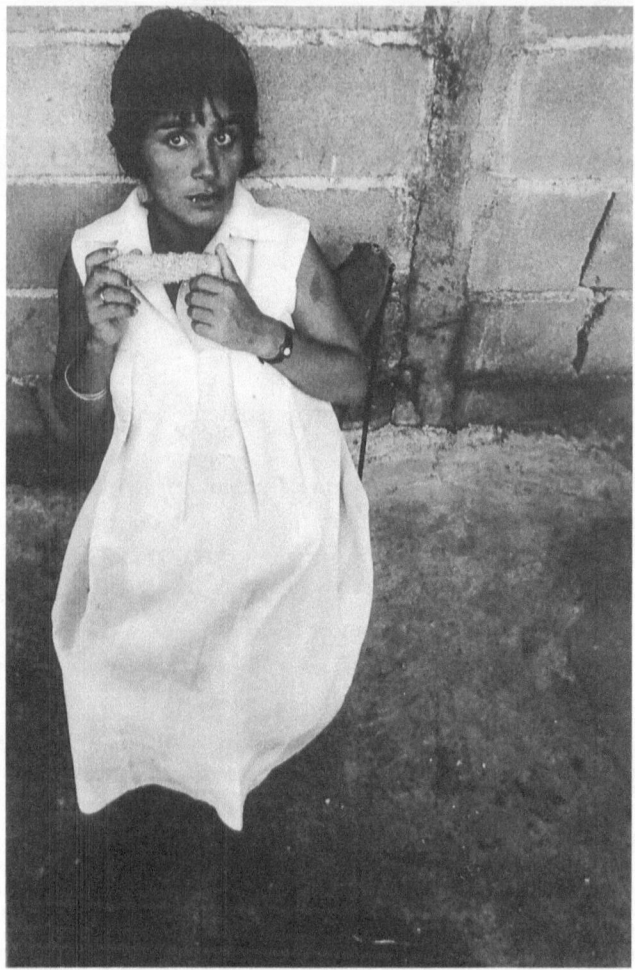

FIGURE 6.3. The JCUS–CVG team retained the services of an American photographer, Donald Wright Patterson, to shoot portraits of the new migrants to Ciudad Guayana. More candid and ambivalent than any of the official imagery produced along the way, they might have served as illustrations for Lisa Peattie's *The View from the Barrio* (1968) had she not published it outside the Joint Center's book series. Here, a *guayacitana* snacks on an ear of corn. "Photographs by Donald Wright Patterson" folder, Lloyd Rodwin Papers, MC 490, Massachusetts Institute of Technology Institute Archives and Special Collections.

or otherwise. All of these authors, in different ways, had forgone the basically liberal faith in improvability that had understood the future metropolis as a place capable of being envisioned, known, and eventually materialized in three dimensions. Yet their alternative was not, as is often alleged of the long 1970s, a simple disavowal of futurity and foresight. All, instead, had opted to inquire into the variable, unequal workings of future-orientation.

FIGURE 6.4. A shopkeeper leans in, framed by miscellaneous goods whose arrangement defies the geometries typically on display in official CVG communications. "Photographs by Donald Wright Patterson" folder, Lloyd Rodwin Papers, MC 490, Massachusetts Institute of Technology Institute Archives and Special Collections.

"Too Far Gone": New York and the Temporalities of Ruin

None of the Joint Center's concepts stood still; none could be confined once and for all to a single bounded city or national territory. Every aspect of the center's intellectual output was at least potentially poised to traverse transnational circuits of exchange whose connectivity only increased with use. Appleyard's circumnavigation of Boston was every bit as much a commentary on mobility at Ciudad Guayana; his attempted cartography of the Venezuelan mind, in turn, courted a readership inclined to relate its findings to the anonymous American wanderers Lynch had interviewed on the Rockefeller dime. Peattie distributed her critiques of aloof urban experts between the Americas, indicting configurations of power that luxuriated in transnational comparison while they reinscribed hierarchies between North and South. Banfield's fulminations on Black demonstrators were always already interleaved with his ad hoc moral ethnography of Italian village life, research that he had undertaken in the first place to adumbrate the dynamics of poverty back home. In digesting this body of work, it makes little sense to assign the sort of causality that moves in just one direction, with clear source and destination. North and South America found themselves in what many of the principals surely would have labeled a feedback loop. Northern priorities set limits on how the center intervened in the developing world, but the complexities and frictions they encountered abroad, in places chosen precisely for their potential as laboratories, had an integral role in both shaping and calling into question the core insights of any general theory of urban life. Its Southern exposure continually made and remade the Joint Center.

Most often, the group's attempts to repatriate concepts and conclusions they had refined overseas nominated "the American city," that vague but durable aggregate, as the target for this new expertise. Sometimes its insights were further specified to Boston, Cambridge, and their suburban hinterland. For a great many scholars in the Joint Center's midst, however, the implicit referent was always New York. This made some sense given the center's core personnel and their provenance: Rodwin and Meyerson were natives, as were Glazer, Handlin, Abrams, Frieden, and still others. Ford and other major funders were based there. Raymond Vernon's NYMRS had generated enough data, now carefully filed away on Church Street, to sustain another generation's worth of Gotham-oriented scholarship. New York was, then as now, by far the largest and densest, and thus facially the most urban, American metropolis.

New York was even more central at the end of the 1960s to the group's theorization of time's passage than it was at the outset—more conspicuous a harbinger of a future in putative ruins, more explicitly the final and highest-stakes explanandum for the Joint Center's interdisciplinary labors. The question is not why it became so, but how. To answer it, the career of Glazer and Moynihan's *Beyond the Melting Pot* (1963; rev. ed. 1970) is worth revisiting. Therein, between the lines of what could pass for a static, atemporal inventory of ethnic groups, New York went on display as the cautionary, uniquely futureless metropolis.

A seasoned doubter, Glazer had been publishing essays with titles such as "Is New York City Ungovernable?" as early as 1961. ("Why City Planning Is Obsolete," which included some discussion of New York, dated to 1958.)[112] Specters of crisis and chaos haunt *Beyond the Melting Pot*: New York's incipient depopulation; industrial flight at least to the suburbs and often well beyond them; degradation of the city's housing stock through subdivision and overcrowding; large-scale in-migration (in a world before Hart–Celler) from, especially, the Caribbean and the American South, the source of simmering conflicts along lines of complexion and class; and the foundational issues of governance that stemmed from all these. Officially, its chapters appear in no meaningful sequence, but it is difficult not to conclude that the authors have ranked their five groups in ascending order of perceived cultural soundness and potential for assimilation. Jewish and Irish populations bring the book to its conclusion. The authors' justification for leading off the book with a discussion of "the Negroes" is astonishingly facile: "We begin, as the visitor might, with what immediately strikes the eye, and proceed from there."[113] Visual analysis plays no acknowledged role in the book, which is unillustrated, and Glazer and Moynihan refrain from detailed analyses of buildings and other material artifacts, despite their well-demonstrated interest in the topic. There is, however, an assumed gradient of whiteness and blackness, visible lightness and darkness, that imparts the book a structure and anchors its more invidious intergroup comparisons.[114]

In ways that harmonize closely with Appleyard and especially Banfield—both echoing his Italian hours and anticipating the rawest stretches of *The Unheavenly City*—Glazer and Moynihan prove amenable to classifying their five New Yorks in terms of time orientation. They commit to none of the faux formalism that Banfield's epigones held up as evidence of his methodological sophistication, and there is no chapter or even subheading flagging time as such. At crucial moments, however, a rigid politics of temporal difference shows through. Glazer and Moynihan often index time orientation to microeconomic behavior. They allege "the failure of [native-born] Negroes to develop a pattern of saving"; various "frustrations," they write, refocus Black attention on the "search for pleasure in consumption." Puerto Ricans populate the book's second chapter, and there they are depicted as "amazingly fertile," both as organisms capable of reproduction and as economic actors "spawning small stores" in increasingly densely settled neighborhoods. If the latter group is economically successful, the authors imply, it is not because it is economically rational. To support this hunch, Glazer and Moynihan cite the overrepresentation of so-called crimes of passion as a percentage of Puerto Rican "delinquency."[115]

To these two groups, Glazer and Moynihan oppose the Jewish case, again on grounds of divergent time orientation. Glazer had aired similar themes in *American Judaism* (1957), a semipopular historico-sociological survey text that enjoyed a wide readership and went through multiple editions. There, working to counter reductive Marxian approaches, his aim was to argue that working classes, in the plural, had to be differentiated at least by ethnicity and religion, and that the Jewish working class in America had always "had a broader horizon" than other fractions.[116] By 1963, due only in part to far-flung projects on the order of Ciudad Guayana, the comparative impulse in social science was even better entrenched. So was Glazer's pugnacity, and rather than let this unfalsifiable remark stand on its own, he pivoted from it to stinging criticisms of the supposedly low mental acuity of darker, newer New Yorkers.

"This is a beginning book," Glazer and Moynihan state at the outset of *Beyond the Melting Pot*, purely a "book of prefaces" (with no apparent apologies to

Mencken for pilfering his words). But prefaces to which future—and whose? By the second chapter, we hear that for those urbanites "at the bottom of the scale things are too far gone for anything to break the circle."[117] *Too far gone*—the phrase encodes a charged, highly specific politics of time and tense, one that imbues the entire book's argumentation without ever being straightforwardly declared or justified. Persons, places, and things, it implies, are not simply on the road to ruin, but already there—and the only future that can thus be methodically inferred from the decaying present consists of further decline and debasement. The alreadyness of urban collapse and, thus, the belatedness of any proposed intervention—this maneuver, conceptually distinct from anything directly proffered by Banfield (being Banfield), Appleyard (in his comparative mode), or Peattie (in her less guarded moments), defines the deepest recesses of *Beyond the Melting Pot* as a commentary on urban time. It marks out the rhetorical path that the Joint Center's rightmost offshoots would follow in years to come.[118] *Beyond the Melting Pot* and other work contemporaneous with the planning of Ciudad Guayana set out developmental criteria that the New Town project would always fail to meet, and its argumentation prefigured the diverse senses of futurelessness endemic to American politics a decade hence.

That was in 1963. Celebrated upon its arrival, the book emerged in a second edition seven torrid years later—a new ninety-page introduction the clearest sign that minds had changed. "In New York," Glazer and Moynihan write, "the 1960s ended much worse than they began." Full stop. As evidence, the authors air a litany of common neoconservative complaints: blockheaded Urban Renewal of the Robert-Mosaic variety, rioting in the streets and on the campuses (notably Columbia's), the Great Society as symptom and efficient cause, New York's robust local welfare state as hypertrophic instance thereof. They were introducing a book on race and ethnicity specifically, though, and focused their ire on new, "purely divisive groups and philosophies," especially those who sensed "white ethnic racist" impulses coursing through studies such as their own. Black studies, which had intellectual roots in Black Power politics as articulated most prominently in Harlem, had quickly been added to the menu of college subjects following dramatic acts of resistance at San Francisco State University; Glazer and Moynihan called for coequal scholarly attention to Poles, Italians, and Southern whites, among other groups.[119] Without claiming the label, Glazer had become one of the most articulate first-person explainers of the neoconservative drift. "On Being Deradicalized" (1970), published that same year in *Commentary*, was his first attempt to take stock, and it would not be his last.[120]

The reactive Glazer and Moynihan of 1970 remain conceptually invested in using time orientation as a proxy for race, class, and worldview. In *Beyond the Melting Pot*'s second edition, though, their interest manifests in new ways. Their concern is no longer simply to distinguish future- from present-oriented subcultures. Now the authors unleash on Black and Puerto Rican populations for their supposed impatience, their inability to wait for anything but immediate parity with white groups—their attempt, in a sense, to short-circuit the ordinary sequencing of assimilation to some imagined "mainstream." "Everyone else has."[121] The sanctimony grates. The shift in temporal reasoning, however, is more subtle. In the aftermath of the 1960s, conservatives looking to defuse urban and otherwise social reform learned from Glazer and Moynihan's rhetoric, and to oppose proposed measures it became common to claim that they would arrive too fast, too soon in the developmental sequence to do much good. After about 1968, right-facing critics increasingly appealed to notions of the proper timing and pacing of political intervention, and what they recommended was a strategy of perpetual, indefinite deferral. Deferral is the quintessence of "logical governance," wrote their interlocutor Karl Deutsch, who insisted that every impulse favoring immediate action be tempered with the "positive repressive force of the past."[122] Wait—not yet.

Two competing temporalities, then, coexist across the career of *Beyond the Melting Pot*. One, reliant on *too soon* and *not yet*, maintains a belief in at least the possibility of planning: the future meaningfully exists as concept and object, and opportunities for its betterment lie somewhere on the horizon. The presence of these tropes in 1970 could be taken as evidence of a late-blooming swell of hope, cautiously reasserting planning-as-futuring on the far side of a decade that had so threatened that ideal. But the first edition had preemptively closed down that possibility. The city of 1963 was already ruined and beyond saving (and the main body of the original text remained unaltered upon its 1970 reissue; only the prolix introduction was new). Then, things had (somehow) gotten "much worse." One begins to wonder if, through these injunctions to slow down, hold out for the right moment, and let time do its work, Glazer and Moynihan had been running interference. *Not yet* meant *never*. *Too soon* conjured a future already written out of existence by *too far gone*.

In the mid-1970s, moral anguish at the mention of New York City became a commonplace feature of American discourse. *Death Wish*, *The Warriors*, *Pelham 123*, "mugged by reality," "the Bronx is burning"—for several years on either side of the calamitous 1975 fiscal default ("Ford to City . . ."), lay prophets of decline made profligate reference to the city as a "negative definer of America," as Joshua Freeman has put it.[123] In *The Politics of Neglect* (1975), the Joint Center's Bernard Frieden and Marshall Kaplan, New Yorkers both, noted the city's perverse utility to scholars and pundits as a "striking" example of "deterioration," pockmarked with vast areas rendered newly "unlivable."[124]

There was arson, and there was rubble—quite a bit of it—especially in the South Bronx, where "whole neighborhoods literally dematerialized" as landlords calculated that insurance payouts would exceed anything they could garner from rent collection. Hundreds of acres of that resolutely mid-rise borough lay vacant, their buildings carved open to the wind or reduced to ashes. The *New York Times* began to publish a daily count of the fires, which was referred to informally as the "Ruins Section." In a 1977 episode whose photographic record has come to illustrate too many histories of this era, President Jimmy Carter walked an incinerated block of Charlotte Street and vowed to rebuild, calling the "ruins" of the Bronx "as crucial to an understanding of American urban life as Auschwitz is crucial to an understanding of Nazism."[125] In the 1980s, the novelist and native Leonard Kriegel would write that "only in dying has the Bronx been collectivized into an American object lesson."[126] For whom? By and large it was the right who made New York's ruins didactic, either—from across the American heartland—to indict the too-diverse, too-permissive city for alleged sins that could well have been confabulated a century prior, or—among disaffected natives—to scale up from the mess Moses made and demand far more pitiless rollbacks of social services.

The term *ruin* participates in a complex temporality, uneasily poised between past and present, inheritance and eventuality, form and its erosion. It carries a Romantic conceptual heritage: to call a site a ruin is, more often than not, to contrast its present condition with a bygone state of stability and to induce mourning or nostalgia for what once stood. *Ruin* thus signals a way of diagnosing urban ills by shuttling among the tenses. It identifies deviations from the usual progressive sequence past–present–future and, discursively at least, punishes infractions from what the Joint Center and its peers had installed as the temporal framework for expert commentary on urban change. *Too late* and *too soon* depend on this normative sequence as a point of reference. The same might be said of *obsolescence*, a concept often used to further qualify abandoned urban scenes. Notions of the obsolete and anachronistic proved useful for those looking to flag architectural holdovers so as to render them further expendable. Urban reformers and complainers of all sorts had uttered the word for decades, often alongside the slipperier *blight*.[127] The precise manner in (and ease with) which these terms colonized urbanist discourse in the 1970s testifies to the influence of organized urban research and its manner of demarcating time and tense. This language also underwrote the entire resentful sociology of differential time orientation that Banfield perfected but *Beyond the Melting Pot* had helped normalize for urban studies. Its divisive glossary sounded technical but was shot through with moral condemnation and disavowal, and it became indispensable to the temporal weaponry of neoconservative urbanists.

Rightists, however, had no monopoly on premonitions of apocalypse.[128] In his reelection-year memoir, *The City* (1973), for instance, John Lindsay conjured visions of Brownsville, where rowhouses could be seen to "sag in vacant lines, the tin in their windows staring harshly over the sidewalks." He closed the book asserting, in language concordant with so much of the era's tensed social science, that "time has run out." (Unlike the *Beyond the Melting Pot* authors, he then pled for action: "Our cities will either be saved—now—or they will not be saved at all.")[129] Some years earlier, the "New York, N.Y." (1961) issue of reliably socialist *Dissent* aired its own intimations of death and decay, whether in "The City," Robert Nichols's poem that led off the volume ("Consider: a city wasted at the guts . . ."), or Edward T. Chase's polemic, which argued that traffic congestion, and the Port Authority's apparent insouciance about combating it, was the main toxin. His title was "New York Could Die."[130]

The bard of Brownsville, Alfred Kazin, also spent the 1970s dwelling on ruination. Working on the third and longest of his memoirs, *New York Jew* (1978), he visited the neighborhood yet again and found it "a foreign country now, a forbidden country. . . . It was a poison spot on the New York map."[131] *A Walker in the City* (1951) had hardly been unequivocal in exalting the past; indeed, it is precisely the oscillation between nostalgia and disavowal that gives Kazin's text its complexity and makes his tendentially left politics so difficult to classify. (At no point did he indulge Trotskyism, like most of his classmates, or embrace conservatism except of the cultural sort—in this last respect like his brother-in-law, the sociologist.)[132] *A Walker in the City*'s arc—go back to Brooklyn, wind through the streets, and leave—can give the sense that Kazin is remembering in order to forget, immersing himself one last time in order to reenact the very processes of abandonment and flight "beyond! beyond!" that make his memoir legible as a microhistory of Jewish American mobility. (Hence his fixation on Brownsville's borders and edges, and the maniacally precise social geography, charting block-by-block gradations of "Americanness" en route to what many Brooklynites still call "the city": Manhattan.)[133]

By the 1970s, though, the ruins begin to strike him differently. No longer the still-warm husks of a still-vital past, they become indices of a far more encompassing decline. "In the empty spaces of Brownsville we laid out our future," Kazin writes in *Our New York* (1989), a heavily illustrated book (with photographer David Finn) that reworks several passages from the memoirs. "Now there are a lot of empty spaces again, but it is the vacancy of breakdown." Streets that once spirited along the eager walker now host "street people" who "seriously impede traffic."[134] He notes that *Brownsville* has lately entered circulation as a metonym for urban desperation, quoting Boston mayor Kevin White's remark that there, on a tour hosted by John Lindsay, he had seen "the first tangible sign of the collapse of our civilization." Kazin had pored over the ruins of postwar Cologne, "loose mounds of brick . . . squashed houses with their insides open to the street." His German hosts were uniformly of the belief that "ruins meant a new start." In Europe, he reported, ruins offered "freedom from history."[135] Not so in the United States.

"The more the city seems to hang by a nail—the more we approach 'the last days of New York'—the wittier and more knowing the commentary," writes Kazin, scare-quoting the simplistic anti-urbanism that was ubiquitous by decade's end. "We are the best historians of our own death."[136] In the 1970s, he became a collector and comparer of "ruins." He was also, however, an ironist, reflexive about the category and the finality it implied. Few in American letters were ever more obsessed with reinhabiting the past, more credulous in the mystical power of a walk, a scent, a sound, a book, a bridge to transport the unsuspecting urbanite across vast stretches of time. In the 1970s, the landscapes left behind by large-scale abandonment seemed, at last, to prove Kazin's point, the temporal substrate of all his writing. We are not decoupled from history, nor were we ever. The ruins said so.

Urbanists inclined to culturalize the drivers of poverty tended to downplay the visual and tactile dimensions of the city. They generated nothing like Kazin's experience-near accounts, no learned psychogeographies that—without attempting to diagram it in any technical way—describe space richly and give a clear sense of urban morphology's emotional grip. Nonetheless, amid the neoconservative turn there were telling exceptions. Throughout his career but especially from the 1970s forward, Nathan Glazer maintained an acute if nonspecialist interest in urban architecture. It was New York's unmatched "heritage of variousness" that most compelled him. The city "has uniquely made itself and renews itself, often in surprising ways," he wrote in the 1990s. "In an age when this [dense, pre-automotive] form will never be seen again, it exerts its own fascination."[137] In a 1984 issue of *The Public Interest* devoted to architecture and public space, he opposed complex and polychronic Paris, a "city that works," to the "extravagant and awful" Albany abruptly etched into existence at Nelson Rockefeller's Empire State Plaza.[138] Paris, however, was a sideshow, and, realistically, Albany's built environment could anger a Downstater only so much. New York City lore was the one topic on which Glazer allowed himself the luxury of romanticism.[139] New York, he insisted all his life, had a past worth defending, and that past was of interest precisely because of the futures it harbored. As he wrote in 1992, the city "has served for eighty years or more as the defining image of the future."[140] "The historical city,"

Glazer wrote in 2007, using words whose patrimony runs straight through the Joint Center, "is not of one time, but of many times."[141]

Glazer's most particulate accounts of architecture arise in essays that oscillate between rage and dismay. Never content merely to score rhetorical points by announcing that ruin stalks the land, Glazer conjures the American city in three dimensions and attempts (with mixed results) to delineate exactly how specific cracks and crevices in its physical plant create or exacerbate social problems. Typical is his phrasing in the "Negroes" chapter of *Beyond the Melting Pot*, which describes "the psychic assaults of a hundred awful sights"; for him, the nonhuman environment is active, affecting unsuspecting bodies by way of the visual encounter.[142] (Ruins act, too. Attrition, weathering, and decay are activities; slowly collapsing is one of the main things that buildings can be said to do of their own accord.) In an infamous 1979 essay attacking graffiti in New York, Glazer extends this animism to walls bearing artists' tags, which, on his telling, "assault" the senses and "encourage" crime. "The mind," he writes, "will go on" in response, quickly inferring the city's deeper institutional brokenness and calculating that punishment will not be forthcoming. Disorder "reaches and affects every" passerby, and it instills "a prevailing sense of the incapacity of government."[143] Reading Glazer the conservative architectural critic, it can seem that every single urban mass, surface, or aperture might somehow emit an unwelcome charge, conditioning even more criminality than someone convinced prima facie of poverty's pathological "tangle" might be primed to expect of those living within its thrall. A single, if crooked, line runs from the early Glazer to the embittered late.

This did not mean that Glazer was an environmental determinist exactly, at least in the classic mold. He took pains to reason probabilistically: nothing is ever entirely certain, causation can only be inferred from scattered evidence, and buildings' design and upkeep make "significant" but nonetheless "indirect contributions" to the degree of civic "order" observable in local behavior.[144] The same could not be said of James Q. Wilson, the Joint Center's director when *Beyond the Melting Pot* was released and a beacon of disbelief who identified as a conservative years before his colleagues' apostasies. Following his schematic but influential *Varieties of Police Behavior: The Management of Law and Order in Eight Communities* (1968), Wilson cut a path from urban studies into criminology, and it was Wilson who, having digested the same stereotyped images of the "inner" city's "bombed-out" acres, went public on a massive scale with "Broken Windows" (1982, with George Kelling of Rutgers), the *Atlantic* article that launched a thousand punitive policing regimes mouthing "quality of life" and taking "order" as their highest value. (Measured in terms of uptake by policy makers, this magazine piece has likely had the broadest impact of any single publication with intellectual roots at the Joint Center.) The broken, punctured, deformed built environment nonverbally generates a steady stream of "communication," "messages" that solicit further disorder through sustained exposure. So argue Kelling and Wilson, flashing their cybernetic pedigree and catapulting over the wall that postwar debates had erected to separate physical and social, object- and subject-centric, approaches to planning. Ruined buildings, in short, produce ruined people.[145]

On July 30, 1975, at the very nadir of Gotham's fiscal woes, the *New York Times* ran a curious feature titled "18 Urban Experts Advise, Castigate, and Console the City on Its Problems." Pithy pull quotes, drawn from what had to have been fairly extensive conversations, covered the page. (The convener, reporter Israel Shenker, was a celebrated interviewer with an uncommon interest in Yiddish lexicography.) Together, they were meant to represent the full range of expert or otherwise authoritative opinion on the prospects for the nation's alpha metropolis. Conspicuous among the voices were scholars who had burnished their credentials at the Joint Center, and in every case, they lined up to castigate, not console. Robert C. Wood was among the eighteen. It had been quite a while since his year in charge, but, in a clear indication of the group's public profile, he was identified as the one-time director of the Joint Center, not, say, as a veteran of early HUD. Raymond Vernon resurfaced, credited with steering the NYMRS all those years ago. Concerned that there were now some 2,100 governments to set in order, not the mere 1,400 that Wood's volume had found, he urged New Yorkers to resign themselves to depopulation and make room for more corporate involvement in redevelopment. Nathan Glazer complained about fiscal fallout from the growing clout of public-sector unions. Edward Banfield averred to the paper of record that New York's revival was simply "not possible." This core message was echoed by the former optimist Jane Jacobs and also by her sparring partner Lewis Mumford, whose counsel was as follows: "Make the patient as comfortable as possible; it's too late to operate."[146]

First the center had augured impending urban collapse, claiming that it alone, in ways beyond the ken of ordinary city-dwellers, had the methods and cognitive bandwidth to make inferences about what lay over the horizon for New York and many lesser American cities. Now the center announced that the catastrophe had come, more or less on schedule—Q.E.D.—and lined up to issue itemized commentary explaining why it was forever insoluble. A decade and a half into what Rodwin and Meyerson had hatched as a liberal experiment encouraging far-reaching inquiry into "the city" so called, the center narrowed course, instead touting its own bona fides as the nation's indispensable experts on the city in crisis.[147] Founded to specify the relationship between systematic knowledge and the practice of planning, the Joint Center for Urban Studies and its alumni now disavowed the possibility of either. No future, indeed.

Coda
A Forward Signal

In the Reagan years, following on from its period of diminished expectations, exhausted prognoses, profuse budget cuts, and the attendant administrative and methodological restructuring toward economism, the Joint Center waned still further. It had able leadership, from 1982, in the person of H. James Brown, an energetic and well-connected microeconomist with the occasional Georgist streak, but its topical focus narrowed to the exclusive study of housing. Housing questions are fundamental, of course, but now even the gentlest suggestion that the center make moves toward a fully interdisciplinary account of the urban condition would have met with a chorus of disapproval. In 1985, it was renamed the Joint Center for Housing Studies. In 1988, MIT severed ties. Leadership kept the word *Joint* but redefined it to denote the center's shared affiliation with Harvard's GSD and the Kennedy School (formerly the Graduate School of Public Administration) rather than the two universities. The end of the high urban-studies era arrived with little fanfare, little open controversy, and no notable denunciations or embittered memoirs; there is no sense in trying to inject narrative drama where none resides. Well into the twenty-first century, the Joint Center for Housing Studies persists, a source much consulted by journalists, policy makers, and certain kinds of scholars for its quantitative data and the methodical but scarcely visionary forecasts such numbers equip.[1]

Ciudad Guayana, too, persists—its place in the annals of urban visioning periodically noted by scholars and largely ignored by locals. The city grew even beyond the population figures its patrons had projected, with some 877,000 residents as of the 2015 census, and it remains a distinctly sprawling second-tier metropolis, Venezuela's sixth largest, with state-owned steel and aluminum plants working away out beyond the ceremonial center. The percentage of residents dependent on automobiles for everyday mobility is higher than the Venezuelan average, even as only a minority can afford to buy their own. Commuters commonly rely on buses and a loosely regulated network of jitneys, and those commutes can balloon to two hours in each direction as workers traverse the twenty-five–mile linear city of Willo von Moltke's dreams. Industrial jobs remain concentrated west of the river while population skews to the east, at least a fifth of it sheltered in substandard circumstances. (The share of strictly informal—in the sense of unrecognized—housing is lower in Ciudad Guayana than in other Venezuelan cities because the CVG, in a move that fascinated Charles Abrams as an instance of self-help, early on devised a program by which to regularize squatters' tenancy.) Ordinary high-speed roads, executed with none of the breathless excitement that Avenida Guayana inspired in designers, connect it with Caracas, but the place still strikes most Venezuelans as fairly remote—a workaday industrial city nestled in scenic countryside but seldom a destination unto itself for purposes unrelated to business. Its turn as the future metropolis has long since passed.[2]

When referring to their hometown, few residents honor the nomenclature that Betancourt's planners devised. A 2019 newspaper article published on the fifty-eighth anniversary of the New Town's founding dubbed "Ciudad Guayana" *el nombre que nadie usa*—the name that nobody uses. *Guayacitanos* claim allegiance to the Guayana region, but when pressed, the relevant local toponyms are Puerto Ordaz, San Félix, Castillito, and other options that well predated Betancourt. The city has suffered as much as any in Venezuela during the half-century since developmentalism crested and Latin America became the test case for policies of structural adjustment that rolled back the lion's share of statist provision for which the New Town was such a ready signifier.[3]

When Hugo Chávez, the assertive socialist president whose every initiative was monitored closely from the north, came to power in 1998, he inherited an acute housing shortage. It outlasted him, even as Chávez continued the modern tradition of Venezuelan presidents initiating New Towns as vehicles for and monuments to their political ideals. In 1997, Rafael Caldera, the Christian Democrat (and philosophically anti-Marxist) president, had a small settlement called Ciudad Sucre built near the Colombian border to help repel guerrillas. In 2006, Chávez inaugurated Caribia, just west of Caracas, and the next year, atop the ruins of a major earthquake in Peru, sponsored the town of Simón Bolívar to house the displaced and instill goodwill.[4]

Formally, Ciudad Guayana's extant protocols for planning stress decentralization and citizen participation, with neighborhood associations officially recognized since 1977 and popular elections for municipal council a reality as of 1989. Yet its urban texture is radically uneven, with shacks marking the perimeter of elite subdivisions built for factory managers and CVG civil servants. Those inequalities have only deepened since 2013 under the *chavista* Nicolás Maduro. Since crippling shortages of food and gasoline began around 2016—and poverty rates nationwide ballooned upward of 80 percent, part of a catastrophe well beyond this book's scope—Ciudad Guayana's immiseration has been less often televised than that of Caracas, but it is no less severe. In an era defined by famine and something very close to existential crisis, the Venezuelan state has had concerns other than the founding of New Towns.

"Like generals," William Alonso wrote in 1963 at the peak of the Urban Renewal order, "city planners may be fated always to fight the day's battles with the outworn ideas of their last war." On this logic, state action would always arrive too late to realize the alternatives that its advocates had envisioned. This did not, however, mean that the future had been discarded as a cognitive horizon. Quite the opposite. Alonso continued: "Every plan is tentative, both because information is imperfect and because there is no final stage: there is always a future beyond the stage projected."[5] Marshall Kaplan made a compatible point in 1973, at Renewal's dusk. "We do not *yet* have" the ability to make reliable predictions, he wrote, arguing that, in fact, it may be the "marginal state of the planner's knowledge" about the "long range" that sustains the profession's signature future-orientation.[6] For Stephan Thernstrom, the same had to be said of the organized social research that, owing in large part to the Joint Center's powers of persuasion, planners had come to expect as a prelude and accompaniment to their programs of intervention. Urban social science had its own inertia—"Why stop now?"—and, in Thernstrom's view, survived only by way of its indefinite deferrals: "research now, freedom later," he quipped.[7]

For Alonso, Kaplan, and Thernstrom—just three examples of what by 1975 was a pervasive tendency—skepticism reigned. Along intellectual circuits that span the Northern and Southern Hemispheres, the Joint Center's pessimists arrived at a complex if self-exculpatory political temporality that fundamentally recast the terms of debate on the viability of the American city as a collective endeavor. Doubt achieved uncontested primacy over belief, as Rodwin had learned from Morris Cohen all those years ago but never applied with such single-minded, deflationary intent.[8] If doubt had already assumed pride of place in a self-critical, Trillingian liberalism, now it served to undercut just about any predictive or projective claim about the city to come. *Not yet* was the skeptics' temporal bulwark against more accelerated paths to urban repair that tacked at least as far left as the Great Society. As a conservative strategy of deferral, it worked to defuse reform while conspicuously dangling the possibility that expert knowledge—theirs—might, at some unknown moment, constellate in ways that would merit translation into concrete programs of provision and (re) distribution. Between 1959 and 1975, in short, the Joint Center's fundamental temporal operation shifted from planning to waiting, and to making others wait for tomorrows that would never come. Again, it misstates the political temporality of urban expertise, and of the straitened, diminished 1970s in the round, to charge that the future as such ever disappeared from calculation—that a pure presentism dislodged it or ever could have.[9] Urbanists known for knowing continued to invoke *the future metropolis, future-orientation*, and a host of cognate concepts with regularity as variables to explore. Rather than working to draw the future near, however, they now deployed concepts that let them push it farther and farther away, casting doubt on the robustness of their claims and dividing up the sorts of human minds capable of assessing their plausibility.

Not yet could disable the planning imagination out of hand. It became a vernacular way of hedging against the confidence projected by either staid, credentialed experts or those elements of the postwar left then attempting to induce rupture and reconstruction. Recoded, however, it could just as easily supply the temporal and political foundation for planners' last best hopes. Amid the great diversity of liberal skepticisms and skeptical conservatisms that the dominant styles of postwar urbanism proved able to encompass, the one label that no one seemed willing to claim was "utopian"—Rodwin with his jabs at the British New Towns and the American decentralists who loved them, Meyerson with his calls to "reform reform," and far more caustic critics who saw in Ciudad Guayana a mere retread of Brasília, von Moltke's preemptive denials to the contrary. Yet, as Ernst Bloch put it in *The Principle of Hope* (1938–1947)—an oracular, expressly utopian text that, along with *The Spirit of Utopia* (1918), entered the repertoire of the New Left in translation—"thinking means venturing beyond." The "Not-Yet" (*Noch-Nicht*), for Bloch, propels all thought worthy of the name; it issues "a forward signal which enables us to overtake" the inertial past and present.[10] It became an indispensable category not only for the postwar right, but also for precisely the twentieth-century utopians they subjected to such ridicule.

"True action in the present," reads *The Principle of Hope*, is "unenclosed both backwards and forwards." Every bit as much as the doyens of urban studies, Bloch called attention to the power of explanations that straddle the tenses.

Unlike them, he understood the integrated sequence of past, present, and future to be a "totality" (*Gesamtheit*) in the specifically Marxist sense: "Marxist philosophy is that of the future, therefore also of the future in the past." Yet, rather than ventriloquize vulgar leftisms given to telic guarantees about outcomes, Bloch savored the future's very unknowability, letting it give momentum to his thought and politics. On his telling, the "Not-Yet-Conscious" (*Noch-Nicht-Bewusst*) and "Not-Yet-Become" (*Noch-Nicht-Geworderi*) are not (yet) even concepts, but they still exert a pull: "The world," he writes, "is full of propensity towards something, tendency towards something, latency of something" that by its nature cannot be named in advance.[11] Utopians worth reading, that is, know that they do not know in any recognizably positivist way. It is precisely by deferring its closure that they propose to make the future.[12]

This book has expressed hesitation when discussing instrumental approaches to the writing of urban history, those born of the expectation that mastery of some demarcated past will afford straightforward projections onto present affairs and those to come. Yet this has, throughout, been not only an intellectual history of the urban future as surmised and administered, but a future-oriented history that itself resists closure and connects in multiple and tentacular ways with debates that roil urban life in the twenty-first century. The Joint Center for Urban Studies has passed, but its work reverberates. It haunts the conceptual repertoire of urban studies as well as the array of organizations chartered in its name: the intertwined forms and forums of urban knowledge, ideas and institutions, the atmosphere and the network. In ever more specialized styles of research on cities and in loose-lipped public discourse on the same, deep grammars established by the Joint Center live on, even or especially as their principles contradict.

In organizational terms, it has heirs all across the urbanist academy. Some of the research units formed just after the war remain active and are fixtures in the alphabet soup of interdisciplinarity even as the methods and lingo of what passes for urban studies have changed (and the supersession of traditional disciplines, ascendant at midcentury, no longer seems at all novel or in much need of justification). Newer studies centers still pay titular homage to the *urban*, *metropolitan*, or *regional*, but many look elsewhere for their thematic unity. Their scalar imaginaries, moreover, tend to eclipse national borders. They embed instances of urban life within far broader spatial constellations and acknowledge the priority of global explanations approached "from the South" in ways that the Joint Center and its peers never seriously considered—least of all at Ciudad Guayana, which the vast majority of the Cantabrigians treated as a submissive theater for Northern intervention even as its people and ecologies actively fed back on the planners. Comparative urban research between presumptively bounded cities or nations—along with studies that purport to use a single case study as a scalable proxy for other, ontologically coequal places—has given way to more relational perspectives in which the transnational, power-laden movement of ideas among distant spatial units sits firmly in the foreground.[13]

One of the more conspicuous recent attempts at reorganization has been the Urban Theory Lab (UTL) that opened at Harvard's GSD in 2014 and then, in 2020, moved to the University of Chicago. In its ambitions to generality, its collaborative mode of work, and much else besides, the experiment sounds decidedly postwar, an ORU *après la lettre*. And yet the UTL's conceptual foundations reside in director Neil Brenner's much-debated attempt to explode what some have called "methodological cityism." The UTL's alternative approach refocuses inquiry on "planetary urbanization," tracing global processes and "operations" which touch down in territorial entities that pass for *the city* but refusing to dignify its boundaries as a spatial container of much consequence. (One of the group's appealing features has been its commitment to geovisualization, but its scholars seem disinclined to publish a map that shows any one city in detail.) The scale has changed; indeed, scale as a concept has become the object of much theoretical contestation. Yet the midcentury moment has not been sealed off entirely. Brenner's notion that theory—theory?—is best pursued in a lab has always seemed like an off-modern in-joke, which no one seems to get, about the longstanding impulse to organize research.[14]

The case of the Joint Center, a group Brenner never names despite his institutional location, allows us to consider reperiodizing the development of urban theory across the long twentieth century. In this historiography, the postwar period remains somewhat enigmatic. It has been abundantly studied, but as a matter of intellectual history, it is far harder to distill into a single dominant dispensation, diagram, or school akin to Robert Park and the Chicago sociologists, whose prominence crested in the 1920s; the postmodern Los Angeles School, whose rejection of Chicago's hegemony was conspicuous by the end of the 1980s; or the itinerant UTL. Perhaps this book has furnished the materials to nominate the Joint Center for that role. Spatial scale is a useful heuristic through which to organize the usual sequence of urban-theoretic begats: the Chicago sociologists ontologized *the city* as the naturally given, bounded (if expanding) unit, categorically distinct from its hinterland; the Joint Center and its peers thematized the spreading *metropolis* or *metropolitan region*, which enlaced the urban core with its many and jurisdictionally chaotic suburban fringes; the Angelenos posited a multicentered *post-metropolis* of megaregional scope, responsive to the foundational influence of the automobile in imparting structure to their base of operations; and the Brenner circle, building on a selective reading of Henri Lefebvre, has scaled up to the entire *planet* and charged all foregoing schools with sedentism.[15] In this sequence, the basic unit of study and object of intervention has only grown larger in horizontal extent, with the postwar shift from city to metropolis marking the first key dilation.

When theorists acknowledge it at all, the timescale of planning tends to covary with spatial scale: "comprehensive" planners elaborating "whole" new cities and regions have seemed to be inveterate long-termists, while local, neighborhood, or community planners set more modest, near-term goals. It seems significant, then, that one of the central institutions urging an expansive metropolitan focus for nominally urban studies at midcentury came to proliferate forms of social science that would foreshorten the planner's time horizon—a paradox that has tacitly underwritten this entire book.

Politically, the Joint Center's legacy provokes ambivalence. In its variegated career can be found antecedents to both the most self-assured contemporary voices presuming to steer the urban future and those most allergic to systematic foresight.

Echoes of the early, system-building Joint Center resound today in planning's halls of power. In an age of big data generated without pause by "users" of urban space, *smart cities* has become the label applied to a wide range of basically techno-optimist programs attempting governance through and by that data. Algorithms and other technologies of automated prediction have become the predominant ways of knowing cities and visualizing their impending development. *Expertise* is no longer by any means the prevailing watchword, but it has new synonyms. Smart technologies presume quantitative reasoning without ever seriously questioning its descriptiveness; they place a premium on calculability, even as absolute epistemological certainty about the future has become something only the gauche own up to desiring. As engines of prediction, urbanists' new tools are probabilistic through and through—they optimize without perfecting, manage risk without ever annulling it—but they nonetheless entrench the sense that every urban phenomenon worth caring about could be quantified and known within a specified interval of confidence. The Joint Center's early advocacy for computational methods and the theory of "large-scale social systems" still informs planning's technocratic frontline, narrowly reconstituted some decades after the despairing and defunded pronounced planning's death.[16]

Time and the future, as conceptual preoccupations, came onto midcentury planners' agenda because of perceived shifts in the pace and extent of urban change. Since the turn of the millennium, popular discourse on urbanization has become dominated by questions of what since Ruth Glass—who led her own Centre for Urban Studies, founded 1958, at University College London—we have learned to call gentrification. The most common way of euphemizing that cycle of displacement and replacement is to say, without specifying agents or apportioning blame, that cities "are changing."[17] Knowing that change is occurring, however, does not substitute for asking how or why, and on the pages of newspaper real-estate sections everywhere, it has become an inexhaustible pastime to speculate about which "up-and-coming" districts of a given city are next in line. Forecasting has taken the place of a richer, counterfactual urban futurism informed by history, able to question the temporal dynamics at play, and willing to intervene when catastrophe looms. Forecasters predict, but they do not consciously prefigure alternative futures.[18]

The Joint Center's immanent critique of planning, too, has had implications in domains seemingly distant from urban development and at scales beyond the putative cityism of postwar research. Two decades into the twentieth century, mainline American debates over social policy once again invoke the New Deal and Johnson's Great Society, even if these histories are routinely subject to mendacious misrepresentation and preening disavowal. The suite of policies envisioned under what has come to be called the Green New Deal has as yet functioned mainly as a provocation, but in many rhetorical and some concrete ways, plans and planning, futures and foresight, are again touchstones in at least one big tent of American politics; see, if nothing else, the infrastructure debates of the early Biden administration, the bipartisan reassessment of industrial policy, and the persistent if embattled Warrenite imperative to have "a plan for that." Their opponents, too often defaulting to a planless nihilism, reprise antisocial styles of politics that broke open under Reagan but truly took shape during the postwar standoffs between organized researchers and organized resistance, those who prefer to know the city and those who prefer not to.

Crisis or no crisis? Future or no future? These two axes mark out the terrain of admissible discourse on urban life during the period lent structure by the Joint Center. In rough outline, they underlie the familiar shift from Great Society liberalism to neoconservative critique that this book has sought to recast. The terminology may seem anachronistic in the 2020s, when neither *neoconservative* nor *neoliberal*, its economistic successor, seems adequate any longer to encapsulate the forces that animate the American right wing. A consuming, disconsolate politics that traffics in malice and racialized conspiracy has ushered out the range of postwar conservatisms fed on social science and at least able to disentangle an earned skepticism about solutions from an unearned dismissal of the very solidarities that urban problems were said to threaten in the first place.

Yet there are clear continuities as well. Crisis talk has been resurgent. The new "silent majority"—a phrase exhumed, unreconstructed, during the 2016 election cycle—has often sounded Banfieldian in the extreme, with its figurehead invoking superannuated specters of utter degradation in blue Chicago ("living in hell"), Philadelphia (where "bad things happen"), and, always, New York ("dying"). The performative anti-urbanism of the new radical right adduces *crisis* when it seems expedient, and in this respect, it is revivalist to the core. With the fiftieth anniversary of *The Unheavenly City* as a pretext, even its untouchable author has lately enjoyed a wave of veneration. In 2020, in the wake of remarkable nationwide demonstrations against racialized police violence prompted by events in South Minneapolis, veteran conservative Thomas Sowell argued for the book's contemporary relevance in the pages of the *Claremont Review*, redoubt of the bellicose "West Coast Straussians" and longtime employer of Banfield's son, Elliott, as its principal illustrator.[19] That same year in *City Journal*, organ of the rightist Manhattan Institute, Kevin Kosar announced the arrival of "another era of urban crisis" defined by wanton street crime and emboldened forms of left resistance. Past was prologue: Banfield, Kosar averred, wrote in "a time much like our own." Kosar dubbed *The Unheavenly City* a "Socratic" book in a uniquely Banfieldian sense: if there was indeed a crisis, its author had considered "all possible solutions" and found them, to the one, inoperable. Kosar's title was "The Perils of 'Doing Something.'"[20] This rhetoric, too, is the Joint Center's bequest.

Its bifurcated legacy—plan or no plan?—maps intuitively enough onto the center's earlier and later stages, with the break occurring around 1965 under Wilson. Yet the critical point is not simply that minds changed or, more prosaically still, that new personnel supplanted old under the same institutional moniker. Rather, the theoretical unity, epistemological confidence, and overriding optimism projected in *The Future Metropolis* did not mask but showcase a commitment to doubt as the first principle. Rodwin, Meyerson, and their circle earnestly believed that the systems and generalizations definitive of any scientific urban studies had been built up to, earned, only by way of a skepticism more basic than any other fact or value. This was precisely what social science was supposed to be adding—enriching while checking less self-aware Modernisms. Thus, when that skepticism radicalized, undercutting the claims on futurity that the center had broadcast as evidence of its own legitimacy, the shift came from within. It was a dilation of that commitment to ambivalence— a will to believe always tempered by a readiness to disbelieve and disavow—that Lionel Trilling, most famously, had counted as the indispensable hallmark of the liberal imagination.[21]

Now, planners' premonitions of the future are dominated by the realities of planetary climate change and by a set of ecological phenomena to which the Joint Center—and the rest of urban studies, pre-McHarg—paid essentially no mind.[22] (In 1972, two years after the first Earth Day, Robert C. Wood could still scorn as mere "escapism" the displacement of "the city" by "the environment" as the leading object of consternation.)[23] As sea levels rise and anthropogenic "natural" disasters increase in frequency, a new and still-piecemeal regime of anticipatory governance has made the projection of genuinely catastrophic futures, titrated by fractions of a degree Celsius, an ordinary feature of political debate. Climate politics are a politics of time, denominated in decades but always nested within very long-term thinking, geologists' "deep time," that routinely projects conditions some ten thousand years into the future.[24] Bruce Braun, following Bruno Latour, has argued that climate crisis has at last put an end to the linear developmental temporalities that freeze past, present, and future in the ordinary sequence assumed by clock time or grammatical tense. On a planet whose occupation is under existential threat, they contend, time now originates with "what is coming": in the French, *l'avenir* as distinct from *le future*. The future intervenes anew on the present. Climate science assists in "the revelation of things that are coming toward us."[25]

Amid climate anxieties, cartography, too, has become differently futurist, lately granted a ubiquity in political calculation last seen during the Second World War.[26] Grim documents visualizing the probable spatial distribution of either fire or flood correspond to scenarios empirically substantiated by tens of thousands of scientists—change will continue, nostalgia only distracts, and there exists no pristine planetary nature to go back to—but their projections also serve a rhetorical function foreign to the early Joint Center (and certainly to Raymond Vernon's inertial forecasting study prepared in the run-up). Climate visualizations depict darkened, chaotic futures, but they do so precisely in order to stave them off. Such projections are "counter-performative" instruments in Donald MacKenzie's sense, engines rather than mere cameras, in whose confirmation no forecaster could possibly take pleasure.[27] Their affective register is that of dread; dread shades into anger; anger, they wager, galvanizes forms of action that, once codified in international law, will lessen or reverse the planet's disruption.

Perhaps. Although shared if uneven global exposure to catastrophe would plausibly seem like the occasion for the triumph of long-termism—a universally held, solidaristic future-orientation that Banfield assured us could never obtain across class and color—climate change has instead called forth a new species of American nihilism predicated on refusals to plan, think ahead, or much care what the future holds, even or especially when experts suggest we should. Here, climate politics have revived and intensified the full range of postwar maneuvers against foresight as a habit of mind. Denial of climate crisis in word and deed, a move lifted directly from the political manual of the late Joint Center and other professional skeptics they cultivated, has become a core conviction of the long-since-neoconservative right. From it follow redoubled efforts to discredit even the most modest attempts to invest, now, in the mitigation of impending threats to urban life: sea walls, sponge cities, managed retreat from known floodplains, densification of settlement, electrification of transit, or the global compacts on emissions that would compel some combination of these. *Not yet.*

Time, wrote Marc (not Ernst) Bloch just before his death in the war whose cessation opened the horizons that this book's protagonists spent entire careers seeking to harness, is "the very plasma in which events are immersed." No special justification is needed for undertaking a history of urban temporality rather than urban events. By necessity, as Bloch further observed, historians of every kind arrive belatedly to their subjects. That belatedness, and with it the disjuncture across which we attempt to establish our grip on the past, is an inbuilt feature of historical writing.[28] It cannot be otherwise. There is no reason, however, to conclude, as the Joint Center so often did, that the belatedness of the diagnosis must somehow ensure the futility of action prescribed in response—that maneuvers made late in the imputed sequence of development will always come too late to remake what lies ahead, unformed, unwritten. In fact, as too few since that war have let themselves admit, there are only urban futures, in the plural, and there has never been one central point from which to watch them all draw near.

Acknowledgments

"Passaic seems full of holes," wrote Robert Smithson in late 1967, having boarded a bus outbound from New York's Port Authority with time on his hands, "and those holes in a sense are the monumental vacancies that define, without trying, the memory-traces of an abandoned set of futures." Scholarship can feel this way—each gap, each archival silence or oversight, potentially opening onto another book entirely. If this book, conceived not altogether far from Passaic, holds together, it is due in large part to the trust and generosity of others.

It has benefited from the support, financial and otherwise, of several institutions. A semester at Dumbarton Oaks, formally part of Harvard University but sited on unreasonably pleasant grounds in the Georgetown section of Washington, DC, marked an inflection point in the book's development. There, supported by the Mellon Initiative in Urban Landscape Studies, John Beardsley convened and energized a remarkable interdisciplinary group. Thanks, in particular, to Jeanne Haffner, John Dean Davis, Deirdre Moore, Abbey Stockstill, Sara Jensen Carr, Hartmut Troll, Verena Conley, Margot Lystra, and Anatole Tchikine.

A shorter Nunis Fellowship at the Huntington Library in San Marino, California—also set within an impressive garden—afforded access to useful materials in the history of city and regional planning. Later on, a month-long McColl Fellowship at the American Geographical Society Library, once a denizen of Audubon Terrace in Manhattan but proudly housed since the late 1970s at the University of Wisconsin–Milwaukee, was just as valuable.

During the last full semester before the pandemic, Cornell University's Department of City and Regional Planning, and specifically its Clarence S. Stein Institute for Urban and Landscape Studies, was a generous patron and host. The company of Jeff Chusid, Nick Klein, Tom Campanella, Aaron Sachs, and Austen Torres Davis made this book better: Jeff over numerous symposia and meals, Aaron on two critical laps around Beebe Lake, and Austen on the home front. During that same fall term, Jeffrey Blankenship devoted a memorable day to schooling a novice on the landscapes of Rochester. "Some things can be done as well as others."

Since 2021, this work has been sustained by the University of Southern California and the Berggruen Institute. At Berggruen, amid LA's "ruins in reverse," Nils Gilman has cultivated fellowship in the truest sense. Jonathan Blake and Claire Isabel Webb have organized complex thought on the planet and its futures. During its final stages, the book benefited from the heterodox insights of Stuart Candy, Devika Dutt, Vincent Ialenti, Dominic Boyer, Anna Weichselbraun, Lois Rosson, Cameron Brinitzer, Naomi Oreskes, Alexander Clapp, Harpreet Sareen, Inho Choi, Ziyaad Bhorat, Gabriel Kahan, Boris Shoshitaishvili, Leila Lorenzo, Amelia Sargent, and Jennifer Bourne. Mike McCarthy asked the hard questions.

USC's Center on Science, Technology, and Public Life has become an interdisciplinary crossroads of considerable excitement thanks to the acumen of Andy Lakoff and Emily Rose Anderson, who cohosted most of the Berggruen fellows named above. Many colleagues have since 2022 made USC's School of Architecture a second home on campus: Alison Hirsch, Alex Robinson, Esther Margulies, Aroussiak Gabrielian, Takako Tajima, Jessica Henson, Sascha Delz, Faiza Moatasim, Ginger Nolan, Alvin Huang, Vittoria Di Palma, Trudi Sandmeier, and Amy Murphy. Elsewhere in the USC orbit, Meredith Drake Reitan, Phil Ethington, Paul Lerner, Vanessa Schwartz, Juan De Lara, David Sloane, and Marlon Boarnet have been key interlocutors. A generous grant from USC's Center for City Design helped defray production costs.

For recollections of some of the events discussed in the later chapters, thanks go to Bish Sanyal, Phillip Clay, Alan Altshuler, and Tridib Banerjee, as well as to Larry Vale for his willingness to forge some of these connections and for his overall enthusiasm about the project.

Many portions of this book are the better for having been dissected at conferences and workshops, including those of the Urban History Association, the Society for American City and Regional Planning History, the Society for US Intellectual History, the Society for the History of Recent Social Science, the American Association of Geographers, the Regional Studies Association, and the annual Researching New York conference in Albany. At UHA and SACRPH, conversations with Alison Isenberg, Owen Gutfreund, Robert Fairbanks, Kara Schlichting, Kristian Taketomo, Brian Tochterman, and Mika Mäkelä have been especially beneficial. There and at the Vernacular Architecture Forum, contact with Matt Lasner, Francesca Ammon, and Brian Goldstein has also been instructive. Garrett Dash Nelson, a region unto himself, has been a valued confidant and collaborator.

ACKNOWLEDGMENTS

At S-USIH, the perspectives of Ethan Schrum, Hunter Heyck, Lawrence Glickman, Steven Conn, Christian Christiansen, Elizabeth Tandy Shermer, and Mario Rewers helped refine the book's arguments. The HISRESS circle, first in Toronto and then in Uppsala, subjected portions of this book to the fine-grained scrutiny for which its workshops have become known. Sincere thanks to Jeff Pooley, Jamie Cohen-Cole, Per Wisselgren, Mark Solovey, Andy Jewett, David Engerman, Chris Loss, Philippe Fontaine, Leah Gordon, and Bregje van Eekelen.

Audiences at San José State University's Institute for Metropolitan Studies and the University of Pittsburgh's Humanities Center were notably generous in the days immediately preceding the pandemic. Thanks are due to Gordon Douglas and Anthony Raynsford at SJSU. Dan Kubis and Drew Armstrong were superior hosts at Pitt, where Michael Glass, Nida Rehman, and Jean-Paul Addie supplied incisive commentary.

Portions of chapters 3 and 4 were originally published in the journal *Planning Perspectives* and the book *Infrastructural Times: Temporality and the Making of Global Urban Worlds* (eds. Addie, Glass, and Nelles). For permission to reproduce that material, thanks to Taylor & Francis Ltd. and Bristol University Press, respectively.

Thanks to Taylor & Francis Ltd. for permission to reproduce fig. 2.2, from Kevin Lynch and Lloyd Rodwin, "A Theory of Urban Form," *Journal of the American Institute of Planners* 24 (1958): 201–214. Copyright © 1958 by the American Planning Association, Chicago, Illinois.

Thanks to MIT Press Journals for permission to reproduce fig. 3.5, from Kevin Lynch, "The Pattern of the Metropolis," *Daedalus* 90, no. 1 (Winter 1961): 79–98; and fig. 4.11, from Edmund Bacon, "Urban Process," *Daedalus* 97, no. 4 (Fall 1968): 1165–1178. Copyright © 1961 and 1968 by the American Academy of Arts and Sciences.

Thanks to MIT Press for permission to reproduce fig. 4.8, from Donald Appleyard, Kevin Lynch, and John R. Myer, *The View from the Road*, p. 60. Copyright © 1965 by the Massachusetts Institute of Technology.

Thanks also to MIT Press for permission to reproduce figs. 4.5, 4.6, and 4.10, from Donald Appleyard, *Planning a Pluralist City: Conflicting Realities in Ciudad Guayana*, figs. 7.40 (p. 139), 8.30 (p. 186), and 9.18 (p. 203). Copyright © 1976 by the Massachusetts Institute of Technology.

Thanks *also* to MIT Press for permission to reproduce figs. 4.4, 4.9, and 6.2, from Lloyd Rodwin and Associates, *Planning Urban Growth and Regional Development: The Experience of the Guayana Program of Venezuela*, figs. 6.8 (p. 135), 23.1 (pp. 425–427), and 23.2 (p. 437). Copyright © 1969 by the Massachusetts Institute of Technology.

260 ACKNOWLEDGMENTS

And thanks to Harvard University Press for permission to reproduce fig. 5.3, from the cover of James Q. Wilson, ed., *The Metropolitan Enigma: Inquiries into the Nature and Dimensions of America's "Urban Crisis."* Copyright © 1967 by the Chamber of Commerce of the United States of America. Copyright © 1968 by the President and Fellows of Harvard College.

Numerous archivists and librarians have assisted this project, performing essential labor that too often recedes from view. Thanks to those at the American Geographical Society Library, University of Wisconsin–Milwaukee; Rare Book and Manuscript Library, Columbia University; Division of Rare and Manuscript Collections, Cornell University Library; Special Collections, Frances Loeb Library, Graduate School of Design, Harvard University; Harvard University Archives; Manuscript Division, Library of Congress; Massachusetts Institute of Technology Institute Archives and Special Collections; University Archives and Records Center, University of Pennsylvania; and Rockefeller Archive Center, Sleepy Hollow, New York. Of these, special thanks go to Inés Zalduendo at Harvard's GSD, Georgia Brown and Marcy Bidney at the AGSL in Milwaukee, and Jack Meyers, who enriched a short visit to the Rockefeller Archive Center with warm conversation and a tour of the Cold War bunker where its materials are kept.

It was Michael McGandy who first welcomed manuscript and author into the fold at Cornell University Press—and turned up for a decisive meeting when the latter happened to spend a full semester on fellowship in Ithaca. After the seemingly irreplaceable Michael departed the press, it was Mahinder Kingra who assumed the project, and he, too, has been an attentive, wise reader and advocate. Both fundamentally get it. Also on the editorial side, India Miraglia has been a great help, as have Karen Hwa, Michelle Scott, and Amanda Montes de Oca during the production process. Amron Lehte prepared the index with care. Thanks are due as well to Rosemary Wakeman and Samuel Zipp for farsighted comments on the first draft.

This book is not based on a dissertation, but it took shape on the edges of one produced within the Department of Geography at the University of California, Berkeley. The late Paul Groth, who chaired that project, was the first to call its author a geographer. Sub rosa, his mind and eye have informed this venture in intellectual history. He is sorely missed. Jake Kosek vitalized the project through his camaraderie and constant questioning. Louise Mozingo, of the Department of Landscape Architecture and Environmental Planning, sustained it with careful readings and wonderful repartee.

Elsewhere in the department and across Berkeley's campus, contact with Nathan Sayre, Michael Johns, Dick Walker, Teresa Caldeira, Margaretta Lovell, Michael Dear, Marion Fourcade, and, perhaps crucially, John Lie helped formulate questions to which, several years later and many degrees removed, this book offers some answers.

Those years at Berkeley would have been far less pleasant without the company of friends and scholars including John Elrick, Alexander Arroyo, Kevin Block, Lance Owen, Will Payne, Alex Werth, Rebecca Elliott, Ben Shestakofsky, Alex Roehrkasse, Sarah Cowan, Sunmin Kim, Sujin Eom, Carlos Bustamante, Carter Koppelman, Beth Pearson, Jonah Stuart Brundage, Kappy Mintie, Elaine Brown Stiles, and Ghigo DiTommaso. All of the conversations we began then will continue indefinitely across vast tracts of space and time.

During a second spell at Berkeley, Seth Lunine, John Isom, Nick Anderman, Xander Lenc, Evangeline McGlynn, and the indelible Josh Mandel enriched the project through expansive conversation, collaboration, and immanent critique. With Nick, the itinerary has since swerved by countless containers and cranes in Oakland, Long Beach, San Pedro, and the greater Great Lakes.

During the writing process, Brant Palko and Ryan Rodier's solid-state history lessons helped keep time, as did Scott Miller, Glenn Mercer, Arthur Russell, Frank Boscoe, and Lawrence.

Philip Bartholomew Rocco has had a singular role in this entire body of work. Our itinerary began in the summer of 2010, inland, and we have spent the years since establishing a language to make sense of the American scene.

My brother and brother-in-law—in Chicago and of the Region—continue to expand the map with each passing year. They are models of urban curiosity: the very business we are in.

My parents are readers, and this work bears the traces of an upbringing, surrounded by books, in which reading was by consensus one of the basic responsibilities and delights. They have given this author a great deal.

In the final analysis, this book, and everything else, belongs to Katherine.

Notes

Abbreviations

- AAGR   Association of American Geographers Records, AGSL MSS 23, American Geographical Society Library, University of Wisconsin–Milwaukee
- CAP   Charles Abrams Papers, #3086, Division of Rare and Manuscript Collections, Cornell University Library
- CGR   Joint Center for Urban Studies, Reports on Ciudad Guayana (1960–1965), Reginald R. Isaacs Files, Special Collections, Frances Loeb Library, Graduate School of Design, Harvard University
- CSP   Clarence Stein Papers, #3600, Division of Rare and Manuscript Collections, Cornell University Library
- CUL   Rare Book and Manuscript Library, Columbia University
- DHC   Departmental Histories Collection, AGSL MSS 25, American Geographical Society Library, University of Wisconsin–Milwaukee
- DPMP   Daniel P. Moynihan Papers, Manuscript Division, Library of Congress
- DRP   David Rockefeller Papers, Rockefeller Archive Center, Sleepy Hollow, New York
- FFR   Ford Foundation Records, Rockefeller Archive Center, Sleepy Hollow, New York
- GECC   Grady E. Clay Collection, Special Collections, Frances Loeb Library, Graduate School of Design, Harvard University
- GPR   Joint Center for Urban Studies, Records of the Guayana Project, AC 292, Massachusetts Institute of Technology Institute Archives and Special Collections
- GSDH   GSD History Collection: Academic Affairs, Special Collections, Frances Loeb Library, Graduate School of Design, Harvard University
- JEBP   John Ely Burchard Papers, MC 76, Massachusetts Institute of Technology Institute Archives and Special Collections
- KLP   Kevin Lynch Papers, MC 208, Massachusetts Institute of Technology Institute Archives and Special Collections
- LRP   Lloyd Rodwin Papers, MC 490, Massachusetts Institute of Technology Institute Archives and Special Collections
- MMP   Martin Meyerson Papers (UPT 50 M613M), University Archives and Records Center, University of Pennsylvania
- OMRR   Office of the Messrs. Rockefeller Records, Rockefeller Archive Center, Sleepy Hollow, New York

PIH   Pioneers in Housing: An Oral History Project, Manuscript Division, Library of Congress
PNYP   Papers of Paul N. Ylvisaker, HUGFP 142, Harvard University Archives
RPAR   Regional Plan Association Records, #2688, Division of Rare and Manuscript Collections, Cornell University Library
RRIP   Reginald R. Isaacs Papers, #8468, Division of Rare and Manuscript Collections, Cornell University Library
TPP   Papers of Talcott Parsons, HUGFP 15.xx and HUGFP 42.xx, Harvard University Archives
WVMP   Papers of the Estate of Willo von Moltke, Special Collections, Frances Loeb Library, Graduate School of Design, Harvard University
WZP   Wilbur Zelinsky Papers, AGSL MSS 32, American Geographical Society Library, University of Wisconsin–Milwaukee

Introduction

1. Alfred Kazin, "March 22, 1946," in *Alfred Kazin's Journals*, ed. Richard M. Cook (New Haven: Yale University Press, 2011), 91.
2. Alfred Kazin, *New York Jew* (New York: Knopf, 1978), 152.
3. Alfred Kazin, "December 15, 1958," in *Alfred Kazin's Journals*, 238.
4. Kazin, "March 22, 1946," 91.
5. Alfred Kazin, "May 5, 1942," in *Alfred Kazin's Journals*, 36; Alfred Kazin, *On Native Grounds: An Interpretation of Modern American Prose Literature* (New York: Reynal & Hitchcock, 1942). City and *suburb* are relative terms, and their definitions have varied considerably since the nineteenth century. Brownsville, along with many other Brooklyn neighborhoods south and east of Prospect Park, could plausibly have been called *suburban* just two decades before Kazin wrote; see, for example, Lewis Mumford, "The Wilderness of Suburbia," *New Republic*, September 7, 1921.
6. Alfred Kazin, *A Walker in the City* (New York: Harcourt, 1951). On Kazin, Richard M. Cook, *Alfred Kazin: A Biography* (New Haven: Yale University Press, 2007), is comprehensive; and on *Walker in the City*, see capable commentary by Edward Mendelson, *Moral Agents: Eight Twentieth-Century American Writers* (New York: New York Review Books, 2015), 49–77; and Stephen Miller, *Walking New York* (Bronx: Fordham University Press, 2015), 162–177. Irving Howe writes vividly of his own youthful walks in the Bronx; see *A Margin of Hope: An Intellectual Autobiography* (New York: Harcourt Brace Jovanovich, 1982), 27, 45, 46; see also Irving Howe, "New York in the Thirties," *Dissent* 8 (Summer 1961): 241–250. His *World of Our Fathers* (New York: Harcourt Brace Jovanovich, 1976) is the *locus classicus* of postwar Jewish American nostalgia. Kazin is typically discussed in the company of the "New York Intellectuals," whose tribulations dominated an earlier generation of scholarship in US intellectual history. Quite a number of commentators have asked whether Kazin can be called representative of the larger group. For Irving Howe, "The New York Intellectuals," *Dissent* (October 1969): 29–51, at 29, Kazin was "more or less typical" despite his "distinctive outcroppings of temperament." Daniel Bell deemed Kazin, his brother-in-law, the ideal-typical "New York Intellectual"; Daniel Bell and Pearl Kazin Bell, interview by William R. Keylor, April 1972, Richard Hofstadter Project, CUL. Alan M. Wald, *The New York Intellectuals: The Rise and Decline of the Anti-Stalinist Left from*

the 1930s to the 1980s (Chapel Hill: University of North Carolina Press, 1987), 11, 360, claims that he was "only peripherally involved" and that his biography bears "many uncharacteristic features." Morris Dickstein, *Double Agent: The Critic and Society* (New York: Oxford University Press, 1992), 151, 154, noting a "breathless aphoristic brilliance" that puts Kazin stylistically in league with the group, considers his abiding interest in the past unusual; Howe calls it the "style of brilliance" (41). William Barrett, *The Truants: Adventures among the Intellectuals* (New York: Doubleday, 1982), 69–74, makes the case for Philip Rahv, the editor of *Partisan Review*, and notes that circle's dislike of Kazin (46).

7. Richard Cook notes that Kazin forever after referred to the 1942–1945 period as "the break," both in history's larger arc and in his personal affairs; *Alfred Kazin's Journals*, 41.

8. Kazin, *Walker in the City*, 41.

9. Kazin, "May 8, 1949," in *Alfred Kazin's Journals*, 129. Here Kazin was likely channeling authors such as Stephen Crane and Henry James, both of whose attempts to personify the built environment he discusses in Alfred Kazin, *A Writer's America: Landscape in Literature* (New York: Knopf, 1988), 117, 127, 171–173. Although it appeared late in his life, Kazin conceived of this book in the 1950s, with the working title *The Western Island*; *Alfred Kazin's Journals*, 152.

10. Kazin, *New York Jew*, 210, 155.

11. Kazin, *Walker in the City*, 171, 172. Delmore Schwartz found Kazin's paeans to the past unbearable and called him a "psalm-singing peasant"; James Atlas, *Delmore Schwartz: The Life of an American Poet* (New York: Farrar, Straus & Giroux, 1977), 256. William Barrett, recalling a boyhood in Queens, wrote, "I am not a walker in the city seeking narcissistically to capture myself"; *The Truants*, 24. "The surest sign of any group's demise," wrote James Atlas in 1985 amid a torrent of them, "is the appearance of memoirs"; "The Changing World of New York Intellectuals," *New York Times Magazine*, August 25, 1985.

12. Alfred Kazin, *Starting Out in the Thirties* (Ithaca, NY: Cornell University Press, 1965), 135; Lewis Mumford, *The Brown Decades* (New York: Harcourt, Brace, 1931).

13. Kazin, *Walker in the City*, 170.

14. Kazin, *Starting Out*, 136.

15. Kazin, "March 10, 1959"; in *Alfred Kazin's Journals*, 242.

16. Kazin, *New York Jew*, 73.

17. Kazin, "May 13, 1960," in *Alfred Kazin's Journals*, 261.

18. Transcript, Tamiment Conference on the Metropolis, 1960, box 4, "Daedalus, 1960" folder #2; Outline for "The Metropolitan World: Nature and Potentials," July 24, 1958; Outline for "Mastering the Metropolis," November 1958, box 4, "Daedalus, 1958–1959" folder #1, LRP; "The Future Metropolis," *Daedalus* 90 (Winter 1961). Both social science and the built environment were areas that *Daedalus* had thus far neglected. One index of their inattention is as follows: when asked on a questionnaire required of all new editors which "additional main topics should be covered" in the future, Rodwin could plausibly nominate "the social sciences," "architecture today," and "race problems today." Lloyd Rodwin, "Information Concerning Associate Editors" questionnaire, September 17, 1958, box 4, "Daedalus, 1958–1959" folder #1, LRP.

19. Lloyd Rodwin, ed., *The Future Metropolis* (New York: Braziller, 1961). The architect William Wurster materialized at Tamiment, as did the planners Kevin Lynch and Charles Abrams, the historian Oscar Handlin, the sociologist Nathan Glazer, and the

political scientist Edward Banfield, along with Aaron Fleisher, a technically savvy scholar with a background in meteorology who joined MIT's planning department in 1960. Rodwin's original vision for the conference entailed a highly eclectic group: from established urbanist circles, Catherine Bauer Wurster, William H. Whyte, and Lewis Mumford; from other social sciences, Robert Merton and, curiously, the psychoanalytic Marxist Erich Fromm; and from the top tier of the literary life, Lionel Trilling of Columbia and W. H. Auden, who wintered in New York during the 1950s.

20. Stephen R. Graubard, "Prefatory Note to the Issue 'The Future Metropolis,'" *Daedalus* 90 (Winter 1961): 3.

21. Martin Meyerson, "Utopian Traditions and the Planning of Cities," in *The Future Metropolis*, ed. Lloyd Rodwin (New York: Braziller, 1961), 233–250, at 237, 235. *Daedalus* later brought out a whole issue: "Utopia," *Daedalus* 94, no. 2 (Spring 1965); republished as Frank E. Manuel, ed., *Utopias and Utopian Thought: A Timely Appraisal* (Boston: Beacon, 1967). Contributors included Lewis Mumford, Northrop Frye, Crane Brinton, Judith Shklar, Paul Sears, Bertrand de Jouvenel, Mircea Eliade, and Paul Tillich.

22. Kevin Lynch and Lloyd Rodwin, "A World of Cities," in *The Future Metropolis*, ed. Lloyd Rodwin (New York: Braziller, 1961), 9–16, at 16, 11.

23. Meyerson, "Utopian Traditions," 236.

24. This book uses the word *planners* to designate people affiliated with all of these fields and *planning* to describe their work insofar as it involves claims about the future. Use of the word *design* will also crosscut discipline and profession, but it is reserved for proposals that include at least some visual component.

25. Carl E. Schorske, "The New Rigorism in the Human Sciences, 1940–1960," *Daedalus* 126 (Winter 1997): 289–309. See also Hayward Keniston, "The Humanities in a Scientific World," *Annals of the American Academy of Political and Social Science* 249 (January 1947): 160–168. The New Criticism then remaking some literature departments was often invoked as scientism incarnate.

26. For exceptions, see especially Dowell Myers and Alicia Kitsuse, "Constructing the Future in Planning: A Survey of Theories and Tools," *Journal of Planning Education and Research* 19 (2000): 221–231; Lucie Laurian and Anthony Inch, "On Time and Planning: Opening Planning by Cultivating a 'Sense of Now,'" *Journal of Planning Literature* 34 (2019): 267–285; Timothy J. Dixon and Mark Tewdwr-Jones, eds., *Urban Futures: Planning for City Foresight and City Visions* (Bristol, UK: Bristol University Press, 2021); Andrew M. Isserman, "Dare to Plan: An Essay on the Role of the Future in Planning Practice and Education," *Town Planning Review* 56 (1985): 483–491; Martin Wachs, "Forecasting versus Envisioning: A New Window on the Future," *Journal of the American Planning Association* 67 (2001): 367–372; Seymour J. Mandelbaum, "Temporal Conventions in Planning Discourse," *Environment and Planning B: Planning and Design* 11 (1984): 5–13; from midcentury, Britton Harris, "Plan or Projection: An Examination of the Use of Models in Planning," *Journal of the American Institute of Planners* 26 (1960): 265–272; and Britton Harris, "Inventing the Future Metropolis," in *Shaping an Urban Future*, eds. William W. Nash Jr. and Bernard J. Frieden (Cambridge, MA: MIT Press, 1969), 179–203. David J. Connell, "Planning and Its Orientation to the Future," *International Planning Studies* 14 (2009): 85–98, takes Koselleck at face value and leans too hard on the vocabulary of "modernity" and "postmodernity." Samuel Stein, *Capital City* (New York: Verso, 2019), 13, in passing, defines planning as "the way we shape space over time."

27. Garrett Dash Nelson, "Rexford Guy Tugwell and the Case for Big Urbanism," *Places* (January 2018), https://placesjournal.org/article/rexford-guy-tugwell-and-the-case-for-big-urbanism/; Le Corbusier, *The City of To-Morrow and Its Planning* [1929], trans. Frederick Etchells (New York: Dover, 1987); Thomas S. Hines, *Burnham of Chicago* (New York: Oxford University Press, 1974); Jane Jacobs, *Vital Little Plans: The Short Works of Jane Jacobs*, eds. Samuel Zipp and Nathan Storring (New York: Random House, 2016); and Daniel Immerwahr, *Thinking Small: The United States and the Lure of Community Development* (Cambridge, MA: Harvard University Press, 2015). Modernism's assertive futurism, best expressed in the manifesto form, has loomed over intellectual histories written by both acolytes and detractors. See, for example, Peter Hall, *Cities of Tomorrow: An Intellectual History of Urban Planning and Design in the Twentieth Century*, 3rd ed. (Malden, MA: Blackwell, 2002).

28. Myers and Kitsuse, "Constructing the Future in Planning," 225.

29. Jon A. Peterson, *The Birth of City Planning in the United States, 1840–1917* (Baltimore: Johns Hopkins University Press, 2003), is methodical in distinguishing City Beautiful planning (with Burnham's work at the 1893 Columbian Exposition as its conventional origin point) from the City Scientific, City Practical, or City Efficient alternatives articulated by 1909, the year of the first National Conference on City Planning. From 1909, the profession took further steps to brand itself a science: journals, conferences, (quantitative) methods, and a commitment to holding the city "under observation"—yet a de-emphasis on the city's visible form. See George B. Ford, "The City Scientific," *Engineering Record* 67 (May 17, 1913): 551–552. This period also saw land-use zoning displace architecture as the planner's characteristic instrument, with major codes introduced in Los Angeles (1908), Baltimore (1910), and, above all, New York (1916). On the transatlantic character of these conversations, Daniel T. Rodgers, *Atlantic Crossings: Social Politics in a Progressive Age* (Cambridge, MA: Harvard University Press, 1998), especially 181–208, remains essential.

30. Keller Easterling, *Organization Space: Landscapes, Highways, and Houses in America* (Cambridge, MA: MIT Press, 1999), 13–53. See also Roy Lubove, "Homes and 'A Few Well Placed Fruit Trees': An Object Lesson in Federal Housing," *Social Research* 27 (1960): 469–486; Kristin M. Szylvian, "Industrial Housing Reform and the Emergency Fleet Corporation," *Journal of Urban History* 25 (1999): 647–689; Christian Topalov, "Scientific Urban Planning and the Ordering of Daily Life: The First 'War Housing' Experiment in the United States, 1917–1919," *Journal of Urban History* 17 (November 1990): 14–45; Gail Radford, *Modern Housing for America: Policy Struggles in the New Deal Era* (Chicago: University of Chicago Press, 1996), 37–43; and Eran Ben-Joseph, "Workers' Paradise: The Forgotten Communities of World War I," Massachusetts Institute of Technology, accessed February 22, 2024, http://web.mit.edu/ebj/www/ww1/ww1a.html.

31. David A. Johnson, "Regional Planning for the Great American Metropolis: New York between the World Wars," in *Two Centuries of American Planning*, ed. Daniel Schaffer (Baltimore: Johns Hopkins University Press, 1988), 167–196; and, for example, Stephen Child, "The Regional Planning Organization of the Ruhr Adapted to the Bay Region," *Architect and Engineer* 90 (September 1927): 70–71, and 91 (October 1927): 49–52. Under the New Deal, drawing from a different intellectual lineage, "regional planning" took hydrology, ecology, and landforms into account; the river basin became the

classic unit to which an agency might scale its interventions; *Regional Planning* (Washington, DC: Government Printing Office, 1938).

32. Barbara Wootton, *Plan or No Plan* (London: V. Gollancz, 1934). Wootton acknowledged the "achievements and possibilities" of the Russian model.

33. Hans Speier, "Freedom and Social Planning," *American Journal of Sociology* 42 (1937): 463–483, at 470.

34. Lewis Mumford, foreword to *Planned Society: Yesterday, Today, Tomorrow*, ed. Findlay MacKenzie (New York: Prentice-Hall, 1937), viii; Robert Wojtowicz, ed., *Sidewalk Critic: Lewis Mumford's Writings on New York* (Princeton, NJ: Princeton Architectural Press, 1998).

35. Andrew M. Shanken, *194X: Architecture, Planning, and Consumer Culture on the American Home Front* (Minneapolis: University of Minnesota Press, 2009), vii, 17.

36. John Friedmann, "Introduction," *UNESCO International Social Science Journal* 11, no. 3 (1959): 327–339, at 327, 329, 331.

37. Lionel Trilling, "The Function of the Little Magazine" [1946], in *The Liberal Imagination* (New York: Viking, 1950), 93–103, at 97, 98.

38. Leo Raditsa, "On Paul Goodman—and Goodmanism," *Iowa Review* 5, no. 3 (1974): 62–79, at 79.

39. Kazin, *Starting Out*, 166.

40. Daniel Bell, "The Mood of Three Generations: The Once-Born, the Twice-Born, and the After-Born" [1957], in *The End of Ideology* (New York: The Free Press, 1960), 299–314, at 300.

41. Jan Morris, *Manhattan '45* [1986] (Baltimore: Johns Hopkins University Press, 1998), 8, 11. Morris was not present in New York during that year; in her 1987 acknowledgments, she reports "thirty-three years of bewitched association" (273) with the city. On Morris's life as an openly transgender woman, see Stephanie Burt, "The Conundrum of 'Conundrum,'" *Paris Review*, January 29, 2019, https://www.theparisreview.org/blog/2021/01/29/the-conundrum-of-conundrum/.

42. Louis Menand, *The Free World: Art and Thought in the Cold War* (New York: Farrar, Straus & Giroux, 2021), supplies an unsurprisingly New York–centric synthesis of cultural and intellectual life between 1945 and 1965. See also Jed Perl, *New Art City: Manhattan at Mid-Century* (New York: Knopf, 2005); and David Reid, *The Brazen Age: New York City and the American Empire* (New York: Pantheon, 2016). Michael Johns, *Moment of Grace: The American City in the 1950s* (Berkeley: University of California Press, 2003), borrows its title from Morris, *Manhattan '45*, 12.

43. David C. Engerman, "Introduction: Histories of the Future and the Futures of History," *American Historical Review* 117 (2012): 1402–1410; Jenny Andersson, "The Great Future Debate and the Struggle for the World," *American Historical Review* 177 (2012): 1411–1430; Jenny Andersson, *The Future of the World: Futurology, Futurists, and the Struggle for the Post–Cold War Imagination* (Oxford: Oxford University Press, 2018); Jamie L. Pietruska, *Looking Forward: Prediction and Uncertainty in Modern America* (Chicago: University of Chicago Press, 2017); Martin van Creveld, *Seeing into the Future: A Short History of Prediction* (London: Reaktion, 2020); and Reinhart Koselleck, *Futures Past: On the Semantics of Historical Time*, trans. Keith Tribe (New York: Columbia University Press, 1985).

44. Peter Osborne, *The Politics of Time* (London: Verso, 1995), explores some of these concerns within the Western Marxist tradition. See also Carol J. Greenhouse, *A*

Moment's Notice: Time Politics Across Culture (Ithaca, NY: Cornell University Press, 1996), which engages legal theory; and Dan Edelstein, Stefanos Geroulanos, and Natasha Wheatley, eds., *Power and Time: Temporalities in Conflict and the Making of History* (Chicago: University of Chicago Press, 2020).

45. Pitrim A. Sorokin and Robert K. Merton, "Social Time: A Methodological and Functional Analysis," *American Journal of Sociology* 43 (1937): 615–629, at 615, 618, 620–621, 628; Pitrim A. Sorokin, *Sociocultural Causality, Space, Time: A Study of Referential Principles of Sociology and Social Science* (Durham, NC: Duke University Press, 1943). See also Lewis Coser and Rose Laub Coser, "Time Perspective and Social Structure" [1973], in *A Handful of Thistles: Collected Papers in Moral Conviction* (New Brunswick, NJ: Transaction, 1988), 167–179, which distinguishes "time reckoning," a conceptual matter, from "time perspective," which for the Cosers emerges only from experience.

46. Wilbert E. Moore, *Man, Time, and Society* (New York: Wiley, 1963).

47. E. E. Evans-Pritchard, "Nuer Time-Reckoning," *Africa* 12 (1939): 189–216; Edmund R. Leach, "Two Essays Concerning the Symbolic Representation of Time," in *Rethinking Anthropology* (New York: Humanities Press, 1961), 108–116; Marian W. Smith, "Different Cultural Concepts of Past, Present and Future," *Psychiatry* 15 (1952): 395–400. For a wide-ranging earlier work that resists summary, see Wyndham Lewis, *Time and Western Man* [1927] (Boston: Beacon, 1957). On the sociological and anthropological literatures glimpsed here, see Barbara Adam, *Time and Social Theory* (Cambridge, UK: Polity, 1990). On the time–temporality distinction, David Couzens Hoy, *The Time of Our Lives: A Critical History of Temporality* (Cambridge, MA: MIT Press, 2009), is an effective philosophical introduction.

48. But see Rosemary Wakeman, *Practicing Utopia: An Intellectual History of the New Town Movement* (Chicago: University of Chicago Press, 2016); Gabrielle Esperdy, *American Autopia: An Intellectual History of the American Roadside at Midcentury* (Charlottesville: University of Virginia Press, 2019); Samuel Zipp, *Manhattan Projects: The Rise and Fall of Urban Renewal in Cold War New York* (New York: Oxford University Press, 2010); Samuel Zipp, "The Cultural Structure of Postwar Urbanism," *American Quarterly* 66 (2014): 477–488; Christopher Klemek, *The Transatlantic Collapse of Urban Renewal* (Chicago: University of Chicago Press, 2011); Jamin Creed Rowan, *The Sociable City: An American Intellectual Tradition* (Philadelphia: University of Pennsylvania Press, 2017); and Hall, *Cities of Tomorrow*. Thomas Bender, *Intellect and Public Life* (Baltimore: Johns Hopkins University Press, 1997), 3, notes how 1970s rifts between social and intellectual history ensnared the field of urban history and consigned it to the former camp, reducing systematic attention to the "spatial structures of intellectual life." One of Bender's main exceptions is Carl E. Schorske, *Fin-de-Siècle Vienna: Politics and Culture* (New York: Knopf, 1979). Also germane are many post-Habermasian studies of Enlightenment coffeehouses as spaces that encouraged intellectual exchange; for perspective, see Charles W. J. Withers, *Placing the Enlightenment: Thinking Geographically About the Age of Reason* (Chicago: University of Chicago Press, 2007).

49. Robert J. Brym, "Intellectuals, Sociology of," *International Encyclopedia of the Social and Behavioral Sciences*, 2nd ed., vol. 12 (Amsterdam: Elsevier, 2015), 277–282, at 281.

50. Peter Burke, *What Is the History of Knowledge?* (Cambridge, UK: Polity, 2016).

51. Gil Eyal and Larissa Buchholz, "From the Sociology of Intellectuals to the Sociology of Interventions," *Annual Review of Sociology* 36 (2010): 117–137, at 129, 132;

Scott Frickel and Neil Gross, "A General Theory of Scientific/Intellectual Movements," *American Sociological Review* 70 (2005): 204–232, at 205; Bell, "The 'Intelligentsia' in American Society," 125; Karl Mannheim, "The Sociology of Intellectuals" [1932], trans. Dick Pels, *Theory, Culture, and Society* 10 (1993): 69–80. See also Charles Kurzman and Lynn Owens, "The Sociology of Intellectuals," *Annual Review of Sociology* 28 (2002): 63–90, on the class debates; Jerome Karabel, "Towards a Theory of Intellectuals and Politics," *Theory and Society* 25 (1996): 205–233; and Lewis Coser, *Men of Ideas* (New York: Free Press, 1965), still highly valuable for its portraits, which span the eighteenth, nineteenth, and twentieth centuries. In *No Respect: Intellectuals and Popular Culture* (New York: Routledge, 1989), 229, Andrew Ross notes that by the end of the 1980s, commentaries lamenting the "decline of the public intellectual" had amounted to their own cliché-ridden genre.

52. Nils Gilman, *Mandarins of the Future: Modernization Theory in Cold War America* (Baltimore: Johns Hopkins University Press, 2003), 21, 113.

53. Hunter Heyck, *Age of System* (Baltimore: Johns Hopkins University Press, 2015), 195.

54. H. C. Darby, "The Problem of Geographical Description," *Transactions and Papers (Institute of British Geographers)* 30 (1962): 1–14.

55. John A. Kouwenhoven, "What's 'American' About America" [1955], in *The Beer Can by the Highway* [1961] (Baltimore: Johns Hopkins University Press, 1988), 37–73, at 66.

56. Kouwenhoven, "What's 'American' About America," 72. For perspective on the travels of the grid form, see Dan Stanislawski, "The Origin and Spread of the Grid-Pattern Town," *Geographical Review* 36 (1946): 105–120; Edward T. Price, "The Central Courthouse Square in the American County Seat," *Geographical Review* 58 (1968): 29–60; and Reuben Rose-Redwood and Liora Bigon, eds., *Gridded Worlds: An Anthology* (Cham: Springer, 2018). For a valuable critique of "origin" narratives, see Reuben Rose-Redwood, "Genealogies of the Grid: Revisiting Stanislawski's Search for the Origin of the Grid-Pattern Town," *Geographical Review* 98 (2008): 42–58. Typical of anti-grid critique are Jill Grant, "The Dark Side of the Grid: Power and Urban Design," *Planning Perspectives* 16 (2001): 219–241; and Peter Marcuse, "The Grid as City Plan: New York City and Laissez-Faire Planning in the Nineteenth Century," *Planning Perspectives* 2 (1987): 287–310. More complex appreciations are Paul Groth, "Streetgrids as Frameworks for Urban Variety," *Harvard Architecture Review* 2 (Spring 1981): 68–75; Dell Upton, "The Grid and the Republican Spatial Imagination," in *Another City: Urban Life and Urban Spaces in the New American Republic* (New Haven: Yale University Press, 2008), 113–144; and Leslie Martin, "The Grid as Generator," in *Urban Space and Structures*, eds. Leslie Martin and Lionel March (Cambridge, UK: Cambridge University Press, 1972), 6–27.

1. Centers and Their Edges

1. David Popenoe, "Urban Studies Reconsidered: Present Trends and Future Prospects," *Urban Education* 6 (1971): 6–31, at 7.

2. Louis Menand, "Pulp's Big Moment," *New Yorker*, January 5, 2015.

3. Jason Epstein, *Book Business* (New York: Norton, 2001), 64; Kurt Enoch, "The Paper-Bound Book: Twentieth-Century Publishing Phenomenon," *The Library Quar-*

terly 24 (1954): 211–225, at 214. There was a vigorous nineteenth-century market for paperbacks; the Copyright Act of 1891 chilled it until the late-1930s revival. On social science in public, see Peter Mandler, "The Language of Social Science in Everyday Life," *History of the Human Sciences* 32 (2019): 66–82; and Peter Mandler, "Good Reading for the Million: The 'Paperback Revolution' and the Co-Production of Academic Knowledge in Mid–Twentieth-Century Britain and America," *Past & Present* 244 (2019): 235–269. On postwar shifts in publishing and bookselling, see Kenneth C. Davis, *Two-Bit Culture: The Paperbacking of America* (Boston: Houghton Mifflin, 1984); Evan Brier, *A Novel Marketplace: Mass Culture, the Book Trade, and Postwar American Fiction* (Philadelphia: University of Pennsylvania Press, 2010); Paula Rabinowitz, *American Pulp: How Paperbacks Brought Modernism to Main Street* (Princeton, NJ: Princeton University Press, 2015); Laura J. Miller, *Reluctant Capitalists: Bookselling and the Culture of Consumption* (Chicago: University of Chicago Press, 2006); Hayden Carruth, "The Phenomenon of the Paperback," *Perspectives USA* 15 (1956): 192–204; and Cecil Hemley, "The Problem of the Paperbacks," *The Commonweal* 61 (1954): 95–97.

4. Nathan Glazer, "From Socialism to Sociology," in *Authors of Their Own Lives*, ed. Bennett M. Berger (Berkeley: University of California Press, 1990), 190–209, at 197, 201.

5. Peter L. Laurence, *Becoming Jane Jacobs* (Philadelphia: University of Pennsylvania Press, 2016), 248.

6. Laurence, *Becoming Jane Jacobs*, 190, 202. Architectural Forum had undergone a reorganization in 1952, broadening its definition of the "urban" in imitation of the British publication *Architectural Record*; Clément Orillard, "The Transnational Building of Urban Design: Interplay between Genres of Discourse in the Anglophone World," *Planning Perspectives* 29 (2014): 209–229.

7. Martin Weil, "Frederick Gutheim Dies," *Washington Post*, October 4, 1993.

8. Martin Weil, "Wolf von Eckardt Dies at 77," *Washington Post*, August 28, 1995.

9. Ada Louise Huxtable, *Will They Ever Finish Bruckner Boulevard?* (Berkeley: University of California Press, 1989), 2, 1.

10. Grady Clay, *Right before Your Eyes* (Washington, DC: Planners Press, 1987).

11. Grady Clay, *Close-Up: How to Read the American City* (Chicago: University of Chicago Press, 1972).

12. Peter Ekman, "Diagnosing Suburban Ruin: A Prehistory of Mumford's Postwar Jeremiad," *Journal of Planning History* 15 (2016): 108–128. Paul Goodman was another New Yorker with interwar foundations, decentralist prescriptions, and a biophilic, utopian bent who achieved a high profile in the postwar period. On Mumford at Penn, see Robert Wojtowicz, "A New Yorker in Philadelphia," in *Lewis Mumford at 100: Sticks, Stones, Cities, Culture* (Philadelphia: University of Pennsylvania, 1995), 7–16.

13. Bruce Kuklick, "Myth and Symbol in American Studies," *American Quarterly* 24 (1972): 435–450; and, on some of the field's funders, Deborah Cohn, *Cold War Humanities: Modern Language Study, American Studies, and the National Interest* (Sleepy Hollow, NY: Rockefeller Archive Center, 2019).

14. "Too much has been written" on the New York Intellectuals, Morris Dickstein could assert by 1977; *Gates of Eden: American Culture in the Sixties* (New York: Basic Books, 1977), 253. Mark Greif, *The Age of the Crisis of Man: American Thought and Fiction, 1933–1973* (Princeton, NJ: Princeton University Press, 2015), 65, calls them "the most studied group in midcentury" America. On the set's literary, political, and social thought, see

especially Irving Howe, *A Margin of Hope*, 119–151, at 122, which disputes that they were ever a coherent community or movement, finding only "filaments of sensibility"; Irving Howe, "The New York Intellectuals," *Dissent* (October 1969): 29–51; Daniel Bell, "The 'Intelligentsia' in American Society" [1977], in *The Winding Passage* (Cambridge, MA: Abt Books, 1980), 119–137; Alexander Bloom, *Prodigal Sons: The New York Intellectuals and Their World* (New York: Oxford University Press, 1986); Neil Jumonville, *Critical Crossings: The New York Intellectuals in Postwar America* (Berkeley: University of California Press, 1991); Alan M. Wald, *The New York Intellectuals: The Rise and Decline of the Anti-Stalinist Left from the 1930s to the 1980s* (Chapel Hill: University of North Carolina Press, 1987); Hugh Wilford, *The New York Intellectuals: From Vanguard to Institution* (Manchester: Manchester University Press, 1995); Harvey M. Teres, *Renewing the Left: Politics, Imagination, and the New York Intellectuals* (New York: Oxford University Press, 1996); Stephen A. Longstaff, "The New York Intellectuals: A Study of Particularism and Universalism in American High Culture" (PhD diss., University of California, Berkeley, 1978); Thomas Bender, *New York Intellect* (New York: Knopf, 1987), 78–90, on events before 1930; and *Arguing the World*, directed by Joseph Dorman (1998; New York: First Run Features). Omnibus studies of this sort dropped off in the early twenty-first century, just as the tradition of "little magazines" in the *Partisan Review* tradition underwent a revival. On the fraught gender dynamics within the group—which included Hardwick, Sontag, McCarthy, Diana Trilling, and many more in addition to the prodigal *sons*—see Ronnie Grinberg, *Write Like a Man: Jewish Masculinity and the New York Intellectuals* (Princeton, NJ: Princeton University Press, 2024); and David Laskin, *Partisans: Marriage, Politics, and Betrayal among the New York Intellectuals* (Chicago: University of Chicago Press, 2000). On the circle's racial outside, the ongoing work of Tobi Haslett, for example, "Moving On Up," *Bookforum* (April–May 2017), has been instructive. Bloom, *Prodigal Sons*, 311, 313, posits that the group's geographic dispersal—to university campuses across the country, to California, to the Cape—marked its end. Bloom does not venture to explain the inverse: what about New York as an urban environment had kept them together. Russell Jacoby, *The Last Intellectuals: American Culture in the Age of Academe* (New York: Basic Books, 1987), makes a similar point about the decline of urban bohemias. On Jewish migration west, see Deborah Dash Moore, *To the Golden Cities: Pursuing the American Jewish Dream in Miami and L.A.* (Cambridge, MA: Harvard University Press, 1994).

15. "A Note from the Editors," in "New York, N.Y.," *Dissent* 8 (Summer 1961), front matter; Brian L. Tochterman, *The Dying City: Postwar New York and the Ideology of Fear* (Chapel Hill: University of North Carolina Press, 2017), 102–121, at 104. *Dissent* often featured social scientists in its pages. The sociologist Daniel Bell, who had married Alfred Kazin's sister, Pearl, the year before, appeared in the special issue, pronouncing on political economy. Kazin was notably absent from the issue. The majority of the New York Intellectuals were literary and humanistic in orientation; for Kazin, social science was an affront to that ethos. In the 1970s, he would remember "Charlie"—C. Wright—Mills as "a kind of gadfly to us, whom we didn't always take seriously. . . . It may be my literary inability to take sociologists seriously." He was equally wary of Bell's work: "My brother-in-law you know fancies himself a sociometrical technical expert, which I think is a lot of crap"; "Recollections of Alfred Kazin, 1972," May 1, 1972, Richard Hofstadter Project, CUL. In his journals, Kazin would record similar impressions of Nathan Glazer: "Fundamentally, so non-literary that he has the skeptical look of the City College chem-

istry major in the face of the English[-]department intellectuals." Kazin was "dutifully" invited by Irving Howe to contribute to the 1987 sequel to the "NY number (whatever that is)," but he declined; Alfred Kazin, "June 20, 1959" and "January 7, 1987," in *Alfred Kazin's Journals*, ed. Richard M. Cook (New Haven, CT: Yale University Press, 2011), 251, 532; "In Search of New York," *Dissent* 34 (Fall 1987).

16. Lionel Trilling, "The Function of the Little Magazine" [1946], in *The Liberal Imagination* (New York: Viking, 1950), 93–103, at 93.

17. Janet Mendelsohn and Chris Wilson, eds., *Drawn to Landscape: The Pioneering Work of J. B. Jackson* (Staunton, VA: George F. Thompson Publishing, 2015); Helen Lefkowitz Horowitz, *Traces of J. B. Jackson: The Man Who Taught Us to See Everyday America* (Charlottesville: University of Virginia Press, 2019); Jeffrey D. Blankenship, "Reading *Landscape*: J. B. Jackson and the Cultural Landscape Idea at Midcentury," *Landscape Journal* 35 (2016): 167–184; Jeffrey D. Blankenship, "Midcentury Geohumanities: J. B. Jackson and the 'Magazine of Human Geography,'" *Geohumanities* 4 (2018): 26–44; Jamin Creed Rowan, *The Sociable City: An American Intellectual Tradition* (Philadelphia: University of Pennsylvania Press, 2017), 116–123; and Paul Groth, "J. B. Jackson and Geography," *Geographical Review* 88, no. 4 (1998): iii–vi.

18. J. B. Jackson, "The Domestication of the Garage" [1976], in *Landscape in Sight*, ed. Helen Lefkowitz Horowitz (New Haven, CT: Yale University Press, 1997), 118–125, at 118.

19. Carl O. Sauer, "'Now This Matter of Cultural Geography': Notes from Carl Sauer's Last Seminar at Berkeley" [1964], ed. James J. Parsons, in *Carl O. Sauer: A Tribute*, ed. Martin S. Kenzer (Corvallis: Oregon State University Press, 1987), 153–163, at 156; Peter Ekman, "'This Scene Is Itself Living': Buildings as Landscapes in Transatlantic Human Geography, 1870–1970," *History of the Human Sciences* (2021): 336–361.

20. J. B. Jackson to Wilbur Zelinsky, August 15, 1966, and June 27, 1967, box 6, folder 34, WZP.

21. Roger L. Geiger, "Organized Research Units: Their Role in the Development of University Research," *Journal of Higher Education* 61 (1990): 1–19, at 10, 9, 5, 3; Hunter Heyck, *Age of System* (Baltimore: Johns Hopkins University Press, 2015), 51–80; Christopher P. Loss, *Front and Center: Academic Expertise and Its Challengers in the Post-1945 United States* (Philadelphia: University of Pennsylvania Press, forthcoming). Paul Warde, Libby Robin, and Sverker Sörlin, *The Environment: A History of the Idea* (Baltimore: Johns Hopkins University Press, 2018), 166, use the language of "aggregated expertise." Centers became "hubs" where a range of nonacademic institutions made contact, per Mitchell L. Stevens, Elizabeth A. Armstrong, and Richard Arum, "Sieve, Incubator, Temple, Hub: Theoretical Advances in the Sociology of Higher Education," *Annual Review of Sociology* 34 (2008): 127–151. As Geiger notes, *center* connoted a more academic, theory-building orientation, with members usually retaining departmental affiliations. *Institute* often signaled obeisance to outside funders. Cornell's vast new School of Industrial and Labor Relations, founded 1945, was a conspicuous example of that model; schools necessarily include teaching.

22. Mark Solovey, *Shaky Foundations: The Politics–Patronage–Social Science Nexus in Cold War America* (New Brunswick, NJ: Rutgers University Press, 2013), 20–55, 148–187; David Paul Haney, *The Americanization of Social Science: Intellectuals and Public Responsibility in the Postwar United States* (Philadelphia: Temple University Press, 2008), 30–38.

23. Heyck, *Age of System*, 200.

24. Roger E. Backhouse, "Economics," in *The History of the Social Sciences since 1945*, eds. Roger E. Backhouse and Philippe Fontaine (New York: Cambridge University Press, 2010), 38–70, at 49; Andrew Abbott, *Department and Discipline: Chicago Sociology at One Hundred* (Chicago: University of Chicago Press, 1999), 213–214.

25. Solovey, *Shaky Foundations*, 56–102; Ethan Schrum, *The Instrumental University: Education in Service of the National Agenda after World War II* (Ithaca, NY: Cornell University Press, 2019); Theodore M. Porter, *Trust in Numbers: The Pursuit of Objectivity in Science and Public Life* (Princeton, NJ: Princeton University Press, 1996); Theodore M. Porter, "Speaking Precision to Power: The Modern Political Role of Social Science," *Social Research* 73 (2006): 1273–1294. Porter's political histories of quantification backdate the impulse to the middle nineteenth century, noting the etymological link between statistics and the state.

26. Samuel A. Stouffer et al., *The American Soldier*, 2 vols. (Princeton, NJ: Princeton University Press, 1949); Libby Schweber, "Wartime Research and the Quantification of American Sociology: The View from *The American Soldier*," *Révue d'Histoire des Sciences Humaines* 6 (2002): 65–94. Stouffer's work became the touchstone for a new kind of publication: the methods textbook.

27. Jennifer S. Light, *From Warfare to Welfare: Defense Intellectuals and Urban Problems in Cold War America* (Baltimore: Johns Hopkins University Press, 2003); Joy Rohde, *Armed with Expertise: The Militarization of American Social Research during the Cold War* (Ithaca, NY: Cornell University Press, 2013).

28. Roger E. Backhouse and Philippe Fontaine, "Toward a History of the Social Sciences," in *The History of the Social Sciences since 1945*, 184–233, at 207, 208, 216; David Hounshell, "The Cold War, RAND, and the Generation of Knowledge, 1946–1962," *Historical Studies in the Physical and Behavioral Sciences* 27 (1997): 237–267; Christian Dayé, *Experts, Social Scientists, and Techniques of Prognosis in Cold War America* (Cham: Palgrave Macmillan, 2020); Daniel Bessner, *Democracy in Exile: Hans Speier and the Rise of the Defense Intellectual* (Ithaca, NY: Cornell University Press, 2018), 139–155, 205–224, and passim. Bessner calls RAND "the model Cold War think tank" (10).

29. Nils Gilman, *Mandarins of the Future: Modernization Theory in Cold War America* (Baltimore: Johns Hopkins University Press, 2003); David C. Engerman et al., eds., *Staging Growth: Modernization, Development, and the Global Cold War* (Amherst: University of Massachusetts Press, 2003); Michael E. Latham, *Modernization as Ideology: Social Science and "Nation Building" in the Kennedy Era* (Chapel Hill: University of North Carolina Press, 2000); Bessner, *Democracy in Exile*, 195–203; and see Nils Gilman, "The Cold War as Intellectual Force Field," *Modern Intellectual History* 13 (2016): 507–523. Ithiel de Sola Pool, a CENIS mainstay, called the social sciences "the new humanities of the Twentieth Century"; Jill Lepore, *If Then: How the Simulmatics Corporation Invented the Future* (New York: Liveright, 2020), 212. Haney, *Americanization of Social Science*, 65, deems 1951 the turning point for social science qua science, while Heyck, *Age of System*, 81–125, makes sport of "the magical year 1956, plus or minus one." Haney stresses social scientists' retreat from public engagement, a contention that is only partially borne out by his evidence.

30. Roger L. Geiger, *American Higher Education since World War II: A History* (Princeton, NJ: Princeton University Press, 2019), 78, 94, 126; Stuart W. Leslie, *The Cold War*

and American Science: The Military–Industrial–Academic Complex at MIT and Stanford (New York: Columbia University Press, 1993); Daniel Lee Kleinman, *Politics on the Endless Frontier: Postwar Research Policy in the United States* (Durham, NC: Duke University Press, 1995); Naomi Oreskes and John Krige, eds., *Science and Technology in the Global Cold War* (Cambridge, MA: MIT Press, 2014); Audra Wolfe, *Freedom's Laboratory: The Cold War Struggle for the Soul of Science* (Baltimore: Johns Hopkins University Press, 2018). On MIT's military outputs, see John Burchard, *Q.E.D.: M.I.T. in World War II* (New York: Technology Press, 1948); and John Burchard, ed., *Mid-Century: The Social Implications of Scientific Progress* (New York: Wiley, 1950). Burchard was MIT's first dean of humanities. On prewar contract research, primarily in the hard sciences, Larry Owens, "MIT and the Federal 'Angel': Academic R&D and Federal–Private Cooperation before World War II," *Isis* 81 (1990): 188–213, is valuable.

31. Paul Erickson, "Mathematical Models, Rational Choice, and the Search for Cold War Culture," *Isis* 101 (2010): 386–392, at 392; and see Paul Erickson et al., *How Reason Almost Lost Its Mind: The Strange Career of Cold War Rationality* (Chicago: University of Chicago Press, 2013); Joel Isaac, "The Human Sciences in Cold War America," *The Historical Journal* 50 (2007): 725–746; Jamie Cohen-Cole, *The Open Mind: Cold War Politics and the Sciences of Human Nature* (Chicago: University of Chicago Press, 2014); and Schrum, *Instrumental University*, 5–9.

32. Geiger, *American Higher Education*, 95.

33. Geiger, "Organized Research Units," 12.

34. Schrum, *Instrumental University*, 54.

35. Clark Kerr, "The Idea of a Multiversity," in *The Uses of the University* (Cambridge, MA: Harvard University Press, 1963), 1–45, at 20. As Louis Menand has written, some interdisciplinary work amounted to a "predictable and aimless eclecticism." And did calls for *inter*disciplinarity, as opposed to *trans*- or *post*-disciplinarity, actually advance "the institutional ratification of the logic of disciplines"? Louis Menand, *The Marketplace of Ideas* (New York: American Council of Learned Societies, 2001), 20, 15. On *inter*-, *trans*-, *post*-, and *anti*-, see Peter Osborne, "Problematizing Disciplinarity, Transdisciplinary Problematics," *Theory, Culture & Society* 32(5–6) (2015): 3–35. For a defense of disciplines, see Jerry A. Jacobs and Scott Frickel, "Interdisciplinarity: A Critical Assessment," *Annual Review of Sociology* 35 (2009): 43–65. For other accounts, see Andrew Barry and Georgina Born, eds., *Interdisciplinarity: Reconfigurations of the Social and Natural Sciences* (London: Routledge, 2013); Harvey J. Graff, *Undisciplining Knowledge: Interdisciplinarity in the Twentieth Century* (Baltimore: Johns Hopkins University Press, 2015); Hugh David Graham and Nancy Diamond, *The Rise of American Research Universities: Elites and Challengers in the Postwar Era* (Baltimore: Johns Hopkins University Press, 2004); and Loss, *Front and Center*.

36. Kerr, "Idea of a Multiversity," 14; Schrum, *Instrumental University*, 19–32, 40–50. "Governmental research" and "municipal research" were important forerunners of postwar urban studies.

37. "Trading zones," after Peter Galison, *Image and Logic: A Material Culture of Microphysics* (Chicago: University of Chicago Press, 1997).

38. Margaret Mead, "Values for Urban Living," *Annals of the American Academy of Political and Social Science* 314 (1957): 10–14, at 13.

39. Sam D. Sieber, *Reforming the University: The Role of the Social Research Center* (New York: Praeger, 1972), 68, 5. On scientificity and specialization, 1870 to 1930, Dorothy A.

Ross, *The Origins of American Social Science* (Cambridge, UK: Cambridge University Press, 1991), endures.

40. Paul F. Lazarsfeld, foreword to Sieber, *Reforming the University*, ix, v; Sieber, *Reforming the University*, 148; Paul F. Lazarsfeld, "The Sociology of Empirical Social Research," *American Sociological Review* 27 (1962): 757–767; Allen H. Barton, "Paul Lazarsfeld and Applied Social Research," *Social Science History* 3 (October 1979): 4–44.

41. Barton, "Paul Lazarsfeld," 33, 20.

42. Abbott, *Department and Discipline*, 37–39.

43. Charles Camic, "Three Departments in Search of a Discipline: Localism and Interdisciplinary Interaction in American Sociology, 1890–1940," *Social Research* 62 (1995): 1003–1033. On Berkeley as the fourth great department—built up after the war by attracting refugees from Chicago, Columbia, and Harvard—see Michael Burawoy and Jonathan VanAntwerpen, "Berkeley Sociology: Past, Present and Future," Public Sociology, Berkeley, https://publicsociology.berkeley.edu/intro/berkeleysociology/berkeleysociology.pdf.

44. Talcott Parsons, interview by Isabel S. Grossner, March 22, 1967, Carnegie Corporation Project, CUL. After 1945, Yale essentially opted out of the top tier of social science. On Parsons's contact with the "Pareto circle" and interwar Harvard's "interstitial academy," see Joel Isaac, *Working Knowledge: Making the Human Sciences from Parsons to Kuhn* (Cambridge, MA: Harvard University Press, 2012); and, for a visualization of these tangled networks, see Lawrence T. Nichols, "Merton as Harvard Sociologist: Engagement, Thematic Continuities, and Institutional Linkages," *Journal of the History of the Behavioral Sciences* 46 (2010): 72–95, at 77. On Parsons's theories of economy, see Howard Brick, *Transcending Capitalism: Visions of a New Society in Modern American Thought* (Ithaca, NY: Cornell University Press, 2006), 121–151.

45. Lawrence T. Nichols, "Social Relations Undone: Disciplinary Divergence and Departmental Politics at Harvard, 1946–1970," *American Sociologist* 29 (1998): 83–107, at 89, calls 1951–1956 its "peak" period.

46. George C. Homans, *The Human Group* (New York: Harcourt, Brace, 1950).

47. "Departments of Geography Which Give Work toward a Ph.D." (1945), box 303, folder 13, AAGR. The schools were Berkeley, Clark, Chicago, Columbia, Harvard, Johns Hopkins, Minnesota, Michigan, Nebraska, Ohio State, Syracuse, Washington, and Wisconsin–Madison.

48. David N. Livingstone, *The Geographical Tradition* (Oxford: Blackwell, 1991), 177. Neil Smith refers to this same ideal as the "unity myth"; "'Academic War over the Field of Geography': The Elimination of Geography at Harvard, 1947–1951," *Annals of the Association of American Geographers* 77 (1987): 155–172, at 169.

49. Kirk H. Stone, "Geography's Wartime Service," *Annals of the Association of American Geographers* 69 (1979): 89–96; Evelyn S. Pruitt, "The Office of Naval Research and Geography," *Annals of the Association of American Geographers* 69 (1979): 103–108; Trevor J. Barnes, "The Discipline That Came In from the Cold: American Human Geography Becomes a Cold War Social Science," *Environment and Planning F* 1 (2022): 145–167; Light, *From Warfare to Welfare*.

50. Harold M. Mayer, "A Half Century of Urban Geography in America: Retrospect and Prospect," in *Harold M. Mayer: Fifty Years of Professional Geography*, eds. Lutz Holzner and Jeane M. Knapp (Milwaukee: American Geographical Society Collection,

1990), 1–9; Harold M. Mayer, "Urban Geography and Chicago in Retrospect," *Annals of the Association of American Geographers* 69 (1979): 114–118; Ron Johnston, "Human Geography," in *The History of the Social Sciences since 1945*, eds. Backhouse and Fontaine, 155–183, especially 163–168; Livingstone, *Geographical Tradition*, 304–346; Elvin Wyly, *Geography's Quantitative Revolutions: Edward A. Ackerman and the Cold War Origins of Big Data* (Morgantown: West Virginia University Press, 2019). On regional science specifically, see Walter Isard, *Location and Space-Economy* (Cambridge, MA: MIT Press, 1956); and Walter Isard, *History of Regional Science and the Regional Science Association International: The Beginnings and Early History* (Berlin: Springer-Verlag, 2003).

51. Smith, "'Academic War'"; Clive Barnett, "Awakening the Dead: Who Needs the History of Geography?" *Transactions of the Institute of British Geographers* 20 (1995): 417–419. For further perspective, see Saul B. Cohen, "Reflections on the Elimination of Geography at Harvard, 1947–51," *Annals of the Association of American Geographers* 78 (1988): 148–151, by the rare figure who experienced the department as both an undergraduate and a graduate student; and Geoffrey J. Martin, "On Whittlesey, Bowman, and Harvard," *Annals of the Association of American Geographers* 78 (1988): 152–158. For an account, published the year of the Harvard closure, that admits "a real need for institutes of research" but lyrically defends town "anatomy" and "morphology" as the quintessence of urban geography, see Robert E. Dickinson, "The Scope and Status of Urban Geography: An Assessment," *Land Economics* 24 (1948): 221–238.

52. Compare Wilbur Zelinsky to Lester Klimm, "Department of Geography," April 8, 1957; with Zelinsky to Klimm, "Professor of Geography," January 11, 1958; box 7, folder 16, WZP.

53. Eric Robsky Huntley and Matthew Rosenblum, "The Omega Affair: Discontinuing the University of Michigan Department of Geography (1975–1982)," *Annals of the American Association of Geographers* 111 (2021): 364–384.

54. Marvin Mikesell to Wilbur Zelinsky, September 12, 1986, box 9, folder 3, WZP.

55. Geoffrey J. Martin, "Geography, Geographers, and Yale University c. 1770–1970," in *Geography in New England*, eds. John E. Harmon and Timothy J. Rickard (New Britain, CT: New England/St. Lawrence Valley Geographical Society, 1988), 2–9.

56. Arch Gerlach to Joseph E. Spencer, February 7, 1963, box 306, folder 3, AAGR.

57. Michael Porter, "Lost in the Shadows: The History of the Columbia University Geography Department" (2002; unpublished), box 1, folder 20, DHC. On Jane Jacobs's undergraduate studies in economic geography at Columbia, see Laurence, *Becoming Jane Jacobs*, 52–55.

58. Nichols, "Social Relations Undone," 89, 90; Talcott Parsons, interview by Isabel S. Grossner, March 22, 1967.

59. Barton, "Paul Lazarsfeld," 15, 10.

60. Roger L. Geiger, "American Foundations and Academic Social Science, 1945–1960," *Minerva* 26 (1988): 315–341, at 341, 335.

61. Waldemar Nielsen, *The Big Foundations* (New York: Columbia University Press, 1972). Solovey, *Shaky Foundations*, 4, sees "a single, albeit loosely integrated system" of patronage; Heyck distinguishes two systems of patronage, federal and philanthropic, that share one "common sense."

62. Geiger, "American Foundations," 319.

63. Talcott Parsons, interview by Isabel S. Grossner, March 22, 1967.

64. David Riesman, interview by Isabel S. Grossner, December 6, 1967, and January 9, 1968, Carnegie Corporation Project, CUL; David Riesman, with Nathan Glazer and Reuel Denney, *The Lonely Crowd* (New York: Oxford University Press, 1950); Geiger, "American Foundations," 322.

65. Martin Bulmer and Joan Bulmer, "Philanthropy and Social Science in the 1920s: Beardsley Ruml and the Laura Spelman Rockefeller Memorial, 1922–29," *Minerva* 19 (1981): 347–407, at 371. On Carnegie and Rockefeller's interwar activity, see Mark C. Smith, *Social Science in the Crucible: The American Debate over Objectivity and Purpose, 1918–1941* (Durham, NC: Duke University Press, 1994). Bulmer and Bulmer also acknowledge pre-1920s philanthropy by the Russell Sage Foundation (beginning with the Pittsburgh Survey of 1907–1908), the early years of the Carnegie Institution (from 1900), and the Carnegie Corporation (from 1911, distinct from the Institution), which supported research on education.

66. Robert E. Kohler, "The Management of Science: The Experience of Warren Weaver and the Rockefeller Foundation Programme in Molecular Biology," *Minerva* 14 (1976): 279–306, at 283.

67. Bulmer and Bulmer, "Philanthropy and Social Science," 384, 386.

68. Kohler, "The Management of Science," 282; David Riesman, interview by Isabel S. Grossner, December 6, 1967, and January 9, 1968.

69. Merle Curti, "The History of American Philanthropy as a Field of Research," *American Historical Review* 62 (1957): 352–363, at 357. Curti's paper was occasioned by a 1956 Russell Sage conference on the topic. In 1958, he would exalt the Carnegie–Rockefeller–Ford approach as offering a uniquely "American equivalent for socialism," a "middle way" between state and society; Merle Curti, "American Philanthropy and the National Character," *American Quarterly* 10 (1958): 420–437, at 436.

70. Christopher Tunnard and Boris Pushkarev, *Man-Made America: Chaos or Control?* (New Haven, CT: Yale University Press, 1963); Ian Nairn, *The American Landscape: A Critical View* (New York: Random House, 1965); Edmund N. Bacon, *Design of Cities* (New York: Penguin, 1967). What Nairn called "subtopia" in Britain, he simply called "goop" in the United States—"the goulash of environment." On Bacon's visions, see Alexander Garvin, "Philadelphia's Planner: A Conversation with Edmund Bacon," *Journal of Planning History* 1 (2002): 58–78; Doug Hassebroek, "Philadelphia's Postwar Moment," *Perspecta* 30 (1999): 84–91; Gregory L. Heller, *Ed Bacon: Planning, Politics, and the Building of Modern Philadelphia* (Philadelphia: University of Pennsylvania Press, 2013); and his public-relations star turn, the film *Form, Design, and the City* (1961; Richmond, VA: Reynolds Metal Company), which diagrams his proposed reconstruction of Philadelphia's historic core across an enormous whiteboard, accessible only with the aid of wheeled stepladders and a cadre of silent assistants.

71. Here and throughout the postwar period, signal contributions came from Europeans and European émigrés. Although their reliance on European aesthetic standards was not embraced equally by all of their American interlocutors, Nairn and Pushkarev were not exceptions by virtue of their foreignness. Bacon's story cannot be told without reference to Oskar Stonorov and I. M. Pei. "American" urban research and social science were deeply transnational.

72. Eric Mumford, *Defining Urban Design: CIAM Architects and the Formation of a Discipline, 1937–69* (New Haven, CT: Yale University Press, 2009); Eric Mumford, *The*

CIAM Discourse on Urbanism, 1928–1960 (Cambridge, MA: MIT Press, 2000); Clément Orillard, "Tracing Urban Design's 'Townscape' Origins: Some Relationships between a British Editorial Policy and an American Academic Field in the 1950s," *Urban History* 36 (2009): 284–302; Tim B. Mueller, "The Rockefeller Foundation, the Social Sciences, and the Humanities in the Cold War," *Journal of Cold War Studies* 15, no. 3 (2013): 108–135. Penn had begun a combined degree program in city planning and architecture in 1956. It evolved into a degree in urban design, but only after 1960; Witold Rybczynski, *Makeshift Metropolis* (New York: Scribner, 2011), 127.

73. Peter L. Laurence, "The Death and Life of Urban Design: Jane Jacobs, the Rockefeller Foundation, and the New Research in Urbanism, 1955–1965," *Journal of Urban Design* 11 (2006): 145–171. Jacobs's main contact was with Rockefeller's life-sciences division, particularly Warren Weaver.

74. Orillard, "Tracing Urban Design's 'Townscape' Origins," 297; Gordon Cullen, *Townscape* (New York: Architectural Press, 1961).

75. Jean Gottmann, *Megalopolis: The Urbanized Northeastern Seaboard of the United States* (Cambridge, MA: MIT Press, 1961). On his keyword, see Elizabeth Baigent, "Patrick Geddes, Lewis Mumford and Jean Gottmann: Divisions Over 'Megalopolis,'" *Progress in Human Geography* 28 (2004): 687–700; and Helen Meller, "Some Reflections on the Concept of Megalopolis and Its Use by Patrick Geddes and Lewis Mumford," in *Megalopolis: The Giant City in History*, eds. Theo Barker and Anthony Sutcliffe (London: Palgrave Macmillan, 1993), 116–129. See also *Megalopolis: Cradle of the Future* (1962; Wilmette, IL: Encyclopedia Britannica Films).

76. Luca Muscara, "The Complete Bibliography of Jean Gottmann," *Cybergeo: European Journal of Geography*, Document 64 (1998), https://doi.org/10.4000/cybergeo.1849; Smith, "'Academic War,'" 162.

77. *About the Ford Foundation* (New York: Ford Foundation, 1961), 15, 16; Stuart W. Leslie, "Richard Macksey and the Humanities Center," *Modern Language Notes* 134 (2019): 925–941; and see François Cusset, *French Theory: How Derrida, Deleuze, & Co. Transformed the Intellectual Life of the United States* [2003], trans. Jeff Fort (Minneapolis: University of Minnesota Press, 2008). The Humanities Center at Hopkins also drilled into questions of "method" with a vengeance. Its founding director would quote words written by Charles Sanders Peirce in 1882 while on Hopkins's faculty: "This is the age of methods, and the university which is to be the exponent of the living condition of the human mind must be the university of methods"; Leslie, "Richard Macksey," 933; Charles Sanders Peirce, "Introductory Lecture on the Study of Logic," *Johns Hopkins University Circular* 2 (November 1882): 11–12.

In the early Cold War, the Rockefeller Foundation proved more amenable than Ford to sponsoring work on intellectual history and political theory, including some with a Western Marxist flavor, and these became important channels through which it could integrate European émigrés into American academia; Mueller, "Rockefeller Foundation," 110, 124.

78. *About the Ford Foundation* (1972).

79. Geiger, "American Foundations," 321.

80. Francis X. Sutton, "The Ford Foundation: The Early Years," *Daedalus* 116 (1987): 41–91, at 46, 44; *Report of the Trustees of the Ford Foundation* (New York: Ford Foundation, 1950).

81. Roger L. Geiger, *American Higher Education since World War II: A History* (Princeton, NJ: Princeton University Press, 2019), 106.

82. Dwight Macdonald, *The Ford Foundation: The Men and the Millions* (New York: Reynal, 1956), collects a series of acerbic, left-facing profiles by the *New Yorker* writer and former editor of *Politics*. The foundation's Modernist building, completed in 1967 a block from the United Nations on East 42nd Street, has long been an object of fascination. On its vegetated atrium alone, see Danielle Narae Choi, "Risk and Fun: Dan Kiley's Interior Landscape for the Ford Foundation," *Studies in the History of Gardens and Designed Landscapes* 40 (2020): 95–109; and David Gissen, *Manhattan Atmospheres: Architecture, the Interior Environment, and Urban Crisis* (Minneapolis: University of Minnesota Press, 2014), 71–82.

83. Geiger, "American Foundations," 331, 332.

84. Geiger, "American Foundations," 327; Emily Hauptmann, "The Ford Foundation and the Rise of Behavioralism in Political Science," *Journal of the History of the Behavioral Sciences* 48 (2012): 154–173; Emily Hauptmann, *Foundations and American Political Science: The Transformation of a Discipline, 1945–1970* (Lawrence: University of Kansas Press, 2022); and Solovey, *Shaky Foundations*, 103–147, on the BSP's "rocky" history.

85. Alice O'Connor, *Poverty Knowledge* (Princeton, NJ: Princeton University Press, 2008), 103–106.

86. Solovey, *Shaky Foundations*, 129.

87. Sutton, "Ford Foundation," 72, 55; Jefferson D. Pooley, "A 'Not Particularly Felicitous' Phrase: A History of the 'Behavioral Sciences' Label," *Serendipities* 1 (2016): 38–81.

88. Arnold Thackray, "Notes toward a History," *CASBS Annual Report* (1984), 59–71; Bessner, *Democracy in Exile*, 177–194.

89. Geiger, "American Foundations," 329. Units set up by Ford used a variety of terms to name their field of study. CASBS was the most celebrated example by a wide margin. Hopkins organized a Department of Social Relations, following the Parsonian nomenclature. "Self-study" programs assessing preparation to do research (and attract funding) in the behavioral sciences went ahead at Chicago, Harvard, Michigan, North Carolina, and Stanford. "Self-study" was a practice Ford had encouraged before, and not only at these interdisciplinary crossroads: in 1951 and 1952, Chicago's Department of Sociology produced an intensive self-inventory that reified disciplinary boundaries as the outer limits of the possible; Abbott, *Department and Discipline*, 34–79.

90. Sutton, "Ford Foundation," 83.

91. *Metropolis* (New York: Ford Foundation, 1959), 7, 2, 4, 15.

92. And cf. Holly Case, *The Age of Questions* (Princeton, NJ: Princeton University Press, 2018), on the "question form" motivating nineteenth-century social inquiry.

93. "Program Submission Concerning Future Program Activities" (Spring 1962), box 6, "Ford Foundation—Public Affairs Program—Special Committee Materials, 1961–1962" folder, PNYP.

94. "Report on the Urban (Metropolitan) Program" (March 1957), box 6, "Ford Foundation—Reports on Programs" folder, PNYP.

95. Paul Ylvisaker to Dyke Brown, February 14, 1958, box 6, "Ford Foundation—Public Affairs, 1958–1966" folder, PNYP.

96. *Metropolis*, 18–62; "Report on the Urban (Metropolitan) Program" (March 1957), box 6, "Ford Foundation—Reports on Programs" folder, PNYP. Penjerdel, funded to

the tune of $900,000, was active from 1960 through 1963; "A Proposed Program of Research for Penjerdel" (September 1960); "Penjerdel . . . in brief" (August 1960); and the newsletter *Penjerdel Roundtable* (slogan: "All Levels Working Together"), 1961–1963; box 69, folder 17, RPAR.

97. *The Ford Foundation and St. Louis* (New York: Ford Foundation, 1958), 3, 18, 20, 7.

98. *The Ford Foundation and St. Louis*, 18, 27, 28, 4, 8, 6, 7; emphasis added. Products of the survey include Henry J. Schmandt, Paul G. Steinbicker, and George D. Wendel, *Metropolitan Reform in St. Louis: A Case Study* (New York: Holt, Rinehart, and Winston, 1961), especially 66–70; and John C. Bollens, ed., *Exploring the Metropolitan Community* (Berkeley: University of California Press, 1961). On Cleveland, see Jane Jacobs, "Metropolitan Government" [1957], in *Vital Little Plans*, eds. Samuel Zipp and Nathan Storring (New York: Random House, 2016), 87–106.

99. *The Apprentice Experts* (New York: Ford Foundation, 1960), 20–21; *Metropolis*, 51–53; William N. Cassella, "The New York Metropolitan Region Study Program," *American Behavioral Scientist* 1 (1958): 36–37. Students came primarily from Columbia, but also from Yale, Chicago, and Princeton. The one Chicago graduate was a young Frances Fox Piven.

100. Ylvisaker to Brown, February 14, 1958.

101. *Bergen Evening Record*, editorial, "Making a Science of City Resurrection," July 17, 1959.

102. Richard Magat, *The Ford Foundation at Work: Philanthropic Choices, Methods, and Styles* (New York: Plenum, 1979), 99; *About the Ford Foundation* (1961), 18.

103. Magat, *Ford Foundation at Work*, 100. By 1974, Ford claimed to have helped found three hundred new centers of urban studies, some departments, and some entire schools. The program officer William Pendleton admitted, however, that the foundation had touched only two segments of higher education's "trinity": research and service, with only "negligible" efforts on teaching. On this, and on the extension programs' "mixed results," see William C. Pendleton, *Urban Studies and the University: The Ford Foundation Experience* (New York: Ford Foundation, 1974), 3–7, 17; Joel Fleishman, "The Teaching Function of Urban Centers," in *The Role of University-Based Urban Centers* (Cambridge, MA: Joint Center for Urban Studies, 1971), 48–89; and John E. Bebout, "Urban Studies: Higher Education and the Urban Community," *Urban Education* 6 (1971): 76–105. One exception to Ford's reticence on curriculum design arose at historically Black Morgan State University, in Baltimore.

104. "Program Submission Concerning Future Program Activities."

105. Ylvisaker to Brown, February 14, 1958.

106. Virginia M. Esposito, "Paul Ylvisaker: A Biographical Profile," in *Conscience and Community: The Legacy of Paul Ylvisaker*, ed. Virginia M. Esposito (New York: Peter Lang, 1999), xv–xxxvi; Paul N. Ylvisaker, *Intergovernmental Relations at the Grass Roots: A Study of Blue Earth County, Minnesota, to 1946* (Minneapolis: University of Minnesota Press, 1946).

107. "Public Affairs Program: Evaluation (1950–1961)."

108. Ylvisaker to Brown, February 14, 1958.

109. Paul Ylvisaker memo, "Social Science (and Humanities?) Centers," May 27, 1959, box 6, "Ford Foundation—Public Affairs, 1958–1966" folder, PNYP.

110. *About the Ford Foundation* (1972).

111. Schweber, "Wartime Research," 73; Daniel Bell, "The Idea of a Social Report," *The Public Interest* 15 (Spring 1969): 72–84.

112. United States National Resources Planning Board, *Our Cities: Their Role in the National Economy* (Washington, DC: Government Printing Office, 1937). On cities understood as "resources," see Jennifer S. Light, *The Nature of Cities: Ecological Visions and the Urban Professions, 1920–1960* (Baltimore: Johns Hopkins University Press, 2009).

113. Avigail Sachs, "Research and Democracy: The Architectural Research Division of the Tennessee Valley Authority," *Journal of Architecture* 24 (2019): 925–949, at 935.

114. Charles E. Merriam, "Urbanism," *American Journal of Sociology* 45 (1940): 720–730; Louis Wirth, "Urbanism as a Way of Life," *American Journal of Sociology* 44 (1938): 1–24; and see Christopher Klemek, *The Transatlantic Collapse of Urban Renewal* (Chicago: University of Chicago Press, 2011), 52–57, 263n7.

115. Schrum, *Instrumental University*, 32–40. Before the war, only four universities offered programs in planning: Harvard, MIT, Columbia, and Cornell. By the end of the 1940s, Illinois, North Carolina, Berkeley, and others had joined the ranks.

116. Robert M. Lillibridge, "City Planning Research in the United States," *Journal of the American Institute of Planners* 23 (January 1953): 296–307. On Merriam's outfit, see the deathlessly strange Jo Hindman, *Terrible 1313 Revisited* (Caldwell, ID: Caxton Printers, 1963), a conspiratorial account from the right that identified Chicago public-administration scholars as the fulcrum of large-scale statist repression.

117. Lillibridge, "City Planning Research," 301, 307.

118. Schrum, *Instrumental University*, 95–102. This was a competition among mostly elite universities. See Klemek, *Transatlantic Collapse*, 53: "Such developments require locating an intellectual history with specific cultural prestigious institutions, namely, elite centers of higher education, which act as a kind of fulcrum for the influence of particular ideas upon society at large. To put it another way, Ivy League universities began credentialing modern urbanists—planners, city architects, and urban designers—before most Americans even knew they needed such services (beyond a handful of high-profile turn-of-the-century City Beautiful projects)."

119. Reginald Isaacs, report for ACTION, September 16, 1954, box 11, folder 11, RRIP. On ACTION, see Light, *Nature of Cities*, 148–151; Martin Meyerson, Barbara Terrett, and William L. C. Wheaton, *Housing, People, and Cities* (New York: McGraw–Hill, 1962); and Martin Meyerson, with Jaqueline Tyrwhitt et al., *Face of the Metropolis* (New York: Random House, 1963). ACTION was one of the urban agencies Ford supported, in addition to its research projects and university-based centers.

120. Minutes, Study Group on Metropolitan Problems, June 14–16, 1956, Reel L-7, Log L55–282 ["Log Files": failed grant proposals]; Minutes, board meeting, March 22–23, 1957, Reel L-7, Log L55–282; Coleman Woodbury to Paul Ylvisaker, September 22, 1956, Reel L-7, Log L55–282; Conference proceedings, October 10–11, 1956, Reel L-7, Log L55–282; FFR. This application came in through Ford's Metropolitan Areas Program, from 1955 to 1958 a funding stream formally distinct from Urban and Regional.

121. Weil, "Frederick Gutheim Dies"; and see *Community Renewal Program Experience in Ten Cities* (Washington, DC: Washington Center for Metropolitan Studies, 1964), conference proceedings illustrative of the work of the Washington Center for Metropolitan Studies.

122. For example, Raymond Vernon, *The Changing Economic Function of the Central City* (New York: Committee for Economic Development, 1959).

123. Lowdon Wingo Jr., *Cities and Space: The Future Use of Urban Land* (Baltimore: Johns Hopkins University Press, 1963), is one synthesis that emerged from a Resources for the Future conference.

124. Joseph R. Passonneau, "Emergence of City Form," in *Urban Life and Form*, ed. Werner Z. Hirsch (New York: Holt, Rinehart, and Winston, 1963), 9–27, at 24, 23; Leo F. Schnore, "Urban Form: The Case of the Metropolitan Community," in *Urban Life and Form*, 169–197; William L. Weismantel, "A New Vision in Law: The City as an Artifact," in *Urban Life and Form*, 29–58.

125. F. Stuart Chapin Jr., "Foundations of Urban Planning," in *Urban Life and Form*, ed. Werner Z. Hirsch (New York: Holt, Rinehart, and Winston, 1963), 217–248, at 233, 220, 245.

126. David Popenoe and Robert Gutman, "Centers for Urban Studies: A Review," *American Behavioral Scientist* 6 (1963): 48–54, at 48, 54. In some ways, this prefigures the arguments of Noortje Marres, for whom "issues" and "problems" precede and give rise to "publics." See "No Issue, No Public" (PhD diss., University of Amsterdam, 2005); and "The Issues Deserve More Credit: Pragmatist Contributions to the Study of Public Involvement in Controversy," *Social Studies of Science* 37 (2007): 759–780.

127. David Popenoe, "Urban Studies Centers in Institutions of Higher Education: Some Thoughts on Their Structure, Functions and Problems," *Urban Affairs Quarterly* 5 (1969): 143–150, at 148, 147. The third in the series was Popenoe, "Urban Studies Reconsidered."

128. John Friedmann, "The Uses of Planning Theory: A Bibliographic Essay," *Journal of Planning Education and Research* 28 (2008): 247–257, at 254.

129. Harvey S. Perloff, *Education for Planning: City, State, and Regional* (Baltimore: Johns Hopkins University Press, 1957), 4; Joseph L. Arnold, *The New Deal in the Suburbs: A History of the Greenbelt Town Programs* (Columbus: Ohio State University Press, 1971).

130. The historical literature on PERP is scattered, but see Jean-Louis Sarbib, "The University of Chicago Program in Planning: A Retrospective Look," *Journal of Planning Education and Research* 2 (1983): 77–81; Light, *Nature of Cities*, 108–111, 242–245; Robert A. Beauregard, *Planning Matter: Acting with Things* (Chicago: University of Chicago Press, 2015), 194; John Friedmann, "A Life in Planning," in *The Prospect of Cities* (Minneapolis: University of Minnesota Press, 2002), 119–157, at 119–122; John Friedmann, "Harvey Perloff: Explorer, Pioneer," *Journal of the American Planning Association* 50 (1984): 79–82; Mayer, "Urban Geography and Chicago"; Martin Meyerson, Remarks to ACSP, October 1982, box 124, folder 48, MMP; and Perloff, *Education for Planning*. A PERP student, Janet L. Abu-Lughod, *New York, Chicago, Los Angeles: America's Global Cities* (Minneapolis: University of Minnesota Press, 1999), viii, recalls learning "a then-new approach to planning being honed."

131. Perloff, *Education for Planning*, 135. Peter Hall dates the split between planning theory and planning practice to around 1955. Whereas there had always been some theory in planning, Hall claims, the theory of planning became autonomous after 1955; *Cities of Tomorrow: An Intellectual History of Urban Planning and Design in the Twentieth Century*, 3rd ed. (Malden, MA: Blackwell, 2002), 355.

132. Rexford G. Tugwell, "The Study of Planning as a Scientific Endeavor," *Fiftieth Annual Report of the Michigan Academy of Sciences, Arts, and Letters* (1948): 34–48, at 43; emphasis added.

133. Martin Meyerson, "Research and City Planning," *Journal of the American Institute of Planners* 20 (1954): 201–205, at 202, 201, 203. As Meyerson noted, the antiplanning ideas of Friedrich Hayek, Ludwig von Mises, Milton Friedman, and Michael Polanyi were already ascendant in Chicago's economics department.

134. Martin Meyerson, "What a Planner Has to Know: III," in *Planning 1946* (Chicago: American Society of Planning Officials, 1946), 167–172, at 171.

135. Martin Meyerson and Edward C. Banfield, *Politics, Planning, and the Public Interest* (Glencoe, IL: The Free Press, 1955), 280. Meyerson had moved to Penn by 1955, but the book was very much a Chicago product.

136. Edward C. Banfield, "Ends and Means in Planning," *UNESCO International Social Science Journal* 11, no. 3 (1959): 361–367.

137. Perloff, *Education for Planning*, 18.

138. Melville C. Branch Jr., "Coordinative Planning and the Architect," *Land Economics* 26 (1950): 78–81, at 79. See also his *City Planning and Aerial Information* (Cambridge, MA: Harvard University Press, 1971).

139. Meyerson, "What a Planner Has to Know," 169.

140. Martin Meyerson, "Building the Middle-Range Bridge to Comprehensive Planning," *Journal of the American Institute of Planners* 22 (1956): 58–64, at 60.

141. Melville C. Branch Jr., "Concerning Coordinative Planning," *Journal of the American Institute of Planners* 16 (1950): 163–171, at 163, 165. For excellent nineteenth- and early-twentieth-century context, see Jamie L. Pietruska, *Looking Forward: Prediction and Uncertainty in Modern America* (Chicago: University of Chicago Press, 2017).

142. Rexford G. Tugwell, "The Fourth Power," *Planning and Civic Comment* (April–June 1939): 1–31, at 1, 26.

143. Walter Friedman, *Fortune Tellers: The Story of America's First Economic Forecasters* (Princeton, NJ: Princeton University Press, 2013).

144. Timothy Mitchell, "Econometality: How the Future Entered Government," *Critical Inquiry* 40 (2014): 479–507. Mitchell and others have adapted these insights from the work of Michel Foucault. When "one works on probabilities," Foucault writes, then "one works on the future . . . a future that is not exactly controllable, not precisely measured or measurable." According to his well-known framework, this future-orientation typifies a concern with power as *security* rather than either penal–surveillant *discipline* or the *sovereignty* typical of early-modern statecraft; Michel Foucault, *Security, Territory, Population* [1978], trans. Graham Burchell (New York: Picador, 2007), 19, 20. Foucault traces these shifts to the late eighteenth century, when quantitative rates, ratios, "forecasts, statistical estimates, and overall measures" were durably integrated into the machinery of governance. As geographers have detailed, Foucault extended these insights to the governance of "environment" and "the urban problem"; for example, Michel Foucault, *"Society Must Be Defended"* [1976], trans. David Macey (New York: Picador, 2003), 243–246.

145. Rexford G. Tugwell and Edward C. Banfield, "Governmental Planning at Mid-Century," *Journal of Politics* 13 (1951): 133–163, at 163.

146. Paul Ylvisaker, "The Brave New Urban World" [1961], in *Conscience and Community: The Legacy of Paul Ylvisaker*, ed. Virginia M. Esposito (New York: Peter Lang, 1999), 107–124, at 119.

147. Paul Ylvisaker, "Conscience and the Community" [1964], in *Conscience and Community: The Legacy of Paul Ylvisaker*, ed. Virginia M. Esposito (New York: Peter Lang, 1999), 34–41, at 35.

148. Paul N. Ylvisaker, "Innovation and Evolution: Bridge to the Future Metropolis," *Annals of the American Academy of Political and Social Science* 314 (1957): 156–164, at 156. Martin Meyerson himself edited this issue of the *Annals*, which addressed "images of the future"; Martin Meyerson and Barbara Terrett, "Metropolis Lost, Metropolis Regained," *Annals of the American Academy of Political and Social Science* 314 (1957): 1–9.

149. Ylvisaker, "Conscience and the Community," 40; Paul Ylvisaker, "Quality of Life in 1980" [1965], in *Conscience and Community: The Legacy of Paul Ylvisaker*, ed. Virginia M. Esposito (New York: Peter Lang, 1999), 42–57, at 42, 43. The 1964 essay had first appeared in *Television Quarterly*.

150. Paul Ylvisaker, "The Shape of the Future: Urban Life," address at the New School for Social Research, October 26, 1961, box 120, CAP.

151. Harvey S. Perloff, "Planning Concepts and Regional Research," *Social Forces* 32 (1953): 173–177.

152. Tugwell, "Study of Planning," 41, 40; emphasis added. On Heidegger, see David Couzens Hoy, *The Time of Our Lives: A Critical History of Temporality* (Cambridge, MA: MIT Press, 2009), 1–93 and passim.

153. Ylvisaker, "Conscience and the Community," 40. Invoke the future to justify intervention on the present: a number of scholars have explored the political predicates of this temporal reasoning. Some see it as the quintessential Cold War politics of time. Game theory, scenario planning, and other RAND-identified techniques placed a premium on prediction and preemption, with nuclear attack in mind as the particular future to be averted. See, inter alia, Jenny Andersson, *The Future of the World: Futurology, Futurists, and the Struggle for the Post–Cold War Imagination* (Oxford: Oxford University Press, 2018), 49–121; S. M. Amadae, *Rationalizing Capitalist Democracy: The Cold War Origins of Rational-Choice Liberalism* (Chicago: University of Chicago Press, 2003); Limor Samimian-Darash, *Uncertainty by Design: Preparing for the Future with Scenario Technology* (Ithaca, NY: Cornell University Press, 2022); Erickson, "Mathematical Models." Joel Isaac suggests that Cold War politics sought *control* of the future but not genuine *planning*; "Human Sciences," 739.

154. Clark Kerr, Introduction to "Opening Session," in *The Metropolitan Future* (Berkeley: University of California, 1965), 1–3, at 2; Martin Meyerson, Remarks on "The Future of California," in *The Metropolitan Future*, 189–192, at 191. Bacon seconded Meyerson's thoughts: fragmentation was the "failure of our educational institutions," just as it had failed the American metropolis; Edmund S. Bacon, "In Defense of Big Cities: Urbanity or Suburbanity?," in *The Metropolitan Future*, 26–32, at 26. On Bauer and this meeting, see H. Peter Oberlander and Eva M. Newbrun, *Houser: The Life and Work of Catherine Bauer, 1905–64* (Vancouver: UBC Press, 1999), 296–300.

155. Earl Warren, "A Vision for California," in *The Metropolitan Future*, 203–210, at 207.

2. The Atmosphere and the Network

1. *Metropolis* (New York: Ford Foundation, 1959), 54. Coequal with sections titled "Demonstration Projects" and "Related Urban Projects Abroad," this publication allots an entire subheading to the Joint Center, the only institution so honored. Ford considered it the premier center of urban studies and funded it accordingly.

2. Historical accounts of the Joint Center, with varying emphases and degrees of sympathy, include Eugenie L. Birch, "Making Urban Research Intellectually Respectable: Martin Meyerson and the Joint Center for Urban Studies of Massachusetts Institute of Technology and Harvard University, 1959–1964," *Journal of Planning History* 10 (2011): 219–238; Lawrence J. Vale, *Changing Cities: 75 Years of Planning Better Futures at MIT* (Cambridge, MA: SA+P Press, 2008), 30–36; Christopher Klemek, *The Transatlantic Collapse of Urban Renewal* (Chicago: University of Chicago Press, 2011), 179–184, 202–207; Eric Mumford, "From Master Planning to Self-Build: The MIT–Harvard Joint Center for Urban Studies, 1959–1971," in *A Second Modernism: MIT, Architecture, and the "Techno-Social" Moment*, ed. Arindam Dutta (Cambridge, MA: MIT Press, 2013), 288–309; and Christopher Loss, "Remapping the Midcentury Metropolis: The Ford Foundation and the Joint Center for Urban Studies of MIT and Harvard University," Rockefeller Archive Center Research Reports Online, March 10, 2014, http://rockarch.org/publications/resrep/loss.pdf.

3. Joint Center for Urban Studies, *The First Five Years* (Cambridge, MA: The Center, 1964), 7.

4. JCUS proposal to Ford Foundation, September 28, 1965, Reel 3006, Grants L–N (FA 732E), FFR.

5. Nils Gilman, *Mandarins of the Future: Modernization Theory in Cold War America* (Baltimore: Johns Hopkins University Press, 2003), is compatible as microhistory. In its argumentation through the case of one interdisciplinary center (the Special Operations and Research Office) housed at one university (American), Joy Rohde, *Armed with Expertise: The Militarization of American Social Research During the Cold War* (Ithaca, NY: Cornell University Press, 2013), has also been instructive, as has Martin Bulmer, *The Chicago School of Sociology: Institutionalization, Diversity, and the Rise of Sociological Research* (Chicago: University of Chicago Press, 1984), the biography of a vital precursor from whose example the Joint Center's divergences are telling.

6. *Metropolis*, 21.

7. Anna Vallye, "The Middleman: Kepes's Instruments," in *A Second Modernism: MIT, Architecture, and the "Techno-Social" Moment*, ed. Arindam Dutta (Cambridge, MA: MIT Press, 2013), 144–185, at 162. The School of Architecture's first ORU was founded in 1936 with money from the Bemis Foundation, and Burchard directed it for a decade; Brendan D. Moran, "Toward a 'Nation of Universities': Architecture and Planning Education at MIT circa the 1940s," in *A Second Modernism*, ed. Dutta, 686–713, at 709. Moran usefully stresses the interplay of "two complex unities simultaneously": the home institution and the "decentralized network" of other universities, departments, and interdisciplinary entities.

8. CURS minutes, June 7, 1951, box 55, "Committee on Urban and Regional Studies, 1951–1954" folder #1, LRP.

9. "Summary—Urban Research Discussion," October 7, 1952, box 55, "Committee on Urban and Regional Studies, 1951–1954" folder #1, LRP.

10. CURS minutes, June 25, 1951, box 55, "Committee on Urban and Regional Studies, 1951–1954" folder #1, LRP.

11. CURS minutes, October 2, 1952, box 55, "Committee on Urban and Regional Studies, 1951–1954" folder #1, LRP.

12. *Regional Plan of New York and Its Environs, Volume One: Graphic Regional Plan* (New York: Regional Plan of New York and Its Environs, 1929); *Regional Survey of New York and Its Environs*, 8 vols. (New York: Committee on Regional Plan of New York, 1929–1931); Regional Plan Association, *From Plan to Reality*, 3 vols. (New York: Regional Plan Association, 1933–1942); David A. Johnson, *Planning the Great Metropolis: The 1929 Regional Plan of New York and Its Environs* (London: Routledge, 1995); Robert Fishman, "The Regional Plan and the Transformation of the Industrial Metropolis," in *The Landscape of Modernity: New York City, 1900–1940*, eds. David Ward and Olivier Zunz (Baltimore: Johns Hopkins University Press, 1992), 106–125; R. L. Duffus, *Mastering a Metropolis* (New York: Harper and Brothers, 1930).

13. Rexford G. Tugwell, "The Study of Planning as a Scientific Endeavor," *Fiftieth Annual Report of the Michigan Academy of Sciences, Arts, and Letters* (1948): 34–48, at 51; CURS minutes, June 7, 1951; Moran, "Toward a 'Nation of Universities,'" 709; Charles R. Walker, *Steeltown: An Industrial Case History of the Conflict between Progress and Security* (New Haven, CT: Yale University Press, 1950).

14. CURS minutes, June 7, 1951.

15. CURS minutes, June 7, 1951.

16. CURS minutes, June 25, 1951. On the Regional Planning Association of America's political visions, see, from among an extensive literature, Garrett Dash Nelson, "Regional Planning as Cultural Criticism: Reclaiming the Radical Wholes of Interwar Regional Thinkers," *Regional Studies* 55 (2021): 127–137; and Carl Sussman, ed., *Planning the Fourth Migration: The Neglected Vision of the Regional Planning Association of America* (Cambridge, MA: MIT Press, 1976). On Stein's postwar efforts, see Kristin E. Larsen, *Community Architect: The Life and Vision of Clarence S. Stein* (Ithaca, NY: Cornell University Press, 2016), especially 218–228.

17. H. Peter Oberlander and Eva M. Newbrun, *Houser: The Life and Work of Catherine Bauer, 1905–64* (Vancouver: UBC Press, 1999), 228–229.

18. CURS minutes, June 7, 1951.

19. Progress report, November 27, 1951; "Progress Report: A Center for Urban and Regional Studies," January 18, 1952; box 55, "Committee on Urban and Regional Studies, 1951–1954" folder #1, LRP.

20. "Lloyd Rodwin, 80, MIT Urban Studies Professor, Extended the Field of Planning to Social Sciences and the Third World," *MIT News*, December 8, 1999; Lloyd Rodwin, interview by Morton Schussheim, June 11, 1994, PIH; Lloyd Rodwin, "Information Concerning Associate Editors" questionnaire, September 17, 1958, box 4, "Daedalus, 1958–1959" folder #1, LRP. The standard account of Cohen is David A. Hollinger, *Morris R. Cohen and the Scientific Ideal* (Cambridge, MA: MIT Press, 1975). City College comes up in every omnibus treatment of the New York Intellectuals. Many invoke the alcoves. The most exacting description of their physical layout and appropriation as "turf" is Irving Kristol, "Memoirs of a Trotskyist," *New York Times Magazine*, January 23, 1977. Rodwin's interest in specifically American intellectual traditions was notable; it was his wife, Nadine, who introduced him to European high culture later in life.

21. Lloyd Rodwin, interview by Morton Schussheim, June 11, 1994; Charles Abrams to Lloyd Rodwin, March 23, 1945, box 10a, CAP. On Abrams as a public figure, see A. Scott Henderson, *Housing and the Democratic Ideal: The Life and Thought of Charles Abrams* (New York: Columbia University Press, 2000).

22. For Abrams's account of antisemitism in the profession, see "The Reminiscences of Charles Abrams," April 26, 1964, CUL. For a similar discussion between two other stars in the firmament of urban research, Reginald Isaacs to Harvey Perloff, April 24, 1967, box 10, folder 39, RRIP: "inherited religious designation" kept Isaacs from owning a home in certain parts of greater Boston.

23. Lloyd Rodwin, "Garden Cities and the Metropolis," *Journal of Land and Public Utility Economics* 21 (1945): 268–281, at 271, 278, 281. On Rodwin's ensuing debate with Bauer and Mumford, which attracted attention and led to his being awarded a fellowship and admission to the doctoral program at Harvard, see Oberlander and Newbrun, *Houser*, 230–235.

24. Lloyd Rodwin, *The British New Towns Policy: Problems and Implications* (Cambridge, MA: Harvard University Press, 1956), 201, 166; emphasis added.

25. When Greendale, the Greenbelt town outside Milwaukee, was sold off in 1948, Rodwin did not mourn: it was "no longer Utopian"; Abrams "to whom it may concern" re: Lloyd Rodwin, March 29, 1957, box 10a, CAP; Rodwin to Abrams, December 22, 1948, box 102, CAP.

26. Lewis Mumford, "Garden Cities and the Metropolis: A Reply," *Journal of Land and Public Utility Economics* 22 (1946): 66–69, at 69; Lloyd Rodwin, interview by Morton Schussheim, June 11, 1994.

27. Catherine Bauer memo, October 12, 1948, box 8, folder 16, CSP.

28. Rodwin to Gerald Holton, February 24, 1959, box 4, "Daedalus, 1958–1959" folder #1, LRP; Lewis Mumford, *Technics and Civilization* (New York: Harcourt, 1934). Many historians of modern temporality have seized on Mumford's (12–18) discussion of fourteenth-century monasteries and the mechanical clock; for example, Kevin Birth, *Objects of Time: How Things Shape Temporality* (New York: Palgrave Macmillan, 2012).

29. "The Case for a Research Center for Urban and Regional Studies at MIT," December 14, 1956, box 56, "Harvard–MIT Federation Discussions, 1957–1963" folder #1, LRP. Christopher P. Loss, "'The City of Tomorrow Must Reckon with the Lives and Living Habits of Human Beings': The Joint Center for Urban Studies Goes to Venezuela, 1957–1969," *Journal of Urban History* 47 (2021): 623–650, is very informative on the 1957–1959 period but says little on the events of 1951–1957.

30. Vale, *Changing Cities*, 27.

31. "The Physical Environment of City and Region," September 20, 1957, box 5, "Proposed Focus for the Center, 1957–1959" folder, LRP; CURS minutes, June 7, 1951; Kevin Lynch, "A Proposal for a Center Program on City Form," December 11, 1958, box 55, "Rockefeller Project" folder, LRP.

32. Clément Orillard, "Tracing Urban Design's 'Townscape' Origins: Some Relationships between a British Editorial Policy and an American Academic Field in the 1950s," *Urban History* 36 (2009): 284–302, at 292. Lynch had also received Ford money that year for a more narrowly defined study of Italian cities.

33. Kevin Lynch, *The Image of the City* (Cambridge, MA: MIT Press, 1960); Tridib Banerjee and Michael Southworth, "Kevin Lynch: His Life and Work," in *City Sense*

and City Design (Cambridge, MA: MIT Press, 1990), 1–29; Anthony Raynsford, "Civic Art in an Age of Cultural Relativism: The Aesthetic Origins of Kevin Lynch's *Image of the City*," *Journal of Urban Design* 16 (2011): 43–65; Hashim Sarkis, "Disoriented: Kevin Lynch, around 1960," in *A Second Modernism: MIT, Architecture, and the "Techno-Social" Moment,* ed. Arindam Dutta (Cambridge, MA: MIT Press, 2013), 394–433. Districts, nodes, and edges rounded out Lynch's fivefold typology of form, one of the most familiar catechisms of planning education.

34. Inter alia, San Francisco Department of City Planning, *Existing Form and Image* (San Francisco: Department of City Planning, 1970); Los Angeles Department of City Planning, *The Visual Environment of Los Angeles* (Los Angeles: Department of City Planning, 1971); Meredith Drake Reitan and Tridib Banerjee, "Kevin Lynch in Los Angeles: Reflections on Planning, Politics, and Participation," *Journal of the American Planning Association* 84 (2018): 217–229. "People are hungry for such visions," Ed Bacon believed; Edmund S. Bacon, "In Defense of Big Cities: Urbanity or Suburbanity?," in *The Metropolitan Future* (Berkeley: University of California, 1965), 26–32, at 31. Rodwin, for his part, remained sufficiently attached to the image framework that he brought out an edited volume as late as 1984: Lloyd Rodwin and Robert M. Hollister, eds., *Cities of the Mind: Images and Themes of the City in the Social Sciences* (New York: Plenum, 1984), spanned the disciplines, expanded Lynch's insights beyond the domain of "large-scale architecture" (160), and used *image* to signify Gestalt, paradigm, or prior assumption.

35. Kevin Lynch, "The Form of Cities," *Scientific American,* April 1, 1954, 54–63, at 60, 62, 63, 55.

36. Kevin Lynch and Lloyd Rodwin, "A Theory of Urban Form," *Journal of the American Institute of Planners* 24 (1958): 201–214, at 202, 201, 203, 213. For an episode in which a pre-functionalist Robert Merton sought to ascertain the effects of neighborhood layout on behavior, see Kenneth Fox, "Sociology Applied to Planning: Robert K. Merton and the Columbia–Lavanburg Housing Study," *Journal of Planning History* 19 (2020): 281–313, at 296, 303, 304. As the first research editor of the *Journal of the American Institute of Planners,* Meyerson cited Merton's study.

37. Vallye, "The Middleman," 146, 172. For Kepes's first major statement to this effect, see György Kepes, *Language of Vision* (New York: Theobald, 1944); and also the highly critical John R. Blakinger, *György Kepes: Undreaming the Bauhaus* (Cambridge, MA: MIT Press, 2019).

38. Eugenie L. Birch, "ACSP Distinguished Educator, 1996: Martin Meyerson," *Journal of Planning Education and Research* (2018): 490–492. Sert also went by José Luis, the Castilian Spanish version of his Catalan given name.

39. Eugenie L. Birch, "Reviving the Art of Biography: The Emblematic Life of Martin Meyerson," *Journal of Planning History* 10 (2011): 175–179, at 177; Ellen Shoshkes, "Martin Meyerson and Jaqueline Tyrwhitt and the Global Exchange of Planning Ideas," *Journal of Planning History* 9 (2010): 75–94, at 83.

40. Marcia Marker Feld, "Martin Meyerson: Building the Middle-Range Bridge to Educate Professional Planners," *Journal of Planning History* 10 (2011): 239–248, at 241; Michael B. Teitz, "Martin Meyerson: Builder of Institutions," *Journal of Planning History* 10 (2011): 180–192, at 181.

41. Martin Meyerson to Abrams, May 29, 1946, box 102, CAP. On Telesis, see Francis Violich, "The Planning Pioneers," *California Living,* February 26, 1978, 29–35.

42. Regional Development Council of America, "Regional Dispersal for Defense and Peace" (1950), box 8, folder 13; Catherine Bauer memo, October 12, 1948, box 8, folder 16, CSP.

43. Shoshkes, "Martin Meyerson and Jaqueline Tyrwhitt," 89, 79, 85.

44. Birch, "ACSP Distinguished Educator, 1996," 490.

45. Meyerson, "Middle-Range Bridge," 63.

46. Loss, "'City of Tomorrow,'" 5–9.

47. "Memorandum on Proposed Research Policy," box 55, "Harvard–MIT Federation Discussions, 1957–1963" folder #1, LRP.

48. Loss, "'City of Tomorrow,'" 5–9.

49. Paul Ylvisaker to Dyke Brown, February 14, 1958, box 6, "Ford Foundation—Public Affairs, 1958–1966" folder, PNYP. MIT was obviously the more scientific of the two universities, but see Clark A. Elliott and Margaret W. Rossiter, eds., *Science at Harvard University: Historical Perspectives* (Bethlehem, PA: Lehigh University Press, 1992). On Harvard generally, see Morton Keller and Phyllis Keller, *Making Harvard Modern: The Rise of America's University* (New York: Oxford University Press, 2001); and on the GSD, see Anthony Alofsin, *The Struggle for Modernism: Architecture, Landscape Architecture, and City Planning at Harvard* (New York: Norton, 2002).

50. "Proposed Agreement of Collaboration," February 24, 1958, box 56, "Harvard–MIT Federation Discussions, 1957–1963" folder #1; Memorandum of Agreement, March 26, 1958, box 56, "Harvard–MIT Federation Discussions, 1957–1963" folder #1; Memo, September 22, 1958, box 55, "Harvard–MIT Federation Discussions, 1957–1963" folder #1, LRP; and "Grant PA58-391: MIT," Reel 3006, Grants L–N (FA 732E), FFR. Between 1952 and 1958, Ford had given $12 million to Harvard social scientists and $3.5 million to the MIT counterparts; Roger L. Geiger, "American Foundations and Academic Social Science, 1945–1960," *Minerva* 26 (1988): 315–341, at 332.

51. Loss, "'City of Tomorrow,'" details this sequence. Loss presents Ylvisaker as domineering and plots the story as one in which "Cambridge would succumb to New York" (631). This may overstate the case. Another geographic matter: Loss writes that the Joint Center's shared office space was located "away from both campuses" (624). In actuality, it was clearly in Harvard's part of town, two blocks from Harvard Yard but fully two subway stops from MIT.

52. But contrast this office, its selection subject to the whims of commercial real estate, to the purpose-built Social Sciences Building, "1126," that, through the adjacencies written into its floor plan, both reflected and helped sustain the Chicago School's vaunted interdisciplinarity; Bulmer, *Chicago School*, 195–197.

53. "Grant PA58-391: MIT."

54. Martin Meyerson, "Report to the Visiting Committee of the Joint Center for Urban Studies," June 1963, box 14, folder 9, FFR. The governance structure of the Joint Center comprised a faculty committee (drawn from Harvard and MIT equally), an administrative committee (same), and a visiting committee, whose ranks during the first five years included major financiers such as David Rockefeller, urban civil servants such as Robert C. Weaver of the Housing and Home Finance Agency (and eventually HUD), politicians such as Joseph Clark (Ylvisaker's mentor and by then a Pennsylvania senator), and, as chair, Thomas Cabot, of the Boston Brahmin family by that name.

55. Joint Center for Urban Studies, *First Five Years*, 5. See also Joint Center for Urban Studies, *The First Two Years* (Cambridge, MA: The Center, 1961).

56. Joint Center for Urban Studies, *First Five Years*, 5, 10.

57. Meyerson, "Report to the Visiting Committee."

58. Using Lazarsfeld's typology, the Joint Center was a "subject-specialized" center, as opposed to one committed to formulating theory; Allen H. Barton, "Paul Lazarsfeld and Applied Social Research," *Social Science History* 3 (October 1979): 4–44, at 40; Paul F. Lazarsfeld, "The Sociology of Empirical Social Research," *American Sociological Review* 27 (1962): 757–767, at 763–765.

59. Joint Center for Urban Studies, *First Five Years*, 9, 8, 10, 50; Meyerson, "Report to the Visiting Committee"; JCUS final report to Ford Foundation, December 31, 1970, Reel 3006, Grants L–N (FA 732E), FFR. Jamie Cohen-Cole, *The Open Mind: Cold War Politics and the Sciences of Human Nature* (Chicago: University of Chicago Press, 2014), provides beneficial context regarding the understandings of cognition advanced in postwar meditations on free-flowing intellectual exchange.

60. John Delafons, *Land-Use Controls in the United States* (Cambridge, MA: MIT Press, 1962).

61. A. Scheffer Lang and Richard Soberman, *Urban Rail Transit: Its Economics and Technology* (Cambridge, MA: MIT Press, 1962).

62. George Sternlieb, *The Future of the Downtown Department Store* (Cambridge, MA: Harvard University Press, 1962), 2, 188–189, 4. For a complete roster of research members, fellows, visiting associates, and research assistants, see Joint Center for Urban Studies, *First Five Years*, 57–62.

63. Richard L. Meier, *A Communications Theory of Urban Growth* (Cambridge, MA: MIT Press, 1962).

64. The center also issued reports—typically unbound, policy-oriented white papers—and reprints of journal articles by core faculty that seemed likely to interest audiences beyond the academy. The latter included Lynch's (1954) and Lynch and Rodwin's (1958) statements on urban form.

65. Some books with roots at the Joint Center appeared with commercial presses. An example is Serge Chermayeff and Christopher Alexander, *Community and Privacy: Toward a New Architecture of Humanism* [1963] (New York: Anchor, 1965). Alexander was a doctoral student in architecture at Harvard. Chermayeff was a lecturer at both Harvard and MIT. Architectural scholarship was not in the Joint Center's mainstream.

66. William Alonso, *Location and Land Use: Toward a General Theory of Land Rent* (Cambridge, MA: Harvard University Press, 1964).

67. Charles M. Haar, ed., *Law and Land: Anglo-American Planning Practice* (Cambridge, MA: Harvard University Press, 1964), the proceedings of a joint conference with Brookings.

68. Charles Abrams, *Man's Struggle for Shelter in an Urbanizing World* (Cambridge, MA: MIT Press, 1964).

69. Bulmer, *Chicago School*, 3, 4, 16. Generalization from empirical research defined what Bulmer calls "the Chicago approach to theory." The Chicago School's monograph series was univocal in its commitment to theory-building. The range of admissible argument seemed circumscribed by departmental priorities: most volumes carried an

introduction by Robert Park, and Ernest Burgess's concentric-circle diagram, presented as the ground truth underlying empirical inquiry, had a way of showing up in just about every student's first book. There, the publication program was even more central to the enterprise; indeed, the University of Chicago Press had been founded concurrently with the university itself, a mark of total dedication to research.

70. "Publications of Urban Studies by Members of the Joint Center," March 1965, box 13, folder 5, FFR.

71. Ralph W. Conant, ed., *The Public Library and the City* (Cambridge, MA: MIT Press, 1965); Everett Hughes to Talcott Parsons, June 20, 1963, JCUS folder, TPP. Samuel Stouffer, who died in 1960, was the first sociologist on the committee; Joint Center for Urban Studies, *First Five Years*, 57–58.

72. Martin Meyerson to Thomas J. Wilson and Lynwood Bryant, November 19, 1959, JCUS folder, TPP. Formally, the publisher is The MIT Press.

73. Meyerson to Wilson and Bryant, March 19, 1962, JCUS folder, TPP. The Joint Center also provided "back-up services" for its scholars. These included research assistance (by paid undergraduates) and clerical work, including the typing of manuscripts. Its funds also paid part of the salaries of twenty-five faculty members. See Meyerson, "Report to the Visiting Committee"; Joint Center for Urban Studies, *First Five Years*, 6.

74. Faculty Committee minutes, November 6, 1962, JCUS folder, TPP.

75. James Q. Wilson memo, July 18, 1963, JCUS folder, TPP.

76. Lloyd Rodwin, *Housing and Economic Progress: A Study of the Housing Experiences of Boston's Middle-Income Families* (Cambridge, MA: Harvard University Press and The Technology Press, 1961), 127.

77. For accounts critical of Gray Areas, see Alice O'Connor, "Community Action, Urban Reform, and the Fight against Poverty: The Ford Foundation's Gray Areas Program," *Journal of Urban History* 22 (1996): 586–625; Robert Halpern, "Neighborhood-Based Initiatives to Address Poverty: Lessons from Experience," *Journal of Sociology & Social Welfare* 20 (December 1993): 111–135; Ananya Roy, Stuart Schrader, and Emma Shaw Crane, "'The Anti-Poverty Hoax': Development, Pacification, and the Making of Community in the Global 1960s," *Cities* 44 (2015): 139–145; G. William Domhoff, "The Ford Foundation in the Inner City: Forging an Alliance with Neighborhood Activists," Who Rules America?, September 2005, http://www2.ucsc.edu/whorulesamerica/local/ford_foundation.html; and Karen Ferguson, *Top Down: The Ford Foundation, Black Power, and the Reinvention of Racial Liberalism* (Philadelphia: University of Pennsylvania Press, 2013). Raymond Vernon, *The Changing Economic Function of the Central City* (New York: Committee for Economic Development, 1959), is the origin of the term.

78. Rodwin, *Housing and Economic Progress*, 37, 108–114, 122. Hoyt is complex in ways that Rodwin and other critics missed; see Robert A. Beauregard, "More Than Sector Theory: Homer Hoyt's Contributions to Planning Knowledge," *Journal of Planning History* 6 (2007): 248–271. See also Homer Hoyt, *The Structure and Growth of Residential Neighborhoods in American Cities* (Washington, DC: Federal Housing Administration, 1939); Ernest W. Burgess, "The Growth of the City: An Introduction to a Research Project," in *The City*, ed. Robert E. Park, (Chicago: University of Chicago Press, 1925), 47–62; and Elaine Lewinnek, "Mapping Chicago, Imagining Metropolises: Reconsidering the Zonal Model of Urban Growth," *Journal of Urban History* 36 (2010): 197–225.

79. Bernard J. Frieden, *The Future of Old Neighborhoods: Rebuilding for a Changing Population* (Cambridge, MA: MIT Press, 1964), 1, 2, 49, 120, viii. By 1970, ten of seventy-nine Joint Center–aligned dissertations had been published in the book series; JCUS final report to Ford Foundation.

80. Joint Center for Urban Studies, *First Five Years*, 5–6.

81. Joint Center for Urban Studies, *First Five Years*, 42–49; Herbert J. Gans, *The Levittowners: Ways of Life and Politics in a New Suburban Community* (New York: Random House, 1967); and on New Haven, especially Francesca Russello Ammon, *Bulldozer: Demolition and Clearance of the Postwar Landscape* (New Haven, CT: Yale University Press, 2016), 140–181.

82. Joint Center for Urban Studies, *First Five Years*, 57–61. From 1965, Handlin headed the new Charles Warren Center for American History—which university historians Morton Keller and Phyllis Keller denigrate as a "lesser add-on" to the area-studies centers organized before 1960. The Joint Center, they contend, also merits this description. See *Making Harvard Modern*, 414.

83. After Michel Callon, "Some Elements of a Sociology of Translation: Domestication of the Scallops and the Fishermen of St. Brieuc Bay," *Sociological Review* 32 (1984): 196–233.

84. Helen Kistin, *Urban Economic Research: Improving the Accessibility and Utilization of Literature, Data, and Data Sources* (Cambridge, MA: Joint Center for Urban Studies, 1961), 40, 15. Formally, the report was done for the Joint Center, but it was addressed to Resources for the Future.

85. Lazarsfeld, "Sociology of Empirical Social Research," 766. Lazarsfeld, following Robert Lynd, held that, in its openness to a multiplicity of uses, basic research was "research for the future."

86. Cf. the vision outlined in Joel Isaac, "Epistemic Design: Theory and Data in Harvard's Department of Social Relations," in *Cold War Social Science*, eds. Mark Solovey and Hamilton Cravens (New York: Palgrave Macmillan, 2012), 79–95, whereby the postwar emphasis on diagrams, models, tables, and types led to an "increasingly holistic empiricism" (92).

87. David Greenstone, *A Report on the Politics of Detroit* (Cambridge, MA: Joint Center for Urban Studies [JCUS], 1961); Martha Derthick, *City Politics in Washington, D.C.* (Cambridge, MA: JCUS, 1962); James Q. Wilson, *A Report on Politics in Los Angeles* (Cambridge, MA: JCUS, 1959); Robert Binstock, *A Report on Politics in Manchester, New Hampshire* (Cambridge, MA: JCUS, 1961); Robert Binstock, *A Report on Politics in Worcester, Massachusetts* (Cambridge, MA: JCUS, 1960); Mark K. Adams, *A Report on Politics in New Castle, New York* (Cambridge, MA: JCUS, 1961). Note slight variations in the wording of the titles. Derthick's volume also names the Washington Center for Metropolitan Studies on its cover.

88. Kenneth E. Gray, *A Report on Politics in Kansas City* (Cambridge, MA: JCUS, 1959), I-6; Bertil Hanson, *A Report on the Politics of Milwaukee* (Cambridge, MA: JCUS, 1961), I-10; Kenneth E. Gray, *A Report on the Politics of Houston* (Cambridge, MA: JCUS, 1960), I-22; and Robert L. Freedman, *A Report on Politics in Philadelphia* (Cambridge, MA: JCUS, 1963).

89. Edward C. Banfield and Martha Derthick, eds., *A Report on the Politics of Boston* (Cambridge, MA: JCUS, 1960).

90. Bertil Hanson, *Stockholm Municipal Politics* (Cambridge, MA: JCUS, 1959); for a complete list, see Joint Center for Urban Studies, *First Five Years*, 66–68.

91. Alan Altshuler, *A Report on Politics in Minneapolis* (Cambridge, MA: JCUS, 1959); Alan Altshuler, *A Report on Politics in St. Paul* (Cambridge, MA: JCUS, 1959); and Alan Altshuler, personal communication, January 14, 2020. With sixty years of hindsight, Altshuler described his work as "fairly slapdash," even as it laid the groundwork for a dissertation that became *The City Planning Process* (Ithaca, NY: Cornell University Press, 1965).

92. See front matter to virtually any report named above. The findings are too miscellaneous to address in any depth, but amusing minutiae lurk in the cracks of basic science. Some reports border on cultural geography, invoking the built environment to shed light on a city's "ethos." Salt Lake City is commended for the regularity of its grid, in which streets are assigned numbers and cardinal directions but not names, because "You can't get lost"; Dixie S. Huefner, *A Report on Politics in Salt Lake City* (Cambridge, MA: JCUS, 1961), I-16. The volume on San Diego, of all places, counts intellectuals as one of the core interest groups; David Greenstone, *A Report on Politics in San Diego* (Cambridge, MA: JCUS, 1962). Many authors report with gusto the anomalies of certain (white) ethnic groups, as in Manchester, "a city of paradox," whose phone directory is said to be saddled with pages upon pages of names beginning with *Mc*, *O*, *La*, and *Du*—Irish and French Canadian, the majority of its textile workforce; Binstock, *A Report on Politics in Manchester*, I-17, I-18. Other reports attend quite seriously to questions of racism and segregation—for example, Mark K. Adams and Gertrude Adams, *A Report on Politics in El Paso* (Cambridge, MA: JCUS, 1963), which devotes twenty pages to Hispanic matters; and Altshuler's twin reports. "I was told that race questions have not affected public housing plans," he relates, but "I cannot help but notice that all of the public housing projects are close together"; Altshuler, *A Report on Politics in Minneapolis*, VI-13. Race "is not a major issue" in St. Paul, he is told, but some 14 percent of the African American population had already been displaced by new highways. "In this, there is probably the making of an issue." Black leaders, he writes, call it "ghettoization." See *A Report on Politics in St. Paul*, V-11, V-12.

93. Joint Center for Urban Studies, *First Five Years*, 21. Banfield was going to publish "a volume of condensed revisions" with a trade publisher. This never came to pass. He did, however, bring out a textbook, Edward C. Banfield, ed., *Urban Government: A Reader in Administration and Politics* (New York: Free Press, 1961), with a second edition in 1969, that reprinted work by Altshuler; Norton Long of Brandeis, a Joint Center regular; and various other authors, such as Robert Dahl, Nelson Polsby, and Floyd Hunter, who depicted politics in terms of a plurality of groups competing for "influence."

94. Edward C. Banfield and James Q. Wilson, *City Politics* (Cambridge, MA: Harvard University Press, 1963), n.p., 2, 1–32, 329–346, and citations of the reports on 31, 34, 41, 94, 134, 135, 160, 180, 182, 288, 307, 317; Wilson, *A Report on Politics in Los Angeles*.

95. Meyerson and Banfield, *Politics, Planning, and the Public Interest*, 12; for Banfield's single-authored "Note on Conceptual Scheme," labeled a "supplement" to the main text, see 302–329.

96. Grady Clay, address to Nieman Conference, Cambridge, MA, May 8, 1960, box 8 (DL245A), GECC. Later in the 1960s, a Nieman Fellowship allowed Robert Caro to launch what became *The Power Broker: Robert Moses and the Fall of New York* (New York: Knopf, 1974); Robert Caro, *Working* (New York: Vintage, 2019), 14.

97. Grady Clay to Martin Meyerson, April 18, 1960, correspondence box 2 (CB2) of 6; Joint Center to Clay, November 4, 1960, CB2 of 6; Clay to Meyerson, October 16, 1961, CB2 of 6; GECC.

98. One excellent account of this "lost" project is Alison Isenberg, *Designing San Francisco: Art, Land, and Urban Renewal in the City by the Bay* (Princeton, NJ: Princeton University Press, 2017), 276–299. Isenberg does not much dwell on the role of the Joint Center.

99. GC notebook, October 24, 1960, to November 25, 1960, box 4 (DL225PP), GECC. Clay's funds were technically disbursed through MIT, but Meyerson was his primary host and interlocutor.

100. Grady Clay, draft of "The Competitors" (unpublished book manuscript), box 11 (DL245F); GC notebook, November 26, 1960, to December 9, 1960, box 4 (DL225PP), GECC.

101. Edward Logue to Clay, February 5, 1962; Logue to Clay, February 15, 1962; Clay to Logue, February 22, 1962; CB2 of 6, GECC. On Logue's work in New Haven, Boston, and New York, Lizabeth Cohen, *Saving America's Cities: Ed Logue and the Struggle to Renew Urban America in the Suburban Age* (New York: Farrar, Straus & Giroux, 2019), is essential. Logue began his stay in Boston in 1960 and had contact with Harvard and MIT faculty, including at the Urban Design Conferences (192–193). Later in the 1960s, he himself spent time as a formal associate of the Joint Center (474n143).

102. Grady Clay, *Right before Your Eyes* (Washington, DC: Planners Press, 1987), collects his columns; and Grady Clay, *Crossing the American Grain* (Louisville, KY: Butler Books, 2003), compiles page-length pieces he read aloud on Louisville's National Public Radio affiliate.

103. GC notebook, August 22, 1961, to December 2, 1961, box 5 (DL225NN), GECC; emphasis added.

104. Clay to Meyerson, January 15, 1962, CB2 of 6, GECC.

105. Meyerson to William Wheaton, August 20, 1962; Clay to William Wheaton, August 20, 1962; Meyerson to Clay, September 17, 1962; CB2 of 6, GECC.

106. Clay to Wheaton, September 20, 1962, CB2 of 6, GECC.

107. Clay to Robert C. Mitchell, n.d., 1962; Wheaton to Clay, September 21, 1962; CB2 of 6, GECC.

108. Meyerson to Clay, April 15, 1963; Russell Lynes to Clay, October 22, 1962; CB2 of 6, GECC.

109. Meyerson to Clay, April 15, 1963; Meyerson to Clay, June 19, 1963; CB2 of 6, GECC.

110. James Q. Wilson to Clay, December 26, 1963; Curley Bowen to Clay, January 14, 1964; CB2 of 6, GECC.

111. Grady Clay, *Close-Up: How to Read the American City* (Chicago: University of Chicago Press, 1972), 17–22, begins with a chapter on urban analysis as a "wordgame."

112. Grady Clay, summary of "New Towns for Appalachian America," address to Harvard Urban Design Conference, April 13–14, 1962, box 8 (DL245A), GECC.

113. "New Directions in American Landscape Architecture," Harvard Graduate School of Design, February 5, 1964, box 8 (DL245A), GECC.

114. Clay's attempt at a comparative case-based social science may have arrived too soon to be legible to his audience. Comparative historical analysis as a method in sociology was not widely recognized until the later 1960s, following Barrington Moore Jr.,

Social Origins of Dictatorship and Democracy (Boston: Beacon, 1966). Yet Clay's work was clumsy in some respects. He began his manuscript on design competitions with a definition of the word *competition*—albeit one drawn from the *Encyclopedia of Social Science*, not the dictionary.

115. Skip Lowney and John D. Landis, eds., *Fifty Years of City and Regional Planning at Berkeley* (Berkeley: NSQ Press, 1998).

116. Meyerson, "Report to the Visiting Committee."

117. Lloyd Rodwin, "Images and Paths of Change in Economics, Political Science, Philosophy, Literature, and City Planning: 1950–2000," in *The Profession of City Planning: Changes, Images, and Challenges, 1950–2000* (New Brunswick, NJ: Transaction, 2000), eds. Lloyd Rodwin and Bishwapriya Sanyal, 3–23, at 19, 16; Bish Sanyal, personal communication, October 22, 2019.

118. Paul Ylvisaker, "Information Paper: Urban Study and Consulting Centers," November 9, 1962, box 13, folder 5, FFR.

119. Paul Ylvisaker memo, October 3, 1962, box 13, folder 5, FFR.

120. Robert J. Havighurst et al. to Paul Ylvisaker, March 30, 1962, box 353, folder 008330, FFR.

121. Homer C. Wadsworth to Paul Ylvisaker, May 18, 1961, box 353, folder 008329, FFR.

122. Malcolm Moos to W. McNeil Lowry (on behalf of Moos, Louis Winnick, and Francis E. Rourke), August 11, 1965, box 13, folder 5, FFR; emphasis added.

123. Ford memo on James Q. Wilson, 1965, box 14, folder 9, FFR.

3. "Our Retrospection Will All Be to the Future"

1. Nathan Glazer and Daniel Patrick Moynihan, *Beyond the Melting Pot: The Negroes, Puerto Ricans, Jews, Italians, and Irish of New York City* (Cambridge, MA: MIT Press, 1963).

2. On Glazer's trajectory, see Nathan Glazer, "From Socialism to Sociology," in *Authors of Their Own Lives*, ed. Bennett M. Berger (Berkeley: University of California Press, 1990), 190–209; and Nathan Glazer, "My Life in Sociology," *Annual Review of Sociology* 38 (2012): 1–16.

3. On Moynihan, the literature is quite extensive. For one useful cross section, see Robert A. Katzmann, ed., *Daniel Patrick Moynihan: The Intellectual in Public Life* (Washington, DC: Woodrow Wilson Center Press, 2004), especially Nathan Glazer's contribution, "Daniel P. Moynihan on Ethnicity," 15–25.

4. Glazer and Moynihan, *Beyond the Melting Pot*, 16, 17, 3, 2; emphasis original. Gordon had trained at Columbia, and while Glazer (and Moynihan) granted that its sociology department was "of equal distinction" to Chicago's, midcentury Columbia's "had almost nothing to do with New York." Chicago was "far more closely studied" due to Robert Park and the ethnographic tradition he created; see Ulf Hannerz, *Exploring the City: Inquiries toward an Urban Anthropology* (New York: Columbia University Press, 1980), 19–58. Perhaps Gordon had been trained not to mine New York's panoply of neighborhoods in search of social facts; perhaps if he had, he would have uncovered evidence with which to dispel the myth of the melting pot. Yet *Beyond the Melting Pot* did not blame him for the oversight—New York was too vast to master sociologically. "Big as it was, Chicago still offered a structure and scale that could be more easily compre-

hended." Scholars in New York "tended to shy away" from becoming scholars of New York.

5. Nathan Glazer, "Beyond the Melting Pot Twenty Years After," *Journal of American Ethnic History* 1 (1981): 43–55, at 43–44. The ubiquitous Talcott Parsons, no expert on ethnicity, served as one of the manuscript's reviewers; Martin Meyerson to Talcott Parsons, August 20, 1962, JCUS folder, TPP.

6. Nathan Glazer to Daniel Patrick Moynihan, September 9, 1963, box I:52, folder 6, DPMP; emphasis added.

7. Glazer to Moynihan, September 25, 1963, box I:52, folder 6, DPMP.

8. Martin Meyerson, with Jaqueline Tyrwhitt et al., *Face of the Metropolis* (New York: Random House, 1963); Clarence Stein to Martin Meyerson, October 11, 1963, box 15, folder 28; Meyerson to Stein, December 13, 1963, box 15, folder 28, CSP.

9. Moynihan to Bernard Frieden, June 19, 1972, box I:176, folder 6; James Q. Wilson memo to faculty, March 23, 1966, box I:176, DPMP.

10. Alan Altshuler, personal communication, January 14, 2020; Godfrey Hodgson, *The Gentleman from New York: Daniel Patrick Moynihan* (Boston: Houghton Mifflin, 2000), 129–133.

11. Leonard Fein memo, December 18, 1968, box I:176, folder 8, DPMP. When *Time* ran its cover story "Urbanologist Pat Moynihan," among the images was a photograph of Moynihan mid-seminar, captioned "Salvation in the Jersey Meadows or a Prison in Sherwood Forest"; "Cities: Light in the Frightening Corners," *Time*, July 28, 1967.

12. Robert A. Peck, "Daniel Patrick Moynihan and the Fall and Rise of Public Works," in *Daniel Patrick Moynihan: The Intellectual in Public Life*, ed. Robert A. Katzmann (Washington, DC: Woodrow Wilson Center Press, 2004), 68–97.

13. James M. Beshers, ed., *Computer Methods in the Analysis of Large-Scale Social Systems* [1965], 2nd ed. (Cambridge, MA: MIT Press, 1968). For a very different history of computing, see Evangelos Kotsioris, "The Computer Misfits," in *Radical Pedagogies*, eds. Beatriz Colomina et al. (Cambridge, MA: MIT Press, 2022), 314–317, on Harvard's Laboratory for Computer Graphics (and Spatial Analysis).

14. David M. Heer, ed., *Social Statistics and the City* (Cambridge, MA: Joint Center for Urban Studies, 1968).

15. "Lloyd Rodwin, 80, MIT Urban Studies Professor, Extended the Field of Planning to Social Sciences and the Third World," *MIT News*, December 8, 1999; Tridib Banerjee, personal communication, February 8, 2022.

16. Report of first student–faculty committee meeting, Harvard GSD, November 28, 1967, box I:166, folder 10, DPMP.

17. These developments were, of course, not confined to Harvard or MIT, nor did they represent the apogee of quantification for its own sake. Ethan Schrum, *The Instrumental University: Education in Service of the National Agenda after World War II* (Ithaca, NY: Cornell University Press, 2019), 183–214, details the founding of the University of California, Irvine, in 1965 as a specialized campus devoted to the newest, hardest social science. Its core curriculum revolved around a small collection of basic models, and its School of Social Sciences consisted only of topical centers, to the exclusion of discipline-defined departments.

18. Lloyd Rodwin memo, n.d., box 58, "Policies and Focus of the Joint Center, 1957–1965" folder, LRP.

19. Robert C. Wood, *The Necessary Majority: Middle America and the Urban Crisis* (New York: Columbia University Press, 1972), 6. General accounts include Roger Biles, *The Fate of Cities: Urban America and the Federal Government, 1945–2000* (Lawrence: University Press of Kansas, 2011); and Mark I. Gelfand, *A Nation of Cities: The Federal Government and Urban America, 1933–1965* (New York: Oxford University Press, 1975).

20. Rodwin memo, n.d.

21. JCUS proposal to Ford Foundation, September 28, 1965, Reel 3006, Grants L–N (FA 732E), FFR.

22. Robert C. Wood, *Whatever Possessed the President?: Academic Experts and Presidential Policy, 1960–1988* (Amherst: University of Massachusetts Press, 1993), 68, 57, 69, 75–77, 79–81, 83–84. Few new policies came of the task forces on suburbia or New Towns, but see the elaborate, if delayed, *Final Report of the President's Task Force on Suburban Problems*, ed. Charles M. Haar (Cambridge, MA: Ballinger, 1974). Meanwhile, certain Joint Center affiliates, such as Martha Derthick and John Burchard, worked for Republicans.

23. Joint Center for Urban Studies, *The Effectiveness of Metropolitan Planning* (Washington, DC: United States Government Printing Office, 1964), 115, 148. This was one of three reports the subcommittee had lined up to address the topic. The others were prepared by the HHFA and the United States Advisory Commission on Intergovernmental Relations, which itself tapped Joint Center scholars.

24. Wood, *Necessary Majority*, 5.

25. Paul Ylvisaker to McGeorge Bundy, April 1966, box 6, "Ford Foundation—Public Affairs, 1958–1966" folder, PNYP. Paul Davidoff, "Advocacy and Pluralism in Planning," *Journal of the American Institute of Planners* 31 (1965): 331–338, is the key text in the participatory turn.

26. From among legions of commentary, see James T. Patterson, *Freedom Is Not Enough: The Moynihan Report and America's Struggle over Black Family Life from LBJ to Obama* (New York: Basic Books, 2010); Greg Weiner, *American Burke: The Uncommon Liberalism of Daniel Patrick Moynihan* (Lawrence: University Press of Kansas, 2015); Joe Klein, "No Easy Answers," *New York Times Book Review*, May 23, 2021; and Ta-Nehisi Coates, "The Black Family in the Age of Mass Incarceration," *The Atlantic*, October 2015, a qualified defense written from within an Afropessimist tradition. The most comprehensive account of the "culture of poverty" thesis in all its permutations is Alice O'Connor, *Poverty Knowledge* (Princeton, NJ: Princeton University Press, 2008); on Moynihan, 203–210.

27. Nathan Glazer and Daniel Patrick Moynihan, "Introduction to the Second Edition: New York City in 1970," in *Beyond the Melting Pot: The Negroes, Puerto Ricans, Jews, Italians, and Irish of New York City*, 2nd ed. (Cambridge, MA: MIT Press, 1970), vii–xcviii.

28. James Q. Wilson to Morton Schussheim, August 25, 1964, box I:91, folder 14, DPMP.

29. Moynihan memo, "Urban Studies at MIT: A View from the Social Sciences" (1967), box I:199, folder 1, DPMP.

30. Wilson to Nathan Pusey, December 26, 1966, box I:165, folder 3, DPMP. Frazier, it must be noted, was African American.

31. Lee Rainwater and William L. Yancey, eds., *The Moynihan Report and the Politics of Controversy* (Cambridge, MA: MIT Press, 1967).

32. David Riesman to Moynihan, July 3, 1968, box I:191, folder 3, DPMP.

33. Homer C. Wadsworth to Paul Ylvisaker, May 18, 1961, box 353, folder 008329, FFR.

34. Robert J. Havighurst et al. to Paul Ylvisaker, March 30, 1962, box 353, folder 008330, FFR.

35. Malcolm Moos to W. McNeil Lowry (on behalf of Moos, Louis Winnick, and Francis E. Rourke), August 11, 1965, box 13, folder 5, FFR; JCUS proposal to Ford Foundation, September 28, 1965; Ford memo on James Q. Wilson, 1965, box 14, folder 9, FFR.

36. Wadsworth to Ylvisaker, May 18, 1961. Martin Bulmer, *The Chicago School of Sociology: Institutionalization, Diversity, and the Rise of Sociological Research* (Chicago: University of Chicago Press, 1984), 24, credits the Chicago School's policy orientation to the social commitments of George Herbert Mead, who took inspiration from the Pittsburgh Survey and in 1912 proposed opening a central statistical bureau for Chicago's lawmakers.

37. Moos to Lowry, October 11, 1965.

38. Malcolm Moos memo, May 4, 1965, box 13, folder 5, FFR. The visiting committee was rebuking Rodwin and Meyerson. Rodwin wanted to avoid having to provide "straight service functions," mere "operating services" for local governments, but he and Meyerson were nonetheless open to doing some applied work.

39. R. C. Sheldon to William McPeak, October 5, 1962, box 13, folder 5, FFR. On campus–city dynamics, see LaDale Winling, *Building the Ivory Tower: Universities and Metropolitan Development in the Twentieth Century* (Philadelphia: University of Pennsylvania Press, 2018); Margaret Pugh O'Mara, *Cities of Knowledge: Cold War Science and the Search for the Next Silicon Valley* (Princeton, NJ: Princeton University Press, 2005); Blake Gumprecht, *The American College Town* (Amherst: University of Massachusetts Press, 2008), 268–276, on postwar attempts to brand Ann Arbor the "Research Center of the Midwest"; Schrum, *Instrumental University*, 90–125, on Penn, the University City project, and the West Philadelphia Corporation, to which Meyerson contributed; and Michael Carriere, "Fighting the War Against Blight: Columbia University, Morningside Heights Inc., and Counterinsurgent Urban Renewal," *Journal of Planning History* 10 (2011): 5–29.

40. Joint Center for Urban Studies, *The First Five Years* (Cambridge, MA: The Center, 1964), 21, 50. On Route 128 and its university connections, see AnnaLee Saxenian, *Regional Advantage: Culture and Competition in Silicon Valley and Route 128* (Cambridge, MA: Harvard University Press, 1994).

41. Bernard Taper, *The Arts in Boston* (Cambridge, MA: Harvard University Press, 1970), n.p., 98, 4, 5, 9, 2, 1; Martin Meyerson and Edward C. Banfield, *Boston: The Job Ahead* (Cambridge, MA: Harvard University Press, 1966), 9; and, of course, Edward C. Banfield and Martha Derthick, eds., *A Report on the Politics of Boston* (Cambridge, MA: Joint Center for Urban Studies, 1960). The profile of Abrams is Bernard Taper, "A Lover of Cities," *New Yorker*, February 4 and 11, 1967. On Kepes's center, see Elizabeth Goldring and Ellen Sebring, *Centerbook: The Center for Advanced Visual Studies and the Evolution of Art–Science–Technology at MIT* (Cambridge, MA: SA+P Press, 2019).

42. Taper, *The Arts in Boston*, 115–125, 149–156; quotation on page 121. The Joint Center assisted the BRA on less design-centric projects as well. In 1965, representatives consulted on how best to redress the racialized displacement introduced by one project pitched as a gateway to Boston's South End; MacDonald Barr memo, November 9, 1965, box 2, "Joint Center Committees, May 1965–June 1966" folder, LRP. In 1966, it

proposed research on the soon-to-be-explosive question of crosstown busing programs intended to create racial balance in public schools. The research would assist in "selecting the types of white residential communities which would be most desirable"; "Evaluation of Measures to Deal with Racial and Social Class Imbalance in the Boston Public Schools," box 2, "Joint Center Committees, May 1965–June 1966" folder, LRP.

43. Donald Appleyard, Kevin Lynch, and John R. Myer, *The View from the Road* (Cambridge, MA: MIT Press, 1964), 3, 4, 18.

44. Grady Clay, *Close-Up: How to Read the American City* (Chicago: University of Chicago Press, 1972), 108.

45. Appleyard et al., *View from the Road*, 18, 27, 83; Gabrielle Esperdy, *American Autopia: An Intellectual History of the American Roadside at Midcentury* (Charlottesville: University of Virginia Press, 2019), 225–235; Margot Lystra, "Envisioning Environments: Designs for Urban U.S. Freeways, 1956–1968" (PhD diss., Cornell University, 2017), 132–185; László Moholy-Nagy, *Vision in Motion* (Chicago: Theobald, 1947). Esperdy situates this text alongside two other 1960s inquiries into the driver's-eye view: Lawrence Halprin, *Freeways* (New York: Reinhold, 1966); and portions of Christopher Tunnard and Boris Pushkarev, *Man-Made America: Chaos or Control?* (New Haven, CT: Yale University Press, 1963).

46. Michael Southworth and Kevin Lynch, "Designing and Managing the Strip," Working Paper 29 (1974), Joint Center for Urban Studies, Harvard University and Massachusetts Institute of Technology, 5, 2, 46, 26. See also Michael Southworth, "The Sonic Environment of Cities," *Environment and Behavior* 1 (1969): 49–70.

47. "Proposed Program for the Use of Design Talent in Improving the Urban Environment in the Boston Area," November 23, 1965, box 2, "Joint Center Committees, May 1965–June 1966" folder, LRP. Logue later adjudged Boston's version of Urban Renewal "terrible," "Corbusian," and "useless," wedded to fantasies of "total clearance." "There's no city like that," he said. "It's more comprehensive than any place in the country by a wide margin." Bacon in Philadelphia, by contrast, championed preservation in tandem with rebuilding, and by the 1990s, Logue deemed that approach much preferable; Edward J. Logue, interview by Morton Schussheim, May 24, 1995, PIH.

48. Moynihan memo, "The Future Role of Urban Studies at MIT, with Special Reference to the Department of City Planning," December 1966, box I:199, folder 1, DPMP.

49. American Academy of Arts and Sciences materials, April 5, 1964, box 55, "Boston Metropolitan Regional Planning, 1961–1965" folder #1, LRP.

50. MAPC materials, box 55, "Boston Metropolitan Regional Planning, 1961–1965" folder #2, LRP.

51. Joint Center for Urban Studies, *Economic Development in the Boston Area* (Cambridge, MA: Joint Center for Urban Studies, 1965), 43.

52. Joint Center for Urban Studies, *Planning Metropolitan Boston* (Boston: Metropolitan Area Planning Council, 1967), 1, 20, 30, 21.

53. *Planning Metropolitan Boston*, 28, 29, 13, 35; emphasis added. "Our cartoon of Utopia" came from Lowdon Wingo of Resources for the Future. Meyerson's "middle range" entailed between five and ten years of foresight; Martin Meyerson, "Building the Middle-Range Bridge to Comprehensive Planning," *Journal of the American Institute of Planners* 22 (1956): 58–64, at 62. See Jennifer S. Light, *The Nature of Cities: Ecological Visions and the Urban Professions, 1920–1960* (Baltimore: Johns Hopkins University

Press, 2009), 70, on debates over the "timing and sequencing" of Renewal projects; and Dowell Myers and Alicia Kitsuse, "Constructing the Future in Planning: A Survey of Theories and Tools," *Journal of Planning Education and Research* 19 (2000): 221–231, at 225–226, on the tendency for longer timescales to correspond to larger spatial scales.

54. Michel de Certeau, *The Practice of Everyday Life* [1980], trans. Steven Rendall (Berkeley: University of California Press, 1984), 94, is the source of this unlovely but useful term.

55. Robert J. Havighurst, "The Quality and Significance of the Research of the Harvard–MIT Center," June 1962, box 13, folder 5, FFR. The NYMRS counted as one of Ford's "specialized area projects."

56. Civic Interests, Series D (FA313), box 39, folder 313, OMRR; Grant PA 56–210, Reel 156 (FA732F), FFR; Grant PA 62–103, Reel 392 (FA732F), FF; RPA to Merrill Foundation, January 9, 1957, box 63, folder 4; Harold Osborne to Bernard L. Gladieux, February 23, 1954, box 63, folder 8, RPAR.

57. Front matter, Edgar M. Hoover and Raymond Vernon, *Anatomy of a Metropolis* [1959] (Garden City, NY: Anchor, 1962), ii. This citation represents the Anchor paperback edition. The other NYMRS volumes to receive the paperback treatment are similarly cited. Each was initially published in hardcover with Harvard University Press in the year indicated between square brackets.

58. David Rockefeller to Nathan Pusey, December 23, 1959, box 12, folder 145, DRP. On the elite composition of the RPA's board of directors, see Forbes B. Hays, *Community Leadership: The Regional Plan Association of New York* (New York: Columbia University Press, 1965), 38, 45–51; of the NYMRS's board, 105.

59. "Regional Fact-Finder: Raymond Vernon," *New York Times*, June 1, 1959; Edward S. Mason to Charles McKim Norton, November 28, 1955, box 68, folder 6, RPAR.

60. Osborne to Dana Creel, November 18, 1955, box 68, folder 6, RPAR.

61. "Progress Report to the Project Management Committee," May 1955, box 68, folder 7, RPAR.

62. Barbara R. Berman, Benjamin Chinitz, and Edgar M. Hoover, *Projection of a Metropolis* (Cambridge, MA: Harvard University Press, 1960).

63. Hoover and Vernon, *Anatomy of a Metropolis*. On the suburbanization of New York's industries, see inter alia James B. Kenyon, *Industrial Localization and Metropolitan Growth: The Paterson–Passaic District* (Chicago: University of Chicago Department of Geography, 1960); and Richard Harris, "Industry and Residence: The Decentralization of New York City, 1900–1940," *Journal of Historical Geography* 19 (1993): 169–190.

64. Oscar Handlin, *The Newcomers: Negroes and Puerto Ricans in a Changing Metropolis* [1959] (Garden City, NY: Anchor, 1962).

65. Raymond Vernon, *Metropolis 1985* [1960] (Garden City, NY: Anchor, 1963).

66. Robert C. Wood, with Vladimir V. Almendinger, *1400 Governments: The Political Economy of the New York Metropolitan Region* [1961] (Garden City, NY: Anchor, 1964), 1.

67. On "Boroughitis," see Alan J. Karcher, *New Jersey's Multiple Municipal Madness* (New Brunswick, NJ: Rutgers University Press, 1998), by an ex–state assemblyman.

68. Wood, *1400 Governments*, 214, 192–193, 188, and, on Moses, 178–181 and passim; Robert Moses, "Are Cities Dead?," *The Atlantic*, January 1962. On RPA v. Moses, see Hays, *Community Leadership*, 63–67. For other contemporary debates on metropolitan coordination, see inter alia Luther Gulick, "Metropolitan Organization," *Annals*

of the American Academy of Political and Social Science 314 (1957): 57–65; Victor Jones, "The Organization of a Metropolitan Region," *University of Pennsylvania Law Review* 105 (1957): 538–552; and Robert Coldwell Wood, *Metropolis against Itself* (New York: Committee for Economic Development, 1959).

69. Max Hall, "Three Industries on the Move," in *Made in New York: Case Studies in Metropolitan Manufacturing* (Cambridge, MA: Harvard University Press, 1959), 1–18, at 3. More recent accounts of some of the same geographies of production are Joshua B. Freeman, *Working-Class New York: Life and Labor since World War II* (New York: The New Press, 2000), 3–22; and Aaron Shkuda, *The Lofts of SoHo: Gentrification, Art, and Industry in New York, 1950–1980* (Chicago: University of Chicago Press, 2016), 12–41. Hall's collection also includes a chapter on the nascent electronics industry.

70. Benjamin Chinitz, *Freight and the Metropolis* (Cambridge, MA: Harvard University Press, 1960). On containerization then and since, see Marc Levinson, *The Box* (Princeton, NJ: Princeton University Press, 2006); and Deborah Cowen, *The Deadly Life of Logistics: Mapping Violence in Global Trade* (Minneapolis: University of Minnesota Press, 2014).

71. Martin Segal, *Wages in the Metropolis* (Cambridge, MA: Harvard University Press, 1960); Robert M. Lichtenberg, *One-Tenth of a Nation* (Cambridge, MA: Harvard University Press, 1960); Sidney M. Robbins and Nestor E. Terleckyj, *Money Metropolis* (Cambridge, MA: Harvard University Press, 1960).

72. "America's Front Office: N.Y.M.R.S. Vol. No. 11"; Vernon to Norton, 1959, box 143, folder 3, RPAR.

73. *Jeanyee Wong: Calligrapher, Cartographer, Designer, Illustrator, Letterer & Teacher*, at http://jeanyeewong.blogspot.com, offers a partial compendium of her illustrations and cover art. The UCLA geographer Howard Nelson commended the study's focus on shifting spatial distributions but faulted H. I. Forman's simplified thematic maps, "sometimes, perhaps apologetically, labeled 'charts,'" as well as the small surface area of the paperback pages displaying them. "Pocket" paperbacks had their shortcomings. This critique was particularly salient in the case of Handlin's *The Newcomers*, which described an immense number of spatial shifts enacted over time by mobile ethnic and racial groups. Any reader outside New York, if broad accessibility was the goal, would have benefited from basic maps distinguishing, for instance, the (Jewish) Lower East Side from the Garment District from the Grand Concourse, (African American) Harlem from Bedford–Stuyvesant from Brownsville, and finer-grained distinctions at the scale of the block. Alas, Nelson wrote, "publishing attitudes and possibilities" had changed since 1929, when the RPNY had issued forth on more spacious pages. Howard J. Nelson, "Megalopolis and New York Metropolitan Region: New Studies of the Urbanized Eastern Seaboard," *Annals of the Association of American Geographers* 52 (1962): 307–317, at 311.

74. Richard Magat, *The Ford Foundation at Work: Philanthropic Choices, Methods, and Styles* (New York: Plenum, 1979), 121; Paul Ylvisaker memo, "The Gray Areas" (1963), box 5, "Ford Foundation—Gray Areas, 1963 (January–June)," PNYP. Ylvisaker called it a "new phrase" to designate "an exceedingly old fact of urban life." He deemed it "neutral language"; Ford Foundation, Oral History Project, interview of Paul N. Ylvisaker by Charles T. Morrissey, September 27, 1973, and October 27, 1973, box 5, PNYP. Alice O'Connor notes the "veiled reference to . . . racial composition"; *Poverty Knowledge*, 130. Ylvisaker imagined Ford establishing Gray Areas Programs abroad, in countries with centralized governments used to rapid implementation of new social policies.

He suggested pilot programs in Calcutta, The Hague, Athens, Delhi, Lagos, Rio de Janeiro, Warsaw, Mexico City, and Cairo; "Program Submission Concerning Future Program Activities" (Spring 1962), box 6, "Ford Foundation—Public Affairs Program— Special Committee Materials, 1961–1962" folder, PNYP.

75. Hoover and Vernon, *Anatomy of a Metropolis*, vii, 198–226, 56, 184.
76. "Regional Fact-Finder."
77. Berman, Chinitz, and Hoover, *Projection*, 1, 2, 3, 23, 32.
78. Berman, Chinitz, and Hoover, 245.
79. Berman, Chinitz, and Hoover, front matter, 32.
80. Vernon, *Metropolis 1985*, 241, 247, 255.
81. Andrew M. Shanken, *194X: Architecture, Planning, and Consumer Culture on the American Home Front* (Minneapolis: University of Minnesota Press, 2009), especially 1–58; and on the distinction, see Britton Harris, "Plan or Projection: An Examination of the Use of Models in Planning," *Journal of the American Institute of Planners* 26 (1960): 265–272.
82. Oscar Handlin, "The Modern City as a Field of Historical Study," in *The Historian and the City*, eds. Oscar Handlin and John Burchard (Cambridge, MA: MIT Press, 1963), 1–26, at 25; emphasis added.
83. Vernon, *Metropolis 1985*, 252–253, 243.
84. Wood, *1400 Governments*, 191, 192; cf. Robert C. Wood, "1400 Governments on the Road Toward Greenbelt and Graybelt Economies," address to RPA annual conference, October 7, 1961, box 143, folder 4, RPAR.
85. "Progress Report to the Project Management Committee" (1955), box 68, folder 7, RPAR.
86. Hoover and Vernon, *Anatomy of a Metropolis*, 245–246; emphasis added. "A List of Issues Calling for an RPA Position," September 21, 1959; draft of RPA position, October 21, 1959, box 63, "Comments on Books" folder, RPAR; Stanley Tankel, "RPA Position on Issues Raised in *Anatomy of a Metropolis*" (January 1960), box 143, "Miscellaneous Papers: NYMRS" folder, RPAR.
87. Regional Plan Association (RPA), *The Second Regional Plan: A Draft for Discussion* (New York: Regional Plan Association, 1968); RPA, *Spread City: Projections of Development Trends and the Issues They Pose: The Tri-State New York Metropolitan Region, 1960–1985* (New York: RPA, 1962), 2, 33. See also RPA, *The Region's Growth* (New York: RPA, 1967); RPA, *The Lower Hudson* (New York: RPA, 1966); RPA, *Public Services in Older Cities* (New York: RPA, 1969); Rai Y. Okamoto et al., *Urban Design Manhattan* (New York: Viking, 1969); RPA, *Public Participation in Regional Planning* (New York: RPA, 1969); RPA, *Goals for the Region Project*, 5 vols. (New York: RPA, 1963). The RPA earnestly tried to coin "Spread City," always capitalized, as a popular catchphrase, but in public consciousness it lost out to Gottmann's "Megalopolis," William H. Whyte's "Exploding Metropolis," or simply "sprawl."
88. RPA, *Region's Growth*, 26.
89. William A. Caldwell, ed., *How to Save Urban America* (New York: New American Library, 1973); William B. Shore et al., *Listening to the Metropolis* (New York: Regional Plan Association, 1974); Kristian Taketomo, "'Town Meetings by Television': Regional Plan Association's 'CHOICES for '76,'" *Gotham: A Blog for Scholars of New York City History*, October 4, 2018, https://www.gothamcenter.org/blog/town-meetings

-by-television-regional-plan-associations-choices-for-76; *Regional Plan News*, no. 84 (May 1967), box 119, RPAR.

90. John Keith to C. McKim Norton, June 17, 1960, box 69, folder 13, RPAR; Memo on meeting with "Bud" Schlivek, March 23, 1962, box 69, folder 13, RPAR; Keith to Norton, October 25, 1961, box 69, folder 13, RPAR; Louis Schlivek, "Preliminary Outline," May 15, 1960, box 69, folder 13, RPAR.

91. Louis B. Schlivek, *Man in Metropolis* (New York: Doubleday, 1965).

92. Norton to Samuel Vaughan, May 26, 1960, box 69, folder 13, RPAR; Norton to Keith, March 29, 1962, box 69, folder 13, RPAR.

93. Several other large-scale collaborative studies drew influence from its example. The multivolume Pittsburgh Economic Study began in 1959, and Benjamin Chinitz offered his services there too, penning a semilegendary paper, "Contrasts in Agglomeration" (1961), that pit Pittsburgh's industrial structure against that of the more diversified New York. Edgar Hoover served as the Pittsburgh Study's director. "The productivity of the staff" in Pittsburgh, Chinitz wrote to the RPA's John Keith, "has been enhanced by the capital accumulated in the course of the New York Study." *Region with a Future*, one component volume, went to even greater lengths than Vernon's team to defend "projection" as an essential scientific commitment while insisting that the uncertainties baked into that genre of social science were inherently the most interesting part. Prophecy had become a term of abuse; by the early 1960s, in expert circles, it seemed a "delusive" mode of thinking about the future. Far more sharply than had Vernon and his economists, Hoover and the Pittsburgh group stated that "hopefully" the projections would incite action and "help to provoke their own invalidation." Benjamin Chinitz, "Contrasts in Agglomeration: New York and Pittsburgh," *American Economic Review* 51 (1961): 279–289; Chinitz to Keith, April 21, 1960, box 63, "Comments on Books" folder, RPAR; Pittsburgh Regional Planning Association, *Region with a Future* (Pittsburgh: University of Pittsburgh Press, 1963), 3, 5, 10; Ira S. Lowry, *Portrait of a Region* (Pittsburgh: University of Pittsburgh Press, 1963). From the Community Renewal Program that succeeded the Pittsburgh Economic Study, see Ira S. Lowry, *A Model of Metropolis* (Santa Monica, CA: RAND Corporation, 1964). See also Patrick Vitale, *Nuclear Suburbs: Cold War Technoscience and the Pittsburgh Renaissance* (Minneapolis: University of Minnesota Press, 2021).

94. It would be off base to see the NYMRS as just so many exercises in regional science, but the linkages are hard to miss. Edgar M. Hoover, Vernon's immediate subordinate on the NYMRS, was a regular at the earliest meetings (from 1950) that gave rise to the Regional Science Association (chartered 1954), and his contributions to location theory were among the new field's theoretical cornerstones: Edgar M. Hoover, *Location Theory and the Shoe Leather Industries* (Cambridge, MA: Harvard University Press, 1937); and Edgar M. Hoover, *The Location of Economic Activity* (New York: McGraw–Hill, 1948). While housed at MIT, Isard himself had collaborated with the RPA in 1953 and 1954 and devoted a third of his work time to a projection project that predated the NYMRS—and diverted some funding that had been allocated for research on Puerto Rico, reasoning that the island's economic connections to New York could justify his shift in focus; Walter Isard to Norton and Henry Fagin, August 1, 1953, box 66, folder 9, RPAR. Two NYMRS volumes, *Wages in the Metropolis* and *Money Metropolis*, bear subtitles that identify them as studies in "location."

95. *Metropolis* (New York: Ford Foundation, 1959), 38–40; notes on meeting with Paul Ylvisaker, February 26, 1958, box 66, folder 6, RPAR. Ford denied the RPA a second grant in 1958.

96. Paul N. Ylvisaker, "Innovation and Evolution: Bridge to the Future Metropolis," *Annals of the American Academy of Political and Social Science* 314 (1957): 156–164, at 156.

97. Raymond Vernon, *The Myth and Reality of Our Urban Problems* [1962] (Cambridge, MA: Harvard University Press, 1966), v.

98. Nathan Pusey and Julius Stratton to David Rockefeller, November 2, 1959, box 12, folder 145; Rockefeller to Pusey, December 23, 1959, box 12, folder 145, DRP.

99. JCUS, *Effectiveness of Metropolitan Planning*, 22. They also approved of the Pittsburgh work (4).

100. Meyerson to Norton, July 15, 1960, box 63, "NYMRS Books: Correspondence, Etc., 1959–" folder, RPAR.

101. Hannerz, *Exploring the City*, 28. On the oscillation between the placeless "laboratory" and situated "field" research within Chicago sociology, Thomas Gieryn, "City as Truth-Spot: Laboratories and Field-Sites in Urban Studies," *Social Studies of Science* 36 (2006): 5–38, is instructive; and see Robert E. Kohler, *Landscapes and Labscapes: Exploring the Lab–Field Border in Biology* (Chicago: University of Chicago Press, 2002).

102. Robert S. Lynd and Helen Merrell Lynd, *Middletown: A Study in Modern American Culture* (New York: Harcourt, Brace, 1929); Robert S. Lynd and Helen Merrell Lynd, *Middletown in Transition: A Study in Cultural Conflicts* (New York: Harcourt, Brace, 1937); Sarah E. Igo, *The Averaged American: Surveys, Citizens, and the Making of a Mass Public* (Cambridge, MA: Harvard University Press, 2007), 23–102, at 39, 85. Robert Lynd also took on a high-level position at the Social Science Research Council.

103. Robert A. Dahl, *Who Governs?: Democracy and Power in an American City* (New Haven, CT: Yale University Press, 1961), v, vi; Nelson W. Polsby, *Community Power and Political Theory* (New Haven, CT: Yale University Press, 1963), vii; Raymond E. Wolfinger, *The Politics of Progress* (Englewood Cliffs, NJ: Prentice–Hall, 1973). Wolfinger's book, initially meant to come out with Yale, was delayed. Dahl also received funding from Ford and the Social Science Research Council, in addition to the year at CASBS. This research took shape within the network of organized research detailed in previous chapters, even as Yale as an institution had largely opted out. Ford's officers were aware of Dahl and his team, and in his critical 1965 evaluation of the Joint Center, Malcolm Moos noted that Yale seemed to have gotten perfectly adequate results without funding a dedicated center for urban studies; Malcolm Moos to W. McNeil Lowry (on behalf of Moos, Louis Winnick, and Francis E. Rourke), August 11, 1965, box 13, folder 5, FFR. The second edition of Polsby's book elevated questions of method and generalizability still more, as indicated in its subtitle: Nelson W. Polsby, *Community Power and Political Theory: A Further Look at Problems of Evidence and Inference* (New Haven, CT: Yale University Press, 1980). On Lee's carefully staged promotional photographs, which showed him with a Cheshire-cat grin behind the steering wheel of a wrecking ball, see Francesca Russello Ammon, *Bulldozer: Demolition and Clearance of the Postwar Landscape* (New Haven, CT: Yale University Press, 2016), 140–143.

104. Lizabeth Cohen, *Saving America's Cities: Ed Logue and the Struggle to Renew Urban America in the Suburban Age* (New York: Farrar, Straus & Giroux, 2019), 72, 83, 92, notes

that Ylvisaker established Gray Areas only upon visiting New Haven, that Lee and Logue drafted the first ever "urban platform" for the 1960 Democratic convention, and that a "diaspora of New Haven veterans" coursed through the field of urban planning.

105. Polsby, *Community Power and Political Theory*, 7. Polsby (5n3) cited Morris Cohen to establish his definition of scientific verifiability. Not everyone was convinced by a methodology built on case studies, however. Casework became the pedagogical trademark of Harvard Business School, whose curriculum attracted scorn from Clark Kerr and Herbert Simon. To begin with an example, they felt, was inimical to truly general theory, which had to "stand above the case"; Schrum, *Instrumental University*, 75.

106. W. Lloyd Warner and Paul S. Lunt, *The Social Life of a Modern Community* (New Haven, CT: Yale University Press, 1941), is the first of five.

107. August B. Hollingshead, *Elmtown's Youth* (New York: Wiley, 1949). New Haven itself is known as the Elm City. Warner organized his own study of Morris and renamed it "Jonesville": W. Lloyd Warner et al., *Democracy in Jonesville: A Study of Quality and Inequality* (New Haven, CT: Yale University Press, 1949).

108. Floyd Hunter, *Community Power Structure* (Chapel Hill: University of North Carolina Press, 1953).

109. For complete citations of these works—articles, not monographs—see Polsby, *Community Power and Political Theory*, xiii–xiv.

110. E. Digby Baltzell, *Philadelphia Gentlemen* (Glencoe, IL: Free Press, 1958). See also Caroline F. Ware, *Greenwich Village, 1920–1930* (Boston: Houghton Mifflin, 1935), which stated an allegiance to the Lynds' "community study" tradition but introduced a far more historical method.

111. Polsby, *Community Power and Political Theory*, 117, 115.

112. Paul F. Lazarsfeld, "Evidence and Inference in Social Research," *Daedalus* 87 (Fall 1958): 99–130; Erik H. Erikson, "The Nature of Clinical Evidence," *Daedalus* 87 (Fall 1958): 65–87; Raymond Aron, "Evidence and Inference in History," *Daedalus* 87 (Fall 1958): 11–39, at 19, 38; Daniel Lerner, "Preface to the Issue 'On Evidence and Inference,'" *Daedalus* 87 (Fall 1958): 3–10, at 5, 9.

113. Transcript, Tamiment Conference on the Metropolis, 1960, box 4, "Daedalus, 1960" folder #2, LRP. For this characterization of Banfield, see James Q. Wilson, "A Connecticut Yankee in King Arthur's Court: A Biography," in *Edward C. Banfield: An Appreciation*, ed. Charles R. Kesler (Claremont, CA: Henry Salvatori Center, 2002), 31–80.

114. "The Future Metropolis," *Daedalus* 90 (Winter 1961); Lloyd Rodwin, ed., *The Future Metropolis* (New York: Braziller, 1961); see especially Kevin Lynch and Lloyd Rodwin, "A World of Cities," 9–16; Kevin Lynch, "The Pattern of the Metropolis," 103–128; György Kepes, "Notes on Expression and Communication in the Cityscape," 190–213; Edward C. Banfield, "The Political Implications of Metropolitan Growth," 80–99; and Raymond Vernon, "The Economics and Finances of the Large Metropolis," 42–63. Note that the book appeared not with either university press, but with George Braziller, the trade press responsible for many popular introductions to architecture and urbanism. Anna Vallye notes that Kepes contributed to two other *Daedalus* issues, "The Visual Arts Today" (1960) and "Science and Culture" (1965); this series of "themed interdisciplinary seminars" and publications culminated in his *Vision and Value* series of 1965–1966. Kepes was not primarily an urbanist, but work with urban-

ists abetted his larger agenda; Anna Vallye, "The Middleman: Kepes's Instruments," in *A Second Modernism: MIT, Architecture, and the "Techno-Social" Moment*, ed. Arindam Dutta (Cambridge, MA: MIT Press, 2013), 144–185, at 171, 179–180.

115. Martin Meyerson, "Utopian Traditions and the Planning of Cities," in *The Future Metropolis*, ed. Lloyd Rodwin (New York: Braziller, 1961), 233–250, at 249.

116. Preface to *The Historian and the City*, eds. Handlin and Burchard, vi. Another contemporary look at the problem of inference is Louis Gottschalk, ed., *Generalization in the Writing of History* (Chicago: University of Chicago Press, 1963), prepared by the Social Science Research Council's Committee on Historical Analysis. See also Peter Winch, *The Idea of a Social Science and Its Relationship to Philosophy* (London: Routledge Kegan Paul, 1958), a text much discussed at the time; H. Stuart Hughes, "The Historian and the Social Scientist," *American Historical Review* 66 (1960): 20–46; and William H. Sewell Jr., *Logics of History* (Chicago: University of Chicago Press, 2005).

117. Handlin, "Modern City," 1. This analogy between physical and disciplinary disorder recurred in 1962 comments by Ed Bacon (see chapter 2), and there was already a long transnational history of planners and social scientists using aerial views to suggest full comprehension; see, for example, Jeanne Haffner, *The View from Above: The Science of Social Space* (Cambridge, MA: MIT Press, 2013).

118. John Burchard, "Some Afterthoughts," in *The Historian and the City*, eds. Oscar Handlin and John Burchard (Cambridge, MA: MIT Press, 1963), 251–269, at 265, 260; emphasis added. Burchard was parroting comments made by Carl Schorske.

119. Handlin, "Modern City," 26; emphasis added.

120. Burchard, "Some Afterthoughts," 261, 262.

121. Lewis Mumford, *The City in History* (New York: Harcourt Brace, 1961), 574; emphasis added. Reinhart Koselleck, too, distinguishes projection and forecasting (or "prognosis") from prophecy. He notes versions of this split emerging in fifteenth- and sixteenth-century Italy, and then elsewhere in Europe during the Enlightenment. "The rational forecast, the prognosis, became the counterconcept of contemporary prophecy." Prophets do not doubt, and their certainty becomes destructive: "Prognosis produces the time within and out of which it weaves, whereas apocalyptic prophecy destroys time through its fixation on the end." Reinhart Koselleck, "Modernity and the Planes of Historicity" [1965], in *Futures Past: On the Semantics of Historical Time*, trans. Keith Tribe (New York: Columbia University Press, 1985), 9–25, at 18, 19. On "public prophecy" during the eighteenth and nineteenth centuries, see Arthur M. Schlesinger, "Casting the National Horoscope," *Proceedings of the American Antiquarian Society* 55 (1945): 53–94; and Greil Marcus, *The Shape of Things to Come: Prophecy and the American Voice* (New York: Picador, 2006). Leon Festinger, Henry W. Riecken, and Stanley Schachter, *When Prophecy Fails* (New York: Harper, 1956), is the crucial postwar study of why even discredited predictions have a way of begetting more predictions.

122. Handlin, "The Modern City," 18. Handlin's introductory essay also displayed his familiarity with the burgeoning literature in the sociology of time (by Sorokin and Merton), the history of timekeeping in factories and prisons (while leaving out Mumford on the monastery), and the "tempo" of mercantile and otherwise economic life (13–18). On the production of "the past" as a domain separate from the present and thus amenable to study, see Michel de Certeau, *The Writing of History* [1975], trans.

Tom Conley (New York: Columbia University Press, 1988); and Zachary S. Schiffman, *The Birth of the Past* (Baltimore: Johns Hopkins University Press, 2011).

123. Alfred Kazin, *New York Jew* (New York: Knopf, 1978), 36.

124. Burchard, "Some Afterthoughts," 268.

125. Burchard, "Some Afterthoughts," 257; emphasis added. Seymour Mandelbaum notes the epistemological asymmetry of past (knowable) with future (not). Still, Mandelbaum argues, in practice, planners are constantly cross-referencing the tenses, performing "loops through time within each judgmental step and the varied sequence of steps"; Seymour J. Mandelbaum, "Temporal Conventions in Planning Discourse," *Environment and Planning B: Planning and Design* 11 (1984): 5–13, at 6, 11. Together, they amount to a version of what Martin Jay has called "longitudinal totality" and noticed in ancient Greek thought, Enlightenment philosophy, Marx, and many of his Western epigones; *Marxism and Totality* (Berkeley: University of California Press, 1986), 26, 31, 64–66, and passim.

126. Oscar Handlin, "The Social System," in *The Future Metropolis*, ed. Lloyd Rodwin (New York: Braziller, 1961), 17–41, at 17. The title was surely a nod to Parsons.

127. Burchard, "Some Afterthoughts," 265, 269. Schlesinger Sr.'s key urban writings are Arthur M. Schlesinger, *The Rise of the City, 1878–1898* (New York: Macmillan, 1933); and Arthur M. Schlesinger, "The City in American History," *Mississippi Valley Historical Review* 27 (1940): 43–66.

128. Blake McKelvey to Rodwin, November 18, 1957, box 58, "Early Joint Center Correspondence" folder, LRP.

129. Bayrd Still and Diana Klebanow, "The Teaching of American Urban History," *Journal of American History* 55 (1969): 843–847; Bayrd Still, *Mirror for Gotham: New York as Seen by Contemporaries from Dutch Days to the Present* (New York: New York University Press, 1956); Bayrd Still, *Milwaukee: The History of a City* (Madison: State Historical Society of Wisconsin, 1948). The racial tinge of "frontier"—repurposed to describe increasingly Black cities rather than the indigenous American West—went undiscussed. The authors noted that "institutes, centers, and programs" were helping to "re-inforce" historical writing with social-scientific methodology, but they found no centers of urban history worth naming. The textbook is Charles N. Glaab and A. Theodore Brown, eds., *A History of Urban America* (New York: Macmillan, 1967).

130. John Harwood, "How Useful?: The Stakes of Architectural History, Theory, and Criticism at MIT, 1945–1976," in *A Second Modernism: MIT, Architecture, and the "Techno-Social" Moment*, ed. Arindam Dutta (Cambridge, MA: MIT Press, 2013), 106–143, at 113, adjudges the Joint Center "scientific and political, and not historical, in character." Eric Mumford acknowledges but downplays this work; "From Master Planning to Self-Build: The MIT–Harvard Joint Center for Urban Studies, 1959–1971," in *A Second Modernism*, ed. Arindam Dutta, 288–309, at 296–297. Jennifer Light sees in Joint Center "another" example of the "type of urban expertise" on offer at RAND's New York office; *From Warfare to Welfare*, 71.

131. Joint Center for Urban Studies, *First Five Years*, 25.

132. Meyerson to Chadbourne Gilpatric, December 6, 1962, JCUS folder, TPP.

133. Moos memo, May 4, 1965; emphasis added.

134. Sam Bass Warner, *Streetcar Suburbs: The Process of Growth in Boston, 1870–1900* (Cambridge, MA: Harvard University Press, 1962).

135. Robert A. Woods and Albert J. Kennedy, *The Zone of Emergence: Observations of the Lower Middle- and Upper Working-Class Communities of Boston, 1905–1914* [1905–1914] (Cambridge, MA: MIT Press, 1962).

136. Robert M. Fogelson, *The Fragmented Metropolis: Los Angeles, 1850–1930* (Berkeley: University of California Press, 1967).

137. Richard Sennett, *Families against the City: Middle-Class Homes of Industrial Chicago, 1872–1890* (Cambridge, MA: Harvard University Press, 1970).

138. JCUS final report to Ford Foundation, December 31, 1970; Joint Center for Urban Studies, *First Five Years*; Roy Lubove, ed., *The Urban Community: Housing and Planning in the Progressive Era* (Englewood Cliffs, NJ: Prentice–Hall, 1967); Frederick J. Adams and Gerald Hodge, "City Planning Instruction in the United States: The Pioneering Days, 1900–1930," *Journal of the American Institute of Planners* 31 (1965): 43–51; Marvin Lazerson, *Origins of the Urban School: Public Education in Massachusetts, 1870–1915* (Cambridge, MA: Harvard University Press, 1971); Ira Marvin Lapidus, *Muslim Cities in the Later Middle Ages* (Cambridge, MA: Harvard University Press, 1967). Most Joint Center–associated dissertations in history came out of Harvard, not MIT, and most were chaired by either Oscar Handlin or, after 1962, Stephan Thernstrom.

139. Stephan Thernstrom, *Poverty and Progress: Social Mobility in a Nineteenth-Century City* (New York: Atheneum, 1969), 4, 6, 192, 193, 194; Stephan Thernstrom, *Poverty and Progress: Social Mobility in a Nineteenth-Century City* (Cambridge, MA: Harvard University Press, 1964). See also Stephan Thernstrom, *The Other Bostonians: Poverty and Progress in the American Metropolis, 1880–1970* (Cambridge, MA: Harvard University Press, 1973); and Bruce M. Stave, "A Conversation with Stephan Thernstrom," *Journal of Urban History* 1 (1975): 189–215.

140. Thernstrom, *Poverty and Progress*, 237, 239, 228. Thernstrom declared himself "markedly" less "pessimistic" (238) than Warner on the prospects for social mobility.

141. Morton and Lucia White, *The Intellectual versus the City* (New York: Mentor, 1964), n.p.; Morton and Lucia White, *The Intellectual versus the City* (Cambridge, MA: Harvard University Press, 1962); Morton White, *A Philosopher's Story* (University Park: Pennsylvania State University Press, 1999).

142. Thernstrom, *Poverty and Progress*, 1–2.

143. Warner, *Streetcar Suburbs*, 165, 166. The second edition's preface is even more explicit; Sam Bass Warner, *Streetcar Suburbs: The Process of Growth in Boston, 1870–1900*, 2nd ed. (Cambridge, MA: Harvard University Press, 1977), vii–xvi.

144. Fogelson, *The Fragmented Metropolis*, 2.

145. Sennett, *Families against the City*, 237. Sennett's reliance on psychoanalytic theory—the "family disease," so called, "could have passed down" over the generations—was unusual in the Joint Center context (as was his polemical tone), but it bore the stamp of Harvard's Department of Social Relations in its post-Parsonian moment. In the appendix, meanwhile, Sennett referred "professional readers who can make further use of the census materials" (243) to the office at 66 Church Street.

146. White and White, *The Intellectual versus the City*, 13. Their parting suggestion— "All the world's a city now and there is no escaping urbanization, even in outer space" (238)—anticipates a tangled and ongoing set of twenty-first–century debates on "planetary urbanization"; for example, Neil Brenner, ed., *Implosions/Explosions: Towards a Study of Planetary Urbanization* (Berlin: Jovis, 2014).

147. Reinhart Koselleck, "'Space of Experience' and 'Horizon of Expectation': Two Historical Categories" [1976], in *Futures Past: On the Semantics of Historical Time*, trans. Keith Tribe (New York: Columbia University Press, 1985), 255–275, at 258; emphasis added.

4. "A Documented Experience"

1. Malcolm Moos memo, May 4, 1965, box 13, folder 5, FFR.

2. Walter McQuade, "Urban Renewal in Boston" [1964; originally "Boston: What Can a Sick City Do?"], in *Urban Renewal: The Record and the Controversy*, ed. James Q. Wilson (Cambridge, MA: MIT Press, 1966), 259–277, at 260, 261, 266; and see David Monteyne, "Boston City Hall and a History of Reception," *Journal of Architectural Education* 65 (2011): 45–62.

3. Walter Muir Whitehill, *Boston: A Topographical History* [1959], 2nd ed. (Cambridge, MA: Harvard University Press, 1968), 189, 191. On "the Pru" specifically, see Elihu Rubin, *Insuring the City: The Prudential Center and the Postwar Urban Landscape* (New Haven, CT: Yale University Press, 2012).

4. Lizabeth Cohen, *Saving America's Cities: Ed Logue and the Struggle to Renew Urban America in the Suburban Age* (New York: Farrar, Straus & Giroux, 2019), 211, 181, 151. On the West End, see Herbert J. Gans, *The Urban Villagers* (New York: Free Press, 1962); Herbert J. Gans, "The Failure of Urban Renewal," *Commentary* (April 1965): 29–37; Chester Hartman, "The Housing of Relocated Families," *Journal of the American Institute of Planners* 30 (1964): 266–286; and Marc Fried, "Grieving for a Lost Home: Psychological Costs of Relocation," in *Urban Renewal: The Record and the Controversy*, ed. James Q. Wilson (Cambridge, MA: MIT Press, 1966), 359–379. For other treatments of Urban Renewal in Boston, see Thomas H. O'Connor, *Building a New Boston: Politics and Urban Renewal, 1950–1970* (Boston: Northeastern University Press, 1993); Lawrence W. Kennedy, *Planning the City upon a Hill: Boston since 1630* (Amherst: University of Massachusetts Press, 1992), especially 157–215; Gerald Gamm, *Urban Exodus: Why the Jews Left Boston and the Catholics Stayed* (Cambridge, MA: Harvard University Press, 2001), on population loss; and Karilyn Crockett, *People before Highways* (Amherst: University of Massachusetts Press, 2018), on resistance. On the region's postwar economic restructuring, see AnnaLee Saxenian, *Regional Advantage: Culture and Competition in Silicon Valley and Route 128* (Cambridge, MA: Harvard University Press, 1994). Cohen points out that, in addition to the summary demolition for which federal urbanism is most remembered, Boston's Section 221(d)(3) program of building rehabilitation was the nation's largest; *Saving America's Cities*, 210.

5. Cohen, *Saving America's Cities*, 169, 149, 192, 191; Monteyne, "Boston City Hall," 48. The Citizens' Seminars held at Boston College, Cohen (156) argues, were another crucial venue—that school, albeit Catholic, functioning as a neutral ground where Yankee and Irish factions (state and city politicians, respectively) could learn to get along.

6. Whitehill, *Boston*, xv. Whitehill closed the third edition citing Meyerson and Banfield's 1966 *Globe* series as an invitation to savor the city's architectural variety.

7. This chapter embeds the center's domestic agenda in a broader circuitry, granting its Southern exposure a formative role. Attempts to theorize urban studies "from the South" have proliferated in the early twenty-first century to such a degree that any

enumeration would be partial. Trenchant statements on transnationalizing urban history include Stephen V. Ward, *Planning the Twentieth-Century City: The Advanced Capitalist World* (New York: Wiley, 2002), on the "negotiated imposition" of Northern forms and policies; A. K. Sandoval-Strausz and Nancy H. Kwak, eds., *Making Cities Global: The Transnational Turn in Urban History* (Philadelphia: University of Pennsylvania Press, 2017); Rosemary Wakeman, "Rethinking Postwar Planning History," *Planning Perspectives* 29 (2014): 153–163; Clément Orillard, "The Transnational Building of Urban Design: Interplay between Genres of Discourse in the Anglophone World," *Planning Perspectives* 29 (2014): 209–229; and Ellen Shoshkes, "Martin Meyerson and Jaqueline Tyrwhitt and the Global Exchange of Planning Ideas," *Journal of Planning History* 9 (2010): 75–94. On expertise and its border crossings, see Mark Solovey and Christian Dayé, eds., *Cold War Social Science: Transnational Entanglements* (Cham: Palgrave Macmillan, 2021); Donna Mehos and Suzanne Moon, "The Uses of Portability: Circulating Experts in the Technopolitics of Cold War and Decolonization," in *Entangled Geographies: Empire and Technopolitics in the Global Cold War*, ed. Gabrielle Hecht (Cambridge, MA: MIT Press, 2011), 43–74; Johan Heilbron, Nicolas Guilhot, and Laurent Jeanpierre, "Toward a Transnational History of the Social Sciences," *Journal of the History of the Behavioral Sciences* 44 (2008): 146–160; and Edward Baring, "Ideas on the Move: Context in Transnational Intellectual History," *Journal of the History of Ideas* 77 (2016): 567–587.

8. Julius Stratton to Lloyd Rodwin, February 26, 1964, box 55, "Boston Metropolitan Regional Planning, 1961–1965" folder #1, LRP. And see "Laboratories for Urban Studies," box 4, "Long-Range Plans, 1965–1966" folder, LRP: "The real world," Rodwin wrote to his departmental colleagues, "must remain our ultimate laboratory."

9. Agenda from visit of August 31–September 2, 1966, box 6, "Guayana, MIT Visits" folder, GPR. This visit brought three consecutive directors—Rodwin, Wilson, and Moynihan—to town on a single plane. For a complete roster of Joint Center staff working on-site, up to 1964, see Joint Center for Urban Studies, *The First Five Years* (Cambridge, MA: The Center, 1964), 63–64.

10. Frederik Schulze, "In Search of El Dorado: U.S. Experts and the Promise of Development in the Guayana Region of Venezuela," *History and Technology* 35 (2019): 338–363, the best extant source on the political context, notes, at 352, that Betancourt and the CVG adjusted population projections several times. The figure six hundred thousand dates from 1963; in 1961, they projected two hundred thousand residents. On Colombia, see Amy C. Offner, *Sorting Out the Mixed Economy: The Rise and Fall of Welfare and Developmental States in the Americas* (Princeton, NJ: Princeton University Press, 2019), 79–111; and, on the Alliance for Progress generally, Michael E. Latham, *Modernization as Ideology: Social Science and "Nation Building" in the Kennedy Era* (Chapel Hill: University of North Carolina Press, 2000), 69–108, which does not mention Venezuela. As Offner writes, the United States was clearly unlike Colombia, but it seemed to contain "little Colombias" (11) where Southern lessons might apply. Ciudad Kennedy, a case of "aided self-help housing" by which the state formalized the ownership structure of existing informal settlements, began construction in 1962 and now houses a million people, more than a tenth of Bogotá. The Colombian analogue to the CVG was the Cauca Valley Corporation, also partially modeled on the TVA; David Lilienthal called the Cauca his "second-favorite valley" (22).

11. Lloyd Rodwin, interview by Morton Schussheim, June 11, 1994, PIH; David Ekbladh, "'Mr. TVA': Grass-Roots Development, David Lilienthal, and the Rise and Fall of the Tennessee Valley Authority as a Symbol for U.S. Overseas Development," *Diplomatic History* 26 (2002): 335–374.

12. Lloyd Rodwin, interview by Morton Schussheim, June 11, 1994.

13. Eric Carlson memo, April 1959, box 4, "Lloyd Rodwin's Private Consulting for Venezuela, 1958–1960" folder, LRP.

14. Lisa Peattie, *Planning: Rethinking Ciudad Guayana* (Ann Arbor: University of Michigan Press, 1987), 35, 36.

15. Arturo Almandoz, "Towards Brasília and Ciudad Guayana: Development, Urbanization and Regional Planning in Latin America, 1940s–1960s," *Planning Perspectives* 31 (2016): 31–53, at 44. An official nationwide framework of regions was adopted in 1969. For one book-length account by a Cordiplan employee, see Maritza Izaguirre, *Ciudad Guayana y la estrategia del desarrollo planificado* (Caracas: Ediciones SIAP, 1977).

16. Peattie, *Planning*, 27–29; Christopher P. Loss, "'The City of Tomorrow Must Reckon with the Lives and Living Habits of Human Beings': The Joint Center for Urban Studies Goes to Venezuela, 1957–1969," *Journal of Urban History* 47 (2021): 623–650, at 633. Simone Rots and Ana María Fernández Maldonado, "Planning Ciudad Guayana, an Industrial New Town in Oil-Rich Venezuela," *International Planning Studies* 24 (2019): 353–368, focuses on the CVG. Other productive discussions include Ijlal Muzaffar, "Fuzzy Images: The Problem of Third World Development and the New Ethics of Open-Ended Planning at the MIT–Harvard Joint Center for Urban Studies," in *A Second Modernism: MIT, Architecture, and the "Techno-Social" Moment*, ed. Arindam Dutta (Cambridge, MA: MIT Press, 2013), 310–341; Eric Mumford, "From Master Planning to Self-Build: The MIT–Harvard Joint Center for Urban Studies, 1959–1971," in *A Second Modernism: MIT, Architecture, and the "Techno-Social" Moment*, ed. Arindam Dutta (Cambridge, MA: MIT Press, 2013), 288–309; Schulze, "In Search of El Dorado"; Robert H. Kargon and Arthur P. Molella, *Invented Edens: Techno-Cities of the Twentieth Century* (Cambridge, MA: MIT Press, 2008), 113–123; and Felipe Correa, *Beyond the City: Resource Extraction in South America* (Austin: University of Texas Press, 2016), 89–110.

17. John Friedmann, *Regional Development Policy: A Case Study of Venezuela* (Cambridge, MA: MIT Press, 1966), 155, 154, 160, 152. Broader treatments of the Venezuelan state during this era include Miguel Tinker Salas, *The Enduring Legacy: Oil, Culture, and Society in Venezuela* (Durham, NC: Duke University Press, 2009); Fernando Coronil, *The Magical State: Nature, Money, and Modernity in Venezuela* (Chicago: University of Chicago Press, 1997); and Rómulo Betancourt, *Venezuela: política y petróleo* (Mexico City: Fondo de Cultura Económica, 1956). On its cities, see Marco Negrón, *Ciudad y modernidad, 1936–2000: El rol del sistema de ciudades en la modernización de Venezuela* (Caracas: Instituto de Urbanismo, 2001); Elisenda Vila, *La planificación en Venezuela* (Caracas: Instituto de Urbanismo, 1985); and Arturo Almandoz, *Modernization, Urbanization, and Development in Latin America, 1900s–2000s* (London: Routledge, 2015).

18. Friedmann, *Regional Development Policy*, 159.

19. Carlos Brillembourg, "Sowing the Oil: Brutalist Urbanism, Ciudad Guayana, Venezuela, 1951–2012," paper delivered to the X Seminário Docomomo Brasil (October 15–18, 2013), 6, 7.

20. Almandoz, "Towards Brasília and Ciudad Guayana," 46.

21. Charles Abrams, *Man's Struggle for Shelter in an Urbanizing World* (Cambridge, MA: MIT Press, 1964), 13, 53; Talton F. Ray, *The Politics of the Barrios of Venezuela* (Berkeley: University of California Press, 1969). In 1947, Venezuela was the site chosen for the international Conference on Tropical Housing; Nancy H. Kwak, *A World of Homeowners: American Power and the Politics of Housing Aid* (Chicago: University of Chicago Press, 2015), 97.

22. Almandoz, "Towards Brasília and Ciudad Guayana," 36; Francis Violich, "A Planner Reports on Latin America," *The Planners' Journal* 8 (1942): 19–25; Francis Violich and Juan B. Astica, *Community Development and the Urban Planning Process in Latin America* (Los Angeles: Latin American Center and Centro Latinoamericano de Venezuela, 1967); Francis Violich, *Urban Planning for Latin America: The Challenge of Metropolitan Growth* (Boston: Oelgeschlager, Gunn & Hain, 1987). On Robert Moses in Latin America, see Marcio Siwi, "The Making of New York's Avenue of the Americas: Transnational Circuits of Urban Renewal," *Journal of Urban History* 47 (2021): 85–110.

23. Correa, *Beyond the City*, 65–88.

24. Minutes, June 7, 1951, box 55, "Committee on Urban and Regional Studies, 1951–1954" folder #1, LRP; David E. Snyder, "Ciudad Guayana: A Planned Metropolis on the Orinoco," *Journal of Inter-American Studies* 5 (1963): 405–412, at 405. Roosevelt's Good Neighbor Policy lubricated these contacts. For an earlier example, see Greg Grandin, *Fordlândia: The Rise and Fall of Henry Ford's Forgotten Jungle City* (New York: Macmillan, 2009). On US Steel at Ciudad Guayana, see Manuel Shvartzberg Carrió, "Infrastructures of Dependency: US Steel's Architectural Assemblages on Indigenous Lands," in *Architecture in Development: Systems and the Emergence of the Global South*, ed. Aggregate Architectural History Collective (London: Routledge, 2022), 217–236.

25. For critical histories in which Ford figures prominently, see Inderjeet Parmar, *Foundations of the American Century* (New York: Columbia University Press, 2012); Daniel Immerwahr, *Thinking Small: The United States and the Lure of Community Development* (Cambridge, MA: Harvard University Press, 2015); Kwak, *A World of Homeowners*; George Rosen, *Western Economists and Eastern Societies: Agents of Change in South Asia, 1950–1970* (Baltimore: Johns Hopkins University Press, 1985); and Matthew Connelly, *Fatal Misconception: The Struggle to Control World Population* (Cambridge, MA: Harvard University Press, 2008). The Rockefeller Foundation is not this chapter's focus, but Nelson Rockefeller was an investor in and frequent visitor to Venezuela between the 1930s and the 1950s; Darlene Rivas, *Missionary Capitalist: Nelson Rockefeller in Venezuela* (Chapel Hill: University of North Carolina Press, 2002).

26. *About the Ford Foundation* (New York: Ford Foundation, 1963), 19.

27. *The Ford Foundation and Pakistan* (New York: Ford Foundation, 1959); Eugene S. Staples, *Forty Years: A Learning Curve: The Ford Foundation Programs in India, 1952–1992* (New Delhi: Ford Foundation, 1992); *Roots of Change: The Ford Foundation in India* (New York: Ford Foundation, 1961), 46 and passim; *The Ford Foundation and Foundation-Supported Activities in India* (New York: Ford Foundation, 1955); *Architects of Order* (New York: Ford Foundation, 1959); Program, Calcutta Conference, June 1–2, 1961, box 5, "Ford Foundation—Calcutta" folder, PNYP. Meyerson, Raymond Vernon, and Edgar Hoover were present at Ford's 1961 conference on Calcutta; Andrew Rumbach, "'Between the Devil and the Bay of Bengal': The Ford Foundation and the Politics of Planning in Post-Independence Calcutta," *Planning Perspectives* 36 (2021): 1025–1051.

On Ford's work in Eastern Europe and the Balkans, on which Meyerson and other Joint Center figures consulted, see Vladimir Kulić, "Ford's Network: The American–Yugoslav Project and the Circulation of Urban Planning Expertise in the Cold War," *Planning Perspectives* 37 (2022): 1001–1027.

28. Staples, *Forty Years*, 52.

29. Sam Collings-Wells, "Developing Communities: The Ford Foundation and the Global Urban Crisis, 1958–66," *Journal of Global History* 16 (2021): 336–354, at 340, 336; Immerwahr, *Thinking Small*; Odd Arne Westad, *The Global Cold War* (Cambridge, UK: Cambridge University Press, 2007).

30. Stuart W. Leslie and Robert Kargon, "Exporting MIT: Science, Technology, and Nation-Building in India and Iran," *Osiris* 21 (2006): 110–130.

31. Ethan Schrum, *The Instrumental University: Education in Service of the National Agenda after World War II* (Ithaca, NY: Cornell University Press, 2019), 126–163.

32. Shoshkes, "Martin Meyerson," 79, 89, 80; Ines Tolić, "News from the Modern Front: Constantinos A. Doxiadis's *Ekistics*, the United Nations, and the Post-War Discourse on Housing, Building and Planning," *Planning Perspectives* 37 (2022): 973–999; Mark Wigley, "Network Fever," *Grey Room* 4 (Summer 2001): 82–122. Meyerson attended Delos in 1964, from 1967 to 1969, and in 1972. For Meier's political economy, see Richard L. Meier, *Science and Economic Development: New Patterns of Living* (Cambridge, MA: MIT Press, 1956).

33. The literature is vast, but see, for example, Constantinos Doxiadis, "Ecumenopolis: Tomorrow's City," *Britannica: Book of the Year 1968* (Chicago: Encyclopedia Britannica, 1968), 16–38. On the 23 de Enero, see Alejandro Velasco, *Barrio Rising: Urban Popular Politics and the Making of Modern Venezuela* (Berkeley: University of California Press, 2015).

34. Lloyd Rodwin, interview by Morton Schussheim, June 11, 1994.

35. Meyerson to Rodwin, July 6, 1960, box 55, Martin Meyerson folder, LRP.

36. Friedmann, *Regional Development Policy*, 134, 136, 147, 137. By 1960, a majority of Venezuela's population was living in spaces classified as urban. Abrams was struck by the public housing towers "standing like monumental tablets proclaiming their superiority to the makeshift ranchos nearby" on the hillsides. When it rained, Abrams wrote, "a lava of human excrement" sped downhill from the ranchos; *Man's Struggle*, 53, 17.

37. Velasco, *Barrio Rising*, 25–26, 21–22, 36, 98–105. Velasco identifies Betancourt with an "anti-urban strategy," although it might better be described as decentralist.

38. Friedmann, *Regional Development Policy*, 170; Snyder, "Ciudad Guayana," 409.

39. Anthony H. Penfold, "Ciudad Guayana: Planning a New City in Venezuela," *Town Planning Review* 36 (1966): 225–248, at 225, 230.

40. "The Guayana Development Program," March 1965 (Report B80), box 1, CGR. Early on, the Joint Center retained the consultancy Arthur D. Little to identify the five to seven industries it should prioritize. Arthur D. Little advised against leather, woodworking, metalworking, and food processing, all "sectors considered to be sick"; Arthur D. Little proposal, March 17, 1962 (Report E12), box 1, CGR. The new steel mill, or *siderúrgica*, began production in 1964, aluminum broke ground in 1965, and pulp in 1966; Penfold, "Ciudad Guayana," 237. Consumer products were manufactured using the Guayana's raw materials in cities west of Caracas. Flood control was the other ma-

jor impetus for damming the river; two million acres of land were thereby reclaimed for agriculture.

41. Charles Abrams, "Report on the Development of Ciudad Guayana in Venezuela," January 25, 1962 (Report A5), box 1, CGR. One observer, noting "sharp contrasts" between neighboring pockets of development, called Ciudad Guayana "in many ways suggestive of Panama inside and outside of the Canal Zone, but, of course, on a much smaller scale"; Snyder, "Ciudad Guayana," 410.

42. Friedmann, *Regional Development Policy*, 157, 137. To differentiate things further, Friedmann (144) described an overarching spatial structure of five east–west economic bands, progressing stepwise south from the oceanfront: fishing, then agriculture, then forest, cattle, and arid land. See also Corporación Venezolana de Guayana (CVG), "Guayana: Cornerstone of the Development of Venezuela" (n.d.); CVG, "Developing Venezuela's Guayana" (1963); and CVG, "Guayana: Economic Program Key to the Development of Venezuela" (1965); box 6, "Ciudad Guayana Informational Materials" folder #2, GPR.

43. Guayana Project, Work Outline, October 13, 1961, box 1, GPR, 17, 35.

44. Doxiadis, "Ecumenopolis," 16.

45. Guayana Project, Work Outline, 1.

46. Norman Williams Jr., "Planning the Guayana," address to Fourth International Planning Congress, San Diego, November 1962, box 1, GPR, 13.

47. Lisa Peattie would later point out that, in practice, the project was less than fully interdisciplinary. Urban designers, who spoke constantly of "the site," and economists, who fixated on dollars and population counts, called most of the shots; *Planning*, 46, 51.

48. Roderick Peattie and Lisa Peattie, "Immediate Steps toward Civic Consciousness," June 7, 1962 (Report C13), box 5, GPR.

49. Guy Kelnhofer and Anthony Penfold, "Revised Statement of Tentative General Goals for the City," February 20, 1963 (Report D25), box 3, GPR, 5.

50. Abrams, "Report on the Development of Ciudad Guayana in Venezuela." Abrams paid multiple visits to Ciudad Guayana between 1962 and 1964, each of which resulted in a memo: Norman Williams to Charles Abrams, January 17, 1962, box 42, "Studies: Venezuela, 1962" folder; Antonio Alamo to Abrams, January 24, 1962, box 42, "Studies: Venezuela, 1962" folder; Williams to Abrams, January 17, 1962, box 42, "Studies: Venezuela, 1962" folder; Abrams, report on Ciudad Guayana, January 25, 1962, box 42; Abrams, report to Lloyd Rodwin and James Q. Wilson, December 20, 1963, box 42; Abrams, notes on Materiales Mendoza, December 1963, box 42, "Studies: Venezuela, 1963" folder; Abrams, report on Ciudad Guayana, May 14, 1964, box 42, "Studies: Venezuela, 1964" folder; CAP. Snyder, "Ciudad Guayana," 407, puts the figure for 1960 at forty thousand, up from the 1950 count of five thousand.

51. Williams, "Planning the Guayana," 2.

52. Guayana Project, Work Outline, 42.

53. Penfold, "Ciudad Guayana," 235.

54. Roderick Peattie and Lisa Peattie, "Tourist Facilities," May 17, 1962 (Report C14), box 5, GPR. Nor, Abrams noted, was Venezuela's tradition of philanthropy particularly strong. Wealthy citizens and major banks showed little interest in speculating on large-scale housing developments. One exception was Eugenio Mendoza, who began

a nonprofit concern in 1961, accrued American contacts, and by 1964, with the assistance of Charles Abrams, secured fifteen separate loans from the Development Loan Fund. Abrams persuaded him to switch over to the savings-and-loan model, which US-AID officials favored; Abrams, *Man's Struggle*, 152.

55. Guy Kelnhofer, "Report on Trip to the Guayana," December 4, 1962 (Report F50), box 2, CGR.

56. See Rosemary Wakeman's vigorously transnational *Practicing Utopia: An Intellectual History of the New Town Movement* (Chicago: University of Chicago Press, 2016). See Ann Forsyth, *Reforming Suburbia: The Planned Communities of Irvine, Columbia, and The Woodlands* (Berkeley: University of California Press, 2005), for three leading US examples; Roger Biles, "New Towns for the Great Society: A Case Study in Politics and Planning," *Planning Perspectives* 13 (1998): 113–132; and, for a 1970s case, Yonah Freemark, "Roosevelt Island: Exception to a City in Crisis," *Journal of Urban History* 37 (2011): 355–383.

57. Abrams, *Man's Struggle for Shelter*, 135.

58. Guy Kelnhofer, "Planning and Administration of New Towns," June 1963 (Report D29), box 3, GPR; Joseph L. Arnold, *The New Deal in the Suburbs: A History of the Greenbelt Town Programs* (Columbus: Ohio State University Press, 1971).

59. Martha Derthick, *New Towns In-Town* (Washington, DC: The Urban Institute, 1972). Many of these examples remain reference points for urbanists—for example, Tim Bunnell et al., "Points of Persuasion: Truth Spots in Future City Development," *Environment and Planning D: Society and Space* 40 (2022): 1082–1099.

60. Alan Turner and Jonathan Smulian, "New Cities in Venezuela," *Town Planning Review* 42 (1971): 3–27, at 3, 4; Edward Lynch, "Propositions for Planning New Towns in Venezuela," *Journal of Developing Areas* 7 (1973): 549–570, at 550; Correa, *Beyond the City*, 72–74; and Ervin Y. Galantay, *New Towns: Antiquity to the Present* (New York: Braziller, 1975), 48–51.

61. Lloyd Rodwin, *The British New Towns Policy: Problems and Implications* (Cambridge, MA: Harvard University Press, 1956), 162, 85. In Rodwin's widest-circulation article on the topic, he opted for the term "new city": Lloyd Rodwin, "Ciudad Guayana: A New City," *Scientific American* 23 (1965): 122–132.

62. Box 5, "Round Table Conference on the Planning of New Towns, 1964" folder, LRP.

63. Abrams, "Report on the Development of Ciudad Guayana in Venezuela"; and see "An American Ruhr," *Fortune* (October 1933), depicting the Tennessee Valley.

64. Lisa Peattie, travelogue from Mexico, August 1962 (Report C16), box 1, CGR. This was Lisa Redfield Peattie, daughter of Robert Redfield, the prominent cultural anthropologist of "folk society" who had made a career studying Mexico.

65. James Holston, *The Modernist City: An Anthropological Critique of Brasília* (Chicago: University of Chicago Press, 1989), is the most comprehensive account, especially of the copious informal housing that cropped up on the edges of the seemingly airtight city plan.

66. Willo von Moltke, in Boletín de la Asociación Cultural Humboldt (1965), box 9 (DL24HC), WVMP; Penfold, "Ciudad Guayana," 238. The Joint Center's records include a 1961 clipping of an article from the *Jornal do Brasil*, soon republished as F.G., "Crisis in Brasília," *Ekistics* 14, no. 83 (October 1962): 143–146. The marginalia: "Be we prepared!"

67. Willo von Moltke, Lecture in Brasília, May 1964, box 6 (DL24HB), WVMP. See also Ervin Y. Galantay, "Ciudad Guayana: New Town and Regional Growth Pole," *Swissair Gazette* (October 1988): 39–41; and *Big City 1980 with Garry Moore* (1961; New York: CBS Television) for a prime-time program, featuring John Burchard, that cuts between Brasília—"bursting into tomorrow from yesterday"—and redevelopment politics on the streets of Philadelphia.

68. Holston, *Modernist City*, passim; Rodwin, *British New Towns Policy*, 129.

69. Bruno Taut, "A Programme for Architecture" [1918], in *Programs and Manifestoes on 20th-Century Architecture*, ed. Ulrich Conrads (Cambridge, MA: MIT Press, 1971), 41–43, at 41. For other examples of this rhetoric of speed, obsolescence, and violent discontinuity with the past, see, anthologized in the same volume, Antonio Sant'Elia and Filippo Tommaso Marinetti, "Manifesto of Futurist Architecture" [1914], 34–38; Walter Gropius, "Programme of the Staatlische Bauhaus in Weimar" [1919], 49–53; Erich Mendelsohn, "The Problem of a New Architecture" [1919], 54–55; and the all-important Le Corbusier, "Towards a New Architecture: Guiding Principles" [1920], 59–62. The CIAM's 1933 Charter of Athens, which scaled these principles up from the building to the city, was somewhat more measured in tone.

70. Willo von Moltke, "Santo Tome de Guayana," *Ekistics* 15, no. 87 (February 1963): 113–115, at 113.

71. Jenny Andersson, *The Future of the World: Futurology, Futurists, and the Struggle for the Post–Cold War Imagination* (Oxford: Oxford University Press, 2018), 49, 27; Nils Gilman, *Mandarins of the Future: Modernization Theory in Cold War America* (Baltimore: Johns Hopkins University Press, 2003); Jill Lepore, *If Then: How the Simulmatics Corporation Invented the Future* (New York: Liveright, 2020), 205–254, on MIT activities in Vietnam. The field of industrial relations was also preoccupied with the timing and pacing of development in the postcolonial world, where scholars were convinced that moving too fast would generate social "dislocation" and a receptiveness to socialist remedies; Schrum, *Instrumental University*, 64, 68.

72. Friedmann, *Regional Development Policy*, 127, 86, 194.

73. Arthur H. Fawcett and James N. Kise, "Alternative Forms for Ciudad Guayana," July 14, 1962 (Report E54), box 1, CGR.

74. Appleyard, "The Future Form of Santo Tomé," December 1962, box 57, Donald Appleyard folder, LRP.

75. "Form Studies," National Capital 2000 AD Planning Commission Regional Council, box 1, "Guayana Planning Reference Material, 1958–1965" folder, GPR.

76. Frank Martocci to Norman Williams, March 16, 1962 (Report E38), box 2, CGR.

77. Meyerson to Rodwin, July 6, 1960. Bacon was John Burchard's preferred candidate.

78. Williams, "Planning the Guayana," 11.

79. Willo von Moltke, "The Evolution of the Linear Form," in Lloyd Rodwin and Associates, *Planning Urban Growth and Regional Development: The Experience of the Guayana Program in Venezuela* (Cambridge, MA: MIT Press, 1969), 126–146, at 134, 135.

80. Memo on CIAM, March 3, 1962, (Report E16), box 1, CGR.

81. Williams, "Planning the Guayana," 11.

82. Willo von Moltke, "The Visual Design of Ciudad Guayana" (June 1965), box 1, Wilhelm von Moltke folder #1, GPR.

83. Willo von Moltke and Edmund N. Bacon, "In Pursuit of Urbanity," *Annals of the American Academy of Political and Social Science* 314 (1957): 101–111.

84. Penfold, "Ciudad Guayana," 246.

85. Abrams, *Man's Struggle*, 112n15, 112, 139n8, 147.

86. Penfold, "Ciudad Guayana," 240, 238, 239; William L. Porter, "Three Episodes, Three Roles," in *A Second Modernism: MIT, Architecture, and the "Techno-Social" Moment*, ed. Arindam Dutta (Cambridge, MA: MIT Press, 2013), 740–769, at 750, 743.

87. Donald Appleyard to Lloyd Rodwin, April 16, 1964, box 57, Donald Appleyard folder, LRP.

88. Appleyard to Rodwin, June 11, 1965, box 57, Donald Appleyard folder, LRP; Donald Appleyard, Kevin Lynch, and John R. Myer, *The View from the Road* (Cambridge, MA: MIT Press, 1964), 83. The notion that landscapes "unfold" as one moves through them is a commonplace in the history of Qing-era Chinese garden design. In the 1960s, many Chinese and Western landscape architects began to write of that period's interest in the mobile eye as if it had prefigured Modernist understandings of spacetime; Andong Lu, "Lost in Translation: Modernist Interpretation of the Chinese Garden as Experiential Space and Its Assumptions," *Journal of Architecture* 16 (2011): 499–527.

89. Donald Appleyard, "Motion, Sequence and the City," in *The Nature and Art of Motion*, ed. György Kepes (New York: Braziller, 1965), 176–192, at 189, 185, 190; Appleyard to Rodwin and Wilson, March 3, 1965, box 57, Donald Appleyard folder, LRP. Appleyard reproduces elements of a design by George Kurilko, one of his students at MIT. He also makes passing reference to Caracas as an automobile-dominated city.

90. Willo von Moltke, Lecture in Ciudad Guayana, 1972, box 6 (DL24HB), WVMP.

91. Von Moltke, Lecture in Ciudad Guayana.

92. Von Moltke, Lecture in Ciudad Guayana; von Moltke, "Evolution of the Linear Form," 142–144; Loss, "'City of Tomorrow,'" 638–640. The city's first "comprehensive" design plan appeared in 1964. In 1965, von Moltke began amending it, and the dual-boulevard scheme for Alta Vista came about. The design was part of a broader attempt to sequence both the district's development and its selective abandonment. According to what has variously been called an "inside-out" or an "outside-in" scheme, von Moltke wanted first to fill the swath, six hundred feet wide, with commercial establishments to the point of overcrowding. Then, once it seemed ready to overspill its boundaries, planners would encourage businesses to move either north or south of the Avenida; the CVG would not renew their leases or court new businesses to take their place. This would depress land values at the center of Alta Vista, and once they were low enough, the CVG would replace the short-lived commercial blocks with a sunken highway enjoying fewer visual distractions and faster traffic. "This development strategy," von Moltke wrote, "uses the principle of planned obsolescence."

93. "The Guayana Development Program"; Robert Jungk, *Tomorrow Is Already Here* (New York: Simon and Schuster, 1954). "Past, present, and future are joined," Appleyard wrote in "Motion, Sequence, and the City" (182). "Each experience is relative" to the whole complex—"each event, set against the remembered past."

94. Von Moltke specifically asked that the road be illuminated at night and that "temporary sheds for [the CVG's] exhibition purposes" line the road; Willo von Moltke, "Visual Development of Ciudad Guayana" (1965), box 9 (DL24HC), WVMP. On the distinction between arrival (at a parking lot) and entry (into a building), see Douglas

Suisman, *Los Angeles Boulevard: Eight X-Rays of the Body Public* [1989] (Novato, CA: ORO Editions, 2014), 75–78. On period mantras that "history is a highway," see Eric Avila, *Popular Culture in the Age of White Flight: Fear and Fantasy in Suburban Los Angeles* (Berkeley: University of California Press, 2004), 185–223. David C. Engerman, "West Meets East: The Center for International Studies and Indian Economic Development," in *Staging Growth: Modernization, Development, and the Global Cold War*, eds. David C. Engerman et al. (Amherst: University of Massachusetts Press, 2003), 199–223, at 217, notes the use of subway analogies by American economists: postcolonial leaders should "take the local" rather than the "express train to modernity."

95. Kevin Lynch, "The Pattern of the Metropolis," in *The Future Metropolis*, ed. Lloyd Rodwin (New York: Braziller, 1961), 103–128, at 120. And see György Kepes, *Language of Vision* (New York: Theobald, 1944), 53: "Vision is the work process of the eye.... [It] needs both action and repose."

96. A point elaborated in Hashim Sarkis, "Disoriented: Kevin Lynch, around 1960," in *A Second Modernism: MIT, Architecture, and the "Techno-Social" Moment*, ed. Arindam Dutta (Cambridge, MA: MIT Press, 2013), 394–433.

97. Philip Thiel, "A Sequence-Experience Notation for Architectural and Urban Spaces," *Town Planning Review* 32 (1961): 33–52, at 33.

98. John Ely Burchard, "The Urban Aesthetic," *Annals of the American Academy of Political and Social Science* 314 (1957): 112–122, at 118, 119.

99. Kevin Lynch, "Some Notes on the Design of Ciudad Guayana," July 22, 1964 (Report E90), box 3, GPR. Even if the mill concisely encapsulated the modernization process and rewarded drivers' expectations, it would likely not have inspired wonder as outlined by Philip Fisher, *Wonder, the Rainbow, and the Aesthetics of Rare Experiences* (Cambridge, MA: Harvard University Press, 1998), 21: "So important is the visual, the sudden, and the unexpected within the experience of wonder that within the arts wonder is almost uniquely possible within architecture, sculpture, painting, and within grand projects of engineering like the George Washington Bridge where, in every case, a sudden experience of the whole is possible. The arts of time—narration, dance, and music—are never present as a whole in an instant of time. They also depend on controlled expectations, followed by surprise against the backdrop of what we have been led to think will happen next. Wonder does not depend on awakening and then surprising expectations, but on the complete absence of expectation."

100. Lynch, "Some Notes."

101. Kevin Lynch, *What Time Is This Place?* (Cambridge, MA: MIT Press, 1972).

102. Kevin Lynch, *Managing the Sense of a Region* (Cambridge, MA: MIT Press, 1976), 49, 28.

103. Lynch, "Some Notes."

104. Penfold, "Ciudad Guayana," 234; Julián Ferris to Reginald Isaacs, March 14, 1960, box 1, folder 18, RRIP. Isaacs, among other Joint Center members, consulted on its organization.

105. Lloyd Rodwin, Introduction to *Planning Urban Growth and Regional Development*, 3, 5; Lloyd Rodwin, "Reflections on Collaborative Planning," in *Planning Urban Growth and Regional Development*, 468.

106. Williams to Daniel Lerner, January 19, 1962 (Report C12), box 1, CGR.

107. Daniel Lerner, May 21, 1962 (Report C8), box 3, GPR.

108. Roderick Peattie and Lisa Peattie, "Some Notes on the Organization of the Joint Center Guayana Project," July 19, 1962 (Report F25), box 5, GPR.

109. Lloyd Rodwin, interview by Morton Schussheim, June 11, 1994.

110. Noel F. McGinn and Russell G. Davis, *Build a Mill, Build a City, Build a School: Industrialization, Urbanization, and Education in Ciudad Guayana* (Cambridge, MA: MIT Press, 1969); Richard M. Soberman, *Transport Technology for Developing Regions: A Study of Road Transportation in Venezuela* (Cambridge, MA: MIT Press, 1966). There was also the unpublished dissertation John R. Dinkelspiel, "Administrative Style and Economic Development: The Organization and Management of the Guayana Region Development of Venezuela" (PhD diss., Harvard University, 1967); and see Martin Meyerson, "Planning for Movement in Developing Countries," in *Regional Planning* (United Nations Department of Economic and Social Affairs, 1958), 85–93, which the Joint Center reprinted.

111. Frank Martocci, "The Physical Regional Plan," 1962 (Report F21), box 2; Willo von Moltke, "Urban Design," 1962 (Report F22), box 2; William Doebele, "Legal Implementation," 1962 (Report F23), box 2; "Political Organization," 1962 (Report F24), box 2; CGR. Eric Mumford, *Defining Urban Design: CIAM Architects and the Formation of a Discipline, 1937–69* (New Haven, CT: Yale University Press, 2009), 166, claims that urban design's consolidation as a field was "advanced by" Ciudad Guayana.

112. Rodwin, "Reflections on Collaborative Planning," 467.

113. Donald Appleyard, *Planning a Pluralist City: Conflicting Realities in Ciudad Guayana* (Cambridge, MA: MIT Press, 1976). Von Moltke's manuscript morphed into "Urban Design Intent: Three Case Studies"—namely, Ciudad Guayana, Philadelphia, and Istanbul. No draft was complete until 1981, and von Moltke made revisions as late as 1983. It was still unpublished at the time of his death in 1987. The GSD's then dean, Gerald McCue, urged against its publication but in 1991 disseminated the draft: "It captures a sense of both the intellectual excitement and the methodology developed in the formative years of the new profession." See Willo von Moltke, "Urban Design Intent: Three Case Studies" (unfinished book manuscript), box 9 (DL24HC), WVMP.

114. John Friedmann and Clyde Weaver, *Territory and Function: The Evolution of Regional Planning* (Berkeley: University of California Press, 1979), 130; John Friedmann, "A Life in Planning," in *The Prospect of Cities* (Minneapolis: University of Minnesota Press, 2002), 119–157, at 129, 130, 128; Friedmann, *Regional Development Policy*, viii. Friedmann did, in truth, honor Walter Isard's contributions. At the midpoint of the Guayana project, working to stabilize the field of regional planning by pruning its canon, he brought out a thick reader of classic theoretical statements—entirely post-1950 save for one by August Lösch—and dedicated it to Isard; John Friedmann and William Alonso, eds., *Regional Development and Planning: A Reader* (Cambridge, MA: MIT Press, 1964). See also John Friedmann, "Regional Planning as a Field of Study," *Journal of the American Institute of Planners* 29 (1963): 168–175, at 169, which leads with Ciudad Guayana; and, for further theoretical development, John Friedmann and John Miller, "The Urban Field," *Journal of the American Institute of Planners* 31 (1965): 312–320.

115. Peattie, *Planning*, 34, 33.

116. Friedmann, *Regional Development Policy*, 14, 253. The concept first appeared in François Perroux, "Notes sur la notion de 'pôle de croissance,'" *Economie Appliqué* 7 (1955): 307–320.

117. Friedmann, *Regional Development Policy*, 78, 173, 8, 123, 160; emphasis original. On "regions of lasting difficulty," Friedmann cited the British geographer H. J. Fleure; and see Richard C. Wade, *The Urban Frontier: The Rise of Western Cities, 1790–1830* (Cambridge, MA: Harvard University Press, 1959).

118. Friedmann, *Regional Development Policy*, 174, 43.

119. Arthur H. Fawcett, "Comments on the Delineation of a Planning Region," June 30, 1962 (Report E44), box 1, CGR; and also Blair T. Bower, "A Note on the Definition of the Region," August 22, 1962 (Report E55), box 1, CGR.

120. Inter alia, Anssi Paasi, "The Institutionalization of Regions: A Theoretical Framework for Understanding the Emergence of Regions and the Constitution of Regional Identity," *Fennia* 164 (1986): 105–146. For Friedmann's earliest theorizations, see John R. P. Friedmann, "The Concept of a Planning Region" and "Locational Aspects of Economic Development," *Land Economics* 32 (1956): 1–13 and 213–227. For a more recent intellectual history, see Liane Lefaivre and Alexander Tzonis, *Architecture of Regionalism in the Age of Globalization* (London: Routledge, 2011). Human geography's sharp turn in the later twentieth century from the "regional" to the "spatial" awaits a full-scale intellectual history of its own.

121. Friedmann and Weaver, *Territory and Function*, 6, 125.

122. Bish Sanyal, "A Planners' Planner: John Friedmann's Quest for a General Theory of Planning," *Journal of the American Planning Association* 84 (2018): 179–191, at 181; Karl Mannheim, *Man and Society in an Age of Reconstruction* [1935], revised ed., trans. Edward Shils (New York: Harcourt, Brace, 1940). On Mannheim's influence on a range of midcentury American and German-émigré intellectuals, see Daniel Bessner, *Democracy in Exile: Hans Speier and the Rise of the Defense Intellectual* (Ithaca, NY: Cornell University Press, 2018), 20–25 and passim. Daniel Bell called *Ideology and Utopia* "probably the crucial book of my college years," offering a "much more sophisticated Marxism"; Daniel Bell and Pearl Kazin Bell, interview by William R. Keylor, April 1972, Richard Hofstadter Project, CUL.

123. H. Wentworth Eldredge, "Aesthetics," in *Taming Megalopolis: What Is and What Could Be*, vol. 1 (New York: Anchor, 1967), 269; Wilhelm von Moltke, "The Visual Development of Ciudad Guayana" [1965], in *Taming Megalopolis*, 274–286. Eldredge thrilled to the work of Lynch, Kepes, and Appleyard on "note-taking devices" and "perception quantifiers" (268).

124. Lloyd Rodwin, *Nations and Cities: A Comparison of Strategies for Urban Growth* (Boston: Houghton Mifflin, 1970), 25, 31, 67; and see geographer David J. Robinson, "The City as a Center of Change in Venezuela," in *Cities in a Changing Latin America*, eds. David Fox and David J. Robinson (London: Latin American Publications Fund, 1969), 23–48. Rodwin had consulted on urban affairs in Turkey, and also in Morocco, Egypt, Indonesia, Malaysia, Mexico, and Japan; Lloyd Rodwin, interview by Morton Schussheim, June 11, 1994. See also Lloyd Rodwin, *Urban Planning in Developing Countries* (Washington, DC: Department of Housing and Urban Development, 1965), a brief publication Rodwin prepared for the Agency for International Development as part of HUD's "Ideas and Methods Exchange" series. Again Ciudad Guayana was the lone example, despite his title's generality.

125. Lloyd Rodwin, interview by Morton Schussheim, June 11, 1994. For other instances of Cold War programs being tested in Latin America and then exported north,

see Stuart Schrader, *Badges without Borders* (Oakland: University of California Press, 2019), on counterinsurgency; Siwi, "The Making of New York's Avenue of the Americas"; Lepore, *If Then*, 209, on collaboration between the Simulmatics Corporation and CENIS at the Centro de Estudios de Desarrollo in Caracas; and Offner, *Sorting Out the Mixed Economy*, who rightly notes the "detours," "blocked passages," and circuitous pathways of influence (288). Lepore (259–260) describes the US Army's counterinsurgent Project Camelot, begun 1964, as a "Venezuela study writ large." Simulmatics formed a domestic Urban Studies Division in 1964 at the urging of board member Pat Moynihan and set about developing techniques of riot prediction. For instances of nineteenth-century European experimentation with urban form in the colonies with an eye to remaking social life in the metropole, see Paul Rabinow, *French Modern: Norms and Forms of the Social Environment* (Chicago: University of Chicago Press, 1989); and Gwendolyn Wright, *The Politics of Design in French Colonial Urbanism* (Chicago: University of Chicago Press, 1991). See also Alexander Arroyo, "Making the Earth Count: From Living Laboratory to Laboratory Planet," *Scapegoat* 11 (Winter 2017–Spring 2018): 9–18.

126. Snyder, "Ciudad Guayana," 411.

127. Reginald Isaacs, report on Center of Studies for the Planning of Development, April 4, 1960, box 10, folder 27; Reginald Isaacs, "The Development of the United States Virgin Islands" (n.d.), box 3, folder 20; RRIP. One cannot overstate "how decisive Latin American experience proved to be for the development of regional planning doctrine"; Friedmann and Weaver, *Territory and Function*, 129.

128. Correa, *Beyond the City*, 109.

129. Faculty Committee minutes, May 17, 1963, JCUS folder, TPP.

130. Joint Center for Urban Studies, *First Five Years*, 41, 35; Friedmann and Weaver, *Territory and Function*, 153.

131. Case Study Workshop syllabus, 1971, box 1, Wilhelm von Moltke folder #1, GPR.

132. Donald Appleyard, "Selected Bibliography: Environmental/Behavioral Factors and Urban Design" (Berkeley: Department of City and Regional Planning, 1969); Donald Appleyard, *The Urban Environment: Selected Bibliography* (Monticello, IL: Council of Planning Librarians, 1972). On Appleyard's turn toward three-dimensional simulation as a pedagogy and "perceptual bridge" to citizen participation, see Anthony Raynsford, "Simulating Spatial Experience in the People's Berkeley: The Urban Design Experiments of Donald Appleyard and Kenneth Craik," *Design and Culture* 6 (2014): 45–63; and Donald Appleyard, Peter Bosselmann, Randy Klock, and Alexander Schmidt, "Periscoping Future Scenes: How to Use an Environmental Simulation Lab," *Landscape Architecture* 69 (1979): 487–488, 506–510.

133. Francis E. Rourke to Malcolm Moos, March 25, 1965, box 13, folder 5.

134. Galantay, "Ciudad Guayana."

135. Lynch, "Propositions for Planning New Towns in Venezuela," 560, 563.

136. Abrams, "Report on the Development of Ciudad Guayana in Venezuela."

137. Lawrence J. Vale, *Changing Cities: 75 Years of Planning Better Futures at MIT* (Cambridge, MA: SA+P Press, 2008), 33. On tensions between the Americans and the CVG staff, who perceived them as arrogant, see Schulze, "In Search of El Dorado," 348–350.

138. Rodwin, *Nations and Cities*, 68, 67.

139. Lloyd Rodwin, interview by Morton Schussheim, June 11, 1994.

140. Peattie, *Planning*, 42.
141. Williams, "Planning the Guayana," 1, 2.
142. Friedmann and Weaver, *Territory and Function*, 114, 174.
143. John Friedmann to William Porter, December 20, 1965, box 1, John Friedmann folder, GPR.
144. Peattie and Peattie, "Some Notes on the Organization of Ciudad Guayana."
145. Roderick Peattie and Lisa Peattie, "Planning Problems," May 15, 1962 (Report E26), box 5, GPR.
146. Lisa Redfield Peattie, *The View from the Barrio* (Ann Arbor: University of Michigan Press, 1968), n.p. On Peattie's broader legacy, see Bish Sanyal, "ACSP Distinguished Educator, 1999: Lisa Peattie," *Journal of Planning Education and Research* 39 (2019): 520–522. Had it been included in the Joint Center series, the book might have seemed like matter out of place. Peattie took her business to Michigan.
147. Peattie, *View from the Barrio*, 1, 6, 21. Peattie did not devote much attention to gender divisions within the town, but this question would animate several Marxian studies written in the 1980s (and focused on events in the 1970s): Cathy A. Rakowski, "The Planning Process and the Division of Labor in a New Industrial City: The Case of Ciudad Guayana, Venezuela," in *Capital and Labour in the Urbanized World*, ed. John Walton (London: Sage, 1985), 195–223; Cathy A. Rakowski, "Women in Steel: The Case of Ciudad Guayana, Venezuela," *Qualitative Sociology* 10 (1987): 3–28; Cathy A. Rakowski, "Evaluating Development: Theory, Ideology, and Planning in Ciudad Guayana, Venezuela," *International Journal of Contemporary Sociology* 26 (1989): 71–92.
148. Peattie, *View from the Barrio*, 90, 9, 74, 77, 85, 87, 81, 89. Peattie identified three distinct "poles of force" (11) with which dwellers were contending: local commercial elites, American corporations, and the CVG. It was not only the "public interest" that Peattie decomposed analytically into smaller moving parts. The CVG itself lacked unity. It planned; it provisioned; it sought to coordinate. But it was only a "congeries of particular functions . . . unarticulated dispersed efforts" (72). Ray, *Politics of the Barrios*, broadcasts no obvious radicalism but explores parallel struggles over service delivery in two informal settlements, one in Maracaibo and one in western Caracas; Ciudad Guayana, populated by an "aspiring class" (66–67), comes up only briefly. Tinker Salas, *Enduring Legacy*, details the complex multiracial communities thrown together in the oil camps of the pre-Betancourt period and comprising inter alia Chinese, Mexican, West Indian, and British people, in addition to a large Venezuelan-born labor force and managers from the United States.
149. Peattie, *View from the Barrio*, 27, 28, 8, 15–18, 10. Peattie (28) noted that American corporations had imposed new forms of temporal discipline on *barrio* life. Not only were work hours fixed and lateness punished, but because work and home were separated by zoning, workers had to allocate time for their roughly twenty-minute commute, and, to self-regulate, workers began purchasing watches, an uncommon possession up to that point, recalling E. P. Thompson, "Time, Work-Discipline, and Industrial Capitalism," *Past & Present* 38 (December 1967): 56–97.
150. Peattie, *View from the Barrio*, 7, 138, 25, 24, 21; emphasis added.
151. Peattie, *View from the Barrio*, 134, 143, 4, 3. Venezuelan planning scholars in the late 1980s also cast a critical look back at the town's origins: *Guayana 25 años después: Teoría y práctica de la planificación urbana* (Caracas: Sociedad Venezolana de Planificación, 1987).

152. Wood, *1400 Governments*, 70, 4.

153. Robert C. Wood, "The Contributions of Political Science to the Study of Urbanism" [1963], in *Taming Megalopolis: What Is and What Could Be*, vol. 1, ed. H. Wentworth Eldredge (New York: Anchor, 1967), 191–220, at 196, 220.

154. Robert C. Wood, "Science: The Good Urban Witch," in *Cybernetics and the Management of Large Systems*, ed. Edmond M. Dewan (New York: Spartan Books, 1969), 123–131, at 125, 124.

155. Robert Wood, "Academe Sings the Blues," *Daedalus* 104 (1975): 45–55, at 54. On the ASC, see Ronald R. Kline, *The Cybernetics Moment* (Baltimore: Johns Hopkins University Press, 2015), 185, 190. The group was founded in 1964 with CIA backing in order to close a perceived "cybernetics gap" with the Soviet Union.

156. Norbert Wiener, Karl Deutsch, and Giorgio de Santillana, "How U.S. Cities Can Prepare for Atomic War," *Life*, December 18, 1950, 77–82. See also Matthew Farish, "Disaster and Decentralization: American Cities and the Cold War," *Cultural Geographies* 10 (2003): 125–148; Robert Kargon and Arthur Molella, "The City as Communications Net: Norbert Wiener, the Atomic Bomb, and Urban Dispersal," *Technology and Culture* 45 (2004): 764–777; and Peter Galison, "War Against the Center," *Grey Room* 4 (Summer 2001): 5–33.

157. Norbert Wiener, *The Human Use of Human Beings: Cybernetics and Society* [1950], revised ed. (Boston: Houghton Mifflin, 1954). Wiener did not actively forge links with social scientists. They came to his ideas, a bit belatedly; Kline, *Cybernetics Moment*, 95.

158. Magoroh Maruyama, "Heterogenistics and Morphogenetics: Toward a New Concept of the Scientific," *Theory and Society* 5 (1978): 75–96, at 76. See also Magoroh Maruyama, "Human Futuristics and Urban Planning," *Journal of the American Institute of Planners* 39 (1973): 346–357. Bacon sent Meyerson a draft of the latter article by Maruyama, "in whom I am most interested"; Bacon to Meyerson, June 16, 1972, box 34, folder 41, MMP.

159. Kline, *Cybernetics Moment*, 78, 82, 71, 96, 98, 198, 4; on its basis in analogy, 1, 39, 44, 45, 96. Kline's is the most ecumenical account. For other useful treatments of cybernetics as theory, practice, mood, and fad, see Steve J. Heims, *The Cybernetics Group* (Cambridge, MA: MIT Press, 1991); Peter Galison, "Ontology of the Enemy: Norbert Wiener and the Cybernetic Vision," *Critical Inquiry* 21 (1994): 228–266; Andrew Pickering, *The Cybernetic Brain: Sketches of Another Future* (Chicago: University of Chicago Press, 2010); Orit Halpern, *Beautiful Data: A History of Vision and Reason since 1945* (Durham, NC: Duke University Press, 2014); and Poornima Paidipaty, "'Tortoises All the Way Down': Geertz, Cybernetics, and 'Culture' at the End of the Cold War," *Anthropological Theory* 20 (2020): 97–129. "Systems theory" was often invoked in the same breath. Howard Brick writes that the language of systems "appeared promiscuously throughout elite culture" in the 1960s. "The system," of course, became radicals' all-purpose opponent during that same decade, but, as Brick notes, "one still needed a concept of 'system' to fight a system." Among technocrats and leftists alike, "the temptation was to exaggerate the degree of order that actually prevailed"; *Age of Contradiction: American Thought and Culture in the 1960s* (Ithaca, NY: Cornell University Press, 1998), 124, 131, 133.

160. Jay Forrester, *Urban Dynamics* (Cambridge, MA: MIT Press, 1969).

161. Kline, *Cybernetics Moment*, 193.

162. Avigail Sachs, *Environmental Design: Architecture, Politics, and Science in Postwar America* (Charlottesville: University of Virginia Press, 2018), 7, 10, 43, 27, 28. On landscape architecture, see Margot Lystra, "McHarg's Entropy, Halprin's Chance: Representations of Cybernetic Change in 1960s Landscape Architecture," *Studies in the History of Gardens and Designed Landscapes* 34 (2014): 71–84; Kathleen John-Alder, "Processing Natural Time: Lawrence Halprin and the Sea Ranch Ecoscore," *Studies in the History of Gardens and Designed Landscapes* 34 (2014): 52–70; Sonja Duempelmann and Susan Herrington, "Plotting Time in Landscape Architecture," *Studies in the History of Gardens and Designed Landscapes* 34 (2014): 1–14; Larry D. Busbea, *The Responsive Environment: Design, Aesthetics, and the Human in the 1970s* (Minneapolis: University of Minnesota Press, 2020); and Michel Conan, Introduction to *Landscape Design and the Experience of Motion*, ed. Michel Conan (Washington, DC: Dumbarton Oaks Research Library and Collection, 2003), 1–33.

163. Edmund N. Bacon, *Design of Cities* (New York: Penguin, 1967). See also Edmund N. Bacon, "Urban Process," in *The Conscience of the City*, ed. Martin Meyerson (New York: Braziller, 1970), 75–88. On Bacon, "systems," and "feedback," see Andrew M. Shanken, "Plot Lines: A Story about Edmund Bacon," *OASE: Journal of Architecture* 98 (2017): 9–20.

164. Jennifer S. Light, *From Warfare to Welfare: Defense Intellectuals and Urban Problems in Cold War America* (Baltimore: Johns Hopkins University Press, 2003), 45–54; Garry D. Brewer, *Politicians, Bureaucrats, and the Consultant: A Critique of Urban Problem Solving* (New York: Basic Books, 1973); John W. Elrick, "Simulating Renewal: Postwar Technopolitics and Technological Urbanism," *Environment and Planning D: Society and Space* 38 (2020): 1120–1137. See also Daniel J. Elazar, *Opening Cybernetic Frontiers* (New Brunswick, NJ: Transaction, 2004), 394, 396; and Melvin M. Webber, "The Post-City Age," in *The Conscience of the City*, ed. Martin Meyerson (New York: Braziller, 1970), 1–20.

165. *Region Manual: Urban Systems Simulation* (Washington, DC: Washington Center for Metropolitan Studies, 1968). Allan Feldt of Cornell was involved, having released the Community Land Use Game to acclaim.

166. Albeit not as directly so as argued by Reinhold Martin, *The Organizational Complex* (Cambridge, MA: MIT Press, 2003), 79, who claims that Kepes worked "in strict compliance with the imperatives of the organizational complex" puppeteered by corporations. M. Christine Boyer, "The Two Orders of Cybernetics in Urban Form and Design," in *Companion to Urban Design*, eds. Tridib Banerjee and Anastasia Loukaitou-Sideris (London: Routledge, 2011), 70–83, also overstates Kepes and Lynch's interests in "control." Halpern, *Beautiful Data*, 96, 97, 115, is closer to the mark: Kepes can be read as something like a contemporary affect theorist, while Lynch and other urbanists sometimes "take liberties" with cybernetic thinking.

167. Karl W. Deutsch, "On Social Communication and the Metropolis," in *The Future Metropolis* (New York: Braziller, 1961), ed. Lloyd Rodwin, 129–143; Karl W. Deutsch, *The Nerves of Government: Models of Political Communication and Control* (New York: The Free Press, 1963); Karl W. Deutsch and Richard L. Meier, "The Confederation of Urban Governments: How Self-Controls for the American Megalopolis Can Evolve," Working Paper 77 (1968), Institute of Urban and Regional Development, University of California, Berkeley; Hayward R. Alker, "The Powers and Pathologies of

Networks: Insights from the Political Cybernetics of Karl W. Deutsch and Norbert Wiener," *European Journal of International Relations* 17 (2011): 351–378.

168. Richard L. Meier, *A Communications Theory of Urban Growth* (Cambridge, MA: MIT Press, 1962), 129, 174, 138. For a large-scale application of cybernetics to socialist ends in Latin America, see Eden Medina, *Cybernetic Revolutionaries: Technology and Politics in Allende's Chile* (Cambridge, MA: MIT Press, 2014). Chile became a net exporter of "second-order" cybernetic theory in the late 1970s, mainly via Humberto Maturana and his student Francisco Varela.

169. Meier, *Communications Theory*, 170.

170. See, for example, Lisa Peattie to Norman Williams, June 20, 1962 (Report C10), box 1, CGR.

171. Lisa Peattie, "People Becoming a City," July 9, 1962 (Report F20), box 2, CGR.

172. John Friedmann, "Planning as Social Learning," Working Paper 343 (February 1981), Institute of Urban and Regional Development, University of California, Berkeley, 1, 2.

173. Lloyd Rodwin, "Planning Guayana: A General Perspective," in *Planning Urban Growth and Regional Development*, 9–26, at 16, 25; Rodwin, "Reflections on Collaborative Planning," 488; Bish Sanyal, personal communication, October 22, 2019.

174. Rodwin, "Reflections on Collaborative Planning," 482.

175. Penfold, "Ciudad Guayana," 245.

176. Willo von Moltke, May 21, 1962 (Report F12), box 2, CGR; Fumihiko Maki, "The Harvard Years, 1955–1969" [1983], *Ekistics* 52, no. 314–315 (1985): 436–441; Ellen Shoshkes, "Jaqueline Tyrwhitt: A Founding Mother of Modern Urban Design," *Planning Perspectives* 21 (2006): 179–197, at 190, 194. Recall that Maki had spent time at Washington University's architecture school and Institute for Urban and Regional Studies.

177. Norman Williams, "Notes on the Mitchell Report," June 20, 1962 (Report F17), box 2, CGR.

178. Peattie, "Notes on the Concept of 'Disjointed Incrementalism' as Applied to Regional Planning," November 7, 1962 (Report C18), box 1, CGR.

179. John Friedmann, "Introduction to 'The Study and Practice of Planning,'" *UNESCO International Social Science Journal* 11, no. 3 (1959): 327–339, at 337.

180. John Friedmann, "Intention and Reality: The American Planner Overseas" (April 1968), box 6, "Ford Foundation Seminar on Social Science, 1966–1968" folder, LRP. See also Staples, *Forty Years*, 1, written on behalf of Ford in India, which begins, "Indian philosophy teaches us that progress is not linear, a wise thought to keep in mind when considering economic and social change."

181. Von Moltke, May 21, 1962.

182. J. N. Kise to staff, April 14, 1962 (Report E12), box 1; on "inscrutable" methods, Klaus Herdeg, in "The Harvard Years," 438.

183. Lynch, "Some Notes."

184. Appleyard, "Motion, Sequence, and the City," 181, 176; Donald Appleyard, "The Environment as a Social Symbol," *Ekistics* 278 (1979): 272–281, at 279. At this later date, Appleyard likened the environment to a language with syntactic and semantic structure. In the 1960s, he generally did not.

185. Abrams, "Report on the Development of Ciudad Guayana in Venezuela."

186. William Alonso, "Concerning Some Aspects of the Projected Guayana City," 1962 (Report A6), box 1, CGR; emphasis added.

187. Wood, "Contributions of Political Science," 215. In the same work, he calls the very notion of a case study into question. Its epistemology is "episodic, expensive, and debatable." Yet he admits the following: "In competent literary hands the case study can always refute an overly enthusiastic generalization" (212).

188. Abrams, "Report on the Development of Ciudad Guayana in Venezuela"; Norman Williams, June 12, 1962 (Reports F15 and F16), box 2, CGR.

189. Martin Jay, *Songs of Experience: Modern American and European Variations on a Universal Theme* (Berkeley: University of California Press, 2005), appeals to German thought to distinguish two senses of the English word *experience*. *Erlebnis* names something like raw, immediate experience in the moment. *Erfahrung* is the sense by which one can be said to have had an experience—or to be an "experienced" person as a result.

5. Reoriented

1. Agenda from visit of August 31–September 2, 1966, box 6, "Guayana, MIT Visits" folder, GPR; Outline of Moynihan remarks in Caracas, September 2, 1966, box I:196, folder 6, DPMP.

2. Karl W. Deutsch, John Platt, and Dieter Senghaas, "Conditions Favoring Major Advances in Social Science," *Science* 171 (February 5, 1971): 450–459, at 457. They did not single out the Joint Center by name, but they were clear that "a small number of interdisciplinary centers" had demonstrated the "environmental group conditions for creative success," and that fully half of them were based in either Cambridge, New York, or Chicago (450, 458). The authors itemized discrete "advances," several of which the Joint Center had a major role in consolidating: input–output analysis, "economic development," cybernetics, simulation techniques, and quantitative approaches to political science—all substantially achieved by 1966.

3. David Popenoe, "Urban Studies Reconsidered: Present Trends and Future Prospects," *Urban Education* 6 (1971): 6–31, at 7, 9, 11.

4. Christopher Tunnard and Henry Hope Reed, *American Skyline* (Boston: Houghton Mifflin, 1955), 252.

5. Martin Anderson, *The Federal Bulldozer: A Critical Analysis of Urban Renewal, 1949–1962* (Cambridge, MA: MIT Press, 1964), 191, 174, 208, 230; emphasis original. On the antinomies of "blight," see Wendell E. Pritchett, "The 'Public Menace' of Blight: Urban Renewal and the Private Uses of Eminent Domain," *Yale Law and Policy Review* 21 (2003): 1–52; Themis Chronopoulos, "Robert Moses and the Visual Dimension of Physical Disorder: Efforts to Demonstrate Urban Blight in the Age of Slum Clearance," *Journal of Planning History* 13 (2014): 207–233; and Richard Brandi, "San Francisco's Diamond Heights: Urban Renewal and the Modernist City," *Journal of Planning History* 12 (2012): 133–153, at 137.

6. Anderson, *Federal Bulldozer*, 73, 9, 88, 163, 179. In the introductory chapter, Anderson claimed the usual project duration was ten years, not twelve. Note that Anderson writes "urban renewal" without initial capital letters. The present account capitalizes the phrase—the better to distinguish references to work sponsored by the

federal Urban Renewal Administration from more casual usages that might naturalize its sense of the verb "to renew."

7. Francesca Russello Ammon, *Bulldozer: Demolition and Clearance of the Postwar Landscape* (New Haven, CT: Yale University Press, 2016), 146. Many arch-conservatives did address aesthetics. The sociologist Ernest van den Haag—best known for his enthusiastic defense of the death penalty—wrote that Renewal only deposited new slums "built as slums," and that "neophilia" must be resisted at all costs; "Notes on New York Housing," *Dissent* 8 (Summer 1961): 277–281, at 277, 279. Alfred Kazin, for his part, saw a different temporality of architectural "waiting" in midcentury New York, where "urban removal and burial are everywhere." Scanning the "rows of low red houses (soon to be demolished)" along Fulton Street in downtown Brooklyn, he generalized: "What has not been torn down is waiting to be torn down"; *New York Jew* (New York: Knopf, 1978), 210. In his first memoir, he marked time by contrasting Brownsville's New Deal-era public housing with the speculative dwellings nearby: "so many of the old tenements have been left undisturbed on every side of the project, the streets beyond are so obviously just as they were when I grew up in them, that it is as if they had been ripped out of their original pattern and then pasted back again behind the unbelievable miniatures of the future"; Alfred Kazin, *A Walker in the City* (New York: Harcourt, 1951), 14.

8. Steven Conn, *Americans against the City: Anti-Urbanism in the Twentieth Century* (New York: Oxford University Press, 2014), 160; James Q. Wilson, Letter to the editor, *Harvard Today* (Spring 1965).

9. George H. Nash, *The Conservative Intellectual Movement in America since 1945* [1976], 3rd ed. (Wilmington, DE: Intercollegiate Studies Institute, 2006), 354, 282, 281.

10. Irving Kristol, "Forty Good Years," *The Public Interest* 159 (Spring 2005): 5–11, at 9; Irving Kristol, "Utopianism, Ancient and Modern" [1973], in *Neoconservatism: The Autobiography of an Idea* (New York: The Free Press, 1995), 184–199, at 185, 186. Kristol was borrowing the cemetery example from William H. Whyte.

11. James Q. Wilson, "Urban Renewal Does Not Always Renew," *Harvard Today* (January 1965); Robert C. Weaver, "Urban Renewal," Godkin Lecture, March 30, 1965, box 13, folder 5, FFR.

12. Malcolm Moos memo, March 29, 1965; Francis E. Rourke to Malcolm Moos, March 25, 1965; box 13, folder 5, FFR. His infamy did not prevent Anderson from a long and consequential career spent at the highest levels of Republican politics. He served as Nixon's director of policy research, and after advising two Reagan campaigns, in 1976 and 1980, he signed on as the actor's chief advisor on domestic policy. The specter of Urban Renewal haunted a far broader set of cutbacks in federal spending.

13. Charles Abrams to Dwight Macdonald, December 20, 1961, box 102, CAP.

14. James Q. Wilson, ed., *Urban Renewal: The Record and the Controversy* (Cambridge, MA: MIT Press, 1966), xiii–xix, at xvi, xiv.

15. Herbert J. Gans, "The Failure of Urban Renewal," *Commentary* (April 1965): 29–37; Marc Fried, "Grieving for a Lost Home: Psychological Costs of Relocation," in *The Urban Condition*, ed. Leonard J. Duhl (New York: Basic Books, 1963), 151–171; Chester Hartman, "The Housing of Relocated Families," *Journal of the American Institute of Planners* 30 (1964): 266–286.

16. Charles Abrams, "Some Blessings of Urban Renewal" [1965], in *Urban Renewal: The Record and the Controversy*, ed. James Q. Wilson (Cambridge, MA: MIT Press, 1966),

558–582, at 582; see Charles Abrams, *The City Is the Frontier* (New York: Harper and Row, 1965).

17. Roger Montgomery, "Improving the Design Process in Urban Renewal" [1965], in *Urban Renewal: The Record and the Controversy*, ed. James Q. Wilson (Cambridge, MA: MIT Press, 1966), 454–487, at 456, 476; the original is Roger Montgomery, "Improving the Design Process in Urban Renewal," *Journal of the American Institute of Planners* 31 (1965): 7–20.

18. Robert C. Weaver, "New Directions in Urban Renewal" [1965], in *Urban Renewal: The Record and the Controversy*, ed. James Q. Wilson (Cambridge, MA: MIT Press, 1966), 663–672, at 671.

19. Gans, "Failure of Urban Renewal," 538, 539.

20. Wallace F. Smith, "*The Federal Bulldozer*: A Review," *Journal of the American Institute of Planners* 31 (1965): 179–180.

21. Bernard J. Frieden, *The Future of Old Neighborhoods: Rebuilding for a Changing Population* (Cambridge, MA: MIT Press, 1964), 4, 154, 153; emphasis added. In *Neighborhood Renewal* (Lexington, MA: Lexington Books, 1979), Phillip L. Clay, Frieden's advisee and MIT faculty from 1975 on, would extend the study of renovation in a skillful early analysis of gentrification.

22. Langley C. Keyes Jr., *The Rehabilitation Planning Game: A Study in the Diversity of Neighborhood* (Cambridge, MA: MIT Press, 1969), 191, 202, 22, 154. See also Langley C. Keyes Jr., *The Boston Rehabilitation Program: An Independent Analysis* (Cambridge, MA: Harvard University Press, 1970); Lizabeth Cohen, *Saving America's Cities: Ed Logue and the Struggle to Renew Urban America in the Suburban Age* (New York: Farrar, Straus & Giroux, 2019), 214, 239; John H. Spiers, "'Planning with People': Urban Renewal in Boston's Washington Park, 1950–1970," *Journal of Planning History* 8 (2009): 221–247; and Edward J. Logue, "A Look Back at Neighborhood Renewal in Boston," *Policy Studies Journal* 16 (1987): 335–346, which calls attention to programs of rehabilitation rather than demolition. Keyes called Boston "an old city built for another century, as her narrow winding streets, abandoned waterfront, and weed-filled railroad yards testify. Despite her age and relatively small size, Boston is not a geographically or historically integrated community" (25). It had grown by annexing existing towns, and especially in Charlestown, the identity as other-than-Boston seemed unchangeable. See Garrett Dash Nelson, "Making the Single City: The Constitutive Landscape and the Struggle for 'Greater Boston,' 1891–1911," *Landscape Research* 42 (2017): 243–255.

23. Keyes, *Rehabilitation Planning Game*, 1, 7, 18–19, 96, 92, 235–236, 8, 9, 212, 196.

24. Keyes, *Rehabilitation Planning Game*, 203–204.

25. Keyes, *Rehabilitation Planning Game*, 32, 222.

26. Richard Magat, *The Ford Foundation at Work: Philanthropic Choices, Methods, and Styles* (New York: Plenum, 1979), 120, 121. Noting the "ambiguity of progress," Jeanne R. Lowe headed the last section of her popular book "The Good but Complex Life"; *Cities in a Race with Time* (New York: Vintage, 1967), 576, 577.

27. Charles E. Lindblom, "The Science of 'Muddling Through,'" *Public Administration Review* 19 (1959): 79–88. For reviews specific to the planning profession, see Ernest R. Alexander, "After Rationality, What?: A Review of Responses to Paradigm Breakdown," *Journal of the American Planning Association* 50 (1984): 62–69; and Richard E. Klosterman, "Arguments for and against Planning," *Town Planning Review* 56 (1985): 5–20.

28. Lisa Peattie, "Notes on the Concept of 'Disjointed Incrementalism' as Applied to Regional Planning," November 7, 1962 (Report C18), box 1, RRIP.

29. William Alonso, "The Unplanned Paths of Planning Schools," *The Public Interest* 82 (Winter 1986): 58–71, at 65, makes this distinction. "Planning in general had always been a suspect activity" for conservatives, while city planning retained "broad political support."

30. Cohen, *Saving America's Cities*, 236–238, 223, 224–225, 385. Logue counted the North Harvard episode among his failures.

31. Nathan Glazer, "The Schools of the Minor Professions," *Minerva* 12 (1974): 346–364, at 362. Other prominent "anti-planners" in his viewshed were Ivan Illich, Saul Alinsky, and Father James Groppi of Milwaukee. All were at odds with the "model hunger" that had lately defined the profession. On anti-highway activism in Boston, see Karilyn Crockett, *People before Highways* (Amherst: University of Massachusetts Press, 2018).

32. Peter L. Laurence, *Becoming Jane Jacobs* (Philadelphia: University of Pennsylvania Press, 2016), 289, 294; Kristol, "Utopianism," 186; and on the Jacobs–Hayek affinity, see also Roger Scruton, "Public Space and the Classical Vernacular," *The Public Interest* 74 (Winter 1984): 5–16, at 9, 11; and Anthony Fontenot, *Non-Design: Architecture, Liberalism, and the Market* (Chicago: University of Chicago Press, 2021). On Jacobs in Toronto, see Christopher Klemek, *The Transatlantic Collapse of Urban Renewal* (Chicago: University of Chicago Press, 2011), 139–142, 170–172, 219–243. Samuel Zipp and Nathan Storring have characterized Jacobs's ideal as "markets without capitalism"; Introduction to *Vital Little Plans* (New York: Random House, 2016), xxxii. Among ardent capitalists, Hayek, too, questioned attempts to know the future, most succinctly in Friedrich A. Hayek, "The Use of Knowledge in Society," *American Economic Review* 35 (1945): 519–530. Whereas Hayek did not disparage all uses of foresight—he opposed centralized planning by states of their economies—his Austrian confrere Mises questioned private-sector permutations as well; see Ludwig von Mises, "The Plight of Business Forecasting," *National Review*, April 4, 1956. On Hayek's distinctions, see Nash, *Conservative Intellectual Movement*, 3, 16, 171. On traditionalist conservatism, the libertarian alternative, and the possibility of "fusionism," see Mark C. Henrie, "Understanding Traditionalist Conservatism," in *Varieties of Conservatism in America*, ed. Peter Berkowitz (Stanford, CA: Hoover Institution, 2004), 3–30; Patrick Allitt, *The Conservatives* (New Haven, CT: Yale University Press, 2009); and Nash, *Conservative Intellectual Movement*, 79, 325, 328, 351, 352, and passim.

33. Jane Jacobs, *The Death and Life of Great American Cities* (New York: Random House, 1961), 428–448; Laurence, *Becoming Jane Jacobs*, 297; Jane Jacobs, *The Nature of Economies* (New York: Modern Library, 2000), 95, 102–104.

34. Klemek, *Transatlantic Collapse*, 111; Lloyd Rodwin, "Neighbors Are Needed," *New York Times Book Review*, November 5, 1961.

35. Jane Jacobs, "A Living Network of Relationships" [1958], in *Vital Little Plans* (New York: Random House, 2016), 131–144, at 143. On the "natural strength of the unfinished situation seeking closure," see her contemporary Paul Goodman, *Five Years* (New York: Brussel and Brussel, 1966), 185; and Paul Goodman, *The New Reformation: Notes of a Neolithic Conservative* (New York: Random House, 1970). The "semi-lattice" form proposed in Christopher Alexander, "A City Is Not a Tree," *Architectural Forum* 122 (April 1965): 58–62, also drew on network thinking and achieved remarkable influence among designers.

NOTES TO PAGES 187–191   331

36. Lawrence Halprin, *Cities* [1963], revised ed. (Cambridge, MA: MIT Press, 1972), 194, 208–215, 7. Alison Bick Hirsch, *City Choreographer: Lawrence Halprin in Urban Renewal America* (Minneapolis: University of Minnesota Press, 2014), 180, explores Halprin's "inability to resolve the issue of flexibility." For broader intellectual histories of planning for the "small," see also Daniel Immerwahr, *Thinking Small: The United States and the Lure of Community Development* (Cambridge, MA: Harvard University Press, 2015); and Benjamin Looker, *A Nation of Neighborhoods: Imagining Cities, Communities, and Democracy in Postwar America* (Chicago: University of Chicago Press, 2015).

37. Paul Goldberger, "A Design-Conscious Mayor: The Physical City," in *Summer in the City: John Lindsay, New York, and the American Dream*, ed. Joseph Viteritti (Baltimore: Johns Hopkins University Press, 2014), 139–160, at 158, 157; and see *The Social Life of Small Urban Spaces*, directed by William H. Whyte (1979; New York: Municipal Art Society), which celebrated pedestrian "choice" and took shape in the wake of New York's 1961 rewrite of its zoning code. For a more recent iteration of the putatively "unplanned," see Daniel Campo, *The Accidental Playground: Brooklyn Waterfront Narratives of the Undesigned and Unplanned* (New York: Fordham University Press, 2013).

38. John V. Lindsay, *The City* (New York: Norton, 1969), 131, 116.

39. Emanuel S. Savas, "City Halls and Cybernetics," in *Cybernetics and the Management of Large Systems*, ed. Edmond M. Dewan (New York: Spartan Books, 1969), 133–146, at 136, 139.

40. Regional Plan Association, *Public Participation in Regional Planning* (New York: Regional Plan Association, 1969); William A. Caldwell, ed., *How to Save Urban America* (New York: New American Library, 1973); William B. Shore et al., *Listening to the Metropolis* (New York: Regional Plan Association, 1974); Kristian Taketomo, "'Town Meetings by Television': Regional Plan Association's 'CHOICES for '76,'" *Gotham: A Blog for Scholars of New York City History*, October 4, 2018, https://www.gothamcenter.org/blog/town-meetings-by-television-regional-plan-associations-choices-for-76; and see Regional Plan Association, *Regional Plan Association: 50 Years* (New York: Regional Plan Association, 1979).

41. Horst W. J. Rittel and Melvin M. Webber, "Dilemmas in a General Theory of Planning," *Policy Sciences* 4 (1973): 155–169, at 159.

42. After Greg Castillo et al., eds., *Hippie Modernism: The Struggle for Utopia* (Minneapolis: Walker Art Center, 2015).

43. Robert Goodman, *After the Planners* (New York: Simon and Schuster, 1971), 91, 205, 204, 202, 67, 147, 103–106, 82, 163, 168, 164. For a recognition that "'no plan' always means in fact some inherited and frequently bad plan," see other Goodmans: Paul and Percival Goodman, *Communitas: Means of Livelihood and Ways of Life*, 2nd ed. (New York: Vintage, 1960), 10. On Paul Goodman's distinctive, embattled anarchism–conservatism, see Lewis Fried, *Makers of the City* (Amherst: University of Massachusetts Press, 1990), 159–206; and Kingsley Widmer, *Paul Goodman* (Boston: Twayne, 1980).

44. Stephan Thernstrom, *Poverty, Planning, and Politics in the New Boston: The Origins of ABCD* (New York: Basic Books, 1969), xii, 132, 12, 17, 26. Norton Long was the editor for this abortive series; at the time of writing, Thernstrom, too, was on faculty at Brandeis.

45. Thernstrom, *Poverty, Planning, and Politics*, 168, 104, 175, 191, 185, 130, 165, 186; emphasis added. (Strictly, "action–research," in joining two elements nonhierarchically,

calls for an en dash, not a hyphen.) Seymour Martin Lipset, a friend of the Joint Center, later made the case that social science is by its nature conservative: it is multivariate, and it favors the null hypothesis; "The Prescient Politician," in *Daniel Patrick Moynihan: The Intellectual in Public Life*, ed. Robert A. Katzmann (Washington, DC: Woodrow Wilson Center Press, 2004), 26–43, at 29, 35.

46. Martha Derthick, *New Towns In-Town* (Washington, DC: The Urban Institute, 1972); Martha Derthick, "Defeat at Fort Lincoln," *The Public Interest* 20 (Summer 1970): 3–39. For a similar analysis gestated at the Washington Center for Metropolitan Studies, see Paul Peachey, *New Towns, Old Habits: Citizen Participation at Fort Lincoln* (Washington, DC: Washington Center for Metropolitan Studies, 1970). To the Joint Center series, Derthick also contributed *The Influence of Federal Grants: Public Assistance in Massachusetts* (Cambridge, MA: Harvard University Press, 1970), on the "professionalization" of social reform—a favorite Moynihanian theme—in the Great Society.

47. William Alonso, "The Mirage of New Towns," *The Public Interest* 19 (Spring 1970): 3–19, at 3, 4, 19, 11, 13, 14, 16, 17. Alonso was a seasoned regional scientist, and he cited with approval that field's lack of interest in urban "form" or "image" (16). See also Thomas Healy, *Soul City: Race, Equality, and the Lost Dream of an American Utopia* (New York: Macmillan, 2021).

48. William Alonso, "Beyond the Inter-disciplinary Approach to Planning," Working Paper 90 (1968), Center for Planning and Development Research, University of California, Berkeley, 12, 13. For a less despairing statement, see Karen S. Christensen, "Coping with Uncertainty in Planning," *Journal of the American Planning Association* 51 (1985): 63–73, at 71; Urban Renewal is one of her key examples.

49. Andrew Hartman, *A War for the Soul of America* (Chicago: University of Chicago Press, 2015), 38–39. "I am not sure how much you will like your country when you get back," Moynihan wrote to Rodwin as the latter embarked on a vacation in 1966. "Things seem to be changing." This statement appeared in the letter with which Moynihan accepted the appointment as Joint Center director. Moynihan to Rodwin, February 18, 1966, box I:176, folder 4, DPMP.

50. Nash, *Conservative Intellectual Movement*, 342; and see Seymour Martin Lipset, "Neoconservatism: Myth and Reality," *Society* 25 (July–August 1988): 29–37. Greg Weiner, *American Burke: The Uncommon Liberalism of Daniel Patrick Moynihan* (Lawrence: University Press of Kansas, 2015), 21–22, 43–45, identifies Moynihan with "policy liberalism" as distinct from "program liberalism."

51. Mark Gerson, *The Essential Neoconservative Reader* (Reading, MA: Addison–Wesley, 1996), xiii–xvii, at xiv; Peter Steinfels, *The Neoconservatives: The Men Who Are Changing America's Politics* (New York: Simon and Schuster, 1979), 300. See also Gary Dorrien, *The Neoconservative Mind: Politics, Culture, and the War of Ideology* (Philadelphia: Temple University Press, 1993); and Justin Vaïsse, *Neoconservatism: The Biography of a Movement*, trans. Arthur Goldhammer (Cambridge, MA: Harvard University Press, 2010).

52. Irving Kristol, "Human Nature and Social Reform," *Wall Street Journal*, September 18, 1978. Kristol, an experienced editor at Basic Books, was well known to Moynihan by way of *The Public Interest*, the skeptical, social science–forward magazine he founded in 1965. By 1967, Moynihan was recommending him to direct Harvard University Press; Moynihan to Franklin Ford, March 27, 1967, box I:177, folder 8, DPMP. On *The Public Interest* worldview as a "revisionist liberalism," not a purist or apocalyp-

tic conservatism, see Nash, *Conservative Intellectual Movement*, 338, 344. On its decision to focus only on domestic affairs, see Kristol, "Forty Good Years," 351; on the absence of economists on its editorial board, Irving Kristol, "American Conservatism: 1945–1995," *The Public Interest* 121 (Fall 1995): 80–91, at 88.

53. Klemek, *Transatlantic Collapse*, 204–206; "Retired MIT Professor Rosenblith Dies at 88; Pioneered Use of Computers to Study Brain," *MIT News*, May 3, 2002.

54. Bernard Frieden, Marshall Kaplan, and Charles Haar, "Analysis of Federal Role in the Model Cities Program: A Case Study in Policy Analysis" (1971), Grant PA72–65, Reel 1749, Grants L–N (FA 732E), FFR. The authors secured funding from the Ford Foundation; note that this was project-specific funding, separate from the recently extinguished grant that had supported the center as a whole. At first, Model Cities was known as Demonstration Cities, but the 1966 bill that committed funds changed course. "By that time," Frieden and Kaplan wrote, "city demonstrations had an unpleasant overtone"; Bernard J. Frieden and Marshall Kaplan, *The Politics of Neglect: Urban Aid from Model Cities to Revenue Sharing* (Cambridge, MA: MIT Press, 1975), 64–65.

55. Thernstrom, *Poverty, Planning, and Politics*, viii.

56. Keyes, *Rehabilitation Planning Game*, 230, 232.

57. Frieden and Kaplan, *Politics of Neglect*, 36–39, 201, 204–205, 207, ix. For a detailed timeline of Model Cities, as well as its financial structure and the list of participant cities, see 258–275. Charles Haar, the third scholar on the grant and himself a former assistant secretary at HUD, broke away to write his own book, which advanced a more conciliatory narrative that would have sat uneasily with the mid-1970s Joint Center: Charles M. Haar, *Between the Idea and the Reality: A Study in the Origin, Fate, and Legacy of the Model Cities Program* (Boston: Little, Brown, 1975).

58. Frieden and Kaplan, *Politics of Neglect*, 3, 68, 8, 21, 14, 25, 234, 238, 240, 186, 184, 65. "We are all decentralists now," wrote Irving Kristol in "Decentralization for What?," *The Public Interest* (Spring 1968): 17–25, at 19, taking Model Cities as his leading example. That ideal is now pursued with "the same kind of enthusiastic abstractness they once brought to centralization."

59. Jeffrey L. Pressman and Aaron Wildavsky, *Implementation* [1973], 3rd ed. (Berkeley: University of California Press, 1984), 1, 2, 141; Walter Dean Burnham and Myron Weiner, "Jeffrey L. Pressman," *PS: Political Science and Politics* 10 (1977): 273–274. On war and containerization, see Deborah Cowen, *The Deadly Life of Logistics: Mapping Violence in Global Trade* (Minneapolis: University of Minnesota Press, 2014); and on Oakland, the Oakland Project (briefly), and the transnational "urban crisis," see Ananya Roy, Stuart Schrader, and Emma Shaw Crane, "'The Anti-Poverty Hoax': Development, Pacification, and the Making of Community in the Global 1960s," *Cities* 44 (2015): 139–145. Other Oakland Project volumes include Frank Levy, Arnold J. Meltsner, and Aaron Wildavsky, *Urban Outcomes: Schools, Streets, and Libraries* (Berkeley: University of California Press, 1974); and Jeffrey L. Pressman, *Federal Programs and City Politics* (Berkeley: University of California Press, 1975). Pressman's work with Joint Center affiliates includes Francine Rabinovitz, Jeffrey Pressman, and Martin Rein, "Guidelines: A Plethora of Forms, Authors, and Functions," *Policy Sciences* 7 (1976): 399–416. Program officials at Ford read Wildavsky in the years before the foundation cut funding for urban studies; William C. Pendleton, *Urban Studies and the University: The Ford Foundation Experience* (New York: Ford Foundation, 1974), 13, quotes *Implementation*

at length to argue that academics should intervene in public policy only if they have special competency in the issues at hand.

60. Pressman and Wildavsky, *Implementation*, xxii–xxiii, xv, xviii, xxi (Roman-numeral citations include the prefaces to both the 1973 and 1984 editions), 138, 136, 126, 143.

61. Aaron Wildavsky, "If Planning Is Everything, Maybe It's Nothing," *Policy Sciences* 4 (1973): 127–153, at 131, 132, 128, 129, 145, 138. Wildavsky's lengthy musings on the category of "rationality" exceed our scope. He skillfully if irascibly renders it synonymous with a set of what had been technical-sounding watchwords—*system, efficiency, coordination, consistency*—and declares it a "secular faith" that lacks meaning. By 1973, Wildavsky could also write, echoing Rittel and Webber, that the "thermostatic" (133) or cybernetic model of learning-while-doing had become the profession's default. On antipathy to expertise since the 1950s, see Michael J. Brown, *Hope and Scorn: Eggheads, Experts, and Elites in American Politics* (Chicago: University of Chicago Press, 2020).

62. James Q. Wilson, ed., *The Metropolitan Enigma: Inquiries into the Nature and Dimensions of America's "Urban Crisis"* [1966], revised ed. (Cambridge, MA: Harvard University Press, 1968).

63. Marshall Kaplan, *Urban Planning in the 1960s: A Design for Irrelevancy* (New York: Praeger, 1973). Kaplan's investment in the Joint Center as a unit seems to have been low. In a 2020 interview, he recalled a meeting in Cambridge at "the Urban Institute, I think it was called"; Marshall Kaplan, "A First-Hand Account of the History of HUD," Trailblazers Impact, July 2020, https://trailblazersimpact.com/2020/07/marshall-kaplan/. Moynihan was a friend, however, and was so taken with Kaplan's own analysis of implementation in Oakland that he enjoined his entire staff to read it. Kaplan had also chaired a HUD Task Force on Simplification and Consolidation, and here he quipped that, due to the byzantine structure he was describing, his final write-up was "the only book on simplification that took five hundred pages" to do the job.

64. Marshall Kaplan, "The Planner, General Planning, and the City" [1964], in *Urban Planning in the 1960s: A Design for Irrelevancy* (New York: Praeger, 1973), 14–23, at 18.

65. Marshall Kaplan, Preface to *Urban Planning in the 1960s: A Design for Irrelevancy* (New York: Praeger, 1973), v–vii, at vii.

66. Marshall Kaplan, "New Communities and Public Policy" [1970, with Edward Eichler], in *Urban Planning in the 1960s: A Design for Irrelevancy* (New York: Praeger, 1973), 24–42, 39. For his fullest account of New Towns before the Great Society, see Edward P. Eichler and Marshall Kaplan, *The Community Builders* (Berkeley: University of California Press, 1967).

67. Marshall Kaplan, "Random Thoughts on Planning, Problems, and Approaches: Small Cities" [1970], in *Urban Planning in the 1960s: A Design for Irrelevancy* (New York: Praeger, 1973), 104–108, at 107. For more on this motif, clearly a preoccupation for Kaplan, see 61, 62, 65, 92, 107, and passim.

68. Kaplan, "New Communities and Public Policy," 40. Weiner, *American Burke*, 129, 131, identifies Moynihan, too, with a Burkean disinclination to look more than "just a little bit ahead into the future," lest one breach society's "contract" with the past.

69. Marshall Kaplan, "Comments on the Demonstration Cities Program" [1966], in *Urban Planning in the 1960s: A Design for Irrelevancy* (New York: Praeger, 1973), 80–84, at 84; Kaplan, "An Overview and Summary," in *Urban Planning in the 1960s*, 129–130, at 130.

70. A similar notion of intervention in the "here and now," contra any politics of deferral, is a staple of anarchist thought—for example, Simon Springer, *The Anarchist Roots of Geography* (Minneapolis: University of Minnesota Press, 2016), 3, 7, 13, and passim. See also Lucie Laurian and Anthony Inch, "On Time and Planning: Opening Planning by Cultivating a 'Sense of Now,'" *Journal of Planning Literature* 34 (2019): 267–285, who appeal to Walter Benjamin's concept of a redemptive *Jetzzeit* out of which the future "explodes."

71. Alonso, "Beyond the Inter-disciplinary Approach," 18.

72. Keyes, *Rehabilitation Planning Game*, 219.

73. Kaplan, Preface to *Urban Planning in the 1960s*, vi, vii.

74. Marshall Kaplan, "Advocacy and Urban Planning" [1968], in *Urban Planning in the 1960s: A Design for Irrelevancy* (New York: Praeger, 1973), 63–79, at 77–78.

75. Marshall Kaplan, "The Roles of the Planner and Developer in the New Community" [1965], in *Urban Planning in the 1960s: A Design for Irrelevancy* (New York: Praeger, 1973), 85–103, at 98. For a theoretical argument that planners need to establish a "usable present," a "public temporal order" within which to look ahead, see Seymour J. Mandelbaum, "Temporal Conventions in Planning Discourse," *Environment and Planning B: Planning and Design* 11 (1984): 5–13, at 9, 5. Planners, on this view, are "sensitive arrangers responding at the unfolding edge of events"; Seymour J. Mandelbaum, "Historians and Planners: The Construction of Pasts and Futures," *Journal of the American Planning Association* 51 (1985): 185–188, at 188.

76. "The Five-Year Plan: 1978–1983," August 1978, box 20, folder EA024, GSDH.

77. Arthur P. Solomon, *Housing the Urban Poor: A Critical Evaluation of Federal Housing Policy* (Cambridge, MA: MIT Press, 1974). Solomon soon departed academia to work in real estate. In 1981, an internal review credited his book with having "helped lay the groundwork for the streamlining of the federal housing subsidy programs . . . after 1979." It was just one of "a number of reports and critiques" of federal allowances coming out of the center; "Report to the Joint Center for Urban Studies Advisory Committee by the Program Review Committee," May 1981, box 20, folder EA015, GSDH.

78. Martha Derthick, *Between State and Nation: Regional Organizations of the United States* (Washington, DC: Brookings Institution, 1974).

79. Robert Schafer, *Mortgage Lending Decisions: Criteria and Constraints* (Cambridge, MA: Joint Center for Urban Studies, 1978); Robert Schafer and Helen F. Ladd, *Discrimination in Mortgage Lending* (Cambridge, MA: MIT Press, 1981). Schafer claimed to have found no discrimination at work in Albany and "little" in Buffalo. He wrote as a self-appointed debunker: one chart classified his opponents' arguments as either "supported," "equivocal," or "contradicted." In 1981, realizing that redlining, past and present, was a "sensitive" topic, the center set up a special advisory committee to discuss it; "Report . . . by the Program Review Committee."

80. Bernard J. Frieden, *The Environmental Protection Hustle* (Cambridge, MA: MIT Press, 1979).

81. "Report . . . by the Program Review Committee." Their diction oscillated between "economics" and "development." For one last act of physical planning with the Joint Center's seal of approval, see *Lessons from Local Experience: CDBG/Urban Environmental Design* (Washington, DC: United States Department of Housing and Urban

Development, 1983); and *Urban Environmental Design Research: Case Studies of Ten Cities* (Washington, DC: United States Department of Housing and Urban Development, 1981). These volumes reported on contract work completed for HUD and touched on disparate cases: Cambridge; Cincinnati; Salem, Massachusetts; San Diego; Savannah; Charleston, South Carolina; Hudson, New York; Seattle; Los Angeles; Dallas; Denver; Decatur, Georgia; Mankato, Minnesota; Minneapolis; Pittsburgh; and Baltimore.

82. Sar A. Levitan, *Work and Welfare Go Together* (Baltimore: Johns Hopkins University Press, 1972).

83. Martin Rein and Lee Rainwater, *From Welfare State to Welfare Society: Some Unresolved Issues in Assessment* (Cambridge, MA: Joint Center for Urban Studies, 1981).

84. Mary Jo Bane, *Here to Stay: American Families in the Twentieth Century* (New York: Basic Books, 1976). Levitan, Rein, and David Marwick also collaborated on a report titled "Challenging Welfare Myths"; "Joint Center for Urban Studies of the Massachusetts Institute of Technology and Harvard University" (brochure, ca. 1979), box 20, folder EA013, GSDH. By 1981, "physical environment" was officially no longer one of the center's foci; "Report . . . by the Program Review Committee."

85. Mary Jo Bane and David T. Ellwood, "The Dynamics of Dependency: The Routes to Self-Sufficiency" (Report to the United States Department of Health and Human Services, 1983); Alice O'Connor, *Poverty Knowledge* (Princeton, NJ: Princeton University Press, 2008), 252, 295. Both served in the Department of Health and Human Services during the 1990s.

86. Phillip Clay, personal communication, September 20, 2023. Clay postulates that the Joint Center's longevity and influence owe, in part, to its lack of identification with any one dominant personality.

87. "The Five-Year Plan: 1978–1983." This was substantially the same reason that the Joint Center's contract research held appeal for those in the building industry: insight into the scale and rate of "household formation" would allow them to predict demand for glass, brick, appliances, and many other products; Phillip Clay, personal communication, September 20, 2023.

88. Henry Rosovsky to McGeorge Bundy, July 31, 1974; Bundy to Rosovsky, October 1, 1974; Reel 1859, Grants L–N (FA 732E), FFR; *The Role of University-Based Urban Centers* (Cambridge, MA: Joint Center for Urban Studies, 1971); and Pendleton, *Urban Studies and the University*, 7, 9. Pendleton projected disappointment: "It is not clear that the involvement of two prestigious universities added a new dimension to either the direct output of the center or the field of urbanism in general." The sociologist Charles Lemert's summary of the 1970 Joint Center conference noted participants' reluctance to claim that urban studies counted as its own discrete subject. "The larger, metaquestions were frequently commuted into middle-range variants" and "bilateral avoidance of the extremes" seemed to be the "state of the art"; "What Has Athens to Do with Jerusalem?," in *The Role of University-Based Urban Centers*, 118–128, at 108, 107. At that conference, however, Sam Bass Warner—by then based in Ann Arbor—made a proposal unusual in official Joint Center proceeding: he called for such units to refashion themselves as explicit critics of society. For too long, he insisted, centers of urban studies had suffered "imprisonment" as "service agencies for entrepreneurs of every age and ambition," "buffers" between town and gown, and instruments by which to "legitimize" foregone conclusions about the course of private development. The term

"center," Warner argued, unlike "department," has "communal and informal connotations," and they should cut against its conscription to for-profit schemes. "The Role of University Urban Centers as a Focus for Research, Teaching, and Criticism," in *The Role of University-Based Urban Centers*, 8–19, at 14, 10, 13.

89. Minutes of Faculty Executive Committee, December 16, 1981, box 20, folder EA014, GSDH; JCUS final report to Ford Foundation; Joint Center for Urban Studies, *The First Five Years* (Cambridge, MA: The Center, 1964).

90. "The Five-Year Plan: 1978–1983."

91. "Urban M.I.T., 1967–1969," box 1, folder 33, JEBP.

92. John P. McNichols, *New England's Paper Mill Industry: Survival through Plant Maintenance and Product Specialization* (Cambridge, MA: Joint Center for Urban Studies, 1979); Margaret R. Clark, *The Transformation of an "Old" Industry: Private Investment and Technological Change in Commercial Printing in New England* (Cambridge, MA: Joint Center for Urban Studies, 1979); Thomas A. Barocci, *Disinvestment in Massachusetts: A Case Study of the Personal and Economic Impacts of a Chemical Plant Closing* (Cambridge, MA: Joint Center for Urban Studies, 1979). Also included in the 1979 initiative toward "studies of specific regions" was an economic "policy analysis model" of Alaska. Language last seen in Friedmann's pre-critical work on Venezuela reappeared. "Because of its relative simplicity," Alaska afforded "a useful laboratory or prototype" of regional development; "The Five-Year Plan: 1978–1983," 39–40. On the "uneven," the key text to emerge from this generation of radical geography is Neil Smith, *Uneven Development: Nature, Capital, and the Production of Space* [1984], 3rd ed. (Athens: University of Georgia Press, 2008).

93. Minutes, December 16, 1981. The workshops lavished developmental attention on Boston's waterfront and the Harbor Islands, the latter characterized as a "frontier." George Masnick presented work attributing the city's woes to declining birthrates, not suburban flight.

94. "The Five-Year Plan: 1978–1983"; Alan Altshuler, personal communication, January 14, 2020.

95. "Joint Center for Urban Studies of the Massachusetts Institute of Technology and Harvard University"; "Report . . . by the Program Review Committee"; Jerold S. Kayden, *Privately Owned Public Space: The New York City Experience* (New York: Wiley, 2000). In undertaking these economistic shifts, the center was in no way unique. In the twenty-first century, such accommodations to market forces, the corresponding retrenchment of state social provision, and the increased capture of philanthropy's putative "third sector" by less-than-public interests have been favorite themes of a vast (if redundant and often underspecified) historiography that posits the rise of "neoliberal" governance, thought, and subjectivity as the epochal shift of the late twentieth century to which all else must be found subsidiary. The oil crisis of 1973 is a commonly cited point of origin or inflection. In its stress on the economics of social policy and urban development, some but not all Joint Center work of the late 1970s and early 1980s may merit the addition of this label (which evokes nineteenth-century British, not twentieth-century American, usage of the term "liberal") to the neoconservative carapace. The best intellectual history of free-market advocacy is Angus Burgin, *The Great Persuasion: Reinventing Free Markets since the Depression* (Cambridge, MA: Harvard University Press, 2013), which situates the 1970s eruption in decades of fine-grained debates fraught with

internal tensions. A useful recent effort to link the dueling *neos*—rather than to separate them and prioritize market talk de facto, a tendency of too much history and theory written with critical aspirations—is Melinda Cooper, *Family Values: Between Neoliberalism and the New Social Conservatism* (Brooklyn: Zone Books, 2017).

96. Robert C. Wood to Martin Meyerson, February 24, 1969, box 18, folder 6; Jerome Wiesner to Meyerson, February 29 [*sic*], 1973, box 18, folder 7; Wiesner to Meyerson, July 24, 1974, box 18, folder 7; MMP.

97. Martin Meyerson, "The University Community and the Urban Community," in *The City and the University* (Toronto: Macmillan, 1969), 1–17, at 4, 11. He also brought organized research to Buffalo as a matter of policy, proposing seven permanent institutes (corresponding to the university's seven faculties), each empowered to create centers and launch projects, and three interfaculty centers including a Center for Urban and Regional Studies; Martin Meyerson, "Proposed Policy for Organized Research," June 23, 1968, box 121, folder 23, MMP.

98. Roger L. Geiger, *American Higher Education since World War II: A History* (Princeton, NJ: Princeton University Press, 2019), 142, 194–195; John L. Puckett and Mark Frazier Lloyd, "Martin Meyerson's Dream of 'One University': The Penn Presidency, 1970–1981 and Beyond," *Journal of Planning History* 10 (2011): 193–218. See also Ethan Schrum, *The Instrumental University: Education in Service of the National Agenda after World War II* (Ithaca, NY: Cornell University Press, 2019), 90–125; and Ann L. Strong and George E. Thomas, eds., *The Book of the School: 100 Years: The Graduate School of Fine Arts of the University of Pennsylvania* (Philadelphia: University of Pennsylvania, 1991). Meyerson was the first Jewish president of an Ivy League school.

99. Brochure on MIT Special Program for Urban and Regional Studies (September 1967), box 10a, CAP. As early as December 1962, Rodwin had taken part in a Conference on the Training of Planners for Work in Developing Countries. The north–south exchange of knowledge outlasted the Guayana contract.

100. Magat, *The Ford Foundation at Work*, 100.

101. "GSD: New Trends, New Processes," 1966, box 19, folder DC013, GSDH.

102. "Influencing the Future of New York City," brochure, Urban Action and Experimentation Program, Institute of Urban Environment, Columbia University, October 17, 1967, box 120, CAP.

103. Rodwin to Abrams, May 5, 1969, box 10a, CAP. Harvard's Department of Urban Planning and Design continued to stress Modernist physical interventions. Since Meyerson's departure, it had had little independent contact with the Joint Center or MIT, and thus there was no assumption that it would change over to the DUSP model; Charles Abrams, "Memorandum on Harvard's Planning Division," June 18, 1968, box 120, CAP. In 1968, the GSD established its own Center for Environmental Design Studies, "an administrative umbrella" meant to coordinate all things interdisciplinary but intra-Harvard; "The School Today," 1968, box 19, folder DB023, GSDH. As for the field of architecture, John Burchard returned to MIT from Berkeley—"thank God," he wrote to Wilson—in the critical year of 1968, but there, too, he found himself "much disturbed" by the new politics visible among trainees. Students struck him as "antihero," "anti-pro," and "disinterested in much save talk." Faculty were complicit, producing not architects but "amateur politicians, amateur social psychologists, amateur revolutionaries"; John Burchard to James Q. Wilson, March 30, 1970, box 3, folder 10;

Burchard to William Wheaton, July 2, 1971, box 2, folder 33. Burchard was particularly sour in his conservatism, but, like Wilson, he was no *neo*: he had been voicing these sorts of complaints since the 1950s; John E. Burchard, "My Worries about the Education of Architects," *Journal of Architectural Education* 10 (Spring 1955): 5.

104. "The School Today." Professional associations made similar moves; from human geography, see Proposal, Task Force on Urban Problems and the Use of Urban Space (1971), box 274, folder 8, AAGR.

105. "Research in Progress as of November 1, 1968, According to Major Areas of Investigation," box 19, folder DB026, GSDH. This document gives a sense of the leftmost research that GSD faculty and graduate students were undertaking: on the Civil Rights Movement, on squatters in Lima and Bogotá, on race and the American suburb (by the unlikely pairing of Lisa Peattie and Bernard Frieden), and more. On "busing," see Matthew F. Delmont, *Why Busing Failed: Race, Media, and the National Resistance to School Desegregation* (Oakland: University of California Press, 2016); and, for a careful recent oral history, "Fiasco: The Battle for Boston," *Luminary Podcasts*, accessed February 22, 2024, https://luminarypodcasts.com/listen/leon-neyfakh/fiasco-luminary-premium/8607a31a-cab7-4c9f-9df8-b6110ba93b52.

106. Joint Center for Urban Studies, *How the People See Their City: Boston 1969* (Cambridge, MA: Joint Center for Urban Studies, 1970).

107. Schrum, *The Instrumental University*, 220–221. Nisbet scorned this entrepreneurial quality as "academic capitalism"—no neoliberal, he.

108. A sociological overview is Thomas Medvetz, *Think Tanks in America* (Chicago: University of Chicago Press, 2012); on the microeconomics-driven Urban Institute, the Manpower Development Corporation, and the tank-incubated Charles Murray, see O'Connor, *Poverty Knowledge*, 228, 232, 247–250; and see also Alice O'Connor, "The Privatized City: The Manhattan Institute, the Urban Crisis, and the Conservative Counterrevolution in New York," *Journal of Urban History* 34 (2008): 333–353.

109. Alonso, "Unplanned Paths," 66, 67. The Association of Collegiate Schools of Planning and the American Planning Association also grew apart in the 1970s, staking respective claims to theory and practice.

110. Robert C. Weaver, interview by Morton Schussheim, December 19, 1985, PIH.

111. Alexander, "After Rationality, What?," 62.

112. Alonso, "Unplanned Paths," 69.

113. David L. Birch et al., *America's Housing Needs, 1970–1980* (Cambridge, MA: Joint Center for Urban Studies, 1973).

114. Bernard J. Frieden et al., *The Nation's Housing, 1975–1985* (Cambridge, MA: Joint Center for Urban Studies, 1977).

115. "Joint Center for Urban Studies of the Massachusetts Institute of Technology and Harvard University."

116. Minutes, December 16, 1981.

117. Seen from 1973, the farthest horizon was 1980; an equivalent jump from 1977 would have placed the target on the still-unacceptable year of 1984.

118. "The Five-Year Plan: 1978–1983"; Minutes, December 16, 1981. The center also published Barbara Brenzel, *Daughters of the State: A Social Portrait of the First Reform School for Girls in North America, 1856–1905* (Cambridge, MA: MIT Press, 1983), by a PhD from Harvard's education school—a case study of Lancaster, Massachusetts, a

small town subject to forces at work in Worcester and Boston, too, but located well outside either city.

119. Martin Meyerson, ed., *The Conscience of the City* (New York: Braziller, 1970). This volume had its roots in a 1967 conference put on by the recently formed Urbanism Committee (or Subcommittee) of the American Academy of Arts and Sciences; "Transcript (and related papers)," Project 1976: Urbanism Committee, February 15–16, 1967; "Rough notes from Martin Meyerson," Shaping the American Future: Subcommittee on Urbanism, box 149, folder 6; MMP.

120. Fred C. Doolittle et al., *Future Boston: Patterns and Perspectives* (Cambridge, MA: Joint Center for Urban Studies, 1982). Kresge's major research work with the Joint Center, based in part on the Alaska study noted above, was David Kresge et al., *Regions and Resources: Strategies for Development* (Cambridge, MA: MIT Press, 1984), the book series' last entry.

121. Ira Lowry, in *The Prospective City: Economic, Population, Energy, and Environmental Developments*, ed. Arthur P. Solomon (Cambridge, MA: MIT Press, 1980), 127; emphasis added. From the same generation, see also Richard P. Coleman, *Attitudes Toward Neighborhood: How Americans Choose to Live* (Cambridge, MA: Joint Center for Urban Studies, 1978), 41–44, which marshals survey data to assert the following "lay prophecy": "downtown can't be saved," the suburban approximation of "Ruralia" is the only viable future, only 8 percent of suburbanites even consider moving back to the nearest city, and "decline is the unquibbling prediction"—the last statement followed by an invocation of the racial makeup of those who are moving to big cities.

122. Arthur P. Solomon, "Shaping the Future Metropolis: The Role of Public Policy," in *The Prospective City: Economic, Population, Energy, and Environmental Developments* (Cambridge, MA: MIT Press, 1980), 347, 344.

6. The Belated City

1. Irving Howe, *A Margin of Hope: An Intellectual Autobiography* (New York: Harcourt Brace Jovanovich, 1982), 328.

2. Daniel T. Rodgers, *Age of Fracture* (Cambridge, MA: Harvard University Press, 2011); Fredric Jameson, "Postmodernism, or The Cultural Logic of Late Capitalism," *New Left Review* 146 (July–August 1984): 53–92; Jefferson Cowie, *Stayin' Alive: The 1970s and the Last Days of the Working Class* (New York: The New Press, 2010); Simon Reynolds, *Rip It Up and Start Again: Post-Punk, 1978–1984* (New York: Penguin, 2006). Jameson's essay draws sustenance from the Joint Center, famously invoking Kevin Lynch's mental maps to develop a broader argument about temporal, spatial, political, and economic disorientation. "The important sound of things falling apart" heads a chapter of Cowie's book and references the Akron, Ohio, quintet Devo ("de-evolution"), on whose historicity see Theo Cateforis, *Are We Not New Wave?: Modern Pop at the Turn of the 1980s* (Ann Arbor: University of Michigan Press, 2011). Accounts of 1970s economic restructuring on both sides of the Atlantic are legion; for one synthesis, see Judith Stein, *Pivotal Decade: How the United States Traded Factories for Finance in the 1970s* (New Haven, CT: Yale University Press, 2011).

3. Jenny Andersson, *The Future of the World: Futurology, Futurists, and the Struggle for the Post–Cold War Imagination* (Oxford: Oxford University Press, 2018), 223.

4. For instance, Matthew Worley, *No Future: Punk, Politics and British Youth Culture, 1976–1984* (Cambridge, UK: Cambridge University Press, 2017); and Franco Berardi, *After the Future* (Oakland, CA: AK Press, 2011). For a remarkable musicological account of punk's roots in the blues—one that, incidentally, disputes its standing as a full-fledged youth movement—see Evan Rapport, *Damaged: Race and Musicality in Early American Punk* (Jackson: University Press of Mississippi, 2020).

5. Rodgers, *Age of Fracture*, 9, 191, 64.

6. Niklas Luhmann, "The Future Cannot Begin: Temporal Structures in Modern Society," *Social Research* 43 (1976): 130–152, at 141, 151, 150, 152.

7. François Hartog, *Regimes of Historicity*, trans. Saskia Brown (New York: Columbia University Press, 2015), xv, 196; Rodgers, *Age of Fracture*, 244.

8. Morris Dickstein, *Gates of Eden: American Culture in the Sixties* (New York: Basic Books, 1977), 107. Socialist Irving Howe wrote, "It was hard to trust a future constructed by those who knew so little about the past"; *A Margin of Hope*, 333. He also noted, correctly, that the New Left's anti-liberalism focused its ire entirely on the postwar American variety, on "Clark Kerr, not John Dewey; Max Lerner, not John Stuart Mill"; Irving Howe, "New Styles in 'Leftism,'" *Dissent* 13 (Summer 1965): 295–317, at 316.

9. Simon Reynolds, *Retromania: Pop Culture's Addiction to Its Own Past* (New York: Farrar, Straus & Giroux, 2011), xxii.

10. Peter Fritzsche, *Stranded in the Present: Modern Time and the Melancholy of History* (Cambridge, MA: Harvard University Press, 2004), 5, 201, and passim. On the sensation of being "stuck" in present configurations of power, see Jordan Alexander Stein, *Avidly Reads Theory* (New York: NYU Press, 2019), 99–124.

11. Irving Kristol, "Old Truths and the New Conservatism," *Yale Review* 47 (May 1958): 365–373, at 373.

12. Simone Abram, "The Time It Takes: Temporalities of Planning," *Journal of the Royal Anthropological Institute* n.s. 20 (2014): 129–147, questions narratives that announce the "end" of planning, the "loss" of the future, or other such epochal shifts. The late twentieth century, she argues, was marked more by a creeping pastlessness than a futurelessness. See also Simone Abram and Gisa Weszkalnys, "Anthropologies of Planning: Temporality, Imagination, and Ethnography," *Focaal: Journal of Global and Historical Anthropology* 61 (2011): 3–18; and the much-cited Jane I. Guyer, "Prophecy and the Near Future: Thoughts on Macroeconomic, Evangelical, and Punctuated Time," *American Ethnologist* 34 (2007): 409–421, at 409, which defends the near future as the domain of "struggles for specific goals," neglect of which severs the necessary sense of continuity between history and the long term.

13. Bernard J. Frieden and Marshall Kaplan, *The Politics of Neglect: Urban Aid from Model Cities to Revenue Sharing* (Cambridge, MA: MIT Press, 1975), 243, 257.

14. Lloyd Rodwin, *Nations and Cities: A Comparison of Strategies for Urban Growth* (Boston: Houghton Mifflin, 1970), 284–285; emphasis added.

15. Andrew M. Isserman, "Dare to Plan: An Essay on the Role of the Future in Planning Practice and Education," *Town Planning Review* 56 (1985): 483–491, at 483.

16. Andrew M. Isserman, "Projection, Forecast, and Plan: On the Future of Population Forecasting," *Journal of the American Planning Association* 50 (1984): 208–221, at 209, 219. Like the NYMRS's many critics, Isserman faulted planners for relying too much on projections, which tended to overstate the inertia of existing trends. The point

was to "develop a counter-trend mentality" (219). See also Graham May, "The Argument for More Future-Oriented Planning," *Futures* 14 (1982): 313–318.

17. Isserman, "Dare to Plan," 491, 485; emphasis added. See also Martin Wachs, "Ethical Dilemmas in Forecasting for Public Policy," *Public Administration Review* 42 (1982): 562–567; Dowell Myers and Alicia Kitsuse, "Constructing the Future in Planning: A Survey of Theories and Tools," *Journal of Planning Education and Research* 19 (2000): 221–231; Dowell Myers, "Symposium: Putting the Future in Planning," *Journal of the American Planning Association* 67 (2001): 365–367; and Martin Wachs, "Forecasting versus Envisioning: A New Window on the Future," *Journal of the American Planning Association* 67 (2001): 367–372. Myers echoes Isserman: "The future is the only topic that other professions have ceded to planners as relatively uncontested turf. Perhaps because it is uncontested, planners take this topic for granted" (366).

18. "Future studies" and "futures studies" were both in use. Kaya Tolon, "Futures Studies: A New Social Science Rooted in Cold War Strategic Thinking," in *Cold War Social Science*, eds. Mark Solovey and Hamilton Cravens (New York: Palgrave, 2012), 45–62, at 46, contends that the pluralized version—a precursor of theoretical syntax dominant in the humanities since the rise of post-structuralism—marked a deliberate attempt to distinguish more utopian, left-identified intellectuals from hidebound Cold Warriors. Andersson, *Future of the World*, concurs: 1960s futurists were progressive, 1970s futurists were not, and Toffler's book, which Andersson mostly ignores, stands between them. For general treatments, see Edward Cornish, *The Study of the Future* (Bethesda, MD: World Future Society, 1977); and Wendell Bell and James A. Mau, eds., *The Sociology of the Future: Theory, Cases, and Annotated Bibliography* (New York: Russell Sage Foundation, 1971). Alvin Toffler's 1969 course at the New School also purported to survey "the sociology of the future." For one contemporary critique, see Bettina J. Huber, "Some Thoughts on Creating the Future," *Sociological Inquiry* 44 (1974): 29–39.

19. Alvin Toffler, *Future Shock* (New York: Random House, 1970), 10, 11, 1, 3, 5. He coined the phrase in *Horizon* magazine in 1965. On Toffler's ubiquity, see Rodgers, *Age of Fracture*, 107–109. Against the thesis of universal acceleration, see Sarah Sharma, *In the Meantime: Temporality and Cultural Politics* (Durham, NC: Duke University Press, 2014).

20. Toffler, *Future Shock*, 447, 471, 530, 365. He was at least a consumer of scholarship in urban studies. Toffler cited "leading urbanologist" Scott Greer, Richard Meier, and a host of others with ties to MIT. For one explicit attempt to bridge futures studies and planning, see Sam Cole, "Dare to Dream: Bringing Futures into Planning," *Journal of the American Planning Association* 67 (2001): 372–383, also part of the Myers symposium. Cole claims an "essential symbiosis" between the two: "Planning is the vehicle whereby futures studies is manifest in physical and social reality" (373).

21. Toffler, *Future Shock*, 531.

22. Wallace Hamilton, "Proposals and Ideas, Past and Present, for Higher Education in Columbia" (1967/1968), Reel 1859, Grants L–N (FA 732E), FFR. "'Applied futurism,'" wrote Hamilton, a Rouse Company representative, "is getting to be a very big thing these days."

23. Oscar Handlin to Daniel Patrick Moynihan, October 17, 1966, box I:152, folder 1, DPMP. By no means did the Joint Center take a turn toward popular Tofflerian forms of futurology. Kevin Lynch independently attended a "futures workshop" that had participants construct a "photo wall" and engage in free-associative mind mapping; Kevin

Lynch, "Talking About the Future," 1978, report on workshop of the Comprehensive Planning Organization, box 14, KLP.

24. Daniel Bell, *The Coming of Post-Industrial Society* (New York: Basic Books, 1973), 20; Daniel Bell, "Ten Theories in Search of Reality: The Prediction of Soviet Behavior in the Social Sciences," *World Politics* 10 (1958): 327–365; Daniel Bell, "Twelve Modes of Prediction—A Preliminary Sorting of Approaches in the Social Sciences," *Daedalus* 93 (1964): 845–880; and see Daniel Bell, "The Study of the Future," *The Public Interest* 1 (Fall 1965): 119–130. Bell's article on Sovietology discusses Harvard's Russian Research Center. On the Cold War roots of futurology, see Andersson, *Future of the World*; and Eglė Rindzevičiūtė, "A Struggle for the Soviet Future: The Birth of Scientific Forecasting in the Soviet Union," *Slavic Review* 75 (2016): 52–76. Jenny Andersson, "The Great Future Debate and the Struggle for the World," *American Historical Review* 177 (2012): 1411–1430, at 1420, 1417, claims that forecasting studies in the United States became popular as a response to the Soviet tradition of *prognostik*, and that they should be understood as a genre of modernization theory.

25. Daniel Bell, ed., *Toward the Year 2000: Work in Progress* (Boston: Houghton Mifflin, 1967).

26. Andersson, *Future of the World*, 120.

27. Daniel Bell, *The Winding Passage* (Cambridge, MA: Abt Books, 1980), xiii.

28. For example, Robert L. Heilbroner, "Futurology," *The New York Review of Books*, September 26, 1968, who lamented the group's "curiously bland, inconclusive, unimpressive" work, wracked by Bell's signature ambivalence and more able to "establish limits . . . than targets, [to] depict interactions rather than clearcut trajectories." See also Jenny Andersson, "Prediction and Social Choice: Daniel Bell and Future Research," in *The Decisionist Imagination*, eds. Daniel Bessner and Nicolas Guilhot (New York: Berghahn, 2018), 250–271. His son underscores that Bell did not identify as a futurist and that he mocked Toffler as so much "Future Schlock": David A. Bell, "Remembering Daniel Bell: Two Perspectives," in *Defining the Age: Daniel Bell, His Time and Ours*, eds. Paul Starr and Julian E. Zelizer (New York: Columbia University Press, 2022), 31–58, at 55; and Daniel Bell, "The World and the United States in 2013," *Daedalus* 113, no. 3 (Summer 1987): 1–31, at 5.

29. Toffler, *Future Shock*, 447, 448, 451, 469.

30. Tolon, "Futures Studies," 51; Andersson, *Future of the World*, passim; Krishan Kumar, *Prophecy and Progress: The Sociology of Industrial and Post-Industrial Society* (London: Pelican, 1978), 186. Kumar deems Bell "intellectually bolder and tougher by far" (7), and better informed about history, than anyone else parading futurist credentials in the 1970s.

31. Toffler, *Future Shock*, 478. A progressive form of this field lives on in the twenty-first century. See, for example, Stuart Candy and Cher Potter, eds., *Design and Futures* (n.p., 2019). Candy and Potter make recourse to Ashis Nandy's sense of futures studies as "a game of dissenting visions"—"dissent from the existing ideas of normality, sanity, and objectivity"; "Bearing Witness to the Future," *Futures* 28 (August 1996): 636–639, at 637.

32. Toffler, *Future Shock*, 4. This textual strategy—to induce a line of questioning in the reader—is essentially what Mark Greif has called the "maieutic" discourse in postwar letters; *The Age of the Crisis of Man: American Thought and Fiction, 1933–1973* (Princeton, NJ: Princeton University Press, 2015), 24–26.

33. Bell, *Post-Industrial Society*, 14, 44, 4; emphasis added. Even Nixon's recent federal budget, he noted, pursued economic policy based on an "as if" structure of reasoning about future occurrences (25). See also Daniel Bell, *The Social Sciences since the Second World War* (New Brunswick, NJ: Transaction, 1982), 43–44.

34. Bell, "Study of the Future," 122.

35. Peter Steinfels, *The Neoconservatives: The Men Who Are Changing America's Politics* (New York: Simon and Schuster, 1979), 197, and, on Bell's politics generally, 174–183. Howard Brick, *Daniel Bell and the Decline of Intellectual Radicalism* (Madison: University of Wisconsin Press, 1986), stresses the centrality of ambivalence and paradox to Bell's "modernist" social thought. In "Government by Commission," *The Public Interest* 3 (Spring 1966): 3–9, at 7, Bell argued that Johnson's many advisory commissions on technology, automation, and so forth were primarily an opportunity for "the Government informally to explore the 'limits' of action."

36. Peter Osborne, *The Politics of Time* (London: Verso, 1995), 200.

37. Edward C. Banfield, *The Unheavenly City: The Nature and the Future of Our Urban Crisis* (Boston: Little, Brown, 1970), vii, viii, 23–44. For sales figures, see Patricia McLaughlin, "Is the Author of *The Unheavenly City* Really Diabolical?," *Pennsylvania Gazette*, November 1973. On Meyerson and Banfield's friendship, see Rodwin to Abrams, March 14, 1966, box 10a, CAP; Meyerson to Banfield, May 25, 1986, box 34, folder 45, MMP; and Martin Meyerson, Eulogy for Edward Banfield, Memorial Church, Harvard University, December 9, 1999, box 34, folder 45, MMP.

38. Richard Bernstein, "E. C. Banfield, 83, Maverick on Urban Policy Issues, Dies," *New York Times*, October 8, 1999.

39. James Cramer, "Banfield Redux," *Harvard Crimson*, September 15, 1975. This is the same Jim Cramer who would loudly join CNBC in the early twenty-first century, first on *Kudlow & Cramer* and then on *Mad Money*.

40. Banfield, *Unheavenly City*, 4, 1, 5, 261; emphasis added. See also Edward C. Banfield, "A Critical View of the Urban Crisis," *Annals of the American Academy of Political and Social Science* 405 (January 1973): 7–14; Irving Kristol, "Is the Urban Crisis Real?" [reply to Jerome Zukofsky], *Commentary* (November 1970): 40–48; on the diversity of this phrase's uses between the 1950s and the 1970s, Timothy Weaver, "Urban Crisis: The Genealogy of a Concept," *Urban Studies* 54 (2017): 2039–2055; and, on its temporality, Janet Roitman, "The Stakes of Crisis," in *Critical Theories of Crisis in Europe: From Weimar to the Euro*, eds. Poul F. Kjaer and Niklas Olsen (London: Rowman and Littlefield, 2015), 17–34.

41. Banfield, *Unheavenly City*, 6, 12, 240, 17; emphasis added. See also Irving Kristol and Paul Weaver, "Who Knows New York?—and Other Notes on a Mixed-Up City," *The Public Interest* 16 (Summer 1969): 41–59.

42. Martin Meyerson and Edward C. Banfield, *Boston: The Job Ahead* (Cambridge, MA: Harvard University Press, 1966), 3; and see James Q. Wilson, "The Independent Mind of Edward Banfield," *The Public Interest* 150 (Winter 2003): 63–88, at 82–83. Richard Bolan's work for the Joint Center also cited Banfield in its discussion of "time horizons in planning"; Joint Center for Urban Studies, *Planning Metropolitan Boston* (Boston: Metropolitan Area Planning Council, 1967), 28–29.

43. Raymond Vernon, *The Myth and Reality of Our Urban Problems* [1962] (Cambridge, MA: Harvard University Press, 1966). He charged liberal decision-makers with "inar-

ticulate, scarce-comprehensible murmurings" (54) about "bad-but-not-quite-critical" (10) conditions.

44. James Q. Wilson, "Urban Problems in Perspective," in *The Metropolitan Enigma: Inquiries into the Nature and Dimensions of America's "Urban Crisis"* [1966], revised ed. (Cambridge, MA: Harvard University Press, 1968), 351–372, at 352. A year prior, petitioning Ford, he had made a similar point in a more hopeful way, not to defuse research agendas but to haul in more funding and refine them: "The true 'crisis' in urban affairs is not that cities are about to be destroyed by the problems but that the concepts, knowledge, and intelligence necessary for dealing with the problems which do exist are in such critically short supply"; JCUS proposal to Ford Foundation, September 28, 1965.

45. Moynihan memo, "The Proposed Harvard Urban Seminar" (1971), box I:199, folder 2, DPMP.

46. Horst W. J. Rittel and Melvin M. Webber, "Dilemmas in a General Theory of Planning," *Policy Sciences* 4 (1973): 155–169, at 160.

47. Edward C. Banfield, "Ends and Means in Planning," *UNESCO International Social Science Journal* 11, no. 3 (1959): 361–367, at 365, 367.

48. Edward C. Banfield and James Q. Wilson, *City Politics* (Cambridge, MA: Harvard University Press, 1963), 4, 344, 346.

49. Edward C. Banfield, "The Political Implications of Metropolitan Growth," in *The Future Metropolis*, ed. Lloyd Rodwin (New York: Braziller, 1961), 80–99, at 99.

50. Abrams to Rodwin, March 4, 1966, box 10a; Rodwin to Abrams, March 14, 1966; CAP; hyphens added. "Really, we cannot do anything" has always been the default position for most Americans, wrote Paul Goodman, *Utopian Essays and Practical Proposals* (New York: Vintage, 1964), xii. John Burchard cherished a compatible line from Plato: "To refrain from what can be done is the true mark of the intellect." "Quotations, 1949–1959," box 3, folder 38, JEBP.

51. Robert A. Beauregard, *Voices of Decline: The Postwar Fate of U.S. Cities* (Oxford: Blackwell, 1993), 204, 203.

52. Daniel Patrick Moynihan, in James S. Coleman et al., "Social Science: The Public Disenchantment," *The American Scholar* 45 (1976): 335–359, at 350, 348. The stimulus to this symposium was Robert Nisbet, "Knowledge Dethroned," *New York Times Magazine*, September 28, 1975. Wood would date the arrival of a full-fledged, "strong" Banfield-descended "academic school of thought that protests the validity of urban studies and urban policy at all" to 1978; Robert Wood, "Present before the Creation: Lessons from the Paleozoic Era of Urban Affairs," *Journal of Urban Affairs* 13 (1991): 111–117, at 115. For an intriguing forerunner to Banfield's performance of non-knowledge, see Edward C. Banfield, *The Case of the Blighted City* (Chicago: American Foundation for Continuing Education, 1959), an illustrated work of short fiction written in the first person that was included in a series designed to introduce the general reader to debates in public affairs. Banfield's narrator hears from a variety of actors with competing visions of Urban Renewal before concluding, "The trouble was I couldn't make up my own mind on the basis of the facts I had. There were too many angles" (38).

53. Banfield, *Unheavenly City*, 105, 102, 119, 126, 125, 130, 73.

54. Banfield, *Unheavenly City*, 68–69, 79–80, 86.

55. Banfield, *Unheavenly City*, 47, 48, 53, 54.

56. Banfield, *Unheavenly City*, 112. For a partially consonant argument about age and future-orientation, see Lewis Coser and Rose Laub Coser, "Time Perspective and Social Structure," [1973], in *A Handful of Thistles: Collected Papers in Moral Conviction* (New Brunswick, NJ: Transaction, 1988), 167–179, at 174–175.

57. Banfield, *Unheavenly City*, 54; emphasis original.

58. Banfield, *Unheavenly City*, 59, 60, 62. On "the duality of planning and accident that was the study of his career," see Samuel P. Huntington et al., "Memorial Minutes: Edward C. Banfield: Faculty of Arts and Sciences," *Harvard Gazette*, January 18, 2001.

59. Edward C. Banfield, *The Unheavenly City Revisited* (Boston: Little, Brown, 1974), vii; Edward L. Glaeser, "The Life of the City," *New York Sun*, May 14, 2008; Banfield, *Unheavenly City*, 218. *The Unheavenly City Revisited* sought to rebrand Banfield's position on the temporality of class as "an heuristic hypothesis, but it was taken by many readers as an assertion of fact." In 1974, Banfield admitted he had no data—and had never had data—that would demonstrate the explanatory power of time horizon (vii). He qualified some of his more inflammatory claims as being only "plausible," sketches of ideal types of social action and actors (54, 73), but this seemed only to embolden him on questions of race: "it is not implausible to conjecture that some genetic factor may influence" IQ, even as Banfield personally stressed other causes. "Cultural difference . . . and conceivably even biological ones as well . . . account in some degree for the special position of the Negro, as they do for every ethnic group. If there is something about Jewish culture that makes the Jew tend to be upwardly mobile, there may be something about Negro culture that makes the Negro tend not to be" (84). Also new in the 1974 edition was a tendentious distinction between the "Census Negro," who underperforms on every measure, and what Banfield calls the "Comparable Negro" (80–84); and a tone-deaf thought experiment on "how matters would change if overnight all Negroes turned white." Resistance to these "New Whites," Banfield argues, would persist on cultural grounds—and his thinking resonates in preventable ways with the backlash politics of "white ethnics" experiencing "indignities and humiliations not so different from those to which the Negro is now subject" (85–87).

60. Banfield, *Unheavenly City*, 216–218, 46, 222; B. Jeffrey Reno, "Rethinking Horizon Theory: Culture vs. Nature," *Perspectives on Political Science* 36 (2007): 84–90, at 86, 87. In the 1974 revision, Banfield excised the typology of "cognitive," "situational," and "volitional" types of present-orientation.

61. Basil Bernstein, "Some Sociological Determinants of Perception: An Enquiry into Sub-Cultural Differences," *British Journal of Sociology* 9 (1958): 159–174, at 161, 168, 169; Banfield, *Unheavenly City*, 275. Banfield admitted it was at least plausible that the poor could conceptualize the future, but he reemphasized that population's lack of control in planning for it (274). See also Lawrence L. LeShan, "Time Orientation and Social Class," *Journal of Abnormal and Social Psychology* 47 (1952): 489–492; and Louis Schneider and Sverre Lysgaard, "The Deferred Gratification Pattern: A Preliminary Study," *American Sociological Review* 18 (1953): 142–149.

62. David Epley and David R. Ricks, "Foresight and Hindsight in the TAT," *Journal of Projective Techniques and Personality Assessment* 27 (1963): 51–59; Banfield, *Unheavenly City*, 305. On the Thematic Apperception Test, see Rebecca Lemov, *Database of Dreams: The Lost Quest to Catalog Humanity* (New Haven, CT: Yale University Press, 2015), 27–40.

63. Banfield, *Unheavenly City*, 211.

64. Banfield, *Unheavenly City*, 159, 169, 162, 189, 187, 195. His naïveté on suburban landscape—on spatial order as apparent guarantor of social order—is all the more surprising in light of his acquaintance with James Q. Wilson, "A Guide to Reagan Country: The Political Culture of Southern California," *Commentary* (May 1967): 37–45, which Banfield (277) cites. Wilson was a native-born Californian, and on homes and cars, this is one of his more perceptive pieces. See also Lisa McGirr, *Suburban Warriors: The Origins of the New American Right* (Princeton, NJ: Princeton University Press, 2001). On the longstanding "segregated diversity" of suburban America, and on the blurriness of the city–suburb distinction, especially in California, the literature is now vast; for overviews, see Richard Harris and Robert Lewis, "Constructing a Fault(y) Zone: Misrepresentations of American Cities and Suburbs, 1900–1950," *Annals of the Association of American Geographers* 88 (December 1998): 622–639; Richard Harris and Robert Lewis, "The Geography of North American Cities and Suburbs, 1900–1950: A New Synthesis," *Journal of Urban History* 27 (March 2001): 262–292; and Greg Hise, *Magnetic Los Angeles: Planning the Twentieth-Century Metropolis* (Baltimore: Johns Hopkins University Press, 1997). On similar acts of resistance, some of them suburban, since Banfield wrote, see Elizabeth Hinton, *America on Fire: The Untold History of Police Violence and Black Rebellion since the 1960s* (New York: Liveright, 2021).

65. Banfield, *Unheavenly City*, 244–246, 178. Banfield only dug in as the decade ripened. His tone became ever more polemical; his positions were unchanged. By 1977, in an edited volume of criminology, he was calling present-orientation a form of "psychopathy" and turning to Henry Mayhew's lurid survey of Victorian London for support; Edward C. Banfield, "Present-Orientedness and Crime," in *Assessing the Criminal*, eds. Randy E. Barnett and John Hagel III (Cambridge, MA: Ballinger, 1977), 133–142. In his 1974 revision, there are thirteen proposals, not twelve. The newest of them calls for "equal access" to polling places and various "markets"; Banfield, *Unheavenly City Revisited*, 269.

66. Irving Kristol, "The Cities: A Tale of Two Classes," *Fortune* (June 1970); Richard Todd, "A Theory of the Lower Class: Edward Banfield, the Maverick of Urbanology," *The Atlantic* (September 1970); "Environment: Rethinking Cities," *Time*, June 1, 1970.

67. Duane Lockard et al., "Banfield's *Unheavenly City*: A Symposium and Response," *Trans-Action* 8 (1971): 69–78; Theodore R. Marmor, "Banfield's 'Heresy,'" *Commentary* (July 1972): 86–88.

68. James Nuechterlein, "The Unheavenly Urban Philosopher," *First Things* 98 (December 1999): 7–8; Patrick Allitt, *The Conservatives* (New Haven, CT: Yale University Press, 2009), 208; Jeffrey Hart, "The City and the Alchemist," *National Review*, May 19, 1970; George H. Nash, *The Conservative Intellectual Movement in America since 1945* [1976], 3rd ed. (Wilmington, DE: Intercollegiate Studies Institute, 2006), 340–342. Nuechterlein claims that Banfield's book answered questions implanted in his mind since 1967, when as a young white Detroiter he had seen (footage of) the city's Black neighborhoods in flames.

69. See, for example, Beauregard, *Voices of Decline*, 210.

70. Robert C. Weaver, interview by Morton Schussheim, December 19, 1985, PIH.

71. Marmor, "Banfield's 'Heresy,'" 88. Marmor's review was otherwise broadly sympathetic—this was *Commentary* in the 1970s—but he denied Banfield's genuine "brilliance," something his defenders had without exception "exaggerated."

72. Richard Sennett, "Survival of the Fattest," *New York Review of Books*, August 13, 1970.

73. William Ryan, "Is Banfield Serious?," *Social Policy* 1 (November–December 1970): 74–76; William Ryan, *Blaming the Victim* (New York: Pantheon, 1971).

74. Robert C. Wood, *The Necessary Majority: Middle America and the Urban Crisis* (New York: Columbia University Press, 1972), 16, 14; Robert Wood, "Academe Sings the Blues," *Daedalus* 104 (1975): 45–55, at 48, 52, 47. Wood clarified that "I differ professionally" from Banfield and Moynihan, "but in the context of genuine admiration and personal friendship"; *Necessary Majority*, x. Moynihan, however, considered Wood's 1975 article libelous. He circulated a letter to Nathan Glazer, James Q. Wilson, Christopher Jencks, Norman Podhoretz, Clark Kerr, Seymour Martin Lipset, and representatives of the American Academy of Arts and Sciences seeking to have Wood, "not . . . a man to be taken seriously," publicly censured: "I turn to the Academy for redress." Even the usually conciliatory Martin Meyerson weighed in from Penn, calling Wood's work "lightweight." See Moynihan to Gino Ballotti, December 16, 1974; Moynihan to Clark Kerr, February 28, 1975; Robert C. Wood to Moynihan, February 3, 1975; box I:201, folder 7, DPMP. Wood's sharpest criticisms of Moynihan centered on Daniel P. Moynihan, *Maximum Feasible Misunderstanding: Community Action in the War on Poverty* (New York: The Free Press, 1969), which he read as asserting the biological inevitability of racial inequality.

75. Charles D. Aring, "Review of *The Unheavenly City*," *Archives of Internal Medicine* 129 (March 1972): 502–505; Leonard J. Duhl and Stephen R. Blum, "Review of *The Unheavenly City: The Nature and Future of Our Urban Crisis* and *Blaming the Victim*," *American Journal of Orthopsychiatry* 41 (1971): 853–855.

76. Julian H. Levi, "Review of *The Unheavenly City*," *Perspectives in Biology and Medicine* 14 (Winter 1971): 341–344.

77. Cramer, "Banfield Redux"; "Banfield Quits Harvard, Takes Position at Penn," *Harvard Crimson*, December 2, 1971; emphasis added.

78. Mark J. Penn, "Urban Expert Edward C. Banfield to Return to Government Department," *Harvard Crimson*, July 29, 1975; James Cramer, "Banfield's Back," *Harvard Crimson*, August 1, 1975; Cramer, "Banfield Redux"; McLaughlin, "Diabolical?"; Tom Lanctot and Andrew Vought, "Banfield Deserves Forum at Penn," *Daily Pennsylvanian*, April 11, 1973. McLaughlin held that Banfield's list of proposals was only half serious, a spur to discussions of the policy-making process. The ringleader behind Banfield's "award" ceremony, Bonnie Blustein, had been suspended from Harvard for her antagonism of Richard Herrnstein, the psychologist notorious for positing racial differences in IQ. It was only during her leave of absence that other radical groups brought Banfield, the "real racist," to her attention. Conveniently, by 1973–1974, she was a master's student at Penn.

79. Jon Ziomek, "Protestors Disrupt Prof's U. of C. Talk," *Chicago Sun–Times*, March 21, 1974; Edward C. Banfield, "The City and the Revolutionary Tradition," April 11, 1974, https://www.aei.org/research-products/book/the-city-and-the-revolutionary-tradition/. On Banfield, federalism, and the Federalists, see Kimberly Hendrickson, "Edward Banfield on the Promise of Politics and the Limits of Federalism," *Publius: The Journal of Federalism* 34 (2004): 139–152, which disputes his standing as a full-fledged conservative.

80. Alan Altshuler, personal communication.

81. "Research in Progress as of November 1, 1968, According to Major Areas of Investigation," box 19, folder DB026, GSDH.

82. "Christopher DeMuth Transcript," Conversations with Bill Kristol, March 19, 2014, https://conversationswithbillkristol.org/transcript/christopher-demuth-transcript/. DeMuth has become one of the major caretakers of Banfield's legacy in the think-tank world. In 1974, he celebrated Banfield's "saint-like restraint" in not using *The Unheavenly City Revisited* as a vehicle to seek vengeance on his critics; Christopher DeMuth, "Banfield Returns," *The Alternative*, November 1974. DeMuth's notion that Banfield now "had the data," however, strikes the careful reader as risible: Banfield had plumped up the text with many more citations, due in large part to *The Unheavenly City*'s widespread adoption in college courses, but on the crucial nexus of class and time he was, by his own admission, still in "essay" mode; *Unheavenly City Revisited*, 302–303n6. On Banfield as a critic of the New Deal, see Daniel DiSalvo, "Edward Banfield Revisited," *National Affairs* 32 (Summer 2017): 171–187, at 173.

83. Charles L. Leven, "The Emergence of Maturity in the Metropolis," in *The Mature Metropolis* (Lexington, MA: Lexington Books, 1978), 1–19, at 19, 3. This group, too, had given itself over to partnerships with private industry.

84. Edward C. Banfield, *The Moral Basis of a Backward Society* (Glencoe, IL: Free Press, 1958), 164, 175–186; Numa Denis Fustel de Coulanges, *The Ancient City* [1864], trans. Willard Small (Garden City, NY: Anchor, 1956), 15. This was perhaps not "the Global South" as scholars now define it, the "Orient," or certainly the Eastern Bloc, but one author has argued that Banfield's use of the Mezzogiorno to exemplify a premodern social world belongs to a period literature on the not-quite-Western "Cold War Mediterranean": Jane Schneider, "Anthropology and the Cold War Mediterranean," *Urban Anthropology and Studies of Cultural Systems and World Economic Development* 41 (2012): 107–129; and see David H. Price, *Cold War Anthropology* (Durham, NC: Duke University Press, 2016). Schneider's other leading example is Julian Pitt-Rivers, *The People of the Sierra* (Chicago: University of Chicago Press, 1954), a study of a pseudonymous Andalusian village. The *questione meridionale*, or Southern Question, has preoccupied Italian political theorists since at least Gramsci.

85. Banfield, *Moral Basis*, 166–167, 10, 85; emphasis added.

86. O'Connor, *Poverty Knowledge*, 115, notes his "stunningly facile leap" from case to population.

87. William Muraskin, "The Moral Basis of a Backward Sociologist: Edward Banfield, the Italians, and the Italian-Americans," *American Journal of Sociology* 79 (1974): 1484–1496. Muraskin's leading examples were Herbert Gans, Gerald Suttles, and Humbert Nelli. Banfield's rendition of "backward" Chiaromonte has long provoked debate in Italian social science but, unsurprisingly, found few adherents; Emanuele Ferragina, "The Never-Ending Debate about *The Moral Basis of a Backward Society*: Banfield and 'Amoral Familism,'" *Journal of the Anthropological Society of Oxford* 1 (2009): 141–160. For one mystifying example of a contemporary Italian political movement that appeals to his work, and his alone, to chart a path forward, see "Edward Christie Banfield: Un americano nel Mezzogiorno," Montegrano Revolution, accessed February 22, 2024, http://montegranorevolution.weebly.com/edward-c-banfield.html.

88. A considerable literature theorizes differential temporalities as construed along lines of gender and sexuality as well. Here, too, we see the denial or withholding of

tenses other than the present to populations labeled deviant, inexpert, or irrational. A number of authors have sought to embrace temporalities that resist the linear scheme—past, present, future—so basic to the varieties of planning and social science discussed thus far. Classic articulations of feminist temporality include Rita Felski, "Telling Time in Feminist Theory," *Tulsa Studies in Women's Literature* 21 (2002): 21–28; Joan Tronto, "Time's Place," *Feminist Theory* 4 (2003): 119–138; and Julia Kristeva, "Women's Time," trans. Alice Jardine and Harry Blake, *Signs* 7 (Autumn 1981): 13–35. A recent meditation on the phenomenology of time not passing is Lisa Baraitser, *Enduring Time* (London: Bloomsbury, 2017). These authors all elevate themes of repetition, cyclicality, rhythm, and persistence—"without cleavage or escape," Kristeva (16) writes—against the telic visions of progress and development, coded masculine, that oriented the preponderance of postwar social science. Compatible works of queer theory—for example, Lee Edelman, *No Future* (Durham, NC: Duke University Press, 2004)—have predicated their refusal of received notions of futurity on biopolitical grounds. "The future" as usually invoked, Edelman and others argue, is a reproductive future that dubiously assumes the inevitability of childbearing and generational succession.

89. Lisa Redfield Peattie, *The View from the Barrio* (Ann Arbor: University of Michigan Press, 1968), 104, 119, 123.

90. Lisa Peattie to Norman Williams, July 1, 1962 (Report C11), box 1, CGR.

91. Left renditions of the "culture of poverty" thesis were far more common than most scholarship written since the Reagan years tends to foreground. The most influential example from this era, published exactly as Peattie traveled to Venezuela, is Michael Harrington, *The Other America: Poverty in the United States* (New York: Penguin, 1962), written by a founder of the Democratic Socialists of America and championed by John F. Kennedy in designing what Johnson would dub the War on Poverty. "They do not plan ahead" (130), Harrington wrote of the poor. They lack a "culture of aspiration" (141). "They cannot see [ahead]; they cannot act." The poor are, in short, presentist by nature, "beyond history, beyond progress" (155).

92. Edward C. Banfield, ed., *Urban Government: A Reader in Administration and Politics*, 2nd ed. (New York: Free Press, 1969). The first edition appeared in 1961.

93. Lisa Peattie, *Planning: Rethinking Ciudad Guayana* (Ann Arbor: University of Michigan Press, 1987), 170.

94. Peattie, *View from the Barrio*, 47, 48. She also likened working-class Venezuelans' strategies of thrift to those "prevailing in some American Indian tribes which developed social systems in some ways similar as a response to the uncertainties of a hunting and gathering economy" (52).

95. Peattie, *Planning*, 170. The 1987 book preserves, evens dials up, Peattie's focus on inequalities between the present- and future-oriented. Her main political point, however, concerns the non-contemporaneity of the CVG planners with the inhabitants of Ciudad Guayana, not intracity class divisions; see 3–4, 53, 61, 69, 148.

96. A sense of transnational policy contagion also suffuses *Man's Struggle for Shelter in an Urbanizing World*, the UNESCO-commissioned, Joint Center–published volume that allowed Charles Abrams to collate Venezuela's urban situation with data on dozens of other nations. Intellectual influence ran in several directions: North–South, South–North, North–North, and (albeit less fully realized in his text) South–South. Abrams believed fervently in the export of American policies promoting homeown-

ership. He was also transparently worried about the domino-like implications of even a single successful example of nationalized housing provision in the developing world. "There is no more fertile ground for revolutionary propaganda than the beleaguered cities of the underdeveloped nations" (287), he wrote in the book's peroration. "Time is essential . . . if today's masses are not to become tomorrow's mob." Southern instability readily "threatens world stability" (296). More and better urbanization, he argued, citing Friedrich Ratzel's Nazi-appropriated concept of *Lebensraum* (293), could reduce the centrifugal forces that lead to territorial conflict between nation states. Unlike hardened Cold Warriors, however, he was wise to the lessons in self-sufficiency that squatters and other "slum"-dwellers could impart to credentialed planners on a case-by-case basis. Abrams pushed for land reform and redistribution—just not on the Soviet model then gaining ground. "Land dearth amid land plenty" (25) anywhere was a matter of global concern. Charles Abrams, *Man's Struggle for Shelter in an Urbanizing World* (Cambridge, MA: MIT Press, 1964). The other Latin American states Abrams discusses in depth are Chile, Ecuador, Peru, Colombia, and the Dominican Republic.

As Eric Mumford and Ijlal Muzaffar have explored, Abrams was not alone among the Ciudad Guayana team in his enthusiasm for squatting, self-building, and "sweat equity" as alternatives to state-directed Modernism. Indeed, from 1963, the Joint Center's designers began setting aside land and allocating aid for squatters. By 1964, Arthur Fawcett was laying out a "minimum[-]control approach" to site planning—the better to let the private sector assume most of the investment once the center departed. Architectural researchers, especially from MIT, drew up prototypes for "self-help" neighborhoods in addition to those pitched to the "technical and managerial groups." "It was . . . becoming clear that the shacks had to be seen as part of the process by which people were adapting the urban environment to suit their needs instead of as a sickness of the city," according to William Porter. "Interestingly enough, the unplanned areas of the present city came much closer to [our] image of the future environment than the planned." Abrams, *Man's Struggle*, 18, 137, 236; Lloyd Rodwin, interview by Morton Schussheim, June 11, 1994, PIH; Eric Mumford, "From Master Planning to Self-Build: The MIT–Harvard Joint Center for Urban Studies, 1959–1971," in *A Second Modernism: MIT, Architecture, and the "Techno-Social" Moment*, ed. Arindam Dutta (Cambridge, MA: MIT Press, 2013), 288–309; Ijlal Muzaffar, "Fuzzy Images: The Problem of Third World Development and the New Ethics of Open-Ended Planning at the MIT–Harvard Joint Center for Urban Studies," in *A Second Modernism: MIT, Architecture, and the "Techno-Social" Moment*, ed. Arindam Dutta (Cambridge, MA: MIT Press, 2013), 310–341; Fawcett, "Implementation of the Physical Plan," September 15, 1964 (Report E95), CGR; William Porter, "Changing Perspectives on Residential Area Design," in Lloyd Rodwin and Associates, *Planning Urban Growth and Regional Development: The Experience of the Guayana Program in Venezuela* (Cambridge, MA: MIT Press, 1969), 252–269, at 254, 257, 263, 268. On Colombia, and also Puerto Rico, another leading "laboratory" for these programs at the behest of Americans, Amy C. Offner, *Sorting Out the Mixed Economy: The Rise and Fall of Welfare and Developmental States in the Americas* (Princeton, NJ: Princeton University Press, 2019), is remarkably thorough.

97. Donald Appleyard, *Planning a Pluralist City: Conflicting Realities in Ciudad Guayana* (Cambridge, MA: MIT Press, 1976). John S. MacDonald, *Planning, Implementation, and Social Policy: An Evaluation of Ciudad Guayana, 1965 and 1975* (New York: Pergamon,

1979), by a researcher present in the 1960s, also arrived in the late 1970s. Some things change: in 1974, the CVG finally opened its Alta Vista headquarters building, sited where the Avenida split in two and drivers were encouraged to rubberneck. Some stay the same: most of the CVG staff stayed put in Caracas and managed the main steel mill remotely. Peattie, *Planning*, 48.

98. Donald Appleyard, "Styles and Methods of Structuring a City," *Environment and Behavior* 2 (1970): 100–117, at 100.

99. Appleyard, *Pluralist City*, 281.

100. Appleyard, *Pluralist City*, 1, 232, 231, 42, 190. Lisa Peattie conducted the first round of Appleyard's interviews.

101. Appleyard, *Pluralist City*, 289, 291, 4, 5, 200, 201. In this last quotation, Appleyard meant literally *where*: the proximate task was to make the case to residents of the eastern *barrios* that the westerly extension toward Alta Vista, steel mill, and airport was inevitable. In unpublished work with Lynch, he drew more attention to the potential frictions between drivers' view *from* and neighbors' view *of* the road; Donald Appleyard and Kevin Lynch, "Sensuous Criteria for Highway Design" [1966], in *City Sense and City Design*, eds. Tridib Banerjee and Michael Southworth (Cambridge, MA: MIT Press, 1990), 563–578.

102. Porter, "Changing Perspectives," 264–265; emphasis added.

103. Appleyard, *Pluralist City*, 44, 233, 223, 245, 243; Los Angeles Department of City Planning, *The Visual Environment of Los Angeles* (Los Angeles: Department of City Planning, 1971); Meredith Drake Reitan and Tridib Banerjee, "Kevin Lynch in Los Angeles: Reflections on Planning, Politics, and Participation," *Journal of the American Planning Association* 84 (2018): 217–229.

104. Magdalen Dorothea Vernon, *The Psychology of Perception* (London: Pelican, 1962); Fred Attneave, "Some Informative Aspects of Visual Perception," *Psychological Review* 61 (1954): 183–193; Jean Piaget and Bärbel Inhelder, *The Child's Conception of Space* [1948] (New York: Norton, 1967); Edward C. Tolman, "A Psychological Model," in *Toward a General Theory of Action*, eds. Talcott Parsons and Edward Shils (Cambridge, MA: Harvard University Press, 1951), 279–361.

105. Rudolf Arnheim, *Art and Visual Perception* (Berkeley: University of California Press, 1964); Ernst Gombrich, "On Physiognomic Perception," *Daedalus* (Winter 1960): 228–241; Kenneth Craik, "Environmental Psychology," in *New Directions in Psychology* 4 (New York: Holt, Rinehart, and Winston, 1970), 1–121; Harold Proshansky et al., *Environmental Psychology: Man and His Physical Setting* (New York: Holt, Rinehart, and Winston, 1970); David Lowenthal, ed., *Environmental Perception and Behavior*, Department of Geography Research Paper No. 109 (Chicago: University of Chicago, 1967); Roger M. Downs and David Stea, eds., *Image and Environment: Cognitive Mapping and Spatial Behavior* (Chicago: Aldine, 1973); Peter Gould and Rodney White, *Mental Maps* (Middlesex, UK: Penguin, 1974); Aldous Huxley, *The Doors of Perception* (London: Chatto & Windus, 1954).

106. Appleyard, *Pluralist City*, 158–159, 161, 163. He shows that the master distinction is native to Lynch's work: in *The Image of the City*'s famous fivefold scheme, paths and nodes are sequential, while landmarks, districts, and edges are spatial (182). And the typology continues: crosscutting the two "styles" are three "methods" by which people imaginatively structure the city: "associational," "topological," and "positional" (167).

107. Appleyard, *Pluralist City*, 210, 211, 205, 206, 221; George Santayana, *The Sense of Beauty* (New York: Scribner, 1896). Appleyard did not claim that non-elites denied that growth and change were in the offing. In talking about the future, however, the working and lower classes seldom moved the conversation beyond population figures, whereas middle-class respondents tended to speculate on housing, infrastructure, economic trends, and administrative decisions (194).

108. Appleyard, *Pluralist City*, 218, 223.

109. Johannes Fabian, *Time and the Other* (New York: Columbia University Press, 1983), 33, 80; Eric R. Wolf, *Europe and the People without History* (Berkeley: University of California Press, 1982). Berber Bevernage, "Tales of Pastness and Contemporaneity: On the Politics of Time in History and Anthropology," *Rethinking History* 20 (2016): 352–374, alleges Fabian's own metaphysics of presence. On Fabian and geopolitics, see Ian Klinke, "Chronopolitics: A Conceptual Matrix," *Progress in Human Geography* 37 (2012): 673–690. For the claim that late-Enlightenment concepts of Europe and the United States as "contemporaries" denied the coevalness of "most of the rest of the rest of the world," see Fritzsche, *Stranded in the Present*, 217, 258n3.

110. Donald Appleyard, ed., *The Conservation of European Cities* (Cambridge, MA: MIT Press, 1979); Donald Appleyard, "The Environment as a Social Symbol," *Ekistics* 278 (1979): 272–281; Donald Appleyard, *Livable Streets* (Berkeley: University of California Press, 1981). The first posthumous summary of his work, in what had become his home journal, calls *Planning a Pluralist City* "important" but treats it primarily as an "application" of Lynch's imaging method; Kathryn H. Anthony, "Major Themes in the Work of Donald Appleyard," *Environment and Behavior* 15 (1983): 411–418, at 412.

111. The literature on non-Western understandings of time itself experienced a boom in midcentury anthropology. Many authors alleged that their "primitive" subjects either had abnormally short time horizons or, due to cyclical rather than linear understandings of time's passage, had no horizons at all. On this trend, see Barbara Adam, *Time and Social Theory* (Cambridge, UK: Polity, 1990), 96; and on Piaget and Lévi-Strauss specifically, see Jacques Le Goff, *History and Memory* [1977], trans. Steven Rendall and Elizabeth Claman (New York: Columbia University Press, 1992), 4, 7. For leading postwar examples, see Edmund R. Leach, "Two Essays Concerning the Symbolic Representation of Time," in *Rethinking Anthropology* (New York: Humanities Press, 1961), 108–116; and Marian W. Smith, "Different Cultural Concepts of Past, Present and Future," *Psychiatry* 15 (1952): 395–400. These studies had roots in prewar anthropology—chiefly, E. E. Evans-Pritchard, "Nuer Time-Reckoning," *Africa* 12 (1939): 189–216; and A. Irving Hallowell, "Temporal Orientation in Western Civilization and in a Pre-Literate Society," *American Anthropologist* n.s. 39 (1937): 647–670.

112. Nathan Glazer, "Is New York City Ungovernable?," *Commentary* 32 (September 1961): 185–193; Nathan Glazer, "Why City Planning Is Obsolete," *Architectural Forum* 109 (July 1958): 96–98, 160. Brian L. Tochterman, *The Dying City: Postwar New York and the Ideology of Fear* (Chapel Hill: University of North Carolina Press, 2017), 102, notes that "ungovernable" was "a New York–specific term." Its circulation only increased during the Lindsay administration, on which see Vincent Cannato, *The Ungovernable City: John Lindsay and His Struggle to Save New York* (New York: Basic Books, 2002).

113. Nathan Glazer and Daniel Patrick Moynihan, *Beyond the Melting Pot: The Negroes, Puerto Ricans, Jews, Italians, and Irish of New York City* (Cambridge, MA: MIT Press,

1963), 23. On the flight of manufacturing plants and corporate headquarters at this time, see Lizabeth Cohen and Brian Goldstein, "Governing at the Tipping Point: Shaping the City's Role in Economic Development," in *Summer in the City: John Lindsay, New York, and the American Dream*, ed. Joseph Viteritti (Baltimore: Johns Hopkins University Press, 2014), 163–192. In "Is New York City Ungovernable?," Glazer granted that New York's great spatial extent—and surfeit of low-rise housing in the outer parts of the outer boroughs—meant that many instances of quasi-suburban middle-class flight from the center actually landed families within city limits. A move of eight or ten miles, in any direction, from downtown Boston—or Pittsburgh, San Francisco, Washington, or Baltimore, all of whose municipal borders are drawn far closer in—was almost certain to spell depletion of the city's tax base.

114. Noel Ignatiev, *How the Irish Became White* (New York: Routledge, 1995), is the classic work on that group's path to racial reclassification, which began earlier than its Jewish or Italian analogues.

115. Glazer and Moynihan, *Beyond the Melting Pot*, 33, 112, 122. On one unavoidable representation of *Nuyoricans* at this time, see Julia L. Foulkes, *A Place for Us: West Side Story and New York* (Chicago: University of Chicago Press, 2016). At least one writer, the rare Puerto Rican with ties to the "little magazines" and the only one included in *Dissent*'s "New York, N.Y." issue, signaled at least surface-level endorsement of the idea that her community had an allochronic relationship to the "New York minute": "We can't keep up with things here," wrote Eileen Diaz in "A Puerto Rican in New York," *Dissent* 8 (Summer 1961): 383–385, at 384. Daniel Bell, Glazer's good friend and eventual Harvard colleague, would put a slightly different spin on the temporal sensibilities of the presumptively Hispanic poor. For him, the telling slogan he had overheard was "There is always *mañana*" (i.e., sloth arises from perceptions of a lack of urgency, which itself stems from perceptions of a wide-open but unquantified future); Bell, *Post-Industrial Society*, 473.

116. Nathan Glazer, *American Judaism* (Chicago: University of Chicago Press, 1957), 80.

117. Glazer and Moynihan, *Beyond the Melting Pot*, v, 120.

118. Was this sense of belatedness "postmodern" avant la lettre? Jonathan Arac posed this question in 1986 and concluded that the much-contested term was "originally a pejorative from those who attributed to others a belatedness that was also their own"; *Postmodernism and Politics* (Minneapolis: University of Minnesota Press, 1986), xxxix. Mark Greif has extended the claim to every other era labeled *post-*. Postmodern, posthistoric, posthuman—"the abstract belatedness," he writes, somewhat cryptically, "came long ago, and was constituted by the chronology of newness, beginnings, and progress"; *The Age of the Crisis of Man*, 326. David Couzens Hoy, *The Time of Our Lives: A Critical History of Temporality* (Cambridge, MA: MIT Press, 2009), 180, makes a similar point. For a vibrant discussion of earlier encounters with "ruins so soon!"—Tocqueville's remark upon seeing the already-abandoned towns that failed speculators had planted along the Erie Canal—see Nick Yablon, *Untimely Ruins: An Archaeology of Urban Modernity, 1819–1919* (Chicago: University of Chicago Press, 2009).

119. Nathan Glazer and Daniel Patrick Moynihan, "Introduction to the Second Edition: New York City in 1970," in *Beyond the Melting Pot: The Negroes, Puerto Ricans, Jews, Italians, and Irish of New York City*, 2nd ed. (Cambridge, MA: MIT Press, 1970), vii–

xcviii, at lxxvi, lxxxvii, lxxxi; Fabio Rojas, *From Black Power to Black Studies: How a Radical Social Movement Became an Academic Discipline* (Baltimore: Johns Hopkins University Press, 2010).

120. Nathan Glazer, "On Being Deradicalized," *Commentary* 50 (October 1970): 74–80. The essay notes the importance of Urban Renewal's shortcomings in altering his views of state intervention. Glazer and Banfield both contributed advance praise on the back cover of Charles Murray, *Losing Ground: American Social Policy, 1950–1980* (New York: Basic Books, 1984). On Glazer's evolution, see Philip Kasinitz, "The Sociologist as Intellectual," *City & Community* 18 (2019): 433–438, at 435, 434, 433, which calls the second edition of *Beyond the Melting Pot* "extreme" and "overwrought" but credits Glazer with resisting the "dogmatic" cast of mind typical of other New York neoconservatives. His politics sat somewhere "between the Irvings": Kristol on the right, Howe on the left. See also Richard Alba, "Beyond the Melting Pot," *City & Community* 18 (2019): 446–450. The conservative Peter Skerry, in "Nathan Glazer: An Appreciation," *National Affairs* 27 (Spring 2016): 178–191, at 185, refuses to place Glazer in the Banfieldian anti-expert camp: "experts," he felt, "are colleagues presumptively worthy of a hearing." On Glazer's labile politics, see also James Traub, "Nathan Glazer Changes His Mind, Again," *New York Times Magazine*, June 28, 1998. Most of the New York Intellectuals who moved right took measures to minimize or deny their former positions. "People change their view," wrote Irving Kristol, "and, inevitably, rewrite their autobiographies—sometimes with no awareness of duplicity"; "Memoirs of a 'Cold Warrior,'" *New York Times Magazine*, February 11, 1968. On these themes, see Alexander Bloom, *Prodigal Sons: The New York Intellectuals and Their World* (New York: Oxford University Press, 1986), 24, 51, 169, 386; and see Alan M. Wald's comments on memoirs and the "politics of memory" in *The New York Intellectuals: The Rise and Decline of the Anti-Stalinist Left from the 1930s to the 1980s* (Chapel Hill: University of North Carolina Press, 1987), 7, 13. From this group, the most infamous use of memoir to disavow former selves remains Norman Podhoretz, *Making It* (New York: Random House, 1967).

121. Glazer and Moynihan, "Introduction to the Second Edition," lvi. Matthew Frye Jacobson sees such attempts to differentiate white ethnics' stepwise assimilation stories from the "illegitimate impatience" of Black people as "the hallmark of neoconservative writing"; *Roots Too: White Ethnic Revival in Post–Civil Rights America* (Cambridge, MA: Harvard University Press, 2006), 190, 191. Kristol, he notes, saw Black people as "latecomers" (181) to New York. See also Irving Kristol, "What Is a 'Neo-Conservative'?," *Newsweek*, January 19, 1976: "Neo-conservatives are well aware that traditional values and institutions do change in time, but they prefer that such change be gradual and organic." "He worked to make it. Why can't *they*?" is what Joshua B. Freeman calls "the 'my grandfather' question"; *Working-Class New York: Life and Labor since World War II* (New York: The New Press, 2000), 281, emphasis original. The best monographic study of white-ethnic backlash in New York is Jonathan Rieder, *Canarsie: The Jews and Italians of Brooklyn against Liberalism* (Cambridge, MA: Harvard University Press, 1985), based on a dissertation whose committee included Glazer; Rieder notes the "gentler, softer" (42) backlash rhetoric used by Jews. See also Eli Lederhendler, *New York Jews and the Decline of Urban Ethnicity, 1950–1970* (Syracuse, NY: Syracuse University Press, 2001); and Will Herberg, *Protestant–Catholic–Jew: An Essay in Religious Sociology* (New York: Anchor, 1955), by a future neoconservative of note. Benjamin Balint, *Running Commentary*

(New York: PublicAffairs, 2010), 213, argues for "the Jewishness of neoconservatism" and claims that it derives from the "dual inclination to be both different and the same, and the awkward space between acceptance and rejection." Russell Jacoby, *Picture Imperfect: Utopian Thought for an Anti-Utopian Age* (New York: Columbia University Press, 2007), seeks to root a uniquely Jewish opposition to "blueprint utopias" in the long-standing prohibition on "graven images." For the most caustic of the New York Intellectuals, see Lionel Abel, "New York City: A Remembrance," *Dissent* 8 (Summer 1961): 251–259; and cf. Lionel Abel, *The Intellectual Follies* (New York: Norton, 1984), 281–289. For an analysis that decenters explicit backlash as the cause of post-bankruptcy retrenchment, see Benjamin Holtzman, *The Long Crisis: New York City and the Path to Neoliberalism* (New York: Oxford University Press, 2021).

122. On Deutsch, see Orit Halpern, *Beautiful Data: A History of Vision and Reason since 1945* (Durham, NC: Duke University Press, 2014), 187, 189; and cf. Karl Mannheim, *Ideology and Utopia* [1929], trans. Louis Wirth and Edward Shils (New York: Harcourt Brace Jovanovich, 1936), 189: "The very quintessence of political knowledge seems to us to lie in the fact that increased knowledge does not eliminate decisions but only forces them farther and farther back." One critic summarized Banfield's belief in "no crisis that can't be corrected by that conservative weapon of time . . . time and only time"; James Cramer, "Banfield's Back," *Harvard Crimson*, August 1, 1975. At the time of his involve with "CY2000," Daniel Bell spoke in similar terms, telling an interviewer, "You have to learn to control and plan for, anticipate, offset, determine whether you want it or not"; "Reminiscences of Daniel Bell, 1965," June 6, 1966, Socialist Movement Project, CUL. *You* could apply equally to individuals and institutions.

123. Freeman, *Working-Class New York*, 336; Kim Phillips-Fein, *Fear City: New York's Fiscal Crisis and the Rise of Austerity Politics* (New York: Metropolitan Books, 2017), 277–282. On the subsequent displacement of that fear beyond city limits, see Kyle Riismandel, *Neighborhood of Fear: The Suburban Crisis in American Culture, 1975–2001* (Baltimore: Johns Hopkins University Press, 2020). On its religious contours, see Bench Ansfield, "Unsettling 'Inner City': Liberal Protestantism and the Postwar Origins of a Keyword in Urban Studies," *Antipode* 50 (2018): 1166–1185.

124. Frieden and Kaplan, *Politics of Neglect*, 244.

125. Freeman, *Working-Class New York*, 274; Joe Flood, *The Fires* (New York: Riverhead, 2010), 14. Flood's book provides essential background on how restructuring within the New York Fire Department—abetted by algorithms courtesy of "urban RAND"—ended up imposing service cuts in some of the city's most vulnerable neighborhoods. On greater Charlotte Street, see Evelyn Gonzalez, *The Bronx* (New York: Columbia University Press, 2004), 121–129; Peter L'Official, *Urban Legends: The South Bronx in Representation and Ruin* (Cambridge, MA: Harvard University Press, 2020); and Lizabeth Cohen, *Saving America's Cities: Ed Logue and the Struggle to Renew Urban America in the Suburban Age* (New York: Farrar, Straus & Giroux, 2019), 349–383 (on the Ruins Section, see 354).

126. Leonard Kriegel, "In the Country of the Other," *Dissent* 34 (Fall 1987): 207–212, at 208. In the same number of *Dissent*, Jerome Charyn, also a Bronx-born novelist, made compatible remarks about Harlem, citing a different war and likening it to a "burnt-out Vietnamese village"; "'The Rough Adventure of the Street . . . ,'" *Dissent* 34 (Fall 1987): 214–216, at 216.

127. On the distinction between ruin, which in Romantic fashion presumes some bygone form, and rubble, which does not, see Gastón R. Gordillo, *Rubble: The Afterlife of Destruction* (Durham, NC: Duke University Press, 2014), an anthropological study sited in Argentina.

128. For a fuller lineage, see Daniel Abramson, *Obsolescence: An Architectural History* (Chicago: University of Chicago Press, 2015).

129. John V. Lindsay, *The City* (New York: Norton, 1969), 146, 233. He also indulged Moynihanian language of the "dependent" (158) "underclass" (156) and Banfieldian warnings that current policies might "make the problem infinitely worse" (148).

130. Robert Nichols, "The City," *Dissent* 8 (Summer 1961): 219–221, at 219; Edward T. Chase, "New York Could Die," *Dissent* 8 (Summer 1961): 297–303. For another contemporary declensionist analysis steeped in biomedical language, see Mitchell Gordon, *Sick Cities* (New York: Macmillan, 1963). There was also, always, the "Civic Cassandra" Lewis Mumford, whose politics are difficult to categorize but who spent the 1960s insisting that, as Robert C. Wood put it, "our situation is already out of hand" and "our present spread cities . . . are essentially incomprehensible"; "Government and the Intellectual: The Necessary Alliance for Effective Action to Meet Urban Needs," in *Governing Urban Society: New Scientific Approaches*, eds. Stephen B. Sweeney and James C. Charlesworth (Philadelphia: American Academy of Political and Social Science, 1967), 3–14, at 5.

131. Alfred Kazin, *New York Jew* (New York: Knopf, 1978), 154.

132. Alfred Kazin, "July 8, 1976," in *Alfred Kazin's Journals*, ed. Richard M. Cook (New Haven, CT: Yale University Press, 2011), 444.

133. Alfred Kazin, *A Walker in the City* (New York: Harcourt, 1951), 87, 88, 92, 165, 5.

134. Alfred Kazin and David Finn, *Our New York* (New York: Harper and Row, 1989), 73, 204. This was a photo book, sized for the coffee table, and David Finn, the photographer, claimed that his subjects in the South Bronx believed that images could compel action: "Show 'em how bad it looks! Maybe they'll do something about it" (222).

135. Kazin, *New York Jew*, 293, 215, 216, 218. On the racial dimensions of these concepts, see Wendell Pritchett, *Brownsville, Brooklyn: Blacks, Jews, and the Changing Face of the Ghetto* (Chicago: University of Chicago Press, 2002). It is difficult to make a summary statement on Kazin and race. In *A Walker in the City*, he claims, of Brownsville's *shvartze* (Black) population dwelling three to four blocks away, "We just did not think about them." When he did overhear elder Jews expressing racial anxiety, he understood it to be "some strange, embarrassed resentment" from people otherwise steeped in the best universalism of the socialist tradition. The young Kazin perceived an estrangement from the clichés his neighbors would mouth: "They were moving nearer and nearer. They were invading our neighborhood"; *Walker in the City*, 141.

In the 1980s, writing from the Upper West Side, Kazin wrote that "I have never lived so close to blacks before." Three blocks in prewar Brooklyn could separate completely distinct lifeworlds. In Manhattan, he had Black neighbors within the building, and in the elevators, all parties displayed "an anxious civility": "There is proximity but no relating." Kazin was quite friendly with Richard Wright, Ralph Ellison, James Baldwin, and other prominent Black writers, but, as he admitted, that was the extent of his crossover; Kazin and Finn, *Our New York*, 164. Elsewhere, in his private journals, Kazin on a few occasions indulged the ugliest tendencies of racial backlash, in 1957 bemoaning "the naked, shabby, serf-like quality" of Latin American migrants to the West Side. "What lowness, what cravenness, are in these people." His journals also record one sideways glance at "the Blacks playing saxophones in the torrid, Calcutta subway." "Calcutta" as modifier—if Cologne was one stock reference in the transnational ruin-gazer's repertoire, now the postcolonial world was another; "August 11, 1957" and "May 28, 1976" in *Alfred Kazin's Journals*, ed. Richard M. Cook (New Haven, CT: Yale University Press, 2011), 222, 443.

136. Kazin, *New York Jew*, 294.

137. Nathan Glazer, "Amenity in New York City" [1995, 1996, 2002], in *From a Cause to a Style: Modernist Architecture's Encounter with the American City* (Princeton, NJ: Princeton University Press, 2007), 192–227, at 211, 227, 223. Elsewhere, Glazer contrasted stylistically various New York with the (partial) uniformity of Washington, DC. A conservative commentator has defined the "Glazerian status quo ante" as "the unplanned city and the architecture that it spawns." The brownstones of Glazer's native Harlem represent "nondesign," "simple adaptation" to circumstances; Howard Husock, "Nathan Glazer's Warning," *City Journal* (Summer 2011). His preference for brick, stone, and wood over concrete stemmed in part from the fact that these materials "naturally broke down into small units"; Glazer, "Introduction," in *From a Cause to a Style*, 36.

138. Nathan Glazer, "Paris—the View from New York," *The Public Interest* 74 (Winter 1984): 31–51, at 32, 43. Already in 1958, writing against Modernism, Glazer was championing "the minor virtues in design," looking to Italian cities as examples of aesthetic "jumble" and "free play"; Glazer, "Why City Planning Is Obsolete," 98. It was amid the "ruins" of Urban Renewal that historic preservation as a profession and policy domain assumed its modern form. The National Historic Preservation Act passed in 1966; the National Trust had formed under Truman in 1949.

139. Kasinitz, "Sociologist as Intellectual," 438.

140. Nathan Glazer, "Planning for New York City: Is It Possible?" [1992], in *From a Cause to a Style: Modernist Architecture's Encounter with the American City* (Princeton, NJ: Princeton University Press, 2007), 228–251, at 228.

141. Glazer, "Introduction," 15. This little-cited volume merits attention. Despite certain blinkers, Glazer is underappreciated as an architectural critic.

142. Glazer and Moynihan, *Beyond the Melting Pot*, 64. Recent attempts to theorize the nonhuman agency of buildings include Steven Cairns and Jane M. Jacobs, *Buildings Must Die: A Perverse View of Architecture* (Cambridge, MA: MIT Press, 2014); Spyros Papapetros, *On the Animation of the Inorganic: Art, Architecture, and the Extension of Life* (Chicago: University of Chicago Press, 2012); Bruno Latour and Albena Yaneva, "Give Me a Gun and I Will Make All Buildings Move: An Ant's View of Architecture," in *Explorations in Architecture: Teaching, Design, Research* (Basel: Birkhäuser, 2008), 80–89; and Graham Harman, *Architecture and Objects* (Minneapolis: University of Minnesota Press, 2022). Contrast these works with the more anthropocentric Thomas Gieryn, "What Buildings Do," *Theory and Society* 31 (2002): 35–74; Neil Harris, *Building Lives: Constructing Rites and Passages* (New Haven, CT: Yale University Press, 1999); Stewart Brand, *How Buildings Learn* (New York: Penguin, 1994).

143. Nathan Glazer, "On Subway Graffiti in New York," *The Public Interest* 54 (Winter 1979): 3–11, at 4, 7, 5, 11, 10; and, for similar language, Nathan Glazer, "The South-Bronx Story: An Extreme Case of Neighborhood Decline," *Policy Studies Journal* 16 (1987): 269–276.

144. Glazer, "Paris," 4.

145. James Q. Wilson, *Varieties of Police Behavior: The Management of Law and Order in Eight Communities* (Cambridge, MA: Harvard University Press, 1968); George L. Kelling and James Q. Wilson, "Broken Windows," *The Atlantic* (March 1982): 29–38. Christopher P. Loss, "The Making of a Neocon," *Modern American History* 5 (2022): 263–287, argues persuasively that Wilson's own experience within complex organizations—campus, committee, center, department—conditioned shifts in his thinking about organizations and complexity. For other basically pro-police scholarship with Joint Center ties, see David W. Abbott et al., *Police, Politics, and Race: The New York City Referendum on Civilian Review* (New York: American Jewish Committee, 1969), with an introduction by Moynihan and an allergy to acknowledging either racism or police brutality as generators of public fearfulness. Sam Collings-Wells, "From Black Power to Broken Windows: Liberal Philanthropy and the Carceral State," *Journal of Urban History* 48 (2022): 739–759, details the work of the Police Foundation, established in 1970 with Wilson on its board of directors, and the origins of this research agenda within Ford's community-action programs. Characteristically, Kazin the pedestrian fixated on the malign agency of "broken sidewalks": "New York is dying. I am on my last mile, etc.—but the overabundance of people, orange baseball caps, broken sidewalks, potholes in the gutter—all swallow you up like the most severely unimpressible process of nature"; "May 28, 1976" in *Alfred Kazin's Journals*, 443. David Finn, his photographer, would write, seven years after Wilson and Kelling, "The cancer originates in those burned-out buildings, the piles of rubble and decay. . . . It is now metastasizing to the rest of the country"; *Our New York*, 200. Finn's impetus for writing was personal: in 1979, his brother had been murdered, seemingly at random, in the Riverdale section of the Bronx. His killers had come from middle-class backgrounds, and so for Finn, the usual sociological explanations could not suffice. The built environment, his photographic subject, had to be at fault.

146. "18 Urban Experts Advise, Castigate, and Console the City on Its Problems," *New York Times*, July 30, 1975; Margalit Fox, "Israel Shenker, 82, Reporter with the Instincts of a Scholar, Dies," *New York Times*, June 17, 2007.

147. As a marker of their prestige and visibility, note that in 1974, a literary critic revisiting the 1959 novel by Paul Goodman could remark, "Had our politicians read *The Empire City* . . . they would have known an urban crisis was upon them before the *New York Times* announced it as reflected in the latest MIT studies"; Leo Raditsa, "On Paul Goodman—and Goodmanism," *Iowa Review* 5, no. 3 (1974): 62–79, at 68.

Coda

1. "Joint Center Renamed," *Joint Center Review* (October 1985), box 168, folder 13, MMP; Joint Center for Housing Studies, "Our History," accessed February 22, 2024, https://www.jchs.harvard.edu/about/history; Alan Altshuler, personal communication, January 14, 2020; Phillip Clay, personal communication, September 20, 2023. There was talk of having the Kennedy School fully absorb the Joint Center (along with Harvard's planning program, which had entered receivership); the Taubman Center for State and Local Government was another proposed home. The rationale for MIT's departure remains somewhat unclear, even to those who bore witness, but among the factors were its administrators' loss of interest in the diminished center and the Harvardians'

increasing assertiveness about its priorities. It was in the process of organizing events to mark the center's twenty-fifth anniversary, in fact, that Phillip Clay, associate director, first appreciated the degree of tension. Harvard's city-planning program lost its accreditation in 1981, complicating the jointure for a time before the GSD established a new degree, renamed urban planning, effective 1984. By 1985, Clay recalls, most faculty were "long gone" from the Joint Center.

2. On Ciudad Guayana since the 1970s, see especially Clara Irazábal, "A Planned City Comes of Age: Rethinking Ciudad Guayana Today," *Journal of Latin American Geography* 3 (2004): 22–51; Thomas Angotti, "Ciudad Guayana: From Growth Pole to Metropolis, Central Planning to Participation," *Journal of Planning Education and Research* 20 (2001): 329–338; Arturo Almandoz, *Modernization, Urbanization and Development in Latin America, 1900s–2000s* (London: Routledge, 2015); and Lisa Peattie, *Planning: Rethinking Ciudad Guayana* (Ann Arbor: University of Michigan Press, 1987).

3. Yessika Muñoz, "Ciudad Guayana: el nombre que nadie usa," *Nueva Prensa*, July 2, 2019.

4. Irazábal, "Planned City Comes of Age"; Simon Romero, "Urban Paradise in Venezuela Can't Escape Country's Woes," *New York Times*, August 13, 2007. Irazábal associates the Chávez era with a "return to developmentalism," signaled by the much-recited slogan promising that his administration would "re-found the Republic" (39).

5. William Alonso, "Cities, Planners, and Urban Renewal" [1963; originally "Cities and City Planners"], in *Urban Renewal: The Record and the Controversy*, ed. James Q. Wilson (Cambridge, MA: MIT Press, 1966), 437–453, at 453, 439.

6. Marshall Kaplan, *Urban Planning in the 1960s: A Design for Irrelevancy* (New York: Praeger, 1973), 129; emphasis added.

7. Stephan Thernstrom, *Poverty, Planning, and Politics in the New Boston: The Origins of ABCD* (New York: Basic Books, 1969), 191, 149.

8. For Daniel Bell, City College Class of 1938, "The claims of doubt are prior to the claims of faith"; *The End of Ideology* (New York: The Free Press, 1960), 16. On its producers, see Naomi Oreskes and Erik Conway, *Merchants of Doubt* (New York: Bloomsbury, 2010).

9. Life itself, Giorgio Agamben notes in a discussion of what Walter Benjamin called messianic time, can be thought of as a process of "continuous deferment or delay." He invokes the grammatical distinction between tense (past, present, future) and aspect (whether any one of these has yet been accomplished). *Not yet* preserves the future tense but shifts its aspect. "The Time That Is Left," *Epoché* 7 (2002): 1–14, at 6, 9.

10. Ernst Bloch, *The Principle of Hope* [1938–47], vol. 1, trans. Neville Plaice, Stephen Plaice, and Paul Knight (Cambridge, MA: MIT Press, 1995), 4, 9; Ernst Bloch, *The Spirit of Utopia* [1918], trans. Anthony A. Nassar (Stanford: Stanford University Press, 2000).

11. Bloch, *Principle of Hope*, 9, 18; emphasis added. Since Fredric Jameson, *Marxism and Form* (Princeton, NJ: Princeton University Press, 1971), 116–159, commentators friendly to Bloch have foregrounded his play with tense and aspect; see Jamie Owen Daniel and Tom Moylan, eds., *Not Yet: Reconsidering Ernst Bloch* (London: Verso, 1997). "Future in the past" is itself the technical name of a grammatical construction familiar to historians: "He *would soon* find out. . . ."

Many philosophically minded anthropologists have explored hope as a conceptual category. See Vincent Crapanzano, "Reflections on Hope as a Category of Social and Psychological Analysis," *Cultural Anthropology* 18 (2003): 3–32; Vincent Crapanzano, *Imaginative Horizons* (Chicago: University of Chicago Press, 2004); Hirozaku Miyazaki, *The Method of Hope* (Stanford: Stanford University Press, 2004); Hirozaku Miyazaki, "The Temporality of No Hope," in *Ethnographies of Neoliberalism*, ed. Carol Greenhouse (Philadelphia: University of Pennsylvania Press, 2010), 238–250; and Rebecca Bryant and Daniel M. Knight, eds., *The Anthropology of the Future* (Cambridge, U.K.: Cambridge University Press, 2019).

12. Reinhart Koselleck, "The Temporalization of Utopia," in *The Practice of Conceptual History: Timing History, Spacing Concepts*, trans. Todd Presner (Stanford, CA: Stanford University Press, 2002), 84–99.

13. For example, Jennifer Robinson, "Comparative Urbanism: New Geographies and Cultures of Theorizing the Urban," *International Journal of Urban and Regional Research* 40 (2016): 187–199.

14. Neil Brenner, ed., *Implosions/Explosions: Towards a Study of Planetary Urbanization* (Berlin: Jovis, 2014), is the most representative collection.

15. Inter alia, Robert E. Park and Ernest W. Burgess, *The City: Suggestions for Investigation of Human Behavior in the Urban Environment* (Chicago: University of Chicago Press, 1925); Allen J. Scott and Edward W. Soja, eds., *The City: Los Angeles and Urban Theory at the End of the Twentieth Century* (Berkeley: University of California Press, 1996); Michael Dear, "The Los Angeles School of Urbanism: An Intellectual History," *Urban Geography* 24 (2003): 493–509; David Wachsmuth, "City as Ideology: Reconciling the Explosion of the City Form with the Tenacity of the City Concept," *Environment and Planning D: Society and Space* 32 (2014): 75–90; Hillary Angelo and David Wachsmuth, "Urbanizing Urban Political Ecology: A Critique of Methodological Cityism," *International Journal of Urban and Regional Research* 39 (2015): 16–27; and Hillary Angelo, "From the City Lens toward Urbanisation as a Way of Seeing: Country/City Binaries on an Urbanising Planet," *Urban Studies* 54 (2017): 158–178.

16. Laura Kurgan and Dare Brawley, eds., *Ways of Knowing Cities* (New York: Columbia Books on Architecture and the City, 2019); Shannon Mattern, *A City Is Not a Computer: Other Urban Intelligences* (Princeton, NJ: Princeton University Press, 2021); James M. Beshers, ed., *Computer Methods in the Analysis of Large-Scale Social Systems* [1965], 2nd ed. (Cambridge, MA: MIT Press, 1968).

17. Ruth Glass, *London: Aspects of Change* (London: MacGibbon & Kee, 1964); Ruth Glass, "The Centre for Urban Studies: Extracts from the Quinquennial Report," *Town Planning Review* 34 (1963): 169–184.

18. Jill Lepore, *If Then: How the Simulmatics Corporation Invented the Future* (New York: Liveright, 2020), 324–328, notes the ahistoricism of the political-prediction industry. On "prefiguration" as opposed to "anticipation," compare Craig Jeffrey and Jane Dyson, "Geographies of the Future: Prefigurative Politics," *Progress in Human Geography* 45 (2021): 641–658; with Ben Anderson, "Preemption, Precaution, Preparedness: Anticipatory Action and Future Geographies," *Progress in Human Geography* 34 (2010): 777–798; and, for example, J. Peter Scoblic, "We Can't Prevent Tomorrow's Catastrophes Unless We Imagine Them Today," *Washington Post*, March 18, 2021. See also Stephen J. Collier and Andrew Lakoff, *The Government of Emergency: Vital Systems, Expertise, and the*

Politics of Security (Princeton, NJ: Princeton University Press, 2021); and Mary L. Dudziak, "The Future as a Concept in National Security Law," *Pepperdine Law Review* 42 (2015): 591–606.

19. Thomas Sowell, *"The Unheavenly City* at Fifty," *Claremont Review of Books* (Fall 2020). Strauss and Banfield were colleagues and allies at Chicago in the 1950s; see Leo Strauss, "Remarks at Farewell to E. C. Banfield on Departure from Chicago, 1959," Edward C. Banfield: An Online Resource, https://edwardcbanfield.wordpress.com/2011/02/19/leo-strauss-%e2%80%9cremarks-at-farewell-to-e-c-banfield-on-departure-from-chicago-1959-2/. In 2002, Elliott Banfield solicited advice from Martin Meyerson on how to gain readmission to Columbia, the school he had dropped out of in 1968 (one week before the May uprising) amid political currents he disliked. (He had briefly enrolled in the architecture program at Washington University in St. Louis but fled "a rank modernism which I rejected.") Elliott Banfield to Martin Meyerson, September 23, 2002, box 34, folder 46, MMP.

20. Kevin R. Kosar, "The Perils of 'Doing Something,'" *City Journal*, December 31, 2020.

21. For the latest in a series of critiques of Trilling and his interlocutors, see Samuel Moyn, *Liberalism against Itself: Cold War Intellectuals and the Making of Our Times* (New Haven, CT: Yale University Press, 2023).

22. This was so despite the publicity that attended Rachel Carson's *Silent Spring* (1962), published in Boston by Houghton Mifflin and extensively covered by the *Boston Globe*, who presented Carson as a hometown author; Priscilla Coit Murphy, *What a Book Can Do: The Publication and Reception of* Silent Spring (Amherst: University of Massachusetts Press, 2005), 57–88, 133–135.

23. Robert C. Wood, *The Necessary Majority: Middle America and the Urban Crisis* (New York: Columbia University Press, 1972), 8, 9; Ian McHarg, *Design with Nature* (Garden City, NY: Doubleday, 1969). Of course, there is a more complex history at stake; Paul Warde, Libby Robin, and Sverker Sörlin, *The Environment: A History of the Idea* (Baltimore: Johns Hopkins University Press, 2018).

24. Marcia Bjornerud, *Timefulness: How Thinking Like a Geologist Can Help Save the World* (Princeton, NJ: Princeton University Press, 2018); Vincent Ialenti, *Deep Time Reckoning: How Future Thinking Can Help Earth Now* (Cambridge, MA: MIT Press, 2020).

25. Bruce P. Braun, "A New Urban *Dispositif*?: Governing Life in an Age of Climate Change," *Environment and Planning D: Society and Space* 32 (2014): 49–64; Bruce Braun, "Futures: Imagining Socioecological Transformation—An Introduction," *Annals of the American Association of Geographers* 105 (2015): 239–243, at 239; Bruno Latour, *Down to Earth: Politics in the New Climatic Regime* (Cambridge, UK: Polity, 2017); Dipesh Chakrabarty, "The Planet: An Emergent Humanist Category," *Critical Inquiry* 46 (Autumn 2019): 1–31.

26. On wartime mapping, see Susan Schulten, *The Geographical Imagination in American, 1880–1950* (Chicago: University of Chicago Press, 2001), 204–238.

27. Donald MacKenzie, *An Engine, Not a Camera: How Financial Models Shape Markets* (Cambridge, MA: MIT Press, 2006). On the maps FEMA produces in order to set rates on flood insurance, Rebecca Elliott, *Underwater: Loss, Flood Insurance, and the Moral Economy of Climate Change in the United States* (New York: Columbia University Press, 2021), clarifies. For other temporally minded scholarship, see Liz Koslov, "How Maps

Make Time: Temporal Conflicts of Life in the Flood Zone," *City* 23 (2019): 658–672, also on New York; Kasia Paprocki, "All That Is Solid Melts into the Bay: Anticipatory Ruination and Climate Change Adaptation," *Antipode* 51 (2019): 295–315, on Bangladesh; Ruth Fincher et al., "Time Stories: Making Sense of Futures in Anticipation of Sea-Level Rise," *Geoforum* 56 (2014): 201–210; and Daniel Tubridy et al., "Managed Retreat in Response to Flooding: Lessons from the Past for Contemporary Climate Change Adaptation," *Planning Perspectives* 36 (2021): 1249–1268. In human geography, climate futures loom over much theoretical work on temporality; for a review, see Elaine Lynn-Ee Ho, "Social Geography I: Time and Temporality," *Progress in Human Geography* 45 (2021): 1668–1677.

28. Marc Bloch, *The Historian's Craft* [1941], trans. Peter Putnam (New York: Vintage, 1953), 141, 27.

Index

Note: Page numbers in *italics* refer to illustrative matter.

abandonment, 5, 201, 221, 241–42, 318n92
Abrams, Charles, 61, 66, 71, 203–4, 217; on Urban Renewal, 181, 182; on Venezuela, 140–42, 149, 162, 174–75, 247, 350–51n96
ACTION (American Council to Improve Our Neighborhoods), 44, 90
Action for Boston Community Development (ABCD), 190–91
After the Planners (Goodman), 188–89
Agamben, Giorgio, 360n9
Alexander, Christopher, 291n65
Alliance for Progress, 133
Alonso, William, 71, 73–74, 191, 198, 248
American Academy of Arts and Sciences, 3, 117, 213
American Enterprise Institute (AEI), 205, 223–24
The American Landscape (Nairn), 31
The American Soldier (Stouffer), 23
Anchor Books, 18, 88, 104
Anderson, Lawrence B., 57, 131
Anderson, Martin, 178–83, 222, 327n6
Appleyard, Donald, 99, 233; at Ciudad Guayana, 145, 150, *152–54*, 173, 235; *Planning a Pluralist City*, 228–233; on time orientation, 230–33; *The View from the Road*, 98–99, *151*
Architectural Forum (publication), 19, 271n6
automobility, 99, *109*, 118, 145–56, 161, 173–74, 318n92
Avenida Guayana, 145–56, 173–74, 247, 318n92. *See also* Ciudad Guayana, Venezuela

Bacon, Edmund, 31, 52, 82, 137; Ciudad Guayana proposals, 146, *147*; *Design of Cities*, 31, 169
Bane, Mary Jo, 200

Banfield, Edward, 48, 50, 118, 193, 227–28, 235, 254, 347n65; *City Politics*, 77–80, 217; *The Moral Basis of a Backward Society*, 224–26, 233, 349n87; on time orientation, 218–22; *The Unheavenly City*, 215–23, 254, 346n59
Banfield, Elliott, 254, 362n19
basic research, 23, 63–64, 70–71, 77–84; vs. applied research, 95–97
Bauer, Catherine, 52, 57, 59, 61–62
behavioral sciences, as field, 34–36, 156
Bell, Daniel, 9, 12, 25, 89, 213–15, 272n15
Belluschi, Pietro, 67, 131
Betancourt, Rómulo, 133, 134, 137, 247. *See also* Ciudad Guayana; Corporación Venezolana de Guayana (CVG); Venezuela
Beyond the Melting Pot (Glazer and Moynihan), 87, 88–89, 94, 184, 236–38, 240
blight, as term, 92, 178, 240
Bloch, Ernst, 249–50
Bloch, Marc, 256
Bolan, Richard S., 101–102, 196
Bollens, John C., 38, 39
Boroughitis, 106
Boston, greater: Ford Foundation and, 56–57; 127, 185–99, 329n22; Joint Center studies of, 59, 63, 73–74, 81–83, 95–102, 201–2, 204, 207, 217; Urban Renewal in, 130–32, 178, *180*, 197
Boston College, 37, 96, 310n5
Boston Redevelopment Authority (BRA), 82, 97, 131
Bowman, Isaiah, 27, 32
Branch, Melville C., Jr., 42, 47, 48–49, 52
Brasília, Brazil, 142, 146, 161
The British New Towns Policy (Rodwin), 61
"Broken Windows" (Kelling and Wilson), 243–44
Brown, H. James, 246

INDEX

Brownsville, Brooklyn, 1–2, 60, 241, 264n5, 328n7
Buckley, William F., Jr., 186
Burchard, John, 57, 75, 120–23, 154, 179, 189
Bureau of Applied Social Research (BASR; Columbia University), 25, 29
Bureau of Public Administration (Berkeley), 24, 52
Bureau of Urban Research (Princeton University), 42
Burgess, Ernest, 74, 114

Caracas, Venezuela, 133–39, 141, 158, 162, 247, 318n89. *See also* Venezuela
Carnegie Mellon University, 23
Carnegie philanthropy, 29–31, 33, 201
Carter, Jimmy, 200, 240
Cass, Melnea, 190
center, as organizational form. *See* organized research units (ORUs)
Center for Advanced Study in the Behavioral Sciences (CASBS), 36
Center for Advanced Visual Studies (MIT), 97, 100
Center for International Studies (CENIS; MIT), 23, 76, 136, 161
Center for Urban and Regional Studies (CURS; MIT), 57, 59–60, 62–64
Center for Urban Studies (CUS; Harvard), 65
centers of urban studies, 22, 41–46, 273n21. *See also* organized research units (ORUs)
Centre for Urban Studies (University College London), 252–53
Chapin, F. Stuart, Jr., 46, 58
Charlestown, Boston, 183–84
Chase, Edward T., 241
Chávez, Hugo, 247–48
Chiaromonte, Italy. *See* Montegrano
Chicago Housing Authority, 48, 65
Chicago Land Clearance Commission, 43
Chicago School (sociology), 12, 84, 88, 92, 96, 103, 114, 291–92n69
CHOICES for '76 (RPA project), 188
The City in History (book by Mumford), 20, 121
"The City in History" (conference), 120, 122
city planning. *See* planning, overview
City Politics (Banfield and Wilson), 77–80, 217
Ciudad Guayana, Venezuela, 132, 137–45, 156–75, 227–33, 247–48, 320n114. *See also* Avenida Guayana; Corporación Venezolana de Guayana (CVG); Venezuela

Ciudad Kennedy, 133, 311n10
Claremont Institute, 205, 254
Clay, Grady, 19, 20, 80–84, 124
Clay, Phillip, 336nn86–87, 360n1
climate change, 255
cultural geography. *See* geography, as discipline
cognitive mapping, 63, 163, 230, *231*, 352n106
Cohen, Morris Raphael, 60, 127, 248
Collins, John F., 131
Colombia, 133
Columbia, Maryland, 141, 161, 213
Columbia University, 25, 28, 29, 39, 58, 66, 203–4
The Coming of Post-Industrial Society (Bell), 213
Commentary (publication), 20, 88, 182, 222
Commission on Civil Disorder. *See* Kerner Commission
Committee on Juvenile Delinquency and Youth Crime, 190
Committee on Urban and Regional Studies. *See* Center for Urban and Regional Studies (CURS)
comparative analysis, 120, 237, 251, 295–96n114; in urban studies, 71, 74, 77–80, 88–89, 183–84
The Competitors (Clay), 80–84, 113, 124
Compton, Karl, 33–34, 35
Computer Methods in the Analysis of Large-Scale Social Systems (ed. Beshers), 90–91
Conference on the Metropolitan Future, 52–53
Congrès Internationaux d'Architecture Moderne (CIAM), 32, 142–43
The Conscience of the City (ed. Meyerson), 206, 216, 340n119
Corporación Venezolana de Guayana (CVG), 132–34, 137–40, 150–66, 247–48, 311n10, 318n92, 323n148, 352n97. *See also* Ciudad Guayana, Venezuela
Corrada, Rafael, 134, 176
Costa, Lúcio, 142
cultural geography. *See* geography, as academic discipline
Curti, Merle, 31
CVG. *See* Corporación Venezolana de Guayana (CVG)
cybernetics, 166–74, 184–88, 191, 204, 226

Daedalus (publication), 3, 62, 117–18, 265n18
Dahl, Robert, 115–16, 183, 305n103

INDEX

Darby, H. C., 14
The Death and Life of Great American Cities (Jacobs), 19, 32, 186, 187
decentralism, 61, 139, 143, 158, 167, 187, 333n58
deindustrialization, 2, 5, 56, 107, 201, 209, 236
Delafons, John, 70
DeMuth, Christopher, 224
Department of Housing and Urban Development (HUD), 45, 93
Department of Social Relations (Harvard), 26
Derthick, Martha, 72, 78, 113, 191, 195, 199
Design of Cities (Bacon), 31, 169
Deutsch, Karl, 119, 169
Dissent (publication), 20
Doxiadis, Constantinos, 75, 136
Dunlop, John T., 202

Eldredge, H. Wentworth, 160
Emergency Fleet Corporation, 7
Empire State Plaza (Albany), 242
environment, as concept, 192, 255
environmental design, as field, 32, 168
environmental psychology, 230
Epstein, Jason, 18–19
Evans-Pritchard, E. E., 11
The Exploding Metropolis (ed. Whyte), 19, 224

Fabian, Johannes, 233
Face of the Metropolis (Meyerson et al.), 90
Families against the City (Sennett), 123–24
The Federal Bulldozer (Anderson), 178–83, 222, 327n6
Fogelson, Robert, 124, 213
Ford Foundation, 4, 29; Behavioral Sciences Program, 34–36; as funder of Joint Center, 54, 190, 193, 200–1; headquarters, *35*; Public Affairs Program, 44; public image of, 34; support of international projects by, 135–36; Urban and Regional Program, 36–41, 56–57, 281n103
forecasting, 10, 49–50, 213, 253, 255, 307n121, 341n12. *See also* futurism; projection
Forrester, Jay, 168
Foucault, Michel, 284n144
foundations, philanthropic, 17, 29–46, 104, 135–36, 200–1. *See also* names of specific institutions
The Fragmented Metropolis (Fogelson), 124
Frazier, E. Franklin, 94
Frieden, Bernard, 74, 182, 193, 199, 206, 239

Friedmann, John, 8, 47, 172–73; Ciudad Guayana and, 134, 138, 139, 143–45, 157–59, 162–63, 171; as critic of Joint Center, 162–63; on regions, 157–59, 165
frontier, as concept, 123, 158–59, 182, 308n. *See also* resource frontier, as concept
The Future Metropolis (ed. Rodwin), 4, 119–20, 122, 206, 217, 254
Future Shock (Toffler), 212–15
futures studies. *See* futurism
futurism, 4, 143, 206–7, 212–15, 267n27, 342n18. *See also* forecasting; projection
futurology. *See* futurism

Gaither, H. Rowan, *33*, 35
Gans, Herbert, 21, 75, 131, 182
"Garden Cities and the Metropolis" (Rodwin), 61
Garden City movement, 61, 120, 141, 149, 174
Geddes, Patrick, 8, 66, 122
gentrification, 178, 183, 252–53, 329n21
geography, as academic discipline, 21, 26–28, 43, 159, 212
George Washington University, 20, 45
Gestalt psychology, 6, 51, 65, 230
Glass, Ruth, 252–53
Glazer, Nathan, 18–19, 66, 92, 93, 118, 186; *American Judaism*, 237; *Beyond the Melting Pot*, 87–90, 236–240; on Modern architecture, 242–43
Gómez, Juan Vicente, 137
Goodman, Paul and Percival, 20
Goodman, Robert, 188–89
Gottmann, Jean, 32–33, 126
Government Center (Boston), 130, *131*, *197*
Graduate School of Design (GSD; Harvard University), 58, 65, 76, 91, 131, 203–4, 246, 251
Graduate School of Public Administration (Harvard University). *See* Kennedy School (Harvard University)
Gray Areas Program, 73, 92, 107, 302n74, 306n104
Great Depression, 7, 11, 21, 84
Greater Boston Chamber of Commerce, 201–2
Great Society programs, 92–93, 141, 192–94, 216, 224, 253
Grebler, Leo, 43, 52, 58
Greenbelt program, 47, 61, 141
Green New Deal, 253
Greer, Scott, 39, 52, 342n20

INDEX

grid plan, 15–16, 63, 173
growth poles, theory of, 139, 158–59
Guayana region. *See* Ciudad Guayana, Venezuela; Corporación Venezolana de Guayana (CVG)
Guiding Principles for Federal Architecture, 90
Gulick, Luther, 41, 45
Gutheim, Frederick, 19, 20, 45, 120

Haar, Charles, 71, 92–93, 113
Halprin, Lawrence, 187
Handlin, Oscar, 89–90, 104–6, 110, 120, 121, 213, 293n82
Harrington, Michael, 20, 94
Harris, Chauncy, 47
Hartman, Chester, 182, 186
Harvard University: Business School, 70, 306n105; Department of Geography, 27–28; Department of Social Relations, 26, 29, 220; Faculty Club, 90; graduate program in urban design, 5, 32; GSD, 58, 65, 76, 91, 131, 203–4, 246, 251; Kennedy School, 200, 246; organized research units of, 24, 25, 26, 28, 43; Russian Research Center, 23, 30; School of City Planning, 42. *See also* Ciudad Guayana, Venezuela; Joint Center for Urban Studies
Havighurst, Robert, 85, 95, 103
Heald, Henry T., 34
Heidegger, Martin, 51
Hirsch, Werner Z., 39, 45, 52
The Historian and the City (eds. Handlin and Burchard), 120–21, 206
Hoffman, Paul G., 34, 35
Homans, George, 26
Hoover, Edgar M., 104, 110–11
Hoover, Herbert, 42
Housing and Economic Progress (Rodwin), 73–74
Housing and Home Financing Agency (HHFA), 45, 88, 94
Howard, Ebenezer, 61, 141
Howard, John Tasker, 44, 57
Howe, Irving, 20, 209, 341n8
Hoyt, Homer, 73–74
human geography. *See* geography, as academic discipline
Hutchins, Robert Maynard, 25, 35
Huxtable, Ada Louise, 19, 20
Hynes, John, 57, 130

Illinois Institute of Technology, 47
The Image of the City (Lynch), 63, 71–72, 87, 98, 153–54, 230, 352n106

industrial location, 7, 27, 104–8, 134–39, 141–42, 157–59, 201–2
inference, as problem in social research, 71, 77–84, 113–18, 120–122, 124–28, 133, 156–63, 232
Institute for Research in Social Science (University of North Carolina), 31, 43
Institute for Urban and Regional Studies (IURS; Washington University), 45, 195, 224
Institute for Urban Land Use and Housing Studies (Columbia University), 43, 58
Institute of Human Relations (Yale University), 26, 31
Institute of International Relations (University of California, Berkeley), 24
Institute of Urban Studies (IUS; University of Pennsylvania), 44, 65, 282n118
intellectual, as term. *See* public intellectual, as term
The Intellectual versus the City (White and White), 126–27
Inter-American Housing Center, 133
interdisciplinarity, as ideal, 17–26, 29–36
Isaacs, Reginald, 161
Isard, Walter, 41, 58, 71
Isserman, Andrew, 211–12

Jackson, John Brinckerhoff, 21, 27, 62, 98
Jacobs, Jane, 19, 32, 80, 186, 187, 244
James, William, 156
Johns Hopkins University, 24, 33
Johnson, Lyndon B., 227
Joint Center for Housing Studies, 246. *See also* Joint Center for Urban Studies
Joint Center for Urban Studies: establishment of, 54, 57–67; overview of, 4–5, 10–16; refinancing and recession of, 199–208. *See also* Harvard University; Joint Center for Housing Studies; MIT (Massachusetts Institute of Technology); *names of specific leaders and projects*; Ciudad Guayana, Venezuela
Jouvenel, Bertrand de, 214

Kaplan, Marshall, 193–94, 196–99, 206, 239, 248, 334n63
Kazin, Alfred, 1–5, 241–42, 264–65n6; as "New York Intellectual," 264–65n6; *New York Jew*, 241; *On Native Grounds*, 1; *Our New York*, 241; on social science, 272n15; and Tamiment Conference, 5; *A Walker in the City*, 1, 3, 241, 265n9, 357n135; on WWII, 9
Kennedy, John F., 25, 88, 92, 133, 161

INDEX   369

Kennedy School (Harvard University), 200, 246, 359n1
Kepes, György, 63, 65, 97, 100, 119, 150, 169, 306n114
Kerner Commission, 92, 204
Kerr, Clark, 24, 52, 202–3
Key, V. O., 76, 124
Keyes, Langley C., Jr., 183–84, 193, 198
Kiley, Dan, 35
Killian, James T., 23, 57
Kise, J. N., 173
Kistin, Helen, 76, 78
Kosar, Kevin, 254
Koselleck, Reinhart, 10, 128, 307n121
Kouwenhoven, John, 15–16
Kresge, David, 207
Kriegel, Leonard, 240
Kristol, Irving, 179, 186, 192, 211, 332n52
Kubitschek, Juscelino, 142, 143

laboratory, city as, 39, 57, 95–97, 103, 130–132, 160–61, 190
La Laja neighborhood, 154, 157, 163–65, 186, 227, 228
Lander, Luis, 133, 137
Landscape (publication), 21
Lang, A. Scheffer, 70
Latour, Bruno, 255
Laura Spelman Rockefeller Memorial, 30, 31, 114
Lazarsfeld, Paul, 25, 29, 58, 117
Lee, Richard C., 115
Lerner, Daniel, 117, 125, 156–57
Levitan, Sar, 200
The Levittowners (Gans), 75
Lewis, Oscar, 94, 218
Lindblom, Charles, 185, 193, 197
Lindsay, John V., 187, 212, 241
Little, Arthur D., 169, 314n40
Llewelyn-Davies, Richard, 141
Logue, Edward J., 97, 115, 131, 135, 186
Lomax, Alan, 25
London School of Economics, 31
The Lonely Crowd (Riesman et al.), 18–19, 30, 66, 87
long-term planning. *See* timescale, in urban planning
Los Angeles School (urban studies), 251–52
Lowry, Ira, 200, 207
Luhmann, Niklas, 210
Lydon, John, 209
Lynch, Kevin, 4, 6, 57, 62–65, 71–72, 91, 150, 163; on Ciudad Guayana, 154–56; *The Image of the City*, 63, 71–72, 87, 98, 153–54, 230, 235, 352n106; "The Pattern of the Metropolis," 118, *119*, 152–53; "A Theory of Urban Form," 63–64; *The View from the Road*, 98, 102, 150, *151*, 229
Lynd, Robert Staughton and Helen Merrell, 114

Macdonald, Dwight, 181
Maduro, Nicolás, 248
Mahwah Assembly, *108*
Maki Fumihiko, 46, 172, 173, 326n176
Man and Society in an Age of Reconstruction (Mannheim), 159
Manhattan Institute, 205, 254
Man-Made America (Tunnard and Pushkarev), 31
Mannheim, Karl, 12, 159
Man's Struggle for Shelter in an Urbanizing World (Abrams), 71, 141
Marshall Plan, 34, 104
Martocci, Frank, 146, 157
Maruyama, Magoroh, 168
Marxist thought, 12, 166, 184, 250, 308n125, 321n122
McGinn, Noel, 157, 176
Mead, Margaret, 8, 24
Megalopolis (Gottmann), 32
Meier, Richard, 136, 169
Merriam, Charles, 42–43, 44, 282n116
Merton, Robert C., 11, 207, 289n36
metropolis, as geographic unit, 4, 7, 101, 251–52
Metropolitan Area Planning Council (MAPC; Boston), 100–2, 196
Metropolitan District Commission, 96–98
The Metropolitan Enigma (ed. Wilson), 196, *197*, 206, 216
Metropolitan St. Louis Survey, 38–41, 45, 112, 135
Meyerson, Martin, 4–5, 44, 52, 65–67, 190, 216, 217, 249; international work of, 136–37, 157; as Joint Center director, 68–70, 72, 77–85, 89–90, 93, 96, 113; as planning theorist, 47–49, 101, 102, 119, 211; as university president, 202–3, 223
Middletown (Lynd and Lynd), 37, 114
MIT (Massachusetts Institute of Technology): CAVS, 97, 100; CENIS, 23, 76, 136, 161; CURS, 57, 59–60, 62–64; city and regional planning at, 43, 58, 74, 104, 204; Cold War and, 23; Ford Foundation and, 33–34; SPURS, 91, 203. *See also* Ciudad Guayana, Venezuela; Joint Center for Urban Studies

370 INDEX

Mitchell, Robert Clair, 44, 58
Model Cities Program, 92, 193–94, 333n54, 333nn57–58
Modernism, 23, 42, 47, 57, 159, *197*, 267n27; CIAM and, 32, 142–43; critiques of, 178; in landscape architecture, 35, 76, 187–88, 280n82, 318n88; temporality of, 142–45; in Venezuela, 135–137, 150
modernization theory, 23, 142–45, 156–57, 225, 227
Moholy-Nagy, László, 66
Montegrano, Italy, 224–26, 233, 349n87
Moore, Wilbert, 11
Moos, Malcolm, 85–86, 95–96, 124, 181
The Moral Basis of a Backward Society (Banfield), 224–26, 233, 349n87
Morris, Jan, 9, 268n41
Moses, Robert, 106, 135
Moynihan, Daniel Patrick, 75, 88–91, 93–95, *138*; on architecture, 90, 100, 189; *Beyond the Melting Pot*, 87–89, 94, 184, 236–38, 240; Ciudad Guayana and, *138*, 176–77; as Council for Urban Affairs director, 192–93; as Joint Center director, 94–95; "The Negro Family" report, 94–95; as "neoconservative," 192, 217–18; public persona, 90
Mumford, Lewis, 8, 20, 61–62, 121–22, 123, 244
Municipal Manpower Commission, 97, 201
Muñoz Marín, Luis, 161

Nairn, Ian, 31
Nash, George H., 179
National Commission on Urban Problems, 91, 92
National Institute of Mental Health, 22
National Resources Planning Board, 42
National Science Foundation, 22, 30, 41
The Nature and Art of Motion (ed. Kepes), 150
Nelson, Howard J., 302n73
neoconservatism, 192–208, 211, 214, 215–26, 236–40, 242–45, 355–56n121
New Deal, 7–8, 42, 47, 61, 141, 224, 253, 267–68n31
New Haven, Connecticut, 75, 115–16, 305n103, 305–306n104
New School for Social Research, 51, 60
New Town projects, 42, 141–43, 161–62, 213, 247–48; critique of, 174, 181, 191; study of, 80, 93, 161. *See also* Ciudad Guayana, Venezuela; Garden City movement

New York Metropolitan Region Study (NYMRS), 103–13, 167, 193, 236, 244
New York Times (publication), 240, 244
Nichols, Robert, 20, 241
Nieman Foundation, 75, 80
Nisbet, Robert, 204–5
Nixon, Richard, 90, 192, 222

Oakland Project, 195
Odum, Howard, 31
Office of Naval Research, 22
Office of Strategic Services, 23
organized research units (ORUs), 22–28, 41–46, 204–5, 286n7. *See also names of specific institutions*
Our Cities (National Resources Committee), 42

paperback publishing, 17, 18–22, 88, 104, 302n73
Paramus, New Jersey, *109*
Park, Robert, 12, 26, 84, 114
Parsons, Talcott, 11, 26, 72, 213
Partisan Review (publication), 20, 265n6
"The Pattern of the Metropolis" (Lynch), 118, *119*, 152–53
Peattie, Lisa, 140–42, 157, 158, 186, 235; *The View from the Barrio*, 163–66, 169, 171, 226–28, 323nn146–49
Peattie, Roderick, 140, 163–64, 227
Pendleton, William, 200–201
Penfold, Anthony, 138
Penjerdel, 37
Pérez Jiménez, Marcos, 133, 137
Perloff, Harvey, 45, 47, 51, 58
Peterson, Jon C., 125, 213
Philadelphia, 38–39, 44, 142, 146, 203
Pittsburgh Economic Study, 304n93
Planned Society (ed. MacKenzie), 8
planning, overview, 6–9, 11–13
Planning a Pluralist City (Appleyard), 228–34
Planning, Politics, and the Public Interest (Meyerson and Banfield), 48, 78
planning theory, as subfield, 47–48, 283n131
Plan or No Plan (Wootton), 7
Point Four Program, 136
policy, as term, 195
The Politics of Neglect (Frieden and Kaplan), 193, 198, 211, 239
Polsby, Nelson, 115, 116
Popenoe, David, 17–18, 46, 177
Porter, William L., 150, 230
postmodernity, 209, 251, 340n2, 354n118

Poverty, Planning, and Politics in the New Boston (Thernstrom), 190
Poverty and Progress (Thernstrom), 125
presentism, 210–15
Pressman, Jeffrey, 194–95
Program for Education and Research in Planning (PERP; University of Chicago), 46–50, 55, 65, 79, 84, 159, 216
projection, 49, 103–113, 206–7. See also forecasting; futurism
prophecy, 61, 66, 122, 304n93, 307n121
Public Affairs Program (Ford Foundation), 44
public intellectual, as concept, 11–12, 269n48, 270n51
publishing industry, 17, 18–22
Pusey, Nathan, 94, 104

quantification, in social research, 22–23, 27, 90–91, 111–112, 252

Rainwater, Lee, 95, 200
RAND Corporation, 23, 58, 169, 285n153
Ravard, Rafael Alfonzo, 133, 134
region, as geographic unit, 7, 36, 48, 111, 157–59, 251–52, 267–68n31
REGION (game), 169, *170*
Regional Plan Association (RPA; New York), 7, 58, 100, 103–13, 187–88
Regional Planning Association of America (RPAA), 61, 66, 141
Regional Plan of New York and Environs (RPNY), 58, 103, 302n73
regional science, 27, 40, 71, 200 304n94
The Rehabilitation Planning Game (Keyes), 183, 193
Rein, Martin, 200
A Report on Politics series, 77–79, 294n92
Resettlement Administration, 47
resource frontier, as concept, 132, 158–59. See also frontier, as concept
revitalization, as term, 178
Riesman, David, 19, 30, 66, 87
Rittel, Horst, 188, 217
Roche, Kevin, *35*
Rockefeller, David, 104, 113, 290n54
Rockefeller Foundation, 29–33, 63, 104, 279n77, 313n25
Rockefeller Urban Design Conferences, 32, 63, 66, 83, 187
Rodwin, Lloyd: *The British New Towns Policy*, 61; departure from Joint Center, 90–91, 100, 203–4; "Garden Cities and the Metropolis," 61; *Housing and Economic Progress*, 73–74; as Joint Center director, 3–5, 57–68, 72, 84, 118–19, 159, 176; *Nations and Cities*, 160, 211; on "systematic doubt," 60, 61, 248; "A Theory of Urban Form," 63–64; Venezuela project and, 132–37, *138*, 141–43, 156–57, 160, 162, 171
Rosenblith, Walter, 193
Rostow, W. W., 23, 143, 145
Rouse, James, 52, 202, 213
Roxbury (Boston), 183–4, 186, 190
Ruhr Valley (Germany), 142
ruin, as category, 9, 53, 140–41, *180*, 238, 239–245
Russian Research Center (Harvard University), 23, 30
Rutgers University, 39
Ryan, William, 223

San Francisco Bay Area, 99, 161, 187, 195, 196. See also Oakland Project
sanitary reform, 7
Sasaki, Hideo, 76
Sauer, Carl, 21, 32
Savas, E. S., 187
Schafer, Robert, 199, 335n79
Schapiro, Meyer, 66
Schlivek, Louis, 111
Schmandt, Henry, 39
School of Humanities and Social Sciences (MIT), 23, 57
Schorske, Carl, 24, 120, 126
Second Regional Plan of New York, 111
Sennett, Richard, 124–25, 127, 222–23, 309n145
sequencing: of economic development, 143–145, *144*; of visual perception, 145–56, *151*, *152*, *153*, 173–74. See also modernization theory; *The View from the Road* (Appleyard et al.)
serialization of knowledge, 67–70, 78–79
Sert, Josep Lluís, 81, 131, 135, 137, 289n38
Shenker, Israel, 244
Shils, Edward, 26
short-term planning. See timescale, in urban planning
Sieber, Sam, 25
Simon, Herbert, 23
Skidmore, Owings & Merrill, 135
Sloan School of Management (MIT), 201
smart cities, 252
Soberman, Richard, 70, 157

372 INDEX

Social Science Research Council, 30, 43
Social Statistics and the City (ed. Heer), 91
sociology and anthropology of time, 10–11
Solomon, Arthur, 199, 207, 335n77
Sorokin, Pitrim, 11
Southeastern Michigan Metropolitan Community Research Corporation, 37
South End (Boston), 183–84, 190
Southworth, Michael, 99
Sowell, Thomas, 254
Special Program for Urban and Regional Studies (SPURS; MIT), 91, 203
Speier, Hans, 8
sprawl. *See* urban form and formlessness
Stein, Clarence, 59, 90
Steinfels, Peter, 215
Sternlieb, George, 70–71
Stevenson, Adlai, 133
Stouffer, Samuel, 23, 76
Stratton, Julius, 67, 132
Strauss, Leo, 224, 254, 362n19
Streetcar Suburbs (Warner), 124
Study Group on Metropolitan Problems, 44
Survey Research Center (University of Michigan), 23, 24
Symposium on Library Functions in the Changing Metropolis, 72
systems theory, 324n159

Tamiment Conference on the Metropolis (1960), 3, 4, 50, 118, 265n18, 265n19
Taper, Bernard, 97
Task Force on Urban Problems, 193
Taut, Bruno, 143
Taylor, Frederick Winslow, 48
Tejera Paris, Enrique, 134
Tennessee Valley Authority, 42, 132, 161
tense and aspect, grammatical, 360n9, 360n11
Thematic Apperception Test, 224, 225
"A Theory of Urban Form" (Lynch and Rodwin), 63–64
Thernstrom, Stephan, 124, 125–26, 190–91, 206, 248
Thiel, Philip, 154
think tanks, 205, 224
time orientation, as research subject, 218–22, 224–26, 230–34
timescale, in urban planning, 6, 101–2, 196–99, 252, 255
Toffler, Alvin, 212–13, 342n20, 342n23
Toward the Year 2000 (ed. Bell), 213
TransAction (publication), 95, 222

Trilling, Lionel, 8, 21, 66, 254
Tucker, Raymond, 38
Tugwell, Rexford, 47, 48, 49–50, 51–52, 58, 61, 133
Tunnard, Christopher, 31, 120, 178
Turner, Frederick Jackson, 123, 158
Twentieth Century Fund, 32, 104, 126
Tyrwhitt, Jaqueline, 136, 172

UNESCO (United Nations Education, Scientific, and Cultural Organization), 25
The Unheavenly City (Banfield), 215–23, 254, 346n59
United States Housing Corporation, 7
University of California, Berkeley, 21, 24, 52, 83, 99, 161, 194–95
University of Chicago, 25–26, 28, 42, 46–50, 62, 77, 96, 251. *See also* Chicago School (sociology); Program for Education and Research in Planning (PERP)
University of Michigan, 23, 28
University of Pennsylvania, 44, 47, 65, 202–3, 223
Urban and Regional Program (URP; Ford Foundation), 36–41, 56–57, 281n103
urban crisis, as term, 37, 91–95, 136, 196, 203–4, 215–18, 254, 345n44
urban design, as field, 5, 32
Urban Design Conferences. *See* Rockefeller Urban Design Conferences
urban economics, as subfield, 40, 85
urban form, 31, 62–65, 99, 100, 111, 118–19, 121, 127, 140; of Ciudad Guayana, 140, 145–56, 165; and formlessness, 20, 31, 36, 40, 52–53, 107–8, *109*, 111
urban history, as subfield, 120–28
urbanisme, as term, 42
Urban Life and Form (ed. Hirsch), 45
Urban Planning Aid (organization), 186
urban problem, as term, 36–37, 56, 94, 113, 127–28, 181, 193, 216–18
Urban Renewal: Anderson on, 178–85; as Clay's manuscript subject, 80–84; conference on, 75; in greater Boston, 130–32; Jacobs on, 80, 178, 186–88; Joint Center debates on, 178–85; Keyes on, 183–85; landscapes of, 179, *180*, *197*; opposition to, 178–99, 222, 226, 238; as term, 178; temporal aspects of, 178–85; Toffler on, 212–13
urban studies, origins as academic field, 22, 29–46. *See also names of specific institutions and programs*

Urban Theory Lab (UTL), 251–52
The Urban Villagers (Gans), 131, 182
utopia, as concept, 4, 249–50

Venezuela. *See* Ciudad Guayana, Venezuela; Corporación Venezolana de Guayana (CVG)
Vernon, Raymond, 73, 76, 119, 193, 255; on "gray areas," 73, 107; NYMRS and, 103–13; on "urban problems," 217, 244
The View from the Barrio (Peattie), 163–64, 171, 227–28
The View from the Road (Appleyard et al.), 98, 102, 150, *151*, 229
Von Eckardt, Wolf, 19
von Moltke, Willo, *138*, 142, 146–50, *148*, 172, 176, 318nn92–93, 320n113

Wade, Richard, 158
Wadsworth, Homer, 85, 95
A Walker in the City (Kazin), 1–3, 241, 265n9, 357n135
Warner, Sam Bass, 124, 213
Warner, W. Lloyd, 116, 125
Warren, Earl, 52–53
Washington Center for Metropolitan Studies, 45, 169, *170*
Washington University in St. Louis, 38, 45, 95, 224, 362n19
Watts, Los Angeles, 91–92, 94–95, 203, 221
Wayne, New Jersey, *109*
Weaver, Robert C., 181, 205, 222
Webber, Melvin, 75, 188, 217

Wells, H. G., 36
West End (Boston), 131, *180*, 182, 186
Wheaton, William C., 52, 58
White, Morton and Lucia, 126–27
Whitehead, Alfred North, 48
Whitehill, Walter Muir, 130, 132
Whittlesey, Derwent, 27
Whyte, William H., 19, 224
Wiener, Norbert, 167, 171, 324n157
Wildavsky, Aaron, 194–96
Williams, Norman, Jr., 139–40, 156, 172, 175
Wilson, James Q.: "Broken Windows," 243–44; *City Politics*, 79, 217, 225–26; on Clay's *Competitors*, 113; as Joint Center director, 72, 85, 90, 123–24, 176, 196, 243; *The Metropolitan Enigma*, 196, *197*, 206, 216; on "urban problems," 181; on Urban Renewal, 181–82; *Varieties of Police Behavior*, 243; Venezuela project and, *138*, 161
Wong, Jeanyee, 106, *107*
Wood, Robert C., 72, 97, 113, 166–67, 223, 244, 255; NYMRS and, 104, 106, 110–11; work with federal government, 91–92, 192–93
Wurster, Catherine Bauer. *See* Catherine Bauer

Yale University, 26, 28, 115–17, 276n44, 305n103
Ylvisaker, Paul, 37, 39–41, 44, 93, 107, 112; Joint Center and, 67, 73, 84–85; on time and tense, 50–52